For David
with warm fraternal greetings
Neville Barker Bryer

The Arch and the Rainbow

The Arch and the Rainbow

The Story of the Order of Mark Master Masons and the Degree of Royal Ark Mariner

The Revd.
Neville Barker Cryer

Further titles by the same author:
Masonic Halls of England – The South
Masonic Halls of England – The Midlands
Masonic Halls of England – The North
Masonic Halls of North Wales
Masonic Halls of South Wales

© 1996
The Revd. N. B. Cryer
First Published in England in 1996

Published by IAN ALLAN REGALIA
Coombelands House, Coombelands Lane, Addlestone, Surrey, KT15 1HY
who are members of the Ian Allan Group of Companies.

ISBN 085318 211 6

British Cataloguing in Publication Data
A Catalogue record for this book is available from the British Library.

All rights reserved. No part of this book may be reproduced or transmitted in any form or by any means, electronic or mechanical, including photocopying, recording or by any information storage and retrieval system, without permission of the Publisher in writing.

Filmset by Selwood Systems, Midsomer Norton
Printed in Great Britain by Butler & Tanner Ltd
Frome and London

Contents

List of Illustrations

(The page nos. refer to mention of a person or item in the text)

Foreword

by

R.W.Bro. Peter Glyn Williams, PGJW., GMRAC.
Grand Secretary

R.W.Bro. The Reverend Neville Barker Cryer, Past Provincial Grand Master for Surrey, has asked me to write a short 'Foreword' to this fascinating and instructive volume, and I consider it a privilege to be associated with it not only on account of the intrinsic value of the book, but also because of the Masonic debt I owe the author for his encouragement, wise counsel, and support in all my masonic activities.

The manuscript arrived at Mark Masons' Hall as a tour of duties overseas was about to take place and, dismissing weight allowance restrictions, it was placed in the hand luggage. Once we were airborne I started to read, and found myself reading on and on, completely captivated by the riveting text.

Neville Barker Cryer has the ability to change the tone in a word from one of fearsome indignation to exploding revelation. He is also a prodigiously gifted story-teller who makes full use of his vast vocabulary to create word pictures in an inventive and original manner which enthralls the reader.

Mark Twain said, 'Experience is an author's most valuable asset; experience is the thing that puts the muscle and the breath and warm blood into the book he writes.' That is undoubtedly true, but when experience is combined with a deep abiding love of the subject the finished work develops magical properties and becomes compulsive reading.

The book will speak for itself, but by revealing the orchestrated prejudices, and in presenting an unbiased interpretation of the evidence, R.W.Bro. Neville Barker Cryer has provided the means by which Mark Master Masons and Royal Ark Mariners, as well as other diligent freemasons and masonic researchers, can make a significant and genuine advancement in their masonic knowledge.

This History and Origins of the Mark Degree and the Ancient and Honourable Fraternity of Royal Ark Mariners will confirm the author's worldwide reputation as one of the leading masonic scholars of his day.

30th March, 1996 P.G. Williams

Introduction

HAVE YOU EVER asked yourself any of the following questions:
Whatever is meant by the words 'Ark, Mark, Link and Wrestle'?
What is a Noachida?
Where did the cipher alphabet used in the Mark degree come from?
Why did the idea of a separate Grand Mark Lodge originate in England?
Is there such a thing as a proper Mark penny?
Where does the Royal Ark Mariner degree belong?
Why do Scottish and Irish Masonry insist on the Mark before one enters the Holy Royal Arch?

Certainly these and many other such questions have puzzled me during thirty years and more. And because I am sure that others too want to have some answers to their Mark and Royal Ark Mariner queries this book has been written. It is the result of years of listening to more experienced Mark Masons, reading widely and even researching material that has not hitherto been considered likely to provide solutions. What is certain is that though there have been some attempts to provide a satisfactory 'history' of these two degrees there has never been a book which has tried to give an overall picture of them both – and certainly not under one cover. It is hoped that this book will supply that want.

It has also to be said that the last publication on the subject was written over 30 years ago and even that work is now out of print and only available for the new and younger reader in private or lodge libraries. There were of course earlier works but these too are even less likely to be consulted and each of them tends to concentrate on some individual aspect of the story rather than to try and see the Mark and Ark Mariner degrees as a whole. Having thought for a long time about the subject as a lodge member, an officer, a Past Master, a Grand Chaplain and a Provincial Grand Master, I hope that what I can now share with fellow Mark Masons *and others* will be both interesting and rewarding.

I would like to think that there will be no topic or area in this field which does not receive attention in what follows. I also greatly hope that some matters that have hitherto been thought to have reached a dead end or just been consigned to discreet silence will here be given a new measure of light. Subjects that even twenty years ago had to be the subject of great caution can, in today's more open climate, be treated with new freshness. It will therefore be part of this book's purpose not only to follow the way in which the rituals of Mark

Man and Mark Master developed, and the ceremonial was conducted, but also to examine some of the personalities and events that were involved in that whole process. Some of them, I believe, need looking at in quite a new way. We shall also, of course, have to take into account the charitable concerns of the Mark Benevolent Fund, the various properties which the new Grand Lodge occupied, and the relationships that developed with both Ireland and Scotland. These latter links, it will be seen, have always been closer and more formative than often realised.

Having said that it is important to point out that this is not intended to be a formal history. There must, of necessity, be some opportunity for essential references to be provided for those who want to check up on or pursue some interesting point but it is not the plan to interrupt our story by endless notes. There will also be a booklist at the end for those who want to read in more detail and become acquainted with the work of past years. In view of the book's stated purpose, however, it occurs to me that there may yet have to be a further book of essays at a later date in which those who want to examine some of my suggestions and solutions can do so much more fully. Certainly it would prevent the kind of easier reading which I hope I have provided if there were too many diversions into detailed source material. This book, after all, is meant to be an adventure into the fascinating story of how these two degrees were conceived, emerged, grew and came to us as they are today. What I have tried to provide is a good, though reliable, read.

To produce a book which seeks to cover so much ground and to delve into so many masonic by-ways has required the assistance of a great many people over a long period of time. Some of those who have contributed much in the way of clarifying difficult points or suggesting avenues of discovery are no longer alive to see this book come to birth. Some of our predecessors in the Quatuor Coronati Lodge who have wrestled with the issues here are also no longer available to give their wise judgement on what is written. All I can do here is acknowledge my debt to these earlier friends and guides and declare my lasting gratitude to them.

There are others of course to whom I can express my present thanks and deep appreciation for all that they have contributed to make my efforts worth while. Amongst these are the staff of the Library of the United Grand Lodge in London, the Grand Secretary and his staff at Mark Masons Hall, not forgetting the Brother who has begun to revive the Library collection there and make it more accessible for research; the Grand Scribe E. and his staff in their new home at St. John's Street in Edinburgh; and the Assistant Grand Registrar of the Grand Royal Arch Chapter of Instruction in Dublin. I owe a special debt of gratitude to the members of York Lodge No. 236 in the ancient City of that name, for the generous way in which they have made me welcome as this book was being brought to a finish, and to their Secretary and Heritage Committee who have granted me full and easy access to their remarkable library and museum. No less do I thank many other brethren in Provincial and local Masonic libraries in Newcastle-on-Tyne, Durham, Sunderland, Whitby, Scarborough, Pickering, St. Saviourgate (York), Sheffield, Manchester, Derby, Leicester, Birmingham, Bristol, Norwich, Canterbury, Brighton, Havant, Portsmouth and Newport (Isle of Wight). To so many brethren here I cannot express adequately how much I felt their trust in allowing me to borrow books the study of which would have been impossible otherwise.

Especially do I want to thank my fellow member of the Quatuor Coronati Lodge, No. 2076, Bro. Yasha Beresiner, who not only shared with me his ideas and papers, but also agreed to read my draft chapters and give me his frank and helpful advice. Let me hasten to add, however, that any errors or faulty conclusions in this book are wholly my responsibility and are not to be attributed to anyone but myself. I shall certainly respond to any who might want to write to the author after they have read what is here, for I hope I am still ready and willing to learn.

Nor can I forget to thank the publishers for their ready encouragement to produce this work. They have thus allowed me to express and expand what has been in my mind and heart for many years, and made possible the enjoyment that I have had in preparing for and writing what follows. I trust that in turn those who now read it will feel that it has helped them to make a worthwhile advancement in masonic knowledge and that now they can the better 'mark well'. If so, that will be reward indeed.

Chapter One

The Mark and the Ark

What they mean and how they work

THIS BOOK HAS been written for as wide a range of readers as possible. If you are someone who has perhaps only heard about the Mark and Royal Ark Mariner degrees, and would like to learn more about them before you join, then this book will tell you all you need to know. If you have been a member of one or both of these Orders for some time but have not been able to find something that will explain the background to their ceremonies, and how they come to be part of that Freemasonry to which you belong, then this too will answer your questions. If you are a Preceptor, a Past Master or a Past Commander and you know that you ought to be able to answer the questions that others may ask you, on both regular and rehearsal evenings, then this book has you also in mind. Whether it is why we do, or no longer do, this or that part of our ritual then the answer will be here for you to find.

Again, even if you are long in experience and would consider yourself fairly well informed on the history, the past variations in Mark and Ark ritual, the great personalities, the degrees as practised in other Constitutions than your own, and the way in which Mark and Ark Mariner Masonry are going, I still think that this book could interest you and provide you with some new information on familiar features, some fresh angles on old topics and some surprise interpretations of historical 'chestnuts' for those with the usual traditional views. For the scholarly I hope that there is sufficient to stimulate your reactions and to suggest remaining avenues of worth-while research. Still further this is a book for you whatever your Masonic allegiance, or none, and whatever your land. If you are not a Freemason I hope that this book will help you to appreciate why through 250 years our forebears have been happy and content to belong to these Masonic Orders as we do now: and if, being a Mason, your particular national authority is not mentioned by name you should know that it is from those that are described that your present use or disuse of these two Orders originally derived. Whoever you are then, reader, this book is meant to speak to you. For this is merely another staging post on the journey into discovery that the Mark and Ark degrees provide.

Let me begin, however, by attempting to answer questions about the setting, the significance and the sequence of both the Mark and the Ark Mariner in the pattern of present degrees and then go on to explain how these degrees originated and are controlled by the Masonic governing bodies in England and Wales, Ireland and Scotland. Despite the obvious differences that will appear, the same general answers can be given for most of the bodies that govern Mark and Ark Mariner Masonry so that today a remarkable sense of unity is felt by all that both value and enjoy membership of these degrees. As we shall see there are in these aspects of our fraternity both interesting and worthwhile lessons to be learned.

The Degree or ceremony of Mark Master Mason (M.M.M.) is an initiatory practice of considerable antiquity and has been closely associated with speculative Freemasonry for almost two and a half centuries. Though at one time it was a two-grade rite there is no evidence of its being worked as an initiation ceremony on its own, ie. it was never a means used for introducing a person initially to Freemasonry. It was always seen as belonging to the process which began with the degree system formally begun in the early 18th century and now called either the Craft, St John's or Blue Masonry. As time passed both these degrees, in some places, became attached to Arch or Red Masonry but how that came about and what it has meant for those degrees today is part of the longer and fuller story that is given in other chapters.

Mention has just been made of the Mark ceremony once having been in two parts and this needs to be kept in mind as we learn or ponder the perhaps surprising fact that when a person prepares to become a Mark Master Mason (M.M.M.) he is attired like a Fellow-Craft (F.C.) or Second Degree Mason and enters a lodge where everything seems to be done in that degree, although he is told that he cannot be admitted unless he is a Master Mason or in the Third Degree in the Craft. This is because in the first of the two **original** ceremonies he was treated throughout as a F.C. and became a Mark Man or Mark Mason, whilst in the second he was treated as a Master Mason (M.M.) and became a M.M.M. Today the two steps are treated in one ceremony and what happens may look very illogical, but is in fact a sign of the Degree's great antiquity and the retention of some of its first practices.

Whilst this is the setting for the Mark as far as its **qualifications** are concerned a word needs to be said about its setting in regard to the story of the Degree. As is now sufficiently well known by anyone who takes even the slightest trouble to study Freemasonry, whether from without or as a participant, the theme of Craft Masonry today is the symbolic building of a Temple named after Solomon, the Wise King. The Entered Apprentice Freemason (E.A.) is admitted to the fellowship of those engaged on this task, but it is only as a Fellowcraft (F.C.) that he is provided with the rest of those tools which effectively enable him to prepare a shaped stone, and thus progress to the making of a master-piece. He is now able to operate as a skilled craftsman; he is encouraged to pursue the hidden mysteries of nature and science; he knows the *moral* meanings of the square, level and plumb-rule and he even learns where and in what spirit the craftsmen received their wages.

Yet in the Craft Second Degree today he is no longer allowed to show his skill as an operative mason: he is not allowed to receive his *personal Mark* which enabled the Temple construction to proceed without disturbance; he is not normally shown how to apply the square, level and plumb-line to the actual stones presented for the building; he is not shown how to receive his wages and most important of all he is not made privy to the necessity for that most important stone of all, which completes an Arch and thus leads him naturally and logically to the completion of the M.M. Degree, the Holy Royal Arch. Is it any wonder that there have been those Masons who have contended both that the F.C. Degree has not been completed until the Mark has been taken, and that the M.M. Degree is without an essential part of its complete working until the M.M.M. Degree has revealed that keystone (or capestone) without which the Temple building is not a proper whole.

It is precisely this handling of the very stones that make up the physical structure that adds such significance to this particular Degree. However much we may have heard about rough and smooth ashlars in the E.A. and F.C. Degrees it is in the Mark Degree that we see the finished items being put to use. An oblong or real ashlar for the walls, a cube representing a foundation stone and a keystone as the cape (or cope) stone of an arch or vault. These are the objects around which the drama of this ceremony is constructed. When, above all, the work that is sincerely presented by the Candidate for inspection is apparently unrecognised, and dismissed as of no importance whatsoever, then indeed this Degree begins to come into its own.

Here, as in a kind of cameo, is represented something of true life as most of us experience it. A new idea or a fresh contribution to a project is put forward by us only to be rejected by someone who, through sheer ignorance or with a vested interest, prefers to follow older methods. That might even be the treatment that some parts of this very book you are reading might receive from some experienced brethren.

Naturally we have to be careful to distinguish between what we may consider stupidity, lack of awareness or plain obduracy in those who oppose us, and an appreciation of the fact that others are not bound to appreciate our work as we do. The Mark Degree seeks to encourage the sure confidence that if our work is of true quality then in the end it will be recognised for what it is. Such humility is not easy. It is really part of that Temperance that is spoken of when anyone first enters Freemasonry.

Yet this Degree also helps to set this true humility at the point of rejection in its proper perspective. We are helped to face the moment or period of dismissal with patience. In the Mark Degree as it has now come to us we have the perfect illustration of that well-known phrase, 'Patience is its own reward'.

Moreover this Degree has in its own way 'left its mark' on the whole fabric of the Craft. It is when we experience its proper presentation that we realise where all those other phrases about work 'well-done' came from. We say, 'he has made his mark' in music or painting or one of the professions and we will, if we pause to reflect, realise that such an achievement must have entailed patient endeavour often after heartbreak at one's first efforts. We are so to labour that if what we proffer is genuine and worthwhile it will be so marked out for approval here or hereafter.

There is also another lesson which those who enter this Degree will be able to appreciate. The one who comes bringing his masterpiece is in fact fulfilling the design prepared by a Master whose mantle we have already assumed as a M.M. We thus become an essential link in a much greater and longer chain and find ourselves contributing more than ever may have been thought possible to the Temple that is to be built. In the end we shall appreciate the more the Mark Master's sign of approval.

Such are some of the special lessons to be learned from this distinctive Degree. It is because of this thematic setting and its relevance to the other ceremonies that surround it, that the Mark assumes the position it does in the sequence of degrees in the various countries of the British Isles. In *England and Wales* it may be taken as and when a Master Mason wishes but the recipient must have been raised in a regular Master Mason's Lodge before he can be advanced in the Mark Degree. He then applies to a *separately organised* Mark Lodge for Advancement (the term used by Mark Masons today for receiving their ceremony). In *Ireland* he will not be able, or need, to receive the Mark unless he wishes to proceed to the Royal Arch Degree and then he will be advanced by the Chapter to which he applies for admission (or Exaltation) and a temporary Mark Lodge is formed for that specific purpose. In *Scotland* the same practice is followed for when a Master Mason seeks the privilege of becoming a Royal Arch Mason he is required to be a M.M.M. before he can enter that Degree and he has also to receive another intermediate degree (Excellent Master) before the Royal Arch itself. Yet such are the intricacies of history, as will be explained later, that the Grand Lodge of Scotland also permits a Craft Lodge to confer the Mark Degree as an occasional ceremony and as part of its power under a Craft warrant. This does not mean that the recipient has to move on to the Royal Arch but it does ensure that if he wishes to do so in due course he is already qualified in that regard.

Whilst the procedure thus varies, the relation of the Mark to the other basic Masonic degrees is abundantly clear. It lies most naturally between the M.M. Degree and the Royal Arch whilst in its present working it links both the F.C. and the M.M. as well as the M.M. with the Royal Arch. For anyone who wishes to understand and make a natural progression through these stages of modern Freemasonry the Mark Degree can be seen to have a sensible and useful place.

As regards the government of the Degree on a national level the body that controls it in England and Wales is the 'Grand Lodge of Mark Master Masons with its Districts and Lodges Overseas'. This Grand Lodge has much the same list of Grand Officers as in the Craft save that in the same way as in its private contributing lodges there are Overseers who take their place in between the Wardens and Deacons. In the story that will be told later we shall see how this office developed and became one of the most distinctive features of the Mark Master ceremony. As one might also guess when the mention of people receiving their personal Marks is mentioned there is another officer whose title is Registrar of Marks. Grand Stewards figure no less prominently in the Grand Mark Lodge than they do in the United Grand Lodge of England. The Grand Lodge also has a General Board to which certain Grand Officers are appointed for a period and it is with the assistance of this body that the main work and legislation of the Degree is conducted by the MW the Grand Master.

From a very early time after the formation of the Grand Mark Lodge of England and Wales there was the creation of a Provincial system very similar to that already existing in the Craft and the Holy Royal Arch. Each Provincial Grand Master (PGM) now serves for periods of five years which may be renewed at the discretion of the MW the Grand Master. A PGM is in charge of that Province to which he is appointed and has specific duties that he should perform and privileges which he may exercise. He too has a Grand Lodge for his Province and this should meet annually within his Province. He then appoints his Provincial officers and receives the Annual Accounts and is able to communicate with the leaders of his Province and such visitors from other Provinces as may be invited or wish to attend.

As the solid foundation on which this superstructure is erected there is, of course, the local Mark Lodge with officers, other than the three Overseers and the Registrar of Marks, as in the Craft Lodge. The Lodge is presided over by a Worshipful Master as in the Craft and it is the normal expectation that such a Brother will have served as the WM of a Craft Lodge before he assumes this post just as in the case of becoming a Principal in the Royal Arch Chapter. However, it is also possible for a Master Mason who is eligible for the Mark Chair to apply for a dispensation from his Province so that he may proceed to the Chair before he becomes a Craft Installed Master. It is usually expected that the Brother in question can show that he is either about to enter the Craft Chair or is clearly on the ladder towards it. The opportunity which this gives for Master Masons to experience the task and privilege of ruling a Lodge is often invaluable as a preparation for the usually more demanding Craft appointment.

In Ireland the whole situation is so much simpler. The Mark Degree is under the jurisdiction of the Supreme Grand Royal Arch Chapter there and hence there are no equivalents of the English Grand Mark offices. By the same token (which is, incidentally, another phrase deriving from a Mark Degree practice of giving a token as a symbol of wages) there is no Provincial Mark system and equally no separate Mark Lodge. When the Mark is to be conferred the Companions of the Chapter often withdraw to another room and there the VW Master conducts the Ceremony of Advancement. The office of Very Worshipful Master (VWM) in a Mark Lodge is only granted to a Companion who is eligible for and about to be installed as King (or First Principal) and before proceeding to the latter distinction the Companion must have a duly signed certificate which indicates his having been installed as Master in a Very Worshipful Mark Lodge. His installation ceremony would be quite familiar to those holding the same office in England and Wales. The other officers of the Mark ceremony are the same as the Chapter ones and a clear parallel list is available which shows what office in both Orders is held by the same Companion. Moreover, since 1991 it has been laid down that not only the VWM but all the officers are to be installed in turn at an annual occasion.

In Irish Chapters there follows a similar ceremony to the Scottish Excellent Master but that is practised *within* the Chapter as part of the Royal Arch ceremony. Any qualified English Royal Arch Mason may attend and see the Veils ceremony but he may not be present when the Mark ceremony takes place unless he is already an advanced MMM or arrangements have been authorised for him to be so advanced in Ireland.

In Scotland there is similarly no separate Mark organisation. As we have already remarked there is apparently divided rule over the MMM Degree, but such rule is, let me hasten to add, very happily accepted by both parties. Law 84 in the current Constitutions and Laws of the Grand Lodge of Scotland is in the following terms:

> 'The Degrees of Freemasonry authorized and governed by Grand Lodge are those of Entered Apprentice, Fellow-of-Craft (including the Mark) and Master Mason and no other.'

There is, *unlike the English formula*, no mention of the Order of the Royal Arch.

The only Officers of Grand or Provincial rank are those who discharge their Craft duties in that capacity and they oversee the correct working of the local lodges. It is here that a MM registered on the books of the Grand Lodge has the first opportunity of advancing in the Mark Degree though when he does so at this point it is likely to be the shorter of the two forms of Scottish Mark ceremony that will be followed as there are often many candidates at once. Though we have seen that by one Law the Mark is regarded as being attached to the FC Degree there is another, Law 196, which states that no Scottish lodge is allowed to work more than one ceremony at any one meeting. This incidentally explains why most Scottish lodges meet fairly frequently – perhaps as often as twice a month from October to April, though in Scotland they usually do not meet at all in the summer months. It is at one of these meetings that the Mark Degree will be conferred by the RWM and officers of the Craft Lodge. In such a situation there is no requirement for, or appointment to, the post of Master of a Mark Lodge.

Whilst that is the position in the Scottish Craft the Mark may also be conferred as a preliminary to being exalted into a Scottish Royal Arch Chapter. If the candidate for the Royal Arch has already been advanced to the Mark Degree he does not have to repeat the experience and he may attend the ceremony, which may often be a longer one, for those who have not yet had the Mark secrets. It is worth remarking here that if a Companion of an English

Royal Arch Chapter wishes to attend a Scottish Royal Arch meeting and is also not a MMM he is not required to take that Degree, or the subsequent one of Excellent Master, but he will be asked to withdraw from the lodge room whilst these ceremonies take place. If he is a Mark Mason he is allowed to stay for that part of the ceremonies but unless he is affiliating to the Scottish Chapter he may not apply to be put through the Excellent Master degree. By the concordat reached between the two countries he is perfectly free, on providing proof that he is a qualified Royal Arch Mason, to attend their ceremony of Exaltation.

The most distinctive feature of the Mark in Scotland, apart from the two forms of ceremony, concerns the Installation of a Master in the Mark Chair the ceremony being performed under a Chapter Warrant. This is carried out during the period when the same Companion is at last being Installed as the First Principal in the Chapter, in the presence of First Principals only and in a quite separate room. It is during that ceremony that the installing Z carries out a ceremony very similar to that used in England and Wales for the installation of a WM in a Mark Chair. Hence the closest link between the Royal Arch Chapter and the Mark Degree is here preserved in that *no Craft Master in the Chair is able to confer the Mark Chair secrets* even though he carries out a Mark ceremony as a Craft Installed Master. To be a true Right Worshipful Master (RWM) in the Mark Degree you have to reach the pinnacle of Royal Arch Masonry in a Chapter.

In turning to the degree of Royal Ark Mariner we shall seek to follow the same pattern as with the Mark: to describe the setting, the significance and then the sequence of ceremonies in which it is set.

As will be explained more fully in Chapter 11 the Ark Mariner Degree can rightly claim as distinguished a pedigree in speculative masonry as the Mark can in the operative field. Its story is linked directly with the events recounted in Chapters 6 to 10 of the *Book of Genesis* and all known workings of this degree have kept the flood, the building work of Noah and his sons, the restoration to dry land, the subsequent thanksgiving with God's confirming sign of the Rainbow and the building of the Tower of Babel as the principal features of Ark Mariner ceremonies.

That important lessons were intended to be taught by these remarkable and dramatic stories is unquestioned. The very fact that in early eighteenth century masonic documents the very name given to the Brethren was **Noachidae** suggests that somehow the example and standing of Noah and his family in God's sight were important for Masons.

In this degree, as we have it today, Noah is honoured, with his sons, as the builder of the Ark of Safety, which prevented the extinction of the human race. The construction of the Ark was an act of great faith and the trust in God thus displayed was all the more impressive because it was not merely a matter of words but of very hard labour. Indeed the degree teaches reliance on God's direction and the need for practical prayer in action.

"As I understand it the teaching of the Royal Ark Mariner degree is that by Work character is formed. In the building of the Ark, despite ridicule and discouragement, Noah persevered from the triangle of Wisdom, Strength and Beauty to a new perfection: as the huge marine building grew under his hands so did his character develop and by toiling at its obstinate timbers Noah made smooth many rough edges of his tongue and soul."[1]

In a strange way, because it is by no means certain that this and the Mark Degree were ever intended to be linked, there are some common features that do make them suitable partners. There is the centrality of the triangle, the recognition of work well done, the rescue from possible disaster and the ultimate offering of thankful praise for the satisfying outcome.

Ark Masonry has promoted several songs or verses to commemorate its purpose and here we might usefully hear some words written by one whom we shall meet more fully later in this book, Ebenezer Sibly. These lines were composed at the end of the 18th century:

Within an **Ark Lodge** there can nothing reside
Belonging to **Malice**, base **Envy** or **Pride**;
For old Father Noah, doth teach his sons how,
To shun such Hell Fiends, as their dang'rous **Foe**.

Then let us unite, and Unanimous join,
To establish this Order, as Masons combine;
Then true **Sons** of **Wisdom**, once blind, soon shall see,
The long wish'd for **Zenith**, of ARK MASONRY.

Where does this distinctive and far too neglected degree fit in the Masonic system? Its past treatment, as we shall see later, has been somewhat varied if not erratic. Today its place has been clearly fixed.

In England and Wales the degree has the firm protection and direction of the Grand Lodge of Mark Master Masons and every Royal Ark Mariner lodge is firmly attached to, and can only be sponsored by, an existing local Mark Lodge. It is therefore the normal practice for most MMMs to pass on to become Ark Mariners in an RAM Lodge attached to their own Mark Lodge or to another convenient one. It is not permitted in England and Wales for a Mason to be installed in a Royal Ark Mariner Lodge Chair until he has been through the Chair of the Mark Degree, though in certain cases a dispensation from the Mark Province that controls the RAM can be applied for.

In Ireland the Ark Mariner degree is not now practised and therefore any Irish Mark Mason who might wish to attend a RAM ceremony in England or Wales must apply to become a candidate for the same and fulfil the same conditions as laid down in Grand Mark Lodge regulations.

In Scotland the RAM degree is controlled by the Supreme Grand Royal Arch Chapter of the country. As with the Mark degree the Officers in a Royal Arch Chapter occupy corresponding posts in the conferring of this degree in a

Lodge convened for that purpose. It is very important to note that this right of holding a Lodge of Royal Ark Mariners (or for that matter a corresponding Council of Red Cross Knights) is not an inherent privilege which comes with the Chapter warrant or Charter. To be permitted to confer the latter rites there must be issued a separate Charter to the Chapter allowing that privilege. For the full requirements in working this degree regularly in Scotland consultation of the current Constitutions and Laws of the Supreme Grand Chapter is essential.

Such then is some introduction to the degrees of Mark and Royal Ark Mariner as they exist at the time of this book's publication. The fuller story of how these degrees emerged and developed, of how their several rituals were formed and grew into the ceremonies known today is what will occupy the chapters that follow. It is hoped that the reader will already appreciate that whatever his interest in these topics there will be much here that can satisfy his particular concerns.

Chapter Two

Where did the Mark Degree come from?

IF THERE IS one refrain that is constantly repeated in any previous writing on the Mark degree, it is that this degree, more than any other, is connected with Operative Masonry. Two samples of this claim will have to suffice though they could be easily multiplied. One writer says: "To the question, 'What is the Mark Degree and what are its teachings?' I can at once answer that no degree in the whole Masonic system can lay claim to greater antiquity than this. It forms one of the closest links in the chain which connects the present speculative with the old operative system of Freemasonry."

Another writes: "The Grade of Mark Masonry contains a profound symbolism. It sets out to reinstate Operative Masonry as an essential part of the Craft which is operative only in speculation; but it ends itself in symbolism, and as symbolism it stands almost alone in the treasury of Masonic (practice)."

In the face of these recurring claims the student of Mark Masonry has to answer this question. What evidence is there of any kind of Operative practice with which anything like Mark Masonry could have been connected? Here let me admit at once that this question touches the whole matter of masonic origins in general. Clearly we cannot enter into that whole debate in this book. It may well be, however, that what is said here has to be reconsidered elsewhere in that connection.

AN OPERATIVE BEGINNING

There are those, of course, who hold that the primitive operative craft ritual was of such a simple, bald, unattractive, or so to speak, commonplace character that it was quite incapable of providing any pattern for even the developing forms of the early eighteenth century. Another view is that those who object to the claim of the Operative Free Masons that they were always divided into seven grades, on the grounds that that is too elaborate a division and suggests too involved a ritual for the ancient masons to have invented, is "an argument almost too futile for words."

"Just consider", continues this point of view, "who these ancient masons were and what buildings they erected. These were the men who built our Cathedrals and churches, hundreds of which still stand to testify to their skill (and that of) the bishops, abbots and priests who were associated with these masons (and) were often the architects themselves. That anyone should dare to suggest that such men as these could not invent, or as is more likely, perpetuate and develop a system and ritual such as the present-day Operative Free Masons practise, is incredible to anyone who knows the work these men did and the manner of men they were."[1]

Despite the apparent contrast between these two points of view Bro Gould is on record as saying that "The importance of the Mark Degree as a connecting link with the operative Masons' *customs and traditions* prior to the formation of the premier Grand Lodge is not always fully appreciated, particularly by those Freemasons under the obedience of the English Rite and Constitution." Perhaps Gould has here usefully pointed us to the missing factor in our search for origins. He speaks of 'customs and traditions' *rather than degree ceremonies*, suggesting not that we can derive from some ancient ritual texts an actual form of ceremony such as we are accustomed to today but that, lying-in-wait to be so employed in Speculative Freemasonry, there were long-standing forms of instruction as well as customary practices that could be so shaped. Eric Ward, another distinguished scholar Freemason, wrote in 1962 of a realisation amongst Masons "that material once possessing infinite mystical value had somehow been discarded (and) was capable of revival and expansion into a rite *purporting to restore* the genuine secrets. 'He also went on:' One of the peculiarities of ritual growth is that customs *discarded in one place turn up surprisingly in another* at a much later date." That is a profound insight into the development of speculative masonic practice that deserves much more comment but which again cannot be pursued here.

In the story which we are unfolding it encourages us to look afresh at what are the possible signs, not of *a Mark degree in the distant past* but of customs and teachings which, being perhaps overlooked or even laid aside later, would lead to their being re-adopted and formed into a more ceremonial shape. We also have to remind ourselves that what first emerge as probable material in the late 17th century are not fully fledged degree 'dramas' but collections of questions and answers or 'catechisms'. It we carry these points forward into our search we may be more encouraged by the information that is available.

THE CONTRIBUTION OF THE CRAFT GUILDS

According to an old German tradition stone-cutters were first banded together into a brotherhood at the building of Magdeburg Cathedral which was started in **1211**. Interestingly this date fits closely that mentioned by Milner in his "History of Winchester" where we learn that it was in **1202** that Bishop Lucy established a company of workmen to further the building of that Cathedral. That any such association had rules of entry, regular membership and stages of promotion is certain and by the *end of the thirteenth century* there is evidence that these lodges of stone-masons were separate from the monastic authority that would have been in control before that time.

Findel in his *History of Freemasonry* claims that these associations had their own special signs of recognition and methods of instruction in trade secrets, with their privileges and duties well understood. By 1352, in a statute of Edward III, there is the first official record of 'freemasons' and the acknowledgement of Operative Masons' Guilds. These had their regular procedures by which a lad was admitted as an apprentice, taught his work, and subsequently became entitled to practice his trade. Between 1390 and 1420 we have the oldest of a series of Regulations and Charges used by English freemasons and some eighty of these types of document bridge the period between then and the 18th century.

This, however, is only one aspect of the early years. Another is the existence of actual examinations and requirements for the masons of the 14th and 15th centuries. We shall need to look at these in terms of later Mark practice and instruction.

The training of an apprentice lasted normally seven years, though it might be no more than five and could even be twelve. At the end of this term, and if he had given satisfaction, he became a journeyman and though qualified as a fellow of the craft he was still under the Overseer's rod. He was free to find work wherever he could if none were available locally, but in order to prove his qualifications in a far from literate age – at least for workmen – two essential signs of competence were needed. These were a grip of recognition and a personal mark for placing on his work. Before coming to those specific features, however, it might be of interest to hear some of the questions and answers expected in a lodge of German Stonemasons at this period. A travelling 'Fellow' is applying for admission to a lodge in order to qualify him for local work. Among other questions which he is asked by *the* Warden (W) (*Note the singular*) and answers (A) are:

W. Approach: what is your request?
A: I desire to have my honest name inscribed in the book of the Craft as other honest fellows have done before me.
W. Stranger, are you a letter-mason or a salute-mason?
A: I am a salute-mason.
W. What was the name of the first mason?
A. Anton Hieronymus (Adonhiram) and the working tool was invented by Walkan (Tubalcain)
W. How many words has a Mason?
A. Seven.
W. What is secrecy in itself?
A. Earth, fire, air and snow, through which to honest promotion I go.
W. What is the best part of a wall?
A. Union.

We are also told that in his promise to the Craft on his being made a Fellow he "will disclose or say to no man the greeting or the hand-grip (Handschenk) of a mason, except to one to whom he should rightly say it; and also that he will put nothing thereof in writing".[2]

There is also evidence of a very interesting lodge custom which seems to be of considerable antiquity. "When a mason spoiled a stone it was christened 'Bernhardt' (and) the spoiled stone was carried on a bier to a place, some distance from the lodge, which was nicknamed 'Charnel-house'; all the journeymen accompanied the 'corpse' to its last rest. Next after the bier, as chief mourner, went the author of the crime; and when he came back to the hut he was subjected to a 'Prutsch' (a punishment of blows from his fellow-workers). I believe that the Charnel-house of the lodge at Regensburg has been recently discovered. Pieces of finished stone were found among stone-cutters' refuse, extending to a depth of some 12 feet below the present surface; and the cathedral architect... considers these to be 'evidently rejected masons' work' ". A similar case is quoted " ... of carved work found buried just outside one of the doors of Notre-Dame (Cathedral) in Paris."[3] The practice must surely suggest echoes of a much later Mark Degree practice, albeit not carried out with quite so much ceremony. This seems the reverse of the bald, simple customs of earlier times that some make so much of.

THE REGULATIONS OF THE STEINMETZEN

In the year 1452, Jacob Dotzinger, who was the Master-builder of the work at Strasburg Minster, was successful in uniting the existing lodges of Germany in a general or Grand body and was even nominated Grand Master. In 1459 at Regensburg the statutes and general regulations of the stone-cutters or masons were at last written down and after various revisions they received Imperial approval at the hands of the Emperor Maximilian in 1498.

One of the major revisions took place in 1462 in the Saxon town of Torgau when German stonemasons from the towns of Magdeburg, Meissen, Halberstadt, Hildesheim, Mollburg, Merseburg and the districts of Voightland, Thuringia and Harzland gathered to plan the still better government of the Operative masonic craft. What is significant in their declaration of purpose is that "important *changes had crept into* the masonic organisation and they intended to bring the internal organisation of Freemasonry *back to the established usages* and immemorial customs such as their predecessors had practised from a remote period." The words strangely reflect exactly the same aim of the eighteenth century 'Antient' Masons. Moreover the Constitutions thus agreed was thereafter read publicly at each annual communication of Masters and Fellows and strict conformity to it was required. It is worth remarking that these annual gatherings were actually called 'Chapters' and it was *during them that Fellows received the Grade of Master.* We now need to turn to some of the contents of these Regulations.

Regulation 25: A Fellow who has learned the work may appear before his Master and, on exhibiting proof of his skill, the Master may award him a mark.

Regulation 26: .... the Master shall, within 14 days of his becoming a Fellow, deliver to the new Craftsman his mark or token.

Regulation 30: An Apprentice shall only be permitted a mark if there be no work locally for his employment ... so that he may travel to seek work and obtain wages.

Regulation 59: Each Apprentice shall be given his mark on becoming a Fellow of the Craft.

Regulation 72: All work of a Fellow shall be examined by *the* Warden (see above, p16, and p40) and no mark shall be hewen on any stone unless the stone is found to be in harmony with the plans. If the mark is thus allowed then the craftsman shall be entitled to have his wages.

Regulation 109: If a travelling mason shall request a stone and chisel with which to carve his mark it shall be immediately given.

These extracts from what can be recognised as a highly organised arrangement of craft practices show us at last what took place in the closed recesses of a masons' lodge and also provide the earliest known references to the operative practice of taking and receiving a mark. Such a practice in an age when even basic education was still a privilege confined only to the clergy and certain sons of noble houses was clearly very important indeed. It was for the mason his seal and his diploma.

THE SIGNIFICANCE OF MASONS' MARKS

The study of Masons' Marks both throughout the centuries since Egyptian times and across the world from Ireland to India has been a thriving employment for a host of students. It would be both an impossibility and a digression even to attempt to summarise the main works on the subject. Yet there are three factors regarding the use of marks by stonemasons that should be mentioned because, as with the regulations of Torgau already referred to, they point the reader to elements that will later re-emerge as parts of the Mark ceremonies that are known today.

The first feature of the use of masons' marks is that they were personal. It was customary , in early and late mediaeval times, for each mason to adopt some small device or mark which became his peculiar property, and we know that at least in Germany and Scotland this was generally registered with his name in the book of the lodge. The German stonemasons were required to swear an oath that they would never alter the form of their individual marks, whilst in Scotland the Schaw Statutes of 1598, which were devised by the King's Master Mason for the proper control of the Craft, include the following words:

"That on the day of receiving the said Fellow of Craft or Master *he be orderly booked* and his name and *mark inserted* in the said book". Interestingly, William Schaw followed his own ruling, for at an assembly of masons held at the Lodge of Edinburgh on 8 June, 1600, he attested the minutes of the meeting by appending his personal mark in the minute book.

The minute book of the Lodge of Aitchison's Haven, the oldest extant record of any Lodge (and still preserved in the museum of the Grand Lodge of Scotland) contains an entry for the year 1598, recording the marks adopted by new brethren.

Furthermore, there are other early records in Scotland that indicate that when non-operative members were accepted into an Operative Lodge from 1600 onwards such persons who were devoid of any experience, skill or training in the craft of stonemasonry, were yet permitted to select their distinguishing mark.

One of the most notable examples of such a practice is the Mark Book still preserved from 1670 by the Lodge Aberdeen 1ter (sic). It can be seen there that in 1670 the lodge consisted of 49 Fellowcrafts or Master Masons and 11 Apprentices. Only about 10 of the 49 names in the list of members fall within the definition of operative masons. Whether or not the list of marks began with at least the lodge of 1541 in the town we cannot know. But the fact is that when this book was *re-bound in* 1748 the Boxmaster who undertook the task only pasted into the new volume 28 at least 147 pages of the original Mark book that would thus take it back long before 1670.

Bro. Springett, in writing about Masons' Marks (*The Mark Degree*), has some further useful comments on the matter of personal selection. "The mason did not adopt his mark and device *indiscriminately* nor was it left to his own caprice and invention, for often many strange and bizarre forms would then be found amongst masons' marks and they could not exhibit the same similarity and characteristics which are so noticeable in them."[4] Three courses were apparently open to him:

1) He might adopt his father's mark, but rarely did so.
2) He might adopt one of the old traditional marks common amongst the Masonic Order.
3) He might devise one of his own construction, as he ought rightly to do, but according to a prescribed manner.

In England the only known instance thus far of personal marks being recorded in an operative lodge that was accepting non-operatives is the register of the lodge at Alnwick. Prior to 1680 the Operative Lodge kept records which actually remained extant until 1919 when the widow of the last man to hold them burnt them after his death not realising their importance. Even so there are still available minute books from 1701 and it is these early ones that show us the same situation here as in the books of lodges further north. Sadly, in the Swalwell Operative Lodge meeting on South Tyneside there was not a similar record though, as we shall soon see, that lodge had its own peculiar contribution to make to our story.

The second feature of masons' marks that we need to consider is that they were marks of approval. It may be recalled that the Torgau regulations forbade a mason to engrave his work with his mark until the stone had been inspected and passed by the Master or lodge Warden. With that approval the craftsman is permitted to seal the work lying on his work-bench or stone-bed, called a 'banker', before it left the yard or shed, and thus the 'task-masters' could later verify the amount of weekly work done by each craftsman when pay-day came round. The title 'task-master' given to the supervisor was a very correct one since the qualified mason was engaged in 'task-work', or piece work, and was not paid on a time basis. Thus we have the corporation regulation for London masons of 1356: "That the Master shall oversee that all the journeymen shall take for their hire according as they are skilled and may deserve for their work pieces, and not outrageously". The banker-mark was thus by way of being a business-voucher imposed upon the mason from above; it signified originally, "*You must* sign your work" rather than "*I want to* sign my stone". This approach seems to have changed steadily until such marks became increasingly artistic as if the stone-mason was now showing his great satisfaction with the work he had carried out.

In addition to these 'banker-marks' there were also positioning marks which have been confused with them. Coulton explains this very clearly:

> "The classical example here is that of the west front of Reims Cathedral. At Notre-Dame-de-Paris, a little earlier than this, some of the elaborate statuary had been built into wrong places by the setters, thus confusing the sequence of subjects which had been thought out by the directing authorities and worked out in the lodge.
>
> "The Reims master-mason was evidently determined to have no such confusion; every stone, therefore, was carefully marked. One symbol denoted a particular side of a particular portal, another denoted more exactly the place of the statue or statuette within the lines of this general indication. For instance, the general sign for the north side of the great central portal is a crescent and, as there are five great statues on each side, these are further marked with *one* straight line for the nearest to the door, *two lines* for the next, and so on. The plainest instance, conspicuous in any photograph, is (the statue of) St. Joseph who comes fourth and therefore bears a crescent with 4 lines. So, again, on the south side of the southern portal .... the general sign is a TAU-cross (T) sometimes upright and sometimes reversed; masons often showed great indifference on that score. It can just be traced on the Archangel Gabriel (who is first, whilst the) next figure is clearly marked with a – III on a broad hand fold of the skirt ...." [5]

What is of **further interest** to the Mark Mason in this connection is the fact that "position-marks were more commonly placed on the bed or the joint of the stone, and can therefore only be studied in a ruined building.... At St. Mary Redcliffe, Bristol, the restorers had the good sense to lay the discarded stones of window-tracery in the churchyard." [6]

Despite all this highly organised arrangement for the right forming and placing of stones there is also the astonishing but proven fact that there were both signed *and unsigned* stones in most buildings. Yet, on reflection, we may see that this fits in with the rest of the story. In any large establishment the employees tend to separate into two categories, a permanent staff and a more or less casual section. In a MS register of Canterbury Cathedral from about **1413** we start with the regular servants of the monastery including carpenters, tylers and masons. But after **1428** we have a new heading of 'Lathomi de la Loygge' who came and settled down for a brief period, forming a lodge. Since the banker-mark was a check on quality and the amount of workmanship it is quite likely that once a man's capacity was locally recognised he would cease to mark his stones unless it was, as I earlier suggested, a matter of pride in some special work achieved. The facts submitted by collectors of building marks suggest, however, that the best-cut stones are the least often signed and Coulton says, "plain capitals are seldom marked after the Norman period; and really artistic capitals, so far as my experience goes, *never.*" [7]

We turn thirdly to an understanding of the building marks as a form of cryptic language. When the Fellow-craft freemason devised his own form of mark it was not at all surprising if he used his own daily language or else his name and initials. We know, for instance, that in the early Middle Ages masons in Southern France used their full name as a banker-mark, whilst others spelt their Christian names in capital letters separately or else joined together. Elsewhere it seems most probable that, originally, the mark system used was not that invented by the workmen but was one imposed by local superiors. It was thus very likely to have been created on a definite plan and with clear guide-lines.

Springett refers to a Professor Hoffmeyer who mentions a 'mother-diagram', or key-diagram, upon which was based the marks of the masons found on Strasburg Cathedral, the diagram having been discovered by the architect Arnold of Strasburg. From this key every stone-mason was supposed to have selected conjoined lines as his mark. The Professor also mentions that in the year 1828 a mason named Kirchner of Nuremberg possessed a book which derived all the individual marks from such a common source.

W.H. Rylands in a once well-known work says that this system of derivation has been elaborately worked out by a Professor Rxiha. (The latter)

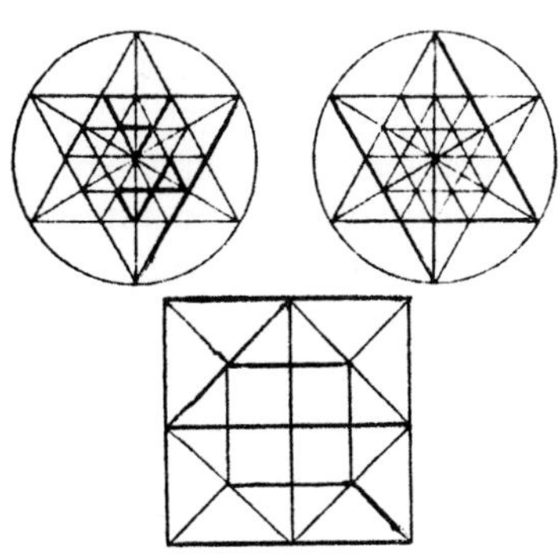

claims that he has discovered the 'mother-diagram' of the Masons of Nuremberg, Prague, Dresden, Strasburg, Cologne, Vienna and other towns.[8] The relevance of this aspect of marks and the studies on it will become more obvious as we pursue the development of the Mark Degree in the eighteenth century and after.

Meanwhile we can usefully consult an article on 'Masonry and Letters' which was written by Sir John Cockburn of Australia. His main claim is "that the association which has always existed between Masonry and the sacred writings may in some measure be explained by regarding the forms of the letters used in the ancient alphabets as derived from symbols composed of elementary forms, such as straight lines, curves, angles, circles and segments similar to those which have at various times been adopted as masons' marks, signs of the Zodiac, planetary signs..."

He continues: "Masons' marks are of extreme antiquity and bear a general resemblance even when found in widely separated countries. Among the masons' marks which have found a place in the Greek and Roman alphabets are:

A Z Δ T N V H θ ʘ

The last of these letters is an ancient form of Theta, so called after Taaut or Thoth, who is credited with the invention of the alphabet. He it was who introduced the worship of the serpent, which is still the symbol of the Letter 's'. Philo states that a coiled serpent with its head in the centre represents the all-seeing eye of God in the world and we are back into some aspect of the Fellow Craft stage of Masonry. Sir John further pointed that although the masonic square appears as the Gamma Γ in the Greek and mediaeval ecclesiastical alphabets, and as L in Latin, it does not seem to have been much used as a mason's mark. As a symbol of deity it was possibly regarded as too sacred for

such a purpose. These right angles, however, combined to form H, a swastika, and the Cross. He therefore judges that the link of Masonry with letters was intimate. This was not only because the marks of masons provided the prototypes of several of the letters of the alphabet but because letters, having a symbolic as well as a phonetic value, could not fail to provide an interesting subject of research for Freemasons[9]. The relevance of this kind of study in marks and letters will appear when we come to the matter of cypher alphabets. Indeed one writer has summed it up in the words, "True masons' marks are merely the cyphers of operative workmen."

We cannot leave this section on marks, however, without noting two other pieces of evidence. F.G. Harmer made the claim from a careful study of marks in various countries that they roughly divide into two classes:

1. Those of the Overseers.
2. Those of the men who worked the stone.

Those in the first class were generally monogrammatic, that is, a single line or two, and those in the second were symbols, eg. trowels, mallets, shoes, etc. It was also generally found that the man who had worked the stone made his mark on the internal face. At the present day we find that the cutter of the stone still places his mark on the inside surface of the stone whilst the builder puts his on the outside.[10]

This latter discovery was further illuminated by part of the lecture given by T.B. Whytehead in 1883 when he told a Bradford audience that even in their day the Operative Masons carried out the same practices as their forebears and in their work could be seen the identical usages that characterised the men who wrought with mallet and chisel upon palaces and temples. He told them how a Bro. Cumberland of York drew his attention to the fact that in the restoration work on York Minster the masons were making use of marks which were of a character and class well known in Speculative Freemasonry. He even described a visit to their workshop (alias Lodge) where the stonecutting was in progress. Here he found the Overseer superintending his Craftsmen with the drawing or tracing board that had the design for the intended structure placed on a table. Each stone bore the mark of the Craftsman who was to be responsible for executing the work in the area.[11]

In regard to the character of the marks that were allowed for the masons' use in operative times there was a distinction that has perhaps been overlooked by those who have imagined, or even claimed, that marks were made by mallet and chisel and that therefore they must of necessity be composed of straight lines. The old ritual of Chapter Esk No 42 in Scotland, however, states clearly that 'straight or curved lines' are permitted and Springett tells us that in Operative days marks were broadly divided into two classes, Square Masons' Marks and Arch Masons' Marks, and generally, whenever a mark is curved, that would be known as an Arch Masons' mark or had come down from Arch Masons in the past. Thus we come to the last but perhaps the most important part of our enquiry into where the Mark Degree came from. We examine the traditional and continuing division of work amongst those who belong to Operative Free Masonry.

It was in 1890 that R.F. Gould stated his case that the Manuscript Consitutions afforded conclusive evidence that the story of Masonry must be looked for in the history of the Craft as it has come down to us. He was also strongly of the opinion that the class of persons who constructed the Craft legend in the fourteenth century or earlier were people who understood much better than we can the symbolism which has descended from ancient to modern masonry. He therefore urged that the study of our written traditions should go hand in hand with a study of our symbolism. It is in the spirit of that wise advice that we move from the exercise and meaning of old symbolic practices to the writings and traditional history of our predecessors.

In a fifteenth century copy of the *History and Articles of Masonry* there is the bald statement that "at the making of the temple in Solomon's time as it is said in the Bible .... Solomon had four score thousand masons at his work. And the King's son, of Tyre, was his master mason."

In the York Roll of the *Constitutions of Masonrie* of 1704 we learn that Solomon "sent for Masons into Divers Countrys (*sic*) and of Divers Lands and gathered them together so that he had Four score Thousand workers of stone and were all named Masons and he chose out of them three Thousand that was Ordained to be Masters and governers of his Worke ..."

In another document which was to provide the figures used in the later historical lecture of the Royal Arch we learn that a vast number of Masons were employed on that building with their names and marks. Besides the 80,000 operatives employed in the quarries and at the Temple, a further 30,000 were in the Forests of Lebanon. These 110,000 men had 1100 lodges with three Masters in each lodge, and the 3,300 Masters had 100 lodges of their own, with 33 in each lodge. As regards their marks each Fellowcraft had his own to distinguish his work and each of the Masters had the same mark of a special kind of which the use was restricted to them and the Overseers.

This evident process of steadily increasing detail was carried one stage further in the year 1769 when Wellins Calcott provided the following list in his *'Candid Disquisition of the Principles and Practices of the Most Ancient and Honourable Society of Free and Accepted Masons'; together with some strictures on the 'Origin, Nature and Design of the Institution'.*

In that work he classified the type and number of the workmen as:

1. HARODIM. Princes, Rulers or Masters. 300
2. MENATZCHIM. Overseers and Comforters of the people. 3300
3. GHIBLIM. Stone squarers, Polishers and Sculptors, with
   ISH GHOTZEB, Men of hewing, and
   BENAI, Setters, Layers, or Builders,
   being able and ingenious Fellow-Crafts 80,000
   THE LEVY out of Israel, appointed to work in Lebanon, one
   month in three, under the direction of **Adoniram** as
   Junior Grand Warden. 30,000
   ISH SABBAI, or Men of burthen, who were the remains of the old Canaanites,
   and are not numbered among Masons. 70,000

Acknowledging his awareness of the previous numbers Calcott added a footnote: 'This gives a much larger number of workmen than is embraced in the usual Masonic enumeration which does not commonly include the 300 Masters nor the 30,000 under Adoniram.'

The question that must now be answered is where did Calcott and the author of the material to be used in the later Royal Arch historical lecture get their information? The answer to this query provides, I believe, the final solution to our quest in this whole chapter.

The material was held by the Operative Free Masons who by the second quarter of the eighteenth century also had their own catechisms, lectures and rituals which embraced the traditions, customs and practices from which the Speculative Masons adapted their own more restricted models. It is not possible here to survey the whole field of masonic development but we must look at those sections of the Operative workings which point to the source of later Mark, and even Royal Ark Mariner, practice. It ought perhaps to be said at this point that nothing that is revealed in this book is being so done for the first time. All the information has been printed in Masonic journals in earlier days and with the express approval of the present Operative Society concerned.

For those who know nothing of the past in this connection it should be noted that a Guild of Operative Free Masons flourished in England until about 1870. It then diminished owing to altered economic conditions and the growing influence of the Trade Unions. By the time of the First World War there were only a few of its lodges existing and it was from a lodge of over 300 members at Bardon in Leicestershire that there came a member, Thomas Carr, who provided much of the material that follows. He was greatly helped in his presentation by Clement Stretton who was a senior member of the Leicestershire Operatives, and it was his copy of the ritual which was eventually presented to myself by a Past Third Grand Master of the present speculative Order who had himself held it for much of his lifetime. It was only in preparing this book that the full significance of what I possessed began suddenly to dawn upon me.

The full title of the originally Operative body with which we are here concerned was "The Worshipful Society of Free Masons, Rough Masons, Wallers, Slaters, Paviors, Plaisterers and Bricklayers." Such a title, comprising so many distinct trades, is perhaps at first sight rather curious but it was not at all an uncommon state of affairs in England in the seventeenth century. In Oxford in 1604 a Company was incorporated that comprised Free Masons, Carpenters, Joiners and Slaters in that city. In Kendal in 1667 the twelfth Trade Company comprised Free Masons, Rough Masons, Wallers, Plaisterers, Slaters and Carpenters.

Yet it is in the City of Durham that we find exactly the same trades combined as in the overall parent Society. In 1594 the Prince Bishop of Durham, Matthew Hutton, had incorporated the Rough Masons, Wallers and Slaters whilst in 1609 Bishop James confirmed the bye-laws and ordinances of a body that had added Paviors, Tylers and Plaisterers, Finally, on 16 April 1638, Bishop Morton, acting in his capacity as a Count Palatine, gave a new charter to "The Company Societie and the Fellowshipp of Free Masons Rough Masons Wallers Slaytors Pavers Plaisterers and Bricklayers". These operatives became Freemen of the City of Durham and many of the gentry of the County became Honorary Members of the Company, regarding it as an honourable distinction.

The same is still true of professional and business men joining the Honourable or Livery Companies in the City of London to this day. In London, by the mid-seventeenth century, the Paviors and Slaters had already become small but separate companies, and the Company of Masons had decided to drop the term 'Free' because all the members of other companies had to be freemen before they could be admitted to 'the Livery'. The term 'Free' in the Masons' case might have had other connotations but the reason they dropped the word in the City was the one stated.

In the year 1677 'The Worshipful Society of the Free Masons of the City of London' (note: not the Company) issued a map of England on which was shown the division of the Operatives into eight districts:-

(1) City of London	(2) Westminster
(3) Southern	(4) Bristol
(5) Chester	(6) Island of Anglesea (*sic*)
(7) Lancaster	(8) York

These divisions may be seen to have a peculiar relevance and interest as our story unfolds.

From their earliest period of existence the Operative Masons were divided into two classes – Straight or Square Masons, and Round or Arch Masons. The reason for this was that the straight work needed less skill, and hence was able to command less wages, than the art of making arches, bridges and all kinds of curved or graved work. The two classes were each divided into seven grades:-

Apprentice to the Craft of Free Mason.
Fellow of the Craft of Free Mason.
Super Fellow, who had his mark.
Super Fellow Erector, who worked on the stone construction.
Super-Intendent of the Craft, or Menatzchim.
Passed Master of the Craft, who had literally 'passed a technical examination' to attain the position of a Master, as Masters of sailing vessels still have to qualify. He was thus a properly certificated Master who was also known, especially in the North east of England, as a Harod (plural: Harodim).
Master Mason, or Grand Master of the Craft of Free Masons.

The traditional reason given why the Operative Free Masons needed to be thus graded was because when Solomon began to build the Temple on Mount Moriah he needed specific persons for its different stages and tasks. Thus he could ensure that 'the house shall be built of stone made ready before it was brought hither: so that there shall be neither hammer nor axe nor any tool of iron heard in the house while it was in building'. That required careful planning and strict administration to ensure that every stone was made to a required size and gauge in the second degree stone-yard. It was then fitted and marked by the Mark Men in the third degree yard so that the erectors on the actual building site could quietly set each stone in its indicated place.

It is thus that the Operative system of employing 'course' and 'base' marks, to ensure correct positioning and accountability, was preserved by the Society until its demise. The system was fallible and there is one Operative story of how a keystone and a North east cornerstone were wrongly marked, with the result that delay was caused just when the Temple was nearly completed. The workers of the stone were however correctly identified and punished.

A man was allowed to belong to only one of the two classes (ie, the Square or the Arch Masons) but he was allowed to transfer from one to the other if the Masters so ordered it.

When a young man was apprenticed, at the age of 14 after **1663,** though previously it had been at 12 or 13 years of age, he chose in which class he wished to serve. It is also to be noted that an apprentice was not regarded as being a member of the Craft. Indeed a General Assembly was held by the Operative rulers in Wakefield on 8 **December 1663,** where they agreed that no person should be accepted a Freemason until he was 21 years of age. (It is worth recording that to this day the Craft in the USA does not accept an apprentice as a full member of the lodge. The influence on Freemasonry as it came to be practised in North America is also part of our story.)

If the young man decided to be a Straight Mason he was given a square and if an Arch Mason the compasses. If therefore you might want to find a hostelry where both classes of working masons would congregate you looked for a inn with the sign: The Square and Compasses. The very combination of these implements in present Freemasonry reveals that materials and customs from both classes were adapted in order to form the new practice after 1717.

The real Secrets and the real Ritual of the Operative 'Masters' could not be given as but few knew them, namely, only those who had actually been one of the three Grand Masters (Seventh degree) by whom the Operatives were ruled and though Dr. Anderson was once a Chaplain in an Accepted Lodge he was *not privy to all its secrets.* The Three Grand Masters were of course the same for both Square and Arch Masonry but their apparent non-involvement in any plans for the newer type of Masonry meant that much was left out that would have helped to explain omissions that were soon noticed by older Operative members. It was this, and Irish tradition, that helped in the formation of Arch Masonry and subsequently the practices of the Antients from the 1750s.

The colour of the Square Mason was blue whilst the Arch Mason was distinguished by red. A lot of time and ingenuity in discussing the origin and appropriateness of masonic colours could have been saved if only this traditional fact were better known. These colours are clearly illustrated if one examines the original Arms of the Society of the Free Masons granted by Edward IV and which eventually had two supporters. The one on the right side was a mason with a *square* in his hand and with blue-facings on his jacket, whilst the figure balancing him on the other side is an Arch Mason with *red* facings and holding a *pair of compasses.* Once again we have aids to our style of regalia, and the ceremonial details that follow will show even more clearly the missing items that were in due time to emerge as parts of the Mark Degree.

THE OPERATIVES AT WORK

The lodge room for the Operatives working up to the old fifth degree was oriented so that the three Grand Masters, sitting side by side as in several of our present masonic ceremonies, were *in the West* in order *to face* the rising sun. The Junior Warden sat *in the North to mark* the sun at its meridian, and the Senior Warden sat in the east so as *to observe* the setting sun. Seeing the sun's light is, after all, quite important in Mark Masonry. This was the same orientation as of the Holy Place in the Temple at Jerusalem and it also explains why Antient Freemasons insisted on this type of lodge formation for the principal officers. The altar was in the centre of the lodge (another Scottish, Irish and American custom still) and there were three Deacons, the Master also being so served.

The entry of the *Apprentice* in such a lodge is to be noted. He was hoodwinked, clothed in a white cloak but he also had a blue cord around his middle, the end held taut by two brethren, one on each side. In addition one man in front and one behind held the ends of another blue cord around his neck. Thus was formed *a diamond of five points* which had not only Operative but subsequent Mark significance. When asked how he hoped to obtain admission he claimed the help of El Shaddai and being 'F.a.o.G.R.'. When he came to his obligation he knelt at the central altar, which had a rough ashlar to the East of it, and placed his left hand flat under the V.S.L. whilst laying his right hand flat upon it. This is of course still preserved in lodges under the Grand Lodge of Scotland as the 'due guard' sign. The candidate then took an obligation which remained the same from when it was first written out and signed by Robert Padgett, Clerk to the Worshipful Society of Free Masons of London in 1686. One copy is supposed to have been taken by Dr. Anderson but is now in the possession of the Lodge of Antiquity. A similar oath is found in the Kilwinning MS No 4, which only serves to emphasize its antiquity. Once again we see the pre-Grand Lodge provenance of Operative practices.

Moving on to the *Fellow of the Craft* degree, the candidate had to prepare a rough dressed ashlar as a specimen of his work and the Inspector of Material had to pass it before he could proceed. He also had to *have this specimen with him* when he entered the lodge and must declare that it was all his own work. He was obligated, given the sign with the right hand flat, and the word, Banai, meaning 'Builder'. The charge that was delivered was one that was also produced by Robert Padgett in 1686 and signed by him for use in all the eight divisions of the country. Two of its provisions are noteworthy:

1) 'You shall honour El Shaddai and his Holy Church: that you use no Heresy, Schism nor Error in your Undertakings, or discredit wise Men's teachings.

4) 'You shall keep Secret the obscure and intricate Parts of the Science, not disclosing them to any but such as study and use the same.'

The candidate now receives the sign and word as above but in addition to the usual tools he is also given another straight edge, the two foot rule and the perfect Ashlar Square. The latter is a wooden frame with overlapping corners which is the exact size of a Royal Cubit. He is now a Free Man and a Free Mason and is directed to begin work in the North-east corner of the yard where he is to make his rough dressed Ashlar into a stone true and polished.

When completed his work has to be submitted for inspection and tried so that, if satisfactory, he might receive the word 'Giblim' which meant 'stone squarer' or 'expert mason'. Interestingly the words of this Operative degree suggest how the adaptation and re-arrangement took place after 1717. It is known that Dr. Anderson was aware of these words because he mentions them in the 1738 edition of the Book of *Constitutions* but because, as we have noted, he had an imperfect knowledge of their place and use he and/or others used them differently.

The Mason having made his test piece he had it approved by the Inspector of Materials and having served another year as a Fellow he was now eligible to apply for the degree of Super Fellow. Notice having been given by a form posted in the yard, and the sign, word and work having been presented, the candidate entered into what the Speculative Mark Mason of today would recognize as the degree of Mark Man. The Super Fellow is allotted his Mark and is charged to produce ' fare work and square'. He is led round the lodge three times and takes his obligation kneeling on his bare knees and on the polished stone he brought with him.

His next step is that of Erector and here we discover a ceremony very close to that of the other half of the earlier Mark Master. It is at this point that an interesting distinction occurs. The stone that is found to be missing amongst Square Masons is the *chief corner stone.* whilst among the Arch Masons it is the *keystone.* The moral that is pointed up is the same in both ceremonies but for the Mark Mason of today we have here a solution of what seems in our present working a surprising confusion about which stone is being sought.

Amongst the Operatives being 'heaved over' refers to the negligent workmen who failed to 'mark well' and, more in accordance with the spirit of biblical times, they were *discarded* over a drop of 30 cubits. The candidate takes his obligation this time kneeling on a perfect polished stone, is led *four* times round the lodge and the word and sign given are those of the degree today. This was as far as most Operative Masons ever went since considerable technical knowledge was required before proceeding further. What is to be noted is that every Operative Mason did have all the MARK knowledge that awaits us today.

In the remaining Operative customs there were, however, some features that we need to take note of. The term 'Superintendent' comes from their fifth degree, thus showing its subordinate status to that of the Grand Master in the Arch class, whilst for Mark Masons the word of the degree, 'Menatzchim', has a more familiar ring.

The 'Passed Master' or sixth degree requires that a candidate shall be able to 'lay schemes, draw plans, and take charge of a department' of the work. With this step defined it can be understood why the Antients insisted that here one had a separate and *essential* degree before moving on to Arch Masonry. Moreover the senior Passed Master was called 'Adoniram' and was, in effect, a General Manager responsible directly to the Grand Masters. The word of this degree was 'Harod' or 'Harodim'. From the limited lodge of 15 members in this grade *three members only* were able to proceed to the long-serving degree of Grand Master. They were led round the lodge room seven times and, according to the class they were in, they represented either the Craft Grand Masters, Solomon, Hiram and Hiram Abiff, or the Three Principals as we know them in a Royal Arch Chapter today (except in Ireland). In the lodge room a new arrangement was now adopted as it had been since the sixth degree started.

The three Grand Masters now sat together in the West but at the top of seven steps. Below the steps sat Adoniram and in the East were the two pillars with Passed Masters behind them, facing west. B...was on the left facing east, and J..... on the right. In addition the Masters were thought to be seated on Mount Moriah, the pillar B... was considered to be Mount Tabor and J..... was Mount Sinai. It is from this arrangement that the names of the situations used in Grand and Provincial Lodge meetings are derived. On the occasion of the Annual Assembly the three Masters do not open their lodge privately behind a veil as usual but do it openly assisted by the Sixth degree Passed Masters. During this ceremony the 18 form into groups of three and say the word of their meeting by syllables. The word is 'SAN – HE – DRIM'.

It was at the Foundation Commemoration Day each year in April that the first Grand Master would quote the passages from 1 *Kings* regarding a levy of 30,000 men and that 'neither hammer nor axe nor any tool of iron shall be heard in the house while building' and thus the need for 'marking well' was underlined.

Such, in outline, were the features of older Operative practices that particularly relate to the Mark degree(s) and when we come later to the development of the Mark rituals in the eighteenth and nineteenth centuries we shall look in still more detail at the actual words of Operative practice. These were preserved first in an old cypher language called 'Turanian' and then transcribed in the late eighteenth century.

I have no doubt that there will be some readers who will query whether the Operative Society did not receive its forms and ritual **from** the Speculatives and not the other way round. *If that were so* then we have two further and apparently insoluble questions to tackle. The first: Where **did the Speculatives get** their original information and basis of practice from? And the second: Why are there differences between the two systems with the Operatives having material that is not used by the Speculatives, and with the latter always employing material that is much more logically explained when set within the larger Operative scheme? Nowhere that I have been able to find is there an attempt to face and wrestle with these necessary issues.

On the contrary there is something else. On 6 January **1911** an historical note was published by the United Grand Lodge of England. It read as follows: 'The Ritual of Freemasonry, as far as the First and Second Degrees are concerned, is IN PART (*sic*) *no doubt derived from the ceremonies of the early Operative Guilds.*' Here at last we have the admission of the sequence and source of derivation and *from the Grand Lodge itself*. One would have thought the author to be more accurate had he added, 'the Third Degree and the Mark' to the Sections which were mentioned but then that might have given the whole game away and in any case officially the Grand Lodge cannot acknowledge the Mark Degree, even as a development of a long lost part of the Second Degree. The author might however have usefully reflected on these words from a *History of Freemasonry* published in 1865.

"Originating from the Fraternity of Operative Masons, the Craft has borrowed its emblems and symbols from the building Corporations to impart to its members moral truths and the rules of the Royal Art." How that happened through the Craft so as to produce the first glimpses of a future Speculative Mark degree is the next part of our story.

Chapter Three

How did the Mark Degree emerge?

"IT IS QUITE certain that when a revised and modified Masonry was founded in the early years of the 18th century there were *many essential points* in Operative Masonry which were not carried over into the newer rituals ... Doubtless some of these omissions were wise and calculated to facilitate the establishment of Moral or Speculative Masonry ... Anderson and those associated with him were chiefly concerned to embody references to such trade methods and tools as to their mind the more readily lent themselves to symbolism and allegory of a moral kind. But *unfortunately much was left out which it is necessary to know* in order to understand some of the symbols themselves and to grasp properly the meaning of some of the references which remain in the ritual."[1]

Whether or no this is a completely correct analysis of the situation around the time of the formation of the first Grand Lodge the result of what then took place was that anything resembling the sections of the Operative 3rd and 4th degrees which referred to Mark practices was omitted. In a precise sense it was not the "Mark" customs and ceremonies that were lost but integral parts of the "Fellow of the Craft" degrees. It is for this reason that so many later students were to declare that 'the Mark belonged to the Fellow Craft degree' or, bearing in mind the Operative system, that 'the Mark was an essential preliminary to Arch Masonry'. It is as we begin to recognise the new context in which this whole subject is set that we can read afresh the intimations of the Mark in the first half of the 18th century. Let us therefore re-view the information we have, even if some of it is fairly well known, and begin with England.

In 1677 the London Masons' Company was incorporated by Charter from the Crown and the control was vested in a Master, two wardens and 24 or more assistants, the latter being chosen for life. As in the previous century the Company continued to exercise trade functions which mainly centred round the preservation of the monopoly of trade in the City and *the search for faulty work*. With the first of these tasks we shall not here concern ourselves but the second is of special interest to any Mark Mason. Knoop and Jones have written as follows about this aspect of the Company.

"There were two types of false work which it was the business of the Company to try to suppress – bad workmanship and the use of defective materials. So far as we can judge, relatively little attention was devoted to the first type; on the other hand, the 'search' of Purbeck stone, in particular, was a not insubstantial source of revenue to the Company ... and Orders for the Company of Freemasons, 1580, laid down special provisions regarding Purbeck stone and Purbeck paving, the use of which was rapidly increasing. Ill-wrought and undersized stones were forfeited and broken by the officials of the Company as late as the beginning of the 18th century ... The last general search which we have been able to trace was held in 1704, when a small quantity of stone was broken."[2]

The particular significance of these facts for our purpose is to emphasise in an Operative setting a practice that would also have been well known to the Accepted members of the lodge that was formed in the 17th century in the London Masons' Company. The rejection or 'heaving over' of work or workmen was a practical reality in the 17th just as much as in the 15th century and as far as the 'Mark' sections of any Operative ceremonies were concerned it was central and necessary. Indeed we shall do well in looking at the material set out in this and the succeeding chapter to keep in mind some very sound advice given by J.A.Grantham in 1935:

"The Mark degree, as now worked, is essentially a 'Rejection' Grade. It should be noted that whilst stones of shapes other than the familiar Key-stone have been employed at various times as the central symbol, the relative rituals were based on the 'Rejection' *motif*... There were other 'Mark' grades in practice in the 18th and 19th centuries which lacked this motif and these must not be confounded with modern Mark Masonry."[3]

By the year 1722 this important factor was referred to in a book translated from the French but published in England. It contains the following lines:

"Ye are living stones, built up (into) a spiritual House, who believe and rely on the chief Lapis Angularis which the refractory and disobedient Builders disallowed ..." Here we have already the beginning of the later intermingling of Key-stone and Cornerstone rejection but in the light of what we learnt in the last chapter we should not be surprised at this double usage. (See p. 29) And the same applies to the term 'Arch'.

In the well-worn passage that occurs in the 1723 edition of the Constitutions of the Grand Lodge of England we read three things:

i) of the '**freeborn** BRITISH NATIONS ... having of late much indulg'd their happy Genius for Masonry of every sort' – which surely meant the practice of Operative *and* Speculative Masonry, not to mention variations or classes of practice within those two main groups;
ii) of how 'this fair **Metropolis** flourishes, as well as other Parts, with several worthy **particular** Lodges, that have a quarterly **Communication**, and an annual **grand Assembly**, wherein the **Forms** and **Usages** of the most ancient and worshipful Fraternity are wisely propagated' – which must refer to at least the burgeoning Grand Lodge at York as well as the many operative lodges north of that city. It is the recognition of a wider and older Freemasonry that was continuing in the country at large despite what happened in London, and of other practices maintained there; and

iii) of how 'the whole Body resembles a well-built **Arch**' – not of course an early reference to any particular Royal Arch legend or ceremony but to the whole panoply of Masonry which, as we have already seen, was thought of as culminating in well-rounded Arch skills ruled over by the three Masters.

Is it then at all surprising that but eleven days before the issuing of these Constitutions there should have appeared in *The Daily Post* of London the following advertisement:

"This Day is publish'd, The FREE-MASONS. An Hudibrastick Poem. Illustrating the whole History of the Ancient Free-Masons, from the Building of the Tower of Babel to this Time, with their Laws, Ordinances, Signs, *Marks*, Messages, Etc. *so long* kept Secret ..."

It was, of course, an attack on the Craft and not the first of its kind that accused it of being 'pretentious' since, as was said in a public letter of 7 July 1722, Masons are 'a Set of Low Gentry among our Artificers'. Certainly this poem made much of the trade connections of the brethren whose

"... sev'ral **Rules** and **Orders** made,
Relating to the Mason Trade,
Shou'd be observ'd as long as Time."

It was not of Masons in their Operative guise but as Speculatives that the writer of this poem addresses his audience. He relates one of the very 'legends' that Anderson will shortly be making public in his History of Freemasonry – the story of the Tower of Babel – and here, says the poem, when the masons could not complete their task however hard they tried,

"They then resolved no more to rome,
But to return to their own Home;
Tho' first they Signs *and Marks* did frame,
to signify from whence they came;
that whereso'er these Men shou'd go,
they always might their Breth'ren know ..."

The nature of the Freemasonry which this critic addressed is made perfectly plain some 15 lines later:

"BUT since, 'tis found, the Masons-Free,
which in our modern Times we see,
Workmen are of **another kind**,
To Sport they're more than Toil inclin'd
they have no Trowels, nor yet Lines,
But *still retain their Marks* and Signs."

For anyone to maintain that the presenting of marks was some kind of ceremony only known in remote areas or certain lodges away from London is surely an untenable view. This was, or was to become, common knowledge about masons of the new kind.

Yet this poem does not only speak of 'marks' as part of the current masonic practice. Having poked fun at certain apocryphal gestures used by Masons he then adds two other features to which we will have to return when we come to the 19th century. The poem speaks of the first one thus:

> "These some are of the Marks and Signs,
> to which each Mason strong inclines;
> And to these Signs I'm here to add,
> what may be deem'd almost as bad.
> Their **Messages**, and scraps of Paper,
> Which are not seal'd with Wax or Wafer,
> nor writ upon, and yet make known
> The greatest Secrets of the Town.
> A MASON, when we needs must drink,
> sends **Letter**, without Pen and Ink,
> Unto some Brother, who's at hand,
> And does the Message understand;
> The Paper's of the shape that's Square,
> thrice-folded with the nicest Care;
> For if 'tis round (which ne'er it ought)
> It will not then be worth a Groat,
> Have any Force or meaning good,
> by which it may be understood…
> And he that can interpret these
> Unwritten Scrolls and Messages,
> It is alone is welcome Guest,
> And fit to be at Mason's Feast."

Of the second we have a shorter description:

> "But there's another Billet-doux,
> Which in times past was much in Use,
> It Paper was, all over writ on,
> By **Spaniard, Swede**, by **Dane**, or **Briton**;
> In antient Language, and each Rover,
> All Masons cou'd the Sense discover:" [4]

What is at least intriguing is that so early in our Mark adventure we should come across the paper missive and the use of cypher.

References to the 'Mark' as a masonic fact come thick and fast in the next five years. In 1723 there had appeared a solitary enquiry in the April edition of *The Flying Post:*

Q. Where does the Master place his Mark upon the work?
A. Upon the S.E. corner.

The discerning reader might at first be confused by this dialogue until we determine that at this stage of speculative masonic development there was no 'Master's degree' and we are still at the point where Fellow of the Craft and Master are the same. Hence the place for his 'mark' fits the case perfectly.

Indeed the receiving of a mark so that it could be used is where it operatively always was – firmly in the Fellow of the Craft degree.

In the publication *A Mason's Examination* we have a whole verse:

> "If a Master Mason you would be
> Observe you well the Rule of Three;
> And what you want in Masonry
> Thy *Mark* and Maughbin makes thee free."

What this reveals is that the Operative influence is still very much in evidence. Remember that in the old working you were not a real *free*-mason until you had passed to the grade of a Fellow of the Craft. There you received your Mark but you were also now allowed to attend the annual Commemoration Ceremony where the 3rd Grand Master was always slain before the edifice of the Temple was completed. I must surely say no more to explain the occurrence of the word 'Maughbin' though it is not often pointed out that here we have but one word when elsewhere it is always two. If we pause to consider that a Union had to take place between two distinct masonic traditions before both words were used we might better understand present practice. In 1723 there was but ONE word.

In 1725 or thereabouts there appeared *A Dialogue between Simon a Town Mason and Philip a Travelling Mason.* It contains a series of Questions and Answers as to how one Mason could make himself known as such to another Mason. There is even reference directly to the differences already appearing between the 'Old Masons' and the 'New Masons under J.T.Desagulier's Regulations' (which of course meant the Masons of lodges now owing allegiance to the Grand Lodge of England). It also contains two diagrams showing respectively 'the form of the old Lodges' and 'the new Lodge under Desagulier Regulation'. Since Knoop and Jones came to the conclusion that Simon and Philip were Operative Masons it seemed that the first of these with the Master and his pedestal in the East and the two Wardens facing him in the West was the oldest form. According to the arrangements described earlier (p. 28) we can see that both methods were possible in Operative meetings save that the orientation was reversed in each case. What the *Dialogue* at least shows is that Operative ideas and influence continue and if this is so then it is hard to believe that where the older practices were still remembered a Mark practice of some kind connected with the Fellow-craft degree did not persist.

We have just such examples of this 'memory' in 1726 and 1727. Though there is a possibility that it was produced a generation earlier (the date given on the document is unclear 1$\overset{2}{7}$6) it is likely that 1726 saw the first appearance of the *Graham MS*. If this is its dating then there is a reference in the text which suggests a 'legendary event' of surprising similarity to later Mark ceremonial practice. The passage is this:

> "... now it is holden fforth by tradition that there was a tumult at this Errection (of the Temple of King Solomon) which should hapened

(sic) betwixt the Labourers and masons about wages and ffor to call me all and to make all things easier the wise king should have had said(,) Be all of you contented ffor you shall be payed all alike(,) yet give a signe to the Masons not known to the Labourours, and who could make that signe at the paying place was to be payed as masons(,) the Labourours not knowing thereof was payed as fforesaid."

Much pondering on the whole MS has already taken place which merits the attention of any interested mason[5] but it is also true that there is no agreement yet as to the MS's place of origin, though the south west of Scotland and Lancashire are possibilities. There is also no clear lead as to whether this valuable and original work is copied from an older document. We are left to speculate and there are some interesting comments that we would do well to record.

The first one is this: "What is very strange is that Noah, Bezaleel and the (incident at the) Warden's Wicket, having been consigned to oblivion, did not stay there. Men who can hardly have heard of Thomas Graham dug them up again, years later, as the basis of additional ceremonies."[6]

A second view by Harry Carr was:

"the legends are almost certainly some part of inherited tradition: indeed two of the legends are introduced 'we have it by tradition' and 'it is holden forth by tradition' and this implies that they belong to the period when only two degrees were practised. It is here that the *Graham MS* makes a major contribution to our study of the evolution of the Masonic ritual, because it not only recounts the legends but shows, by internal evidence, that at least one of them was linked to the early bi-gradal practice."

He continues: "We know ... that under the two-degree system the 'Fellow-Craft or Master' received the F.P.O.F. and a 'word'. It may well be that in the earlier 'operative' days when the ceremonies were characterised by their brevity, those (legendary) elements were communicated *very shortly* and without explanation ... Collectively they seem to represent *a separate store of Craft-lore*, originally unconnected with its ritual practices but *available for adoption* into the ritual."[7]

As a confirmation of this view it is worth looking at a form of ritual which was about to be launched on the English scene by those who sincerely believed that what had happened subsequently to the formation of the first Grand Lodge was an abrogation of ancient and especially Christian Freemasonry. I refer of course to the system now called 'The Royal Order of Scotland' though its origins seem unquestionably English. Its present title is due to later developments.

In the ritual of the Order we have constant allusions to many masonic practices that now appear as separate degrees but which in and after 1730 were clearly considered parts of an older 'whole'. But let the ritual speak for itself:

"Q. How many form a Lodge of Fellow-Crafts?

A. Five.
Q. Why so?
A. ... for three reasons.
Q. What is the third?
A. Because there are five points of fellowship which do or ought to unite Masons.
Q. Name them.
A. Hand to hand, foot....
Q. How many rule a Lodge?
A. Three....
Q. What is the third (reason)?
A. Because there are Three Persons in the Holy Trinity...."

And there is yet a third opinion: "Thomas Graham could have been making a fresh copy of something he himself knew many years before: the hand is of a man who learned to write in the second half of the 17th century. And I agree with Bro. Bernard E.Jones: 'Everything about the *Graham MS* suggests that it reflects the actual working of a lodge or lodges.' "[8]

All these ideas are given even greater weight as far as a possible future Mark degree is concerned when you consider the parallels in other contemporary writings. In the *Dumfries MS* we find the only other early pointer to the 'sign' which distinguished a mason from a labourer at the pay-desk or wicket on the building site. It reads:

"Q. Which way came ye W first about(?) (Word, warranty or wicket?)
A. It was given to King david by report when he was hewing ye stones in ye mount to know ye workmen from ye labourers..."

and the phrase in the *Graham MS* "to obey God and all true squares made or sent from a brother" is more fully dealt with in *A MASON's Confession* from the year 1727:

"if one were in a company, and to send for another mason, he does it by sending a piece of paperr, with a square point folded in at the corner, and suppose he squeze it all in his hand, when it is opened out, the mark where the square point was folded in is the thing that's noticed."

In this same document we also have another clear reference to a Mark custom:

"The day that a prentice comes under the oath (i.e. he becomes a Fellow of the Craft) he gets his choice of a mark to be put upon his tools by which to discern them. So I did chuse this – which cost one merk Scots.

"Hereby one is taught to say to such as ask the question, Where got you this Mark? A. I laid down one, and took up another."

This would seem to mean: when I finished with the Apprentice grade and took up the Fellow-Craft I was then granted the mark.

With all this material to hand two conclusions seem almost inevitable. One is that whatever the actual case may have been *inside* the lodges there was clearly enough impression *outside* them that in some way and at some time

Freemasons received a distinctive mark and sign that was peculiarly theirs. Moreover there were also other masonic practices which were thought to go along with this ancient use and formed part of their privileges or 'Oddities'.

The other conclusion has to be that whether or not there were any ritual acts accompanying the granting of a 'mark' whatever was done was closely related to the older operative procedure and therefore would not at first appear as a separate ritual act. As Mackey lengthily but correctly puts it:

> "The giving of this mark of distinction was (in the Middle Ages) generally accompanied by a banquet, furnished to a certain extent by the Lodge which admitted him (to the Fellow of the Craft grade). But there is not the least allusion in any document extant to the fact that the bestowal of the Mark was accompanied by any secret ceremonies which would give it the slightest resemblance to a degree ... Yet", Mackey continues, "the very instinct of a group of persons engaged in a serious and important ceremony, approving of a certain Mark which was to be preserved for life by the one receiving it and having a use that meant much to everyone in the trade, must have invited and probably suggested a method or ritual to impress upon all present the fullest meaning and purpose of their engagements to one another. If this did not result in a typical and appropriate ceremony the case would be exceptional and opposed to all our experience ... There is no doubt that many of the Operative Masons who had joined forces with the non-operatives took advantage of the opportunity presented to them by their association to suggest a ritualistic formula which would enshrine forever the traditions of centuries of operative craft legends and customs."[9]

This is not a mere theory. Between the years 1725 and 1740 we see the above suggestion put into practice. Not yet in terms of a 'Mark' ceremony as such for that had to be secondary but first as a separate degree for masons who though not 'Masters of Lodges' yet sought a recognition of their capacity for that office in a quite novel degree of Master Mason and the subsequent 'English Masters' lodges. Next, as already mentioned, in a new and definitively Christian degree, or pair of degrees, nowadays known as the Royal Order of Scotland; and finally with the establishment of the Royal Arch as a separate degree to which only Past Masters of lodges could be admitted. With this welter of new masonic creations in *just over a decade* it is hardly to be expected that what was rightly regarded as an adjunct of the Fellowcraft degree would receive much attention. What I hope the reader has begun to appreciate is that the ground was now being prepared for further masonic degrees to appear. One writer has summed up the situation at this stage of the 18th century as follows:

> "English Masonry having, by segregation into Lodges on different levels, departed from the principle that 'All Masons are as Brethren upon the same level', thus sowed the seed which became a tree of many branches.... In the belief that some other degree somehow completed the previous ones, first the Scots Master and then the Royal Arch took shape,

partly by fabrication of new material and partly by resurrecting discarded fragments. We shall also, I think, see that Laurence Dermott's claim to preservation of ancient practice, although much exaggerated, was not wholly without substance." [10]

That shrewd assessment of what was happening perfectly sets the scene for the next stage in the emergence of the Mark as a degree, or pair of degrees, in England, but before we come to that exciting point we need to look at what had been happening in both Scotland and Ireland.

Some mention was made in the previous chapter about the requirement of marks in Scotland from the 16th century and the registering of them in a lodge book such as the copy still retained in Lodge 1ter Aberdeen. Nevertheless it is worth recording here the express regulation laid down in Article 13 of the First Schaw Statutes of 1598. This article recites that no Fellow Craft (or Master) is to be received or admitted to the Lodge except in the presence of six Masters (who must include *the Warden* of the Lodge) and two entered Apprentices. The date of admission must be entered in the Book, and the Candidate's name and his *mark* also inserted. This requirement is of interest in that it

(i) emphasises at this date the place of the 'single Warden' as ruling the lodge rather than a Rt. Worshipful Master;
(ii) makes clear the significance attached to the registered admission of one who is only at this point recognised as a Mason;
(iii) determines the reception party as the Warden and 7 members;
(iv) indicates, especially in view of the presence of the two Apprentices, that there were no 'secret' parts to the occasion, though it is to be noted that the 'candidate' is already 'promoted' to the grade of Fellow Craft/Master.

This regulation was obviously acted upon for in the oldest masonic Minutes as yet known – those of the Lodge of Aitchison's Haven – we read that on 20 November 1599 there is the first use of a mark as a sign-manual, and on 28 December 1603 there is the first registration of a mark adopted by an entrant Fellow.

As was noted in one of the English references the cost of 'his cess for his buking' was one merk Scots, which was two-thirds of a pound Scots or one-eighteenth of a pound sterling, or about a day's pay.

The Lodge of Edinburgh No. 1 has its earliest extant Minute on 31 July 1599 and here we read the judgement of the Lodge on a Mason who confessed to employing a Cowan. The Minute is affirmed by *the* Warden who adds his mark. I would entirely endorse the footnote by J.A.Grantham when he mentions these early mark registrations, It reads:

"Caveat: It is essential to remember that because a Mason used a Mark in, say, 1599, it does not mean that he was ipso facto a 'Key-Stone Mark Mason'."

What it does show, however, is that in Scotland the Operative insistence on a mark presentation was being retained and was recognised as part of masonic practice. This is further emphasised by the entry of 20 December 1674 in Kilwinning Lodge when John Smith was admitted and has paid for his mark, and James Law was (also) booked with his mark. In 1720 (12 July) 'Robert Montgomerie has paid his Mark (whilst) William Montgomerie receives his Mark and promises to pay 1 Merk Scots to the Box on December 20.' It would seem that times were hard for William. A sidelight on such events in lodges of the time is given in the *Edinburgh Register House MS* which informs us that whilst the formal entry of candidates might seem simple *any signs were communicated outside the room* and given by a junior member detailed for that purpose. When a brother became a Fellow Craft the signs, we are told, were increased. One does just wonder whether that practice was not in place earlier and might even fit the description of a century before. Is this not the ground perhaps for the statement made by an examining Committee of the Grand Lodge of Scotland when a complaint had been made against a Glasgow lodge in 1860. The Committee's findings were that "what is generally known under the name of the Mark Master's degree was wrought by the Operative Lodges of St. John's Masonry in connection with the Fellow Craft degree *before* the institution of the Grand Lodge of Scotland (i.e. prior to 1736)....

"That since that date it has continued to be wrought in the Old Operative Lodges, but in what may be called the Speculative Lodges it was never worked at all – or at all events, only in a few.

"That this degree being, with the exception of the Old Operative Lodges above mentioned, entirely abandoned by the Lodges of St. John's Masonry (which meant the three basic degrees), the Supreme Grand Royal Arch Chapter assumed the management of it as the *Fourth Degree* of Masonry in order to *complete the instruction of their candidates in the preliminary degrees* before admitting them to the Royal Arch."

This was a most important declaration and led to the present arrangement in Scottish Freemasonry which was explained earlier (see p. 10). What we need to emphasise in the above statement at this point of our story is that the evidence given by those Glasgow Masons was that they were simply following the practice of the Glasgow Cathedral builders some time prior to 1550. The builders were said to have had two classes of lodges, one for Apprentices, and one for the Fellows and the latter had an Overseer as their Master. This evidence must have been convincing otherwise it is difficult to see how the hard-headed senior Masons on the Committee would have agreed to the findings they published – affirming that some Scottish lodges had practised some form of ceremony for the conferring of the Mark from the early 18th century and that there were even a limited number of Speculative lodges that copied their ancient example. This is, I believe, vital to the story that follows and not only for Scotland. Furthermore, we are here being told that even though the Supreme Grand Royal Arch Chapter was formally brought into being in the early 19th century it soon recognised the need to do something about those Masons who desired to enter the Royal Arch but had not received the Mark in their Craft lodges. This acknowledgement also is very pertinent to our ongoing story.

The contention made by the Glasgow Masons is given further credibility by the discovery that in the year 1707 that a Lodge of Operative Masons was formed under the title of Lodge Journeymen, in Edinburgh, by brethren who had seceded on an issue of trade rights from their mother lodge, Mary's Chapel, now Lodge of Edinburgh, No. 1. They undertook to make only Entered Apprentices and Fellow Crafts but "apparently *the only other degree worked* was that of the Mark Master, who was the Master of the Lodge."[11]

One writer has stated that a copy of an 18th century Mark ritual was in the hands of the Supreme Grand Chapter of Scotland but having made personal enquiry about this item I am assured by the present Grand Scribe E. that no such document is now in their archives though it would obviously be a great discovery if it could be found. We are therefore in the situation where it has to be admitted that whilst the formal presenting of marks was recognised we cannot, as yet, refer to any specific ceremonial that would enable us to connect such procedure with the present form of ceremony.

All that we can rely on for our story by the middle of the 18th century in Scotland are two further references. The first relates to the Ancient Stirling Lodge which is by repute the oldest body in Scotland to have knowledge and practice of Royal Arch Masonry. In this case it is from the year 1743, though of course the Lodge claims a much older ancestry. What is pertinent to our own study is that this lodge holds two unusual brass plates on which are designed features that suggest an early type of tracing board. It is not possible to enter into full examination of them here but only to point out that in addition to the 3 main drawings that obviously relate to the three basic degrees there are some further etchings that refer to other degrees. One of these is the Red Cross or Ark where a dove bearing a cross symbol has left a vessel whose prow is shown behind it; and another is a series of 6 semi-circles forming an arch with a very definite keystone at its head. The significant comment on these engravings is by W.J.Hughan who wrote:

"The singular figures, and the concentric arches at the foot are very suggestive, and though not in my opinion older than about the middle of the last century (and he was writing in 1893) they are very noteworthy and quite unique."[12] The arch motif with its archstone does at least strongly suggest the natural link of some kind of Mark practice as part of the old 'Arch' practices. Why we may not have any guide to these links is revealed in the bye-laws of 1745 where we read:

"... after the Lodge is formed and while it continues, a certain portion of time be spent in the Instruction of prentices in the Royal Art, and in a way not to be expressed in writing." The other reference is in an extract from the bye-laws of Lodge Doric Kilwinning No. 68 in Port Glasgow, which states:

"XII Article, year 1758. That any member that is admitted into the

Lodge as an entrid Apprentice is to pay Nine shillings starling to the Box & sixpence to the Taylor and one shilling and sixpince for passing to a felow Craft and two shillings for Raising to Master and one shilling and a pinie half Pinie for being *made Mark Master.*" The use of the word 'made' suggests some kind of ceremonial activity rather than the earlier Scottish practice of being allotted a mason's mark. The language here is, for example, quite distinct from the three repetitions in the Aberdeen Lodge bye-laws where it says that the apprentice 'pays one merk piece for his measson merk.' (See also p. 40)

By the middle of the century in Scotland, then, we have clear evidence that the operative custom of ensuring that a mason had a mark by the time he became at least a Fellow Craft was still being observed. Not only so but some kind of ritual form was beginning to be used for this occasion. We can see there the ground being prepared for a discernible degree to appear.

What, however, had been happening in nearby Ireland?

Evidence for that country in many spheres of her mediaeval and later history has been lost by the destruction of documents in her civil conflicts. This is reflected in the loss of Ireland's Grand Lodge records until the latter part of the 18th century though happily the spread of Freemasonry in the countryside was so extensive that 'every village almost had its own lodge'. It is from a study of *local* rather than national records that any understanding of what was taking place in the first half of the 18th century is possible.

Dr. Crawley, in his source book for all the early Irish masonic documents that remain, says that "We can safely hold it as proved that the speculative history of today is the continuous and natural development of the Operative Masonry of the mediaeval Guilds."[13] Certainly that was an opinion fully endorsed by the findings of Lepper and Crossle which show that at least as early as 1688, Lodges of operative Freemasons were admitting speculative members "in the new way".

This latter phrase was one used by a student speaker at Trinity College, Dublin in 1688. The occasion was the annual degree-conferring ceremony when, as also at Oxford and Cambridge, a distinctive custom had been established. On this occasion, called 'Initia' or 'Commencements' in Dublin, someone representing the undergraduates was granted "full licence to air the grievances of his fellows, and to inveigh in unmeasured terms against anybody or anything that might excite their wrath." It was by way of being a satirical speech but it clearly dealt with very real and relevant matters of the time. The speaker on this particular Tripos Day, John Jones, not only referred to the lodge held in the College but to the fact that each Freemason *received his mark*. The context made it quite clear that the speaker was fully aware of the value set upon the Mason's mark by the members.

Lepper and Crossle then take up the story afresh by recording how

> ". . . these speculative freemasons, thus admitted, carried the Craft into the most remote corners of Ireland within a very few years. Indeed the rapidity with which the Craft extended was so amazing that in order

to account for its presence in 1732 in districts far removed from the Capital one is tempted to assign a very much earlier date than 1688 for the admission of speculative freemasons in Ireland."[14]

The value of this statement for our purposes is that with the spreading of the Craft went the practice of conferring a mark. The first step was established of recognising, in true operative fashion, that this was the right and the natural progress of Fellow Crafts. Moreover, when the Grand Lodge in Ireland was established and began to issue warrants it became clear that some lodges were seeking authority to 'continue' their working rather than asking to be 'erected'. As J.A.Grantham says: "Evidence points to Irish Masonry having had in its custody a very full Tradition. Masonic lectures were at one time a feature of the Lodges, different portions of the traditional history being taken as subjects, as is testified by old Minute Books. The number of emblems illustrated on old floor cloths and charts also attests the scope of Irish Masonic lore."[15]

When we reflect on the way in which the histories in the Old Charges in England were steadily amplified by additional details it would not seem surprising if the same happened in Ireland or that the very same details were repeated, as we know that English manuals and handbooks were copied and circulated.

One example of this development is the carved stone of 1738 in Newry. The Lodge here, No. 77, obtained a 'continuing' warrant in 1737 and set about marking its presence in a public manner. The first meeting place was thought to be a very modest house at No. 8 Lower North St., and over the entrance door they placed their carved stone. The 'shield' at the centre was carved into two diagonal parts, the top left having a chisel, mallet and gavel, and the bottom right showing a hand holding a trowel upright. The shield was in fact a form of ashlar for in the top of it was what might be a form of cramp, though there is a further pointed spike protruding from the base of the 'shield'. The 'shield' is surrounded by heraldic mantling with the date 1 7 3 8 at the base. At the top of the stone are the letters H.G.M. and these have since been recognised as the initials of the three grades of workmen engaged at the building of King Solomon's Temple – Harodim, Ghiblim and Menatzchim. These names manifestly came from Anderson's footnote in his 1723 Constitutions which has been given in full earlier when we spoke about Wellins Calcott. Lepper and Crossle support this interpretation of the stone by also referring to the contents and picture in "The Pocket Companion and History of Freemasons, London" of 1764 which was much used and copied in Ireland. There we have Hiram showing to the monarch two tablets held by aproned workmen: the one is a plaque with the book's title and the other shows the classes of workmen in their usual numbers.

Apart, however, from such interesting items we must turn our attention to another Irish development.This is the emergence from at least 1730 onwards of the 'Arch' and additional 'degrees'. It must be understood at once that the difficulty in interpreting Irish usage is that we are naturally inclined to want to apply to the terms used in the 18th century all the features that invest similar terms today. As we shall see in what follows this is a misleading tendency and one that we shall have to avoid. To be specific, the word ‘Arch’ that was used to describe one practice at this time was not the same as the Royal Arch ceremony with which we are now familiar and the description of a step as a ‘Mark’ one did not necessarily mean the same as it does today. The matter will become clearer as we proceed.

In his articles for the Irish Lodge of Research Philip Crossle provided evidence, mainly from local sources, for 2 important theses.

The first of these was expressed as follows:

“I never have been able to accept the argument, brought forward by many Masonic students, that the sublime philosophy of what we now call Royal Arch Masonry was an invention. Surely we must admit, in some unostentatious form, that the philosophy must have been known to our Craftsmen of old. I will endeavour to demonstrate it was known to Anderson and Pennell under the name of the Master’s part.”[16] We cannot pursue that argument in this book but he was duly able to affirm that “during the interval 1730–44, between which Pennell’s and d’Assigny’s books were published, the Irish brethren contented themselves ‘with three material steps’, the third of which, Pennell’s Master’s part, undoubtedly included the present doctrine of our Irish RA”(or what he elsewhere calls the “J” legend of the Royal Arch). Moreover, and this is very pertinent to the whole 18th century story which we are following, Crossle makes the following observation:

“As is well-known, Dr. Francis Drake, when Junior Grand Warden (of the Grand Lodge) of All England, delivered an oration at York on St. John’s Day, 27 December 1726, in which he implied three degrees the same as Pennell’s ... Lower down on the same page, Drake refers to the building of Solomon’s Temple, the repairs to it by King Josiah, and the rebuilding of it by Zerubbabel – so that, at one time, there cannot have been much difference between the practice of Masonry at York and Dublin”. Concluding his thoughts on this development the Irish scholar remarks:

“(Up to about 1750) Pennell’s ‘Master’s part’ apparently comprised the essentials of a ceremony subsequently elaborated into our present Irish Installed Master, Royal Arch, and Red Cross Mason.... The change of names seems to have taken place, in some Dublin lodges, after 1744 ... thus:

1. Entered Apprentice and Fellow Craft (one degree) more often referred to as ‘Entered and Crafted’;
2. Master Mason.
3. Royal Arch.”[17]

The second thesis put forward by Crossle developed from this view of the ‘suitcase’ nature of Irish degrees, viz. that under a general name for the

Degrees there were several subsidiary sections waiting to be opened up or, to use his term, 'elaborated'. He describes how

"At one time, Masonic lectures were a feature in an Irish Masonic Lodge at labour, to illustrate which floorcloths and charts were hung on the wall ... Unfortunately, no Irish manuscript survives which would have described the text of the lectures" even if there ever were one at a time when the rituals were not written down. Such is of course still the case for much Irish masonry today. "Our Irish floorcloths and charts vary so much in the emblems displayed; the lectures must have been anything but stereotype. A standard tracing board, with its set lecture, was unknown in Irish lodges. It seems to me, the lecturer took for his text some portion of the traditional history and held forth upon matters well-known to him; and eventually the text, with its explanation, must have been incorporated as one of the subsidiary degrees of this period."

Crossle continues: "We have Irish minute books which contain entries, such as, 'a lecture went round'. This implies an examination by way of question, by one brother, and an answer by another, and so on round the lodge ... For instance, during the (1750–90) period, an esoteric lecture might 'go round' on the legend of the Ark, of the Mark Fellow, of the Mark Master, of the Link and Wrestle, and so forth ... (and) I think a genuine Irish lecture which 'went round' never found its way into print.

"To my mind, there was nothing new to the Craft in the multiplication of degrees ... The legends pertaining to them were well-known. The *novelty* lay in the application of familiar names to component *parts* of the *old degrees*, and of the *lectures*, and in this way specific *subsidiary* degrees were formed."[18]

Two examples of the kind of lodge floorcloth that would assist this 'lecture' process are reproduced in other places (see below) and it is worth noting in both cases that they show an arch with its keystone in great prominence. In the Lurgan cloth of 1763 this feature is firmly covered with a flat coping stone above which is a cubic stone and a level. In the military Lodge No. 205 cloth of about 1770 the keystone is engraved with the monogram of the Irish Grand Encampment, the 'Wondrous Arch' is supported by four pillars, and the Ark of Noah sails triumphantly to one side. In both cloths the Trowel is clearly indicated.[19]

Within such a framework of developing Freemasonry in Ireland we ought to know that from about 1725 onwards one of these subsidiary 'links' was being worked. It was called the 'Arch' and though only a brief ceremony it was initially required before proceeding with the 3rd degree of the *Royal* Arch itself. The probable tool of this 'degree' was the Trowel and in this connection Crossle gives us a very striking illustration.

"When Lord Rosse was installed Grand Master of Ireland in June 1725 the Mason King at Arms ... carrying upon a Velvet Cushion a little Gold Trowel with a Black Ribbon ... marched in Order before the Grand Wardens to the upper end of the Great Hall, where stood the Mystical Table." After being proclaimed he was invested with the trowel and addressed with some such words as these: 'not doubting your Capacity and Care to preserve the Cement of the Lodge and so to spread it that the whole Body may remain as a well-built Arch'. The floorcloths just mentioned have these sentiments written on their respective arches.

"So far as Irish Masonry is concerned the symbolism of the trowel has been lost sight of, because the subsequent Arch degree to which it applied ... has been *re-named* and the *legend proper has passed away from our memory.*"[20] This may also explain why this early aspect of an emerging Mark ceremony has also not been pursued previously.

The jewel of a James Sullivan in the Irish RA Lodge No. 2 in 1795 is also thought to have belonged to this degree. On its obverse is a circle that encloses the letters **H.T.W.S.S.T.K.S.** and also three axes. (See picture).

When we become aware of even the little that is reliably known about this 'degree' we can begin to see some light on the early start of the Irish form of the Mark degree. The ceremony appears to have centred on the candidate placing the arch stone or key-stone into an incomplete arch which was supported by two pillars set out on the lodge floor. On the key-stone were engraved certain hieroglyphs and a possible guide to what these might have been is suggested by Crossle who reproduces a certificate first drawn up by an engraver in Lodge 620 (IC) after 1788. In this document the central portion is illustrated by the following items, starting at the foot of the page:

> *One step* for 'Entered and Crafted', showing not only the three great and lesser lights but also the rough and smooth ashlars *and* the Euclidian proposition on the smooth stone.
> *Two steps* for the Master Mason, with the three main working tools & upended compasses surmounted by the letter G.
> *Three steps* for 'Passed the Chair', showing a black and white board of 3 by 3 squares, with a straight edge diagonally across it and two hands clasped above an All-seeing eye.
> *Four steps* for the Excellent; with a rod entwined by a serpent;
> *Six steps* for a 'well-built Arch', from the bottom of which steps appears a hand extended holding a mallet, whilst at the top of the steps is the Ark with the shekinah above it. Enclosing the Ark is the Arch with its keystone *and all* its stones bearing letters.
> *Seventh:* Above the Arch is a paved black and white flooring with 2 rows of three columns flanking it and in between a 'Glory', with certain letters in masonic *cypher.*

It is when we understand the background to the enlarged Craft Masonry of Ireland that we can begin to appreciate some of the hitherto odd references that we may have come across elsewhere in England. In 1759, for example, William Carroll, an Irish Mason, applied for relief to the Premier Grand Lodge in 1759, on the plea of being an English (if Antients) Freemason. He was refused by the Grand Secretary on the ground that "Our Society is neither *Arch*, Royal Arch nor Antient so you have no right to partake of our charity." We can now better understand this reply if we recognise that it confirms an awareness of this separate 'Arch' or 'near-Mark' section of Masonry, in the very stronghold of the 'new' Speculatives.

Even earlier, in 1757, Laurence Dermott, then the Grand Secretary of the Antients Grand Lodge, explained how his 'Master of the Royal Arch" included some simple ceremony called the 'Arch' which was connected with a Mark. He also changed the last line of a song, that first appeared in Spratt's 1751 Constitutions, when it was printed in the "Ahiman Rezon" of 1756 so that the fourth verse is now as follows:

"The Royal Art, and Word
is kept upon record,
With upright hearts, and pure,
While sun and moon endure;
Not written, but *indented on*
The heart of every *Arch* mason."

As the century proceeded "certain brief ceremonies", says Crossle, "were elaborated into subsidiary degrees so as to embrace the old operative tradition of Masons' Marks".[21] As the Arch did this before the Royal Arch, so the Mark Fellow did it subsequently. Yet there were other ceremonies – the Ark, Mark, and Wrestle – which are often associated with Mark Masonry but which, at least as far as the two latter were concerned, were very dissimilar to anything which we know in our ceremonies today. We shall, however, look at them in the chapter on rituals.

Before we leave the Irish scene in the last quarter of the 18th century there are two other aspects of Freemasonry that cannot be overlooked. I refer first to the matter of Military lodges. It is impossible in this book to do more than point up certain aspects of the subject but as we shall see in later chapters it may well be that this factor in the story of the Mark degree has been somewhat neglected. In view of the evidence available that is a pity.

"It was the Irish invention of the Warrant which made the erection of travelling Lodges possible. There is little doubt that, to the soldier mason the Warrant of his Lodge held a place in his heart second only to the Colours. The first such warrant was one granted by the Grand Lodge of Ireland to the First Battalion, The Royal Scots, on 7 November 1732. The first issued by Scotland was in 1747, to the Duke of Norfolk's Lodge in the 12th Foot, and in England no lodge in a regiment was warranted by either Moderns or Antients till 1755. Little wonder, then, that Ireland issued altogether more than 200 Regtl. Warrants, more than the combined total under the other Grand Lodges." It will already be noted of course that one cannot assume by the name of a Regiment the country in which its lodge was warranted.

It has also to be recognised that "there is hardly a unit of the British Army which has not served in Ireland, some for many years. They came in contact with the local lodges, some formed lodges of their own, and on the outbreak of each war, we find a spate of regimental warrants issued as the units proceeded overseas."[22]

One example of the military lodge whose floorcloth we have just examined may give us some idea of its wanderings and influence. It is first noted in Smith's Pocket Companion of 1735 as having Warrant no. 23 in Col. Hamilton's Regiment, better known to the public as the Royal Inniskilling Fusiliers. The Warrant was dated some time in 1733. In 1739 the Regiment was sent to Porto Bello and the Isthmus of Darien in Central America and out of 600 men only *nine* returned. In 1744 the Regiment was beating up recruits in Yorkshire but it is not surprising that little more is heard of the lodge until 1750 when the number 205 was granted to them. The number was transferred in 1785 to the lodge in the 35th Foot, later the 1st Battalion, The Royal Sussex. The warrant was transferred to Mayo, Co. Tyrone, in 1790 and was doubtless left there with the floorcloth when the troops marched off to war. The lodge was finally erased in 1801.

The connections with Ireland could be for many reasons: an Irish commanding officer, a neighbouring Irish unit in the same garrison or just because they were stationed in the island. It is surprising, for instance, to discover that the famous Black Watch received its first Warrant from Ireland in 1749 though when you learn that it was on duty there from 1747 to 1754 the reason becomes clear.

What is increasingly obvious is that wherever their Warrant may have come from the dispersal of the Regiments, especially when in England, was a significant factor in establishing some real variants in masonic practice. We shall have occasion to notice this when we look at how Mark ritual developed and it will be found that the military input cannot be disregarded.

These lodges, moreover, were dedicated in their labour and obviously revelled in the privilege that most of them enjoyed of being able to practice a range of degrees. Gould tells us that

"At the first recorded meeting of the Royal Arch Lodge – St. Andrews – in Boston, August, 1769, foreign soldiers were chosen as first officers of the lodge and William Davis, of No. 58 (Antients) in the 14th Foot received 'four steps', described as those of 'Excellent, Super-excellent, Royal Arch and Knight Templar'. This is but one of a host of similar incidents.[23]

The regulations covering the rights and responsibilities of military lodges varied according to which Grand Lodge granted a warrant. No restrictions with regard to who might be initiated in a Regimental lodge were ever imposed by Scotland, but by a law of 1768 the Irish Army lodges were prohibited from making any townsman a Mason in a place where there was already a registered lodge. Equally, of course, the town lodges were forbidden 'to initiate any military man where there was a warranted lodge in the regiment, troop or company, or in the quarters' to which he belonged. The powers of *English* Regimental lodges were also not interfered with until after the Union of the Grand Lodges in 1813 and it is worth remarking that even then the restriction imposed was simply that of not '*initiating*' anyone in the 'town or place at which (the military lodge's) members may be stationed.

Any rules were therefore carefully limited and did not unduly prevent local fraternisation. This was important since it allowed the officers and men, especially those latter who were 'impressed' and above the rank of Corporal, to meet the civilians of a garrison town 'upon the level' and be accepted by them in a manner which might not otherwise have been enjoyed. 'Military men' of any rank normally tended to be looked down on by the citizens of any standing. It can also be appreciated that whilst there might be an official ban on 'initiation' of any local lay person there was still ample opportunity for military lodges, with their usually far wider range of 'degrees', to be places of intense interest to many English masons.

Before leaving this brief survey of military Freemasonry it is necessary for our story that we should learn about two more Army lodges that enter our story later. These are the 'Minden' and that in the 6th Inniskiling Dragoons.

The Minden was an Irish lodge No. 63, and in the 20th Foot. It was founded in 1748 and its Warrant was granted to Lord George Sackville, the Colonel and first Master, as well as Lt. Col. the Hon. Edward Cornwallis, and a Capt. Milburne. The title of the lodge was actually adopted after the important battle of Minden in 1759 when the 20th Foot served on the Right of the Line and with due distinction. It was the Regiment of Major James Wolfe who succeeded the Hon. Edward Cornwallis as 2nd i/c and later commanded the expedition against Quebec. Though all other such ranking officers seem to have been Masons we do not have Wolfe's records and therefore do not know whether he joined the lodge.

The Regiment was stationed as follows:

1757/8:	Isle of Wight.
1758–63:	Germany.
1763–69:	Gibraltar.
1769–74:	England.

The lodge, however, faded somewhat in the years around the turn of the century and had to be revived in 1812. It was dormant from 1819 until a revival in India in 1824, and from 1836 to 1844 when it came to life again in Bermuda and remained active until the 1850s. After this it again departed for India but all its jewels and later records were lost in the Indian Mutiny.

Contrary to what one would expect with so Irish a name there is no record of any Irish lodge in the 6th Inniskilling Dragoons. It held Warrants, at different times, from *both Grand Lodges* of England, that is the Moderns and the Antients, as well as from the Grand Lodge of All England at York. It can therefore be understood that this Regimental lodge had a rich and varied range of traditions from which to select its ritual practices. Its English connections are explained when we learn that the Regiment was first raised as the 7th Horse in 1685, during Monmouth's Rebellion. Their facings were changed in 1714 from buff to green and hence they were known as the 'Green Horse' and were placed on the Irish Establishment in 1746. The lodge received its first

English Warrant in 1757 but this was transferred to Cork and they received another, No. 570, in 1780. They were stationed for a crucial period of our story at

Newcastle on Tyne	1765
Berwick on Tweed	1766
Coventry	1767
Worcester	1768
Lewes	1769
Chichester	1770
York	1771/2
Manchester	1773.[24]

We turn finally in this review of Irish Freemasonry to another aspect which will be seen to have relevance for the Mark degree. It is the working of Knight Templary and the eventual establishment of an 'Early Grand Encampment' in the last part of the 18th century.

It is known that independent Encampments, in addition to those attached to Craft Lodges, developed in Ireland and worked the Knight Templar ceremony as the *Ne Plus Ultra* of a varying series of degrees. The earliest known reference to the K.T. ceremony in Ireland is found in a list printed in 1789 which gives the date, 24 March 1765 ... J.H.Lepper stated that the degree was possibly known in Ireland in 1760 which is clearly possible in respect of the 1765 conferral.

Crossle adds an interesting note referring to Knight Templary at this point. "*The Black Mark*, like the Arch of the R(oyal)A(rch) Group, and the two Mark steps of the Red Cross Mason Group ... was conferred in Ireland as early as 1765. (It was) presumably introduced for the purpose of giving Masonic colour to the introduction of Knight Templarism in a Craft Lodge. What its legend purported I do not know. That it was known to the Irish Craft is evinced by a copper-plate certificate engraved in County Tyrone during the 18th century."[25]

It is therefore quite conceivable that encampments had been formed and were at labour by 1770, and not only around Dublin. On 27 August 1775 the 'Knight Templars' of Kinsale, Co. Cork granted a certificate to a James Dennison which contained the following words:

"... the Bearer our well Belov Br Sir James Dennison was by us Install'd and Dub'd a Knight ... having been Enter'd past and Rais'd was a past Master and Royal Arch Excellent Mason ... We also Certifie that ye above Sr James Dennison is a Mark (Square and Compasses) Mason ..." and the two knights who affirm this also have marks, the one of a skull and the other of crossbones.

There were other 'Mark degrees' to come but that development and the spreading of Encampments into Scotland and North-eastern England will be part of our later story. What we have to note here is that in one form or another the Mark legends and the distinctive Operative features were present and continued to survive in 18th century Ireland.

It only remains to tell the story of what happened among English Freemasons before the Mark degree *finally* emerged in a recognisable form. Our account will largely centre on the North-east of England though we shall also begin to lift our eyes to those overseas areas which had by the mid-18th century begun to be equally part of our national concern.

We begin with the previously Operative Lodge at Winlaton in the Tyne Valley, now known as the Lodge of Industry, No. 48. Whether the Lodge existed before the year 1717 cannot now be known. It certainly became known at that date to the Premier Grand Lodge but there are no lodge records extant until 1725, when the old Minute book shows that the members were then in full working order as operative Masons. Many of the members were employed in building the dwellings for the people who had come to work at the Crowley Ironworks that were set up in 1690, and their distinctive gravestones in the parish churchyards of Whickham and Winlaton can still be seen.

The originally Operative nature of the Lodge cannot be stressed too strongly. "A comprehensive survey of Masonry in the North of England of that (1720s) period," writes William Waples, "suggests that the Lodge was an organised centre for a wide area for the purposes of registering Apprentices; of giving them their freedom after having served the statutory seven years of servitude, and for controlling the activities of the Mason trade in North-west Durham according to law and trade usage. Locally there were similar centres at the same period at Durham City, Newcastle-upon-Tyne, Wark, Alnwick, Ford, Wooler, Sunderland, and maybe others not yet traced."[26]

This lodge was still Operative up to 1733 and there is ample evidence to prove the fact. In the 'Orders of Antiquity' still retained by the Lodge we read:

> '1. That every Mason be a True Lodgeman to God and the Holy Church that he use neither Errour nor Heresy, nor desert discreet and wise men's teaching.
> 3. That you keep truly all Council of the Lodge Chamber and Council that ought to be kept concerning Masonry.
> 4. That you call all Masons *ffellows or Brethren.*
> 7. That no Mason take upon him any Lord's work nor any other Mason's unless he knows himself to be Master of the said work.
> 12. That every Master or ffellow give pay unto his ffellow according as he deserves, so that he be not deceived by false workmen.
> 17. That if any have Trespassed against the Craft, he shall stand to and abide the award of the Master and ffellows.
> 18. That every Master and ffellow shall cherish strange ffellows, when they come out of strange countries, and set them on work if they have any and they willing to work . . ."

It should be noted in the above that 'Master' meant the Master of the Lodge, and in this connection it should be recognised that until 1734 the officers were as follows – Master, Warden (only one and he was also Treasurer), and 2

Stewards (or Deacons, though this Lodge still keeps the old names) – and this is underlined in the 'Penal Orders' where we read:

"If any oppose the Master or Warden ... penalty 6d." and also

"If any be found not faithfully to keep and maintain the 3 ffraternal Signs, and all Points of ffellowship and principal matters relating (to) the secret and craft, each ofence penalty 10 shillings." It is in this working lodge that a minute for "7ber 29 (September) 1730, (reads) Then Georg Gilhespy notified to ye Lodge his haveing taken Tho. Clough Apprentice for seven years and promisses to show his Indentures next Quarterly Meeting."

There is however this entry for July 1746:

MEMORANDUM OF THE HIGHRODIAMS

Enacted at a Grand Lodge held that evening that no Bro. Mason should be admitted into the dignity of a Highrodiam under less than ye charge of 2s 6d, or as the "Domaskin" or "Forin" as John Thompson from Gateside (*Gateshead in dialect*), pd. at the same night 5/-.
N.B. The English Masters to pay for entering into the sd. Mastership 2s 6d pr. majority."

We cannot here enter into the full length explanation of this entry which is only one of a great many in the next fifty years of the Lodge's Minutes. Yet a few comments are necessary if we are to see the connection between these 'Highrodiams' and the emerging Mark degree in this part of Britain.

The term 'Highrodiam' is without doubt the transcription of the local 'Geordie' manner of saying the Hebrew word 'Harodim'. For a manual worker Secretary this attempt at a true record is to be commended. The term 'Domaskin or Forin' probably referred to yet another masonic stage beyond the English Masters and Harodim already acquired. Some think it may mean a Templar/Crusader (Damascus) 'rite' that had been imported (foreign) by this time.

This old lodge At Swalwell (for this was its name after 1734) was by no means the only local lodge to benefit from the 'Highrodiam'. Of the list of old masonic centres given above (p. 52) only Wark has not so far provided evidence of the Harodim. In the *History of the Phoenix Lodge, No. 94*, of Sunderland we are told that "the first mention of the Degree being conferred in this Lodge is in December 1756, and the last date is 28 September 1809, during which period no fewer than 150 Brethren were enrolled, many of whom came from Gateshead, Durham, and other towns. As a rule Special Meetings were convened for the purposes of the Degree, but the regular Officers of the Craft Lodge filled the various chairs, if they were members of the Herodim. There are no records of any business transacted (other than) the date of meeting and the Brethren present. Only on one occasion is there a departure, and that occurs in the 1756 Book, which records the progress of members through the Degrees, where Bro. Richard Markham *Raised to the Herodim* has the words

'Passed the Bridge' added to this date. Two other brethren who received the (Herodim) Degree on the same evening have no such entry."[27]

I hasten to say here that this other local variant of the term Harodim simply underlines the 'oral' nature of the experience which is here referred to. For like the old Irish workings which we heard about above the 'Harodim' consisted of a series of lectures which were intended to enlarge and enrich the knowledge of 'past' Masters. We know, for example, that there was a team of senior brethren who could deliver these lectures and hence there is mention of 'the Harodim passing through a place'. These lectures, of which we have later, edited versions, covered aspects of the three fundamental degrees but amplified them to include material that was wholly Christian, using many biblical stories, and providing the foundation for the Mark, Ark and Link, Passing the Bridge (or Red Cross of Babylon), the Royal Arch, the Rose Croix and Crusader Masons. One long-standing Newcastle student of the *Order* – for using 'Degree' here is a misleading term for modern masons – has made some comments that we need to ponder: (he writes in the late 19th century).

> "I have elsewhere shown ... that the old 'Arch' was identical with this Harodim System. This of course does not mean the more recent system which is void of all the mystery of the circle within a Triangle or Vice Versa, and strictly non-Christian, except by accident, but I mean the old Christian 'Arch' or Harodim." (and)
>
> "An interesting feature of these lectures is that parts thereof are incorporated verbatim into more modern workings, the *Mark*, Arch, *Marked Master* (but *not* Mark Master), Temple, Rose Croix and especially the Royal Order of Scotland or Heredom (better Harodim) of Kilwinning ... Like the Royal Order some of these Lectures are in verse and outside of perhaps one other old System, verse does not occur to my knowledge in any except very old Rituals."[28]

It is tempting to be led into more aspects of this fascinating North-eastern form of Freemasonry which seems to have such common roots with a similar Christian and ancient 'revival' in the London area at exactly the same time – the Royal Order of the 1740s. We must resist that temptation here save for asking the important question: Where did the Swalwell Lodge, as the oldest known base for the practice of this system, get it from? That they had it in 1735 seems fairly well proven. Clearly, as soon as they were strong enough to obtain a 'Constitution' for a separate existence, when work was plentiful and members likewise, they had the Assembly of 'Past' Masters and Fellows which would permit them to invite the Chiefs (or Harodim) to visit them. These were the men who examined and passed Fellows, raised such examined Fellows to Geometrick Masters and thus enabled them, when nine such were available, to open a Lodge of Harodim, to hear and benefit from the 'Higher Order' lectures. It would seem that the institution of the Harodim was part of the old Trade Guild System with which we began this book, only now fitting as an addition to the 'newer' Speculative forms of basic Masonry.

For our purposes the crucial thing to know is that the old Lodge at Swalwell was a Time Immemorial offshoot of the Grand Lodge of York. We are getting back to the same roots as those that linked with old Irish Freemasonry and some Military lodges. We are seeing the further seed beds of the emerging Mark ceremonies and their produce is about to bear fruit.

In 1975 F.S.Collier produced a booklet for the centenary celebrations of the Humber Lodge of Mark Masters, No. 182. Its Preface shows signs of very considerable research and makes the interesting claim that "Mark Masonry (associated with Operative Freemasonry) has been practised in Hull for a very long period. It is recorded in a list published in December 1663 that a Lodge of Operative Freemasons, being No. 3 in the York Division, was held in Hull ... and prior to 1705 a similar Lodge, known as No. 4, was in existence in Hull. Then, when *the Mark Degree ritual was elaborated about 1752* and greater prominence was given to *the symbolic aspects of this Degree in a standardised form* it was customary to confer the two degrees of Mark Man and Mark Master under the Craft Warrants issued by the then rival Grand Lodges of England, of Scotland and Ireland ... and thereafter a steady growth of this particular branch of our Order was noticeable. Hull Craft Lodges adopted and practised Mark Masonry as a distinctive degree in 1782 and then periodically to the present time."[29]

I believe this to be a sober and correct description of what was true generally. It has increasingly been the conviction of any who have thought seriously about the development of the Mark as a degree that it was in the 1750s that something that at last looked like a real and distinct ceremony finally emerged.

In his mammoth study of Freemasonry in the Province of Quebec Graham makes the following statement:

"1750: It appears that the Mark degree was conferred in England before the middle of the 18th century" and he continues by declaring that from 1750 onwards the additional degrees, including the Mark, Past Master and Royal Arch, were increasingly practised by the military and other lodges in the Province. Indeed, so well established were the 'Antient' and other traditional forms of Masonry in this area that trouble was bound to arise when their very existence was later threatened. Further south on that Continent we read of a lodge at Savannah which held a Warrant of 1735. It was under the Premier Grand Lodge in the 18th century but despite that body's views on the Royal Arch this lodge conferred that 'degree' from time to time and in 1758 we read that the Worshipful Master, Benjamin Sheftall, wore an apron that "contained a combination of Blue Lodge and Chapter emblems prominent amongst which is a circle which encloses the letter 'G' and in the circle are also the letters **H.T.W.S.S.T.K.S.**" Not only is that date eight years before the formation of the Grand Chapter (Moderns) but those letters are more likely to be known by Mark Masons today than by Royal Arch ones. Of course, if Wor. Bro. Sheftall had had occasion to be introduced by an 'Irish' or 'York' military lodge to the

'Arch' working that preceded the Royal Arch then he might be excused for what to us might look like a mix up of 'degrees'.

Meanwhile back in the 'old country' a lodge in Newcastle was having its own encounter with the 'Mark'. In the possession of the present Provincial Grand Lodge of Durham there is a copy of the 1723 *Book of Constitutions*. Attached to it by binding is a further set of 'Regulations and By-Laws to be strictly observed by the Brethren of this lodge, which shall be held at the house of John Kirton of Newcastle'. The combined volume also bears the name of "Robert Salmon his book 1759 Geathead", whilst the title page of the Book of Constitutions was signed "Ep Thompson this book belongs". The Bye Laws were signed by Salmon as Worshipful Master and the same Ephraim Thompson as Warden. (Does the signing by ONE Warden suggest a lodge like the old Swalwell one was?). It looks as if the volume was transmitted from one Master to a succeeding one for the last page is headed 'Newcastle January 1756'.

What is written on that rear page is most important. "There being met part of the Body of the Lodge they taking in their serious consideration that no member of the saide lodge shall be made a *Mark Mason* without paying the fee of one Scots Mark that for the Propigation of the pedestal."

What is interesting is that in the minutes of this lodge *prior to* 1756 words that are often used are 'Brother X received his Mark' implying that, as had been the case for Scottish lodges during the previous two centuries at least, a brother paid for and received his mark. Was this change of wording the subtle indication that there was now a distinctive 'ceremony' around this act rather than the making of a mere administrative entry? Waples was convinced of it though some of his colleagues in Quatuor Coronati were cautious and dubious. For my part, bearing in mind the whole context of this one example and the evidence that has been provided in this chapter, I agree with Bro. Waples's final reply to his critics. "I cannot accept the view that this entry refers (only) to paying a fee and receiving a mark for it without some brief ceremony ... it may be that here was the germ of something which is today a full-dress ceremonial." Since we found the same development, with identical words and practice, at the same time (1758) in Scotland I think we are able to claim that the long-germinating plant was at last emerging from the ground.

Chapter Four

Where did Dunckerley get the Mark Degree? (1759–1769)

ON 18 SEPTEMBER 1759 the City of Quebec capitulated and the future possession of Canada by Britain was secured. Amongst the many thousands of British regulars and more than 7,000 American Colonial troops present during the siege and fierce battle that preceded this victory there were members of at least fourteen Regimental lodges. How many more there were involved in the subsequent attack on and capitulation of Montreal we are not told. What we do know is that of these lodges one was the very first to be warranted by the Grand Lodge of Scotland, one was an English 'Antients' lodge and the Grand Lodge of Ireland had 10 representatives. Lodge No. 227. (IC) in the 446th Regt. of Foot became the 'Lodge of Antiquity' in the City of Montreal and eventually No. 1 on the Registry of the Grand Lodge of the Province of Quebec.

Also present at Quebec, but serving as a Gunner on board His Majesty's warship *Vanguard*, was a certain Bro. Thomas Dunckerley, who is recorded in the official report of the occasion as 'having behaved so well'. "In fact", says Graham, "to Bro. Dunckerley's excellent markmanship, for he was a 'Master of the Mathematicks on board ship' may have been due the unfortunate demolition of the magnificent Prioral House of the 'Knights Hospitaller of Malta' then standing on the cliff near the present Dufferin Terrace." Years later, when Dunckerley was the head of the Masonic Knights of England, that exploit may have given him food for thought.

What he would also have regretted at the time was having to miss the celebration of the Festival of St. John the Evangelist on 27 December 1759, when most of the Freemasons in the army of the 'immortal Wolfe' gathered for the seasonal festivities and also "to transact important business relating to the interests of the Craft." What this business was is clearly set out in an extract from an old letter book that belonged to the Royal Artillery at Woolwich. It is dated February 1769, but refers to events a decade earlier. It reads:

"In the winter of the year 1759 ... the Masters and Wardens of all the Warranted Lodges held in the Regiments garrisoned there ... assembled together and unanimously agreed to choose an acting Grand Master to preside over them, the better to advance Masonry, regulate their proceedings, and unite them in one common band of brotherly love.

"Agreeable thereto they made choice of Brother Guinett, Lieutenant in the 47th Regt., and of Lodge No. 192 (IC) and drew out, sign'd and seal'd a

Warrant, empowering him and his successors elected, to congregate them together as a Grand Lodge for the intent before mentioned, they having the Constitutions as their chief guide."

"This regulation, together with the charitable collections made and given to the poor widows and orphans of the Army and the distressed Canadians, brought the Craft into such universal esteem that numbers applied to the different Lodges, and was made Masons, in as much as to make them so numerous as to oblige the Grand Master to grant Warrants from under his present authority, until opportunity might offer for them to apply for a greater."[1]

This was very heady stuff and it is hardly surprising that as the fame and size of the Masonic presence in Canada grew so there should be increasing anxiety back in Britain as to the Constitutional implications of these events.

A Capt. John Knox has left a description of this December occasion and it is at least worth recording that a particular masonic friend of Dunckerley's, Col. Simon Fraser, of the famous 78th Highlanders was very much in attendance. Dunckerley's ship had sailed shortly after the capitulation of Quebec and arrived in England early in January 1760. She was, however, ordered to return as soon as her stores could be got on board, in company with several other ships of war, their object being the relief of the capital which was now beseiged by the French. Capt. Swanton in the *Vanguard* was the senior commanding officer and Dunckerley was again his Master Gunner.

On board the *Vanguard*, as she once more ploughed her way back across the Atlantic, there was held the now famous 'Naval Lodge' No. 251 (Moderns) which was warranted almost immediately after Dunckerley's return. Not surprisingly we find that he was the Worshipful Master. What is perhaps more surprising, though not as frequently appreciated, is that the working which he had introduced into this Lodge, and over which he now presided, was that with which he was familiar in his own Mother Lodge, The Three Tuns, at Portsmouth. That was a lodge that dated from as long ago as 1725 and, according to Sadler, "Most of the members seem to have been either naval or military officers of a superior grade, or the higher class of tradesmen." It was a good ancestry and one of which Thomas Dunckerley was rightly proud. Yet Dunckerley's Masonry was not quite what it might seem at first sight and this would appear to be a good moment, as we literally voyage with him to the New World, to look carefully at his position in regard to the conduct of masonic ritual.

In view of the fact that Dunckerley was at this very moment returning to North America with a document in his possession from the Premier Grand Lodge of England it might properly be assumed that he was both a respected and trusted son of that Body. When we learn moreover that this document gave him authority to regulate the affairs of Masonry in the newly conquered Canadian provinces, *or in any other part of the globe that he might visit* where no Provincial Grand Master had as yet been appointed, we can only assume that he was regarded as a totally orthodox and utterly reliable representative.

So as to appreciate just what this might mean in terms of ritual we would do well to hear the words of Dr. Manningham, Deputy Grand Master in 1757, in a letter to a Bro. Sauer at the Hague.

"The only Orders that we know are Three, Masters, Fellow-crafts and Apprentices, and none of them ever arrive at the honour of Knighthood by Masonry."

Quite apart from what that statement says about the prevalence of Masonic knightly practices at this early date it affirms categorically the standpoint of the Premier (or Moderns) Grand Lodge. It was a view which we have heard previously when Samuel Spencer spoke about such matters to an Irish claimant for charity in 1759. There would therefore seem to be little room for manoeuvre as far as allegiance to this Grand Body was concerned. Yet what are the facts in regard to Thomas Dunckerley?

The facts are that Dunckerley's own Mother Lodge at Portsmouth must have practised 'the old working' for it conferred the Royal Arch *Degree*. We have in fact a statement from his own pen:

"I was exalted at Portsmouth in the year 1754." Yet he was only initiated on the 10 January that same year. Such a custom, having Exaltation follow so rapidly upon the heels of the Craft degrees, was exactly what happened in Antients' lodges. Moreover, this was all taking place 3 years before Dr. Manningham's statement, 5 years before the assertion by a Moderns Grand Secretary and 13 years before the establishment of the 'Moderns' Grand Chapter. It surely seems very odd behaviour for a respected son of the Premier Grand Lodge.

Nor is this all. Dunckerley's voyage to Quebec in 1760 offers us yet another clue to his peculiar taste in ritual. "The phrase 'Sublime Degree of a Master Mason' first occurs in the year 1754 in a form of certificate drawn up by the Grand Lodge of Ireland, (of) perhaps several years previously. The same phrase is used in a certificate issued by Lodge No. 11 (IC) in the First Royal Scots Regiment in 1762 ... While it appears in Bristol Minutes in 1768 it is used there *indifferently to describe either the Master Mason or Royal Arch Degree* and can be said **not** to have come into general use in Moderns lodges till approaching the end of the 18th century. Any instance of it before that period I regard as a sign of (the) Antients' ritual having passed that way.

"Very well then: on the 16 October 1760, Dunckerley, as WM of Lodge No. 254 held aboard the *Vanguard*, signed a certificate stating that Bro. Edward Grey "was received and Enter'd Apprentice the second day of October 5760 and Fellow Craft in this Lodge on the Nineth (sic) day of the same Month and Year, and that after having sustain'd with Strength, Firmness and Courage, the most Painfull Works, and Severest Tryalls, we gave unto him the most Sublime Degree of Master." ... Dunckerley (was) responsible for the phrasing ..."[2]

None of this should really be unexpected. The membership of the Three Tuns Lodge must have been, as largely servicemen, accustomed to the ritual used in military lodges, and the vast majority of the Regimental Lodges were 'Antient' in their working. As we have already learnt in the last chapter most of these lodges were Irish in origin and it was not until after 1755 that any English 'military' warrants were issued. As Heron Lepper says, so clearly, "the military lodges generally can be regarded as the great propagators of the old tradition, not only in the Americas but all over the world."[3]

Yet if this explains how Dunckerley might come to be more familiar with Antients working it still does not make clear why someone so obviously recognised and respected by the Premier Grand Lodge leaders should apparently be so disloyal in a matter of masonic practice. "Why" someone has asked, turning the question around, "if Dunckerley was an exponent of Antients ritual did he labour in the mills of the Moderns?" The answer has to be, knowing the man, that he had a plan.

Of Dunckerley's devoted loyalty to the Premier Grand Lodge there cannot be the slightest doubt. He was totally in support of the efforts made by the Grand Lodge to raise the status of the Craft by enforcing a stricter discipline on private lodges, decreeing a minimum fee for Initiation (so as to avoid the haphazard 'Makings for Half a Crown'), and establishing a nobility of leadership and central meeting place. Yet experience had soon taught him that *loyalty to the Antient landmarks in ritual* was not incompatible with devotion to a Grand Lodge which had mistakenly attempted to remove those landmarks. "Forms of ritual, after all, were a matter of choice, chance, or locality. The bulk of English-speaking Lodges preferred, as Dunckerley was well aware, the old forms, and would not change them.... To permit, nay more, *to extend the practice* of (such) ritual in the Moderns lodges would be an effective counter-attack on the arch-enemy, that witty and pestilent fellow (for so Dunckerley would have described Laurence Dermott), who was never done bawling that the *true forms were to be found only in the Antient Lodges*. Why not try a finesse then, and make the best card in his hand, *the card of ritual*, ineffective? ... Above all, let brotherly love prevail, particularly towards an Antient Mason. Build a wide and easy bridge over which Brethren of that persuasion might come with a welcome into the camp of their antagonists; and let them come with drums beating and colours flying and never a hint of a white flag or a white sheet."[4]

Whether or no Dunckerley would have expressed his strategy in quite those terms, or even seen its outline so sharply, this was the way in which he proceeded to act. And the military analogy just given by Lepper was exceedingly appropriate in the Canadian scene to which Dunckerley was once more approaching.

As we might expect from a Mason who had travelled far and wide Dunckerley "held no fantastic theories about the supremacy of the Grand Lodge of England over Freemasonry wheresoever dispersed round the globe." When he again lands in North America he finds the situation described already. There *was* a Provincial Grand Lodge in place in Quebec and members of the four British Grand Lodges were all involved in maintaining and promoting it. So what happened? "Whatever their numbers and whatever their Constitutions, this miscellany of soldier Masons welcomed Dunckerley as 'One of Ours', accepted the document he had brought with him as conferring regularity upon their proceedings and thenceforth all the Masons in Quebec, *both military and civilian, worked under this authorisation....* According to the account given by one who was present at the meeting on the 24 June 1760: 'Bro. Simon Fraser, Colonel of the Highland Regiment, was elected to preside over the Lodges (Guinett's six months was up) and *Bro. Dunckerley honoured them with his approbation of their conduct and installed Bro. Fraser* in his high office."[5] Dunckerley had brought his other great gift into play.

"Dunckerley must have possessed personal charm and pleasant manners to make him welcome in the social circles much higher than his own to which he was admitted from an early age. The friends he made in the higher classes of society were, as we know, of service to him when it came to establishing his true parentage; but we can only surmise what gifts of his had led them to take such an interest in his fortunes ... we are led to conclude that they liked the man for himself ... One thing cannot be disputed: Dunckerley became immensely popular wherever he went (and) That popularity became a weapon of attack used in behalf of his Grand Lodge."[6] One instance some years later will show that this was true.

In 1792 Dunckerley obtained a new *Moderns* warrant for an Antients Lodge in Southampton which had already been in existence for 20 years. It retained its new allegiance until Dunckerley's death, and then reverted to the Antients. This case not only shows the effect of Dunckerley's charm in persuading lodges to alter their allegiance but clearly shows that there cannot have been any essential difference between this lodge's working and that approved by Dunckerley.

It was back into a fascinating masonic melting-pot that Dunckerley returned when the squadron, of which *Vanguard* was part, sailed up the St. Lawrence river in early May, 1760. It was also a fortunate military moment. The ships, says Sadler, "were only just in time to prevent Quebec falling again into the hands of the enemy who had invested the fortress with much spirit by both land and sea. The English ships made short work of the frigates left to defend the approaches, capturing or destroying them under the eyes of the French commander, who seems to have suddenly arrived at the conclusion that after all Quebec was undesirable as a place of permanent residence, for the very same night he hastily left the neighbourhood with all his belongings, forgetting even to leave his address."[7]

The ease with which Dunckerley was once more intimately involved in the masonic activities locally does support the idea that *before* his return to England in 1759 Dunckerley had agreed with the various regimental lodges that they should gather to elect a 'Provincial' Grand Master and that he would obtain a document from Grand Lodge whilst in England to regularise the situation. The idea appears even more likely when we consider that despite the preponderance of Irish, Scottish and even Antient 'lodges' in Quebec they so naturally accepted a Provincial warrant from the Moderns Grand Lodge, as if that were already settled. Or was it a case again of Dunckerley using his charm? What is certain is that from 1761 Col. the Hon. Simon Fraser was for a second time 'deputed' Provincial Grand Master, on this occasion by Lord Aberdour, the Grand Master of England.

Dunckerley was to make four trips to Quebec and back at this time though in March 1761 he was transferred to H.M.S. *Prince*. For this period of masonic work he received another 'extended' authority by which the Grand Lodge granted him the right 'to Make, Pass and Raise Masons, on Board any Ship or Vessel'. Moreover a certificate issued in 1762 is very personal: "Having authority ... *I did receive and enter* our well beloved Brother...." You are in no doubt as to who is in control.

In commenting here on the problems of holding a lodge on board a Man of War in those days a recent biographer of Dunckerley makes another very pertinent point: "Tyling a lodge in a ship crammed with men must have been difficult and finding space amid the stores, sails, ammunition and guns must have been an even bigger problem. It was as well that *there were not the perambulations* of present-day ceremonies ... Captain's permission too was probably obtained, for a number of members of the crew gathering behind closed doors or a secluded corner could suggest a mutinous motive and for this the punishment was stringent."[8]

On land Dunckerley would again encounter that richness of masonic practice that has already been referred to as amongst military masons. A revealing entry in the diary of Lt. John Knox, albeit when this officer was in Annapolis, Nova Scotia, makes the point:

"(12 July 1758) The detachment here is daily at exercise, nevertheless our time passes very heavily; and when the calendar does not furnish us with a loyal excuse for assembling in the evening, we have recourse to a Free-Mason Lodge (sic) where we work so hard, that it is inconceivable to think what a quantity of business, of great importance, is transacted in a very short space of time."[9] This entry certainly suggests that Knox and his fellow-soldiers worked additional degrees which followed rapidly one after the other in any one evening. If this were true of only some of the military or civilian lodges that gathered in Quebec in 1761 and 1762 then Dunckerley would have his first taste of further 'plums' that he might pluck from the rich masonic garden of the Antients. And so that we are in no doubt as to the features of the 'older' forms of ceremony with which Dunckerley would be made so much more familiar let us briefly review them here.

The first feature was the retention of a catechetical type of Lecture. No doubt much of what was in the pre-1717 'lectures' might be considered to be out of date by the 1750s yet 'the archaisms in the text had acquired such sacrosanctity by long usage that their omission would seem sacrilege to a Mason of the old school.' When we come to Dunckerley's own use of ritual shortly we shall see the special relevance of this point.

The second feature was a different way of using Passwords and of course a very strong conviction about how the words B. and J. were to be employed.

A third feature was the insistence on an esoteric and fuller ceremony for the installation of a new Worshipful Master and some linkage between what was done in this ceremony and that of the Royal Arch. Material used here was considered to be pre-1717 in origin.

Fourthly, the St. John festivals of the year were regarded with great respect and kept as important landmarks. As examples of this we might note the following from Bristol between 1750 and 1768.

1750: Lodge 184 held a dinner on both St. John's Days.
1752: Lodge at the Crown, No. 220 elected the WM at both days.
1756: Lodge No. 123 bye-laws stated that the Master, Wardens, Treasurer and Secretary were to be chosen annually on the festivals of St. John. (sic)
1758: The Crown Lodge appointed Deacons on St. John's Day.
1768: The Sun Lo. No. 421 Bye-Laws provide for the election of the Master, Wardens, Treasurer and Secretary biennially on one of these days.

Fifthly, there was the insistence on the retention of the Royal Arch as part and parcel of true Masonry; and

Finally, there was the endeavour to retain the traditional Christian character of the wording and symbolism employed.

If confirmation were needed of Dunckerley's involvement not only with an older form of ritual but with Antients lodges themselves then one need look no further than the words of a nearer contemporary Dr. Oliver. In his book, "The Revelations of a Square", we are told that.

"His views of Masonry were liberal, and he despised sectarian controversy. He frequently visited the Ancient Masons' Lodges for the purpose of ascertaining what was the actual difference between the two systems ... and he carefully culled its flowers, and transplanted them into Constitutional Masonry; for *he actually found* amongst the ancients, *to his undisguised astonishment, several material innovations* in the system of Masonry, including some alteration of the Old Landmarks, and a new application of the Master's Word."

It was faced with these discoveries that Dunckerley set about the task which has already been intimated and which Oliver now spells out. "As John Wesley is said to have observed, when he adopted some popular ditty to his collection of hymns, – 'It is a pity the devil should monopolise all the best tunes', so our Bro. Dunckerley, how loudly soever the self-styled Ancients might blow their schismatical trumpet, and proclaim the exclusive excellence of their schism, resolved that they should not appropriate to themselves a single pearl of any real value towards the *elucidation* of the Craft." *Shedding light* on Freemasonry was something that he quickly set about doing.

Oliver went on to state that Dunckerley was authorised by the Grand Lodge "to construct a new code of Lectures by a careful *revision of the existing ritual*, and a *collation of all the ancient forms*." That Dunckerley did revise some previous workings and adapted older forms is unquestioned but Sadler has shown conclusively that there are no Grand Lodge records to justify Dr. Oliver's assertion. Dunckerley was certainly well fitted for this role of editor. As early as 1757, when 30 years of age and only three years after his initiation, he delivered an address in Plymouth which was so well received that it was later published in a printed form as *The Light and Truth of Masonry Explained* and announced in the Gentleman's Magazine for that year as costing 6d and published by Davey and Law. It is a little known production today and its rotund phrases do not suit our modern ways but anyone who really wants to know the 'oracle of the Grand Lodge', as Oliver called him, has to sample part of this Charge. Three of its paragraphs will have to suffice.

> "Brethren,
>
> Light and Truth being the great essentials of the **Royal Craft**, I shall begin this discourse with that awful message which St. John delivered to the world, **That God is light, and in him is no darkness at all**; and that we are not worthy of the **true Fellowship**, unless we walk in the **Light**, and do the **Truth**. O! sacred **Light**! whose orient beams makes manifest that **Truth** which **unites** all faithful **Masons** in a heavenly **Fellowship**!.
>
> "This sublime part of Masonry is that firm base on which is raised the *shaft* of Faith, that supports a beautiful *entablature* of good works: it is the foundation of a superstructure unbounded as the universe, and durable as eternity. To attempt a description of this stupendous fabrick may seem presumptuous in me, who have been so few years a Mason: but as you, my Brethren, were pleased to request something of this kind, give me leave to assure you that I am truly sensible of the honour...."

Dunckerley concludes:

> "In fine, all good Masons should be pious, prudent, just, and temperate and resolutely virtuous. From what I have *advanced* and from these our ancient charges, I hope it is evident to everyone at the present that it is the duty of every Mason to live soberly, righteously and godly; or, according to the words of the Evangelist, He should walk in the Light, and do the Truth. Continue, my Brethren, to persevere in principles that are disinterested, and I doubt not but you will find this room which we have now opened and dedicated to Masonry constantly resorted to by the wise, the faithful and the good."

After such a delivery one has little trouble in accepting Sadler's description: "Possessing a strong, active mind, with an easy fluent delivery, he was advised in the year 1770 to become a student in the law, and during five years' close application, acquired such a fund of legal knowledge, that in Michaelmas term, 1774, he was called to the bar by the Honourable Society of the Inner Temple." He did not take up the profession but rather joined the Hampshire Militia, being by then also Provincial Grand Master of that county. His non-masonic writings include however several published letters to the notable Earl of Chesterfield, an address at Marlborough in 1769 and a Charge delivered in

Colchester in 1777. He was certainly a man who had a way with words.

It is not surprising to learn, therefore, that whether Dunckerley's talents were used on the national scale or not he certainly used his literary gifts in *adapting* some ritual. In 1764 Dunckerley ended his naval career and became a superannuated R.N. officer. He had joined the Marine Lodge in Plymouth and was its reigning Master in 1765. This, says one of his biographers, "afforded some compensation for the fact that he had missed the opening (of the new Lodge) which he had hoped to perform and for which he had prepared a special ceremony. The Lodge was at that time known as a Geometric lodge, as *Dunckerley's ritual* was based upon that science, and the moral lessons to be learned from it, particularly in *The Fellow Craft degree.*"[10]

The Marine Lodge became the Lodge of Fortitude No. 105 in 1780 and though war and other circumstances greatly depleted its records the work of a Bro. S.J.Bradford during more than 60 years managed to salvage some of the history which was recorded in a short Commemorative booklet. Even more important from our point of view is the recovery of the original Dunckerley workings, not only for the Craft but for most of the additional degrees. Of those workings we shall be speaking shortly.

During 1764, and before Dunckerley was to enjoy a pleasant voyage around the Mediterranean, there took place an event that must have alerted him to the necessity of changing Moderns' attitudes. A Capt. Milborne West, an Irish or Antients Mason, sought admission to the lodge in Bath that is now Royal Cumberland No. 41. He was told that he would be received as a member provided that he was re-initiated, though as he was a Mason of long standing they would do the ceremony 'gratis'.

When one considers that this Brother had been Provincial Grand Master of Quebec from December 1761 to June 1763, and elected to that high office by a Provincial Grand Lodge which functioned by virtue of a power from the Premier Grand Lodge of England brought by Dunckerley, one can begin to appreciate the absurdity of the situation. A Mason who was orthodox enough to govern a Province abroad was not orthodox enough to be a lodge member in England.

The objectors did not remain silent or inactive and by the start of the 1770s the policy of the Moderns Grand Lodge began to be modified. Yet it took action at the highest level to make an impact. On 22 May 1766 Lord Blayney, Grand Master of the Moderns, albeit an Irish peer, went to Wapping to visit Old Dundee Lodge, then No. 9. He witnessed an Initiation ceremony and noticed that Old Dundee had started to abandon some of the Antient forms to which he was accustomed. He said nothing on the day but later sent them a note by the Senior Grand Warden asking them to revert to older practice in just one particular. The lodge agreed, but not without much demur. The details can be read elsewhere but the conclusion from this event is evident – Lord Blayney was determined to restore Masonic ritual to its primitive form at least in some particulars. What *was* being emphasised was that Antients workings in Moderns Constitutional lodges were permitted. The principle was not lost on Dunckerley who was also a member of Old Dundee.

There were other implications for overseas Freemasonry when those who represented the Moderns were less than sensitive to older practice. There had just been a secession of a large body of Freemasons in Philadelphia where the Provincial Grand Master had sought to impose a Moderns form of ritual on a newly warranted lodge that included Irish and Scots as well as English members. Having as Wor. Master a skilled Operative artisan from Belfast the resistance proved too much for the PGM to deal with. It has to be said that this was a sign of the times, and especially of events that would occur in North America into the next century. Those events will affect our story significantly.

Before we come to the year 1769 that especially concerns the student of Mark affairs we must take note of the Royal Arch matters which were absorbing the time and energies of Dunckerley. These too are not irrelevant to our story as I shall soon point out. What is certain is that to someone with a strategic plan, such as Dunckerley clearly had, the settlement of the Royal Arch issue in the Moderns camp was crucial as a stepping stone to the recognition of other degrees. Moreover, efforts to bring about the formation of an authoritative Royal Arch body were so demanding that there was no time for attending to other matters until that was achieved.

"Great as were Blayney's services to Craft Masonry, they were even greater in another (sector) of Freemasonry. He was the first Grand Master of the Moderns to foster the Arch *Degree*, claimed by Laurence Dermott as an appendage belonging solely to the Antients, and his name will be connected for ever with the Supreme Grand Royal Arch Chapter of England, which he founded by the Charter of Compact in 1767."[11]

At the time of this foundation he had not been a Royal Arch Mason for very long for he was exalted in the Caledonian Chapter in London on 11 June 1766 and probably by Dunckerley. This Chapter was composed of members from various lodges who met to help others 'pass the Arch' and by all accounts Dunckerley was 'a new and indefatigable exponent' of the ceremony. This seems proved by a certificate issued to him from a lodge in Plymouth Dock in February 1768. It stated that he had presided as Master for two years 'during which time his Masonic skill, knowledge and experience hath been manifested in the care he hath taken in Governing, *Instructing and Improving* (the) said Lodge in the several degrees of EP . . ., FC . . ., MM . . ., & RA . . .'. It is to be noted that all this was happening in a period prior to the formation of the new Grand Chapter and the issuing of warrants for private Chapters. It was also at the time that the official view regarding the 'degree' was expressed by the Grand Secretary to the Provincial Grand Master of Frankfurt:

"The Royal Arch is a society which we do not acknowledge, and which we hold to be an invention to introduce innovations and *to seduce the Brethren*."

That was in early July 1767 and it was on 22 July that Blayney, certainly encouraged by Dunckerley and others, agreed to lend his name to the constituting the Caledonian Chapter as 'the Grand and Royal Chapter of the Royal Arch of Jerusalem'. That was how the present Supreme Grand Chapter began.

Dr. Oliver had no doubts about Dunckerley's part in these developments. "In one instance, he certainly laid himself open to the charge of building on another man's foundation, for *he reconstructed Dermott's Royal Arch*, and introduced it into the Grand Lodge of England . . . I cannot deny but it was an innovation, for it absolutely disarranged the Landmarks, *by transferring the Master's Word to a subsidiary degree*. But time has effected wondrous changes . . . and the improved Royal Arch Degree is now considered the *perfection* of Masonry."[12]

Lord Blayney had had every opportunity of getting to know Dunckerley well because the latter attended the Committee of Charity (the equivalent of the present Board of General Purposes) as the Master of the Guadaloupe Lodge from 1766, by meeting in the new Somerset House Lodge which was created with the warrant from Dunckerley's naval days, and by their joint interest in the revival of the Lodge of Friendship No. 6. The story of this latter venture is not for telling here save to remark that it again concerned the working of Antients ritual in a Moderns lodge and especially the inner working at the Installation of a new Master.

One of Lord Blayney's last acts as Grand Master was to appoint Thomas Dunckerley as Provincial Grand Master of Hampshire on 28 February 1767. This was the first time that such an officer was appointed there. Sadler has this to say about the office of a PGM at that time:

". . . the appointments were generally made without the slightest regard to either expediency or efficiency, social standing and local influence being the chief considerations. The advent of Dunckerley, and the *earnest and methodical enthusiasm* which he immediately brought to bear upon his new duties, with the *most satisfactory results*, doubtless awakened the authorities to the knowledge that it was possible for a Provincial Grand Master to be a *real help* to the Society, instead of merely an ornamental addition to it."[13]

Sixteen lodges had been formed in Hampshire since 1724 although five of these had already been erased when Dunckerley began his task. We cannot here review his total stewardship though it is evident from the diary of the years 1767–69 that he was maintaining the itinerancy that was to be his hallmark during the rest of his life. He was assiduous in his attendance at the Committee of Charity in London as also at lodges there, but that did not mean that Hampshire was neglected. His involvement in the masonic life of Portsmouth has already been mentioned since he was initiated and exalted there. It was his interest particularly that salvaged the Antiquity Lodge to which he was always so proud to belong and it was on behalf of those members, like himself, who had been 'exalted' in that lodge that he bent his efforts to obtain a Charter for a new Chapter in 1769. On 13 January the Grand Royal Chapter 'passed' 4 chapters and the seal was affixed by 14 July. The warrants were issued on 11

August and "Chapter of Friendship No. 3" was duly inaugurated. It is today the oldest Chapter on the Roll.

In the Bicentenary booklet of this ancient and august Chapter we read the beginning of a remarkable story:

"On p. 4 of his 'History of the Phoenix Lodge Group', published in 1894, W. Bro. A.N.Y.Howell tells us that the wife of his friend W. Bro. G.F. Lancaster had an aunt, a relative of one of the last surviving members of the Lodge of Antiquity, who burned some books (no doubt including minute books) of the Lodge ... This lady described the books as 'Devil's Books'. Again, there was a disastrous 'clearing-up' in 1880, when a large quantity of books and papers was destroyed as rubbish, in a bonfire in the yard, and it was only by good fortune that Lancaster and W. Bro. M.E.Frost rescued two books, in cipher, one of which Lancaster afterwards found to be the first Minute Book of the Chapter. It begins with the minute for the 1 September 1769, recording that Dunckerley himself attended and brought the warrant with him."

In the *Freemason Magazine* for 24 February 1894 a letter from Alexander Howell adds more interesting information about one of these 'finds'. He writes:

"The book is written entirely in cipher, not a single letter being in ordinary writing ... About six years ago (Mark Frost) gave it to me and from that day it has been in my custody without my having the remotest idea what it contained. About 10 days ago, and quite by accident, I discovered that the first page of what had hitherto been considered to be the first minute book of the chapter (commencing in June 1787) had been pasted down to the front fly leaf and that there was writing upon it. After considerable trouble I separated the pages and found that the writing consisted of 19 lines in cipher. I then recollected the book given me by Bro. Frost, and upon comparing the writing found that the cipher used was exactly the same." I must interrupt the story here to say that this narrative has all the marks of being very similar to another one familiar to all Chapter Companions. He continued:

"The difficulty now was to find out what the gibberish was all about, as not the remotest clue was was given anywhere." The reader may here begin to realise how, if this seemed 'gibberish' to a Freemason, it would certainly seem like 'devil's language' to an old lady.

"I copied part of the first page and sent it to Bro. Hughan (a very notable masonic scholar) but he was unable to decipher the writing but told me that the cipher was a combination *unusual in England.* I may say it consists of squares, or parts of squares, angles, and triangles, some of the latter being enriched with a dash inwards from one angle."

"After wasting many hours in trying to work out a key to the problem without the least success I showed the book to a brother who, quite by way of a guess, suggested that certain letters at the bottom of the first page might be the names of the three Principals. Knowing who the first Principals were I found that the number of letters in each line corresponded with the number of letters in each brother's name: the key was found' ... The rest was easy but the reward was great. The book proved to be the first minute book of the Chapter, containing minutes from 1 September 1769, to 7 June 1786."

FRIENDSHIP CHAPTER ENTRY

"At a Royal Arch Chapter held at the George Tavern in Portsmouth on First Septr.Seventeen hundred and sixty nine = PRESENT Thomas Dunckerley, Esq., William Cook, "Z", Samuel Palmer "H", Thomas Scanvill "J", Henry Dean Philip Joyes and Thomas Webb = The "Pro G.M." Thomas Dunckerley bro't the Warrant of the Chapter and having lately rec'd the 'Mark' he made the bre'n 'Mark Masons' and 'Mark Masters'. And each chuse their "Mark", viz...Z. (Interlaced Triangles)....
= He also told us of this mann'r of writing which is to be used in the degree w'ch we may give to others so they be FC for 'Mark Masons' and MASTER M for 'Mark Masters'."

Not only was Thomas Dunckerley present but he was seen to be a Mark Mason and duly made the brethren present Mark Masons and Mark Masters. "And it further appears that we are to thank him for the cipher used in this book. This reference to the Mark degree is nearly (*four*) years earlier than any other (English one) ... In November 1770, we have mention of Excellent and Super-Excellent Masons. And in October, 1778 we find Dunckerley giving the Chapter permission to 'make Knight Templars' ... In the same minute the members are called 'Companions' for the first time being only 8 months after the first use of that word in Royal Arch minutes of which we have any knowledge."

This was indeed a remarkable break-through and it is notable that despite the passage of another century there has not been any other discovery of a like kind to parallel or precede this Mark milestone. Yet if there has been no record of so full a kind it has, I hope, been shown that there was a Mark degree beginning to emerge elsewhere. This was not the only or even the earliest evidence of some kind of Mark practice. Moreover, we are at last in a position to examine this de-ciphered occasion with fresh information that was not available to Howell or to many who followed him. It is now time to see what this entry is trying to tell us, and in order to cover all its implications I shall try to answer five questions.

(i) What exactly was the degree that Dunckerley introduced that day?
ii) Why did he introduce it into a Chapter and a new one at that?
iii) Where did Dunckerley 'receive the Mark' that he now introduced?
iv) Why did he introduce a cypher language and where did it originate?
v) What happened later to this form of the Mark degree?

In providing answers to these questions I believe that we shall not only appreciate 1769 better but will benefit Mark Masonry generally.

i) Ever since Wor. Bro. Howell wrote about the discovery of the cipher written pages of the first minutes of the Chapter of Friendship it seems as if his conclusion regarding the character of Dunckerley's Mark degrees has been accepted without question. He wrote:

"Of what the Mark Degree consisted at that time we have no means of determining, but I should imagine that the ceremony was very slight, probably merely consisting of the selection of a Mark, and intrusting the candidate with some peculiar sign or secret. It will be noticed that Dunckerley stipulated that the Mark Masters Degree was only to be given to a Master Mason, and it is quite possible that this was entirely an idea of his own, and the commencement of a series of regulations for its government."

Such was the impression with which I grew up as a Mark Mason and no alternative to this view seemed ever to be expressed or written about. Certainly there is nothing to dispel this notion in the books written by Grantham, Springett or Handfield-Jones. As none of them, like Howell, ever imagined that there was ritual material connected with Dunckerley which might lift a little more of the veil of the unknown their reticence seems understandable. However, the veil was shortly to be raised substantially.

On 17 February 1954, the Librarian of the Grand Lodge in London received a letter from Shirehall Park, Hendon. It was written by a Freemason, Samuel James Bradford, and read as follows:

> "Dear W. Brother Grantham,
>
> Here are the negatives of the two Degrees of Mark Man or Mark Mason, and Mark Master, or Foreman of the FCs ... both of these *Dunckerley Rituals* are complete ...
>
> The authenticity of these Rituals is beyond doubt.
>
> Our old friend and Brother Songhurst, investigated them *in 1904* and attested to them in 1905. I have a *photostat copy of that attestation* (see below) and could send that along for you to copy ...
>
> I can personally attest them from 1905. Rd. Pearce Couch when near his end, told his wife to take the ritual of John Knight to his friend Capt. Latham. This was done. *His* wife and youngest daughter still survive, and are friends of mine.
>
> In due course Capt. Latham felt that he also was near his end, and instructed his wife to send the Rituals, and other old Certificates etc. *to the Mark Masons* 'on loan'. This was done, and the case duly arrived, but, as the war was on they were not opened, nor have they been opened up since. Capt. Latham's widow is still with us (and we) hope to visit both her and Mrs. Pearce Couch in May next when we take a motor tour down West.
>
> This copy is not from Knight's Copy, but a later one taken *from Dunckerley's original* by Peter Pender when he had completed his Degrees ..."

Enclosed with this letter, as had been indicated, were the photostats of the attestations by Bro. Songhurst. He obviously read two documents which were attached to the Rituals and wrote as follows about them:

i) "The above is copied from a note in the possession of Bro. R.Pearce Couch of Penzance that formerly belonged to his Grandfather Richard Pearce. It is in the handwriting of John Knight and Bro. Couch informs me that it is stated in his family to have been copied by John Knight from a MS lent to him by Thos. Dunckerley.
(signed) W.John Songhurst. 7 January 1905."

ii) "The foregoing is copied from a MS in the possession of Bro. R.Pearce Couch of Penzance. *It* is in the handwriting of John Knight who attests the signature of Bro. R.Pearce (grandfather of Bro. Couch).
(signed) W.John Songhurst. 17 February 1905."

Some comments on these latter documents may be in order before we come to the substance of what they seek to regularise.

A list of candidates for the additional degrees attached to the ritual MSS shows as No. 22 a Richard Pearce aged 25 of Penzance who was admitted on 9 June 1819. This at least confirms the family line by which the information comes to us. At No. 3 in the same list there is Peter Pender, aged 50, of Redruth who was admitted on 17 June 1806. We can add that in 1806 there was already in existence a 'Mark Book' in which John Knight's Mark of 1777 was already entered. Pender and Pearce have their marks duly added.

The 'It' underlined in the second attestation refers of course to the note *with* the MS and not the manuscript itself.

What is it, however, that Bro. Bradford finally handed over, if only in photocopy, to the Grand Lodge library in London? It is a series of almost 100 handwritten pages covering 18 separate degrees though some of the degrees have two parts, 5 points or 4 sections. For our particular purpose the first 6 are the ones that need to be mentioned. They are:–

1) Ent'd Apptce;
2) Fellow Craft;
3) MARK MAN (or Foreman of the F . . . C . . . s);
4) Master Mason;
5) MARK MASTER or MARK MASON;
6) Master of Arts and Sciences.

It ought to be mentioned here that in the *list* of rituals attached there is also mention of 12 "other Masonic Orders" including 'Link' and 'Wrestle' but there is no MS ritual for these. I would assure the reader, however, that we shall deal with these 'orders' in a later chapter.

Whilst a full treatment of the contents of these rituals will be part of the section devoted to Mark rituals there are three things that should be said about them at this stage. The first is that they represent a quite distinct category of Mark ceremony when compared with others that were emerging at this time. They represent the stage of transition from just a series of lectures into an acted drama.

The second thing is that they show an unmistakable connection with the same sort of tradition as the Harodim form of instruction (also called the Geometrick fashion) which has links with either the York Grand Lodge or the Royal Order.

Thirdly, there is a clear distinction between the Mark Man and the Mark Mason/Master steps whereby the former relates to a Fellow Craft and the latter to the Master Mason. Moreover, there seems to be a separation from the Royal Arch because of this attachment, even though these two Mark steps are necessary as one moves towards the Master's chair and thence the Excellent and Super Excellent degrees that precede the Royal Arch.

If, as I am prepared to do, you accept that here at last we have the form of ceremony which Dunckerley introduced at Portsmouth in 1769 then of course we have something much more solid on which to base our ongoing story but we also have to deal with the next issue.

ii) Why did Dunckerley introduce the Mark into *a Chapter* and a new one at that? One immediate answer might well be that that is how the ceremonies were presented when he received them and that what he then had to do was to look for the first available opportunity to repeat the process. If he *had 'lately'* received them, and we shall fully discuss this below, then it must have been a very fortunate circumstance that the opportunity to present a warrant to a brand-new Chapter came so soon.

Whilst that may well be the answer it does not wholly meet all the facts of the case. As has just been pointed out there does seem to be a significant gap here between the Mark sections and the Royal Arch and hence for there to be no necessity for ceremonies linked to the Fellow Craft and Master Mason to be administered in a Chapter. That *does* need explaining. For my part there seems to be only one solution. It was a deliberate ploy by Dunckerley.

Let us consider the situation. Dunckerley is a Provincial Grand Master newly appointed by the Premier Grand Lodge. We know that he has a policy of seeking to filch the best ideas and practices of the Antients and encourage them in Moderns lodges. He has just achieved a very significant breakthrough under the leadership of Lord Blayney so that Royal Arch Chapters may be legitimately warranted and erected. He has actually seen the petition for the Chapter of Friendship safely through the new Supreme Grand Chapter channels. And then he visits some other masonic lodge in which he at last receives the 'secrets' of another growing Antients degree – the Mark. What is he to do?

He has three options. One is to stifle his enthusiasm and let his new-found Masonic knowledge lie fallow. A second is to look for a suitable Moderns lodge in which to plant the new seeds. But thirdly, he has the remarkable opportunity not only of honouring one of the very first warranted Moderns Chapters but of trying out his new 'baby' in a situation where *no-one present* can query the nature of his novel ceremonies nor plead against a break with older tradition. The starting of a Chapter in a Moderns setting was innovation anyway.

It was thus that Thomas Dunckerley came to his decision, being the consummate Masonic politician that he was. The fact that what he did was noted in cypher made the action even more discreet.

iii) Many opinions have been expressed as to where Dunckerley may have obtained the form of Mark ceremony that he communicated to his brethren in the newly formed Chapter of Friendship. The ones I have listed so far are (a) from Scotland, (b) from the North-east of England, (c) from Ireland, (d) from a military lodge, (e) from a Antients lodge, (f) from the Grand Lodge of All England, (g) from somewhere in Hampshire, (h) from America circa 1780 and (i) that he simply created it himself. It is an impressive list of ideas and suggests much ingenuity but in no case where such a suggestion is made is there any *evidence or argument* produced to explain the choice. What is even more interesting is that there is no repetition of one or two of these suggestions as if those were ones with special grounds for selection. One is left wondering in each instance why that particular source was preferred.

We may of course speculate as to the probable reasons for these statements and in doing so we can, I believe, eliminate most of the suggestions, especially if we can accept that what was said above about the nature of the ceremonies that Dunckerley introduced is correct. So let us see where this line of reasoning takes us.

Let me start with the last suggestion that Dunckerley probably created the two degrees himself. In view of the fact that we have no evidence of anything as clear cut as this introduction of *two* distinct 'degrees' anywhere else in Britain before this date it is certainly tempting to imagine that here we have a case of plain innovation. That Dunckerley was both scholarly and literate enough to undertake such a task there can be no doubt. When one is aware of his reputation as a collector and purveyor of Masonic knowledge there can be ready agreement with the view that the task was not beyond him. Just listen to another passage from one of Dr. Oliver's books. It occurs in "The Revelations of a Square" when a Dr. Franco has put forward the thesis that Freemasonry is essentially Jewish.

"Bro. Dunckerley rose, and addressing himself to the chair, observed that he concurred in pronouncing the general construction of Masonry to be cosmopolite, and, consequently, democratic; yet he would submit to the consideration of the Lodge, whether the Lectures which we use are not essentially Christian ... (and) amongst the many hundreds of Christian Lodges, which are spread over the four quarters of the globe, it is very doubtful whether there be a single Jewish Lodge in existence. 'Besides', he added, 'what claim can the Jews, as a nation, have to be conservators of an institution which they certainly never practised, if we except a few Grand Superintendents and the Entered Apprentices, during the 7 years which were occupied in preparing the materials for, and building, the Temple at Jerusalem? The expert Masons, the Fellowcrafts, and Masters, were the Dionysiacs, i.e. Tyrians and Egyptians; and they were ranged in separate Lodges, under Hiram Abiff, Tito, Zadok, and their fellows. When the Temple and Solomon's other buildings were finished, I cannot find that these accomplished men held any further communication with the people of Israel; but spread themselves abroad, and practised the art amongst other nations."[14] Even if Dunckerley never made that speech – *or* revised the Craft Lectures in 1766 – as Dr. Oliver asserts, the important thing is that our Brother was *thought able enough* to do so. He *was* capable of doing such a task but was he *inclined* to do so? It is here that large doubts arise. In all that I have sought to show earlier in this chapter we find in Dunckerley a man with a clear purpose. "Dunckerley fought the Antients by making use of *their own* weapons of ritual (so that) if a bridge could be built by acquiescence or compromise across the gulf of divergent ritual (one) might well hope that in time the *rebels* (for so he regarded them) would cross it and return to the original Grand Lodge of England."

If that was his plan, and nothing less explains his bizarre behaviour as a Moderns 'leader', then there would be no point in creating a hostage to fortune by promoting a couple of degrees that the Antients could demonstrate were never in their repertoire. That would be taking a step (a degree?) too far. Moreover it is worth pondering the question why, if he did create these two degrees 'de novo', he never did anything similar in any other direction. He may have adjusted the Ark Mariner degree (though we shall look at that later, pp. 374ff) and he certainly master-minded the development of the Knights Templar but no-one could suggest that he started them. Indeed he would have lost his case for recommending their acceptance by his fellow-Moderns into the framework of Masonry if such 'engineering' could be proved.

No, the idea that Dunckerley 'contrived' these degrees runs quite contrary to the possible run of play in which he was engaged. What we have to accept, because Dunckerley was an honourable man and only two years previously had been shown to have royal blood in his veins, is that what he said to this new Chapter as the *freshly appointed Provincial leader*, was true. The recorded statement "... having lately *received* the Mark" is what we have to wrestle with.

If the term 'received' is to be a guide it means that Dunckerley was present in a Masonic company where he would be welcomed and fully accepted as a suitable candidate for the Mark. Moreover it had to be a lodge in which there was the practice of distinguishing between a Mark Man and a Mark Master. And thirdly it had to be somewhere that obviously linked the Mark ceremonies in some way with the Royal Arch. These conditions immediately start to limit the field, for these requirements could not be met in Hampshire or the North-East of England. In Hampshire the situation with regard to Atholl or Antients lodges was that Nos. 68 and 101 which met at Portsmouth Common were both erased in 1762 and No. 122 which also met in Portsmouth was erased in 1764. No. 79 met in Gosport and No. 88 in Winchester but there is nothing in their records showing any contact by or with Dunckerley and in any case it is unlikely that, having been Provincial Grand Master for two years prior to the visit to the Chapter of Friendship, he would have gone to either of these local 'rebel' units, one of which was on the doorstep of his own Antiquity lodge. There is, needless to say, no record in either of these lodges of any working of the 'Mark' at this time.

As far as the North-East of England is concerned I am quite aware that Durham was the only part of the North country over which Bro. Dunckerley was to preside as Grand Superintendent of the Royal Arch in the next two decades. We also know that there was already an emergent 'Mark' activity in Newcastle, Sunderland, Durham and Gateshead by this time. There is no information in Sadler's Life of Dunckerley as to his Northern whereabouts in 1767–9, but "we know from the *Freemasons' Magazine* (1793) that he was befriended by many influential gentlemen in the years 1766–68 and may have travelled much throughout England and even to Edinburgh, for General Adolphus Oughton writes to him from that city on 18 November 1767, congratulating him on the pension granted to him that year by the King."[15]

No doubt, were he in these parts, he would seek to prepare the way for what might later be a more prominent role and acquaint himself with all the practice of Freemasonry and not least the Royal Arch and any other degrees beyond the Craft. As Bro. Sharp adds:

"If he did visit Edinburgh he would take the Great North Road from London, through York, Durham, (and) Newcastle and being a most enthusiastic and energetic Freemason, could we not expect him to hear of the Mark degree" wherever he went? The Mark is spoken of as having been present in at least the first and last of those cities by this date and though the first specific evidence of the Mark in Durham is not until 1773 we cannot conclude that that was the very first time anything to do with the Mark there was attempted.

However, even if Dunckerley were made aware of some kind of Mark procedure in Durham or Newcastle, that does not mean that he 'received' anything. I am sure that he did not because, as we shall see in the chapter on Mark rituals, the form in the North-east of England was *a markedly different kind* of ceremony from that which we have already noted as being ascribed to Dunckerley. Of course it is possible to claim that Dunckerley 'received the Mark' in a lodge there but then changed the style of the ceremony to his own liking. This suggestion however carries the same objections as we saw above about 'creating' a new 'degree'. What we have to find is a situation in which Dunckerley could immediately seize upon an Antients working and transfer it into one of his own Masonic units. He could not do that in the North-east.

What are the chances of his having done this in Scotland and Ireland? Again we cannot say categorically that he did not visit these parts of Britain in 1767–9 but I have to submit that it was very unlikely. In 1767 he was very busily engaged with the Soho Chapter and Lodge of Friendship, not to mention the Grand Lodge Committee of Charity, which body he visited every fortnight for most of the year, and in the later part of the year he was in Hampshire trying to rescue his own lodge. No. 35. His concerns there continued into early 1768 when another lodge was erased. In April and May he was in London, involved in the Lodge of Friendship affairs and in dealing with the transfer to a land-base of the Lodge that had been held at sea, so as to become the future Somerset House Lodge. His meetings at Grand Lodge continued and from September to December he was again very busy in the London area after a notable visit to Marlborough in September when he delivered an address which we still have. It is only between May and September that his movements are unknown. By autumn 1769 he was forming the Chapter at Portsmouth and informing them of the Mark he had *lately* received. Did he visit Ireland or Scotland in the summers of 1768/9 and there 'receive the Mark'? It could fit. Moreover, in both these countries, there were definite indications at this date of possible Mark ceremonies and in the case of Ireland they were distinctly linked to the Royal Arch. There is mention of a Mark ceremony which was once in the archives of the Supreme Grand Chapter of Scotland but, as has been said, search for it thus far has proved fruitless. The likelihood of a link here seems to grow until we face two snags. The first is that the Mark ceremonies linked with the Royal Arch in Ireland were distinctly different to the arrangement associated with Dunckerley above and the so-called 'Mark Master' was much more like the ceremony that evolved in Lancashire, Bradford and the North-east of England, than that which Dunckerley acquired. The 'receiving of the Mark' in Ireland would have therefore required the same 'doctoring' by Dunckerley as we saw would create a problem of later acceptance. We do not yet know what the late 18th century working was in Scotland but if it was anything like what came later then again Dunckerley would have had to adapt it to what he offered. The other snag about accepting Ireland or Scotland as the origin of Dunckerley's 'Mark degree(s)' is that even if they were the source they could not be used as the bait for winning over Antients Masons because they were only interested in what their Grand Lodge recognised as *their* legitimate old working – even if the Antients must have first introduced into England traditions known to many of their members from Ireland. No, this is not, I believe, the most satisfactory solution to our problem.

The suggestion that Dunckerley could have obtained the 'Mark' from America in or around 1780 is hardly acceptable since we are faced with the fact that he already had it in 1769, but I want to include the idea of an American 'influence' in the argument that now follows. That argument must deal with the three suggestions that remain and which I propose to take together. These are that he received the 'Mark Man and Mark Master' ceremonies from an Antients and military lodge which had connections with the *Grand Lodge of All England* at York.

That Dunckerley was not only familiar with the military lodges of all the Constitutions but was accepted by them as 'one of ours' we have already seen to be the case in Canada during his visits to Quebec. There is certainly truth in the idea that Dunckerley brought back strong impressions, if not degrees, from his American trips. We also underrate the fact that Dunckerley had all the prestige of being a Serviceman and an officer and was therefore doubly welcome in any military lodge which he might care to visit. His willingness, though 'one of those Moderns', both to acknowledge and *work* the more traditional ritual, must have made him a very acceptable figure. When, no doubt to their delighted surprise, he showed interest in the 'extra' degrees, not least those of Mark, Ark, Excellent, Super Excellent and Knights Templar they would, I am sure, on receiving the required proofs of proficiency, have been willing to admit him to such 'secrets' as they practised and which were not yet known to him.

There were three military lodges in particular that Dunckerley might have used as the place where he could 'receive the 'Mark'. The first was the lodge in the 20th Foot, otherwise known as the Minden Lodge (IC), which had been in Quebec at the time that Dunckerley was present. The Regiment had previously been in barracks at Newport in the Isle of Wight. Indeed we shall see it there again in the next century when its Lodge certainly influenced the formation of the Albany Mark Lodge. After Quebec the 20th Foot was in Germany from 1758–63 and thereafter in Gibraltar until 1769 when it returned to England. The only trouble was that by the time the Regiment returned home the Lodge had temporarily closed and was not opened again for at least another decade. This could not therefore have been the military lodge that Dunckerley used.

The 24th Regiment was commanded by no less a person than the Hon. Edward Cornwallis, a very keen Mason. His second in command was none other than Col. Simon Fraser whom Dunckerley had had the delight of installing as Provincial Grand Master of Quebec for the period 1761/2. That Dunckerley would have been most welcome here is undoubted but the Regiment was in Gibraltar from 1763–9 and was then sent straight to Ireland for the years 1770–4. The dates do not fit the Dunckerley diary.

There remains only one lodge, that in the 6th Inniskilling Dragoons. If we assemble all that has already been stated about this lodge we shall find that it fits all the points of our enquiry with quite astonishing accuracy. It was made up largely of Irishmen but the Lodge had had an Antients warrant, a Grand Lodge of All England (York) warrant and was now in possession of a Moderns warrant. It was thus familiar with a variety of practices and yet was a perfectly proper lodge for a newly appointed Moderns PGM to visit. Moreover, the Regiment was moved to Sussex, and West Sussex at that, throughout 1769 and Dunckerley, let us remember, was shortly to become PGM of that Province also. I can well imagine the lodge here with its Commanding Officer, Col. Cholmondeley, as Wor. Master and one of its Wardens a Lord Kerr, extending a hand of greeting to a prominent Grand Lodge officer whose connection with the Blood Royal was now firmly admitted.

Dunckerley was also doubtless visiting Sussex to acquire new friends and contacts and could so easily have spent an evening in the company of military friends who were working both the Mark Man and the Mark Master according to the Old York style. Indeed I know of no other military lodge that could have known this working that was in any kind of normal reach for Dunckerley at this time. What further underlines the possibility is that in 1852 it was this same military lodge that was to introduce to Masons in the York Lodge at York the very same arrangement of degrees that were here observed by Dunckerley. For my part I find the coincidences too many to dismiss as pure chance. Of course it would be *conclusive* were we able to read of Dunckerley's 'advancement' in an Inniskilling minute. We do not have that, nor is it likely to appear, for military lodge minutes are notoriously rare, many of them having been lost in battle or by dispersal on a Regiment's demise. What I am sure of is that here is the closest answer to our query that we are as yet likely to obtain. At least we have considerably narrowed the field and on this premise Dunckerley *could* say in Portsmouth in September 1769.

"I lately received the 'Mark' and make you, like those brethren made me, 'Mark Masons' and 'Mark Masters'."

iv) Dunckerley went on to introduce a special type of writing. It was introduced with so much emphasis as being the essential accompaniment of the 'Mark' that the members of the Chapter not only used it to record the events of Mark Degree evenings but of all their Chapter evenings as well.

This practice should not surprise us. Such writing had already been used in some Antients documents and I shall discuss these and many other matters regarding the cipher alphabet in a later chapter. Here we are only concerned with the matter in regard to Thomas Dunckerley. For him the mere fact that this was an established Antients practice which particularly fitted his background would have been sufficient to attract his close interest and support.

Most writers on the Mark mention this aspect of 'secret writing' but again no-one seems to have sought in depth for the background to it and certainly no-one has explained why Dunckerley not only used it but introduced a form of cypher that is, so far as we know, unique to the members of Chapter of Friendship. It is here, of course, that I am willing to concede that Dunckerley did make an innovation in 1769. The change was not of principle but of style. There were already variations in the forms of 'square' cipher that were used in Antients lodges or documents and thus it was nothing like as significant a matter for a new Mark body to have its own special cipher. To have had its own 'working' was a change of landmark whereas a variation of 'writing' was an extension of accepted tradition.

Let us turn therefore to the important questions – Why did Dunckerley introduce a cypher mode of writing and where did it come from? The answer to the first part of the question has already been suggested. Because it was part of the emerging Mark practice in the York or Antients tradition and if that was so then Dunckerley was not going to argue with it. But there was something else.

Dunckerley was a naval officer who had obviously had a great deal to do with semaphore and secret battle or sailing instructions. To him the very idea of a 'discreet' manner of communication that was known only to those who had a right to know was part and parcel of his training. It was meat and drink to him and when he discovered that there was actually a part of Freemasonry that still employed not only personal signs, or marks (and he would certainly have known the famous one used by Sir Robert Moray, another serviceman), then I can well imagine him revelling in the opportunity of not only taking up this Masonic practice but making sure that his first communication of it would be distinctive. After all we did hear above how he was disappointed at being absent from the inauguration of a new Lodge in Plymouth because he had devised a 'new form' for that occasion.

If then there is ample reason to explain *why* Dunckerley should introduce the Portsmouth Chapter members to such a custom and stress its special importance we still have to tackle the matter of *where* did he get his system from. Hughan has already been reported as saying that the system was an unusual one and not familiar in England. I shall now attempt to show how right Hughan was and that there was a plan behind the alphabet chosen even though its first solution was achieved only by guess-work.

The first clue to a solution came with the words of W.Bro.Howell in his history:

"Where did (Dunckerley) *learn* the peculiar manner of writing, which he said was to be used in the Degree? He was a very shrewd man, always organising, and trying to improve, and it is equally possible that this again was purely his own idea although *founded* upon the *Marks used by ancient* operative Masons."

I was already clear in my own mind that Dunckerley had only *learnt* one thing. That was that a cipher alphabet was the right accompaniment for the Mark degree. Beyond that he soon realised that it was possible for a student of this 'art' to compose another set of letters if the right pattern of ancient operative forms could be found. It is here that his new-found status as a Royal beneficiary was invaluable. He had been granted a Grace and Favour apartment in Hampton Court and this gave him access to the remarkable library amassed by the founder of the 'palace', Cardinal Wolsey. Not only was Wolsey a great patron of architects and builders but he was a consummate statesman, diplomat and scholar. We shall see later the interesting connection this produced with another cipher system but for the moment we must stay with the array of knowledge placed at his disposal within Hampton's walls. What is clear is that somewhere, and where more likely than Wolsey's library, Dunckerley discovered the same sort of drawings that were mentioned earlier in this book by Bro. J. Rylands (see p. 21). But there was something more. Dunckerley must have lighted upon the oldest and most fundamental of all Operative Masons' symbols – the Square, the Ashlar, the Equilateral Triangle, the Diamond and the Swastika – and saw these as a means of communication.

Just as the graven marks became a sort of language and even assisted in the formation of the letters of ancient alphabets so now he saw that these other ancient forms could serve a similar purpose. Accordingly he must have sat down and pondered how they could be adapted to the kind of cipher system that he would communicate soon in Portsmouth. Did he, I wonder, recall some words that were written a few years before he was born? They have often puzzled me and never been clearly explained. They appear in the pamphlet: "A Mason's Examination."

> "A fellow I was sworn most rare,
> And know the Astler (Ashlar), Diamond, and Square."

No wonder they puzzled me for I was thinking only as a Speculative when these words were still reflecting an Operative past.

To this combination of forms Dunckerley finally added one that has persisted throughout all the Mark cipher systems and which most closely related to the semaphore usage of the Services, the lattice or window shape of crossed bars, but here without a frame.

When most of these shapes are placed in juxta-position and the intervening spaces are allotted to a series of letters from the normal alphabet we then begin to see how the shapes of the Dunckerley cipher were arrived at. As the accompanying diagram shows the lattice has the diamond at its centre with four equilateral triangles within it and four around it and four of the outer squares divided into open ended triangles or semaphore signs. The only symbol that will not fit the whole is that which represents the letters E, G, H and O. They are found in the spaces of a left-facing swastika.

The intricacy of this arrangement, the obvious attempt to engage these ancient shapes and yet the uniqueness of the final arrangement all speak of great care in the alphabet's preparation. It shows the attention that Dunckerley obviously brought to his task and it most certainly proves that he thought the system was one to be prized. It is no wonder that he commended it to the Chapter's attention. It also suggests that when Dunckerley took over Antients working he intended it to be done well in the Moderns bodies to which he brought it.

v) We come therefore to the last query of this period. What happened to this form of the Mark degree? We know that it was 18 years before Dunckerley again appeared in this Portsmouth Chapter and he must have been impressed with the fact that candidates were still being advanced according to this method and the cipher alphabet was still being carefully preserved *and used.* Certainly we have no instance of this same cipher style being employed elsewhere.

We have already seen in relation to the possible workings of the two Mark ceremonies that they were eventually 'retrieved' by Samuel Bradford in the Plymouth area, which was well known to and regularly visited by Dunckerley. There was also mention of a Bro. Richard Pearce in Penzance and a Bro.

Q
A
B
F
M
S
T
L
W
X
C
Z
Y
R
V
U
P
N
D
K
I

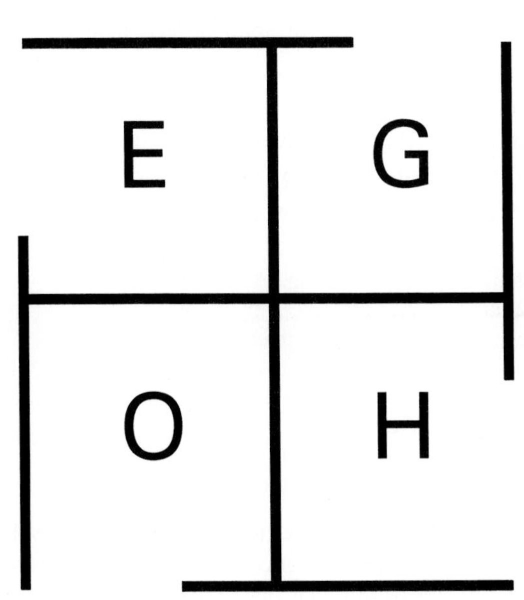
E
G
O
H

John Knight in 1819. We can therefore take it that these areas had knowledge of these 'degrees'.

In regard to John Knight we have two further pieces of information that are relevant to our search. The first is a letter written from Hampton Court Palace by Dunckerley to 'Bro. and Knt. Companion Sir John Knight'. It is dated 27 January 1792. In it occur the following words: "I have also left a Blank for the day on which your first Conclave is to be held. I am *concern'd* that there is so great a distance between us, as it would give me much pleasure to *communicate to every Conclave that I have constituted the Masonic Knowledge* that I have gleaned in Europe, America and Africa for forty years past ... I am not far from 70, yet we intend (with God's permission) to visit the West of England next summer, and (if we should winter at Plymouth) it is probable that I may have the happiness of conversing with some of the Knt. Companions from Exeter, Redruth, and Bideford."[16] This extract only serves to underline the statement by W. Bro. Smyth: "From 1777 onwards Dunckerley's masonic responsibilities grew, until, by 1793, he was concurrently the Provincial Grand Master for 8 Provinces and the Royal Arch Grand Superintendent in no fewer than eighteen, and it must be clearly understood that these appointments were by no means treated by him as sinecures."[17]

Indeed one wonders whether Dunckerley had not already begun his incursion into the South-west of England much earlier when we read the second document concerning John Knight. This is a Minute of a meeting of the following bodies *on the same day*, 17 June 1806.

Druid's Lodge of "Love and Liberality", No. 103.
Druid's Chapter of "Love and Liberality", No. 79.
Masonic Knights Templars (sic), "St. John of Jerusalem", No. 8.

(It is to be noted that the latter body was constituted in 1791).

The Minute reads: "Their Conclave or Field of Encampment, having assembled this day to go thro' the several Degrees, as undermentioned, when the following Brothers Compans.W.Sir Knights were Initiated into the several Degrees, as undermentioned (sic), viz.

	Mark Man.
Knights of Malta.	Mark Mason.
Knights Templars.	Architect.
	Grand Architect.
	Excellent.
	Super Excellent.
	Red Cross.
	Royal Arch 4 Extra Points.
	Royal Ark Mariners or Ark Masons...

(There are three more grades that need not concern us here). It will be immediately obvious that this sequence is the same as that which appears in the 'Knight/Bradford' series that was discussed above (p. 71) surely confirming that these were the same ceremonies that Dunckerley had introduced earlier and elsewhere. Strangely, the first Brother to be mentioned amongst the 'candidates' is John Knight. Yet he cannot have been 'initiated' that day because we know that he was addressed as a Knight Companion in 1792 and here, even more pertinent to our study, he signs himself as follows:

"April 29th – **1777**. John Knight (HIS MARK TO BE SHOWN)"

All the succeeding Knights are dated 17 June 1806 or later, this list clearly being part of a Mark book belonging to the Chapter. It would thus appear that John Knight, being the 'Eminent DGM' of this body, for as such he signs a KT Certificate for a Richard Knight on 29 October 1804, was hitherto the only one to have his name in this book and those taking all the Additional Degrees in 1806 added their Marks to his. We may note the nature of Knight's mark – an equilateral triangle enclosed in a circle, with the letters H A B surmounting IK in the triangle, and a cross on a hill, the square and compasses, and a Maltese cross at each of its sides. The combination of Craft, Arch and KT symbols is very striking.

Whether Dunckerley was able to introduce this series of degrees, starting with the Mark Man and Mark Mason, into other Provinces which he ruled is a topic worthy of more research. The areas needing special attention are Gloucestershire, Herefordshire, Somerset, Dorset, Wiltshire, Essex, Suffolk, Warwickshire and Nottinghamshire. As we shall see in the next chapter Mark Masonry certainly has long roots in the last two of these areas. Did Dunckerley sow the seeds?

Chapter Five

The growth of Mark Masonry before 1813

IT WAS NOT only in the South and South-west of England or under the zealous hand of Thomas Dunckerley that Mark Masonry began to flourish more noticeably in the years after 1770. I would recall the reader to the emergent signs of a Mark ceremony or practice in the North East of England from the 1750s onwards and it is as soon as 1773 that we have the record of a Mark occasion in the Marquis of Granby (Craft) Lodge in Durham. In an entry under 21 December we read:

"Bro. Barwick was also made a Mark'd Mason and Bro. James Mackinlay raised to the Degree of a Master Mason and also made a Mark Mason and paid accordingly."

This is by no means an isolated instance for 2 more brethren were made Mark Masons on 18 January 1774, another at a regular Lodge meeting on 4 July 1775 and another at an Emergency meeting in the same month. There is a still further entry on 21 January 1777. What is of interest is that no-one was admitted to the Mark degree unless he had first been raised to that of a Master Mason and that all this was happening in a lodge which was working under a Moderns warrant. When Thomas Dunckerley became Grand Superintendent in this Province he must have been encouraged to see how the Mark was progressing here. What we do *not* know is whether the reference to a 'Mark'd' Mason suggests a two-stage degree and if here, as in the South or in Scotland, there were two parts to the Mark.

Meanwhile, further North-west, the Journeyman Lodge of Dumfries, now known as the Thistle Lodge, No. 62 (SC) recorded in one of its Minutes for 1770, just a year after Dunckerley's visit to Portsmouth, the earliest Scottish reference to a distinct Mark degree.

This Lodge was constituted on 6 June 1753 and its documents confirm that the degree of the Royal Arch *and all that that implied* was known at a very early period. Sadly several pages of the original Minute Book have been destroyed but there is one page headed, "Record of Royal Arch Masons, and their passing to that." The first name on the list there is under the date, 9 November 1756. For our purposes, however, the most interesting entry is on 8 October 1770 where the steps taken in passing to the Royal Arch are given. These are set out in a certificate which was presented to a candidate 'elevated' to that degree and which read:.

"In the beginning was the Word, and the Light shined in darkness, and the darkness comprehended it not. The bearer hereof ... came to us well

Pre-1813 Locations of Mark Degree
BANFF
EDINBURGH
GLASGOW
ESK
DUMFRIES
WINLATON
NEWCASTLE
SUNDERLAND
DURHAM
SCARBOROUGH
YORK
HULL
BRADFORD
BOTTOMS
RAWTENSTALL
BURY
SHEFFIELD
NOTTINGHAM
BRISTOL
BATH
LONDON
PORTSMOUTH
PLYMOUTH
REDRUTH

recommended, of good report, and free from public scandal. In consequence, we, the Master, Wardens and Brethren of the ... hereby certify and attest to all men enlightened that the said *worshipful brother*, after having been examined and found duly qualified as an Entered Apprentice, Fellow-craft, Master, and *Mark Master Mason* was by us elected *Master of the Chair* and then by us *elevated* to the *Sublime Degree* of Excellent, Super-Excellent, and Royal Arch Mason, and as such we do hereby recommend him..."

The Minute is clearly not the first of its kind though it is the first we have. The lodge was competent to form itself into a Royal Arch body and to confer the appropriate degrees, and the records remaining show that it had been the custom for it so to do previously. If the lost pages were to re-appear who is to deny that we might then have a definite Mark Degree reference that might even pre-date the entry belonging to the St. John's Lodge at Newcastle in 1756. What has especially to be noted here is that the Mark Master degree is placed in its present sequence after the Master Mason, just as in the South and Durham. It was also noticeably separated from the Royal Arch degree whilst apparently being regarded as part of the passage to that goal. The 'Master of the Chair' was of course a degree formed so as to allow those who had not been reigning Masters to proceed to the Royal Arch.

In London in 1777 we see that this practice of a two-stage Mark degree was beginning to be established, for in the Minutes of an 'Antients' lodge, St. Thomas, No. 142 (warranted 1775) we read that "the WM with the following Brothers of that Lodge were made Mark Masons **and** Mark Masters". That was on 9 August and just *five days later* we have, "Regular Lodge night, the WM, the Wardens, the Secretary and Treasurer present worked in the First and Second Degrees. Made the following Brothers Mark Masons *and also* Mark Master Masons." Here the two parts are again separated. If the implication in that Minute seems to be that both steps were taken after the Fellowcraft degree had been worked one has to say that subsequent entries show clearly that the Master Mason degree had to be taken before the MM Mason step could be administered. It could well be that the candidates had *already* been made Master Masons and could therefore be admitted to the Mark steps without again opening in the third degree, strange though that may seem to us. What at least is becoming clear is that there *now were* Mark ceremonies and that it was in order to administer them in a Craft setting, rather than in a Royal Arch one. What does not appear is any mention of the cipher alphabet use.

Back in the North-East of Scotland we have a remarkable parallel to this latter practice. On 7 January 1778 and in the Minutes of the St. John's Operative Lodge, Banff, we see recorded:

"The meeting having under their consideration the state and constitution of the Lodge, that those members *incline to raise themselves* to the Degree of Mark Mason and Mark Master Mason, and that in time past no benefit has accrued to the Lodge.

Therefore resolved that in time coming all members that shall *hereafter raise* to the Degree of Mark Mason shall pay one merk Scots, but not to obtain the degree of Mark Mason before they are passed Fellow-Craft. And those that shall take the Degree of Mark Master Mason shall pay one shilling and sixpence sterling into the Treasurer for behoofe of the Lodge. None to attain to the Degree of Mark Master Mason until they are raised Master."

This full and interesting Minute proves, of course, that the Mark Degree had been worked as two ceremonies prior to 1778 even though no mention whatsoever is made in earlier entries. It shows a similarity of payment for the Mark Mason (or Mark Man) step to that which we find elsewhere but now introduces not only a different but a somewhat larger amount for the second Degree.

We should also note that after this date not only is the same practice followed frequently in *this* lodge but it is copied in Cullen and other towns in the area. When the Royal Arch Masonry also practised in this lodge ceased because a separate Chapter was formed the custom of conferring the Mark *Degree* (sic) was almost exclusively conferred by the new Chapter. The old attachment of Mark with Royal Arch was thus re-affirmed though of course the story of the Supreme Grand Royal Arch Chapter of Scotland and this degree must be told in full later.

What must be mentioned at this point is another fascinating link between the practices in Scotland and Ireland. The forerunner of the Edinburgh Royal Arch Chapter No. 1 was the Grand Assembly of Knights Templar. According to the Minutes of 2 and 4 December 1778 in the books of that body they worked a number of 'steps' in Masonry of which the following are mentioned: Past the Chair, Excellent, Super-Excellent, *ARCH*, Royal Arch, Knights of Malta, Knights Templar. There *were others but they are not here mentioned.* What is to be remarked is the place and presence of an Arch ceremony (see above p. 47f) and the fact that otherwise the series is exactly the same as in the Thistle Lodge of Dumfries in 1770. It must also be recorded that on exactly the same dates in 1778 these degrees were conferred on Brethren by the Lodge Scoon and Perth, now No. 3 (SC). This begins to suggest that there was now a spreading acceptance in Scotland of a firm set of Masonic degrees. In that case and realising the eventual connection between the Mark and the Royal Arch in that land it is only logical to assume that either the 'Arch' section of the above series of the Grand Assembly included Mark elements *or* the Mark degrees were assumed to have been administered already in their Craft lodges to any who were candidates for the 'higher' degrees.

In regard to the manner of taking the degrees it is worth looking at two other places in the South of England about this time. Both of them, as it happens, were associated with Thomas Dunckerley. The first is the Old Dundee Lodge, No. 9 (now No. 18) that met at Wapping and of which he was a member from 1761 to 1768. His signature in their book of Bye-laws for 1764 is still a treasured possession. At the time of Dunckerley's membership it was apparently the custom in this lodge to combine the steps, signs, tokens and instruction of what we would call the Initiation *and* Passing in one ceremony which is described as 'Made a Mason'. There was a fee for this of 2 guineas and to confirm that this was the practice the Lodge still has its 'Portable Tracing Board' that contains small millboard sections which together make up a picture. On one side of these parts there is the lay-out that shows the symbols of the 1st and 2nd degrees thus illustrating a combined procedure. This practice continued in this old Lodge until 1809 when, under the influence of the Lodge of Promulgation, the practice of giving the three degrees separately began.

It is against this background that we take note of two comments by the Lodge's historian, Arthur Heiron, when he remarks that

'It is interesting to note that, although we never gave *our own candidates* the distinctive Degree of a Fellow Craft *by itself* (i.e. until after 1809) we did sometimes confer this Degree on a visitor or a joining Member; it therefore appears that, in such cases, the Brother had either (i) only been made an 'EA' in his Mother Lodge, or (ii) that he (or we) did not consider he had received the Fellow Craft Degree effectively, and so we did it over again, and he had to pay us our fee of 5s for the ceremony; it will be noted, however, that we did not again Initiate him into the degree of an 'EA'.

'Again, Scotland, (where they) continued their Ancient Working, still confers the Degree of a 'Mark Mason', and this 'Mark Degree' can fairly be considered as a glorification or exaltation of the Fellow Craft ... we are apt to forget the great importance our Ancient Brethren originally assigned to the Degree of a Fellow Craft.' And he adds:

"1765. Bro. Gould joined the Lodge and paid for his 'Admission' 10s. 6d. Rec'd of Bro. Gould, on his being Made a Fellow Craft, for which Honour he paid 5s. and Raised a Master, 5s. (He was not Initiated in our Lodge.)

1774, Oct. 13. Proposed That two Brethren should be Initiated into the 2nd Degree of Masonry, carried and they were accordingly 'Made Fellow Crafts', for which Honour they each paid 5s.

"Now as we never gave to our Initiates at this period this Degree of a Fellow Craft separately and distinctly, could *this Degree* refer to that of a 'Mark Mason'? (There are many other similar instances.)"

This is an intriguing situation and one which obviously bemuses even a member of the lodge and its historian. The implications of the idea are not only that here was an earlier instance of conveying instruction in, or a ceremony of, the Mark but that it was in a lodge of which Dunckerley was a fully paid up member until 1768. If this was a case of 'presenting the Mark' after or as a second part of the Fellow-craft degree then that would make sense and be part of the claim made by Dunckerley in 1769 that the Portsmouth brethren should be 'FC for Mark Masons'. Yet it does not explain where he got the idea of *Mark Master* from nor how he came '*lately*' by this knowledge. We know from Heiron that Dunckerley joined "as a Member 'useing the Sea' ... although for the greater part of that period (1761–8) he was *only* a Sea-Member, his duties in the Navy keeping him much away from England." What *could be* a possibility is that, if he learnt that in this old Lodge there was a form of Mark instruction, he would want to acquire it or seek a fuller form of it. As has been suggested in the last chapter he must have heard of the Mark at least in America amongst his military friends. Nevertheless we have here in London a yet further prod in that direction – and if it wasn't the Mark, what was it?

The other body is the ongoing Chapter of Friendship. In July 1771 we learn that 4 brethren were 'made Mark Masons and Mark Masters **also** RA Masons and Excellent and Super-Excellent Masons' whilst in 1778 Bro. John Dance took the mark and chose (a mark, but) declined the Arch." Here we have a further pair of unexpected entries. When the Chapter began the brethren were Chapter Masons who were made Mark, but here they are made Mark Masons before they proceed to the Chapter degrees. This is a much more usual arrangement elsewhere at the time and perhaps suggests that that is what they had been advised to do by Dunckerley who could not start in that way because he was introducing a quite new venture and was, after all, only appointed to bring a Chapter warrant that day. What is much more surprising is the unwillingness of a Brother who enters a Chapter, receives a preliminary 'degree' (or was it degrees?), and then declines the (Royal) Arch, surely the main reason for his entry. Does that mean that the working of the Mark put him off the rest or was it so satisfying that he wanted no more, at least for the time being? It would be good to know. What it certainly tells us is that the 'Mark' was now very much an entity on its own, which serves to confirm the likelihood of the *Dunckerley degrees* being those that carry his name.

As a bit of light relief we might note that in the Minutes for 23 October 1785 there is the following entry:

"Resolv'd that Breaden's boy does not come but only when we give the Mark when he shall have six d".

Howell rightly asks the question, 'But why was the boy to come when they gave the Mark? Were the ceremonies in that degree more arduous for the Janitor than those in the Arch, Excellent, etc.?' It is a very proper query though part of the answer seems to be found when we are told later that a Breaden became Janitor after being exalted. I would suggest that the boy was showing interest in Freemasonry, that the Janitor was probably needed to make up a team or do a part of the Mark ceremony and this lad was a trusty but temporary replacement.

Meanwhile in Hull the Mark degree was given a more solid base in the Minerva Lodge which was founded in 1782. As was shown earlier (p. 55) there had been some kind of Mark practice in that area for 30 years but now we have written evidence to confirm the Degree's existence. As Bro. Ellerby says in his History of the Minerva Lodge, No. 250:

"The early minutes ... in which the Mark records are reported, are conspicuous by their brevity, and according to Grand Mark Lodge Statutes there is *only one other Mark Lodge* under the English Constitution whose records are older than our own. The art of minute writing being either unknown to the brethren (or) certainly not practised, the *barest possible details* were recorded. It is therefore not surprising that little can be gleaned form these records of the working of the Mark Degree." One indeed wonders if that statement does not apply to many of the early references elsewhere.

"The Craft Lodge attracted many candidates from various parts of the country as well as merchants and mariners from foreign countries and members of the militia stationed in the town. Some of these also *took advantage of our Mark Degree* for we find candidates from Grimsby, Lincoln, Wakefield, Norfolk, Dorset, and as far away as Bremen, Hamburg, Lubeck, Stettin, Holland and even the U.S.A."

Some of the distinctive features of the Lodge when working the Mark have come through to us as follows:

"On the 20th November, 1805, *nineteen* candidates were advanced to the Mark degree. On the 2nd March, 1814, a master mariner from Gothenburg was the candidate. The Craft Lodge was *opened in the second degree* – which was our practice in those days – and our friend from Gothenburg was proposed, ballotted for, *initiated*, passed to the second degree, *raised* to the third degree *and the minutes* (sic) then immediately went on to say that *a Mark Masons Lodge was held* and the only Past Master present officiated as Worshipful Master and eight candidates took the degree including the master mariner ... The lodge was then *closed without reverting back* to the Craft degree and it is recorded that the Worshipful Master gave a masterly performance of the Mark degree.

"This is perhaps not surprising when we consider that the only *officers* present for the *Craft* ceremony consisted of Worshipful Master, Senior (and) Junior Warden, Chaplain, Secretary and *two* Tylers ... No information is given as to the form of ceremony such as Secrets, Working Tools, Traditional History or Charge as now practised, and it will be noted *there were NO overseers.*"

What we can say about the working is that it was different even from the quite distinctive usage that Minerva Mark Lodge still employs to this day. We know this because when in 1862 this old Mark Lodge eventually lodged a petition to join the new Grand Mark Lodge a team from the Britannia Lodge in Sheffield came over to 'administer the obligation and rehearse the ceremonies' (i.e. the ritual that had been adopted by the new Mark Grand Lodge). We can also deduce from the meagre information above that a great deal depended on the solo performance of the Master in the Chair and that suggests a form of ceremony not unlike the Dunckerley style that we shall examine in the next chapter.

Whilst still in this part of Yorkshire we ought to take note of the fact stated by Bro. Draffen in his survey of early Mark Masonry:

"The Mark Degree was regularly worked under the authority of the Grand Lodge (of All England), meeting from time immemorial at York." More research has to be done on this topic for it has implications concerning the lodge in the Inniskilling Dragoons, the possible impact on Dunckerley *and* the kind of work done in Hull and some of West Yorks.

Before proceeding with this story of pre-Union Mark Masonry we should perhaps remind ourselves of those areas of the British Isles and beyond where Freemasonry was developing but in which we have not so far encountered traces of the Mark. They are the South-west, the Midlands, Cheshire, Lancashire, West Yorkshire, Northumberland, East Anglia, Ireland and North America (or Canada). Previous surveys of Mark Masonry and its past have either remarked that the degree in the latter 18th century was fairly widespread or present in parts of the North, in London or Scotland, as well as Portsmouth, of course. In what follows we may at last begin to see that practically the whole country was affected by this Masonic development. It is now that we move into a section of our story that has never been told *as a whole* before.

Research reveals that Bro. John Knight of Redruth who was mentioned earlier received the Mark Man and Mark Mason degrees on 27 April 1777. It was the same day as that on which he was also *Exalted* a Knight Templar and installed as a Knight of Malta. In a book on Freemasonry in West Cornwall we read that "he was the principal worker, and an able exponent of the different Rituals, as manuscripts show."

Unfortunately, yet how common, the Minute Book from the opening of (his,) the Druid's Lodge, to 1777 is lost but that the Lodge was in full working order is assumed by the names we have (of) earlier members, and also the entry in the Minutes of the Druid's Chapter which tell us that from February 1754 the Lodge had met *every first and third Tuesday in every month.* In the first Minute Book extant we see that with Right Worshipful Stephen Bell, Esq., in the Chair, R.W.John Knight was the second most senior amongst the members. The Knight Templar degree began here this year so Knight either received the Mark in preparation for entering the further 'degree' or, as seems to have become the case by 1806, those who were Masters through the Chair could move on to another raft of degrees of which the Mark Man and Mark Mason were the first two steps. What we can be sure of is that a Mason of Knight's standing and reputation would not be party to anything that was irregular albeit he was obviously an enthusiastic and eager seeker for 'advancement'. The Mark, we may firmly take it, and not least because of Dunckerley's interest, was appearing in *Cornwall and Devon* by the late 1770s. Hence we read in 1808, in the Redruth Chapter Minutes,

"We stand pretty high in Masonry in Redruth, having a Constitution for Craft Masonry . . . Chapter of the Royal Arch, Conclave of Knights Templars, & c,&c, *and every other Degree in Masonry.*"[1]

"The story of Mark Masonry in *Bath* still remains to be pieced together, if ever its scattered parts can be brought to light." Such was the judgement of John A.Grantham in 1958 and yet he was able to state:

"It has long been accepted as a well-founded tradition that Mark

Masonry was worked in Bath before the Union of the Antients and Moderns in 1813 and continued to be practised afterwards.

"At the General Meeting of the Craft on 30th May 1857 Samuel Lazarus, representing the independent sodality of Mark Masters at Bath, exhibited a Certificate from a Mark Lodge held under the *Antient Grand Lodge* and working sixty or seventy years ago." That means 1787–97.

"Lazarus is also reported as saying that

'He took the Mark *Degree* in the Royal Sussex Lodge, Bath, in 1823. The Royal Sussex Lodge was an *ancient* (sic) Lodge holding Warrant from the York Grand Lodge (but *this* was not the Grand Lodge of All England) which worked *all degrees in Freemasonry.* This Lodge united with the (United) Grand Lodge of England, and the Mark Degree then being excluded, they had worked the Mark under the *sanction of their Old Warrant.*" '[2] This begins to suggest a very steady Mark tradition from the 1780s when, let us remember, Thomas Dunckerley was in charge of the Province. Moreover, Dunckerley was a steady supporter of the Royal Cumberland Lodge, No. 41, and the oldest Mark Lodge in the Province of Somerset is the Royal Cumberland TI Mark. We have the record of a 'very unusual incident on 28 June 1768 (when) at the 'White Hart' the two afore-mentioned candidates and four others were made Fellow Crafts by W. Bro. Dunckerley, PGM for Hampshire.' This ceremony was performed in the presence of Dunckerley's predecessor as PGM for Somerset, and in the 'Bear Lodge'. In 1784 Dunckerley was the local PGM, constituted the Royal Cumberland Lodge and in 1785 the members of the 'Bear' adopted the new Lodge title whilst the new Lodge acquired the furniture that had been used for 50 years. In view of the information given above about the Royal Sussex Lodge which came *after* the Royal Cumberland it seems more than likely that during Dunckerley's time the Mark degrees were introduced to both lodges in the 1780s. The fact that the brethren of the old 'Bear' had performed the Scots Masters degree as early as 1735 suggests that they were not averse to additions to the usual basic run of ceremonies. There is however more to be researched in this area.

If there is no distinctive early and separate Mark working in Bristol that can very easily be explained by the especial way in which Freemasonry there developed beyond the Craft degrees. The story of the Baldwyn Rite from 1772 is not for telling here but it is worth noting that it was only at the time of the Union in 1813 that an independent body or lodge was formed for the express purpose of working the Mark Degree. Could it be that with the requirement of the new Grand Lodge that only the three basic Craft degrees and the Holy Royal Arch were to be acknowledged – and, of course, permission for the 'knightly Orders' – that some element in the previous Craft arrangement – say, the Mark ceremonies attached to Fellow Craft and Master Mason – now had to be provided for separately? It certainly seems as if something like this occurred. Why else was a special body for Mark needed just then? The matter is one that merits still further investigation.

We, however, must move on to the Midlands. populous and important as Birmingham and its surroundings are today it was only beginning to grow as a later metropolis in the late 18th century and its oldest Mark Lodge was not to emerge until the middle year of the 19th. For Freemasonry we have to look first to *Nottingham* and *Derby* and it was in the former that Mark Masonry emerges at this time.

Considering what was written at the outset of our story it is interesting to note that, though "There are no records of the working of any Lodge of Operative Masons in Nottingham and District (yet) the architect who was employed in the building of what is now called the Nottingham Castle – Mr. Wm. Wilson (afterwards knighted by Charles II) was a member of an Operative Society of Masons in London and was (in 1682) initiated into a London Lodge of Speculative Masons (recorded in Elias Ashmole's diary)."[3]

In 1755 there were two lodges in the town and in 1765 one of these accepted a Warrant of Confirmation from the Antients Grand Lodge. Sadly again there are no earlier minutes of this the Newstead Lodge, then No. 44, until 1791 but it is as soon as 1793 that there is the first mention of the Mark Degree. It is stated that "The *Masters Lodge* was closed and a *Mark Lodge* opened, at which three brothers were *advanced*."

"The ceremony of 'giving the Mark' continued to be carried out by the officers of the Craft lodge, who were Mark Masons, until 1802 when a Lodge of Instruction in the Mark Degree was formed and from this date the Mark Lodge met as a separate body and kept their own minutes ... although for many years its membership was almost exclusively confined to Masons of the No. 44 Craft Lodge.

"The fee for 'Giving the Mark' in the Craft lodge was 1/1½d per Brother (which) suggests that the degree came from Scotland where the fee was either 1/1d or 1/1½d which was the equivalent of the old Scottish merk of 13/4d Scots, 1/1½d English.

"The records of the early workings are very meagre and incomplete (so that) the Secretary was contented to make a Minute as follows:

'Masters Lodge closed and Marke Lodge opened, the following brothers *were marked*.... Bros. Richard Calton – William Worthington – Williams Taylor, dated December 2nd 1793.'[4]

The Lodge now demonstrate their 'Old Working' and in the course of it the Junior Warden acting as Inner Guard says to the candidate, 'It is my duty to *put such a mark on you* as will carry to *your grave*.' In so acting and speaking we have another explanation of the above phrase "were marked".

Marks were at first recorded in the Minutes and not in a special book and there is also evidence of some lodges held on a Sunday. One Scottish mason who elected to become a joining member was made Senior Deacon and a Mark Master Mason on the same day. The ritual probably used at this time will be discussed in the chapter on that topic. It was, as we shall see, from this Mark Lodge that the first Mark Lodge in Birmingham developed.

Cheshire is an ancient County and can count the earliest references to the Speculative Craft within its borders. Many of its 18th century lodges, however, ceased to exist before the 19th century got well under weigh and the records that they possessed largely disappeared with them. It would have been helpful, for example, if we could have seen any minutes of the Duke of Devonshire Lodge of Macclesfield, that being the only Lodge in the County constituted by the Grand Lodge of All England at York. It began its life in September 1770 and does not seem to have outlived the Grand Lodge itself which collapsed in 1792. Its workings may well have been revealing.

Instead we turn to the Lodge of Unanimity, which, in the absence of all the Time Immemorial bodies, now ranks as the Senior lodge in the Province. Happily too it possesses all its Minute Books from its constitution in 1754 until the present day. As a further indication of its antiquity the Lodge still has the three magnificent chairs used by the early Masters and Wardens and the gavel wielded by the Master has a plate which reads:

'This Mallet, after being used for laying the first stone of St. John's Church in Manchester, was left here as a memorial by Brother Powell, 1768.'

There is also a perfect Ashlar and its attachments which bears the inscription: "This silver Lewis was presented to this Lodge by the Worshipful Brother Whitehead, Deputy Provincial Grand of this County, and the crane and block by the Worshipful Brother Nabb, 1769."

It was in 1807 that the Lodge finally moved to its present location at Dukinfield and at the second meeting there on 20 April we are given the following details:

"The W.M. Bro. F.D.Astley, was not present, and the chair was taken by

Henry Mills, PM	as WM.
David Torr, of 212 "Integrity"	as SW.
John Chew, of 443 "Union"	as JW.
John Crabtree, of 536 "Minerva"	as SD.
John Redmayne, of 536 "Minerva"	as JD.
John Postlethwaite, PM 585 "Loyalty"	PM.
Saml. Wood	Secretary.

It is worth noting that we can trace the 'Union' and 'Minerva' Lodges to Ashton-under-Lyne which was nearby, but in the Lancashire Province (not yet divided), and the 'Loyalty' Lodge to Mottram which was again quite close. In checking against these lodges we find no mention of the Mark Degree in them and it thus begins to look as if this kind of meeting to carry out a Mark ceremony was a new kind of central activity. This is further confirmed by the other brethren present some of whom were the candidates for the Mark on this occasion. These were:

Squire Butterworth,	602, "Moira";	Wm. Ashton, 536, "Minerva".
Thomas Barber,	602, "Moira";	Thos. Marsland, "Minerva".

John Shaw,	443, "Union";	Martin Dooley, "Minerva.
James Wilson,		Thos. Kershaw.
Jno. Buckley,		Jno. Hussey.

The Minutes continue:

"This being a regular Lodge night, we opened at the hour of 8 o'clock in the evening on the first, second and third degrees of Masonry in peace and good harmony, when the above officers and Brethren were present."

The candidates for Mark Masonry on this evening were the Secretary, Saml Wood, John Shaw from Ashton, and the two from "Moira" Lodge which was in nearby Stalybridge. As there was no other business than the conferring of the Mark it seems right to infer that all the others present were already Mark Masons. Since they were from four other lodges in the area we have to ask the question. 'From where did they get the Mark if this is really the first occasion signalled in Unanimity Lodge?' Could it be, as Armstrong suggests, that "we shall not be far wrong if we recognise in (this meeting) the famous Travelling Mark Lodge of Cheshire, whose centre of operations always seems to have been Dukinfield".[5] Another local masonic historian has gone even further in claiming that Unanimity's "first real activity was to attract an *unattached body* which had been for a number of years working the 'higher' degrees, Mark, Link, Ark Mariner, Wrestle and Red Cross, and which appears to have continued the ultra-Craft work when the old Saddleworth Lodge ... went into abeyance in 1784. From its comparative obscurity in Saddleworth and Mottram, it blossomed forth in Dukinfield."[6]

Though it has generally been understood that the Travelling Mark Lodge in this area began about 1830 there are some more bits of information that support the idea of an earlier start. One is that on 14 September 1807 the Unanimity Lodge was opened for the 'business of Royal Ark Masonry and four of the brethren above mentioned (Shaw, Crabtree, Chew and Dooley) were admitted to that degree'. Members of four lodges were thus involved, for Leggatt, the Tyler of Unanimity, was also a candidate. This reinforces the idea that here was another 'travelling centre' evening. When we learn that shortly afterwards the same body practised Red Cross Masonry the impression is further strengthened.

We also know that John Postlethwaite, who acted as PM at the meeting in April, was the first Master of 'Loyalty' at Mottram in 1798. He was a well-known Mark Mason and his tombstone, erected by the Brethren, was largely inscribed in Mark cipher characters. His ability as a lecturer in the Mark and Royal Ark was especially noted.

All this evidence, together with its subsequent development, means that at least in the eastern part of the Cheshire Province there was a growing and continuous tradition of Mark practice. So far there has not been any proof of a similar outcome in the Chester area.

In *Lancashire* there is rather more evidence of the degree being conferred but in the 18th century it was confined to the Southern part of the

County. Manchester and Salford were only just beginning to expand and flex their Masonic muscles and there were few traces yet of the Mark growth that would occur in Liverpool, Preston and beyond in the 19th century. The independent spirit of the Wigan area had begun to reveal itself in this direction, though it is mainly to the new and flourishing cotton towns that we have to look and the fact that they were juxtaposed with what we have already seen in North-east Cheshire is hardly surprising. Here was the area in which skilled artisans were beginning to take their place alongside tradesmen and the lesser gentry. It was also a setting in which visiting between Masons of different traditions would naturally occur.

In addition to the recognised Royal Arch degree, all "Antient" lodges and many Chapters under the "Moderns" ... worked other degrees from at least 1780. From the Minute books we find meetings described as "Chapter Meeting", "Royal Arch Lodge", "Monthly Arch Night", "Encampment of Royal Arch Masons" and we also find "Knights Templar", "Sons of Babylon", "Ark, Mark, Link and Wrestle", "Order of the Black", "Priestly Order", etc.

Certainly we have actual entries to examine from 1784 when a Register of Marks was begun by a Rawtenstall lodge. Nor is that all. "The minutes of the meetings of the Mark Lodge, which were not held at regular intervals, but simply when required, began in 1785, and are continuous. In the book are two sets of minutes. The first begins at one end of the book and is headed simply 'Mark Masons Lodge'. The first page records the officers for the meetings held on 16 January and 13 March ... and the records continue till 5 April 1865 ... What was this Mark Masons Lodge? The answer is given in the entry for 12 July 1792. It is headed 'Lodge of Tranquility (sic) 549'. This is a Craft lodge. Its number in 1792 was 549 ... and since 1863 it has been 274. In 1810 it transferred to Rossendale (which) is not a township but a long valley containing several townships, of which we need only mention three, Rawtenstall, Newchurch and Stacksteads."[7]

The Lodge of Tranquillity now meets at Stacksteads. The old Mark Lodge was a unit worked by the Tranquillity Lodge and at the end of the above records it was opened at Newchurch in a "Meeting preliminary to reform and Constitute a Mark Masons Lodge" as a separate body. It is perhaps a story for later as to why the new name chosen was "*Rectitude* Mark Lodge".

The oldest lodge in the Wigan area, Lodge of Sincerity, began working in 1787 and was immediately engaged in various degrees beyond the Craft, including the Mark. Norman Rogers has here given us a useful backcloth to this development when he says:

"Probably one of the chief reasons (for this diversity) was the large number of Irish linen merchants who came to Lancashire to sell their wares to the cotton manufacturers (Linen warp and cotton weft went to the making of fustian); these infiltrated the Lodges through Liverpool, bringing their ceremonies with them."[8]

On 22 August 1789 the first lodge opened in Oldham. It was warranted by the Moderns Grand Lodge and amongst the petitioners was a certain Thomas Dunckerley. Other founders were of Irish and Scottish extraction and as one of the lodge's most noted sons, Wor. Bro. Fred L.Pick, remarks "the early members quickly had a finger in every available Masonic pie . . . Our early brethren", he continues, "must have been filled with missionary zeal for within 6 years of the foundation of Friendship, a daughter lodge (now Harmony, 298, of Rochdale) had been formed in Royton, Royal Arch Freemasonry and Knight Templary were in full swing and the Mark Degree was being conferred in Friendship." He also quotes from Hughan:

"The Rev. J.Harrison, historian of Lodge No. 277, Oldham, furnished me with a list of the names of some 20 persons initiated from 1793 to 1799 in that lodge, the dates of taking the several degrees of Apprentice, Fellow Craft, Master Mason, Past Master, and Mark Master, being arranged in five columns." Six brethren were made Mark Masons on 28 October 1795, and further groups in 1798, 1799, and then 1800, 1805, 1808, and 1811. Hughan continues:

"The dates prove that in all cases, save one, the Mark was conferred upon Master Masons, and in that solitary instance the date is left blank, but Bro. Harrison adds, that in a list of members this brother is stated to have been raised on September 23rd, 1795, which was more than a month prior to his taking the Mark Degree. Fewer (brethren) took the 'P(ast) M(aster)' than the Mark probably because the former was worked as introductory to the 'Arch'."[9]

All this sounds fairly familiar and in the Dunckerley 'pattern' particularly when we note the close affinity with the Philanthropy Chapter at Werneth and that some brethren joined the Chapter before taking the Mark. Whilst it is true that there is no mention of a Mark Man degree we should note that the Craft workings were akin to the Antients ritual and the first bye-laws written in 1795 followed an Antients model. There was also clear Irish influence for on the Lodge seal there is the familiar hand holding a trowel.

This Irish 'presence' is something that has to be considered if we want to tackle the question as to what factors governed the working of the Mark Degree in Oldham or what was the nature of the ceremony. One has also to consider the fact that a fair proportion of the Mark candidates were from other lodges or even the Chapter. This, allied to the similar practice in the Dukinfield area some ten miles away, gives support to the view that here again we have an early example of the 'Travelling Mark' idea in which a central point is chosen where Craft or Royal Arch members can attend to receive this particular degree. If this was so then it is likely to have been the working which was later used by the Ashton Travelling Mark Lodge in the 19th century. We shall come to that in a later chapter and its ritual will be discussed along with all the other Mark rituals we possess.

There was also another influence in this area and one that would have interested Dunckerley if what was said in Chapter 3 about the possible source of his working was correct. Within three months of the formation of the Lodge of Friendship several of its members were involved in the founding of a Lodge warranted by the Grand Lodge of All England at York. This was the Lodge of Fortitude to be held at the 'Sun' in Hollingwood. Very interestingly a Lodge with this tradition was admitting brethren to the Mark Degree within weeks of its being constituted and five years before we have any such record in the Lodge of Friendship. Not only were 18 persons admitted to the Mark between 1790 and 1793 but a mark was even bestowed on the Lodge itself. In every case the mark consisted of an initial in the Hebrew or Greek language, often representing the initial of the Brother's name.

It only remains to mention the activity in one other area before we leave Lancashire and move eastwards. A St. John's Lodge No. 303 in Bolton was warranted by the Antients in March 1797 and, says J.A.Grantham, 'it is claimed that Mark Masonry was worked in this Lodge ever since its constitution'. There do not appear to be any 'Mark' minutes in the earliest records of the Lodge and the Chapter Minute book of 1802 is now missing. However, we do know that by the turn of the century another and older Bolton Lodge, Anchor and Hope, No. 37, founded in 1732 had begun to work the Ark, Mark and Wrestle, and we shall see in the early years of the 18th century that along with 2 others in Bolton these four lodges began a system of 'Travelling Mark' ceremonies such as we have already described in Cheshire. When to this development we add the fact that the oldest lodge in Bury, the Lodge of Relief, No. 42, began at the same period to work the Ark and Mark, we can truly say that at least South Lancashire was very well supplied with outlets for those seeking the Mark degree in pre-Union times.

Across the Pennines the oldest encounter with Mark Minutes is made in the Prince George Lodge No.308 held at Haworth in December 1799. On that occasion six brethren 'received the Mark' and this was still the Lodge's practice when it moved to Bottoms, Stansfield, near Halifax in 1812. The Lodge is fortunate in having retained its Minute books intact from 1796 and it is in them that early in the 19th century we read of the degrees referred to as "old Mark" and "Ark, Mark and Link". The writer of a short booklet on this Lodge here comments:

"They have been facetiously named the 1/1½d degree. 1/1½d was the fee for initiation, and this amount is considered to be the British equivalent of half a shekel, a sum considered the least one should offer when appealed to for assistance."[10] For the readers of this book it may also have other echoes in workings elsewhere.

When the Prince George Lodge moved from Haworth in 1812 the Three Graces Lodge No. 408 was left in sole residence there. It had started at Barnoldswick in 1792 and had itself moved in 1806. Since this was a lodge familiar with the ceremony of 'Passing the Chair' to qualify brethren for the Royal Arch degree it should not surprise us that by 1811 we read of yet another brother who 'has received the mark'. This entry clearly indicates that this was by no means the first time that the degree had been given and we note that though not all the brethren took it those who did received it *between the Second and Third Degrees*. We are even told the nature of the Degree as the 'Old mark' and this indication helps us to appreciate why this was also the working in the Prince George Lodge at Bottoms. There is a still further clue when we examine the Freemasonry at Bradford at this same time.

The Lodge of Hope No. 302 in Bradford was warranted in 1794 but it claimed the right to make Mark Masons under an old manuscript Constitution of 1713 that it derived from the Grand Lodge of All England at York. It is still claimed that this document was issued at a meeting in Bradford in 1713 of the 'Ancient and Honourable Society and Fraternity of Freemasons' though neither the exact date nor place of meeting are as yet known. The Minute book was in existence in 1778 and 1779 and a copy of it was referred to by W.J.Hughan.

Bro. Schott continues the story with these words:

"Unfortunately no early Minutes are extant of the Hope Mark Lodge, but Bro. Scholefield, whom we have seen recorded as Secretary at the second meeting, and who was W.M. in 1810, 1830 and 1831 *always asserted that the Mark was conferred* in the Lodge of Hope since its formation ... and it appears that (he) was appointed by the Brethren to represent the Lodge at the Union of the two Grand Lodges in 1813, and to attend the Lodges of Reconciliation to ascertain the position of the Lodge with regard to the Mark Degree, and he reported that *by the authority of the Grand Master*, and arrangements then come to, the Lodge of Hope was entitled to continue to confer the Mark ..."[11]

The only other *Yorkshire* centre that we ought to notice is that of Sheffield. We know, of course, that this was where one of our oldest records of the Royal Arch degree working in England is found and yet there appear to be no contemporary indications of the practice of the Mark Degree. Such record as we have does not emerge until 1870 when we have a 'Register of Marks of the Brethren of the Britannia Mark Masters Lodge No. 53 of the Grand Lodge of Mark Master Masons ...' "This", says the historian of the Lodge, "is a book once belonging to the Lodge 189, which was the number of the Britannia Craft Lodge from 1792 to the Union, 1813–14 ... This book forms a most valuable record as the first pages contain the marks of members of the old Britannia Lodge, which was originally an Atholl Lodge and by its charter from the Antients had the right – which it exercised – to confer the three craft degrees, the R(oyal) A(rch), the Mark, and the K(night) T(emplar).

"The existence of this book is an interesting proof of the continuity of Mark Masonry in Sheffield from early times. It seems likely that this book of Marks had been in the possession of the Craft Lodge and was handed by that Lodge to the founders, four of whom were members of it, by which means the old record was preserved, and the old Mark tradition followed on as a natural course of events." What Bro. Stokes now adds is particularly interesting when set in the fuller context of the whole West Yorkshire scene:

"It is now only a conjecture, but from the way things were done to begin with it certainly looks as if *the founders were reviving an old Mark degree*, the memory of which must have lingered, rather than introducing something totally new."[12]

There is also one more piece of this local jig-saw that ought to be set in place. We are told that the first Minute Book of the Chapter of Paradise is not now to be found after it was known to be in the possession of Companion Ellis in 1875. However, this Companion published extracts from this and other Minute Books in the Masonic Magazine for 1875–6 and there we read:

"Dec. 17, 1809. Bro. James Greenwood (Scribe N) I.
Bro. Thos. Ledger H.
Bro. Thos. Lilley S.
Made Mark Masons this Evening." and then,
"Nov. 18, 1814. G. Fox, Junr. J. Holmes. S. Hall. T. Walton. Made Mark Masons this Evening."

We discover, in fact, that the Mark Degree **was** alive and well in pre-Union days in this part of Yorkshire as elsewhere.

Before heading South once more we ought to bring the situation of the Mark in *Northumberland* up to date. Silence seems to reign between the discovery of evidence of some kind of Mark *activity in Newcastle in 1756 and the Anniversary* meeting of the Mark Masons there in 1852.

That is not the full story and so we begin with the lodge that was formed in the Second Regiment of the Royal Lancashire Militia. This lodge obtained a warrant from the Atholl Grand Lodge (the Antients) on 20 October 1804 and in accordance with the usual custom at that time the warrant was one that had previously been in use by the Black Lion Lodge that met in one of Newcastle's oldest Inns. The new body was called 'The Knight of Malta Lodge No. 120' and at first met in the town.

The Regiment was stationed at Sunderland from 1805 to 1807, in Tynemouth in 1808 and from thence it moved to Hull. During the time it was in Sunderland several townsmen were admitted and it was they who, on the departure of the military lodge for Tynemouth, helped to re-establish the old St. John Lodge No. 94. In 1812 the Knight of Malta Lodge No. 120 appeared on the Atholl Grand Register as a civilian lodge. What matters for our purposes is that throughout its existence until the Union the members practised the 'old mark', Ark and Link degrees. After the Union there is no more mention of them. The memory of this otherwise forgotten lodge was preserved in the minds of the St. John's Lodge members and it was through them that the eventual Union Mark Lodge No. 124 emerged in 1871 but that is part of our later story. What ought also to be mentioned is that wherever this military lodge rested it helped to establish new civilian lodges that continued.

There is another local development that must also be considered. Though the fuller story of Knightly Encampments will be dealt with when we come to the section on Ireland in this chapter it is only right to introduce here the effect of a warrant issued to a Joppa Encampment in Sunderland in either 1806 or February, 1807. This was neither the first nor the last to be issued for a location in England since the EGE records declare that before 1805 "warrants had been granted to different H. Knights Templars in England, Scotland, etc." (e.g. 1799 London) and in 1809 one was issued to brethren in Scarborough. The warrant in this case was sent from Dublin to Edinburgh and then handed over to the 'Joppa' members *after they had taken the necessary degrees*. This latter fact probably accounts for the two dates. The first being the date that the warrant was issued in Dublin and the second that of the conferral of degrees, and the handing over of the authority to work these ceremonies.

What now affects our story is to learn that the degrees included Noachida, and Ark, Mark and Link. So from this data we conclude that all these ceremonies (plus, of course, others) were being performed in and around Sunderland. What is even more to the point is that it was members of Joppa Encampment resident in Newcastle who were to petition in 1812 for the setting up of the 'Royal Kent Encampment' which was to become a veritable stronghold of 'high degree' Freemasonry in North-east England. In 1811 the members of Joppa sought membership of the Royal Grand Conclave (now Great Priory) only to become dormant c.1845. Here again, however, forms of Mark Masonry were being carried out on Tyneside as the century turned.

Yet these neglected aspects of Mark Masonry in Newcastle have also to be set alongside the better known practice of the Mark in this area throughout the early years of the 19th century. When at last the TI Mark Lodge of Northumberland & Berwick-upon-Tweed emerges with a very distinctive Certificate in 1851 it bears Monograms which have a close similarity to those that we shall later see on the same sort of document used by the Travelling Mark Lodge of Ashton-under-Lyne in Cheshire. The two towns that are mentioned in the title also suggest that this was a Mark body that served the whole County and makes one wonder whether in fact this Lodge did have a travelling role. If it did it would only be emulating the manner of the earlier Harodim lecturers, albeit this time it was for one part of extended Masonry only. What adds some credence to this suggestion is that the Master who attests this Certificate is none other than William Punshon, who was recognised as one of the most knowledgeable masons of his time in Northumberland. His lectures and addresses were substantial enough to be reported in the national Masonic magazines.

The designations of the principal officers – RWMkM, WSW and WJW – seem to be copying Scottish practice but the form of ritual that was practised in Newcastle is known to us from a copy still held by the SRIA library in that city. It immediately shows that what held sway here was the more Irish form of ceremony that we have already seen in existence from Cheshire through Lancashire to West Yorkshire. We have confirmation of this, in any case, for when this T.I.Lodge at last began to negotiate membership of the Grand Mark

Lodge there was great reluctance on the part of the Northumberland Mark brethren to give up their 'old working'. It is still, of course, a puzzle as to how exactly the sign of an axe on one of the old chairs in the Berwick Masonic temple might fit into the original degree working in that town. More information regarding the Mark degree in this part of the kingdom would be of great interest to us all.

We now hasten south to *East Anglia*. "In 1795 a third effort was made by Atholl Masons to increase their Norwich lodges. On 24 December a warrant was issued to 7 brethren to hold a Lodge at the Turkey Cock, Elm Hill. This lodge still exists as Perseverance No. 213. 135 brethren joined the Lodge before the Union, and from the Seals of the Lodge ... it is clear that it conferred the Degrees of Royal Arch, Royal Ark Mariner, and Knight Templar from an early date. In addition, the Union Lodge which was warranted in 1732, had by the time of the Union begun to confer the degrees of Royal Arch, Knight Templar, Ark *and Mark* under their Craft Constitution."[13]

One interesting feature of the Norwich scene is a carved tablet of stone that might be worth mentioning here. It is some 2 feet high and displays on one side two fluted columns with an arch linking them above. At the lower part of the arch there is a semi-circle of carved stones with a keystone in the centre and in the space below this there is a very prominent thistle. The space between the columns is occupied by 17 symbolic items as follows:-An all-seeing eye, sun, moon and seven stars, an open book, mallet and chisel crossed, the square and compasses placed as in the Fellowcraft degree with a G between them, a level, heavy maul, trowel, plumbline and rule, star, hammer, a ladder on a coffin bearing skull and crossbones, and three candlesticks. No-one is clear as to what this stone is connected with but it seems not unreasonable to suggest that it was a form of portable 'tracing board' such as we shall again see in use with the Mark travelling lodge in Cheshire. The presence of the thistle must undoubtedly register some kind of Scottish connection and one is thus tempted to imagine that perhaps here we have an item that assisted those who sought to instruct Masons in an Antients form of ritual. It would be one that led the candidate up the *three steps* at the foot of the stone to the threshold stone that clearly lies above them and then through the semblance of an open door that stands above the threshold, and into the fullness of the Fellowcraft degree, which would include the Mark and a raising motif, to the heart of the structure where the Arch completes the whole with its keystone in place. The Scottish touch would be the emphasis on the Fellow-Craft, the inclusion of a Mark section and the relation of the whole to the Royal Arch. In a Masonic setting where, as we shall discuss later in looking at regalia, distinctive *Mark and Ark* jewels were produced by someone who is also registered in the Mark Register that belonged to the Union Lodge we are unlikely to be misled if we see this 'teaching stone' as yet further evidence of *Norfolk* Mark Masonry. It would again be helpful, however, if still more research could be undertaken in this particular field.

Earlier mention of the St. Thomas's Lodge practice of a Mark ceremony seems for many to comprise their appreciation of how extensively the degree was known in the *London* area in the latter part of the 18th century. Looking at the pedigree of the Mallet and Chisel Lodge No. 5 we find that its roots are stated to be in 'old Mark Masonry' and this is borne out by looking at the past experience of two of those who registered the petition for the lodge in 1856. They were Richard Barnes and Richard Edward Barnes, both of them schoolmasters, and both recognised as having 'rendered important services to the Kent (Craft) Lodge for many years.' As we now look at this, the Kent Lodge No. 15 we can begin to realise that Mark Masonry was present in more than one quarter of the capital before 1800.

The historian of the Lodge has given us this extract from the Lodge Minute Book for *Sunday*, 12 January, 1794:

"At a meeting of Master Masons convened under the Warrant of Lodge No. 8 (this being the Atholl Register's number for this lodge) and by a warrant granted under the Patronage of His Royal Highness the Duke of Clarence to Wm. Durisk, Isaac Hoare and Bro. Colcott (PM of No. 2) Opened at 4, when Brs Durisk, Colcott, Witherisk, Wilson and Lewis were dubb'd Ark Brs. Closed at 6 and Opened in the Mark when Brs. Durisk. Wilson, and Lewis were dubb'd Mark Men and Mark Brs. Closed at 7."[14] For the record they then opened in the Excellent and High Excellent degrees and also appointed officers of a 'Royal Ark Vessell' (sic). They also agreed to meet on the 2nd and 4th Sundays in each month. "They closed at 11(p.m.) in Harmony." One feels it was just as well.

On 15 January 1800 the lodge opened at 8p.m. in the Third Degree and three of the brethren present at the previous meeting "dubbed several brethren into the Excellent, High Excellent, Mark Men and Mark Masters degrees. The 12 candidates each chose a mark and the following were the ones selected: A dagger, spinning wheel, shuttle, fleece, a saw, axe, a square, oblong square and a which square (sic). A foul anchor and a tankard were also granted." As can be guessed from some of the 'marks' this lodge met in the heart of the Spitalfields silk-weaving industry. It remained there until about 1830 when French silks were introduced and another 'home' had to be found.

Mention of Kent should also remind us that the Adam's, (Adams or even Adam) Mark Lodge No. 6, of Sheerness took its rise from the 'old Mark working' in the Adam's Craft Lodge which was warranted by the Antients on 4 December 1797. That lodge worked such grades as 'Passing the Chair', 'Ark and Mark', Royal Arch and Knight Templary right up to the Union and beyond. We shall have to return to this lodge at a later point in the book.

Such then was the Mark scene in *England* and *Scotland* as we at present know it prior to 1813. It reveals that practice of a form of Mark degree was varied, persistent and widespread. There are evident similarities in certain areas and there are distinctions between those who recognised two steps in the Mark – Mark Man and Mark Mason (or Mark Master) – and those who clearly did not. There was also separation between those who saw it as somehow related to the Royal Arch and others who saw it as simply an extension of the Craft degrees. In some areas it was administered as part of a local Lodge's intermittent activity whilst elsewhere it was offered at certain central points to members of different local lodges who sought this 'advancement'. It is a diverse and intriguing picture and when we weave into this rich tapestry the similarly differing threads of ritual procedure we may at times wonder if this apparently complex collection of Masonic styles could rightly be described as 'The Mark Degree story'. Whatever might be our eventual judgement on that matter our present concern must be to conclude our pre-1813 survey of the scene. To that end we must move westwards once more and travel to *Ireland.*

We left this part of the then still United Kingdom in 1775 at the point when a certificate issued by the Knights Templar of Kinsale clearly designated one of their number as a Mark Mason. It is, however, to an edition of the 'Antients' renowned handbook, 'Ahiman Rezon', which appeared in Belfast in 1782 that we can turn for confirmation that the two degrees of Mark Fellow and Mark Master were well-known by that time. They appear in a list of toasts of Lodge 257 (IC) that were recorded in this edition. They are:

(Toast) No. 13. All Royal Arch Excellent Free-Masons.
No.14. May *none ever be admitted* Members of this Lodge but such as shall be *found worthy of the MARK.*
No. 15. All MARK-MASONS round the Globe.
No. 16. All Royal Masters who become **Pillars** to each other.

We should note the order. The position of those who receive a Mark and those who are MARK MASONS (the capitals used are in the original document) is *between* the Royal Arch, that in Ireland has a J(osiah) legend about finding the lost Law, and the Royal Masters, with their Z(erubbabel) legend about re-building the Temple. We shall shortly see that this is exactly the order that was adopted around 1810 when a re-alignment of ceremonies took place. What we must register in regard to this printed list of toasts is that they must have become normal and regular before they would be recorded for use or reference by others. That means taking the distinction back to the 1770s.

Attempts to combine and legitimise the desire to work the so-called 'higher degrees' led eventually to the issue in 1781 of a Warrant, No. 584, by the Grand Lodge of Ireland. In its efforts to control these practices the Grand Lodge also insisted on the adoption of a new title – The Early Grand Encampment – by those involved in the administering of the degrees and by 1786 it was declared that this body was 'revived', as though it had existed, as some claimed, in 1705. Perhaps the term 're-organised' would have more correctly described what then took place. It was this body which began to approve warrants for further Encampments in Ireland starting with three undated ones for Dublin and one in June 1793 for Balbriggan. By 1805 there were to be 32 such bodies, including several in Scotland, and some in England.

From our point of view the significant feature that emerged from this re-arrangement of its practices was a series of degrees that were now declared available to members of the EGE. The Red Cross degrees were distinctly separate in Ireland from as early as 1790 and it was with them that the Mark ceremony appears to have been associated. When we discover that it was specially connected to the Red Cross degrees of Knight of the Sword, Knight of the East and Knight of the East and West one wonders if the *pre-1813* arrangement of the Baldwyn Rite was similar, as this would help to solve what was a query when we looked earlier at adjustments in Bristol Masonry. Irish influence, if not example, has always been thought to have played a part in formulating Bristol Masonic procedures.

Irish Red Cross certificates for candidates were issued from 1790 and the wording of them in each degree of the series was very similar. From a Mark point of view the following certificate issued in 1807 has some very interesting phrases:

"... since his **ascending the Ladder** of Faith, he has *placed the Level* of Equity *to all his Works*; ever since he *returned to rebuild the Temple* of the Lord he has been found Upright by the *unerring plumline* (sic) of Righteousness ... the *Chisel and Mallet* have been to him as **faithful monitor** ... His Behaviour Amongst us, has entitled him to this Certificate which, like the **Olive Branch** of Peace, we commit into his Hand and recommend him to all ... *Mark Masters* in the Universe." In this extract from the Certificate the portions in italics will be somewhat familiar to those acquainted with the Mark ceremonies of today (with perhaps one exception) whilst the words in bold will set up echoes for those in other Masonic degrees. The exception just referred to is the mention of a different setting for a Mark Mason, viz. the construction of the *Second Temple* as against the normal suggestion that the events in the degree took place at the erection of *Solomon's* Temple. The import of this variation will become more apparent as we engage with the details of different 'Mark' rituals.

There was a further variation which is revealed in a certificate that was issued in Newry under the sanction of Lodge 706 in May 1791. Issued by the Capt. General and others of the General Assembly of Knights Templars and Knights of Malta the certificate ends with a series of dates that are worth pondering:

Order of Knights Templar	3789	(1998 BC)
Order of Malta	921	
And of *Ark and Mark* Masonry	3798	(2007 BC)
In Royal Arch Masonry.	4138	(2347 BC)
Book of the Law found	2415	(624 BC)

What is this saying to us? We have clearly passed a long way from anything to do with even the *first* Temple of Solomon and are seeing the Mark degree linked with the period of the Ark. Since the EGE was to set the Mark firmly between the Ark and the Link (or Wrestle) the only conclusion can be that here was a ceremony that had some kind of Genesis story as its base. What could that be? Another certificate of the period issued by the Lodge in the Leitrim Militia seems to point us to a solution. It reads:

"We the Worshipfull Grand *Mark'd* Master and Wardens, Representatives of the Three Grand Masters &c K S * * H A * and of the Worshipful Lodge No. 854 Dedicated to the Holy and Undivided TRINITY and under GOD Do recommend our worthy and well Beloved Brother ... a Regular *Mark'd* Mason and as such to be Received into all Regular *Mark'd* Lodges".

The emphasis is on the 'marking' rather than the receiving of a Mark and when we try to attach this to a Genesis story there is only one solution. An article in the Freemasons Quarterly Review for 1834 spells it out for us.

"As the number of the human race increased, their bad passions were called into action; *and Cain*, influenced by envy, apostatised from the principles *of Masonry, and took the life of his brother.* The judgement and sentence of a justly incensed Deity followed, the fratricide and his family were driven forth, Cain being protected from personal violence *by a peculiar mark* which distinguished him from the rest of mankind. Of the nature of this mark or brand many have been the conjectures of the ancients: some have imagined it to have been *the word ABEL imprinted on his forehead*; others the four characters forming the word Jehovah ..."

We can begin to see how one of the 'Mark degree' variants came about and why some series of contemporary ceremonies included a 'Cain's Mark'. And yet that is not the end of this story.

In an article on "Masons Marks", in the same journal but in 1845, another writer tells us that "on the architrave which joins the pillar (of the Apprentice in Roslyn Chapel, near Edinburgh) to a smaller one in the south wall, is an inscription in Gothic characters, containing sentences having a particular reference *to the Red Cross Degree in Masonry*, and amongst the sculptured figures there is a man with a *wound in the centre of his forehead ...*"

When we learn that the Gothic style sentences in Latin read in English:

"Wine is strong. The king is stronger. Women are yet stronger but Truth conquers all" we may begin to see that we are no longer just in one ceremonial variant of the 'marked craftsman' but of yet another that was to figure in many Irish lodges that performed a Mark degree. We shall see all that worked out in the next chapter. At least we can begin to appreciate the increasing complexity of Mark practice and appreciate those words of J.A.Grantham warning any student of this subject that the mere use of the term 'mark' does not mean that we can equate what bears that name in the past with what we do today.

Nevertheless forms of Mark Masonry were practised all over Ireland at this time and three examples of how this presented itself will have to suffice. The first is in Old Lodge 611 at Glasslough, County Monaghan. The most important feature of the Minutes still extant here for the first half of the 19th century is that they reveal how, after the Grand Lodge had attempted to control the additional degrees by authorizing a Grand Chapter and Grand Encampment, a local lodge set about the task of instructing its members in these degrees. hence we read:

> "November 9th, 1802. Lodge met in Dew form the Worshipful High Priest in the Chair when a Royal arch Shuperexcelent (sic) Encampment met..."
> "March 4th, 1805. A fellowcrafts Lecture went round..."
> "September 2nd, 1805. A Master Masons Lecture went round..."
> "November 8th, 1815. When a Master Masons Lodge was opened and lectured on the sum of the degrees..."

The degrees thus lectured on are described as:

> That Magnanimous order of Knights Templars and Knights of Malta.
> That awful degree of a Red Cross.
> The Glorious degrees of Royal Ark Mark and Link Masonry.
> The intricate degrees of Ark Mark and Link Masonry.
> The Sublime Degree of a Royal Arch Superexcellent Masonry.

Since there are other evenings when they did not lecture but worked all the degrees one after another we may truly say that they got carried away – even with their descriptions.

In 1810 a faithful son of Irish Masonry and one whom we shall acknowledge again at a later stage, John Fowler, wrote out a table of all the degrees currently being practised in Ireland. The list is of note because it has no observations on it as if what is written there was so normal and regular that nothing more needed to be said. Coming from such a hand the list is important.

1. Entered Apprentice: Fellow Craft: Master Mason.
2. Past Master: Excellent Mason: Super Excellent Mason: Arch Mason: Royal Arch Mason.
3. Ark Mason: Mark Fellow Mason: Mark Master: Link Mason or Wrestle: Babylonian Pass (or Red Cross of Daniel): Jordan Pass: Royal Order (or Prussian Blue).
4. Black Mark: Templar (Four Grades): Mediterranean Pass: Malta: Red Cross of Constantine: Knight Patmos.

It may perhaps seem unnecessary to set out all these degrees but there are three reasons for doing so. The *first* is that it shows, as mentioned earlier, where degrees with the description 'Mark' were seen to fit in what Crossle called 'The Irish Rite' by this date. *Secondly* it recalls for us the place still retained in Irish Masonry by the 'Arch' degree. I am convinced that this element, as was shown earlier, was vital to the transition which would be made in the next 25 years to another kind of Mark ceremony. This is because it retained three features two of which would be lost to the Royal Arch but incorporated into eventual Mark practice throughout the kingdom. These features were: a skilled but unrecognised Fellow or Master, the keystone he produces and the important place in the Arch that it has to occupy to enable the work to proceed.

When, as appears to have been the case, all that was retained in the Royal Arch ceremony was an Arch with its headstone and aperture the other elements lay idle. They were taken up and *re-designed* (and that was appropriate, as we shall see in the review of rituals) for use in something more like the Mark degree we know today. The 'Arch' degree may have been brief but it was absolutely crucial to our story.

If this is not a correct analysis of the situation that then prevailed I can well understand the frustration of Stephen Forster when he wrote in his 1985 paper on the Mark:

"Examination of Royal Arch certificates of contemporary times (i.e. 1780–1810) similarly fails to produce any mention of the, seemingly elusive, Mark ... Even the famed Kilwinning Lodge at Dublin, long recognised as a proponent of additional degrees, appears not to have worked the Mark degree ... Spasmodic entries in the minute book may refer to conferrals of the Past Master (virtual) and *Arch Degree* but none are found which could be construed to be with respect to the Mark." Was he perhaps looking for the wrong evidence at the wrong time? What he goes on to say I agree with wholeheartedly:

"... the lack of (evidence) tends to suggest that while Templar Encampments were still working *some form of Mark Masonry* circa 1810–1820, the *MMM as is now practised* was not yet introduced into Ireland"[15]. That sounds to me like the real truth of the matter but in this story of ours we are not chasing only the Mark that we have now but the Mark as it evolved.

Thirdly, therefore, the display of all these degrees by Fowler shows us once more how closely linked what **then** were called Mark degrees were with the Babylonian Pass. We shall have ample opportunity to see the significance of this connection very shortly but let us at least keep this link in mind as so plainly portrayed at this date.

The last example of the prevalence of some kind of Mark working also appears in 1810 in the town of Bandon and in Lodge 413. Four certificates given to a William Bishop, as he passed through all the degrees mentioned by Fowler, are still extant. We need only consider the fourth one issued and here again the phrases create all sorts of echoes for those in other degrees. Here is an extract:

> "*Wisdom hath Built her House* she hath Hewn out her *seven pillars*.
>
> We the *Loveing Pillars* of this Royal Sir *Knights Templars Priesthood Order* do hereby Certify that our Loveing Brother Priest Sir. Wm.Bishop has been dubbed a Knight of Malta and of the Priesthood Order and has likewise rec'd the following Degrees in Masonry Vizt: *Ark, Mark, Link*, Meditiaranian Pass (sic), Pursian Blue (sic), Jordan Pass, Red Cross ... to which we *Seven* do put our hands and Seal of our *Royal Union* (in the year) 1810 and of Peace 3783 &c &c".[16]

This is by no means an isolated example of how the 'Mark' was seen in relation to the whole panoply of Freemasonry. In the year 1809 in Edinburgh we have a remarkably similar certificate: 'We the General Assembly of Knights Templars NO. THIRTY ONE holding of the Early Grand Lodge (sic) of Ireland, Have after due Trial and Examination instructed and initiated our said Trusty and Well-beloved Companion and Brother, the Worshipful Sir John Forbes, into all the Mysteries of our Religion, and most Christian Orders ... by installing and Dubbing him a Knight Templar and Knight of Malta, and *expounded unto him all the Secrets of the Ark, Mark and Link Masons* ... Red Cross Knights ... in the year of our Lord M.D.CCC.IX. (1809) (and) of Royal Arch Masonry M.M.M.CC.XCIX (3299 = 1490 BC)..."[17] (with the latter date cf. p. 105)

These two last documents should confirm three things for us as we leave Ireland's shores and sail west. There was some attempt being made to organise the sequence of degrees past the Craft so that they could be taken with a definite goal in view, even if that goal were specifically Christian. Sadly these steps were not coordinated by any one Grand Body for in 1805 the Irish Grand Lodge had severed its ties with the Encampments and even the Chapter work that it had first fostered. And in the midst of all this welter of Masonic activity, under whatever umbrella, something *called Mark degrees* had managed to persist and retain a place in the Masonic structure. It was a vessel in somewhat uncertain waters but it was still afloat and it *was* going somewhere.

Our journey in this chapter at last reaches those shores of *North America* which Dunckerley had navigated in recent years. A long tradition of Freemasonry in that area is testimony to the impact of settlers and military alike and there is no question that in both these cases the influence of Antient Masonry was uppermost. Hence the Mark and Ark degrees had fruitful ground in which to flourish. Bro. Noar (no pun intended) starts us off with a remarkable statement in his non-published papers to the effect that in 1871 a contact in Mark Grand Lodge assured him that 'the Mark degree was conferred in a Mark Lodge in the United States of America *in 1768*.' Certainly Graham in his book affirms that from 1759 to 1781 there were many additional degrees being performed in the Quebec region and some form of Mark was one of these. Whilst Dashwood, in his AQC article on the practices at Middletown, Connecticut, shows that the Chapter there "was to follow the lead of the 'Antients', although St. John's Lodge had been formed by Warrant of the older Grand Lodge, before the 'Antients' came into existence. This was probably due to the *influence of the Regimental Lodges* ... and the establishment of an 'Antients' Provincial Grand Lodge in New York in September 1781, may also have been a contributory factor..."

On the "13th Day of September in the year of our Lord 1783 ... the Subscribers, Members and principal Officers of the Grand Royal Arch Chapter ... assembled ourselves in the Lodge Room at Mrs. Abigal Shaylers and having properly examined each other and finding each and every one of us having been *made a Mark Master Mason* and duly initiated in this *Sublime fourth Degree* in Regular Constituted Mark Lodges; for the purpose of Promoting the Mark *as the Key to the Royal Craft* – Agreed to turn ourselves into a Mark Lodge likewise under sanction of St. John's Lodge. (signed) Oliver Lewis Triangle

John Lewis de Koven Hope and Anchor

Jono Heart Ark

They then opened a Lodge of Mark Master and Mark Wardens, and proceeded to advance (four brethren) for which Marks every one of them paid ... the customary price" which, not surprisingly, was $1/1\frac{1}{2}$d." They then resolved "that this Mark Lodge be and ever remain *for ever* within the *new instituted* Grand Royal Arch Chapter ... and that the Right Worshipful High Priest, Captain General and Senior Grand Master thereof Officiate as the Principal Officers of the said Mark Lodge – Likewise the Treasurer and Scribe of the Chapter as Treasurer and Secretary."

By 1784 there is a footnote to the Chapter meeting of 29 January:

"After closing as above a MARK Lodge was duly Opened & Brother Jared Bunce a Royal Arch Mason was given the Mark as may more fully appear by the Records of the Mark Lodge."

Bro. Dashwood goes on:

"The Mark Lodge minutes confirm this, but the only amplification is the statement that 'the Mark given him is a Wheat Sheaf'. Two facts emerge from this: first, that it was not necessary at this time to be a Mark Mason before acquiring the Royal Arch, and second, that the 'Marks' were not such as we are accustomed to – a few lines that could be cut with a chisel – but were more of the nature of a 'characteristic' which was described in words, not drawn."

It is indeed true that in the Mark minutes of this Chapter no actual Marks are shown and when we read the Marks allotted we understand why. They include Hand in hand, Seven Candlesticks, Five Points, Ship, Bald Eagle, Pulpit, North Pole, a dove descending with an olive branch, a printing press, a Spie Glass and many others. In many cases a motto is appended to the Mark: for instance, the Brother whose Mark is a printing press adds the motto "Defiance to partiality, abstinence from anarchy" whilst the Trowel and Hammer is accompanied by 'Diligence'. One Brother was determined to get his money's worth. He chose as his Mark "The Bible and Heart, Pot of Incence & Letter G" but he only paid the usual thirteen pence halfpenny. The Secretary dismissed one candidate very sharply – "brother George Phillips was marked" is all that appears.

In 1795 we discover that a candidate for the Mark had to be an Installed Master for on 2 January a Master Mason was elected, "whereupon the Mark Lodge was closed and a Masters Lodge opened and (the candidate) was duly Installed and received the Honours of the Chair and then closed this Masters Lodge." The Mark Lodge was then re-opened and the new Master was advanced.

During the next few years the Chapter seems to have lapsed but there was a revival in January, 1795. By February they had even agreed new dates of meeting and fees, though the latter do seem to need some understanding:

"That from and after this Date the Fees for Initiation into this most Super Excellent Royal Arch Chapter shall be the Sum of Two Guineas into the Treasury and one Dollar to the Centinel (sic) – but provided that the Candidate hath Received or does Receive the Degrees of a Mark, and Super Excellent Masters, and Passes on into this Degree of a Most Super Excellent Royal Arch, shall be One Guinea into the Treasury & One Dollar to the Centinel besides the Stated fees recorded in the Mark Masters Records."[18] No doubt they were clear as to what they were doing but whatever the arrangement was at least they were plainly acknowledging Mark Masonry of some kind. Another puzzle here is that whilst the Royal Arch minutes end in 1798 the Mark ones go on to 1812.

It is also intriguing to note that this Chapter, though not Irish, had a H(igh) P(riest) at its head and not a Z(erubbabel). To pursue the implications of that arrangement is not something we can do here but it at least makes a Mark Mason look back at the fourth certificate from Bandon and the earlier dating given at Newry. (See pp. 107f)

This remarkably clear picture of what was happening with the Mark in one North American setting only underlines the task that might face anyone who sought to regulate matters, not only from a distance, but without a clear understanding of how naturally the additional degrees were practised. Especially would this be so, as in the above case, when a lodge and Chapter were involved that were meant to be under the Premier Grand Lodge jurisdiction.

It may seem something of a diversion or even distraction from our main purpose to say more here about North America. Let me assure the reader that what follows is not only indicative of the surprising range of Mark Masonry in the English speaking world of the time but will later be seen to have been crucial to understanding what happened in the middle of the next century.

Graham has graphically painted the scene:

"Among the causes retarding the progress of the "Moderns" in Canada ... may be mentioned: the sparseness of the population, the vast extent of the 'Masonic Jurisdiction' of the Provincial Grand Lodge of the Province of Quebec, the unavoidable infrequency of inter-communication between localities far separated by all but unbroken forests, the American Revolutionary War, the non-adaptability of a foreign Provincial Grand Lodge system of government by deputation ... the great cost and many delays in communicating with the Grand Body, *the concurrent existence of* ***three****, and for a time,* ***four*** *Grand Lodges* in England, engrossing attention at home and distracting it in Canada, *the non-recognition of the 'Moderns'* by the Brethren of Scottish or Irish obedience and by the three 'Ancient' (sic) Lodges in Quebec, 1784–91, and the growing opinion among Masons *in favour of the 'Seceders'* or 'Ancients'."[19]

This formidable mountain of problems meant that by the end of the 18th century there were no lodges left of the 'Moderns' sanction. The implications of this fact for a post 1813 situation may already begin to be imagined.

It was in this context that we must set the following events. On 7 March 1792, the 'Antients' Grand Lodge of England divided their Province of Canada into two parts – Upper and Lower – and appointed two new Provincial Grand Masters, one of whom was no less a person than HRH Prince Edward, 4th son of George III and father of Queen Victoria. We are told that he was "installed with great **éclat**" and under his direction the 'Antients' form of Masonry flourished in those parts and not least because he was resident first in Quebec and then in Halifax, Nova Scotia. Some indication of what this meant for Mark Masonry in that Province can now be given.

1792: In the Minutes of Lodge No. 9 for 7 December: 6 Brethren were *raised* to the degree of a 'Mark Mason'.
1793: Also in No. 9 for 9 August: Bros. Phillips and Scott from No. 5 (Lower Canada) and 'Royal Edward' Lodge, Edwardsburg, (Upper Canada) *received* the degree of 'Mark Master Mason'.
1794: From No. 9 minutes for 14 March: 2 Brethren from No. 7 LC (Lodge of Fidelity, 7th Foot) and 5 Brethren from No. 9 LC (Prevost Lodge, St. Armand) were *made* Master Mark Masons.
1795: Several brethren were made 'Master Mark Masons'.
1798: In minutes for 21 September: 4 Brethren *had the Honour and Degree* of 'Master Mark Mason' *conferred* on them.

Sadly the Minutes of No. 9 are missing from 1809 to 1833. However we have some other sources. The details of the quarterly gatherings of the St. John's Mark Lodge, No. 241 occur with great regularity. We are told that a very considerable amount of work was done and the Marks chosen were generally Craft symbols though there were two of less usual note: quarter moons with either a Passion Cross within or over them. We also note the following:

1801: At a Master Mark Masons Lodge 6 Brethren received the 'Master's Mark' and they choose for Marks respectively the Gavel, Key, Compass, Square, Ladder with three rungs, & Bee-hive.
1805: For 24 September: The Lodge was opened in *the fourth degree* and a Bro. was *marked a member* of this Lodge.
1806: For 16 April: It was resolved that, in future, the money arising from the 'Mark' be deposited in the 'Masters' chest and that the present fund be consolidated in same manner.
1809: For 18 April: Bro. Usher, of No. 2 'Pensilvany' (sic) *prayed to be raised* to the degree of Master Mark Mason.
1810: Note was taken that a new Mark Lodge was warranted in Montreal under the Wellington Persevering Lodge, No. 20 of the Ancient York Masons.
1811: For 18 April: It was voted that no Master Mark Mason residing in Quebec should belong to this Mark Lodge *except he belong to a Masters Lodge.*

That this should be the temporary end also of these minutes is hardly surprising when Graham tells us that the meetings of the Provincial Grand Lodge and of most of the private Lodges were suspended during the war between Great

Britain and the United States, 1812–15, but afterwards "many of the lodges *vigorously resumed work.*"[20]

It is on such a note that this chapter must end. Unhappily, what was meant to be the solving of a conflict between 2 Grand Lodges in England was to begin another kind of battle when the hostilities with the U.S.A. were over. Mark Masonry as we can see was in a flourishing state in its North American home. It was not only going to progress but it was going to have its influence in the old homeland. After all, soldiers had brought the seeds in the first place. Now, as they and new commercial 'combatants' returned to Britain they could display the degree in full flower, or at least some of its variegated species.

Chapter Six

The development of the Mark Ritual

IF THE MARK degree as a separate ceremony or ceremonies took its measured time to emerge, the range of ritual variation, as and when the Mark did appear, presents a very different picture. The seed of ritual components may have seemed to be slow in germinating but the richness of its first and later flowering makes for a fascinating if complex story. What is more, we have the most exciting array of material with which to work. Due to the dedicated efforts of G.W.E.Bridge there is, in the archive of the Grand Lodge of Mark Master Masons in London, a very rich collection of manuscript rituals. Some of these were surrendered by lodge members when the attempt was finally made to introduce an agreed English usage – even if what was then chosen was almost entirely Scottish in origin. Other material has been contributed by wise donors including some from Scotland and further afield. It is time not only that that rich resource should be better known but that students of the Mark to come should be provided with at least a fuller and, I hope, easier guide to its contents.

It is therefore the purpose of this chapter to seek to present a comprehensive survey of this part of our story. This has never been attempted before on such a scale. Springett and Grantham wrote chapters that can only be described as helpful pointers to the subject and though Bridge once produced a private paper entitled 'The Development of the Mark Ritual' it was never seen in print and was acknowledged by the author to be a superficial look at the topic. There have, of course, been papers in both English and Irish masonic research journals looking at one or other individual aspects of the subject but there has never been any attempt to analyse and compare the disparate usages in any coordinated way. Perhaps it was just the sheer complexity of the task that discouraged previous writers. Whilst that was a feeling that certainly beset me as I contemplated writing this chapter what finally prevailed was a sense of amazement at the ingenuity of our forebears together with a growing conviction that this had to be shared more fully than before. I only hope that I can retain the interest, *and* satisfy the desire for discovery, of the reader as the panorama of past Mark rituals unfolds.

Just how to manage the material we have in such abundance is the main problem. To deal with each variant in a strict time scale would be tedious, especially as some of the items can only be dated approximately and their development was not uniform. To try and study them *geographically* would be artificial even though there is some indication that in one or two areas the same pattern did prevail. What has finally seemed best is to select what one can only describe as 'families' of ritual practice and seek to show when, where, how and why they grew as they did. In doing it this way we shall cover the field without, I hope, making it seem too vast. We will also be able to see how elements in these 'families' created the foundation for what was finally adopted up to today.

The three main sections or 'families' of ritual practice which we shall now consider will be as follows:

1) Those deriving from Operative, Guild or Harod(im) workings:
2) Those influenced by Irish Red Cross, Babylonian Pass or Crossing the Bridge workings;
3) Those following the early Scottish (and American) systems.

In addition there will be a subsidiary section in which an explanation will be given of all the *minor degrees* carrying a Mark title or theme. I must also point out that a book of essays is being compiled that will attempt to explain the present day ceremonial features with their origins or meaning and that will, in part, refer back to items being dealt with in what now follows.

SECTION ONE

It should not surprise the reader of this book thus far to have his attention first drawn to the evidence supplied by the workings of the degrees of Operative Craft Masonry. It is not simply the framework of these grades that suggests that they were the foundation for providing a separate dimension to the Craft called 'The Mark' but we have in the rituals of *Guild Masonry* clear pointers to what have now become accepted features of this degree. Let me illustrate.

In the ceremony of 'making a Mason in the Second Degree' we note the following statements:

(a) After having already used the plumbrule and level the candidate is told to "take this Square in your right hand and prove the cubical dimensions of the Perfect Ashlar or Cube Stone."

(b) The letter G is illuminated and this is followed by an explanation of the moral advantages of *Geometry*. For the purposes of continuity we need to hear some of the verse that was then used:

W.M. What means that letter G?
A. My friend, if you pretend to be
Of this fraternity,
You can forthwith and rightly tell
What means that letter G.
By letters four
and Science five
This G erect does stand
With due art and proportion
Thou hast mine answer found....

Our Science free has well composed
A noble structure vast,
A point, a line, a superfice
But a solid is the last.

The catechism continues by asking *what are* a point, a line, a superfice and a solid. (In the extant portions of the Harodim lectures exactly these same words were used, also in verse, but they are there followed by a long historical commentary which begins as follows:

"In this manner was Freemasonry propagated. When our ancient Brethren had finished the Temple at Jerusalem and travelled into foreign parts and lodges were by these means established and masons legally made who were operatives by profession ..." (The significance of all this will in time appear.)

(c) "The Grand Grip of a FC alludes to one of the penal laws of ancient Tyre and is emblematical of the punishment inflicted on the subjects of HKT found guilty of perjury, who were condemned to lose the second finger of the right hand for the second offence of this nature."At the opening of the Guild 3° we read: "They are Mark, and **Marked** Men, and have the arrangement of fitting stones for the Temple, so that the Erectors in the 4°, on the site of the Temple, may know where the stone has to go exactly, being supposed to be Marked with *blue* paint, whilst *Arch* Guild work is marked with *red*...

"As a ceremony the Men are the *Stones to be Marked – living* Stones. When a Fellow of the 2° is to be received he gets in by some means with the crowd, past the Inner Guard. Each Marked Man presents a Stone and when the Order is given 'Every man to his place', all being 'Marked' and knowing their places, they drop into their proper positions." The Fellow finds a blank spot. The Master says he will examine whether the stones are 'complete and perfectly marked' for the Temple work. He finds the Fellow and remarks: 'Here is a stone which has not been fitted to those on either side and is not marked. How did you get here?' The Fellow says he came through the door with others. Despite the consternation this causes they decide that all they can do is recognise him and *mark him*. Thus he becomes a '*Mark Man*' and has an *indelible Mark* imprinted on his *body.*

In the Guild 4° we encounter the Bonai who are setters and erectors. The candidate comes dressed in white (Latin: candidus), bearing himself as a *marked stone* and seeking *advancement*. He is at last permitted to see the partitions removed and the three Grand Masters sitting side by side at the far end of the Temple.

We cannot go into too much detail but four 'strong Masons' now form a close square, foot to foot, shoulder to shoulder, each with a *sword* in the left hand and a different implement in their right. Later they hold four lines grasped at the corners (thus forming rough tassels) with their right hands and with the left they *suspend a plumbline* over the centre thus forming *the five points* of testing a true centre. In the following ceremony HAB is slain and *Adoniram* is elected in his place.

Finally in this particular degree, the great *Corner Stone is lost* and the Master in the 4th Yard sends a messenger to tell those in the 6th Yard that the work is at a standstill because of the loss. The 1st Grand Master makes enquiry and traces its progress through Yards 1, 2 and 3. It is at last found *just outside* the 4th ARCH Yard where it was refused because it was *square* but left intact because it was *wrongly* adorned with a *red mark*. When the man who made that mistake is found it is *he* who is 'heaved over' *from the top of a 30 cubit drop*, thus becoming the sacrifice to crown the edifice.

What we have just read must surely begin to ring bells in the mind of any present day Mark Mason. Nor is it surprising if in the next stage of shaping these ancient operative practices into more speculative forms there was a desire both to preserve the old ways and yet to enhance them in their new setting as non-operative masonic minds got to work on them.

We have already referred briefly to one Harodim embellishment but there were others. There was considerable verse comment on the four great *foundation stones*...

"Who laid the *first* foundation stone of faith?
  On Mount Moriah's highest top
  Abraham an altar did prepare
  As sacrifice to offer there
  His only son....
Who laid the *second*? Jacob.
  He from Beersheba to Pasan (sic) went
  To serve the Lord Jacob was bent
  But the sun having set he sat him down...
  Then Jacob arose in the morning soon
  And took the stone he had laid upon
  Then poured sweet smelling oil in plentiful
  And called the name of the place Bethel....
Who laid the *third*? David.
  On Ornan's the Jebusite's thrashing (sic) floor
  David erected an altar pure...
Pray tell me who the *fourth* may be.
  Christ the Lord. For lo, 'tis said
  Before the Jews from Egypt's land were led
  A Saviour unto them was promised...
  He is the everlasting Corner Stone
  By the builders rejected & by this world disowned..."

This later part was ritual that would return in due course but before then there would be part of the opening of the Harodim 1° lecture:

"WM (asks) Bro. SW. 'Is there anything particular betwixt you and me?' A. 'There is, WM, a Study in Masonry.'

WM. 'What is Masonry?' A. 'The study of Sciences and the practice of virtue ... It comprehends within its circle every branch of useful knowledge and learning, and stamps an *indelible mark* of pre-eminence on its genuine professors'; and it goes on with something that would certainly be re-worked: '... it is a sure foundation of tranquillity amidst the various disappointments of life; a friend that will not deceive, but will comfort and assist in prosperity and adversity, a blessing that will remain with all times, circumstances and places, and to which recourse may be had when other earthly comforts sink into disregard.' With this kind of material around who needed to make up new ritual content? As we shall see the similarity between Operative and Speculative Masonry is too important a feature to overlook.

This was also true of part of the Harodim 2° lecture:

"Why do Five hold a Lodge? In commemoration of the sacred treasures in the Holy of Holies, the Pot of Manna and Aaron's Rod that budded, &c. Your second reason? It alludes to the 5 external senses: hearing, sight, feeling, smell and taste." I forbear to reproduce the extensive explanations then given for these senses but I must remark that not a little of what was used later in this connection owed its first phrasing to the Harodim discourses.

There was reference to an incident probably unknown to most Masons today but which was to re-emerge in a Mark form. The text reads:

"HAB was immediately honoured (at the foundation of the Temple) with the title of Acting and Deputy Grand Master ... and, as the grand superintendent, a Jewel of great value was presented to him from Solomon and what is very remarkable and ought to be written in letters of gold and never effaced from the memory of Free-masons (is) that the singular discovery of this jewel, through the means of the inhabitants of Joppa, was the primary cause of that momentous circumstance which is or ought to be amply elucidated in the third degree." Folk memory was certainly due to work with this incident though it would also be a case of fitting the jewel where it suited best.

There was also this slight but significant amplification of a well-known Fellowcraft question – "Where did our antient (sic) brethren go to receive their wages? A. To *their respective Lodges* in the city of J(erusalem), the quarries of T(yre), the forest of L(ebanon), and the claygrounds of J(udaea) between S(uccoth) and *Z(arthan)*, there to *be paid by the M(aster) or W(arden) in due form, agreeable to the original custom* established by K(ing) S(olomon). Where did they receive them *during the dedication?* In the middle C(hamber) of K(ing) S(olomon's) T(emple)."

In the third section of the Harodim 3° lecture we read something more: "A short time prior to the death of our GM HAB King Solomon issued his Royal proclamation to the Masters of all the Lodges of Masons in Jerusalem setting forth that his royal will and pleasure was, to reward the workmen of each degree, *who came properly recommended*, at the finishing of the Temple; by *honouring them a degree higher*, certified under the hand and seal of these three Grand Masters; to enable them to be sooner employed in foreign countries and also procure *better wages*; which was to have been done by causing all such worthy E.Ap. to be passed to the degree of F.Ct. and so on in regular succession, each degree *advancing* in similar manner, (to) the highest degree (the Superexcellent)...."

Enough has been recorded, I think, to show that here were materials and ideas which, being abandoned by the ordinary Craft ceremonies, could be taken up into the intervening space before or around the Holy Royal Arch. There were those who were already at work adapting such degrees and I have suggested that the military lodges were foremost in such a development.

For anyone who has lingering doubts about this latter process I quote:

"In the 'Ancient' Lodge Room, (Dundee) on 18 February 1773, 'The Ancient Super-Excellent Royal Arch Lodge was duly constituted by Edward Brereton, Grand Master of the Super-Excellent Royal Arch Lodge, No. 52, held in HM 37th Regiment of Foot, with Richard Brodly belonging to the same and Alex Ross, Shipmaster in Dundee.' We have here unmistakable evidence as to how the Royal Arch Degree arrived in Dundee. It came by the hands of *a Military Lodge under the (Antients) Grand Lodge of England*." If that could happen in Scotland it could certainly happen south of the Border.

That is why I am happy to maintain the conviction that what took place in Portsmouth in 1769 was that Thomas Dunckerley, having 'lately' received two new steps in a military lodge conveyed them happily to his naval and commercial brethren in the new Chapter there. By 1777 John Knight, a brother of impeccable masonic probity and long service, was receiving those same degrees at Dunckerley's hands in Cornwall and by his firm testimony we are said to have the documents that show us what the Mark Man and Mark Master of Dunckerley were like.

What are these documents? They are the complete text not only of those two degrees but of the succeeding ones of Excellent, Super-Excellent and Royal Arch, as well as others. They therefore provide the very context in which we have always been told that Dunckerley revealed his new-found ceremonies – and yet we have them so arranged that these degrees could be taken *in any order*, as we know they later were, in Portsmouth itself. I should however like to adjust something that might have been inferred by what was said in Chapter 3 about Dunckerley's possible 'composition' of these Mark Degrees. Whilst I am convinced that Dunckerley received the two forms of Mark as suggested I also have more evidence found in Devon quite recently which would support the view that what Dunckerley may have done was to re-edit the catechetical style of what he had received and shape *them*, and the other degrees in these documents, into something more like an embryonic form of what would later follow. In other words, whilst not *devising* these degrees he certainly *revised* them. Whether he did this work of reshaping before 1769 cannot yet be shown.

What are the degrees like? It will hardly be a surprise to learn that each of them is largely made up of discourse, a Charge and Lecture. In view of their possible provenance and their authentic mid-18th century style (not to mention handwriting and spelling) we should expect little else. Let us look more closely at the first ceremony with its alternative title: "Foreman of the F(ellow) C(rafts)".

The 'lodge' is opened by first getting those present to 'advance' as Ent(ere)d App(renti)ces) and then as Fellow Crafts, in '*the usual Way*' giving the Signs of each. The Master then enquires, 'What is the continual care of a M(ark) M(an).' The JW says, 'To see the Lodge Tiled against those who are not of that Deg(ree)' and *goes himself to the door* to give *two long and two short* knocks. On returning and declaring the Lodge close Ty(led) the Master says. 'To order, Brethren, *as Fellow Crafts*.' And then, **surely no surprise**, he continues:

> "Bro. SW what now Occupies your thought?
> The Grand and Sublime Science of *Geometry.*
> Why did you come here?
> To Study and exercise it.

"GEOMETRY is indeed worthy your Study. It is a Science where your thoughts have a most ample field and can go deeper and with greater certainty than any other. It is divided by us into *two kinds, Operative and Speculative*. Speculative Geometry considers and treats of first principles abstractedly. Operative Geometry applies these considerations to the purpose of Life ... it conducts the Soldier to the field and leads the Seaman through the Wild and pathless Ocean ... Since then it is of such universal service let us adore that being (sic) who frames the mind of Man for exercising this Grand Science whilst we reduce its practice."

The WM gives two long knocks, the SW one short and JW the same. The Brethren are called on to prove themselves Mark Men and the Master ends the Opening with these words:

"... in the name of the Grand Geometrician of the Universe I declare this Lodge duly open in the Degree of Mark Man for the purpose of Improvement and Study." The roots are surely obvious.

The candidate comes hoodwinked but with no other preparation. He is one, says the *SW*, 'who prays to be created a Foreman and comes strongly recommended. He is led round the lodge and at the pedestal in the West the Master says, *inter alia*,

"... Man inspired by his Maker commenced the Study of the Glorious Science by the principles of Geometry ... This Science may justly be considered as the ROCK on which the foundation of the Temple of human knowledge is erected." Then, having spoken of Astronomers, Geographers, Architects and Engineers, the Nile and the preeminence of Egypt, the Master closes this portion by saying, "As a FC the science of Geometry must have been your particular study, therefore, to convince this Lodge of Mark Men that you know the principles, you are requested to give a definition of such figures as shall be proposed to you."

Placing him on a Point the SW then instructs him how to take *4 steps*, at each step having to answer questions such as "What is a point? What is a Line? What is a Superfice? What is a Hexagon?" and many more such. I am

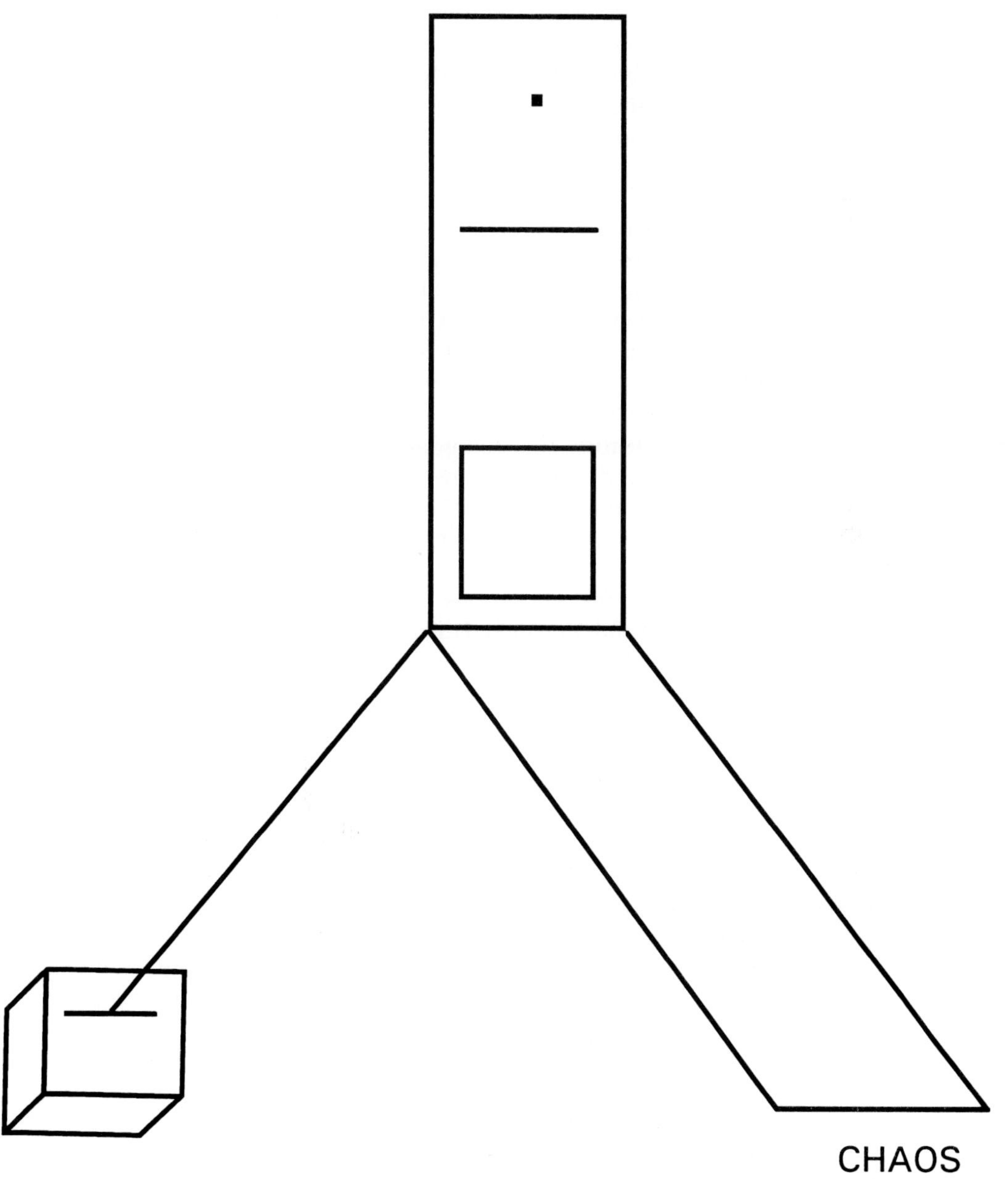

sure that the reader can already discern the obvious links between this and the material we have earlier recorded.

As the Master next speaks he creates an echo of a new kind: "Remember that the road to virtue and vice is like the letter **Y.** A point represents Man in a State of infancy, his mind then being without parts. Man has then but one beaten track in which he travels in his journey thro' life until he arrives at that state represented by the Superficies, in which state his mind becomes expanded and hc is capable of judging Virtue from Vice; here then the road, before plain, branches off into two; the one leading to Perfection, the other darkness, error and confusion – chuse now which you will take remembring (sic) that broad is the way that leadeth to destruction and many there be who find it, but narrow and difficult to proceed on is the right hand path of truth. The path though rough is neither impassable nor untrodden, though the gates stand not so wide as that which opens into Hell, yet, through the narrow gate multitudes have entered and been crowned. Explain the Solid."

No-one who is familiar with the Ark Mariner degree today can fail to wonder if this is not part of the material that helped to form one of its striking features. It certainly disappeared in Mark workings but its significance was too great for it to be wasted.

In the 'Short History' that followed the taking of an obligation the Candidate was introduced to the masons of Egypt, Euclid, Pythagoras, Aristotle, Cambyses 'the Persian Monarch' and Alexander. Whilst we must be selective we cannot pass over the following passages:

"In the Society of Masons of course there must have been Men possessing abilities in different proportions. They therefore found it necessary, without dissolving the bonds that united them, to form themselves into different Sects or Degrees, the highest of which *in those days* were the *Foremen*; each degree to be formed from the most *worthy and deserving of the degree next below.*" Is this by way of seeking to justify the increasingly evident growth of degrees at this time or a recall of Operative tradition?

In explanation of the fearsome penalty attached to the obligation we are told that Euclid, an 'Apostate' for sharing with the Greeks the trade secrets of the Masons, suffered 'an extraordinary death, for an Eagle mistaking his bald head for a *Stone* dropped a tortoise on it to crush the shell.' Do we perhaps smile at this weird use of a classical tale only to realise that cowans today may smile at our words when taken out of context.

The Master now says, "Confiding in your fidelity and trusting that you will not follow the example of the Greeks I shall now proceed to give you the Sign: Like *heaving* a Stone with *one hand* over a Wall or *Precipice* ... the Token: Little fingers coupled, at the same time giving the Entered Prentice grip ... the Word: Mark Well (giving the *Hebrew* word.)". Some of this, we note, is given in code, but not cypher, letters.

In concluding this section we are told that 'of the scattered remains of the Masons some *Emigrated* to the East and settled in China, some *wandered into Europe*, particularly the northern parts, who assumed the name of Druids (who) though they deviated from their original usages and customs ... never committed any of their Secrets in Writing.'

In the Charge that followed the Master describes how 'The first use of the Second degree was before the general Deluge which is commonly called Noah's flood', and thereafter he introduces Lamech, Adah, their children, the pillars they made, and Nimrod the King of Babylon who taught his Craftsmen to 'live truly together and serve their Lord truly *for their pay*'. He introduces Trismegistus and Hermas who invented 'the *sacred writing* of the Egyptians and Hieroglyphics ... and took to him Lords' sons and taught them the Science of Geometry in practice for to work in Stone all Manner of Worthy Work that belongeth to building.' Hermas is commended in that he showed how 'they should call each other his fellow or else Brother and not his Servant or Knave or any foul name and that they should *truly deserve their pay of the Lord* or the Master of the work that they serve ... Nor should they admit another that hath but little cunning and *is not skilled in Geometry* to be a foreman with them in the Lord's work, whereby the Lord should be evil served and they ashamed.' Yet they might make 'the worthiest among them a Governour of the Work (and) call him Master.'

The Lecture simply recapitulates what has been done in 'advancing' the Candidate and the Closing calls on the Brethren to cease their studies. The last words are: 'Brethren, Fidelity, till we meet again.'

Surprisingly the Mark Master or Mark Mason ceremony is shorter but we shall miss several important features unless we follow its given sequence.

In performing the 'most and essential duty' (sic) in opening the Lodge the J.W. again goes to the door and gives the knocks, 1 long, 2 short and 1 long, following which the Master says,

'Brethren, convince our Bro. Wardens that you are all Worthy to remain in a Lodge of Mk. Mas. by giving each to his next Brother the Token of a Mk. Mason.' There is added '(This is to be complied with)'.

The Candidate appears 'having a Square and Compass stuck in the girdle of his white apron' and he is announced as 'made an EP, passed FC, created a Foreman, and raised to the sublime Degree of Master Mason (who) now prays to be entrusted with the Secrets of a Mark Master'.

Whilst he is led slowly round the room the Master *reads 21 verses of the Bible* which relate to the idea of Wisdom whose Seven Pillars were mentioned in the opening. Two verses in particular begin to have especial relevance to what will come later:

"Through Wisdom is an house builded and by understanding it is established. ... *Mark the perfect Man* and behold the upright for the end of that is Peace."

Asked then by the SW how he can prove that he is a Mark Man the candidate points to the 'symbols of Truth and Justice I wear in my Girdle' which he carries 'Because (such) was the custom of our Grand Master HAB when he surveyed the rising Temple and by those Symbols his Body was known when discovered....'

Following an obligation the Master addresses him thus: 'Before we can proceed further it will be necessary for you *to form a Mark or Badge* worn by every Mark Mason, one side of which you ornament with some Masonic device which at your return you are expected to explain to the Brethren ... the other side you are to leave plain to be filled up by my further directions.'

In the ante-chamber thc SW now gives him *instruments with which to form his Mark* and having done this he is re-admitted, taken to the pedestal where he '*lays his Mark* on the Tracing Board which is placed *on the Holy Bible* (sic) and then gives an explanation of the Mark he has chosen. ...' A declaration follows in which he undertakes not to change his mark, adopt a second one or refuse a Bro. Mark Mason if in distress but will lend him the *value of a Mark* (i.e. 13/4d) or more. The Candidate now enters the Mark in the *lodge Mark Book*, and the Master now tells him what to inscribe on the blank side:

"At the death of our worthy GM, HAB, King Solomon, impressed with a grateful sence (sic) of the services rendered to him by that illustrious Artist, ordered the 12 Original Master Masons, under the direction of the noble Prince Adoniram, to prepare a Monument which should hand down to posterity the merits of the Dead and the Gratitude of the living: these 13, proud of the honor done them, resolved to form themselves into a Lodge of *Marked or distinguished Masons* and adopted the Sign, Token and Word which I shall now give you...

Sign: Like the heaving a Stone with *both hands* over a Wall or high place. *Token*: Grasp hands touching Thumb repeat STRENGTH, then turn hands round to form links, the last Sign to throw a Stone over the wall as badly done and of no use. *Word*: Strength.

Jewell: On the one side thereof to be any Mark the Bro. chuses ... on the other side HTSWSS. Viz. Hiram (of) Tyre: Son (of the) Widow: (a) Servant (of) Solomon.' This is, so far as I am aware, the earliest form of the letters that we shall see developed in other workings. The junction of H and T begin to suggest their own tradition and the words that follow in the Master's address about the Funeral Monument begin to add to that tradition.

'The Monument (was) erected in the Garden of KS adjacent to his own Audience Chamber (where) Solomon *held his Chapter* and used to confer with HKT and HAB in *Mystical Matters*.'

The Lecture or Catechism between Master and SW again recapitulates much of what has taken place but there is this special passage:

M. What Supports and beautifies a Mark Masons Lodge?
SW S(even) P(illars).
M. What are they called?
SW Wisdom, Secrecy and Honor support *the dome*: Architecture, Embroidery, Sculpture and Mechanics beautify the Entrance.

M. To what do they refer?
SW To the Moral and Professional excellence of our departed Master"

In closing the Lodge the Master recites a remarkable prayer that has its own resonances in our story:

"Before I dismiss you I recommend you to place your Confidence in that great Being who is a Strength to the needy in his distress, a refuge from the Storm, a Shadow from the heat, when the blast of the *terrible ones* is as a Storm against the Wall, and may your lives actuated by this confidence reflect *honor on the degree of Mark Masons* and by our integrity and purity make us men like that great Man whose *name is inscribed on our Mark....*"

No-one who has followed these ceremonies carefully can be in any doubt as to why the Mark degrees became known at an early stage as 'honorable' nor why they also grew steadily in popularity. Though we shall not enter into most rituals in this section in quite the same detail it was important to see at last how the seeds of the future were sown and to note their obvious links with operative and ancient working. The next stage only serves to underline this fact.

Whilst this was going on in Britain a ceremony was being conducted in Jamaica and also Charleston. What is now disclosed was copied from the 'book of Bro. Fourtaud' which means that it goes back to earlier than 1796, and Bridge in his essay puts it at c.1787. It is called the 5° of the 'Rite Ancien de York'.

The lodge room ought properly to be furnished with *blue* hangings and *sixteen lights* with an altar, on top of which there would be a round white marble stone of considerable thickness. On the stone itself were drawn two concentric circles between which were cut the letters H.T.*W.S.J.*T.K.S. where the italicized letters read 'Wishes (to) Send *Jabulum*'. I would again point out that there is still no fixed form for these letters. Laid on the letters was a Bible, the compasses, three stars and a poignard.

The lodge team is now increased to include *two deacons* but there are *no overseers*, and whilst the deacons carry out the external check on tyling, the Wardens still test the brethren as Mark Masons. The answers of the deacons as to what is their position in the lodge is revealing and relates to what we shall see in other old workings in England. They say: "*Behind* you, Very Wise, (or First Warden) or at your right if you permit it" and they also add "To bear your orders *wherever* it may seem good to you". The Treasurer and Secretary also answer. Before the Lodge is declared open all present have to give the signs of the EP, FC and MM degrees, the latest entries in the Mark Book are read, and the Master asks the SW. "What purpose has brought us together here?" with the response "The Verification of the work of those Brethren who demand an increase in wages." A very operative reply.

The candidate stands prepared in the ante-room. He has his shirt turned down around his waist, he is in short breeches, without stockings or shoes, his hair dishevelled and *a cord around his neck*. Deprived of all metallic items he is attended by one called 'Bro. *Terrible*' who instructs him how to take up as large a stone as he can carry *between the thumb and two first fingers* of his right hand. Bro. Terrible raps 7 times on the door as a Master and they enter.

From the East the Master asks their desire and the reply is: "To make new advancement in Masonry if you find us worthy of it", which leads very naturally to the candidate(s) making *four journeys* round the Lodge and including questions and secrets. Of the latter the most important to remember are:

On the 2nd circuit, the Master asks, "Why have you demanded an increase in pay? A. To acquire new light, and be enabled *the better to relieve the needs* of my Brethren". The SW then gives the candidate(s) the following password *C..H. . . . L..T.* (sic) & the sacred word *K.*.. (See p. 183). On the third circuit the Master asks why they were deprived of all metallic objects... "A. Because at the time of the building of the Temple of Solomon, no noise caused by any working-tools was heard." On the fourth journey the Master asks why they are barefoot, and the reply is: "Because the place by which we have passed is holy ground, for God said to Moses, Take off thy shoes: the place where thou art is holy."

We now discover the reason for the 16 lights since the Master announces that he is reducing the sixteen journeys that should be made to four. He comes down to the altar, examines the stone brought by the candidate, declares it unsatisfactory, and hands it back to the *candidate who*, taking it in two hands, *throws it over* his left shoulder. There is rejection, indeed, but of a surprising kind and the Master now has another surprise for the candidates by asking them for 13 cents each. We are told later that this represents *a day's pay there* and no charity we give should be less than that in amount. When the candidate(s) say that they have no money the Master is scathing: "How is this, my Brethren. Refuse so small a sum for the relief of suffering humanity. The Grand Architect of the Universe will reckon with you for it."

Speaking of money the Deacon urges a candidate to stretch his open hand across the altar as if to receive wages but the JW takes up the poignard, grasps the arm and is about to sever the wrist when the Master intervenes with the question, "Will you take an obligation?" They do so and thereafter the Lodge adjourns for refreshment.

The Lodge resumes work and Bro. Terrible brings the candidates to the foot of the Master's throne. They receive the pass word G..I..B..U..L..U..M.. and the sacred word: H..E..A..V..E.-I..T..-O..V..E..R.. and the first penal sign, the hand sign for wages, and what is now called a 'plumb' sign but was for them 'assistance with lifting a stone'. They are told how to use a token and what to engrave on a medal like the one on the altar, and then they sit for a lecture and a catechism on what has already transpired. Such was the ceremony for making Mark Masons – but it was apparently only the *first of two* Mark degrees.

The second or 6° (called that of 'Marked' Master) was much shorter but introduces three otherwise missing pieces of our growing ritual. First, the candidate, with *a cord tied four times* round his body, brings a 'perfect piece of work' to submit for inspection and this is handed *from the JW to* the SW and thence to the Master. The Master tries it with square *and compasses* but has doubts unless the candidates take an obligation. The idea of *passing the work around* has thus appeared.

Secondly, they are told of a different way of requesting wages, without which their wrist would be cut off. Thus *two ways* of submitting the hand are now registered and the missing second penal sign is given its place in this working.

Thirdly, they are instructed in how, *in addition to* their mark, they should use '*hieroglyphics*, not only incomprehensible to the vulgar, but even to masons of degrees below that of Mark Mason.' Hence we have the introduction not so much of cypher language but of the need to learn it and why. As we proceed we shall see how those who came after fitted all these additions into the structure of their Mark rituals.

Back in England there was at this time a Masonic publicist called William Finch. Born about 1772 he was initiated in the Industrious Lodge No. 326 in 1794 and by 1796 he claimed to be a member of a Royal Arch Chapter. Becoming deeply interested in Masonry, and not least in what may be called the 'appendant degrees', he began to publish works on the subject from 1801. It is in a work of 1802 called "An Elucidation on the Masonic Plates" that we find information that was not only widely circulated but which was re-presented or revived when it might otherwise have been submerged in the revisions at and after the Union of 1813. Let us first of all look at two summaries he gives:

"In the Mark Man degree we are made acquainted with the loss of the **first** KEYSTONE *made* by HAB. A **second** made by … (not disclosed) and what followed thereon. The *loss* of the second and the *finding of both*. What occurred at the laying of the *foundation stone* of the Temple … when King Solomon was congratulating HAB on his discovery of that **famous mathematical figure**. These things ought to be well known by every Mason before he is exalted to the Arch."

This is quite a statement. It maintains the traditional view that the Mark is somehow related to the Royal Arch, continues the theme of an important Temple foundation event, and the 'lost' keystone, whilst at the same time introducing some quite new details. In the, again, quite brief Mark Master degree we "are acquainted with what King Solomon caused to be so eminently displayed on certain occasions in his audience chamber, and what wrought the conversion of his friend and ally, the noble and learned King of Tyre." That is quite new and distinctive and at first sight seems to have little to do with with either previous or present practice. The 'audience chamber' at least recalls a passage about the monument to HAB in the 'Dunckerley' rite.

In Finch's lectures on the first three degrees there are other references that show how his work was a bridge between the past and the future of masonic teaching. In the Second Section of the FC's degree he presents the following:

> "Why were you P(assed) a FC?
> A. To be fully instructed in the letter G.
> What does that G-denote? A. A fund of useful knowledge; but
> in this particular stage of Masonry it means GEOMETRY..."

(He now has a passage on the Nile, Euclid and a lodge of Masons who sought to measure and restore the landmarks, just as in Dunckerley.)

"Explain the Moral Advantages of Geometry. A. Geometry, that noble and godlike science, is the basis on which the superstructure of Freemasonry is erected...." We have here almost the same words and thoughts as appeared in the 'Dunckerley' degree of Mark Man, and just to show that Finch was drawing on the same reservoir of 'ancient knowledge' he ends his lecture on the FC degree, after reaching the Middle Chamber, thus: "Can you define that letter G?

> "A. (There) there stood a letter G
> A letter fair for all to see,
> Many there be ... &c &c." and he continues:
> Give a further definition.
> A. Our science fine
> hath well composed a noble structure vine;
> a point, a line, a superfice, but solid....

and he then goes on to demonstrate what each of these are. The link with the past is clear and obvious and Operative/Harodim influences still thrive. With mention of the 'hand' penalties of Tyre and Sidon and the significance of the five senses that view is confirmed.

Finch, however, has a number of other intriguing items. He speaks of Succoth and *Zarthan*, the ship returning from Ophir and being guided *into port by a light*, every Brother worthy of his hire, a man blowing *a trumpet* by the seaside, and the Rock of Horeb called *Massah*. All these, he assured his readers, were current features of essential masonic instruction. Yet it is only *after* Finch's time that most of them appeared in a Mark working to which we must now turn.

In a small notebook on paper bearing the watermark of 1817 we have a *Mark Man* ceremony that Hughan thought was based on an earlier one of around 1780. If that were so then it would not be surprising if this ritual reflected some of the same features that we have already been looking at.

There are some immediate indications that this is the case. On the cover of the booklet it says 'Mark Man' and under the words 'The Mark' we have two cypher letters making H over T (see p. 124) with an alternative alongside making T over H. Underneath these is a rectangle showing *eight letters* with the rough representation of a jewel at the centre. On the Jewel are the letters

H A B, and around it are T W *S T O D A N* with their meaning given in full – The Widow's Son Tribe Of Dan And Napthali (Finch's spelling). It would seem that by the time of this ritual, called the 'Watson Ms' because it was given to a librarian so named in West Yorkshire, there was still *no fixed series of letters*, but a cypher was used, as recommended by Dunckerley, and the letters H and T have some special significance in a Mark context.

We next notice that the Lodge is opened in the Fellow Craft's degree and, as previously, the work is all done by the Master and Wardens. There is the tyling 'externally' at the door and 'internally' of the members.

The similarity with the past continues in that most of the meeting is occupied by a Lecture given in the form of a catechism between the Master and Senior Warden. It is in the course of this Lecture that certain fresh items appear. It should also be noted that this ritual is very similar to the one published in the 1820s by a *Richard Carlile* of whom more will be said in the next chapter. Before we look at these fresh items that were introduced by the early 19th century let us record the Carlile portions that show its older ancestry.

The SW describes something that happened on the day of the Temple's foundation: "While King Solomon was in the act of *congratulating* our Grand Superintendent, HAB, on the occasion of his having *discovered* the celebrated problem in Masonry and *Geometry*, one of the *precious stones* fell from the royal crown to the ground, which being perceived by the *senior master* of the Order of Mark Men ... he picked it up and returned it to the king. This stone was of the carbuncle kind, and represented the tribe of Judah and our Saviour. It was formed into that great and glorious name, which KS permitted to be used in the test word of this degree ... having been found by one of the chief brethren." Is this why a 'jewel' appears on the bookcover?

The story is, of course, a version of the one earlier met with on p. 118. The circumstances are exactly the same but the event has been tailored to suit another ritual requirement. That this story had such an origin is suggested by the next quotation where the materials for the building of the Temple were brought from Tyre, Lebanon, 'and the clay ground of the Jordan, between the Succoth and *Zarthan*', the very name used in the same source document.

Other earlier features include the forms of the Mark itself. In the Mark Man it is 'The TH, or Tau in ancient characters' but in the Mark Master it is 'the HT reversed and in **ancient Masonic form**'. The earlier *four* great foundations now become *five* 'noble offerings' with a new one associated with the Queen of Sheba. Here too we have not only a mention of the need for the five senses but indications as to *how they were tested*. The candidate repeated a prayer to show he could **hear**; he read from the Holy Bible to demonstrate that he could **see**; the compasses were applied to his throat and chest so that it became obvious that he **felt**; he was invited to distinguish the contents of the pot of manna to evince **taste**; whilst at the altar he described the odour of the incense thus making clear that he could **smell**. This sequence of proofs, given in five perambulations, was to become normal for the next half century.

There were, however, many innovations in this working and some of them need ingenuity to explain.

a) The Candidate is prepared as a Fellow Craft 'with the *additional* characteristic of *this degree* on his apron' and the SW describes these as "The 10 mathematical characters, to correspond with the nine figures and cypher in arithmetic, the signature of HAB and the Mark of this degree." What exactly the first part of these were we are still not certain though obviously the latter items relate to the signs and letters on the cover of this booklet. Were we to find one drawing or picture of such an apron it would obviously be a great step forward. What is somewhat puzzling is why a Candidate for the Mark Man degree should enter already clothed with an apron that bears signs of a degree to which he has not yet been admitted. Especially in this a problem when we hear the next words of the SW regarding this preparation: "To denote the official duties of *this class* of Masons at the building of King Solomon's temple, and the *discovery made by the brethren, when they were repairing the temple*". One is always aware that the Mark degrees have a constant relationship with the Royal Arch and this last phrase already highlights the tension that existed as to whether the Mark related to the First or Second Temple. As we shall see in what follows, both in the repetition of, and variations on, this incident and in what will be introduced in Section Two, we have to keep this dual 'link' in mind if we are to understand some of what is presented.

(b) There may seem to be nothing new in recording 'certain mathematical figures ... which have ever since been denominated the **Freemasons' Secret Alphabet or Mystic Characters**' though this is the first time that such a description is given. What is fresh is the explanation of such an alphabet and how it is represented ritually, and because this will be repeated elsewhere it is as well to rehearse it here.

"WM. Can you describe these characters?

SW. With that circumspection peculiar to Masons I will meet you on the **line parallel**, by giving you one part, leaving you to your own free will in giving the remainder.

WM. I will thank you to proceed.

The SW rises, salutes the WM with the (first penal) sign, advances to him and lays his two penal fingers (first and second) across those of the WM and thus forms the index (sic) to the secret alphabet, by joining the Horizontal parallel to the perpendicular (one).' Whilst we shall look in more detail at the cypher alphabets of the Mark later we need to note here the now increasingly familiar phrase – *lines parallel* – to denote this part of ritual usage.

(c) Another new section in this catechism is the fresh historical account of the degree. It is simplest to reproduce it with italics to bring out the new variations from what has been given previously:

"At the *building* of King Solomon's temple, the valuable and curious keystone, containing many valuable *coins* and the *ten letters* in precious stone work, which HAB took so much pains to *complete*, was lost, supposed to have been *taken away* by some of the workmen, and a reward was offered by King Solomon for the *speedy finding or making* of another to fit the place. An ingenious *Entered Apprentice* made one and *fixed it* in the vacancy in *the arch*, which, being known to some of the *Fellow Crafts*, they conceived it a disgrace to their Order to let *an inferior* bear the palm of honour.

They, therefore, in the heat of jealousy, took it and *threw it and into the Brook Kedron* adjacent to the Temple. A reward was offered for the finding of this second stone, which excited the brother who had made it to *go with two other Entered Apprentices*, in pursuit of it; and when they had found it, they received *equally* among them the last reward and with it *the degree of a Fellow Craft*. The brother who made it received *the first reward* to his own share for his ingenuity, and had the honour *with his two companions* to fix it the second time in the arch, previous to which the brother who made it cut *on the underside the word* **Amasaphus**, and in addition to his former rewards he was honoured with the degree of *Mark Man*, which is done by *going round* the lodge of a Mark Man *putting in his hands* as a fellow craft to receive his wages. (He is acknowledged after stating what he has done.) ... and he being desired to *fetch the said key-stone* he finds it in his way to the arch, *by kicking against the ring of it concealed under ground*, the original key-stone that HAB had made with the proper characters and signatures to it.'[1]

This is a long extract but when compared with the Watson Ms story above it can be seen that many alterations have been introduced. The fuller implications of some of them will appear as we proceed but there is one facet of this story that seems to have puzzled everyone who has previously studied it. I refer to the word **Amasaphus**. Yet the author of this ritual has already attempted to provide his own explanation by saying "we found conspicuous in Hebrew characters the word **Amasaphus**, or as some say, **Amethyst**".

Who the people were who so transposed a proper Hebrew term into such an inadequate English one we are, of course, not told. One could believe that it was an ignorant Masonic informer for only a few months ago a London Mason told the author that the right words of the Chair to be used by a Second Principal in the Royal Arch were 'El Shalimar'. Ignorance works strange changes in Masonic ritual. Let us be quite clear that 'Amethyst' is either misguided or misleading. What is certain is that if the source of this misinformation was a Scottish Mason then either he did not understand his own tradition or he was wanting to conceal it. After recent extensive visits to Scottish Masonic premises I am aware that lack of knowledge does exist, even among Masons there. If, on the other hand, this ritual was compiled on the basis of English hearsay then that too would account for the error. Let me explain.

We must return to the ritual used here to secure our answer.

"WM. What is the chief signature of this degree?

SW. The first is HAB, and the word is S T O D A N."

This word in itself looks odd but if we recall the letters on the cover of the ritual booklet we shall soon see where and how it arose.

"WM. In what manner are they depicted in a Mark Man's lodge?

SW. On the *under surface of the keystone* of King Solomon's Arch which they *discovered* to be a little loosened, at the time that they were inspecting the *subterraneous passages* and making preparations for the *repairs of the temple*.

WM. What else was *there* discovered?

SW. *Round the circle* surrounding the letters HAB and between the other letters forming the remainder of the signature of this degree, we found *conspicuous in Hebrew . . .*"

Notice that we have passed once again from the First Temple scene to the Second Temple needing repair. Search is being made amongst the ruins where a subterranean passage leads to an Arch. I cannot dilate on this matter here but I must ask the reader who is not a Royal Arch Mason to believe me when I tell him that *that is the 'degree'* in which this happens. There a discovery is made and now, with the agreement of the appropriate authority, I will reveal what will answer our 'Mark' problem.

In the Scottish Royal Arch ceremony the candidate is led to a spot where, *under the surface of the ground* he encounters a metal *ring* attached to a slab of stone above the *arch* of a *secret chamber.* On this stone, which covers the main *keystone* of the arch, are words which should be inscribed *in Hebrew letters*. The words transliterated read "Am b'tsaphan" but in most places they read "Am bat saphan" since knowledge of, or acquaintance with, the original Hebrew characters has long wained. Even knowledge of what the original Hebrew meant has been lost and hence it is not considered important that the three latter words on the stone *mean nothing as they stand*. For the record let me tell you that the Hebrew means 'Close to a hidden (or secret) place' which was apt and correctly descriptive of the Solomon situation. Yet if Masons in Scotland today do not fully grasp what "Am b'tsaphan" means then how natural that someone not aware of the significance at that time, or perhaps recording something just overheard, should call it **Amasaphus**. If the word were not so attached to a Royal Arch setting there might be a problem. With the attendant descriptions here there cannot be the slightest question that this is what it refers to. When we come to look more closely at another Hebrew word used in Mark we shall find a similar mis-take.

With these new introductions into growing Mark ritual we might be thought to have said enough about the Watson Ms. Yet we cannot leave it without remarking on the way in which this ritual alone took up the danger signal of the trumpet in the Mark Man degree, and the safety signal of the 'celebrated Light House on the highest point of Mount Lebanon' in the Mark Master ceremony. Both of these, we recall, were mentioned by Finch, but since they are repeated in the Newstead working I shall explain them further there. (See p. 141f)

The ritual also contains a first detailed description of that 'ancient coin', the shekel, and its markings of a *pot of manna, the rod of Aaron budding*, and the names 'Shekel of Israel' and 'Jerusalem the Holy'. But no less interestingly it is here that we have the first English intimation of 'the **link** of a Mark Master', a subsidiary degree that we shall look at before long. Overall, this Watson Ms provides a great deal of fresh material for study of the Mark, and as we shall note again when we consider the Richard Carlile who used or 'marshalled' this material, these ideas were widely circulated. What is therefore the more surprising is how little lasting influence this form of the Mark degrees had on what was practised around the country or under the aegis of the Grand Mark Lodge. Indeed it is just this lack of influence which makes me wonder if this wasn't a 'made-up' or composite ritual which was not actually used anywhere.

It is to Bath and Birmingham that we have to move for our next step in the growth of Mark ritual. Tradition has it that the working which must next occupy our attention was being followed some time before the Union of the Grand Lodges and certainly this could have been the case with the *Antiquity Preceptory* of Knights Templar and the Royal Cumberland Lodge, both in Bath. Since the Howe Lodge in Birmingham was not founded until 1851 that requires another explanation and this will be provided when we look at the Newstead ritual shortly and when we tell the early 19th century story of Mark development in Chapter 7. What is clear is that the rituals of these three bodies were so closely related that they must be examined together. The only major distinction between them is that Royal Cumberland and Howe make extensive use of a cypher alphabet. For greater ease in referring to them we shall use the letters AQ, RC and HW.

Having opened a Lodge in the first two Craft degrees the WM opens a Mark Masters Lodge. Certainly the double tyling, and the sharing of the 'lines parallel' and word 'Adoniram' by the Wardens and Master reflect what had gone before. What is new is that the method of report to the WM by the Wardens is identical with the fashion in which the substituted secrets of the 3° are today communicated. Prayer is in the name of the G.A.o.t.U. (HW, GGOTU) and the Master declares the Lodge open 'to receive reports from the *inspectors of works* (in AQ Inspector)', which clearly refers to the work of examination that comes at the outset of this working.

The Candidate gives proofs of the earlier degrees to a Deacon – SD in RC and HW, JD in AQ – and is told to 'present himself free from cumbersome apparel and ready for work' but whilst he is *given* the pass word we use today in AQ it is *given for him* in RC and HW. We can thus see forms of present day practice developing from older ones.

Once the candidate is led into the lodge room the Junior Deacon assumes the role of fellow-candidate (or 'Steward' in AQ) and presents a cubic stone for testing. The SD acts as Conductor.

We now come to the first fresh input of this ceremony for we meet our *first acting Overseers*. They were known in AQ as 3rd, 2nd and 1st (or Master), but they try the work presented to them with a Square and their remarks already have a familiar tinge.

"3rd. The form of this stone is unusual and cannot be tried with the _|. I cannot pass it without the concurrence of my Bro. Overseer. (and in AQ he *himself passes* the stone to the 2nd Ov.)

2nd. It is curiously wrought. I also cannot prove it but must consult the Master Overseer. Bro. Master Ov. I *bring* this strangely formed stone to you as my Bro. Ov. and myself are unable to test. *You will oblige us* with your opinion of this Bro's work. (The age of courtesy was obviously not over and in RC and HW the S. and M. Ov.s actually leave their posts and meet at the *J. Ov's place* to confer.)

1st. (says to the *Steward* about his stone) Pass and give your stone as a Certificate to the S.W. who will present you to the W.M. (Then, after trying the Candidate's stone) I cannot *perceive the use* to which such a stone is applicable. For what is it intended and where did you *procure* this stone?

Cand. It is a stone which I *found* on my way hither. These Characters ... (and he seeks to explain but is cut short)

1st Ov. ... are not the mark of any of our Craft. This stone was not wrought by you. It is *unfit* for any building. We reject it. (In the AQ working the M. Ov. throws it *on the ground* and cries '**MASSON**'.) Go, your conduct is indefensible. (RC and HW use 'questionable') Lead this Bro. to the W(est) there to await the pleasure of the WM." The Word here used in AQ by the M. Ov. is not by chance though it was not a word that was to be employed in many places. It is almost certainly a form of the Hebrew 'massa' which meant, among other things, 'carry away' and thus referred to the idea of rejection. In addition it is worth recalling that Finch had connected Horeb and *Massah*. Horeb means 'waste or worthless' and the connection of the two terms in the Mark context is too much of a coincidence. When we see two variations of this word that follow shortly the general drift of these words will be obvious.

The JD having now submitted his cube to the SW is rewarded there by *a coin*, the first time such a thing is mentioned in this family of rituals. The Candidate attempts to follow suit, but his hand is siezed by the SW who cries:

"Hold, you betray yourself. Who is this man?"

M. Ov. "One whose work has been rejected." (Candidate is held fast) The W. Master invests the JD with a jewel but defers further remarks as 'important business presses'. He asks the M. Ov. *if any defect shows* in the final erection of the Temple. There is.

"The roof of a *vault beneath the Sanctuary*, being supported in framework which cannot be taken away without endangering its safety, something seems to be wanting to secure it." (The Candidate seeks to solve the problem but is silenced by the SW who holds him.)

It is here that RC and HW have an extra portion not included or even devised by the creators of AQ. It is as follows:

"The SW leaves his place and beckons to JW to follow. They place themselves at the North and South of the WM, select a Plan and confer. The WM and SW in whispers acquaint the JW with the discovery of the *principle of the Arch* by Hiram and its use. They then resume their places." The common working resumes.

WM. "This *portion* of the building was the work of our lamented colleague and was *reserved* to him because of its *connexion with our mysteries* and this drawing represents a stone which would *complete* the structure. It certainly was wrought by him, and Bro. Ovs you must have seen it."

It is now clear that we are more and more shaping the ceremony that we are familiar with though I would emphasise again the constant sense of linking with the Royal Arch. This relationship, I submit, was to continue until the constitutional effects of the English 'Union' and the changes to the English Royal Arch ceremony altered the setting. In the remainder of the ceremony we shall see the 'Arch' motif very firmly underlined, as the following demonstrates:

The detained Candidate is now brought to the W. Master's attention but, on the grounds that his treatment has rendered him 'lost for words', his story is told by the SD (JD in AQ) 'The skilful FC was on his way to the Temple with his masterpiece when he 'observed half-buried in the Channel of a stream (Kedron?) a stone which evidently had been wrought by a Master'. Its curious monogram and shape suggested 'that it might be applied to locking stones together and sustaining them in the position of a full-drawn bow. ... Struck with the vastness of the use to which the discovery would tend he determined to rest upon it his claim to preferment and being unable to convey both' he hid his stone and planned to retrieve it when he had explained the Master's keystone. His subsequent treatment being explained he now sought opportunity to *find his stone or make another* and 'obviate the difficulty which perplexes the builders by fixing the deficient stone and securing the safety of the work they refer to'.

Having approval for such a search 'The candidate is conducted by the JD *slowly round* the lodge to represent *his descent* from the Temple to the Vale of Jehosaphat (RC and HW: 'where the stone would have fallen'). On arriving at the place where the stone was thrown down he *strikes his foot against it* and takes it to the WM'. If anyone wonders where the idea came from of a weaving about around the lodge room as the candidate looks for the stone then here is the answer. Since we have also lost the sense that the heaved over stones (or workmen) were thrown *over a precipice into a valley* it is no wonder that we have also lost all sense of wending our way down the hillside to retrieve the needed masterpiece.

The WM now instructs the Candidate to carve something on the newly-rediscovered stone and to then *place it formally in its rightful place in an Arch*. It is in carrying out these steps that we find variations between the three workings.

(a) In AQ the word carved on the stone is '**MASSON**', in RC it is EMMESEKKA and in HW it is the letters Z S.

(b) Only in RC and HW are we told that this could only be done by 'removing from the stone a *covering which concealed it*'.

(c) In AQ the Master says: 'You will now follow my Deacon who will conduct you to the *crown* of the Arch' (and the Candidate makes *three* perambulations with the Wardens giving specified knocks. The Wardens then flank the Candidate in the East and he ceremoniously sets the Keystone in the crown of the Arch).

(d) In RC and HW there is more detail about how the stone finds its place. The WM says: 'The scaffolding having been removed from the building your way will be *by the winding staircase*.' The Candidate, bearing the keystone, which is held only by the thumb and forefinger, and preceded by the SD, passes *nine times* round and between the three Lights which stand in a line between East and West.

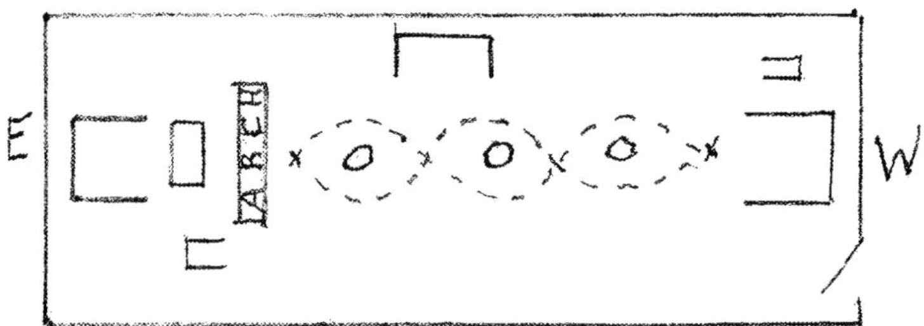

and the keystone is placed in the Arch before the WM. (To complicate matters RC only says: 'thrice round each candlestick')

'Cand. My task is completed and the arch is secured.

WM. You have proved the soundness of your pretensions and established the title to advancement.'

There must, one assumes, have been such a gadget with archstone as is now used in certain Royal Arch ceremonies or the M.E.M. degree in North America, for it may be recalled that in Ireland there was direct mention of an arch raised on two side pillars. The WM (in AQ) even asks the PM to *remove the supports*, so there does seem to have been some kind of structure.

In addition it is worth noting that if the candidate were to make the weaving route down the lodge room as indicated above then the Overseers *cannot have sat permanently where they do now.* We shall see that this was the case in some of the rituals that follow, especially those of Minerva and St. John's No. 1 Bolton. There is clearly more development to note.

The Cand. now took his obligation. The penalty speaks of 'being *cast headlong* from the walls of the Temple (and then amusingly) which I should thereby *render myself unworthy* of working upon.' One might have thought that 'incapable' would be nearer the truth.

The promise is also made in RC and HW 'to conceal the Mark or Grand Cypher (RC, only 'cypher') of the degree from all who are not Mark Masters, and destroying the Key after using it. . . .” The cypher is now much in evidence in these workings as the Signs, Tokens and Grips are shared.

The Mark and Mystic Mark are now conferred and the sign is given by placing the hands on the hips with the thumbs pointing backwards as if one were looking up at a building. The *right hand* is now thrown up as a signal ‘to order the accumulated rubbish to be heaved over the wall into *the valley* beneath’. RC and HW add ‘hence it was removed by the labourers’.

The grip taught here introduces a paper or some other substance with one’s personal mark between the thumb and knuckle joint as if greeting an EA. The word used in AQ is ‘**AMASSON**’ whilst in RC and HW they have ‘**AMETSA** denoting Strength or Power’. This is a right interpretation for in Hebrew ‘**AMATS**’ can mean ‘to make strong’ or ‘be stronger’ and this latter meaning accords well with the attached phrase in the ritual at this point:

“indicating the distinction of the Brethren of this degree who as Overseers have *authority among the workmen* and control over materials.”

The Password is as today but another word is now given which in AQ& RC is ‘**EMESECA**’ and in HW is ‘**EMMASSAKKA**’ but both mean ‘rejected’ being other forms of the word ‘Massa’ which we noticed earlier. This being placed on the keystone meant that this was *the* stone that was refused.

The Candidate is now requested to go to the Registrar to choose his Mark and enter it in the Lodge Mark Book. The Mark may be of ‘any plain geometrical figure’ and an unusual use of the Mark is with a *direction dart* so as to tell other Brethren the way one has taken. If another’s mark is added then he should hasten to reach you. (See p. 189)

The form of making a cypher with a symbol thus ‘X’ is taught and the remaining sign is the ‘lines parallel’ already explained. With his new knowledge the Mark Master is now able to present himself at the SW’s ‘office’ to receive his proper wages, which he does by presenting his hand with his mark on 1st and 2nd fingers. The SW notes the mark, puts a coin on it which the MMM covers with his thumb and the hand is turned over and withdrawn. This turning over seems to be unique to this group of workings along with the Ashton Lodge (see p. 148). The SW now informs the new Mark Master that he is also entitled to know the ‘Grand Cypher’ which is constructed thus # ‘and contains a series of rectangular figures which, when properly arranged, and with the assistance of a point or dot, may be made to express the elementary sounds of every language; this is the key; you must construct it whenever it is necessary to you and destroy it as I do now (tearing it) after using it.’ Reminding the brother of the silent construction of the Temple the SW stresses the ‘language of Signs which we cultivate and preserve’. He therefore points out how with a Mallet and Square the MMM can transmit the letters of the cypher across large distances beyond the reach of normal speech.

One further ‘Grand Cypher of the Monogram (of 3 Gd. Masters)’ is also shown in these rituals as follows:

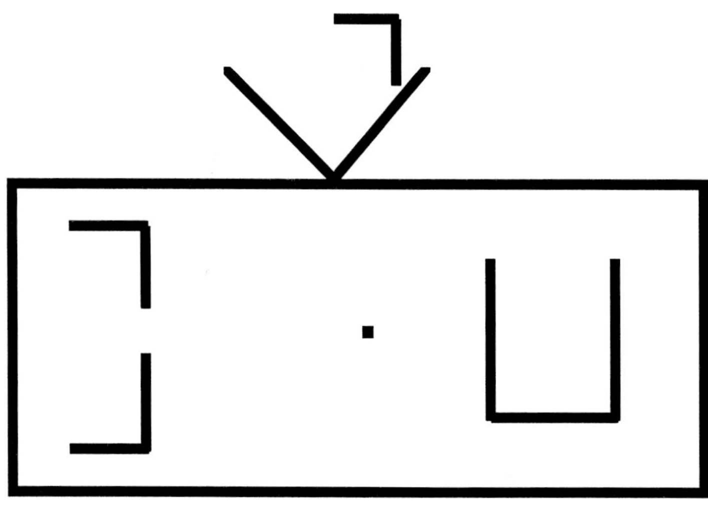

and the explanation is V *S*ulyman (or Solomon) ⌉ *M*elec (King)
⊐ *H*iram ⌉ *M*elec
⊐ *H*iram ⌋ *A*biff

⊔ 3rd letter of Hebrew Alphabet (Gimmel), initial of G. . . .m.

It is a jewel that bears this unusual design with which the new Mark Master is invested and on his restoring himself to his normal dress he returns to hear a lecture, at least in the AQ and HW workings. Though G.W.E.Bridge thought that this must have been a wearisome experience for a candidate the content of what is preserved here is of singular importance to any student of ritual. It also needs to be stated that whilst the general theme of the lecture is the same in both AQ and HW the words used are at times quite different.

Tradition states that during the building of King Solomon's Temple HAB discovered how to create an Arch and (AQ) "consecrated his invention to the *highest uses* by employing it in a part of the Structure prepared for *preserving the written revelation of God to Man*, and the symbols and testimony of Masonic faith *from loss* or destruction." The intention was to put the final keystone of the Arch in place when the builders had all gone away and meanwhile the stone was *left in the Porch* of the Temple for later use.

It was found there by the 15 FCs who thought the strange Monogram was the Master's Mark that they were not to receive. For (HW) "King Solomon being desirous of making Jerusalem the centre of both learning and religion, and the Temple their grand repository, had so arranged that the votaries both of Judaism and Masonry should find it necessary to come up from time to time *for the sake of advancement*." Three of them by envy *removed the stone and concealed it*, hoping to extract terms of agreement on their preferment from its creator.

After his tragic death HAB, being of mixed descent, was buried half in and half outside the Temple precincts. Hence arose the Mark Master's penal sign (AQ) 'which divides the body as half blood divided or gave H(iram) to the kindred both of the Levite and the Gentile'.

As work resumed a stone was missing but was happily recovered.

At this point the two rituals diverge. HW speaks of another Tradition which explains the previous ceremony because Solomon offered a reward to anyone who could make another Arch stone. When an ingenious FC did so his colleagues through envy took it down and threw it *into the brook Kidron*. It was again found by its maker and he carved (in Hebrew) the word '**AMASACH**' (Rejected). However, he placed it, with the help of two friends, once more in the Arch. Later *he stumbled 'against the Lewis'* of the original keystone and this was put where its replacement had been. However, the first part of the story is the one 'we received and accept ... and these may be termed the essentials of our Ceremonies'. The HW version then concludes with moral reflections on the degree.

The AQ version tells us that 2 Grand Masters and Adoniram assisted the new Mark Master to set the keystone 'in its due position and by securing the *mystic arch* and making the work complete (it) became the Chief (corner) stone of the Structure'. But then follows a strange verse:

'Tis the last key stone that makes the Arch
The rest that there are put are nothing
Till that comes to bind and shut
It stands a triumphal Mark. (See however p. 179)

The Lecture continues: "The intention of the 3 Grand Masters of *depositing the Sacred Book and Symbol within the Arch* was carried out by the Royal Survivors and Adoniram and there, after the lapse of ages, *they were again found* as you are told in our Supreme Mysteries. *This degree* supplies a *link essentially necessary* to the completion of the Chain of Masonic influences and an interesting illustration of the *ancient usages* of the Craft. Though among operative Masons many of our customs can no longer be found, that of conferring a Mark still remains. The idea of Speculative Masonry would then *obviously be incomplete* if it wanted (i.e. lacked) that which almost alone of the ancient customs continues to *distinguish its operative parent*. It is however much to be regretted that the Mark rite as it has descended to us has *suffered much from the hand of Man* as well as the touch of time. We have endeavoured to impart it to you in all its pristine state *free from Modern innovations*. It is requisite, however, that you should know what some of these are to facilitate your intercourse with those Mark Masters who practise them" (and the present signs are then given). What is to be noted is that there is still uncertainty about the letters used in the 'modern' lodges. They are here given as HT*WSST*KS or HT*SWST*KS.

This latter Lecture is by way of being a watershed in our story. It clearly recognises that those rituals based on the Operative/Guild customs are now paralleled by different rites that come from another source. What we also see is that in the Bath tradition the link with the Holy Royal Arch is strong and logical. Nowhere else that I am aware of is this connection so plainly expressed though in the Bolton working that we examine in Section Three we shall see the same roots. 'Antiquity' working, said Bridge, has many things in it that point to its being true to its name. The reader can now see that he was right.

In thc Closing, and especially the RC version, there are two short passages that merit recording because of their choice wording. As the Brethren stand to order the WM says:

"Before we separate let us adore the G.O.o.t.U., the parent of all good. May he extend to us his protection, endue us with his strength, enable us to resist temptation and praise Him in our lives." The IPM says, S.M.I.B. and then the SW adds to his usual words "in steadfast hope that we who have laboured in a symbolical, may finally through His mercy be received into the living, Temple not built with hands, eternal in the heavens." We are on the verge of the sentiment as it is expressed today but not quite.

Another antique ritual, this time one of French provenance, was worked around 1802 by the Grand Council of Princes of Jerusalem in Charleston, South Carolina. The principal officers were the *Respectable* Overseer and two Wardens, the latter known as Worshipful Senior and Worshipful Junior, whilst the Deacons were given the titles, Senior Minor and Junior Minor. The altar was a cubic stone on which were the letters we use today. The candidate had to be a Past Master in the Craft but he enters the lodge room carrying a building labourer's hod in which there is a collection of stones of which all, but one, are imperfect in some way. After three perambulations in which he proves himself in the 3 Craft degrees he presents the hod and its contents to the Wor. Senior. The Warden examines the stones and commands all to be heaved over save the one satisfactory piece of work.

The candidate is then invited to receive his wages but the usual 'drama' arises and he has to be exonerated by the Senior Junior who stands up for him before the Respectable Overseer. When the work is at last recognised for its workmanship he is taught how to pick it up with thumb and forefinger, as described earlier. He then takes his obligation and is *admitted a Master Mark Mason* in a manner very similar to today's practice.

In 1849 a Bro. Bassett-Smith wrote as follows:

"I have been to Nottingham and have seen the (Mark) degree conferred there several times and have noted that although the observances were the same at all times the *language used has varied with the candidate*. I have inferred that tradition has handed down the forms without the language and every Master deemed himself justified in using the words he could best remember or thought would be most suitable." In this frank disclosure we have perhaps the reason for what have elsewhere appeared like clear variations in the way certain items were practised. When we reflect on the fact that there were no individual manuals and most of the early Mark ceremonies were largely lectures and charges what Bassett-Smith says could well have been the case. Yet there was another side to this apparent licence in fitting the idiom to the individual. Bassett-Smith concluded by saying:

"This apparent extempore speaking at Nottingham has been joined to a robust jollity in working, which, however calculated to promote fun and good fellowship, does so only at the sacrifice of dignity and effect. The manners of the 18th century do not suit the age yet linger on in too many places in Freemasonry." There speaks the true Victorian. He values tradition but it must be worthy tradition. Not for him the dining table ceremonies of the pre-Union days. He wants authorised and precisely defined ritual and in the Howe ceremony of Birmingham that we have just looked at we see the effect of his hand since he was the one largely responsible for its creation.

Of the Newstead working at the time he was first visiting we sadly have no text but Bassett-Smith has left us some indication of the 'forms' to which he referred. We know, for example, that there was the testing of the five senses as in Howe and that in good operative style they *bound the candidate with a cable tow*, once round the left wrist and three times round the body. In case this practice seems a bit antiquated it is instructive to discover that in the first version of the "Perfect" Mark ceremonies published by Lewis the candidate was still described as being introduced with a cable tow *three times round his neck*. (Cf. p. 146) The stone was brought in by holding it as in Charleston with thumb and forefinger and there was even the same guidance about how to make that practice more possible. As in the Howe ceremony the candidate made *nine* circuits of the lodge to find the stone, thus representing his search as if via a *winding staircase*. There was also the ceremony of fixing the keystone in the arch, and the symbolism of the trumpet, the lighthouse and the rainbow was retained. As I promised earlier to comment on these features at this point let me now deal with the first two. The rainbow will be dealt with in the chapters on the Royal Ark Mariner.

I have made the point in the opening chapter of this book that one of the determining factors in the creation of masonic degrees and their ritual is the existence of legendary or symbolic material that may have no fixed point of reference and can therefore be re-used or re-located. I am sure that this is the case with the trumpet. When it is mentioned by Finch in his 'Elucidation' he specifically describes it as 'a man blowing a trumpet *by the sea-side*' and the tell-tale letters beside that reference are 'KT.' Certainly the use of the trumpet in the oldest methods of opening and closing a KT Encampment is well known and indeed the words used in that ceremony closely ally the context in which the trumpet appears in both the Carlile and Newstead settings.

In the former the First Captain says: "See that this Grand Christian encampment be secure" to which the Second Captain responds "Trumpeter, sound the alarm". In the latter the WM asks, What was that *signal* (of a Mark Man)? SW. The trumpet. WM. Why was it used? SW. To denote the approach of danger." There seems little doubt therefore that we have here a duplication of the same motif for the same purpose. Whether this has something to do with the link of the Mark and KT in those bodies that supplied the material for the Carlile and Newstead rituals or whether Carlile was misinformed and the Newstead ritual was copying Carlile I am not in a position to say. That the trumpet was used in the Temple ceremonies is undoubted (see 2 Chronicles 13.12 ff) and the Mark Man degree is a First Temple ceremony so there is some logic to introducing this as a Mark 'sign' or its explanation. The strange thing is that it was of surprisingly short duration and by 1850 had been dropped by the Newstead working.

The comparatively short life of the 'lighthouse on Mount Lebanon' creates a similar poser. We find it in Carlile's edition of 1825 and a 'Sheet of Masonic Illustrations' issued by John Harris at Bristol in 1839 but it had gone by 1880. Mountains figure regularly in 18th century rituals and most of them have specific associations. If the Lebanon was to be similarly marked then it too had to have some special part to play. The Lebanon was important in Mark Masonry because it was from there that the cedar trees came for the erection of the First Temple. Moreover, in the degree of Secret Master in the Carlile series ('called by Finch the Secret Provost and Levitical Order of Priesthood), we are told that "in this Lodge there is *but one Warden*, who is called Adoniram. It is he who had the inspection of the workmanship done *on Mount Lebanon*, before the death of Hiram Abiff." As it was in Hiram's time that 'the ancient mariners (were) employed in fetching gold, ivory, and precious stones, from Ophir' for the Temple what more natural than that Adoniram should direct their navigation aright by erecting this signal point?

Returning to Newstead, we do have a ritual used there after 1850 and there are still many features of that which had persisted from the earlier time. Most strikingly we now see a Mark ceremony which is in the hands of *Overseers only* and they sit in the places usually reserved to the Master and Wardens. Here too we have at last the terms 'East, West and South Gates'. The Mark Masons present have to prove themselves, and all the other officers – Treasurer, Secretary, Deacons and Tyler – have to answer for their places and duties. In this ceremony too we have more regular use of the term 'G.O.O.T.U.' though the touching opening prayer is addressed to the 'Most Bountiful Creator'. Here too we have an opening Charge which was by now becoming fairly widespread though sadly it has since disappeared from English working. It began with the words: "Wherefore, Brethren, having laid aside all malice and all guile and hypocracies (sic) and envies and all evil speaking ..." What we should further notice is that this Lodge had its own system of knocks. *One* called up the S. and J. Overseers. *Two* called up the officers. *Three* meant that all the members had to stand to order or pay attention. *Four* was the call-sign of the degree.

The candidate entered wearing *a long white apron* with his sleeves rolled up and the ceremony proceeded as today save that when the Overseers tested the stone he brought they remarked on the fact that 'neither has it the regular mark of the Craft upon it'. The real variation begins, however, when, having reached the Master Overseer, the candidate admits that the work is not his own.

> "MO. Where did you get it?
> CAND. I picked it up in the quarry.
> MO. Picked it up in the quarry! – this explains the matter – What! been idling away your time a whole week and now bring up another man's work to impose upon the Grand Or(der or Overseer)? This demands (sic) the sternest punishment."

Further small variants are that the JO speaks of the stone being brought to his *Office*, whilst the MO speaks of 'plans received from our *Grand Master Overseer Hiram*' and then, somewhat lamely, he asks the opinion of his fellow Overseers as to what they should do with the keystone. Having h.i.o. the stone is caught by the J.Ov. who carries it away.

The Brethren are immediately assembled to receive wages with the Candidate *heading* the procession, having been told that the 'last shall be first, and the first last' and it is now that the signs of the previous two degrees are given by all the members as they proceed round the lodge singing the hymn. There is also an interesting rubric.

"While the Ceremony is going on in the Lodge the S.Ov. procures a sufficient number of *pennies* and passes into the *preparation room*, opens *a lattice window in the door* which communicates with the Lodge room, and when the Craftsmen arrive at the Fellowcraft sign each of them in their (next) round puts his hand through the *window in the door* and gives a token. When the hand of the Candidate is seized others who are in the room with the S.Ov. cry out 'Chop off his hand'."

It is at the point where the Candidate's case is being put for him that the difficulty of having one Mason playing two parts begins to show. The M.Ov. has already judged the Candidate and yet has now to act as if he has never heard the case before. When he says, "This young man appears as though he deserved a better fate and as if he might be serviceable in the building of the Temple" you begin to wonder why he did not say all that on a previous occasion. However, he reckons that as the Candidate was never taught how to receive wages properly that somewhat mitigates his crime and he shall retire for further preparation – which consists of being divested of all metals and valuables. (Cf. p. 162)

The Candidate returns and it is as if the present-day ceremony starts all over again with a password given for him and *a Mark put on him 'such as you will probably carry to your grave'*. The 'indelible' mark is still with us. This ritual also preserves an older passage that we have since lost. It reads: "Operative masons make use of the engraving chisel and mallet to cut, hew, carve and indent their work but we, as Free and Accepted Masons make use of them for a more noble purpose. We use them to cut, hew, carve and indent the mind."

Whilst the Candidate is again taken 3 times round the room the M.Ov. reads three passages of Scripture which refer to the stone which was refused by the builders. As the third perambulation ends the brethren start a small disturbance at the J.Ov's pedestal. They lack a keystone and again the curiousness of the M.Ov's position becomes plain.

The S.Ov., in response to an enquiry about seeing the stone, says: "Not liking to take on myself the responsibility of rejecting it I passed it *to the WMO*". Not, we notice, "to *you*, WMO." The M.Ov. admits that he did consult on the matter and rejected the stone but now calls for diligent search to be made for it. He is not deposed for such irrational behaviour, as we have seen happen to earlier officers, but his must have been a most awkward situation. However, he is presented with the stone by the 'drafts*men* who found it', though only the Candidate appears before him, and the latter is told to take '*four* upright regular *steps*' to where he takes an obligation.

Herein he promises not to 'wrong a Brother of this degree to the value of one penny' and where he cannot assist anyone he 'will return him his mark with the value thereof (which is half a shekel of silver equalling 1/-)'. Having sealed his obligation 4 times, a passage from the Book of Revelation (2.17) is read and the M.Ov. adds these words:

"I now present you with *a white stone* on which is written a new name. The initials are H.T.W.S.*S.K.S* ... the Mark of our GMO and at present the General Mark of this degree." It should be noted that there are *only 7 letters* so there is still no definition about how many.

The M.Ov. also carries out a strange form of the Charity Test: he takes the jewel with his mark from his neck and presents it to the Candidate and requests of him some favour such as the loan of 5, 10 or 20 shillings. The Candidate protests his penury but on being repeatedly urged to search his clothing he finds a shilling put there 'slyly' by one of the brethren. He is naturally overcome with embarrassment and protests that he is amazed to find anything. The Master urges him to learn from the experience, gives the explanation of the Chisel and Mallet and closes the ceremony with the Charge as we know it today. In closing the Lodge he uses Ezekiel chapter 4, verses 1, 2, 3 and 5 which have not hitherto appeared.

From the 1830s another working of the Mark degree in which the *Overseers were in charge* was being practised in the Isle of Wight. As we learn elsewhere (see p. 198f) the Albany Lodge was formed by contact with the Minden military Lodge (IC) and the original MS of the ritual is certainly such as to suggest, by its spelling and style of presentation, a much earlier provenance than its date of 1848. In view of its link with Minden this practice may also show us what the Mark degree was like in Ireland in the early 19th century.

The opening ceremony is like the oldest forms in that it is carried out by the three principal officers but there are three features that distinguish it. The first is that it is only after the Tyler has been invited into the Lodge to explain his duties that the M.Ov. in the Chair instructs the brethren 'to be clothed'. We have certainly not encountered this practice before in the Mark but we know that it was a common usage in Antients' Chapters and where, also, the clothing was worn under the jacket in operative fashion. What this particular rubric emphasises is that there was *an apron to be worn* in a Mark Lodge and we certainly know that Albany had aprons because there are some extant in their premises at Newport to this day. (See p. 290) We shall look at clothing and jewels later in this book but it is of real interest to note that from this point onwards the clothing of Mark Masons began to assume a more definite style.

The second feature is that *the Deacons* go round the Lodge to collect the Word of the degree from the members and while they do so the Secretary calls the roll of the officers. This certainly suggests the military character of the working.

The third feature is that the Overseers then answer for their duties and then the Senior and Junior 'receive signs from the SE and NE respectively' after which the M.Ov. makes the following observation:

"Whilst it is considered in many circumstances by some brethren that the Mark Degree is *appended to or intimately concerned with* that of ye FC, it is as regards its peculiar secrets and ceremonies *entirely distinct and separate* from it." Those were highly important words in connection with the whole future of the Mark degree in England and we shall have to weigh them carefully as part of the story that follows in the next two chapters but what matters here is that we see them as reflecting two ancient strands in the development we have been trying to trace. The first is that the Operative practice definitely separated the Fellow of the Craft degree from the Erectors and Builders and thus the general drift of the M.Ov's remarks was correct. On the other hand the ritual material that was shaped into what became a Mark ceremony seems to have been very much part of some Speculative Fellowcraft working. It is this mixed source of origin that also gave rise to the idea referred to first by the M.Ov. of the Mark as an 'appendage' of the FC. What he was really trying to say was that when you see what is to follow you cannot any longer pretend that this is the 'rump' of a past degree. It is a degree recognisable in its own right and with its own distinctive character and contribution. That was a measure of the growth that we have seen taking place and which was to be fiercely defended by those of the Ashton Travelling Mark Lodge whose working we shall shortly examine.

Meanwhile there are two other distinctive aspects of the Albany ritual that deserve our attention.

(a) At first sight the entry of the Candidate would appear to be as today with two other persons in attendance. Here there is a Conductor of Work who leads and carries a stone for inspection, though the SD who accompanies the Mark applicant does not. Once the Conductor has submitted his stone to the J.Ov. and it has been *passed* by him (literally) to the M.Ov. the Candidate and SD go on without him.

(b) The Conductor re-joins the Candidate when the Brethren march two by two to receive their wages. The Candidate is branded an imposter and his plea that he was never instructed in this process is dismissed and he is *banished to the Quarries*. The instructions that are now given are both tantalising and intriguing, and written in shorthand:

"Off(icer)s y(e) w(ill) now inv(es)t ye culp(rit) w(ith) ye PR (does this mean Proper Rope, or Pectoral Rope, or Pectoral Restraint, bearing in mind how earlier we have seen candidates with ropes four or three times round the body?) and low(e)r h(im) thro(ugh) ye Secr(et) P(assage)s (or is it P(art)s?) to ye inner reces(e)s of ye Q(uarries) ther(e) to await (p(ro)p(erly) guard(e)d) until such time as ye MO sh(all) send his mess(e)ng(e)r to recall h(im).

Conductor of Works: Let the guards prepare. IG draws sword.
Senior Deacon. Away with him."

This form of sending the Candidate 'back to the Quarries' is, so far as we know, unique and certainly has the hallmark of military retribution. One cannot avoid the echo of Royal Arch practice, and together with the now familiar 'application for assistance' scene, following the return of the Candidate and his obligation, it does seem as if the military lodge that passed on this working was revealing American influences. This idea is confirmed when we learn that the word of the degree is given as S I R O C. This was a term used in an American High Priestly Order and probably composed of initials that spell out **S**olomon of **I**srael **R**uler **O**f the **C**raftsmen. It is found in one other American 'Mark' ritual but nowhere else in English Freemasonry. This ceremony ends with another long lecture which seems like the original 1° one adapted for the Mark.

By the same period, but in the area of North-east Cheshire, there was a Mark working that was to persist into the last quarter of the 19th century. We have two almost identical copies of it preserved by Bros. Noar and Fitton, the latter being the Secretary of the Lodge that practised this working when it at last joined the Grand Mark Lodge. In addition we have a version called the 'Roe of Dukinfield' manuscript from which some interesting variations will be taken as well as a minute of 1864 which confirms that what follows was the same ritual at that time. For the purposes of identification this is known as the Travelling Mark Lodge ritual (TM).

Since the Travelling Lodge always met under the banner of another Craft Lodge this was opened in the three degrees. A 'Mark Master' now assumed the Chair and opened a Lodge of Mark Master Masons. The JW was asked by what he would be proved and this was his answer:

"By the knowledge of that stone hewn by no mortal hands which was rejected by the builders, but afterwards became the headstone of the corner." It can once more be seen how closely we are approaching the present day wording and even the proving of the brethren is done in a thoroughly modern fashion. The only other difference is that the WM, in declaring the Lodge open includes the passage met already, "I charge you to *lay aside all malice, guile, envy, hypocrisy and all evil speaking*." We should note, however, that he ends by using the name of the G. Overseer.

Since this was a central and occasional working it is no surprise to find the wording: "... at the door of the Lodge are *several Brethren* ... who have made such progress in the *workmanship* of craft masonry as they hope will entitle them to be admitted to the *high degree* of a MMM." The latter term is underlined when they are presented to the SW for this 'high and honourable degree....'

Continuity with what has gone before is shown by the Candidates having the password and pass grip already, bringing an Ashlar (as Mark Men) and knowing the 'trial of strength' by roughening the thumb and forefinger for holding. This still *persistent link with the operative* past is reflected in the WM's words when they have advanced with all the signs. "... it is necessary for you to prove if you are able and expert *bearers of burthens* as well as *hewers of stone*".

To show how ancient this 'trial of strength' was G.W.E.Bridge once revealed that in a book on American Indian Rites there is a stone-lifting contest at Potlatch festivals. A stone weighing some 300 lbs, rounded and greased, was not able to be lifted until a young man advanced who put his hands in his pockets "in which were *some pitch and dry sand*, rubbed his hands together, and *lifted the stone knee-height*. The host (of the potlatch) complimented him thus – 'I admire your strength and the wisdom with which you put pitch and sand on your hands before attempting to raise the stone' and awarded him a prize of (metal) dollars. Here you have the same principle and Bridge comments, "I have not seen this elsewhere." The fact that this was a North American practice makes one wonder whether this custom was known by military lodges in their sojourn there and used in the degree because it *confirmed older operative practices here*. This is perhaps yet another matter for research.

Following the obligation the Master addressed the candidates and some of his remarks are both distinctive and informative:

"Brethren, this degree in Masonry was no less useful in its original intentions, nor were its effects less beneficial to mankind than the former degrees. ... By the aid of these marks the Overseers were enabled without difficulty to ascertain who was the faculty workman so that all deficiencies might be remedied without injuring the credit or diminishing the reward of the industrious and faithful of the Craft." The candidates then chose their marks and the Master began to instruct them carefully in the use of the cypher alphabet "which enables us to correspond with a Bro. MMM in characters unknown to all save those on whom this degree has been conferred." This instruction was perhaps the fullest that had yet been provided in any ritual and its description will be looked at more fully in the chapter on cyphers. It was also *by way of being a peak in the use of such an alphabet* for after the demise of this lodge as a separate unit this aspect of Mark Masonry began to decline and is, today, just a subject for occasional attention and lecture instruction.

The WM had already referred to the Overseers from the 12 Tribes and the marks they used for directing the work at a distance and now the Candidates are shown *the 13 letters* – H K T S T S K I H A T W S – that 'belong to a MM's summons'. Speaking of a summons leads on to the explanation of the 'Paper Missive' which also reaches its culmination in this working (see p. 189). Though this method of communicating is unknown today it is still remarkable to realise that for over 150 years it was part of masonic practice and underlined the point that items neglected in the Craft degrees would emerge alive and well elsewhere.

The practice first noticed in the ceremony at Bath of placing a paper with one's mark on it between hands that join to make the Grip is here repeated and extended to the manner of requesting wages. As we have a practice here that is no longer used it is worth recording it for posterity. The new MMM comes with his 'paper mark' in his hand:

"The SGW immediately cast his eye on a book where all the corresponding M(ark)s were kept, and seeing how much was due to that particular Mark *placed it on the two forefingers* of the Craftsman's right hand, (at which) he puts his thumb down, turned his hand round, and drew it out in the same manner". In the verses that were recited, but *not chanted* at this stage, there was a change of wording. Instead of the present form the lines read – 'But if imposters *be* mixed with the *working* there Caution them to *be aware* of their right hand.'

The Degree now ended with an explanation of the Working Tools and a Charge. The former began with words used today but then passed over into words noted earlier (p. 140) and which were printed in Robert Macoy's 'Masonic Manual' of 1852. It is the form still used by the Ashton District TI Lodge and it closes with an extremely moving extract from Alexander Pope's 'Essay on Man': "Which nothing earthly gives, or can destroy,
The soul's calm sunshine, and the heartfelt joy."

The Charge was one that was also printed in Robert Macoy's Manual and whilst it has many phrases familiar to present MM Masons there are some very pleasant variations. This might be expected to lead to the Closing but this Travelling Lodge prided itself on working the Link and Ark degrees as well. We now have a form of ceremony for them both and whilst we shall look more closely at these forms later there are some things which we should note here.

One is that it is in the Link ceremony of Ashton that we encounter that 'second' stone used in earlier ceremonies which was not carved by the Candidate but was brought up to the builders for their approval. In heaving over this stone we are introduced to a word used in the Jamaican ceremony and shortly to be encountered in that of Bolton. The word is K.B.L.T. and in one American manual it is 'Giblet'. The meaning is given as 'to heave over'. It is a word that merits more thinking about and we shall consider it in connection with the Bolton working. In this ceremony we also have the mention of how this stone was 'put in *the vacant spot which it fitted most exactly*'. The 'Arch' section was thus being reduced to more like what it is today.

We also learn here – not, we notice, in the Mark ceremony proper – that the coin paid for wages was inscribed on one side with S(hekel) of J(erusalem) and a Pot of Manna whilst on the other it had J(erusalem) the H(oly) and Aaron's Rod with its buds. The sign included reference to the penalty and the *Lighthouse of Lebanon* whilst the word 'Omnipotent' was part of the Ineffable Name that was displayed in the centre of Solomon's Audience Chamber. Mention of this name, the audience chamber and the cooperation of the three Grand Masters again suggest RA links. Of the Ark ceremony we shall speak in the Royal Ark Mariner section of this book.

The Closing is almost exactly as at the present day but it has three peculiarities. The first is when the WM asks the JW what he has learned by MM Masonry. He answers: "I have learned three things: my duty towards God, my neighbour and myself" and then proceeds to follow exactly a form of words that we know as part of the first degree Charge. Why we should get this duplication is far from clear and is a matter that might profit from further enquiry. Bridge suggests that this might be a case of the chicken-and-the-egg but since this is not used earlier or elsewhere it is not likely to have originated in the Mark tradition. Since it is alive and well in Craft practice its use here is puzzling.

The Master also uses a form of invocation rather than prayer and since this is also unique it merits repetition here.

"Brethren, As every degree has a tendency to inculcate the principles of pure morality it is invariably a duty incumbent upon us to countenance and encourage it to the utmost of our power, and while we continue faithfully to discharge the duties of that important trust may the favour of Heaven rest upon us, and all regular Masons, to unite and cement us together in the bonds of friendship and brotherly love." The Lodge is then closed to meet next time at *another rendezvous*.

It only remains to examine one more ritual in this Section. In the working of the Minerva Lodge we have something which reveals long-standing traditional ways and yet a Lodge that is still recognisably the same as the one that was founded in 1782. The fact is that here we have the oldest form of working still extant in a regular Mark Lodge whilst it has also made adjustments to suit the Regulations of the new Grand Mark Lodge. It is thus a perfect example of the eventual transition from pre-to post-1856.

What strikes the visitor to this Lodge immediately is the position of the Overseers. They sit with their *backs to the Wardens' pedestals* though with a slight passage behind them. Since the Master has an altar in front of his pedestal the M.Ov. sits as close to the side of it as possible. This arrangement may be usefully compared with that in Bolton in pre-Grand Mark Lodge days (see p. 176) and some American workings. The Overseers also have only a square on their pedestals.

Since this Mark Lodge took its rise in the Minerva Craft Lodge it retains a similar Craft-style opening in which *every* officer is asked his place and duty. It ends with an unusual prayer in that two sections of what follow are said by the Wardens *after the Chaplain's introduction*:

"O Bountiful Creator we acknowledge Thee to be our God, we bow before Thee as our King, we invoke and call upon Thee to be our helper in all trials and difficulties – To Thee we owe whatsoever of good we possess, to Thee we look for every good to come, to Thee we direct our petitions – humbly beseeching Thee to protect our King (or Queen), our Country and our Craft, that so in conformity with the teachings of our Order we may continually confess Thy faith, be strengthened in hope and established in charity."

As the Lodge is declared open the Brethren, all of whom *wear gloves*, discharge the whole penal sign with the right hand flung over the left shoulder. The Bible on the Master's pedestal is left closed but the other Bible on the pedestal of obligation is opened.

The candidate is prepared in a loose fitting 'pyjama-style' suit and wearing a MM's apron. The JD brings a password for him which means 'by the pressure of the mallet' and in the older working still the chisel was actually *applied to his forehead*. Today the candidate enters and gives an old MM sign, a clenched fist with thumb erect and *then applied to the forehead*. He perambulates three times giving proofs of the three degrees to both Overseers *and* Wardens neither of whom give any knocks. *Without receiving a Mark* he is then presented by the SW and is told to take 4 sliding steps towards the altar where another Bible is now opened with *square and compasses* on it. He kneels in a 'meek and humble position'. The obligation is sealed twice, once on the open and once on the closed book.

The candidate withdraws to the Quarries of Tyre and returns with only one companion, the SD and neither of them wear a long apron. They both give a semblance of staggering under the weight of the stones they carry, and they approach the Overseers from the rear as if coming to a gate. (It is worth remarking here that 'gates' are regularly formed in North and East Yorkshire for all ballotting and are therefore a normal feature of Freemasonry.) The SD presents a cube stone.

The response of the Overseers when testing the Keystone is different: "Placed in whatever position I may it does not fit my Square." Yet it is only the J. and S.Ovs. who inspect the stone and when they report their difficulty with it to the M.Ov. he orders the Candidate to retire and the SD to place the offending stone in the centre of the lodgeroom. It is round it that the 3 Overseers now confer and after the usual discussion agree to throw the stone amongst the rubbish, distracting the Candidate's attention so that he does not see where it lands.

The JW then announces that the Brethren are needing their wages and a procession is formed of the two Deacons, the candidate and other Brethren in that order. They circle the lodge three times singing the usual hymn but what follows is distinctive. The *Inner Guard* wields the axe, there is *no wicket*, there is *no receipt* of wages, & no sign manual. The SW discerns the Candidate as not yet entitled to a MMM's wages and thus denounces him as an Impostor. The SD quietly takes him to face the WM who duly reprimands him in different terms to those normally used and even dismisses the Candidate's plea that he was not taught how to claim wages with the words, "A poor excuse". However, as the poor craftsman is dismissed for judgment to be decided, the JW recalls having seen a keystone presented for inspection, but rejected. A search is called for.

The Candidate's bare legs are now covered to protect him from the 'rubble' and in a serpentine fashion he and the SD wander about the lodge to find the stone. It is usually found in the North-east behind the SD's chair and, again 'staggering' under the weight, the Candidate offers it for the WM's inspection and approval.

The password now given is that used earlier but the grip is that which goes with the password used elsewhere today. All that is said of it, however, is that 'this was of help in climbing up a steep bank'. Another distinctive sign is with two fingers across the right wrist in the form of a 'V' whilst the HO sign with two hands joined on the right knee suggests another form used earlier (see p. 183). The *only mode* of receiving wages is that used by MMMs today.

The word 'Mark Well' was now given but accompanied by a form of 'lines parallel' by opening the left palm with the fingers extended and crossing them with three extended fingers of the right which thus make 'M' and 'W'. Another step towards our own demonstration sign is thus taken and the Grand Word which is now given in two forms '*Socoroth*' or '*Kibroth*' raises a fresh interpretation of which I suggested a hint earlier. The former word comes from the Hebrew 'Sok' meaning 'a hidden or covert place or den' and thus has suggestions of both the stone that was hidden and the place that was hidden where the stone belonged. The usual meaning of 'Kibroth' is well known but correspondence with competent Hebrew users convinces me that another viable meaning is 'those who are buried or hidden'. If this is so then the two words have a very similar meaning and properly connect the M Mason and the RA parts of Freemasonry. In the light of what comes shortly in the Minerva ritual this seems to be even more likely the case.

As the WM invests the new MMM with a jewel he explains the letters as meaning 'Hiram The Widow's *Son Sought This Key Stone*' which is clearly not common usage elsewhere. We are with this form still in the era when no fixed form of words was yet agreed. The SW also clothes the Candidate with his MMM apron *on top of* his MM apron and as he does so he says:

"The degree of a MM Mason is superior to that of a MM and it is my duty to inform you that even upon the attainment of this *ancient* degree there is *more to be obtained* if you will *seek* it." Here, as in the Bath workings, we have the explicit connection of the Mark with the Holy Royal Arch and this is further emphasised by placing the Candidate at this point on the very spot where the re-discovered keystone was placed. (It is worth remarking here that in Northumberland to this day the solitary Keystone in the middle of the chamber is still a principal feature of the Royal Arch ceremony. The link is obvious, and yet one wonders why, in Minerva or Northumberland, there is still no form of 'arch' as Bath suggested and most Chapters now have.)

The traditional lecture as now authorised is here given but as an essential part of the ceremony and *not* as an optional extra. The M.Ov. points out that the *candidate is meant to represent* the 'rejected keystone' and is to act as the successor of him *who was such a cornerstone*.

The Candidate is now taken to the Secretary's table where the working tools are explained but with meanings that distinguish them from the Craft usage. He then returns to the centre of the room where a P.Master delivers the present Charge though with some interesting variations. The Lodge is then closed in the more or less normal fashion.

What is fascinating and encouraging as we thus come to the end of this First Section of ritual development is that there are still so many strands from the earliest roots of our ritual still in place in our authorised forms. The fact that there are other Mark Lodges where, as in Minerva, only two Brethren present their stones for proving shows that tradition is alive and well and yet the differences existing between the past of Minerva and our more normal procedure suggest that there were other traditions existing. It is to the next family of those that we must now turn.

SECTION TWO

The next family of Mark rituals is much more compact and distinctive but was also much shorter-lived. Where such a form came from, what was its purpose and why it failed to survive are questions of substance for any serious survey of this degree and it has to be said that only in Springett's book is there any attempt to grapple with these issues, and then somewhat briefly. We are again on new ground and it is hoped that this Section will add materially to our sum of Mark knowledge. Tribute of course has to be paid to G.W.E.Bridge who first gathered together the relevant rituals.

Our story again begins in the North-east with a practice called 'Crossing the Bridge' based on teaching in the Harodim lecture series. Whilst it is not possible or desirable to argue the whole case for this development in this book there are three facts that we have to acknowledge and bear in mind as we look at what follows. The first is that in connection with the Harodim lectures on the Fellowcraft degree there was amplification of the story of the crossing of the Jordan by the stories both of the Jews of the Exodus and of the Ephraimites who were defeated by Jephtha. The passage of the River, or as it increasingly became known, 'Passing the Bridge', was a ritual memory that did not fade. One story there given was that 12 stones were taken out of the foundation of the Bridge at Gilgal in Jephtha's time and used for the creation of a pillar by a flow of water and another in a field of corn. This story is recorded in Irish documents in Crossle's 'Caementaria Hibernica'. It can thus be seen to have been a 'living tradition'.

The second fact is that on the old Swalwell tracing boards *and* on an old board recently restored in Derbyshire we have a clear portrayal of just such a bridge and it also has the arches that so clearly appear on Irish certificates referring to degrees that included this event. We again have a living tradition that persists into the 19th century.

Thirdly, we have in the Royal Order ritual that originated in the first half of the 18th century just such a similar tradition. What is more this was quite a widespread idea because William Waples was given a booklet dated somewhere between 1780 and 1810 which was written by someone in the Sheffield area (it came from a workman's family there) in which the transition 'by the bridge' to the Tower of Refreshment was not only known but was ritually performed in terms that were very similar to those used then in the South and still known today.

A Newcastle Mason of the late 19th century who was immensely knowledgeable about such matters wrote as follows: "This pass was called 'The Passage of the Bridge'. It is entirely immaterial whether or not the bridge in question be from shore to the ship's deck, or from one side of a river to another. (The modern Passage of the Bridge is in Nehemiah's Zerubabbel time.) It was a bridge and it was necessary to cross it, if they wished to proceed on their homeward journey. (Some suppose it a ford of leaping stones like Sh. . .th.)"[2]

There is one other factor mentioned in the last chapter that has also to be taken into account. It was the warranting in Sunderland of an Encampment of the Irish EGE family through an intermediate body in Edinburgh. The date of this was 1807 and part of the package of rites that came with that warrant were the Babylonian Pass (or Red Cross of Daniel), the Jordan Pass and the Royal Order or Prussian (Persian?) Blue. On the whole subject of this 'Cross' series (and here let me emphasise that we are *not talking* about the Red Cross of Constantine or Sepulchre) some words of Crossle are very pertinent:

"The Cross, from which the Red Cross Masons derived their name, is depicted by the annexed woodcuts of old Irish seals. We often find the word '**Veritas**' and sometimes the word '**Libertas**', engraved above or below the cross (of four equilateral triangles). From the more frequent occurrence of the former word one ventures to describe it as a *cross of truth*, symbolical of the truth of the prophecy "to proclaim *liberty to the captives* (Isaiah 61, v.1; 44, vv. 26–28), which was fulfilled through the influence of *Daniel and Zerubbabel* with Cyrus. (Daniel 9, v. 2; 10, v. 13)

With such a background it should hardly be surprising to find that there is a manuscript ritual of circa 1800 and belonging to Sunderland which shows the influence of these several factors. One letter of 1889 says: "This ritual has been used for 55 years by 2 Masons still living, both well known to me, and was in vogue long prior to that. . . ."

The ritual is entitled 'Mark Mason' and has no opening or closing ceremony. The scene is the private chamber of an Eastern monarch and a *Sojourner* stands knocking at the door, The Inner Guard responds and reports to the King. On being admitted the Sojourner reports that he has been in fruitless search of someone amongst the 'Magicians, Astrologers and soothsayers' to interpret the dream which the King has had. He is despatched to search again.

A further report leads the I.G. to say that a 'Captive of the Tribe of Judah' is without who *can interpret* the dream. His name is given as GIBLUM. The King makes an offer;

"The Man who can tell me my dream and give me the interpretation thereof shall be clothed in purple and scarlet, be set upon my own horse and proclaimed before me the third person in my kingdom." This will, for ease of future reference, be called simply 'The Promise'.

The Sojourner and captive are admitted and after greeting the King the Sojourner obviously speaks for his companion. He points out that '*the dream* is not from me but from Him that sent me' when clearly he means the '*interpretation*' of it. He proceeds to describe 'a great Lion standing at thy bedside ready to devour thee and thy household'. The King rises from a couch and admits that this was the dream. He asks for its meaning. The Sojourner tells him that it was 'The Lion of the Tribe of Judah' that will devour him unless he allows 'the children of Israel to go down to Jerusalem to receive *the promise of a Mark Mason*'. The King at once renews 'The Promise' but the Sojourner says that that is not what he asks. Then what is it, asks the King. "Soj. That Thou wouldest pass this man down to Tatnai, Governor on this side of the River, and that Tatnai the Governor *pass him over* to Shethar Boznai and his companions on the other side of the River, and Shethar Boznai pass him down to Jerusalem there to receive the promise of a Mark Mason." This will from now on be called 'The Request'. The King grants the Request adding that he shall have 'Corn, Wine, Oil and Salt for his subsistence while he assists *in re-building the Temple and Holy City* which now lies in ruins, and do as his forefathers have done before him'. It will be noted that all this action is happening at the time after the Exile and in preparation for the Second Temple, thus linking it with the eventual Royal Arch Chapter legend. The time of the events is emphasised by the punishment for disobedience which the King now utters for it comes from the Book of Esther in Persian times. "And whosoever shall alter this my Decree shall have the timber pulled from off his house, it set up, himself hanged thereon, and his house made a dunghill for ever." We shall speak of this as 'The Penalty'.

The scene changes to the riverside and the Sojourner takes the Captive to 'Tatnai, Governor' (TG) and tells him to pass this man over to Shethar Boznai (SB). TG does so and Soj. and Candidate pass over the Bridge. (This was either a ladder or small raised wooden platform laid flat in some Western part of the Lodge.) The Soj. now tells SB that he is to pass 'this man' down to

Jerusalem and SB repeats the terms of the Request and the Penalty.

The Candidate now chooses *a Mark, places it on the Bible* and covers it with his hands as he repeats his obligation. This is in the name of the 'Grand Overseer of the Square' and it is not to be taken *unless* '3, 5, 7, 9, or 11 brother Mark Masons are present' or the Candidate pays thirteen pence halfpenny for his mark. (It was because of this clause that in the North the Mark became known as the '13 pence ha'pny' degree. Those who have followed Section One will understand why that sum was chosen.) The penalty was severing the right hand and slinging it over the left shoulder there to wither and decay. We now begin to see where this sign in Freemasonry came from. The obligation is sealed only twice.

The King now raised the Candidate and explained his Mark in his own words explaining the 'relief' aspect of the Mark whereby another may send his mark and expect a 'half-shekel' (13½d) in return. He now continued with an Historical Lecture.

It is in this Lecture, rather than in any 'drama', that the background to the idea of wages for the various classes of workmen is explained and also the setting up by HAB of 'a place' where hands were submitted to show who should receive what. The Entered Apprentices had no mark and so were soon detected and there was 'a man stationed behind the door with a drawn sword ready to cut off the hands of those in which there were no marks. Those who escaped went away ashamed, rubbing their heads in this Manner (does it) which has since been used as the sign of a Mark Mason'. The sign is not explained but was the precursor to that now regarded as the first part of the penal sign.

The final paragraph of the Lecture is also worth quoting as it illustrates the practices continued in this family of Mark rituals:

"When the stones were brought down to the Temple on which were fictitious marks, consequently not fitting the work, there were men stationed *at the top* of the building, with their hands in this form (right hand over left wrist) and two in this position (constituting the HO sign). These men were also in possession of a word, namely, 'Ekbetain' which was said to mean 'to h.o.' (but see p. 158). They heaved them over and from *the immense height* they had to fall they became rubbish to the Temple in which our Grand Master Hiram was first interred."

We see here the old practice of explaining a degree by lecture rather than by actual performance and some of the signs are still uncertain.

This Sunderland Ms. ritual ends with a series of Questions and Answers which largely rehearse the events of the degree thus far. The secrets not so far rehearsed are important from a survey point of view and are as follows:

Q. Advance to me as a Mark Mason and give me the Secrets.

A. *Sign*: Take one regular step, right hand *as if drawing a sword from its sheath.* Then two fingers behind the ear.

Grip: (is the same as at present given).
Word: Ekbetain.

Q. What further privileges have you as a Mark Mason?
A. That all Mark Masons should wear in the *fifth button-hole* on that part of the garment called a vest or waistcoat, a white ribbon with a pendant or medal hanging thereto.
Q. Why in the fifth button-hole?
A. Because there are *five senses* in Man.
Q. Name them.
A. Hearing, Seeing, Smelling, Tasting and Feeling. (The Penalty is now rehearsed)
Q. Who sought to alter a King's Decree?
A. Haaman, the Jews' enemy.
Q. What became of Haaman? (The Penalty). This ends the manuscript.

We are fortunate also in having various copies of what were called the Old York working that was actively performed in Bradford until the Mark Lodge there joined the Grand Mark Lodge; and in addition we have recently unearthed the version used in Newcastle by the members there. In comparing the few but interesting variations and explanations that these documents give us we shall call them OY and NC.

The OY ritual was almost certainly in existence by the beginning of the 19th century and the NC copy is in the handwriting of a brother living between 1812 and 1830. What we learn from these copies is that the Mark Degree was seen as *belonging between the 2nd and 3rd* degrees of the Craft. One Minute that we have states clearly that after opening in the Fellowcraft degree "the Lodge was *proclaimed open* in the Mark Degree and the *Mark Officers took their respective stations*". This would appear to explain why most copies of this degree show no opening ceremony. There simply was no need. What we do know is that in OY the WM became the King in the East, the JW became TG in the South and SW was SB in the West with 'a bridge between chairs in the South and West'. The Tyler was known as the Outer Guard and the Secretary as Scribe. Every Past Master who was a member of the Mark was also considered a Past Master in this degree and was eligible to be elected as King or to the offices of TG and SB.

Whilst the King and his Governors conducted the first part of the ceremony the latter parts were usually done by a Past Master. The Brethren wore ordinary Craft clothing but had the Jewel representing an old half-shekel on a white ribbon hanging from their 5th button-hole. After the Mark business was concluded the Mark lodge was declared closed and the Craft officers resumed their places to close the lodge in the second and first degrees.

It is salutary to remind ourselves that English Masons have always found the correct retention of Hebrew or other foreign names and terms difficult and this form of the Mark was no exception. One version has Tat*m*ai or Tat*ni* and Sheth*am* Bo*r*nai or Bo*sni* whilst another has *Sether* or Sh*ehar* (NC) and even Shelter Bo*s*nai. One has 'Giblim (alias Daniel)' and another

(OY) 'Gobraim'. Nebuchadnezzar in an OY version is 'Nebucaanezziah'.
Other interesting items that we meet are:

a) In NC the candidate comes *bound head and foot* as a true 'captive'.
b) The Candidate *and* Sojourner pass over bridge NC.
c) In taking the obligation most say 'Great Ov.' but NC has 'Grand Ov.'
d) The penalty in one OY version has 'over my left Breast' rather than 'over my left Shoulder', and another OY has 'wither IN decay'. The sealing 'on the Holy Word' is done twice NC but once OY.
e) One OY version mentions 'aperture' rather than 'hole in the door'.
f) In the Charge the OY versions refer to the scrutiny 'of your Brethren on whom this degree *has not* been conferred' but the NC one speaks of those Brethren 'on whom the degree *has been* conferred'. Watching by each for any example does not seem out of place.
g) In NC they required the TG to be a present or past JW in the Craft, and SB to be a present or past SW.

In some notes on the above forms of this degree G.W.E.Bridge makes the comment that the 'Bridge' ceremony was 'irrelevant to the Mark and not an attractive addition. It seems superfluous that such a long dissertation should be thought a useful way of putting a candidate on the way to Jerusalem where the relevant part of the Mark ritual takes place'. There is justification for these views if you compare what we have now with what was available to those Northern brethren then. Yet I wonder if that is not a wrong way of looking at the matter. Whilst we may now be aware that other methods of practising the Mark were being developed in the country it is not at all sure that those other ways were either known to, or appreciated by, the 'Old Mark' Masons. Above all we have to remember that Irish influence through trade and tradition, not least the 'Red Cross' link with the Royal Arch and the developing Encampments in Scarborough and Newcastle, would tend to dissuade any suggestion that a post-exilic setting for the Mark was either unnecessary or odd. We have seen that even in the first family of Mark rituals there was a persistent strand of 2nd Temple background for this degree and we should therefore be less critical of what may at first seem like an anomaly. What is interesting is that in the 'dream' sequence and the despatch of a Jewish person or group back to Jerusalem by an Eastern monarch we have a masonic feature that, when it was dispensed with as a Mark component, became part of Freemasonry in other places. The principle of 'economy' that we met early on in this book once more came into operation.

Although it has been firmly pointed out that this actual 'scene' in the chamber of Nebuchadnezzar is found only in the Latin Vulgate or Douai version of the Bible used by Irish Catholics, yet individual elements are traceable in the Authorised Version – a king dreams, a Jewish seer interprets, the king releases the Jewish exiles, the Temple has to be re-built with the walls of Jerusalem, there were people called Tatnai and Shethar Boznai and there were classes of builders who used marks. These, as the Book of Ezra in particular demonstrates, show that those who formed the 'Old Mark' ritual were selective. Someone adding notes on the NC version remarks that Susa and *Ecbatana* were ancient Royal palaces and wonders if the latter name was really the origin of an otherwise *strange use of Greek* especially with a word that should have been 'ek*ballein*' meaning 'eject, throw away'. It has also to be remembered that Ecbatana was where Cyrus's decree '*sending forth*' the Jews was found and there may have been other traditions of 'Irish' Masons which the note-maker here was reflecting. Let us hear Crossle once more: "It was largely due to the energy of Irish Masons, and of the EGE at Dublin that these (Red Cross) degrees attained much popularity" and they must have acquired the title 'Red Cross of Daniel' from the tradition such as is recorded in Millikin's Historico-Masonic Tracts, 1848. In this publication we read "that Daniel was an instrument in God's hand, by which Cyrus was urged to the restoration of the Jews and rebuilding of the Temple at Jerusalem. That Daniel was a speculative Mason we can have no doubt, the whole tenor of his long life proves it; he was also an accomplished architect, as we find in Josephus, who speaks of *a famous edifice built by him in Echbatana* in the manner of a castle..."

Millikin goes on to mention the usual RA legend about Zerubbabel but this is the only traditional history of Masonry in which equal prominence is given to *both* Jewish figures.

Further evidence that the memory of Daniel was honoured by the Irish Craft of old is shown by an 1819 certificate from Dundalk which reads:

"O King Darius live for ever (See Daniel 6, v. 21, 28)

Lodge No. 384 on the Grand Registry of Ireland.

We the King and Captain General of the General and Royal Assembly of Knights of the Red Cross having met and assembled ... under the sanction of Lodge 384 ... Certify that Sir Samuel Johnson was initiated into those Magnanimous and Glorious orders of Knights of Patmos, Knights of Jerusalem, Ark & Mark Mason, Link and Chain, Jacob's Wrestle & Mother Word...." We shall need to keep this sort of information in mind as we come to the next stage of this Section.

Reverting to Newcastle the same commentator on their ritual also remarks that whilst HTWSSTKS was explained to the Candidate by the King it had at least *three or even five different* explanations and there were sometimes 8 letters – **M**(ay) **J**(ehovah) **F**(inish) **T**(his) **B**(uilding) **W**(ith) **G**(reat) **J**(oy). When so used this was the inscription on one side of the stone and on the other was the 47th proposition by Euclid together with seven 'eyes'. We meet this latter feature again in Section Three.

It is time, however, to move on to other branches of this 'family' and in this stage of our study we look at the Clough or Perseverance Lodge practice (CP), the Blackburn working (BL) and a close partner of the latter called the Dawson Ritual (DR). There are different opinions as to the dates of these variations but I share Bridge's opinion that CP certainly represents an older form which resembles that of the Old York group. The only certainty we have, however, is that all of them were being worked in the years 1850–70 in the East Lancashire area.

The CL version begins with a *group of* Captives securely bound and standing outside a King's chamber. The knocks given are 2 long and 2 short (but nothing in this ms shows at what point this ceremony occurred in the Perseverance Craft Lodge proceedings.) The Tyler reports that these 'captives of the tribe of Judah seek an audience' with King Nebuchadnezzar and on entering they are placed in the East. A *Deacon* gives the former explanation of the search made for an interpreter of the royal dream and says that one of those present can help. His name is 'Gobraim' (and this may explain why a neighbouring lodge picked up this form). The King's 'Promise' has some variations:

"Gobraim, I have dreamed a dream and the thing is quite gone from me. (He who can help) shall be arrayed in purple and scarlet with a golden chain about his neck, and be placed upon the King's own horse, and led through the streets of the city, and proclamation shall be made before him. Thus shall it be done unto the man whom the King delighteth to honour." The dream is the same as before but the purpose is slightly altered – "to return *to their homes*, even to Jerusalem, there to rebuild the Temple *and the holy sepulchres* which now lie in ruins. …" Despite this clear pointer the King repeats the 'Promise' and G. declines it in favour of the 'Request'. This is granted and it is only now as the King outlines the 'Passing the River' that the return 'to receive the promise of a Mark Mason' occurs. The same 'penalty' is stated. The person who is to see all this carried out is not the Deacon but Gobraim.

On arriving at Jerusalem (which is symbolised by standing in the East before the WM) they are told that if each of them retires and produces a specimen of his skill then he (the WM) will assign to each a portion of the work 'and will admit those who are found worthy to the mysteries and privileges of Mark Masonry'. Saluting (as FCs?) they retire.

Each candidate returns and presents *a rough ashlar* which is rejected. He withdraws and brings in a *perfect* ashlar. The Master is told by the Deacon that "some evil disposed person had taken away the real specimen of our Brother's work and had placed the rough ashlar in its stead" but he submits this stone. The King is impressed:

"I thought that there must be some mistake. This is a stone of a true die and square, and will entitle you to receive the promise of a Mark Mason". If there are other candidates they then enter one by one and when all are through the above ceremony the Questions and Answers follow.

The answers start with the claim that ability to explain the King's dream entitled the Candidate to know himself, or be entitled to the degree of, a Mark Mason, and we then have a passage that shows that the person who enlightened the King was *Daniel*:

Q. How could you make known unto the King a dream which had departed from him?

A. I prayed unto the Lord God of Heaven and he revealed the secret unto me in a night vision. … (See Daniel ch. 2 verse 19, and the earlier verses of this chapter will show where the ritual used here and in Old York came from. For the dream in this chapter see what follows in BL). And now, *new*, "What *was* the promise of a Mark Mason?"

A. That I should, on proof of being found worthy, receive the sign, the Grip or Token and the Word of a Mark Mason. (These are all given)

The Word is 'Gobraim' ('Giblum' in one form of Lancashire dialect could conceivably have sounded near enough to be written like this).

Q. What does this word imply?

A. WW or p.m. (Though not explained WW is probably Worthy Workman and p.m. past master.) The 'Buttonhole pendant' distinguishes a Mk. Mason and in explaining the 5 senses we read: 'three of which are of special use to Mk. Ms, namely Seeing, to see the sign, Feeling, to feel the Grip, and Hearing, to hear the Word given by a Mk. Mason'.

Q. What is Mark Masonry?

A. A peculiar degree in Freemasonry having its own special S, G & W. Every Mark Mason also possesses an Alphabet by which he is enabled to correspond with a Brother Mark Mason. …

As there is no Historical Lecture in this form of the degree we are now told in an answer about how the E.As tried to obtain FC wages and HAB 'laid a scheme to detect it'. The scheme was:

"He had previously ordered *the FCs* to place their *several marks* upon the stones which they had wrought *in the mountains*" to fit in place. "Furthermore, in order that each man might be held responsible for his own work, he now ordered that each FC should place his separate mark *under the thumb* of his right hand thus (shown as in Mark *Man* today) so that when he came to the *middle chamber* of KST and thrust his hand through *the hole in the wall* to receive his wages, the principal *Architect*, on lifting the thumb and finding no mark there, *drew his sword* and struck a violent blow to cut off the hand of the defaulters (shown), in this way originating the *casual* sign of a Mk. Mason."

It can be seen from this quotation that we have here an early explanation of the procedure of 'punishing imposters'. We can also see how the early Operative idea was still around that it was when one became a FC that a Mark was given. Note also the rough form of 'wicket' and the reference to 'drawing a sword' which we met in the Albany working and will again encounter at Bolton in Section 3. We have also dropped a 'casual' sign.

This catechism closes with mention of another King besides Nebuchadnezzar who held the Jews captive. This was Ahasuerus and we hear how Mordecai overheard a plot by Bigthan and Teresh, 2 chamberlains, to murder the King and informed Esther his 'cousin' (the VSL says 'his daughter'). Mordecai was given 'the Promise' and Haaman, the Minister, and the chamberlains between them received 'the Penalty'.

It is worth pointing out once more how in this working the mixture of First and Second Temple setting has emerged. In this ritual they mingle more easily than in some others, especially those that now follow, but it is clearly the Irish origin or influence that is the cause for this.

On opening the pages of the BL version and the Dawson Ritual (DR), we immediately notice some differences from what has gone before. These versions have the Craft Lodge opened first in the 3° (BL) whereas in DR the Craft Lodge is opened in the *Past Master degree.* This latter arrangement suggests three important things: that this working was of much older origin than the mid-19th century, since it is still natural to regard the Installation of a WM as a degree; that the Mark was some stage on beyond the Master Mason; and that there was still the sense that it related to the Royal Arch for which being an Installed Master was essential, which again suggests a date of pre-1840 for this ritual in its original form.

A Mark Lodge being declared it is opened with the usual dialogue between Master and Wardens and the SW then circulates to receive the Password silently from each brother, followed by the JW first declaring the Chisel and Mallet as the tools of the degree and asking the Brethren to show the sign. This done the JW says there are three Principal officers and the SW that there are SIX assistant officers, excluding the Tyler, viz. the Deacons, the Overseers and the IG. We then move as at present to the responses of the Overseers and a final prayer where the WM 'supplicates a blessing from the M(ost) H(igh) God'.

The Candidate enters and has the Password given for him, proves himself in the 3 degrees of the Craft, and assents to taking an obligation. There is no mention of a Mark at this stage or of steps towards the pedestal. The obligation is sealed 4 times. The Conductor is asked to prepare the Candidate for the next part of the ceremony.

The Candidate re-enters with a Keystone *hidden under his apron*. He is led by 4 steps to the J.Ov. (or 4 knocks in DR) who examines it and says: "You see that it is not a square stone – square work is such as is wanted for the building and no others have we orders to receive. Besides, it has no known mark of the Craft upon it. Is the work yours?" On being told that it is not the stone is allowed to be passed to the Senior and Master Ovs. for their opinion. It will be noted that *no other stone* is examined in this working. The M.Ov. remonstrates with the 'young Craftsman' and calling the Ovs. to him *asks them* what shall be done. The J.Ov. proposes that they reject it, the S.Ov. seconds the proposition and the M.Ov. agrees. The J. and S.Ovs. H.I.O.

The M.Ov. then directs the Candidate to be furnished with tools in order to "show the Brethren present how he would begin to work upon the rough ashlar to convert it into a true square." It will be recalled that an earlier but less specific practice was seen at p. 123. It is now the 6th hour of the 6th day and time for the wages so the Brethren are formed into a procession of *three by three* who approach the gate of the SW (BL) and JGW (DR) for what is now the usual form. When taken to the WM he is asked if he is a *FC Mason* and the proper proofs are provided, at which the Master reproves such a 'bright looking Craftsman' for his 'imposing on the Craft' but asks if he has been taught how to receive wages. On being assured that he would do better if so taught the Master sends him out to learn and to bring a better stone.

The Candidate is re-introduced with a square stone because, says his Conductor, "in the *hurry of the moment* he *laid down* his own stone which he had wrought and *took up another* which *accidentally lay near* him and presented it at the office of the M.Ov. as his own work..."

His work is this one. As another day for wages has arrived the Candidate joins others in the procession *and then*....

The WM launches into the story of how Nebuchadnezzar had a dream and threatened the wise men of Babylon with death if they could not explain it. The Conductor asks for time to find someone to do so.

The Candidate who went out with him is now 'bound in chains *representing Daniel*' and is brought in as the 'young man of the Tribe of Judah who was carried away captive by Arioch' and his name is given as above. The catechism that follows about him is entirely based on the facts of the Book of Daniel in the Bible. The Conductor finally gives a Password and 'Daniel is presented to the person representing the King'. Some of the ensuing dialogue is worth noting:

"*Conductor.* O King, live for ever. We have searched thy dominions and fearing thou shouldest think us negligent we have searched *thy very prisons* in one of which we found *our lost Brother*...

King. Art thou Daniel whose name is Beltashazar? Canst thou make known to me my dream...?

Daniel saying he can the *King* tells him to proceed. He does so in two long passages that I will summarise thus:

(a) 'A God in Heaven that revealeth mysteries' has shown the future.
(b) The secret is revealed to Daniel so that the King might learn.
(c) The dream was of a *great statue* which was high and terrible. 'The head of it was pure gold, the breast and arms of silver, the belly and thighs of brass, the feet part of iron and part of clay. This thou saw until *a stone was cut out of the mountain without hands* and it struck the statue upon the feet and broke them to pieces.'
(d) The whole statue disintegrated and was blown away as chaff so that there was no place for its parts 'but the stone which brake it became a *great mountain* and filled the whole earth'.
(e) In interpretation the King is the gold head, and successive kingdoms of silver and brass will follow until a kingdom of iron will subdue them all. The iron and clay feet show a kingdom divided.
(f) Before these kingdoms God set up a kingdom that shall never be destroyed and will subdue all and still stand *like the carved stone.*

The King is overwhelmed and makes 'the Promise' except for the previous 'sitting on his own horse'. 'The Request' is made by Daniel save that there is no 'Promise of a Mark Mason'. Arioch is told to provide the sustinence and pass them over the river to Jerusalem. They give the 'true grip and word' and cross the Bridge **and then**. . . .

We are back in the lodge room and the workmen have no keystone for one of the principal arches. Only the M.Ov. explains what happened to the previous Keystone. When it is found (we know not by whom) the W.Master reads from the Acts of the Apostles chap. 4, verses 1 and 2.

The reading of this passage is a very unusual and unique feature of these two workings. It is one of the rare moments when the Mark ritual is linked with a wholly Christian concept, that of Christ's resurrection, as if the finding of this keystone were an allegory of something much more profound. Of course it can be claimed that the constant use of the phrase 'a stone rejected by the builders' could have such a meaning but there are sufficient Old Testament links to make this only a partial interpretation. Here we cannot avoid the plain inference, and that makes these rituals both distinctive and, in this section of them, probably quite old. Nowhere else that I have encountered however is there anything comparable. This too may be a subject needing further research. Other striking differences are that no Mark is chosen and there are seventeen letters on the stone: **S.K.O.I.S.H.A.B.W.S.T.H.K.O.T.F.R.** The cypher alphabet is now fully explained and all the 'words' following are so written. The penalty, manner of receiving wages at a *lattice window*, and working tools have today's explanation but in re-telling the drama the Candidate is described as having '*discovered* in one of the quarries the keystone *wrought by HAB* and *deliberately thrown away* his own work'. Set alongside the previous 'explanation' this must suggest that two traditional stories have in this ritual become mingled. The reader will doubtless be able to recognise similar stories already given.

Nor can we overlook the following words by the WM: "The keystone was found among the rubbish and afterwards *applied to its intended use*. How it was disposed of *we cannot now inform you*. You must *advance further* in Masonry before you can know." All that we have seen of an 'Arch' ceremony in Section One is here veiled from view presumably because that was, by now, part of a superior degree which it would be wrong to intrude upon. In other words, the 'Arch' which was once part of a whole Rite was by now separate and worked elsewhere.

These words of the WM in BL and DR help us, I believe, to unravel the puzzle regarding this form of the Mark degree which certainly intrigued G.W.E.Bridge right up to the end. What seems to have happened is this. In the early years of the 19th century Irish Masons or Military Lodges communicated to Brethren in Lancashire what Crossle has described tentatively as the Third Group of an Irish progression. This Group was dominated by the Red Cross of Daniel theme (or Babylonian Pass). In Crossle's view this included the Ark, Mark Fellow, Mark Master, Link (or Wrestle), the Babylonian and Jordan Pass, and the Royal Order (or Prussian Blue). These were *not 'side degrees' but part and parcel of RA Masonry.* It was thus that they were communicated, either as a whole or in parts. That tradition persisted in some parts of Lancashire and Yorkshire and hence the apparently bizarre connection between the 'Dream' sequence of Babylon (or Persia) and the elements of different Mark ceremonies. Yet as the Irish degrees were re-ordered after 1810 and the effects of ritual change in England after 1820 took hold the old way of linking Mark forms with either the Royal Arch or the Red Cross of Daniel began to change. New and separate degrees were created so that by 1825 the Encampments, with Finch and Carlile, were reporting a separate Mark Man, Mark Master and Red Cross of Babylon. Most of the previously linked components were now dispersed but in Lancashire and Yorkshire, and perhaps part of the North East, the old ways were preserved and the apparently strange combination continued to be performed. Bridge's query about "*why* the 'dream' passage was inserted into what already looks like the form of the present mark?" is surely answered. It had *always been there* in this family of rituals and it had not been 'rejected'. There is one more piece of the evidence which helps to confirm this conclusion and it is to this that we now turn.

As recently as the 1950s Norman Rogers drew attention to a remnant of Old Mark working that was preserved in a Ms. which had been given to him by the Rev. H.I.Robinson of York. The Ms was said to be in the handwriting of the donor's great great grand uncle, David Moncrieff, a Mason who was linked with the now important Graham Manuscript which we have already encountered.

David Moncrieff died at Hawick in 1834 but much of his Freemasonry was practised *in Lancashire.* In his papers were found his Royal Arch certificate dated 1803 and granted by Lodge No. 310 Antients (Blackburn), now Benevolence No. 226 of Littleborough, and the Craft records show that Moncrieff attended there between 1803 and 1806. The Mark degree was worked at Emergency meetings on 9 occasions between 1813 and 1834 while the Lodge was at Blackburn. The presumption made by Rogers was that the Catechism which was here shown was worked at Blackburn as early as 1803 and that it continued to be worked there because it is very similar to the CP version which we examined above. When the Lodge moved to Littleborough in 1845 the Mark would be worked either by the Lodge or by Perseverance Lodge No. 345. The following comments or extracts show that the CP, BL and DR forms we looked at may have been later versions of something that was composed much earlier.

(a) "How was you prepared to be a Mark Mason?
"Being one of the Captives of Judia (sic) bound hand and foot I was sent for before King Nebukadnezar ... (for he had dreamed dr*eams* that departed from him).

(b) "How could you make known to him his dream and the interpretation ...
I prayed to the God of Heaven to reveal the secret unto me which he did in a Night Vision & I made the Matter known to the King for which he loused (sic)

me from my bands and sent me down to Fatna (later Fatma) Governor on this side of the River (and so down to Jerusalem) to receive my promice (sic) of a Mark Mason.
What was your promice
To keep the secrets of the Mark from every one who is not found worthy of it.
(The signs and words now given)

(c) When asked the meaning of a Mark Mason the answer was that in building the Temple the FCs received *One penny per Day*, whereas the EAs. got "Corn, Salt, Oil and Wine for their Subsistance" but as the EAs tried a fraud, 'A Scheme was found out to know them by', but it is not described.
(d) A second meaning has to do with a buttonhole and five senses.
(e) King Ahasuerus is introduced and Mordecai who tells him of 'Two Ruffins' (sic) who plan to lay hands on him. Mordecai is thus honoured with a Mark, which is the earlier 'Promise', and Hamon suffers the Penalty.

We thus see here in a less developed form all the elements of the later workings and can see the common pattern which they shared. That it was a long standing pattern is also emphasised by the fact that a well-known Mason, John Greenwood, who was installed as *First Master* of the Fearnley Mark Lodge in Halifax, resigned the next month because he felt himself unequal, on account of age, to the task of learning a *new working* of Mark Masonry. Grand Lodge's kind offer to *allow him to work the old way for his year* was apparently of no avail. It does suggest that the change was the real problem rather than age and it shows the attachment felt.

As we approach the end of this Section of our story we ought to look at what happened to the Irish ritual when it was shorn of all other attachments to other degrees. Happily we have such a working that comes from about 1850 onwards and this shows us a reformed Irish rite which was more closely approaching the official form used in Scotland and England at that time. I shall merely indicate the obvious differences.

The Opening is after the 3° and in a very similar form to the present English/Scottish one (ES) save that the JD adds the words to his duties "to prepare and introduce Candidates" and the SD "to receive and *conduct Candidates". The Overseers describe their place as 'in front of* the S/W/E Gate' and the SW ends his response with the phrase "and see that *none depart dissatisfied*". Moreover, when the Lodge is declared open the Overseers put on *red collars with a Square attached.* One cannot but remark here that this seems to echo the Antients custom of having red scarves for the officers in a Chapter and indeed the oldest Chapters in Derbyshire and Devonshire still have such scarves for some officers to this day. In Operative terms it indicated that the working now about to take place had some connection with 'Arch' working.

The Candidate is told to take off his jacket, collar and tie, and to roll up his sleeves but he is not clothed with any apron. The JD gives him a keystone to hold whilst he himself takes a *rectangular* stone but the SD who joins them within the door does not have a stone.

That the Overseers sat as in the Minerva working today seems likely since they are tapped on the shoulder from behind. The Overseer says, "Produce your work" and it is given to him as he holds his hands in the HO position, as though this could be the normal outcome. Eventually the JD's work is approved by the M.Ov. and is 'deposited on the J.Ov.'s table'. The M.Ov. is doubtful about the KS and gets the following reply: "SD. It is *not* his work. He *found it* in the quarries and *adopted* it as his own". He calls the Ovs., tells them "You have both done wrong" and asks them "what shall be done with it?" The S. and J.Ovs together say that it must be h.o. and M.Ov. responds with "Let that be done". The rubric follows: (The stone should not be thrown but passed over the right shoulder of the S.Ov. to JD who conceals it.)

The wages incident is the same with the J.W. now as executioner and when the *Very* WM (a sure Irish trait) discovers that no teaching about how to receive wages was given the penalty is remitted. The SW says there is no KS 'for the completing of the principal arch' and as this was undertaken, says the VWM, "*by our G.M.HAB*" the usual enquiry follows. The Craftsman re-presents the stone and a Chaplain now uses the Scriptural verse: 'The stone which the builders refused. . . .' As the VWM now declares that the Candidate shall retire and be admitted for the degree of MMM there is the hint that what preceded this point was a form of Mark Man ceremony. It is a hint that is shortly confirmed.

When the Candidate returns he has a cable tow firmly placed around his body *four times* and is said to have "passed through all the Degrees of *Ancient Craft Masonry* and now *fraternally* seeks to be advanced." The knocks by the chisel on the left breast are *four* in number, and the Chaplain prays to the G.O.O.T.U. to grant "the Mark of Thy Divine Approval and finally be advanced to an honourable place in Thy Eternal Temple". The Candidate proves himself in 3 degrees, and to supply what was *previously customary* for all FCs, is invited to choose a mark made of '3, 5, 7 or any odd number of lines or salient points joined together', and goes to the Registrar's table to do so. Not only do we again see the present ceremony coming into being but we can appreciate how very long standing features were retained and re-presented. This is shown, for example, when having taught the Candidate how to receive a MMM's wages the SD answers the SW's query about whom he presents: "A *trusty mark man* who has worked well and worthily 6 days or less." The earliest notion of a two-part ceremony is still with us and is further confirmed when in giving the Signs later the sign manual of a Mark Man is distinguished from that of a MMM. The Candidate approaches to make his obligation by 2 long and 2 short steps, whilst the condition he is in is recalled by the words, "and by this Obligation become *further bound* to us as we are to one another." In this ceremony the VWM closes this act with the words: "You will kiss the VSL or in any other manner equally binding on your conscience."

The rest of the ceremony is very like the ES of today save that there was no Charge and the Lecture was optional. There is, however, the first full description of the implement called a Lewis (or cramp) and this would appear to be the place to comment on this feature.

The description of it given in this ritual is almost exactly that provided in any major dictionary and the latter will also provide a derived word 'lewisson'. In more than one place it is suggested that as the present form was invented, or modernised, by a Frenchman in the reign of Louis XIV (1643–1715) it was named after him but that is clearly incorrect for the French word for this item is never 'Louis' and 'Lewis' would not be French.

In Masonic tradition the word has a double meaning as shown in the following late 18th century catechism:

> 'Q. What do we call the son of a Freemason?
> A. A Lewis.
> Q. What does that denote?
> A. Strength.
> Q. How is a Lewis depicted in a Mason's Lodge?
> A. As a cramp of metal...'

In connection with Mark Masonry it is the operative working use of the term 'lewis' that deserves our attention. What does the word actually describe, where did it come from and how did it acquire this meaning?

"The precise purpose of the *lewis* is to allow the hoisting chain of the derrick or crane to *raise* the stone and then *lower* it into its exact, final position in the wall, which could not be effected if chains or ropes passed underneath the stone." It was therefore a form of grapnel, composed of several parts, which was embedded in the upper face of the stone that had to be moved. When ready for use it formed a *loop or hook* through which the end of the lifting gear could be passed. It was this gadget that 'lewis' was meant to describe.

We know that in the Middle Ages the English-speaking masons used several words for some such implement – lowys, lowettis, lewiss, lewisson – and it is from these forms that we have to derive its previous history. Wyld in the Universal English Dictionary and the Old English Dictionary both declare the root of these words obscure or unknown. Bearing in mind that more developed building gear does not seem to have become common until about 1100 and that masons were especially guided by an 'architect' class that was derived from, or educated by, monks it is therefore highly likely that this tool would have been given a name that derived from the contemporary form of Latin. What is interesting is that in the French Compagnonnage (a mediaeval trade guild that included masons) the name for this gadget was 'louve' which derived from 'lupa', the female form of 'lupus'. A Latin derivation for a building usage is therefore shown to have happened and there are some previous writers on this topic who have suggested that as there was a definite French influence in major Church building in England the same derivation might well apply here. If 'lupus' meant 'wolf' (and we still have the literary English word 'lupine') and 'lupa' meant 'She-wolf' then the word 'lewis' came from the same root and was so-named because it could be 'likened to the grip of a mother wolf's fangs'. It is an intriguing suggestion and if the earlier forms of 'lowys' or 'lowes' referred to a form of pincers rather than the present inset shackle then the idea is even more likely. Yet for some reason I cannot explain this suggestion has never completely satisfied me and I had to seek some other solution. With due acknowledgement of what Knoop, Jones and Hamer have written I submit that there are other ways of finding a solution.

What I fully accept in the previous explanation is that the Latin words 'lupus, lupa' were the source of 'louve' in French but what has been overlooked by everyone save the three above is that in any reliable Latin dictionary we are told that 'lupus' *also means 'hook'* or a 'curved piece of metal'. What seems strange is why, with this obvious information, there should continue to be an emphasis on the 'animal' aspect of the Latin term. Why, moreover, should we presume that as this was the way in which the term 'lupus' developed in French the same happened in English? The 3 writers above do face the problem of changing 'lupus' into 'lowys' or 'lewiss' and suggest that 'brouet, brouetz' in Old French became 'brouwys' in Middle English and 'brewis' in Modern English. That seems a parallel but it is not. The letters 'p' and 'b' do not as easily elide as 't, tz', as another example shows.

The word 'loop' comes from the Irish/Gaelic word 'lub' that also means 'a bend, noose, fold or curvature' and originates with Lat. 'lupus'. Incidentally, the Celtic languages made all their words for 'wolf' from the ancient Celtic form 'vailo-s' so the Latin word 'lupus' was not used by them in this sense. On the contrary they took up the other meaning of 'lupus' and formed a word that we still make use of, retaining the original 'up' sound. All this makes the likelihood of 'lowys, lewiss' as a form of 'lupus' difficult to accept but if they were then it was with the meaning of a 'hook' and not a 'wolf', though the Romans knew all about wolves with one of them rearing Romulus and Remus.

The other possibility is that the word derived from 'levare' (pronounced **le-wahre**) meaning 'to lift up, elevate or raise' of which the adjective is 'levis' (pron. **le-wis**) and which also produced the Latin word 'Levatio' which meant 'a lifting or alleviation'. Frankly it seems to me more likely that 'lowys', 'lewiss' and 'lowetton' came from this source rather than 'lupus'. I am aware that Knoop, Jones and Hamer also considered the French verb 'lever' (to raise) and the OED questioned any such link on the ground of wrong sounds. I would agree if the French verb were to be thought the source but if we go *behind the French* to Latin, which did not use the modern 'v' sound, then the story is a different one. We no longer have the same problem as with 'louve', and whilst I am aware that our 3 writers suggested that the French technical term would in medieval England be pronounced '**lou-we**' it is still puzzling why we have to try and prove a Latin/French origin when a straightforward Latin/English derivation will do. That Dr. Anderson in his Scottish dialect transformed the operative 'lowys' into 'lewis', as suggested by Bernard E.Jones, seems to me highly likely as a last stage in the Masonic journey.

It is fitting that with such a reference to a son of Scottish Freemasonry we should shortly pass to the third part of this story of Mark ritual development. Before we do that, however, we have one last ritual to look at in this Section. It is the working currently carried out in Ireland. Obviously it would be undesirable to comment on this at length but the following features are worth mentioning as they show how tradition has been preserved in that land and its Masonic practice.

(a) The Overseers sit very much as in the Minerva working with their gate between their back and a Warden, though the M.Ov. has his back to the N. wall.
(b) Tokens are collected by the Deacons at the opening to prove Brn.
(c) The Overseers state their places to be 'in front of' a Gate.
(d) Only two stones are examined, a cube presented by the JD, and a keystone by the Candidate.
(e) They approach the back of an Overseer and knock on his right shoulder.
(f) To seek approval the cube stone is passed over the shoulder of each Overseer.
(g) When approved by M.Ov. the cube stone is taken to the J.Ov's table.
(h) On enquiry by M.Ov. the SD says the Candidate found the stone and adopted it.
(i) A general search is made for the KS but it is the Candidate who sets it on the VWM's pedestal.
(j) The Cand. on return takes an obligation, obtains signs & grip, is told how to obtain wages and undergoes the Test of Charity.

The Candidate is then invested, receives the usual Charge and is saluted in the North-east corner.

As we reach this point in the story of the Mark Ritual it may well be imagined that we have come very close to the form of working that was to prevail in all the countries of Britain. Certainly the alterations that had taken place in the Irish domain and the influence there of practices that began to blossom across the Atlantic made a significant impact on the shape of the eventual working with which Mark Masons today are familiar. Yet that is not the whole story. Across the Irish Sea, in Scotland, the West and North of England there was yet another family of 19th century workings which was to have the greatest and most lasting influence on what we call the 'Mark Degree' today.

SECTION THREE

In the "Scottish Freemason" of 1895 a Bro. Thompson of Ayr supplied some interesting information about the earliest known forms of the Mark degree in that country and in particular listed the four sections that had existed since the first quarter of the century. They were

1. Fellow Craft Mark (for FCs.)
2. Mark Master (for Masters)
3. Fugitive Mark (for Companions of the Royal Arch)

4. A Hint to a Wayfarer or Christian Mark (for Knights Templar).

At this point in our story we shall concentrate on the first two of these degrees which also appear as the 5° and 6° of the Early Grand Scottish Rite. The story of the body that practised this Rite will be told in chapter 7 but we need to know here that it was operating from about 1810 and it embraced a collection of 41 degrees of which those we shall now consider were the second and third in the series.

The *Fellow Craft Mark* was opened in the Craft 2° and the RWM (a sure sign of Scottish working) then assumed the role of M.Ov. and the Wardens became S. and J.Ov. The working was much the same as today save that the Candidate went *three times round* the lodge room to prove himself, the obligation was only administered *after* the keystone had been rejected, he had been cautioned by the WM to prepare another and then had found the original one carved by HAB. The sign, token and words were similar, but before being designated a *Marks* Man the cypher alphabet was explained and there was a Catechism including these questions: 'By and under what were you marked? – What did you give for your Mark? – Where and how did you receive your wages as a FC Marks Man? – Have you got the key of the Hieroglyphs? – Advance it. – Give me the Blind Mark? – How do you use it? – Who wrought the stone?'

The 6° of the Rite was named 'Marked Master' and was opened from a Master Masons' Lodge, with the principal officers remaining with their normal roles. It was a much shorter ceremony than the former, comprising the Candidate's proofs of proficiency in displaying his Mark, showing his polished ashlar, and demonstrating the signs and tokens of a *Marks Man*. He then took an Obligation and listened to a lecture. It is here that we encounter something significantly different and peculiar to this 'family' of rituals.

The story related how when HAB arrived to take over the supervision of the building of KST he found a relative of King Solomon in charge, and had therefore to take a subordinate position. One day, when HAB was overseeing the laying of a large stone at the top of the North Gate of the Temple enclosure, the stone fell on the Superintendent, who was called **Cavelum**, and killed him. King Solomon was so troubled by this tragedy that, as a memorial, he caused the North Gate to be walled up and never used again.

This *accident*, says the Lecture, was the unwitting cause of HAB's own death for had there been four gates available when HAB sought to escape from the ruffians who attacked him he might well have got away. In Scottish or Continental working this would indeed have been the case for the malcontents placed themselves at the S., W. and E. entrances to the Temple court, but in English practice they used the S., N. and E. It is also worth noting that the Scottish placings are those of the Overseers.

There is more. The smooth ashlar brought by the Candidate is likened to that stone on which the angel with the flaming sword stood when he expelled

Adam and Eve at God's command and it also represented the top surface of the altar used by Abraham for the intended sacrifice of his son, Isaac. The ashlar was also the stone on which Jacob rested when he had his famous dream and finally it became the cap-, cape-or cope-stone of the North-east corner of the Temple and on it King Solomon ordered the 47th Proposition of the First Book of Euclid to be engraved. Around it were added the letters that we saw used earlier in the NC working (p. 158) **M.J.F.T.B.W.G.J.** whilst on the opposite side of the stone were carved 'seven eyes' (cf. p. 191 and the ceremony of the Christian Mark.)

This fascinating exposition continued with the legend that at the re-building of the Temple by Zerubbabel this stone was not used and it in due time became the Stone of Fate (or Destiny) of the old Celtic kings which now resides under the Coronation Chair in Westminster Abbey. The remaining two sides of the stone bore the marks of the FC Marksman, one being the Lines Parallel and letters W) S (K over a T above an H. The other had four 'direction darts' composed of triangular figures with tails. It can thus be seen that in the world of Mark Masonry there were many common motifs that were displayed and explained in several varied combinations. What follows was not communicated by Thompson but was the natural sequence found in the Early Grand Encampment Rite and helps us to appreciate how the 'Mark' sections fitted into the whole.

The 7° was Architect, the 8° Grand Architect, the 9° Master of the Blue and 10° Master of all Symbolic Lodges. As possession of this last degree entitled a Brother to preside over a Craft Lodge it meant that in this arrangement of degrees that privilege was only available to someone who was already a MMM. To this day it is entirely optional for a Brother to take the Mark Degree unless he wishes to enter the Royal Arch and then it is obligatory. The 10° of the EGSR has now become the Installation ceremony of the ES Mark. To link with Thompson's article again the Fugitive Mark was the 12° and the Christian Mark 26°. In 1842 the Supreme Grand Chapter of Scotland took the decision to issue Charters to what were called 'Chair Master Lodges'. Their place in our story will be more fully explained in the next chapter but what is of immediate interest to the reader is the fact that this was a means of communicating the Mark degree in circumstances where it might not otherwise be available. We are fortunate in still having 2 well preserved copies of this working and since only three such Lodges were created this gives us a very clear picture of what took place. The copies belonged to the Lodges of Kinross and the Edinburgh Defensive Band.

The ceremony called 'The Mark or Chair Master's Degree' was first being practised in Kinrosshire as early as 1790 and it was a copy of this ceremony that was obtained around 1845 by William Punshon who was a notable Mark Mason in the Newcastle area. It should be emphasised here that this was quite distinct from the ancient North-east working which we looked at in Section Two, but it is likely that this was the working adopted by the

Newcastle and Berwick TI Lodge and which that Lodge was reluctant to relinquish when it helped to establish the new Grand Mark Lodge. It has features that certainly make it a form of bridge ceremony between those which we examined in Section One and those we are due to look at here. Any variations in the Edinburgh Defence Band working (EDB) will be noted but otherwise they were the same.

As *with the earlier workings* there are *no Deacons* and the opening is carried out between the Master and Wardens though in this instance there is only *one degree* and therefore the opening is as for *a MM's* lodge. The words of the JW in the opening are significant and will be seen to have a link with the Bolton working that comes later (p. 175). He says:"The better to observe the Sun at High Twelve and *therefrom to regulate the time* of the Craft."

The Candidate still comes as a FC though now 'desirous of presiding over a Lodge of operative masons', and whilst being admitted on the edge of the chisel the mallet is raised but not applied. Conducted by the SW he is again asked to show that he is qualified in the previous degrees and since the Master acknowledges the *loss of operative 'mark' practice* the candidate is told that 'as these parts of the ceremony of a FC are usually omitted we shall now supply them'.

The obligation follows that of a Master Mason though it has some distinctive features. It is in the name of 'Almighty God' and includes the words "that when presiding over an Operative or Mark Masons Lodge I will as a Warden pay the wages that are due and as a Master endeavour *to reward merit and suppress jealousy.*" In view of the name of this working such statements are natural and in the light of what we have already seen as the 'dissatisfaction of the workmen and their rejection of their tokens' the duties of the Chair are thus rightly included. The now firmly established 'penalties' connected with the word and grip follow as do the secrets of the pass grip, the sign manual for FCs and a HO sign but one is then puzzled by having the actual penal signs described as 'the way in which the *Mark Masters received wages*'. This suggests that there was still uncertainty about how to explain or introduce such features. The Mark Master's grip is as today and the words which accompany it are given as in Ezekiel chapter 44, verse 5. Much of this information is given in a form of cypher that is unique and which I shall consider with other cyphers in a later chapter. The last 'ancient word' given in cypher is 'Kilbroth' (sic) but, we are told, 'it is seldom used'.

A long Lecture completes this ceremony and the following new features need to be noted:

We now have the categories of craftsmen and workmen named and numbered, as mentioned earlier in Chapter 2 (see p. 24). The terms Harodim and Menatzchim appear but the former name apparently needs to be explained, for someone has inserted in the Punshon edition the words 'Princes and Rulers'. The Ghiblim appear as Stone *cutters and Sculptors* and the Bonai as Builders and Fellow Crafts, and then we have the interesting statement that there were

"3,300 Overseers or Mark Masters (who) are now called Masters and Senr or Junr Wardens". Here, we note, is the recognition of 'Overseers' as an operative office but it was to be some time before it appeared as an actual feature in the working of the degree. Indeed we are told that the Grand Lodge in the days of the 1st Temple had Solomon as Grand Master, HAB as Senior Warden and the noble Adoniram as Jun. Warden. This part of the ceremony particularly suggests how old the original working was.

The Overseers are now said to have their own mark of approval and another mark for setting stones in juxterposition (sic), so the operative practices mentioned at the outset of our story are now being used to create a new ritual. We even have here the first mention of marks having 3, 5, 7, 9, or 11 lines 'joined together to form any figure they pleased except that of a triangle which alluded to the triune essence of the Deity'. The phrase had come to stay. We also have the mention of *Wickets* at *different places*, a practice that will explain what was to follow in some areas.

The JW, here still called the Junior *Harod*, is only described as being on the South side of the Mark Master's wicket to do his duty. The punishment he might inflict was 'an ancient punishment among the Tyrians or Sidonians', another clause that was to persist and also refer back to Guild Masonry.

The Lecture also introduces us to more of our present ceremony by describing how "It was the Mk. Master's duty to prove each stone not only as to its soundness but *as to its finish*, and to see that it was made exactly *according to the Working Plan* with which each Mk. Master was provided: if the stone in every way proved worthy it received the Mk. Master's Mark and was sent to the Temple but if not it was condemned and thrown *over a precipice* among the rubbish."

We now learn that the HO sign came from two FCs standing thus to eject a certain stone that was the subject of the following story. *Every 6th day* the Mk. Masters met with HAB to receive their working plans. One of these plans was mislaid but an ingenious FC either got a glimpse of it, or began to imagine what was on it from the work already done, and he blocked out such a design as he thought was needed. He put *his mark* on it but of course there was no Overseer/Mk. Master's mark and when it was examined by the Overseers at the Temple yard they had no plan and regarded it as 'superfluous' and 'an idling away of the FC's work time'. As the Lecture now states:

"Therefore the FC instead of *honor* received nothing but angry words and reproaches ... and in the heat of passion the overseer ordered the stone to be thrown over the *precipice* which was accordingly done by two men probably well pleased at what they deemed the humiliation of their *companion*'s vanity."

Here we have virtually the stage directions for future ritual practice. We are even given the words the disconsolate FC cried out: 'A.A.m.L.i.l.' which are still used to this day. Moreover the stone so rejected was for Solomon's '*secret* arch' and when it could not be found 'the Overseer of the Builders then sent to the Overseer of the Hewers in the quarries who had received the plans and orders for that part of the building'. (The Operative divisions are still very evident.) There is nothing in his possession and now HAB himself 'not only recollected drawing the plan and writing instructions about this stone, which he wished finished in a particular manner, but of giving them himself to the Overseer of the Hewers'. This poor man is not only reprimanded but *replaced*, after the finding of the stone, by the very FC who made *but does not here re-discover* it.

The Lecture (and the ceremony) closes with these words: "The newly made Mk. Master was now ordered to cut the Mk. Master's Mark on the stone on the side near his own and outside of it *8 letters* relative to which there is *now some doubt* owing to the tradition not having been retained in the original language". They are generally supposed to have been equivalent to H.T.W.S. S.T.K.S. and here they are reproduced not only in their Hebrew but also their *Samaritan* letter counterparts. After this the stone was *conveyed to the Temple with great pomp and parade and when it was fixed in its place* the new Mk. Master in an ecstacy (sic) of joy clapping his hands and looking up cried out T.b.t.G.I.h.m.w. The special version of the Mark Song *sung at the close* will be considered with music later.

At the time when this kind of working was first used much of what has been mentioned was quite new. We have seen how these items in the Mark Ritual continued or were adapted in the other 'families' and we must now see how this happened under other Scottish hands.

We have from 1845 a MS copy of a Mark ritual that was compiled from older Manuscripts by Hector Gairn, the Grand Treasurer of the Supreme Grand Chapter of Scotland. This is the earliest authorised version of the Mark Degree working under that body and its added interest is that this is most likely the form of the Degree as then practised by the Masons in the Inniskilling Dragoons who were stationed in York and who formed the York Mark Lodge in 1852. It is hardly surprising, if this were the case, that what we find here is somewhat different to what Dunckerley may have learnt from that very same Regimental Lodge almost a century previously. What we do know is that this form was provided with more uptodate Opening and Closing ceremonies albeit they still retain a shape that indicates their older origins.

It is still the case that there are no actual Overseers and the RWM and Wardens conduct the whole ceremony. Following the previous ceremony it is interesting to note the JW's words at Opening: "The better to observe the sun at High XII and to beware of and punish impostors." The Candidate is attended by a Conductor but there are no Deacons, no stones to present and a mark is not *chosen*. The emphasis on proving oneself in the previous degrees, taking an obligation, hearing a long lecture and being informed of the secrets has a still remarkable similarity to the 'Dunckerley' rite. The distinctive features are these:

i/ The RWM does not demand the password from the IG.
ii/ Pointing out how FC Lodges no longer give or record their members' marks or teach how to receive wages the RWM says he will repair that loss. "You will go to the SW who will teach you how to put in your hand for wages and *give you a mark*." When the Candidate has his mark he takes it to the RWM who says, "You acknowledge that to be your mark?" The Candidate assents, walks 3 times round the Lodge and makes 4 steps for taking his obligation.
iii/ In the obligation come the words ... 'this Mark Lodge held within the body of the (blank) RA Chapter No. (blank) which I will always acknowledge to be my Mother Lo. of Mk. MS ...' and the same words about rewarding merit and suppressing jealousy appear as before.

In the Lecture that follows the wording is almost identical with the Chair Master's Degree but there are some items that merit attention. We are told of 300 *Harodim* whom HAB himself selected to pay wages: the ancient Word (K. ...) is said 'to *characterise* the people: proving the stones as to their soundness was by 'giving it 3 blows with a maul': the KS was for 'Solomon's secret arch': and the Mark Master's mark was to be placed 'on the *narrow end* – around his own, and outside of it 8 letters...'

A picture of a plug stone showing how this was done is included in the booklet. It is attended by the words "The plugstone above is a representation of the **Keystone** used by the Edinburgh RA Chapter No. 1 since the beginning of the (19th) century"; it is heptagonal in form – agreeing with the description of the vault in another degree. Since the close connection of the Mark and the Royal Arch was established in Scotland by this time the link is not surprising. In the light of what happened elsewhere it is simply the outcome of a traditional bond.

Yet there is another feature of this ritual booklet which contains not only the Mark but the Excellent Master degree. I will not here explain this latter ceremony but in view of the repeated linkage between the Mark and other Royal Arch steps it will perhaps intrigue the reader to remark these brief extracts from what is in the next ceremony:

a) JW in opening: "The better to observe the sun at High XII and *therefrom regulate the time* of the Craft".
b) SW's duty: "To close the Lodge, take charge of the plans when the work of the day is over, and pay the EMs their wages."
c) The Cand. is one who wishes "to avail himself of the decree of Cyrus to return to Jerusalem – to assist in rebuilding a House to the Lord God of Israel (&) now approaches the G.Lo. of Babylon with a request to grant him permission, and such tokens as shall be satisfactory to his Brethren who have already set out from this place and arrived at Jerusalem.
d) RWM says: "You may now proceed *on your journey to J. ...m* (and) on your way thither you will meet with Guards stationed for the purpose of keeping back intruders ..." and the Candidate is given the means of *passing over* on his way.

If ever there were explanation needed to show why the ceremonies in the Section Two 'family' were constructed as they were this Scottish arrangement of much the same period must be some part of the answer. It is only our more modern separation and re-arrangement of the degrees that suggests any oddity. To earlier Masons the cohesion of the whole process was much more evident and hence the apparent interplay of one degree with another.

Whilst this form of the Mark was being introduced to York there were yet other variations being practised in central Lancashire at Bolton. Each of the four texts that we have available for this ritual have their own peculiarities and so we shall indicate these with the letters referring to their titles: Old Bolton (OB), Brockbank (BK), Entwisle (EN) and St. John (SJ).

A) The Officers include a Deputy RWM, a Conductor with that title, an I.G. who is called *Timekeeper*, and even a Chaplain (BK and EN).
B) The Lodge is opened in the 3° and then as a Mark Lodge. The RWM asks for 'the attention and assistance' of the Brethren. The Tyler is *present* in the lodge room from the outset and *only leaves* when he has declared his post and duty.
C) In OB the SW (in BK, EN and SJ the Deacons) then approaches everyone present and requires the Password and Pass grip before reporting to the RWM (as in present 3° closing manner) that all are Mark Masters.
D) In OB the Overseers alone are asked about their Stations and duties and the Lodge is opened in the 'Name of the Most High God'. In BK and SJ *all* the officers are questioned with some interesting answers:

"(Timekeeper). Within the entrance of the *workman's Gate* ... To admit Mk. Mas. on proof, to pass *the workmen to their labours* and to obey the commands of the JW."

"(Ds). In the S (or W) *within hail* of J(S)W ... to carry messages ... and *elsewhere as he may direct.*"

"(Conductor) In the East *within hail of the RWM* To bear all commands of the RW to his Officers, to prepare candidates for advancement & conduct them to the Overseers for the examination...."

"(JW). As the sun is in the South at high twelve, which is the glory of the day, so stands the JW ... (the rest as today)."

It is at this point that a very notable variation has to be mentioned. The arrangement of the Officers at the Opening is with the M.Ov. sitting on the RWM's immediate left and the Conductor on his right. The other Overseers and Deacons also sit on the left and right respectively of their Wardens. It is, as we shall soon see, only at the examination point of the ceremony that the Overseers sit below the Wardens and RWM and after that they return to their original places against the wall. This is quite clearly the transition stage in this 'family' of rituals at which the Overseers move on to the floor as we are accustomed to find them.

Finally the BK and SJ workings have the following prayer before the Lodge is opened in 'due and ancient form' with the present day knocks.

"Let us acknowledge our dependence on the Almighty Architect and Grand Overseer of the Universe. Oh *Most bountiful Creator*, we acknowledge thee to be *our God*, we bow before thee as *our King*, we invoke and call upon thee to be *our helper* in all trials and difficulties. To thee we owe whatever good we possess, to thee we look for every good to come, to thee we direct our petitions humbly beseeching thee to protect and bless our Queen, our Country and our Brethren *wheresoever dispersed over the face of earth and water.*

Grant that *in conformity with the working of the Craft* we may continue to confess thy faith, be strengthened in hope and established in Charity with all mankind. S.M.I.B."

Several candidates might be admitted at once and if so a rubric states that the one later holding the KS represents them all. In the first part of the ceremony the candidate undergoes no preparation but comes in full dress and badge as a Master Mason. For the Examination coats and neckerchiefs (sic) are removed, shirt sleeves are rolled up to the elbow, trousers turned up at the bottom and a large plain leather apron descending to the knees is worn "like the kind of an ordinary operative (BK: working) stone mason".

In the OB the SD acts as Conductor whilst BK, EN and SJ have a separate office. The proofs of being a MM are given *at once* to the RWM (SJ), on going round the room *once* (OB) and going round *3 times* (BK and EN). The ceremony in OB and SJ now followed almost the same practice as today up to the taking of the obligation save that there was no mention of 'Mark Man' but only of being a FC, the Mark to be chosen under the guidance of the SW was still to have 3, 5, 7, 9 or 11 lines, though the triangle was now 'the Mk. M's mark of approval', and the point is again emphasised that these features *should have been part* of the FC degree.

The BK and EN rituals here divert and consist of a long address by the RWM using much of the present Lecture. It includes this paragraph:

"It is even now the custom in some places, particularly in Scotland, for a FC to have a mark presented to him. Have you received ...? NO. Then I have pleasure in *presenting you with such a Mark ...*"

The RWM refers to the "Order, Harmony and Regularity which the original degree maintained" and ended with some words that obviously affected later ritual.

"In a moral sense this degree affords an interesting allusion to that great day when every man's work will be proved, when that which accords not with the square of God's Holy Word will be rejected and cast aside as unfit for the Grand Temple above, into which alone may be admitted that which is just, perfect and true."

There is no taking of an obligation in BK at this point but in OB/SJ the Candidate takes the same steps as we are now accustomed to.

In preparation for the 'Examination' that follows the Overseers move their seats forward to form gates as in 'Minerva' working today. In OB only the KS is brought in for examination and the Candidate makes four gliding steps as he approaches each Overseer. After the Council the stone is h.o. by the S. and J.Ovs.

In the SJ working only two stones are used but BK/EN have the present method of presenting three stones by three similarly clothed persons. The wording is almost exactly the same save that the Ovs. say, "the pass word to the W (or E) gate" and the S.Ov. comments on the KS "altogether different in form and execution to any yet submitted to my examination". When the M.Ov. has told the Candidate (in BK/EN) to 'leave your work with me and stand aside' he rises and stamps on the floor to summon the other Overseers. The stone is duly h.o. by the M. and S.Ov. 'the *Conductor catching* and *quietly laying it down* in an *out of the way place*'. In SJ it is the Deacons who h.i.o. and one of them puts it in a discreet place. The Overseers now resume their former places in all four workings.

Whereas BK/EN have the usual words about "a further specimen of your skill" there is no such remark at this point in SJ, and OB reflects an older working elsewhere (see p. 161f) where the RWM asks him to 'demonstrate to the Brn. how he would set about converting a rough ashlar into a smooth one'.

The Brethren now move noisily about the lodge floor and the usual 'wages drama' is enacted. In OB the Brethren process three by three whereas the other workings have the procession as today. In BK/EN the JW has 'an axe or *heavy sword* and the SW must be provided with a wicket'. This latter rubric plainly indicates that up to this point there was no wicket on the SW's pedestal.

In the OB working the Candidate, having been given a further chance by the RWM, returns with a *cubic stone* which is passed and accepted. This is in addition to the usual procedure of the other workings, viz. the absence of 'a keystone to the secret arch' which is the cause of much commotion at the SW's pedestal and the usual enquiry, search and discovery that follow. It is now in BK/EN that the obligation occurs, with nine steps to the pedestal on which it is taken.

In EN there then follows the now familiar 'Test of Charity' with the Tyler bringing a message asking for the Candidate's help of a Brother in need. The Candidate's discomfiture when he finds a shilling on him has already been noted.

The sharing of secrets that follows is in OB carried out by the SW and not the RWM and is also largely written in cypher. In BK there are three statements which provoke interest. The first is the call to relieve a Brother in need "with at least the value of half a Jewish shekel of silver, *about one shilling* of English money". This is an interesting but close variant of the amounts, especially 1/1½d, of other workings.

The second is the information that in Scotland and America "tho' the p . . . w . . . is the same, the p . . . g . . . is different . . ." and thirdly, the Word of the degree is described as "*literally meaning Companion* (sing.) of the Mark" when the word is manifestly a *plural* Hebrew word.

In completing this part of Section Three we shall be the poorer if we do not take account of three more distinctive passages in these Bolton rituals.

i) In BK and SJ there is an extensive Lecture by the RWM after the secrets are conferred. In it the story of the 'substituted and copied KS' is told and then the Candidate is pointed to the Charter from the Supreme Grand Chapter of Scotland and these words are spoken:

"It is supplied to us for the propagation of pure and legal Mark Masonry until the Supreme Authorities *in this country* shall recognise the degree and, in addition to the terms of your Obligation, in it you are bound in every sense of the word to discountenance all illegal and spurious Mark Master Lodges." This dates these workings fairly accurately and we shall have occasion in the next Chapter to see how such a passage fitted into the story of Mark Masonry's development.

ii) It is noticeable that in all the workings there is no mention of any kind of apron even though there is clear presentation of a jewel.

iii) In OB, BK and SJ the Charge to the Candidate is very close to what we are accustomed to today but it ends in two different ways. In OB we have the RWM telling how 'the placing of the KS in the Arch will be left for a further advance in his masonic knowledge'. A now familiar refrain. In BK and SJ however we have some words that we saw at this point in the Bath workings (see p. 139). The words come after our usual ending about the stone possessing merits unknown and read:

"For it is tho' last (SJ) For this the last (BK)
The Key Stone forms the Arch (SJ) ... perfect Arch (BK)
The rest that there are put (Both)
Are nothing till (Both)
That comes to bind and shut (Both)
Then stands it a Triumphal ARCH (SJ) ... Triumphal Mark (BK)

As to which ending should be deemed the most appropriate I must leave the reader to choose. Did one reflect a Craft and the other a Royal Arch view?

Near as we have obviously come to the emergence of the present day ceremony it has to be admitted that there were still features at Bolton that separate those workings from what was finally accepted. To cross that gap we have to look at one more group of rituals. It is, for instance, striking to note that when you come to the end of the OB working you can turn the MS booklet around and you are presented with a Scottish Mark working that was shortly to prevail. We shall therefore end this Section with the comparison of those rituals that finally helped to produce what we enjoy today. They can be usefully divided into what are called the 'Shorter' and 'Longer (or) Fuller' workings and, since there will be some readers who are not aware of the fact, there are shorter and longer presentations of the Mark ceremony in Scotland to this day.

The Shorter form is no less than the ritual adopted by the Bon Accord Mark Lodge when it was established in London in 1851. It was brought intact from the Chapter in Aberdeen where it had been regularly worked and like the form used in York the Overseers make no appearance in person though they are mentioned in the catechism conducted by the SW. Its being used by the members of a lodge which included the first Grand Master of the new Grand Mark Lodge means that it must have had some influence on what was eventually adopted by that body.

Apart from not questioning any Overseers and invoking the assistance of the *Grand Geometrician* of the Universe the opening is exactly as today. The Candidate comes in with both shirt sleeves and the right corner of his *Royal Arch apron* turned up and is yet announced as a FC seeking advancement. The password is not given to the W. Master but he is 'proved' at the door by the Inner Guard with a *Heavy Maul* and Chisel. The prayer started off as in the FC degree but then became one that is used in Consecration ceremonies today.

Following the Candidate's affirmation of his being a MM the WM made an important declaration:

"As the degree of Mark Master *is not recognised by* the Supreme Grand Chapter of Royal Arch Masons *in England* (though considered one of the principle (sic) steps to Arch (sic) Masonry in Scotland) to prevent interference with the Constitutions of the Supreme Grand Chapter of England the Bye-laws of the London Bon Accord Mark Masters Lodge enact that no person can be here advanced to the secrets and mysteries of this degree unless he be already a Companion of the Royal Arch. Have you attained that high honour?"

To show his attainment the Candidate proceeds *four times* round the Lodge room giving the appropriate sign each time, after which the WM tells him that he should chuse (sic) a Mark which the SD will assist him to do and though it should have an *odd number of lines* and he can use his 'crest' yet "for the sake of despatch" the Mark should rather be some *plain figure* composed of short lines *and curves* as will be *shown you in the Registrar's Book*. What is now evident, as he is taught how to present this Mark, is that already we have the 'Mark Man' ceremony even if that term is not expressed.

Here too we have the 'sign manual' introduced as such and the phrase "a trusty FC who has wrought well and worthily six days or less"; four steps to the East and in the obligation the reference still to one's duty when in charge of a Lodge of Operative Masons; taking the 4th regular step and then hearing a new but fitting lesson from 2 Chrons. 2 verses 11–16. There is even the first mention of 'Chants' and the Chaplain reading from Ezekiel chapter 44 and leaving out verse 4. The secrets are exactly the same but the Ancient Word of the degree is given in reversed form and '*signifying* Companions of the Mark'.

The Wardens test the Candidate and he is duly invested with apron and jewel by the SW with the WM adding his comments on the status attained although warning that one's actions "will be observed and recorded by *the Grand Mark Master* of the Universe". In the Lecture that he delivered we have much common material with the past and the present so that whilst the term 'Harodim' disappears, the h.o. the *precipice* remains, the Candidate is told of an ingenious craftsman who glimpsed the KS drawn by HAB and made a copy but had it rejected, though finding it in the rubbish of the quarry after the Overseers remembered seeing it. The replacement of the thoughtless Overseer by the FC is still retained and as the stone was placed in its proper position the new Mark Master 'clasped his hands together and *looked upwards*' which takes us back to earlier rituals we have examined. What is clear is that we have now lost the older explanations of the Working Tools but the form based on the Craft explanations has arrived.

One interesting feature of this Ritual is that before the closing the WM asks the SW if the dues are all rendered and the wages paid which sounds normal enough but the Brethren are then formed up, sing the Mark Anthem and pass the wicket to *receive their dues*, afterwards saluting the WM in passing and taking their seats. The old use of the Hymn and the new enquiry at the close are thus linked.

It only remains to consider the so-called Longer workings that also incorporated the actual Examination by the Overseers. These are the Pirie ritual of about 1850 (PR), and the Friendship No. 16 TI ritual of Devonport which is copied from an earlier MS but written on paper carrying the 'Pirie' watermark (FP). It was G.W.E.Bridge who commented that PR and FP 'could possibly be the basic structure from which the English Grand Mark Lodge finally created the official version'. Taking that as our final cue I intend to follow these two outlines and to insert where appropriate the alternatives which occur between them.

The Opening ceremony in PR/FP is exactly the same as today save that the Overseers sit in the lodge like other members at this point of the ceremony. In the choice of a Mark under the guidance of the Registrar the candidate was still told that what he chose should be composed of 3 to 11 lines or angles though in the FP booklet there is a separate piece of paper that informs the reader that the new Grand Mark Lodge of England had abrogated this regulation in December 1864. The approach to the East for an obligation was by the present number of steps and the Candidate was then shown how to present his hand at the Warden's wicket. This step in instruction is the nearest we yet get to recognising the Candidate as a Mark Man and certainly he was now allowed to retire to prepare some work for his advancement to the degree of Mark Master.

He was prepared by shedding his jacket, having most of his arms bare, his trousers rolled up and over all he wore a leather apron. On his return to the lodge he would notice the Overseers in places similar to those now occupied by the Minerva Mark Lodge of Hull but, unlike even the Scottish Craft Mark ceremonies, in which only one Deacon presents a cubic stone alongside the Candidate's KS, these ceremonies at last have three stones presented. The full drama of examination takes place, and when the h.o. has occurred the Overseers' pedestals are removed and they resume their places along with the rest of the brethren.

The secrets are communicated as at present save that in FP the old manner of presenting the hand *palm downwards* was employed with it being turned upwards inside the wicket. The word had the form which was common in many Scottish Mark workings – Kebroath – but otherwise all would have been very familiar to modern Mark Masons. We know this to be so because in the appendix to a contemporary Mark ceremony used in Newcastle – the Armstrong MS – we are given a complete description of all the signs, grips and words and they are as if written in a modern ritual. FP here adds the crossed fingers or 'lines parallel' sign and some clear instruction about the cypher alphabet but is otherwise identical.

The two then have a long examination by the SW in the manner familiar at the end of the usual 2° and this seems to replace the older address that was given by the WM. The SW being satisfied as to the Candidate's instruction he is then told to clothe him with an apron which has clearly become normal and decorate him with a jewel which is now bearing the 8 usual letters. The meaning of those letters is the modern one though there is again an interesting variant in one Scottish booklet that says the 'London use is to say that the last 4 letters mean **Sent The Key Stone**'. The Lecture that followed was the same except for the numbers quoted and the Lodge was closed without a hymn and using the dialogue now customary.

We have thus arrived at the threshold of the ceremonies that were generally to be current in Scotland, Ireland and England for the next 150 years. There would be some adjustments, variations and influences between the three jurisdictions and what those were and how they were managed we shall soon go on to explain. What was now certain was that having emerged from a century of experiment in making Mark Men and Mark Masters the future practice was now much clearer. All that remains is for us to examine those additional workings that had clung to the previous presentations of the Mark Degree.

THE ADDITIONAL 'MARK' DEGREES.

When I first encountered the list of these degrees in J.A.Grantham's book I was amazed at their apparent diversity and complexity. That those who devised them were ingenious students of the Scriptures was immediately evident but as we come to examine them more closely we may discover not only that many of them were exceedingly brief in practice but that they had a close knit connection with their parent degrees of the Mark, Ark Mariner, the Royal Arch or some form of Knightly Masonry. They are now either no longer practised or they have been incorporated into the working of those main stream degrees or Orders.

For this, the first exposition of them all together, in full, anywhere in book form, I propose to arrange them in the following groups –

a) Link or Link Mason, Link and Chain, (Jacob's) Wrestle or Sublime Master, (Mark) Link and Wrestle.

b) Mark Fellow Mason or Fellow-Craft Mark, Marked Master, Cain's Mark, Travelling Mark, Arch Mason, Mark, Ark and Link, (Grand) Architect.
c) Fugitive Mark, Babylonian Pass, Jordan Pass.
d) Black Mark, Knight of the Christian Mark.

It will be for the reader who is a Mark Master Mason to determine whether or how the rituals now to be described fit today into the ceremonial which is practised in his Mark Lodge or the Mark ceremony prior to the Royal Arch which he will have experienced.

a) The terms *Link and Link Mason* are interchangeable and refer in *England* to exactly the same ceremony. This was conducted in connection with a Mark ceremony for brethren already advanced. The 'Link' was opened 'by virtue of the power vested in a Mark Master' with the Mark knocks. The candidate was introduced by the password 'Shinar's Plains' and proved himself a Mark Master. A passage from the Book of Genesis was read, Chapter 11, verses 1 to 9, describing the efforts of people in the land of Shinar to make bricks and construct a high tower. Their work ended in a Babel (or babble) of tongues.

This reading is followed by an obligation in which the penalty was to have 'the knuckles twisted off'. The grip was that of linking the small fingers of the hand and aligning the knuckles joint to joint but with the thumbs erect representing a tower. The word was 'Mark'. A short lecture might follow explaining the ceremony and pointing out the need for Mark Masons to work in harmony and employ a common language, a possible reference to the use of the Mark cypher. The ceremony was declared closed.

The story of the *Link degree* is much more complex than this simple description may suggest. A 'Link' was performed in the Ashton Travelling Lodge as was indicated earlier and the content of that ceremony differs from what we have just seen. The explanation there given to Candidates was that when a stone or piece of timber which did not bear either mark or number was brought for examination the Overseers were *united or linked together* in throwing it aside and if it was too large for one to manage then his neighbour was to assist in casting it away. 'Hence the grip and word of a LINK MASON'. The grip was with the hands joined in front of the lower part of the body and the word given at the third swing was K.B.L.T. meaning to 'heave over'. When the Temple was nearly completed the special stone was recalled and the brethren 'linked' together in ensuring that it was placed in its proper position in the structure. It can be well understood, with this interpretation in view, why, in the 1902 Constitutions of the Grand Council of the Allied Masonic Degrees (p. 10) it states: 'Degrees conferred formerly but now not actively worked – The Link or Chain, absorbed by the Mark'.

We are told that the word 'Kibboleth' has been used by the Deacons in Ashton.D.T.I. Lodge from the earliest times, and certainly for more than a century, at the point where the stone is being thrown away. It is also given to the Candidate as a secret when explaining the h.o. sign. G.W.E.Bridge expressed himself unable to trace the word and even asked for help from those he lectured to. I would here like to offer a possible solution to the problem.

My first thought was that as the Ashton working does not make use of the more frequent and similar word met elsewhere – K.B.R.T. – their word could possibly be a mistaken form of that one. In the light of what was said about 'Kibroth' or its variants earlier this would fit the very circumstance with which the word is connected in this ceremony. As the Deacons *link up* to 'bury' this stone in the rubble below they might well employ a term that means 'Companions of that which is marked for burial'.

On the other hand we have already seen two other workings where we have not dissimilar words: in the Jamaica working where we had a Password 'C.H.L.T.' and its Sacred Word 'K.B.R.T.'; and the Blackburn ceremony where the word was 'GIBLET' or 'G.B.L.T'. It was as I was having further thoughts about this that I came across a brief Hebrew glossary that I had once filed. In it was a reference to K.B.L. meaning 'as nothing' and giving a Bible reference: 1 Kings 9 verse 13. This is a very striking passage in which Hiram of Tyre rebukes Solomon for giving him towns that are worthless or 'k.b.l. lands'. If K.B.L. means 'of no account' then it could be appropriate to the h.o. action. G.B.L.T. is used in exactly the same situation as K.B.L.T. and might be a misplacing of G for K. As far as K.H.L.T. is concerned that could mean 'assembly or congregation' and in the Jamaica context would fit well with K.B.R.T. meaning 'sharers'.

In Ireland we find the Link more often referred to as *Link and Chain* or even *Link of the Wilderness*. It introduced quite another ceremony than the ones described above. It took place amongst those who had taken a Mark ceremony and were therefore full Craft Masons. The candidate was brought in and proved in the previous degrees. The passage read was from Genesis chapter 27, verses 11–22 which describe how Jacob was on his journey to Haran when in a desert place he lay down to rest using a stone as his pillow. In a dream he sees a *chain* of angels ascending and descending on a ladder that *links* heaven and earth and on waking realises the holiness of the place. He sets up the stone he rested on, makes a vow to honour the House of God there and to pay a tithe of his possessions to the Lord. This is why in many Irish floorcloths and certificates the degree is depicted as a ladder of Faith with seven steps. An obligation was taken with a penalty referring to death in the wilderness, the password was 'Bethel' and the Grand Word 'Israel'. The grip is not known but the sign seems to have been with fingers extended in a vertical position (as if the rungs of a ladder) and the thumb erect (like the pillar set up).

Yet this was not the end of the story. Just to confuse the issue further the Early Grand Scottish Rite had its own '*Link and Chain*' as the 13° and this was another different but intriguing ceremony which had its own 'links' with what has already been shown in this chapter.

The degree was part of a series called '*Ark, Mark, Link and Wrestle*' and it was, prior to the Encampment's use, conferred in a Royal Arch Chapter. Here the Lodge was opened in the 11°, that of *Knight Ark Mariner* which will be considered in the Ark Mariner section of this book. Noah and his sons are in the principal chairs and the Ark is raised to work in the 13°.

The Guide prepares the Candidate as a Fellow Craft Mark Mason and on entering leads him *5 times* round the lodge room to prove that he has the *five corporeal senses*, in a manner which has been referred to earlier. Here we have one more example of how features that were at one time held together are now separated whilst elsewhere we shall see the reverse process taking place. Another instance of separation follows at once for after the obligation has been taken Noah says:

"This degree was *originally attached to the FC Mark* and its history relates to an event which occurred at the building of the Temple." As Solomon was inspecting the work "he *lost from his crown one of the jewels* forming the sacred name of the Deity." He caused diligent search to be made for it and it was discovered by STODAN, "the same who worked the key-stone of King Solomon's secret arch, and as this stone had not yet been put finally in place" Solomon caused Stodan to carve on it, in addition to the other marks, the name of this jewel, which was an amethyst, or, as our ancient Brethren termed it, "Amasaphus." We are back to the same tradition that was communicated to Finch and Carlile.

The ceremony ends with the secrets being given. The password is Stodan and the meaning of that was given earlier (see p. 129); the Word is Amasaphus which "signifies emblematically a hidden treasure", the sign here is given by offering a hand clenched but with the little finger erect and the grip by linking the same finger of another's hand to form *a chain* thus giving the degree its name. The Mark was the signature of "our Martyr Grand Master given in the ancient form" of H over a reversed T. So ended this form of the Link and Chain, and Noah then adds, interestingly,

"You will now retire while the Lodge is raised to the 14° when you will receive that." Several degrees of this brief nature are thus taken together and not least the 14° because, as we shall now see, it was the 'Sublime Master' or 'Jacob's Wrestle' that completed an ancient sequence.

Turning then to the *Wrestle* degree, which was most often thus joined to the Link in Ireland or in those parts of Northern England that knew Irish influence or contacts, the introductory procedure followed was that a brother had to be a Mark Master and this degree was conferred in that context. Opened again 'by virtue ...' the knocks given were one short and one long. The Candidate was brought in, his state of dress unknown, and there was a reading of Genesis chapter 32, verses 24 to 31. This is the well known story of Jacob sending his household over the river Jabbok but remaining on the other side and *wrestling* with someone who could not overpower him until he damaged Jacob's hip. When Jacob asked his opponent his name he would not disclose it but he told Jacob that *his* name would change and he would be called 'Israel'.

When Jacob limped away next day he called the place 'Peniel (or) Penuel' because he had come face to face with, or had a vision of, God.

In the obligation that followed the penalty was "May I be struck in the hollow of my thigh and the same put out of joint" which in Eastern terms might also mean 'emasculation'. The sign was 'touching the inner part of the upper leg', the grip given as if grappling with someone in a wrestle with the left hand on the other's shoulder and the right hand within the hollow of the other's leg and the word, hardly a surprise, was 'Peniel' with some workings adding 'Thou preservest life'.

The short lecture, beside recapitulating the above events, taught the lesson of not betraying a brother and recognising that we shall have to deal with God for our misdeeds. In Ireland a further lesson was taught. This being part of their Red Cross series the events described by the Bible were applied to predict the subsequent successful *struggle* by Daniel and Zerubbabel, Princes of *Israel, to prevail* with Cyrus and Darius to *preserve Jerusalem* for God's chosen people.

When the ceremony had the alternative title of '*Sublime Master*', as in the EGSR degree, it was held in the Ark Lodge and the Candidate was led in dressed as an Ark Mariner. The Guide took him slowly round the lodge room as *Japhet* read the passage from Genesis. The secrets were exactly as above save that the words "limping thrice" were added to the description of the Sign. A passage in the rare booklet regarding some of these degrees is surely worth recording:

"With this degree is completed the series known to our ancient Brethren as the *Ark, Mark, Link and Wrestle* degrees, interesting to the Masonic student and antiquarian, but which, owing to the ephemeral character of the various bodies at different times claiming jurisdiction over the high grades, have been all but lost, and, were it not for their preservation in the EG Rite, would be known only by the names occurring in some old list, or being mentioned in an encyclopaedia." What that states about this little series could equally be said about the other groups to which we now turn.

b) The *Fellow Craft Mark* was the nearest equivalent to what we now know as the Mark ceremony though it possessed many features that we have already seen in the older workings that have been outlined – the Brethren called Marks-men, an absence of Overseers, having only two stones presented, the stone that is missing being the one "to close in *the arch over the secret vault* of King Solomon and no stone fitting can be found" and four steps to the east. There is also a considerable address by the W. Master and a lecture to follow. Some points in these two sections are worth noting: the 'lines parallel' were given and there is ample reference to the cypher alphabet; a simple form of paper missive is explained; the last four of the normal letters read as 'Sent The Key Stone'; and there is an extensive explanation of the numbers 3, 5, 7, 9 and 11.

It is only right to state that Crossle always contended that in the *Mark*

Fellow Mason degree, which was an even earlier form of Irish working the story told was probably something from the Book of Genesis that linked with the Ark story of the Flood and the Wrestle of Jacob. Whilst there is no document to settle this matter decisively one wonders if, as the Link passage in that country was Jacob's dream, the Mark Fellow theme might not have been the story of the builders of the Tower of Babel which would have fitted between the two and had so many moral lessons to offer including the scattering of the builders across the world. Here again is a subject that might merit more research.

The *Marked Master* is one of those preserved by the E.G.S.R. and is said to bear the same relation to the Master Mason as the Marks-men degree bore to the Fellow Craft. Prior to 1800 it is claimed that this was conferred by one Master Mason on another but that after that date such ceremonies were disallowed in Craft Lodges. What we will see as this working is revealed is that we have here the material that was, or had been, used in some areas of Britain as a form of Mark Master working. To assert that this ceremony was not the real Mark is only true if by that is meant that it is not agreeable to what is accepted today. For some Masons this was their form of the degree.

The password immediately proves the point. It is **M.J.H.F.T.B.W.G.J.** and anyone who wants to know its meaning has only to consult the working on p. 158. In the Lecture that follows a remarkably brief obligation the story told of Solomon's relative, **CAVELUM**, is again given but this time the stone falling upon him from the top of the North Gate was entirely due to the 'culpable carelessness of HAB'. The outcome is as stated earlier but there is a moral lesson here which is all the more surprising in that it refers to one who is otherwise held up as a shining example for all Masons. The passage runs:

"This shows us, my Brother, that the greatest and wisest of earth's children may give way, when led by ambition to temptation, and also our own evil deeds, however long after their committal, will surely work our own punishment." But that is not all. Embellishing the quality of the stone that had been in Paradise, used by Abraham and rested upon by Jacob, it now became not only a 'capestone' of the Temple of Solomon but was preserved from destruction during the rebuilding of the Temple under Zerubbabel, was taken by a colony of Jews under Jeremiah who sailed from Dan to Britain, and there became the Stone of Destiny that was stolen by Edward I of England to become the Coronation stone. Those who knew this Legend are 'Marked Masters' indeed.

At some stage another story from Genesis that involved brothers was used, at least in Irish Masonry, to form a minor degree called 'Cain's Mark'. One of the brothers bore a *mark on his forehead* to remind others of his crime of fratricide. Nothing is certainly known about the details of its working but Genesis chapter 4, verses 1 to 16 would obviously have been read, an obligation administered, and the words used would be 'Cain' and 'Abel'. The sign used in some Mark workings of a clenched fist with the thumb erect and applied to the forehead could have been just the relic of this tradition, limited in time and location as it almost certainly was.

Of the *Travelling Mark* more will be said when we come to the Fugitive Mark in the next group, though there have been several pointers already to the ancient direction markers that were sometimes explained in old Mark lectures. Nor is there much need to expand on the *Arch* degree as so much has been said already in the earlier pages of this chapter (see especially pp. 134f). What can be offered as still extant features of this once important Mark component of 18th century Freemasonry is the fact that to this day there is a wicket used in the old Mark lodge connected with St. Aubyn's in Plymouth that is enclosed within an Arch, and in Saltash they still have the Irish style Arch on pillars into which a keystone is set before the Royal Arch ceremony begins. From both these items and the ritual of Antiquity, Bath, that we have examined it is surely clear that the discovery of a rejected keystone, its formal carrying to the 'secret arch of the vault' and its joyous and careful placing in its proper place was a degree that helped forward some part of the Mark tradition, when the remainder may have been but an undeveloped portion of the 2°. This too is a subject needing much further development.

Of the *Mark, Ark and Link* in its English and Scottish guise something has already been said above. Yet there was another view of these three closely knit degrees. Eric Deane once wrote of how these Irish practices were well known in Scottish ports that had close commercial connections with Ireland or with its military lodges. In these situations the degrees referred, in order, to the building of the *secret* chamber with its vaulted *arch*, the procuring of the *Ark* of the Tabernacle and its being set within the vault, and the erection of the sacred altar as the foundation of the ladder that *linked* heaven and earth. What is certain is that there are still Irish 18th century engravings showing an ark resting upon an altar within an arched vault. Nothing of these ceremonies has yet been found.

Finally there is the degree of *Architect* or *Grand Architect*. Both Carlile and the EGSR have quite full descriptions of these degrees which deal with the conditions immediately after the death of HAB. The loyalty and skill of the Marked Masters is now tested, the disposition of the work force in the plains of *Zarthan* is considered and the offices of RW, Senior and Junior Overseer at last appear. It can thus be seen why they should be in some way associated with the Mark degree.

c) We come now to the degree known as the *Fugitive Mark* which is based on a very old practice but hardly one that links it in anything but name with what we have come to recognise as a Mark degree. Its earliest known connection with Freemasonry is with a practice earlier referred to as the 'paper missive' mentioned in the Hudibrastick Poem of 1723. (See p. 34). Despite this very English connection this working was most prevalent in Ireland though it was taken up by the Irish-influenced 'Mark Lodges' in Lancashire and Cheshire (especially the Ashton Travelling Mark Lodge), and the degree was preserved in Scotland as the 12° EGSR.

It was there worked in an Ark Mariner Lodge (11°) and after the proceedings were declared open for the purpose of making Fugitive Markmen the Candidate took his obligation with his right arm aloft:

"I promise that . . . if I receive the mark of this degree I will immediately go to the sender and, if necessary, lend what assistance I can to him, and that I will never lightly or frivolously send the mark to anyone. This I promise under penalty of having help refused me in my utmost need."

Because this degree was usually employed when travelling away from one's home area it was sometimes called the *Travelling Mark* though this title did not cover the 'paper missive' aspect of the Fugitive. The secrets were as follows. The Sign was given by making a triangle, outwards from the front of the forehead, with the index finger of the right hand. The answer was given with the left hand in the same way. The mark was made by drawing a ▽ with the apex towards oneself and a special feature of this degree was the 'blank mark' which was made by doing the same with a blank piece of paper folded into a triangle and again duly positioned. The words were 'I call' replied to by 'I come'. The 'paper missive' was the despatching of the 'blank mark' by post or messenger to another mason with the sheet folded in a special way (see p. 35).

In the lecture the Candidate is informed that this degree took its special place in days of persecution when 'bigotry and intolerance used every effort at their command to injure our beloved institution'. Thus, if a Mason were to rest in an inn when pressed by pursuers and wanted to find another Mason he might catch another's attention, draw a ▽ on the table with the point towards himself and see whether the stranger did the same. If he did they could withdraw and talk together. Equally, if the Mason had suddenly to flee from the house of a brother he could leave an indication of where he had gone by putting his own mark in a triangle pointing his direction of flight and when possible the Mason who had been left should follow to assist further. It seems desperate stuff but with persecution in Ireland it was highly credible. Indeed it was not only in Ireland but also in Northumberland that there is evidence of this degree being used in circumstances of persecution. What the reader of this book must admit, however, is that this was not truly a Mark degree. It has now completely disappeared though G.W.E.Bridge says that something very similar was, or may still be, practised by the Chinese Hung Society.

It is time to move on to the *Babylonian and Jordan Pass* degrees. A good deal was said about the former of these workings when we looked at the early 19th century practices in Lancashire, Yorkshire and the North East of England. What might be added by way of showing how things developed elsewhere is to remark, first, that by the 1830s Carlile, in his reproduction of many Masonic degrees, showed a Mark Man ceremony that had in it 'Link' features such as the fall of a precious stone from the royal crown and Stodan 'recovering it and restoring it to its proper place' with his workmanship, or a Mark Master degree in which we still have the test of the 5 senses and the threefold descriptive name of the Almighty. – In addition he gives a quite separate and distinct degree of the *Red Cross Sword of Babylon* with a number of features that 19th century North of England Mark Masons would have called theirs. Let me be clear. I am not saying that this latter degree was *exactly like* the contemporary Babylonian Pass section of the Northern Old Mark working. On the other hand we have this rubric in the Carlile practice: 'Scene: *Babylon* with 2 towers, and a *bridge over the River* Euphrates ... A throne is placed in the east and behind it a transparency, descriptive of a *dream* of the *monarch*' (who sits there).

The monarch is now Cyrus but he starts the degree by saying that he has had a dream '*of a lion ready to devour me*, and, at a distance, *Nebuchadnezzar* and *Belshazzar*, my predecessors, in chains' and he intends to liberate the Jews. He therefore calls on his companions to *interpret* what he has seen. Moreover, he has a *visitor* who, though he is called Zerubbabel, makes a *request* for liberty *to return to Judaea* and assist in *rebuilding the Temple*. Need one mention more. For anyone to pretend, in the name of masonic 'amour propre' that these two ceremonies are totally different and distinct is to be wilfully myopic. They *are now* distinct and under different jurisdictions but we must acknowledge that in Irish eyes it was not always so. Once this story had a *Mark* relationship.

The mention of Zerubbabel takes up the second factor about these two Pass workings. Cyrus's decree which is recorded in Isaiah and Ezra enabled a party of Jews to travel safely through Babylon and Syria. Hence the 'Babylonian' name. Trouble ensued after that expedition to Judah and Zerubbabel had to petition a new king, or Darius, for a new passport. All that the king's companions could now do was to sanction the journey up to *the Jordan* (or Jewish) passage and hence the second name and degree. Moreover, when these adjuncts of the Old Mark became detached, they even acquired new names of degrees that I must not here stray into describing. I will simply say that the interested Mason should gain access to the degrees of Knight of the Sword, Knight of the East and Knight of the East and West in Scotland or the Allied degrees in England. He will then discover what these Pass degrees became.

d) Crossle was of the opinion that the *Black Mark* degree served the same purpose for Knight Templary as the 'Arch' ceremony did for the Royal Arch branch and the two Mark steps did for the Red Cross group, namely, to give some kind of *operative colouring* to what might otherwise be considered purely esoteric ceremonies. It seems to have appeared in Ireland as early as 1765 and from some Encampment there it was transferred to Scotland and thus re-appears in the EGS Rite with a complete outline of the ritual. A brief summary of this is as follows:

The Candidate enters in a white robe and with an inkhorn by his side. He is met by three lines of guards who each stop and question him as to his purpose, which is 'to approach the horns of the brazen altar'. The first line say "Pass", the second, "Wormwood" and the third, "Mark Angel".

The Candidate is then led to the Grand Commander for an obligation of which the penalty was 'to be thrust through the middle with a drawn sword'. A passage from Ezekiel is then read, Chapter 9, verses 1 to 8, in which 6 men, including a scribe with an inkhorn, come to execute God's judgement on all except those signed with a mark on their foreheads, and Ezekiel pleads for mercy. As Crossle admitted, the full purport of the passage and its underlying legend are lost in antiquity save that we have in Ezekiel someone firmly linked to the post-exilic scene and also foreshadowing the Christian dispensation.

The sign was as if holding out a sword towards another's middle, the grip is that used today by a Craft Mark Mason in Scotland, the Passwords are "Wormwood" and "Mark Angel" exchanged, and the word is "Ah, Lord God". The meeting was opened and closed in the name of Him who 'sitteth between the horns of the brazen altar'.

If we seem in such a ceremony a long way away from a carefully cut stone that was rejected, found and once more re-instated with its Mark, then at least we should take note that on a rare example of a Black Mark Mason Certificate issued in Edinburgh in 1821 we have a most intriguing Mark incorporating an H, B, rough triple tau and an anchor all surrounded by H.T.W.S. S.T.K.S. Certainly the Grand Master of the Temple in Scotland at the time, Alexander Deuchar, who signed it must have considered that Mark and Templar Masonry were properly juxtaposed.

The '*Knight of the Christian Mark*' (or 'Guard of the Conclave' as it is otherwise called) used exactly the same passage from Ezekiel though one of the knights and not the Candidate has the robe and inkhorn. Bro. Foster, in his paper on the Early Grand Encampments, declared that why this degree was included in any Rite was a mystery. Certainly it seems to have been first created by Pope Alexander for the formation of his personal bodyguard and the selection of its members from the Knights of St. John. The degree was worked in the U.S.A. and West Indies but the normal 'secrets' are not currently available. We do know that there were mottoes used by the Order – 'Christ reigns, conquers and triumphs' and 'King of Kings and Lord of Lords' – and it had a jewel with one old Mark facet, seven eyes engraved on a triangular plate on one side with the letter G in a fivepointed star on the other. Nonetheless this does seem to be on the extreme borderline between Mark and other degrees and is certainly a fitting point at which to end this part of our story.

Chapter Seven

The practice of Mark Masonry (1813–1853)

IT IS NOW time to leave the privacy of the ceremonial chamber and resume our story of how Mark Masonry was faring in the larger world. We saw in Chapter 5 that the Degree, or degrees, had a regular and wide acceptance across the whole of the British Isles as well as in North America. Those who in England followed the practice in Antients or even some Moderns lodges must have hoped that with the happy settlement of all differences between their separate Grand Lodges they would be able to promote still further this and other post-Craft ceremonial.

On 27 December 1813, such Brethren received a far from satisfactory Christmas present. Article II of the Union of the two Grand Lodges was quite explicit: "Pure Ancient Masonry consists of *three degrees* and no more. . . ." It is true that there was an attached clause permitting those in any lodge or chapter who met in the degrees of 'the Orders of Chivalry' to continue their assemblies but it was widely recognised that in England this might well mean the end of any *legal practice* of the Mark Degree in any form. As Handfield-Jones has written, this must have seemed like the start of a 'dark era' in Mark progress.

On the other hand just because the 'Union' agreement did recognise the propriety of the Knightly Orders it was virtually conceding the right within those Orders to practice such 'steps' as were required for admission to them. It has, for example, once more come to light that in the Knight Templar Conclave at Kingston-upon-Hull those who sought to become members had to be 'endowed' first with the degrees of 'Mark Past (or Mark Master), Past Master in the Chair, Superexcellent and Royal Arch'. It is in that context that at least *one major part* of the Mark Degree was preserved and continued after 1813. As J.A.Grantham once affirmed, all was possible provided it was not done openly in Craft..

The reader must have deduced from the range of rituals that have just been considered that it was far from being a time of Mark stagnation. As this Chapter will attempt to show the Mark degree was to reveal a steady will to persist and its practitioners were spread over as many areas as before. Indeed the amount of evidence for the continuing practice of Mark Masonry is so extensive that one cannot pretend to include it all. Yet for what is selected some form of ordered arrangement is necessary or one could be overwhelmed by the sheer volume of facts. I shall therefore tell this part of our story as it

1813-1855 Locations of Mark/Ram Degree
BERWICK
ALL OVER SCOTLAND
NEWCASTLE
DURHAM
SCARBOROUGH
YORK
HULL
WADDINGTON
BRADFORD
BOTTOMS
BOLTON
WIGAN
MOTTRAM
ASHTON
SHEFFIELD
NOTTINGHAM
NORWICH
KING'S LYNN
BIRMINGHAM
WOODBRIDGE
IPSWICH
MILFORD HAVEN
BRISTOL
BATH
LONDON
SHEPPEY
SOUTHAMPTON
PORTSMOUTH
SIDMOUTH
NEWPORT
LISKEARD
PLYMOUTH
REDRUTH

covers 4 regions in England and Wales and then Ireland, Scotland & North America.

(A) THE SOUTH-WEST.

It would seem highly appropriate that the continuance of the Mark degree in Redruth, Cornwall, should have been under the wing of the Knight Templar Encampment there. The Mark Book of St. John of Jerusalem No. 8 (No. 3 in 1824) shows that Brethren were made Mark Men, advanced in the degree of Mark Master, and given their personal mark, not only in 1806 and 1811, but also in 1814, 1816, 1819, 1820 and 1826. It is true that as, according to English custom, the Mark degrees were not required before being exalted as a Royal Arch Mason, so out of 71 Masons installed as Knights Templar in this period only 30 were entered as Mark Masons. What matters however is not the quantity but the fact that not only was Mark Masonry practised but that it was almost certainly performed in the way that had been formulated by Dunckerley. Moreover the loss of the first and last Minute Books of the Druids' Lodge, under which this KT Encampment was held, means that we cannot be sure that there were not more Masons who experienced the Mark step.

Sadly the Druids Lodge and its Encampment went into decline after 1828 when the guiding hand of John Knight was withdrawn with his death that year at the age of 87. It is hard to believe that all the men who had passed through the degrees of the Encampment would have ceased to practise 'higher' Masonry and we know that there were Encampments at Bideford, Barnstaple, Plymouth and Exeter for those willing to make the journey, quite apart from the more local Knights in those places.

There was, moreover, the 'independent' Friendship Mark Lodge that met at Devonport, and its Minute Book also records that not a few Cornish Brethren crossed the Hamoaze and Tamar rivers to be made Mark Masons there. What is even more intriguing is the evidence that some of the Friendship Mark Lodge members, under the leadership of a Bro. John Rogers, formed themselves into a *Travelling Mark 'team'* who would visit lodges in East Cornwall and confer the Mark ceremony under the 'shelter' of a Craft meeting. Two certificates issued by this 'team' are still extant. One of them is for Callington and the other, dated 1846, relates to the St. Martin's Lodge, at the Fountain Hotel, Liskeard. Some of the other wording was as follows: "We the W.C(ommander?), and S. and J.Overseers of the above Lodge do hereby CERTIFY that Edward Lyne ... has been advanced to the honourable Degree of Mark Master; and having received such proofs of his skill as justified us in declaring him worthy of Reward, as of old was apportioned, to the diligent in the works superintended by **H.T.W.S.** who **S.T.K.S.**, we strongly recommend him to all Mark Master Masons, as far as winds blow and waters roll throughout the habitable Globe ..." The Mark chosen is given – an Anchor and Cable – and the principal officer signs his name and office 'W.C.O.'. (See also p. 201)

In all 20 Brethren received the Mark degree in this one lodge alone and between March 1846 and October 1847 there were six meetings held for that purpose. These were held prior to the Craft meeting with John Rogers occupying the Chair 4 times. These meetings were of course in contravention of even the spirit of Article 2 of the Union and it could only be a matter of time before it reached the ears of those in authority in the Province. In November 1847 a letter was received by the Lodge which must have drawn the attention of its members to the nature of their practice and though 22 of the Lodge's 36 members were Mark Masons no further advancements took place and, rightly or wrongly, John Rogers, who had been a most regular attender, never came again. He was not the only one whose feelings on this matter ran high.

Whilst we thus know that the Friendship Lodge of Devonport was seeking to maintain the Mark Degree there are also various certificates issued through the Fortitude Lodge of Plymouth which point to the fact that the Mark was known and followed there even if infrequently. This is in no way to claim that there was a Mark Lodge or that those who carried out these ceremonies regarded themselves as creating such a body. It does suggest, however, that the influence of Dunckerley's original introduction of those ceremonies which were earlier discussed was not forgotten and that to advance to the Mark was part and parcel still of traditional Masonry. The tenacity of the Mark influence was such that a petition was lodged with the new Grand Mark Lodge as late as 1954 to obtain TI status for the present Fortitude Lodge of MMM but it was disallowed on the very proper grounds that practice of the degree long ago did not justify recognising a later unit as a lodge of antiquity. Again, however, we are presented with the fact that a *quarter of a century after the Union* the working of Mark ceremonies was still very much part of the far South-west scene.

In Sidmouth we have a singular example of the presence of the Mark in the period after 1818. It all began when the furniture of a local archaeologist came up for sale in 1883. A Bro. Passmore bought 'a curiously wrought stone' which seemed to have some Masonic connection but as it bore a different number to his Craft Lodge, Perseverance No. 164, he kept it in his own workshop. He presented it to the new Masonic Hall when it opened in 1890 but as it was still not thought to have any link with the Craft Lodge it was kept on a shelf in the Tyler's Room until 1935. In April of that year Bro. T.H.Andrew, who had been asked to uncover the history of the stone, gave a lecture on it to the Perseverance Lodge of MMMs No. 822. Since that date it has been proudly displayed in the Lodge room as a distinctive part of Sidmouth's masonic treasures.

The peculiarities of the stone are its design, its number and the letters A L. The only clue which Bro. Andrew had was the number (268) and if this was a Mark stone, albeit of unusual design, it could not have belonged to Perseverance Mark for that lodge only began in 1926, long after the stone's discovery. It also seemed odd if it belonged to the Mark Lodge presently bearing the same number because that was the Lathom Mark Lodge at Southport in West Lancashire. Some other explanation had to be provided.

The answer came when Bro. Andrews began to surmise that perhaps this stone was first shaped and used for *Mark ceremonies* in a Craft Lodge at Sidmouth in pre-Grand Mark Lodge days. After all, he reasoned, if a local archaeologist had it in his private possession in 1880 then it must have been disposed of, *after its previous use*, and been found or bought, prior to that date. On that reckoning it could easily have been in its original use in the 1850s. What was around masonically in Sidmouth at that time? The answer was: Perseverance Lodge (Craft) No. 164. This seemed a dead end until Bro. Andrew discovered that in 1814 the Perseverance Lodge was shown as No. 268 and meeting at East Stonehouse, Devon. He also realised that the Lodge's candlesticks also bore the No. 268. The Lodge was warranted in June 1813 as No. 213 but became 268 after the Union and moved in 1818 as such to the Cornish Inn, Ordnance Street, in nearby Devonport where we have already had occasion to remark on the ritual and practice of Mark Masonry. In 1824 the Lodge moved to Exmouth where it was known as 'Perseverance' and at last, in 1829, it reached its present home in Sidmouth, though in 1832 its number again changed to 190. The present number of 164 was granted in 1863.

What is evident from the above progress is that the stone obviously took its number in a Craft Lodge between 1814 and 1832. Since the original Lodge was an Atholl Lodge (hence AL) it was naturally allowed to work other than simply the Craft degrees and the fact that there is on some Scottish Mark certificates a shaped stone similar to the one in Sidmouth seems to confirm that this was a stone used in a Mark ceremony after 1814. The connection with the dockyard at Devonport – they first met in the *Golden Marine Inn* – also suggests that it was there, between 1818 and 1824, that such an object was carved and presented. What finally matters is that here again, in another corner of the West Country, we have the continued working of the Mark in a Craft Lodge long after the Union. What is more, we know that the Pirie and Friendship (Devonport) workings of the degree were closely related to Scottish Craft Mark ones and the same diamond shape on the stone is used to this day in the shorter Scottish ceremony. We shall see the same impact of Ordnance depots on a Mark stone when we come to the Isle of Wight.

We had occasion to refer in Chapter 5 to the change that took place in Bristol at the time of the Union when whatever was the arrangement previously for conferring the Mark degree had to be changed to suit the new situation there. In terms of organisation this meant the creation of a 'Mark Lodge' which could operate for that purpose and which was distinct from both the Craft and Knightly Order there. When the present Canynges Lodge of MMM was established in 1857 a resolution was passed that Brethren from the *Old Bristol Mark Lodge* should be 'regularly advanced to the legal rights and position of

MMMs (i.e. be re-advanced) ... the *usual advancement fee* of Two pounds sterling in their respective cases *being absolutely remitted*'.

There is now recent new evidence to suggest that we may learn what the ritual of the post-Union Mark Lodge may have been and thus discover where and how the Bristol Masons were able to establish this new body. What would be even more intriguing to uncover would be the previous arrangement and ritual used for some kind of Mark ceremony.

We know, for example, that in 1809 the Baldwyn Encampment communicated with the Grand Encampment in London and *consented to 'their rule* for so long as the latter kept to the *old customs and usages*. Should any deviation from the regular Proceedings take place, then Baldwyn Conclave would resume their Ancient Independence and Usage as hitherto observed'. One is led to wonder whether their present V° of the East, the Sword and Eagle had, through Irish influence, some section that resembled the 'Old York' working which then had to be altered, or was it that the Royal Clarence Lodge No. 68 had been the host to a Mark degree and it was this that had to change? Research in this is still continuing but what is clear is that Mark Masonry was alive and being practised in the period we are considering.

The same was also true of Bath. We have had ample opportunity to study the rituals of Antiquity and Royal Cumberland so it is evident that Mark activity was afoot in this period. As was said earlier the Antiquity ritual may have related to the degree being worked under the warrant of the Antiquity Encampment of Knights Templar whilst the Royal Cumberland Lodge was noted in a Minute of the Howe Mark Lodge, Birmingham as being, around 1820, 'one of the most distinguished Mark Lodges' in the country.

The Royal Sussex Lodge, Bath, was an Antients lodge that was established as late as 1812. That it practised the Mark is shown by the declaration of a Bro. Samuel Lazarus in 1857 that he took the Mark degree in this lodge in 1823 for, he continued, it 'worked all degrees in Freemasonry' under their Old Warrant. It is true that Mark Masonry did diminish in this city by the 1840s but the fact that there were still Mark Masons in evidence and ready to start a new Mark Lodge in 1857 shows that it never died.

Let us now move to the other end of the region and see what happened in Hampshire at this time. We know, of course, that the Friendship Chapter in Portsmouth continued the practice started by Dunckerley of admitting Brethren to the Mark and we even have the statistics that show how, in the years 1813 to 1844, 44 of some 76 members of the Chapter took the Mark steps. Those who did not were mostly naval and military officers who tended to be mere birds of passage, simply desiring to be exalted before proceeding abroad. From 1844 to 1868 the Chapter Minutes are missing and hence we cannot tell what was happening then other than to say that there must have been an ongoing stream of candidates, because in 1847, when the Mark Lodge was reconstituted, four of the Brethren made declaration, in open lodge and before the Wor. Master, that they had already held the office of WM *in the old Mark*

Lodge. They were thus allowed to resume the rank of Past Master. Two of these Brethren were advanced in 1844 and none of the four were in the Chair of 'Z' until after that year.

If there was a slight diminution of candidates for the Mark in the Friendship Chapter in the 1840s this would be because there were other ways of reaching that step close by. On the Isle of Wight, and in the earlier part of the 19th century, there were various lodges held in Newport, in connection with the military units stationed at the Albany Barracks and at Parkhurst. It was natural that the Brethren of these military lodges should fraternise with their civilian Brethren of the Regular Lodge there, which in 1822 took the name of Albany. It was in its contacts with the Minden Lodge, No. 63 on the Registry of the Grand Lodge of Ireland, that the idea of setting up an Albany Mark Lodge was formed. As was mentioned earlier (see p. 77) the XXth Regiment of Foot (now the Lancashire Fusiliers) had its depot in the island from 1842 to 1851.

The earliest document now possessed by the Albany Mark Lodge is an old dilapidated sheet of Government issue blue foolscap on which the following is written:

"The Officers who presided on this occasion (26 June 1848) assembled in accordance with a notice issued under the Warrant of the Mark Lodge attached to the Minden Lo ... whose members fraternally lent the necessary Ornaments, Furni^re^ and Jewels for the Ceremony, as also the elaborately sculptored (sic) Keystone presented to the Brethren of the XXth Reg^t^ before their leaving Bermuda to embark for Canada."

Consonant with their ritual their officers were 3 Overseers, a Conductor of Works, a Seneschal (sic), a Warder, S. and J. Attendants, an Outer Guard and a Senior Grand Warden (sic). The Key Stone was borne in procession by Mark MMs of the Regiment. The ceremony was opened by an address from the Master Overseer who expressed his conviction "that by fraternising with the Brethren of 176 (Albany) ... permanent and substantial advantages would accrue to the Lodges of the Sister Kingdoms, as whilst 176 could furnish commodious quarters and suitable accommodation No. 63 would reciprocate by advancing to this honourable degree those members of the Albany Lo. who were desirous of participating in the Light which rose from the Emerald Isle." It sounds rather as if the speaker in question, Lieutenant/Paymaster Armitage Eyre, was blessed with the gift of the Blarney.

That there were advantages to be gained is also shown by the other distinctive document in Albany's possession, a Mark Masons' Roll. This is made up of six sheets of parchment bearing the signature of each Brother when he chose his Mark. The top of the Roll is in cypher and then come 276 names for the years 1848 to 1876. The fact that there were 58 soldiers, coming from 20 different Regimental Lodges, and 218 civilians belonging to 53 Private Lodges, shows what a part this Lodge played in disseminating a knowledge of the Mark Degree around the world, at least throughout the British Empire.

The cypher passage on this Roll refers to the establishment of this Mark Lodge by Brethren who had all been enrolled as Mark Masons *abroad*. These included advancements in Canada, Gibraltar and Malta. The first 'muster for the enrolment of Candidates' was on 26 June 1848 and the positions of those taking part are interesting – The Overseers as the usual principal officers, the Seneschal (or Secretary) in the North, the S. and J. Stewards at the *right* of their respective Overseers, the Warder within, and the Tyler outside, *the Gate*.

The presence of these items and the vigour with which the Albany Lodge of MMMs now took off is all the more remarkable when you reflect that this was happening 35 years after a formal Act which was not aimed at confirming or encouraging the Mark Degree in England. What, of course, was also part of the picture was that in Ireland and Scotland the Mark Degree was now under the guidance of some Governing Body, and hence the Mark Masons owing allegiance there could act with both calm and confidence in promoting this ancient aspect of Operative Masonry. It was probably due to the close relations that existed between the Masons at the military depot and of the Albany Lodge that led to an assumption that Albany Mark Lodge had an Irish warrant. Such was not the case. It was a thoroughly independent body and yet it conducted its Mark Masonry with considerable aplomb. In 1850 there was a Minute for 7 March which shows that it was prepared *to re-consider its ritual and the clothing to be worn*, whilst on 17 February 1853 we read of a "general annual Muster of Mark Masons held *in the quarrie* of the Masonic Hall" and the original titles of officers are clearly still in place. We shall see in a later chapter what a *remarkable Tracing Board* they have still preserved. Mark Masonry in Hampshire was alive and well.

Though it is only a sidelight on our story I think it worth relating the later history of the Minden Key Stone. When the Regiment sailed for Canada the stone was left behind and in the keeping of the Lodge at their depot and when that was removed to Aldershot by 1857 the KS was also transferred. The Regiment then took the stone with them when they went to India and it was there, during the Mutiny, that the Lodge lost its warrant, its jewels *and the stone*. That was, in fact, the disaster which ended the Lodge's existence.

Many years later the stone was found in a remote village of Bengal and was restored by a local Mason – surely a very appropriate event for a Mark Keystone. A PM of Albany Lodge made a formal request that the stone might be returned to Newport as Albany was the last surviving Lodge that had a direct interest in it. The District Grand Master there, however, after making careful enquiries about it, decided that the Minden stone should remain as an honourable heirloom of their Grand Lodge. Whether it is still in their care and if so, where exactly, it would be interesting to discover. Considering that the leading figure amongst the Minden Lodge's founders was no less a figure than the Hon. Edward Cornwallis the stone has more than a passing interest for Freemasonry generally.

(B) THE MIDLANDS AND SOUTH WALES.

The Newstead Mark Lodge in Nottingham was already of age when the Craft Union occurred and I find it intriguing that on *the very day after* that significant event Bro. Wm. Ludlow occupied the Chair for the purpose of advancing six Candidates. He was to preside when more Mark Masons were made on 28 June 1814. These months were not mentioned merely by chance for the lodge seems to have met in them regularly thereafter. Indeed, in the December meeting in 1816 we are told that a Brother 'held the line of Mark Mason'.

There were meetings at irregular and infrequent intervals during the 1820s but after 1834 the Lodge resumed much more constant working. After 1838, with a Secretary appropriately named 'Smart', the Minutes are more complete, the times of opening and closing given, the names and *marks* of new members are given in full and we even have details of their Craft Lodges. In April 1839 the Lodge opened at 7, closed at 10 and five Candidates received the Mark Degree, four of them stated as belonging to the 9th Lancers. Like the Lodge in Newport the principal officers here were the Overseers, even if they are recorded as Master and Wardens.

From 1852 the minutes of the Mark Lodge were always signed by the WM of the Craft Lodge even though a Past Master might have occupied the Chair for the Mark business. This serves to highlight something that with all this Mark activity we can easily forget and that is that technically and legally the involvement of Craft Lodges in this Degree was 'ultra vires' and therefore needed to be discreetly veiled. This indeed may account for some of the lack of information that might otherwise be available in the records of older Lodges at this time. What is remarkable is the amount that we can still discover. It is therefore noteworthy when the Craft WM openly endorses these minutes.

For some years a keen Birmingham Mason called Bassett Smith had begun to visit Nottingham with a view to acquiring more Masonic knowledge and it was largely his enthusiasm and personal contacts that led to a quite new Mark development in what was still, at that date, a promising but developing town. In October 1850 a deputation from the Newstead Mark Lodge travelled to Birmingham and opened a Mark Lodge as requested by members of the St. Paul's and Howe Craft Lodges. The Lodge was held at the Town Hall Tavern, Arm Street, Birmingham when 15 members of those lodges – and here the wording is very significant – "were *initiated into and received* the *Mark Mason Degree* and they were *constituted a Lodge of Mark Masons* as belonging and *appurtinant* (sic) *solely to* the Howe Lodge No. 857 … holding their Warrant from the *Grand Lodge of England*." When you ponder for a moment what this meant in the light of Article II of the Union it is hard to believe that it was happening. Certainly it must make any impartial observer realise that contrary to the impression given that Mark Masonry was suffering a steady decline in this century we have here new and vibrant growth and all within the context of regular Craft Lodges.

What is more this new growth in another branch of Freemasonry well reflected the emergence of this great new borough of Birmingham which had just attained that status. So new was the whole Masonic venture there that because the Howe Craft Lodge had yet to establish itself fully the regular meetings of the Mark Lodge did not begin until 1854. That the connection with the Howe Craft Lodge was close is shown by the fact that all candidates for the Mark had to be balloted for there and it was to the Treasurer of the Craft Lodge that all fees and dues were rendered. The Mark Lodge proved an immediate success and Candidates came in a steady stream from Craft Lodges all over the Midlands.

New growth was also evident in South-west Wales during this period. A Bro. Coke who was made a 'Mark Man' in Redruth, Cornwall, is thought to have introduced the Mark to Swansea or the short-lived Mackworth Lodge at Cowbridge. Yet we have further evidence of Mark Masonry's spread.

The Loyal Welsh (Craft) Lodge was constituted at Pembroke Dock in 1824, the founders being mainly from Haverfordwest, close by, and *Devonport*, another naval dockyard. Yet as soon as 1 February 1827 'the Mark Degree was administered in this Lodge by Bros. Hutchings, Chappel and Augustus' to four brethren. Those who formed this first Mark 'lodge' were from the Brunswick and Friendship Lodges of Devonport and we have already seen that Mark Masonry was being practised there. So keen was the interest in this new degree that on 13 February six more Craft Masons were made 'Mark Men' and paid the now statutory fee of 2/6d which was, say the Minutes, 'appropriated on St. Mark's Day for refreshments'.

The officers mentioned in the Minutes for these two occasions were PCO (Thomas), CO (Hutchings), SO (Chappel), JO (Weir), SD (Gale) and JD (Rundell). What is intriguing about this arrangement is that only two of the above were apparently Mark Masons before the meeting began and the others had to be admitted to the Degree in which they were also acting as officers. The fact that Augustus is not mentioned suggests that perhaps he was acting as DC to ensure that all was done aright and doubtless, since we know the working practised at Friendship in Devonport, Bro. Thomas was a PM of the Craft Lodge who could quickly learn what he had to do in the role of P(rincipal)C(ommander)O(verseer). It is interesting that Hutchings was the C(onductor)O(verseer) and hence able to guide the candidates through the ceremony. The JO and Deacons would also be briefed in their modest duties. All would no doubt take the obligation when required.

The Mark Degree seems to have steadily progressed here with senior Brethren from St. Bride's Lodge, Milford Haven and Cambrian Lodge, Haverfordwest attending Loyal Welsh 'to be promoted to this Honourable Degree'. They obviously did not work the ceremony in their own lodges. The Mark meetings were not all minuted in full for reasons already noted elsewhere but there is no doubt that Brethren were being advanced up to the last entry in

1857 which was when the new Grand Mark Lodge had come into existence. A Provincial Grand Master for the Mark in South Wales was appointed and other steps to promote Mark Masonry here and elsewhere began to be taken.

Of further interest here, and to show how carefully records were kept when the Mark was mentioned, we know that the Marks of those who were advanced and the ones adopted by the earliest of the entrants mainly reflect the emblems that appear on the ancient floorcloth that Loyal Welsh is still proud to possess.

We know too that when Brethren were due to be raised to the 3° or advanced to the Mark they had to be proposed by the WM of the Craft Lodge and in each of those cases they were also balloted for afresh. In the beginning Brethren went straight from the MM Degree to the Mark but as time passed it became necessary for them to be PMs and it was in that step that they would encounter a Plumbline ceremony that is now employed regularly by those Installed in the Mark Chair. When this was the rule the candidate came in clothed as a PM with the **TAU** reversed. The evidence of this symbol elsewhere in Mark Masonry, and not least in the Dunckerley working that would have been known in Plymouth and Devonport, has already been drawn to the reader's attention but it is remarkable that to this day the Loyal Welsh Lodge still have W. Bro. Thomas's apron with this feature showing as an impression.

On entering the Lodge Room the candidate would remark its triangular arrangement, for the principal officers sat in the East, South-west and North-west, which has of course been retained in the Ark Mariner Degree. The candidate perambulated five times to prove his possession of the five senses and he was then introduced to the Cypher alphabet by the use of the 'lines parallel' sign and its explanation.

It is of further interest that to this day in West Wales there are some Mark Masons who still use variants of the usual letters seen on the Stone, and in the Mark working at Pembroke Dock the later form was H.T.W.S.S.T.K.S.O., a form then used in some parts of Scotland. In addition there was no lost or rejected keystone but simply a substituted one, yet Bro. Cousins, who has done a great deal of research in this area, recounts how he was given a special type of keystone used in this lodge. It had no lettering, possibly some old marks and one of the lower corners was broken off. Similarly damaged stones are also held by two other local brethren and Bro. Cousins writes: "It is possible that these show that a rejection did occur or the stone was lost in *Sheldron Brook*." One is sorely tempted to believe that 'Sheldron' was a local misappropriation of 'Kidron'. What is also fascinating is that when, before the closing, the WM asked whether any brother had ought to propose for the good of Masonry the Brethren would respond with the loud response 'GOODWILL'. Was this again a local variant of 'MARK WELL'?

We conclude our journey in the Midlands with a visit to Cheshire. That is a fitting thing to do for the work that we are now to describe in this period was that of what is now the "Ashton *District* TI Mark Lodge". Previously it had various names – the Travelling Mark Lodge, the East Cheshire Mark Lodge, the Dukinfield Mark Lodge and, from the fact that its meetings were almost invariably held on a Sunday, the Sunday Mark Lodge. Its most distinctive feature was its mobility. In Cheshire and South-east Lancashire there were some 20 Craft Lodges that received this body of Mark Masons in rotation. When received, its senior members took over the Chairs and conferred the Mark and its appendant degrees. A map of the places visited is given later. (See p. 228).

As was mentioned in Chapter 5 there are references of visits to these Craft Lodges from the latter parts of the 18th century and these are valuable since the earliest records of the Ashton Travelling Lodge have still not been found. What is certain is that from 1830 there were by-laws which confirm the regular existence and functioning of this unit not only as a Masonic instruction body but also as a Friendly Society and Burial Club for its members. Those members may well have been Masons who had hitherto worked the Mark and other ultra-craft degrees in a free-lance manner. One tradition of its foundation was that in the 1790s a non-commissioned officer who had received the Mark degrees in India gathered like-minded East Lancashire and West Yorkshire brethren together to confer these steps on any lodge members who sought their assistance. That tradition still needs further research.

What is much more certain is that this Lodge had a Master and 2 Wardens but no Overseers (as the ritual given earlier showed), it met normally in some location on a Sunday afternoon, and it conferred also the Mark, Link and Ark; Red Cross or Babylonian Pass; and the Wrestle degree.

One of the distinctive local features of this Mark activity is the information gained from cypher-inscribed church memorials that are still extant in this area. One of these is the plaque in the Parish Church of Ashton-under-Lyne which commemorates JOHN POSTLETHWAITE 'who sustained the highest Orders of Masonry without becoming PROUD'. He died in February 1819 'preserved from indigence by the bounty of his friends in 562'. The latter number referred to the Minerva Lodge of the same town, and Postlethwaite was not only WM there but was the first Master of Loyalty Lodge at Mottram-in-Longdendale. Both these lodges were on the regular circuit of the Travelling Lodge.

Yet the most important such record is the tombstone of Thomas Brierley. He grew up as one of nine sons in the neighbourhood of Strines where all of them were eventually employed in the calico printing works that is still functioning there. Thomas was initiated in the Lo. of Benevolence at Marple in 1821 and the Marple historian, Joel Wainwright, states that Brierley 'was very learned and advanced in the mysteries of Masonry'. From our point of view it is worth remarking that both his Lodge and the Lodge of Union at Ashton which he attended for Chapter were also regular visiting points for the Travelling Lodge. Anyone who wonders about the prevalence of the Mark and its cypher language at this stage and in this area should examine not only Brierley's headpiece (he died in 1854) but other items such as the Wilde tombstone in Mottram churchyard, commemorating a father and son who died in 1827 and 1853, and the curiously sculptured stone of 1828 made by Azariah Ollerenshaw for the Lodge of Benevolence. Both these items, like Brierley's, were covered with the characters of a cypher form used only by the Sunday Mark Lodge. In the light of all that has been said about the 'Arch' ceremony earlier it is worth recording that the latter stone depicts two pillars (J and B) *supporting an arch* which contains a prominent Keystone on which is a letter G and on the arch in cypher are the words 'TAKE FAST HOLD OF INSTRUCTION'.

There is more. The Lodge of Benevolence that used to meet at Marple has, beside Brierley's Certificate, a framed drawing known as the Johnson diagram that is recognised as an exquisite piece of penmanship. In the centre are the 5th and 6th chapters of the Book of Ezra, all in the Travelling Mark Lodge cypher. The writing is flanked on either side by numerous Masonic symbols and emblems identifiable with Mark and other grades. There is a Lewis, four steps lead up to the altar, two square pillars *support a rounded Arch* with a very narrow keystone and beneath it is an All-seeing Eye. Was this, one wonders, another form of the kind of 'instruction diagram' that we saw above with Ollerenshaw's stone? Certainly this view is strengthened by the existence of the Pickford Diagram, and the Royal Forest Lodge stone which we shall encounter in the next section.

The Pickford drawing belongs to the year 1838. It is, in its perfect execution, a partner of the Johnson diagram, but it has this important difference, that this deals *with the Mark Degree only*. It uses the Mark cypher of the Travelling Lodge and it has the Master's Mark in a form which is used by no other known Mark Lodge. △ It was so named because the drawing was presented to a Bro. James Pickford of the Lodge of Industry which was again on the roster of the Travelling Lodge.

Since the photograph of this diagram disappeared with J.A.Grantham's personal effects it is good that he once described it.

"At the top of this diagram, which measures $11\frac{3}{4}''$ by 15″, are depicted 12 Masonic emblems in two lines. From left to right in the first line are the VSL; Square and Compasses; Level; Plumb Rule; 24″ Gauge, Compasses and Protractor with irradiated Sun in the centre. From left to right in the second line are the Chisel; Maul; 3 stave Ladder; Hour Glass; Anchor; and Crossed Keys.

"Line three gives the date in AD and AL, whilst line four gives an exposition by diagram of *three forms* of the Mark Cipher which are then explained in lines five, six and seven (The details of this will be given in the chapter on ciphers.) Lines 8 to 11 when decoded read:

"JAMES PICKFORD LODGE/OF INDUSTRY No. 465. GRAPES/INN GEE CROSS CHESHIRE/DECEMBER TWENTY FIFTH 1838."

The Mark letters used in the Travelling Mark are given in line 12. Line 13 gives the numerals 1 to 0 and also depicts *the nine-chamber* and *four-chamber* keys in a manner **which calls to the minds of those conversant, certain arcana formerly connected with the Mark Cipher**. (Quite what Grantham was here referring to has still to be unravelled.)

"The central position of lines 14 and 15 is occupied by the 'Mark Monogram' peculiar to the Travelling Lodge".

Alongside this diagram we also need to place one that was presented by a certain John Ford of Glossop. Ford was a member of Loyalty, at next door Mottram, and he has signed the back of this document but added no date. Though similar to the Pickford in its use of the 12 emblems at the top it is otherwise arranged and certain portions in the original still show traces of colourwash. If we wonder why these 12 symbols were employed the most likely explanation is that they represent the marks of the Overseers of the 12 Tribes of Israel each of whom had his own especial mark.

The oldest example of Sunday Mark certificates that we have as yet is one dated 18 April 1849. This is peculiar because its recipient was a Charles Britnor who was not even *Initiated into the Craft* until Sept. 1849 and the Travelling Lodge did not decide to have this type of certificate printed until January 1858. It was in April 1858 that this kind of Certificate was finally approved during a visit to Loyalty Lodge. Yet Britnor was not then advanced to the Mark. What then does all this mean?

The probability is that when Certificates were being issued on 18 April 1858 Britnor requested that he should have one as a Mark Mason of long standing. This was important as English Lodges working the Mark under warrant from the *Supreme Grand Royal Arch Chapter of Scotland* **and** the *newly-formed Grand Mark Lodge of England* were themselves now issuing Certificates and such a document was becoming increasingly vital. Britnor may well have seen the Secretary about to complete **18 April** *with 1858* and stopped him, pointing out that he was made a Mark Mason soon after his initiation in 1849. The Secretary not wanting to waste one of the new Certificates simply added a different year, **1849**. The circumstance is a salutary one for all masonic students. Do not always take what is written down as final confirmation of what is the case.

The final stage of the Travelling Mark Lodge's story must be told in Chapter 9: but before we leave this County of Cheshire we ought to record the fact that it was Cheshire Brethren, who had entered the Mark Degree at the Sunday meetings, who now desired to start what would eventually be some of the oldest Mark lodges on the new Grand Lodge list. These are the Joppa and Fidelity Lodges of Birkenhead and the Benevolent Lodge at Stockport. Though the members who formed Joppa were to seek a Scottish warrant before they could be established and the Fidelity brethren were to find themselves confronting their 'Mother' lodge, the fact remains that it was due to the instruction they had all received *prior to 1855* that such ventures into a new Masonic phase were due. In maintaining the traditions and precepts of the Mark degree, when it might otherwise have begun to fade, the Travelling Mark Lodge had made an invaluable contribution. That its pupils now sought more stability and identity can only testify to its beneficial influence.

(C) THE NORTH AND NORTH-EAST.

That influence can immediately be detected in this area also. One writer on Freemasonry in Oldham at this time speaks of the Travelling Mark Lodge loading its paraphernalia on to a horse and cart and proceeding to the next place where it was to meet under a Craft Lodge banner. Such was the case with the Lodge of Friendship there. This Lodge had been started in 1789 and, interestingly, the Founders included three Irish and one Scottish mason. The early history of the Lodge presents a distinctly Antients or Irish atmosphere. Whether some of these Brethren felt that they were working under the wrong banner is not known for sure but it is revealing that the WM, an Irishman, and two of the earliest initiates, took an active part in serving the 'Grand Lodge of All England at York' within 15 months of establishing Friendship. It is therefore no surprise to find that after the Union accommodation was made, albeit discreetly, for more than just the Craft degrees.

In 1838 it was at an Emergency Meeting attended by Masons from Denton, Mottram, Ashton-under-Lyne, Dukinfield, Bury and even Liverpool that Friendship entertained a Travelling Lodge team. Of the 7 candidates 'Made Mark Masons' four were members of the Friendship Lodge and three were from the visitors. That was in May, and in August the Minutes record that one of the Friendship Brethren 'Passed the Chair' and took the Mark in the Duke of Atholl Lodge in Denton. Though there are no further references in the Friendship Minutes to such activities we know from the Minutes of the Travelling Mark Lodge that it came regularly, if not frequently, to Oldham for the next 20 years.

In Salford the Minutes of the oldest Lodge there record that on 29 July 1822, *being a regular Lodge night*, 'The Lodge opened on the first, second and third degree of Freemasonry when Bro. Aronbee Past Chair (sic) and Bro. Grundy, Bro. Pinnington, Br. Lee of this Lodge and Bro. Cooke 670 was initiated in the degree arch, mark and link masonry' (sic).

It is a similar story in Bury, with its long tradition of Freemasonry. In three of its oldest Lodges we see the Mark and related degrees being worked throughout this time. The Prince Edwin Lodge Minutes refer to the Ark, Mark and Link ceremonies and there is, not surprisingly, mention of a 'Red Cross Encampment', thus confirming what we have already seen in rituals used in this part of East Lancashire.

In the Lodge of Relief, No. 42, a 'Moderns' Lodge in origin, there are records of 11 meetings between 1834 and 1847, of brethren 'Passing the Chair' and 6 of these also add the Ark, Mark and Link degrees. Two of the latter occasions were joint gatherings with the Prince Edwin members. A sample of what occurred is given on 10 November 1844 when a Lodge of Emergency was called and 9 members 'Passed the Chair & were Saluted in due form, following which 11 members took the Ark, Mark, Link and Wrestle Mason'. The first nine were amongst the latter eleven.

We also note that in the Lodge of St. John, No. 191, we have this entry: "11 June 1846. Lodge then opened to PM Degree at 7 p.m. & the following Brethren pass the chair (3 names). The Lodge then opened in Mark Masonry & same brethren *recd. Mark Masonry at 8.5.* The Lodge was then closed to the Second Degree & Brother Wm. Pitfield passed to the Degree of a Fellow Craft."

At Farnworth near Bolton we have the earliest recorded Minute of the Ark, Mark, Link and Wrestle ceremonies when an Emergency Lodge was opened on 29 April 1821. This was in the St. John's Lodge, No. 325, which was warranted in 1809, and like several other lodges in the Bolton area this was an isolated reference. The suggestion was made by Norman Rogers that this evidence suggests *another Travelling Lodge* which was *based on Bolton* and held meetings between 1818 and 1855. As we have already seen this teaching method used in three parts of the country there is no reason why it should not have been the case and it would be useful to research this matter further.

Certainly we have ample reason to refute any notion that Mark Masonry in some form or another was in decline on the west of the Pennines. We had occasion in the last chapter to examine the ritual at Bolton which was handed on by Bro. Brockbank and he had been advanced to the Ark, Mark and Link as well as receiving the Master's Mark and *Red Cross of Babylon* degree in the Lodge of Charity, Ringley Bridge in 1848. Something of the same must have been true for Bro. Clough whom we mentioned in regard to the distinctive Blackburn working that was worked as late as 1874. We know that in Perseverance Lodge in the 1840s there was the custom for *every* Brother to 'pass the Chair in the fourth degree' and become a Mark Mason. There are repeated references to the symbols chosen and on one occasion there is even a detailed account of how the Mark Masons Lodge was conducted.

In the light of this information we are less surprised when a future Member of Parliament for Pontefract, N.Le Gendre Starkie, announced at his raising in February 1826 that he intended 'to pass the Chair', *in order*, says the Minute, '*to qualify him to become a Mark Mason*'. At that time, says the Lodge historian, an *almost invariable rule.*

As that was happening in Burnley so the same was happening in Colne, which lies next door and on the very border with West Yorkshire. Up to 1814 it seems very likely that in the Royal Lancashire Lodge there the Mark Degree was practised in, or immediately following, the 2° whilst the Exaltation ceremony was linked with the 3°. In 1826 Bros. Hayes and Dyson Passed the Chair and then received the Mark and *both* 'chused' the Square and Compasses for their mark. Here also it was early on Sunday mornings that brethren locally and from Yorkshire attended to receive the Mark, Chapter, KT, the Ancient (and Accepted) Rite, Ark Masonry, Allied and others. It is no wonder that anyone standing in their lodge room today has an evident sense of antiquity. Freemasonry in all its many forms has long impregnated the place where the brethren gather.

Over the Pennines the same impression is in no way abated. We begin in a Craft Lodge which lies on the very edge of the Province of West Yorkshire and has the name Royal Forest 401. It first began at Slaidburn in the Forest of Bowland in 1829 but has now moved to the village of Waddington which is in Lancashire. As one of its precious possessions the Lodge displays 'a curious masonic stone' that used to be kept in a cupboard at Slaidburn and only opened up for certain lodge meetings. The story goes that it was first found discarded in the River Hodder at Slaidburn but no one seems to know why it was left there or what led to its recovery.

The stone, however, which measures 3ft by 2ft is too finely carved, coloured and illustrated to permit its having been made haphazardly and when we set it against other similar carved stones in this part of England there does seem to be a possible reason behind it.

What leads one to believe that it was made for this very Lodge that now possesses it is the 9" high Crown flanked by laurel leaves thus indicating **ROYAL FOREST**. Moreover we are told that the plinth is of York stone and *used to rest on wooden pillars 3' high.* Since the stone's frame is an Arch on two short pillars this has obvious implications, especially when we compare the symbols on this stone with, say, the grave stone of Thomas Brierley of Mottram.

There too we have a pillared Arch with a prominent Keystone, the implements of the Craft degrees, the Mark, the Royal Arch, the Knights Templar, and the Knights of Malta. All these also appear on the Royal Forest Stone. The only significant differences are that Brierley's stone has cypher writing and a sign of the Rose Croix, whilst the Forest stone refers to a Knight of Philippi.

It would seem that this stone was made use of in Slaidburn when a Travelling team came to the Lodge to perform the appendant degrees. That would explain why no mention of the latter is made in the Lodge minutes. Eventually, when either the Travelling team ceased to visit after the formation of the Grand Mark Lodge and other degree bodies or when the Craft Province expressed its displeasure at such ceremonies in a Craft lodge, the stone was discarded in the nearby stream. In true Mark fashion, however, its craftsmanship was later recognised and it was recovered and placed in its honoured position as it is today.

We must move on, however, into another nearby part of West Yorkshire. The story of the Prince George Lodge up to its removal to Bottoms in 1812 was told earlier but following the Union the Mark ceremonies there in no way altered. By 1838 there were separate Minutes for the Mark, and there would eventually be a Prince Edward *Mark* Lodge, but such was the esteem in which the Mark Masons in this place were held that around 1856 the Brethren in London negotiated with them *for their consent* to the founding of the new Grand Lodge. What is of especial importance is that this Lodge was attended by both candidates and visitors from Leeds, Wakefield, Halifax, Huddersfield, and Rochdale. Interest in Mark was widespread and constant.

In Bradford the members of the Lodge of Hope, No. 302 as we learnt in Chapter 5, were firmly of the opinion that under Article II of the Act of Union *the legality of Mark Masonry had been conceded.* Whether one looks at 1794, 1810, 1830 or 1831 the same attitude to the Mark seems to prevail. Bro. Scholefield who attended the Lodges of Reconciliation *to ascertain the position of the Lodge with regard to the Mark Degree*, reported that, by *authority of the Grand Master* and arrangements then come to, *the Lodge of Hope was entitled to continue to confer the Mark* under the authority of the Old York Manuscript Constitution, which has uninterruptedly been done until the Mark Lodge enrolled under the Grand Lodge of MMMs as the Old York TI Lodge. This is impressive evidence and quite apart from the implications for other old Lodges that also continued their Mark ceremonies after the Union it emphasises the immense regard that was afforded to the Mark Degree when all eyes might reasonably have been focussed on the Craft Degrees and the Holy Royal Arch. Is it any wonder that it was in this lodge that a PM refused to take the Chair and work a 'new ritual' when this ancient Mark unit at last joined the new Grand Mark Lodge. What was one of his most grievous concerns was that the new form required a lodge to be opened in the 3° when hitherto the Mark was always given between the FC and MM ceremonies. When he was asked to surrender the Red Cross element as well that was too much to accept. That the tradition was authentic is shown by the inclusion in the 1852 Mark Register of that same Bro. Scholefield who had journeyed to London 40 years before.

As one might have surmised from the list of visitors to the Lodge at Bottoms the Mark Degree had been practised in Leeds throughout the period before us. In a Minute of the Craft Lodge of Fidelity which had been constituted in 1792 we read: '6 September 1821. After the Lodge had been regularly opened in the 1°, 2° and 3°, a Mark Masons Lodge was opened and closed and then the Lodge was afterwards closed in harmony at 11 p.m. (Nine) Brothers received Marks.' Whilst in February 1842 Mark Masons' Certificates were signed in a meeting of the Craft lodge.

Ten years later in York the Union Lodge was meeting at the Merchant Adventurers Hall in Fossgate. The Cavalry Regiment stationed locally was the Inniskilling Dragoons and though at that particular moment, 1852, there was no Lodge in a Regiment which had had a series of 4 previously, there were Officers and NCOs who visited the Union Lodge during that year. Following some conversation there an Emergency Lodge was held 'for the purpose of conferring the Degree of Mark Master Mason'.

The lodge was opened by Captain Barbour as RWM, assisted by 7 other brethren, all of whom were members of the Dragoons. They were Masons from Ireland or Scotland and some were members of both Constitutions. The degree was conferred on 15 members of the Union Lodge and one other military person. The later Minutes are signed by both Capt. Barbour *and* the WM of Union Lodge and they are the only Mark Minutes appearing in the Craft Lodge book. Thereafter a separate Mark record was kept and on 26 September 1853 a Bro. James Melrose was advanced. He was to attain the age of 100 and in 1923 turned up to celebrate his 70 years in Mark Masonry. The lodge at first met when required but eventually met more regularly: it is a lodge that has retained throughout its original music for hymns and chants.

In Kingston-upon-Hull the Minerva Lodge continued, after as before the Union, to advance candidates in a steady stream. It still possesses a full set of Minutes and Registers and shows that any suggestion of a diminution in the practice of the degree is quite misguided. What is striking is that it was not alone in its promotion of the Mark. In addition to Minerva there were 2 other lodges – the Rodney which closed in 1820 and the Phoenix which lasted until 1834. There are references to the Mark Degree in the Minutes of the latter and they show that this ceremony was held on Sunday evenings. Hence we learn how on 31 October 1819, the Lodge was opened in the 2°, when, 'at the request of the WM, Bro. Seymour, late WM of the Humber Lodge No. 73, attended for the purpose of initiating several members of this Lodge into the degree of Mark Mason, when the following brethren accordingly took the same in the most solemn and impressive manner ...' The fee required was 5/-.

The Humber Lodge was clearly well acquainted with the degree and on 2 June 1829 it is recorded in the Craft Minute Book that a MARK lodge was held. What is very revealing, and would probably relate also to the Minerva and perhaps Rodney practice, is that, after 1830, Advancements were made under the Craft Warrant *as a distinctive part of the 2°*, the qualification being that the Candidate was a Fellow Craft. There was also much emphasis laid on MARK MASONRY in the lectures that were given in the Craft Lodge. The fact that the Humber Lodge was an Atholl Lodge and its records are complete from 1809 means that we can see plainly just what the reaction here was to any Union attempt to quash or minimise this distinctive part of Masonry. Of the place and value of the Mark in the other seaside centre of Scarborough we shall hear more when we examine the old Tracing Board that is still preserved there.

Moving further north it has to be admitted that despite the early reference to the Mark in Durham, we do not seem to have any other mention of it in the Marquis of Granby records. It is of course possible that something was being practised in the Fellow Craft degree, as elsewhere in the older lodges, but it may be that those who sought this ceremony were drawn to Sunderland where the Joppa Encampment could provide a form of Mark and other degrees. This too is matter for still further study and research.

In Northumberland the Mark was connected with both Craft and Knight Templary. John Strachan, the Masonic historian here, writes as follows:

"In the early days certain other Orders and Degrees to which Freemasons alone could be admitted, were worked in connection with Lodges and Chapters, and the right of such working is acknowledged by the Articles of Union ... Their history is so interwoven with that of the Craft and Royal Arch that to *ignore their existence and working would not only be a piece of affectation* but would deprive a history of Northumbrian Masonry of much of its value."[1] He went on to illustrate this by showing that on 10 August 1814, at the first meeting of the Provincial Grand Lodge, members of the Craft Lodges were joined by Royal Arch and Knight Templar Masons "that all misunderstanding may be removed ... *so soon after* the Articles of Union had been entered into". Article II, he added, has been frequently misinterpreted.

That the Mark degree was known and practised in and around Newcastle in the post-Union period is now accepted but as there has been no history of either the Royal Kent Encampment or the Northumberland & Berwick-upon-Tweed TI Mark Lodge we are still without any details of how this continuance was maintained. What we do know is that on 30 August 1852 the Mark Masons *held their annual meeting* at the Stockwell Arms, Nelson Street, Newcastle. The fact that this was already an established event shows that the Mark must have been in good heart and well supported and the fact that in 1851 we have an actual example of the Certificates issued to Mark Masons thereabouts also confirms this impression. We do, of course, know of two styles of ritual – the Old Mark, sometimes called 'St. Mark' or 'Holy St. Mark', and the Chair Master's Degree – that were practised in the area in this period, but it would be helpful to be able to relate those more precisely to the bodies that used them. Time has not been available to make further investigation into this portion of our story but that more could be discovered by further research locally I am certain.

(D) EAST ANGLIA & THE SOUTH EAST.

On 23 August 1819 the Duke of Sussex came to Norwich as Grand Master to install the Provincial Grand Master. It seems somewhat ironic that following such a visit, and the Union that his presence represented, we should read in the Minutes of the *Union Lodge* in that City that from this time the degrees of Royal Arch, Knight Templar, Ark and Mark (in that order) were being regularly conferred under their Craft Constitution. Mention was made earlier of Meyer Levi and his mark, as shown in the Mark Register of this lodge, and in a later chapter we shall give details of the jewels he made. What is of interest here is that whilst most of the jewels have 9 letters, **S.K.O.I.H. T.H.W.S.**, two of them have *only 7.* Moreover the letters are almost identical with those used on the Royal Arch pedestal and we can see the logic of that in the light of what was said in the chapter on ritual.

It is simply not credible that what took place in this ancient Lodge was not reproduced in the equally old lodges of Kings Lynn and Great Yarmouth, especially as Philanthropic Lodge at the former place was an Atholl Lodge by origin and was to have a Charter Master who assisted in the formation of the breakaway Grand Lodge of Wigan.

There is certainly no mention of the Mark or similar degrees in the almost complete Minutes of the British Union Lodge No. 114 at Ipswich but the members there were in amity with St. Luke's Lodge in the same town and that was an Atholl foundation. Moreover it is again inconceivable that a place which produced 'Noah' Sibley (see pp. 377) could not have been familiar with the appendant degrees. There was of course a KT 'Encampment of Prudence' at Woodbridge belonging to the Royal York Lodge of Arch Masons and it was only in 1840 that this body was wound up and its effects bought by the British Union Lodge. The intimations of places where the Mark would be practised are therefore present and some more study of these clues may well reveal what has been seen so clearly across the rest of the country where ancient Freemasonry had long flourished.

Even in the Metropolis, where the remit of the Grand Lodge would more surely run, we have the evidence that in the Old Kent Lodge, No. 15, the Mark Degree was regularly practised so that when in 1857 there was a petition to the new Grand Mark Lodge for enrolment the existing 20 members were all granted confirmation of 'their rights and privileges as regularly registered Mark Masters'. Another Mark Lodge of this period was one that met in Southwark and had sought recognition and legitimacy by its appeal to Scotland for a warrant. It was given the number '11' and to this day the Overseers' pedestals, and the aprons used during the examination, bear that number. The lodge also possesses a set of the older type of aprons that were used, here and in the lodge at Newport in the Isle of Wight, and which will be explained in the later section on regalia.

It is therefore not surprising that as we come to the close of this post-Union period there should have been a growing interest in a form of Freemasonry that had been preserved and which seemed to have so much to offer as part of the whole Masonic fabric. The approach to Scotland and the effect that that had on London Masons in particular is part of our next chapter but here we have to underline the fact that it was the incidence and the spread of familiarity with Mark Masonry that made the creation of a Grand Mark Lodge both more possible and more necessary. Had the situation in England and Wales been as bleak as some previous writers, especially Springett and Handfield-Jones, have suggested it is hard to see why its eventual progress should have been so fruitful.

Before we pass to that important moment in the life of the Mark Degree, however, it is essential that we should look at the contributions made to the maintenance of Mark Masonry in Ireland, Scotland and North America.

(i) IRELAND

Continuing the story here from where we left it in Chapter 5 we have to recognise that if we are wanting to discover the Mark degree then we have to accept that it was either disguised under various other titles or was divided amongst several other ceremonies, and these had not so far coalesced as to provide something recognisable as the Mark that we know today. Being separate these 'degrees' bore titles unfamiliar to us and hence the attempt made to explain these in the chapter on ritual. (pp. 156f)

What this explains, of course, is why students of Irish Freemasonry have often been puzzled by the apparent absence of any reference to ceremonies that must surely have been known and worked. Crossle makes the point in regard to the 'Red Cross' degree. This, he says, "is not once referred to in the Minutes of (Lodge) 163, Birr. Yet this old Irish degree was well-known and better preserved at Birr (one of Ireland's oldest lodges) than in any other place in Ireland. With them it was worked under the general name of RA(rch) – witness George Mitchell's certificate dated 1819 and his (reversible) apron of the same period." This latter shows *on one side* a pillared Arch with a strongly outlined Keystone over symbols of everything from Apprentice to Royal Arch including a Maul and chisel, whilst *on the other side* is a bridge over a river, with a serpent-entwined Cross on it, as in the Knight of the East degree at Bristol to this day.

It is this tradition which was one of the strands that Irish Masons brought to Lancashire, and points further East, in the early 19th century and which explains the so-called 'quaint' workings of the Mark with the dream of an eastern monarch, whether Nebuchadnezzar or Cyrus.

Stephen Forster, who has studied this matter constantly over the last decade, has made this point firmly:

"The rituals, ceremonies and degrees worked by Encampments holding of the Early Grand Encampment of Ireland were not of a standardised series, and while the progression of Past Master, Excellent, Super-Excellent, Royal Arch was the common, it was by no means the only, series employed. From existing certificates, a Mark ceremony appears to have been associated with the Red Cross degrees of Knight of the Sword, Knight of the East and Knight of the East and West." He continues: "At the formation of the Supreme Grand Encampment of Ireland in 1836 the Red Cross ceremonies were taken under the protection of that body, and were listed as preceding degrees in the Minutes of 19 July 1837."[2]

Yet he also makes clear that this is not the whole story concerning the Mark in Ireland in this period. Onto the scene of Irish Freemasonry there now stepped a figure of whom it has been claimed that 'he left his mark on Irish Masonry more than anyone either before or since'. His name was John Fowler and he was by profession a Schoolmaster. This no doubt largely accounts for what were to be his gifts of organisation and precision in regard to Irish ritual and administration. In **1818** Fowler was appointed Deputy Grand Master by the Duke of Leinster and he held this office until **1824** when he resigned and assumed the position of Lieutenant Grand Commander of the Supreme Council 33° at the time that that body was warranted. In **1827** he was appointed as Deputy Grand Secretary and held this important administrative post until his death in **1856**. It is his influence throughout this period which affects our story.

Since by 1820 the Encampments were largely responsible for anything resembling Mark ceremonies it is important to realise that they were in some disarray. In 1822 the Dublin Encampment No. 25 proposed that a General Encampment of all Knights Templar in Ireland be formed with a nobleman as its head. This makes clear that the Early Grand Encampment was in decline and when the new proposal was turned down the EGE lasted for only two more years or so. To complete the picture we know that individual Encampments continued to function in Ireland because we have evidence to show this but it was not until 1836, as mentioned above, that an alternative Body under the leadership of the Duke of Leinster was created and Knight Templary with all its appendant degrees could prosper under proper management. That is a story which we need no further pursue.

It was at precisely the point that the EGE was weakest and John Fowler assumed his role in the A. and A. Rite that a letter was sent to him from Charleston in America. We know from his published Letter Book that Fowler had been concerned some years previously that the higher degrees which were practised in Ireland should be recognised in other countries and to this end he was in touch with Dr. Dalcho, the Lt. Grand Commander at Charleston. Fowler and two others were in fact admitted to the 33° by that Supreme Council subject to his taking a solemn obligation in that regard. The obligation was "duly taken with just solemnity in St. Patrick's Cathedral, Dublin, in 1811". Sadly the outbreak of the war between Great Britain and America in 1812 put a temporary stop to further links. The letter we now come to was the sign of such contact resumed.

The letter's contents are highly significant when we realise that the Mark Master Mason (degree) as it is now practised was not yet introduced into Ireland. The writer, Alexander McDonald, said,

"I avail myself of Mr. Cassidy's returning to Ireland to send you the Mark Masters degree for want of which such Irish Royal Arch Masons as Come to the United States Cannot visit the RA Chapters." He went on to mention the Excellent Master degree and the Mediterranean Pass, as well as the Malta degree in lecture form, so we must not think that this was simply or mainly a letter for those interested in the Mark. However he does end up with a PS. "You will find the M(ark) Degree with the Papers sent by the Supreme Council of the 33rd degree".

Upon receiving the MMM ritual Fowler was so impressed that he lost no time in introducing it to his Masonic Lodge, Dublin No. 2. and setting up a

The Coat of Arms of the Worshipful Companie of Free Masons, Rough Masons, Wallers, Slaters, Paviours, Plaisterers and Bricklayers dated 1784 by John Lambert
(Durham University Library)

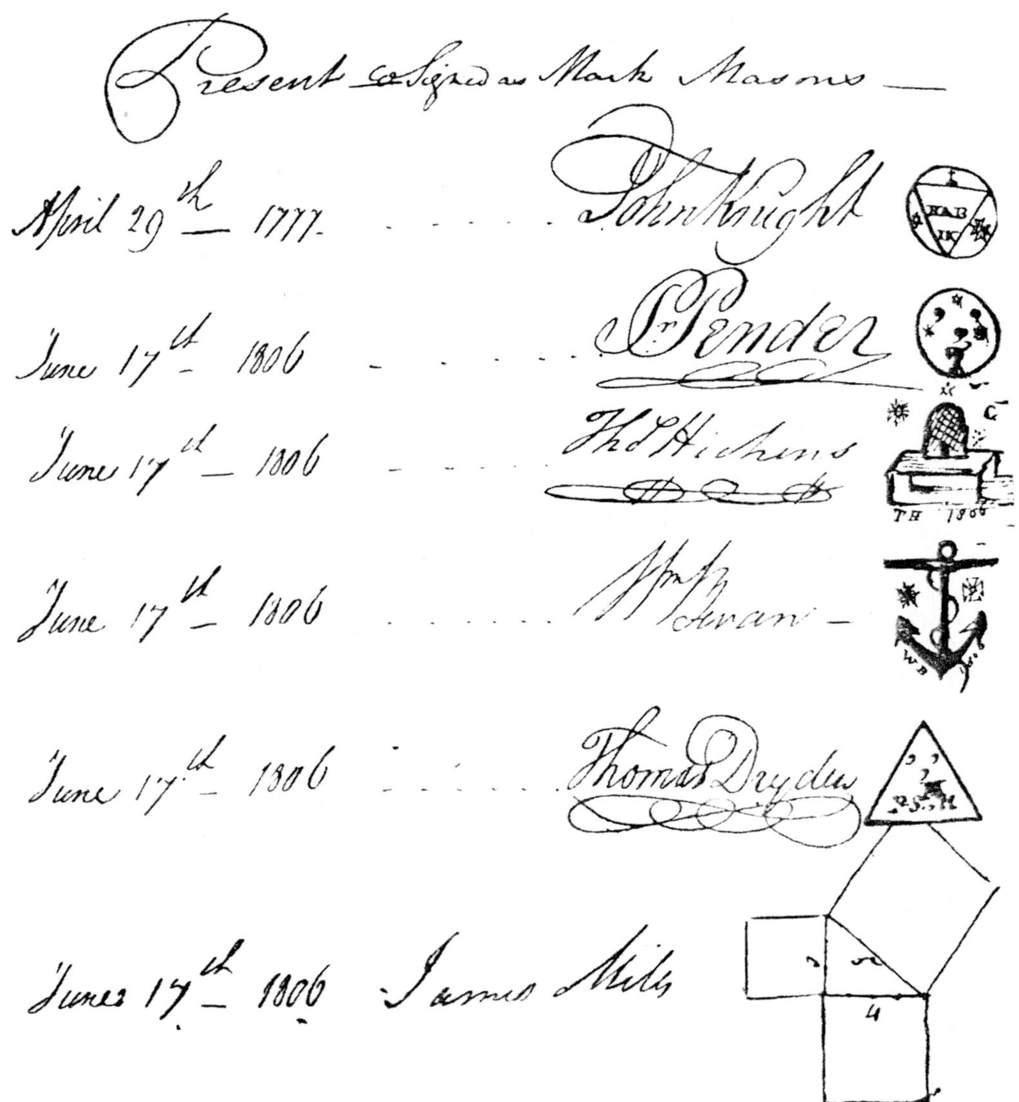
Present & Signed as Mark Masons —

April 29th — 1777 . . . . . John Knight

June 17th — 1806 . . . . . Dr Pender

June 17th — 1806 . . . . . Thos Hichens

June 17th — 1806 . . . . . Wm Evans —

June 17th — 1806 . . . . . Thomas Dryden

Junes 17th — 1806 James Miles

Early Masons Marks used in Druid's Lodge of
'Love and Liberality', No. 103, Redruth, West Cornwall.

Early Mark jewels showing varied emblems. (U.G.L. Museum, London.)

Early Mark Jewels (U.G.L. Museum, London.)

John Fowler, the Irish Ritual reformer.

(Above) *The Minden Keystone made for the Lodge in the XX Regiment.*

An early distinctive Mark apron used in Newport and Southwark which derived its design from that stone.

Rt. Hon. The Lord Leigh, Grand Master 1856–1859

The Rev. Canon G.R. Portal, Grand Master, 1869–1873

M.W. Bro HRH Prince Michael of Kent, Grand Master.

The oldest extant Mark tracing board. Once used by and now held in Albany Lodge in Newport, No. 151, I.O.W.

The 1871 Mark tracing board design by Bro. Rosenthal.

Tracing board of Star of the East Lodge, Scarborough

The official Mark tracing board in use today.

The Johnson 'diagram' once used at Marple, Cheshire in the Lodge of Benevolence No. 336. (Bro. Michael Stratton.)

A Masonic gravestone in Mottram churchyard, Cheshire showing cypher characters.
(Manchester Association of Masonic Research.)

The first Mark Masons' Hall, formerly Bacon's Hotel in Great Queen Street, London.

In the name of the Omnipotent GOD
who created the Earth and the Waters.—
This is to certify, That the Bearer hereof our beloved Brother and Companion Henry Davey has
been regularly admitted to the [illegible] Degree of
Royal Ark Mariner during the time of a just and
careful launch, he having by Fidelity and Courage approved himself worthy of the same. We therefore recommend him to the countenance of all Royal Ark Mariners
on the surface of the Earth and the Waters.—
In witness whereof We the [illegible] of the Vessel
have set our hands, and affixed the Seal of our Order
on board at Leicester, this [illegible] day of March
A.D. 1802, and in the Year of the Flood 3806.
[illegible] M.
John Gale

Henry Davey

An 1802 Ark Mariner certificate. (Leicester Masonic Library)

Ebenezer 'Noah' Sibly.

The Sibley Royal Ark Mariner jewels. (U.G.L. Museum, London.)

Above: *A Royal Ark Mariner tracing board from Dover, Kent.*
Right: *The present official RAM tracing board.*

good working Lodge of MMMs. He kept the record of this Lodge's proceedings in a separate book because the ceremony did not fit in with the sequence of the Irish Rite in 1825. Certainly the letter makes some matters very much clearer. The Irish Royal Arch ceremonies did not at that time include anything like the present Mark Master working and the fact that Fowler was impressed to the extent of setting up a group to work it shows that it was sufficiently different and of such substance as to merit particular attention. The fact that we know, and have shown, this Charleston working (see pp. 125ff) enables us to appreciate what it was that Fowler had read but it also shows that Fowler must have made his own or his group's modifications to the ceremony by adding some of those subsidiary degrees which had hitherto had a 'Mark' relevance in Irish tradition.

Though we have no immediately contemporary ritual of that first Irish group it is clear that what came from Charleston lacked elements which are present by 1844 when the Supreme Grand Chapter of Ireland gave its official protection to the Mark Degree. These elements are most naturally provided by incorporating some of the Babylonian Pass sections that referred to the Mark Mason's return to Jerusalem and his work there, the significant act of the Link with its 'heave over' feature, and the ceremonies of the 'Arch' degree with its keystone and completion of the secret vault. However it actually took place, the fact is that Fowler in his lifetime so organised a system of Mark Masonry that, having the semi-official blessing of the Grand Lodge of Ireland, it began to acquire acceptance and status. On 17 February 1837 we can read the following in the 'Masonic Intelligence':

"A congregation for conferring the degree of MMM was this evening holden under warrant No. 2 (Dublin). The meeting was numerously attended as several respected members of the Grand Master's and other Lodges had expressed their anxiety to be matriculated ... (John Fowler's) Mother Lodge No. 2 continues to confer it on such of the Brethren as are distinguished for their Masonic zeal and moral worth. The ceremonies of this beautiful degree, which is the connecting of the Master's with the Arch, were gone through on the present occasion by Brother Fowler, with his usual correctness, and who communicated to the assembled MARK-MEN the pleasures to be derived from a thorough acquaintance with the pure principles of Freemasonry, impressing on them at the same time, not to lose sight of the solid advantages which can be attained not only by the **knowledge**, but by the **practice** of those obligations which are so well calculated 'To make man like that which is good'."

In November of that same year we have a report in the Freemasons Quarterly Review of a special 'Mark Master Masons congregation attached to Royal Arch Chapter No. 100 in Dublin' whilst in 1839 the Editor of that very journal was himself involved.

"MARK MASONRY. (Dublin) 6 May. – An especial meeting was called for the purpose of giving Bro. Crucefix 'a Mark'. The ceremony, which is interesting and instructive, left a corresponding impression on the mind of the noviciate (sic). Bro. Thomas Wright presided with his usual care, and we hear that Bro. Keek particularly distinguished himself by the *emphatic manner* in which he acted as overseer."

It is revealing that prior to this personal introduction to the Mark Crucefix made no reference to English Mark Masonry. One writer has made the deduction that had Crucefix known anything about the degree in England in the form in which he received it at Dublin surely he would have had something to say about it. This seems to be curious logic. This was, we are led to believe, Dr. Crucefix's first encounter with the Mark Degree and if so how could he compare it with any other form that might exist? If he had been admitted in England in some other way it is then strange that he did not report it in his journal. What is more likely is that he was unaware of the many places where he might obtain 'a Mark' and Dublin was the first intimation of where he might take that step. It was therefore eminently reportable but it is no guide to the prevalence or absence of other forms of Mark workings in England at that time. Why he should go to Dublin for the privilege perhaps the now awaited biography of this notable Mason will reveal.

What was happening in rural Ireland at this time is extremely interesting and a taste of it as it was in the Comber district of County Down is given in a paper printed in 1926. We learn, for example, that most individual lodges there did not confer the 'higher degrees' but their members came to a central spot for that purpose. Hence we learn from the Register of Lodge 165 that in one year in the 1820s 12 brethren took the 'Mark Mason & Rassel' (Wrestle) and 'Princes of the Red Cross', whilst in the '133' records we have 15 brethren made 'Red Cross knights' on 3 March 1818 and 15 made Mark of the Craft and Master. On 7 May 1821 10 brethren were admitted to the 'Mark, Ark and Wrestle' and 8 received 'Cain's Mark'. All these were of course alongside many other knightly ceremonies. The Floor cloth of one of those lodges reveals once more a noticeable similarity to the arrangements of the 'stones' mentioned earlier and shows clearly how all the intermediate and knightly grades were seen as part of one complete whole. This same paper also produces an old Certificate of Lodge 649 at Raffrey, Comber, showing the 'Ark, Mark and Wrestle' degrees as side degrees of Knight Templary.

The official view on all this activity is expressed in a letter of 1822 sent by the Deputy Grand Secretary of Ireland to Lodge 441 held in the 38th Regiment of Foot.

"There is not any warrant issued by the Grand Lodge of Ireland other than that you hold. It has therefore always been the practice of Irish Lodges to confer the Higher Degrees under that authority."

Prior to 1829 there was continual opposition to any change in this arrangement by country Chapters of whom at one time 275 sent in their resolutions to this effect. In this year however a Grand Chapter was created even though it was to be some considerable time before it could exercise full authority. Moreover there was no attempt by this new body to incorporate the

Mark Degree and it was to be 1874 before it became an essential requisite for anyone proceeding to the Royal Arch.

Meanwhile, though the Grand Lodge of Ireland had taken the Mark under its wing in 1844 there was a circular letter issued in 1846 which made clear that from henceforth the warrants issued by that body were for 'Blue Masonry' alone and lodges wishing to work the other degrees must obtain a separate warrant authorising them to do so. It was thus that the Mark and related degrees persisted there for the remainder of the period we are considering. It should be noted that in Ulster there was especially strong resistance to any change from what they regarded as 'time immemorial' methods of working under a Craft warrant. The Mark degree was therefore destined to be preserved in Ireland, and the regulations subsequently issued for Irish Masons taking the Mark degree are recorded in chapter 1.

(ii) SCOTLAND

In August 1817 the Grand Lodge of Scotland reconfirmed the position first made known in May 1800 that henceforth it would only recognise the three Craft degrees of St. John's Masonry. Indeed it went further and prohibited any officer of the 'higher degrees' from sitting in Grand Lodge. That was an even greater restriction than anything considered in England, for the Duke of Sussex was, after all, the Grand Master of the Knights Templar. The future of any degree such as the Mark must, however, have seemed bleak in the wake of this announcement.

There was, however, another important development. Not including the Royal Arch in its remit, as had been done in England, steps to cover this now ancient degree were taken and within three weeks the Supreme Grand Royal Arch Chapter of Scotland had been formed. This meant, of course, that by September 1817 the Mark was neither accepted nor recognised by any Grand Lodge body and while it was still worked by independent Lodges, Chapters and Encampments these were technically illegal for all Craft Masons. The continued existence of Mark Masonry in Scotland was clearly preserved at this time by some Craft Lodges that risked censure by Grand Lodge and by Encampments that were in the full flush of their existence.

Of the sixty Charters granted by the EGE of Ireland nearly a third were issued to Scotland. Indeed in October 1811 the Grand Master in Dublin informed Alexander Deuchar that Charters 36 to 45 had been sent to a Brother who acted as a Provincial Grand Secretary in Edinburgh and these Charters were *blank* so that they could be speedily issued when required. Alexander Deuchar's enquiry was timely because in 1809 he had been appointed as *Provisional* Grand Master of the newly formed Royal Grand Conclave of Scotland at the express invitation of that body's new Patron, HRH the Duke of Kent. What is important to note is that some *nine* of the Encampments which helped to form this new Conclave already owed allegiance to the EGE in Ireland. What is certain, however, is that with the withdrawal of any kind of oversight of more than the Craft degrees by the Grand Lodge of Scotland from 1800 there was an increasing desire by many of the Scottish knights to have a more secure central body in their midst. The Secretary of this new body, for example, wrote in 1810 as follows:

"... (our) plans are not merely confined to the single degrees (sic) of the Templar, but comprehend all the superior degrees of Masonry above that of Master Mason, such as Royal Arch, Ark Mason, Mark Mason, Knight of Malta, etc. etc. in conformity to which plans I am likewise ordered to send copies to all Royal Arch Chapters and to request their support that the improper practices at present in Scotland, of working in that order upon a Master Charter, may be put a stop to ..."

By 1811 the Grand Conclave had been consecrated and established and Deuchar was eager to create a favourable link with the EGE in Ireland. Yet his Conclave's actions created almost as many problems as they solved, for some of the EGE Encampments in Scotland were contemptuous of those whom they regarded as having broken their oaths to Ireland and refused to cooperate in any way.

This disagreement was increased when in 1817, through the efforts once more of Alexander Deuchar, a Supreme Grand Royal Arch Chapter of Scotland was formed to which all Royal Arch Chapters were invited to affiliate. This was too much for the remaining EGE Encampments, and especially those in the West of Scotland. They appealed to Ireland and before the EGE ended its effective life it carried out another important act. It acceded, in May 1822, to the request of the remaining daughter Encampments in Scotland to erect an Early Grand Encampment for that country, and it issued a provisional Warrant to the Scottish representative, Robert Martin, to that effect. That body, with its very extensive array of ceremonies, was to remain in existence until 1895.

Even before this step was taken the fact was that, as far as the Scottish Mark Masons were concerned, there were three Masonic groups that were involved with such additional degrees as the Mark and Ark. There needed to be some resolution of this situation.

In 1818 the Grand Conclave appointed a Committee 'to consider which of the smaller orders of Masonry they authorise to be made under their Charters; and to meet a Committee of the Supreme Grand Royal Arch Chapter of Scotland for the purpose of arranging which of these degrees' each of them should authorise. The decision was communicated in January 1819 and the division was, and is still, of great interest.

The Royal Arch was to control (1) Master Past the Chair; (2) Excellent Master; (3) Super Excellent Master; (4) Arch; (5) Royal Arch; (6) Mark Mason; (7) Ark Mason; (8) Link and Wrestle; (9) Babylonian Pass or the Red Cross of Daniel; (10) Jordan Pass; (11) Royal Order or Prussian Blue; (12) High Priest. Of the Knights Templar degrees we should note the 'Black Mark'.

In view of all that has been said about these additional degrees previously there is hardly much need for comment here but there are three reflections that merit consideration. The first is that here we have the first definite indication of a formal link between the Royal Arch and the Mark and Ark degrees. Of course there was the introduction of the two Mark ceremonies into a Chapter in 1769 and in Ireland any of the earlier forms of the Mark were in such a relationship. Yet these were not official acts of policy and in Ireland the regulation linking the Mark and the Grand Royal Arch Chapter did not occur until 1871.

The second reflection is that in this agreed list there is still a close parallel with the degrees that were obviously brought over by the EG Encampments, even to the extent of maintaining a separate 'Arch' degree, the Link and Wrestle, the title of Red Cross *of Daniel*, and the Jordan Pass. What is more we know that these ceremonies were practised well into the century as, for example, in Edinburgh No. 1 Chapter where a Minute of 28 February 1840 states that certain persons severally received the degrees of Ark, Mark, Link, Jordan Pass, Babylonian Pass and Prussian Blue. None of those ceremonies with those titles would be familiar to Scottish Royal Arch Masons today and yet all the themes which they embodied are still practised under other names. We thus see in this list the strong Irish influence still at work.

Thirdly, there is in the 'Master Passed the Chair' degree the seed that remained from a time when the Royal Arch could only be conferred on those who had passed the Chair of a Craft Lodge and therefore needed a special ceremony to ensure a sufficient number of RA candidates. Yet it was also the seed of a RA device that was introduced for a short time in 1842 though dropped in 1846. A word about this is essential if we are to appreciate what was to follow in a celebrated case.

The crucial point in granting Chair-Master warrants, which additionally empowered the conferring of the Mark Master degree, was to check the irregularity of giving the degree in Craft lodges. The ritual was laid down, only regularly advanced Mark Masons or Past Masters could confer the degree, the Mark had to precede the Past Master degree and of course it was forbidden to use these gatherings for any other purpose than to admit candidates to the Mark. As we enter the next stage of our story we need to remember these requirements even though they were rescinded four years later. We should also note that the seed sown by the Chair Master's ritual, when abandoned, probably provided the ceremony of the Installed Master in the Mark Degree which was eventually adopted by the new Grand Mark Lodge in England.

It can thus be seen that this formation of the SGRA Chapter and its wider remit over several ceremonies was the principal cause of the continuing practice of the Mark Degree in Scotland. Indeed so well did it appear to discharge its oversight in this regard that many Masons **in England** who desired to have a recognisable authority for the conduct of this degree began to look in that direction for help. This was very much the case by the 1850s when the control of the Craft and its practices there were being ever more carefully monitored by a Provincial network that saw no place for the Mark degree.

One result of such a genuine interest in acquiring the degree was set out in an article written by Dr. Robert Beveridge for "The Aberdeen Masonic Reporter" of 1879. Where necessary I shall give the account verbatim but much of it can be summarised. This is his story.

In the year 1850 there were only two RA Chapters still working in Aberdeen. The Chapter of St. George's Lodge was the best working Chapter in the north of Scotland and it had joined Grand Chapter in 1817. Beveridge became a member and having received the Mark Degree from St. George's Lodge he now received the Past the Chair, Excellent and Royal Arch Degrees.

Good as the St. George's working was it was decided by some Companions that another Chapter should be erected to still further improve the ceremonies. Accordingly the Bon Accord Chapter No. 70 was warranted and Dr. Beveridge became SN. The following instructions were given by the Grand SE along with the ritual books that he sent for the Officers. "The Chapter itself works only the Arch degree, but all money transactions and all balloting for new members are done in the Chapter only. The other degrees – MARK, Past, Excellent, etc. – are conferred in Lodges holding of the Chapter. For this purpose the Chapter should issue a Commission or Charter to a member of the Chapter to hold a Mark Lodge along with all who may join him ..." Such lodges were **not independent** but could only act as the Chapter decided. When a candidate had paid the fee to the Chapter Treasurer then the SE issued an order to one designated the "Master of the Mark Lodge" who would confer the degree.

Dr. Beveridge was designated the 'Master of the Mark Lodge' in Bon Accord Chapter, and he was responsible for the keeping of the Minutes in a separate Mark Book. Beveridge thought the rituals inadequate and with the help of a Companion, Dr. Jones, who worked in London, he revised the Mark practice. He did this on the advice of Dr. Walker-Arnott, then the Depute Grand Principal of Scotland, who said in a letter that he 'saw great occasion to change the Mark, and also the Excellent. The Mark, as given by the Edinburgh No. 1 previously, was absurd.' Of course that was *his* opinion. When 5 Companions of Chapter Esk Dalkeith visited the Edinburgh Chapter in 1842 and received the Mark they expressed themselves much gratified with their instruction.

Beveridge took his duties seriously and quotes from his Letter Book to show how the regulations laid down were complied with, including his own warrant to act as a Master of the Chapter's Mark Lodge, in which all the officers had to be "Companions of, and in full order with, Chapter No. 70". The warrant was duly sealed by the Principals and SE.

He then tells us that in the 'autumn' of 1851 he was in London to see the Great Exhibition at the Crystal Palace in Hyde Park. One evening he also attended the Emulation Lodge of Improvement to become acquainted with the best of Craft working and many of the leading London Masons. Several of them "expressed a wish to become acquainted with the Mark degree" and he wrote to Aberdeen to obtain the Chapter's authority to confer the degree upon them.

"The doing so was quite in accordance with masonic custom", he wrote. He was the warranted Master of the Mark Lodge of Bon Accord and Supreme Chapter laws "permitted the working out of Aberdeen, provided there was no interference with any other Chapter. As London was 300 miles at least from any Scottish Chapter or Mark Lodge, and as neither Grand Lodge nor Supreme Chapter in England, nor any other masonic governing body in England took cognisance of the Mark degree" this requirement was met. Nevertheless, to cover any eventuality, the Bon Accord Chapter issued a formal Commission to confer the Mark degree on certain London brethren.

The Commission was issued on *25 August 1851* and named William Jones. "Mark Master of the Bon Accord Mk. M. Lodge, and any other Compn. or Compns., of Bon Accord RA Chapter" as assisting Beveridge "to form, open and hold" the lodge. Compns. Evans, Spencer and Norton were the candidates. The Mark Master degree was conferred on *26 August* so no time was lost.

Dr. Jones, we are told, was an English Companion well-known to the members of Bon Accord Chapter and St. Machar Lodge of Aberdeen, who, "when affiliated into the Bon Accord Chapter, received the subordinate degrees in Aberdeen, obtaining the Mark Master and Past Master degrees. 7 August 1851, and the Excellent Master degree, 12 September 1851."

These facts are important because in 1855, says Dr. Beveridge, the Grand SN (of Scotland) was to state that at that time Dr. Jones was not so affiliated. Yet there was a letter from the Grand SN himself, dated 11 February 1852 acknowledging receipt of the affiliation fee.

"Besides Compn. Jones and myself, there were about that time in London, two other Aberdeen Brethren, Br. Ramage and Br. William Duthie. At the time when the Commissions arrived both these had left ... This necessitated our looking out for another Mark Master to make up the three necessary to confer the degree on at least *one* of the candidates." On enquiry "We found that many knew the degree by name, and thought that they had received it, but were unable to show that they knew it." They even found a Midland Counties Brother who knew of the 'Mark, Ark, Link and Chain' that used to be conferred and an eminent Grand Orient 33° Brother who was upset when his claim was doubted.

"At last, however, a Brother from the Bermudas was found who was a member of Chapter No. 1 Edinburgh and had obtained there the Mark Master degree, and with his assistance a Lodge was duly formed." Compns. Absalom and Graves were added to the previous 3 candidates, "so when I left London a day or two after, there were then six members of the Bon Accord Mark Lodge". As several other London brethren wished to obtain the degree a wish was expressed that Dr. Jones be granted a Commission to confer the degree or to hold a Mark Lodge as Beveridge had been. "This granting of warrants, although afterwards found fault with, was at that time, it will be remembered, in accordance with instructions received from Grand SE."

On 6 September 1851 an Emergency Chapter met in Aberdeen of which the Minutes state that whilst no Commission could be granted to Compn. Jones "steps should be immediately taken to grant a charter or warrant for holding a Mark Master Lodge in London, and Scribe E. was instructed to write Compn. Jones to that effect."

On 11 September a Petition signed by the six London Mark Masters was laid before the Aberdeen Chapter, where it was proposed by P.Z., seconded by P.J. and unanimously agreed that the Charter be granted. **On the following day** Jones was in Aberdeen, received the Excellent degree, "and at the same time the Mark ritual was finally adjusted by the addition of the Charge. He left at once for London – in a day or two the Charter was forwarded and on 18 September the new Lodge, named the London Bon Accord Mark Master Lodge, was opened, and seven candidates advanced. In this manner the Lodge was established..."

There now follow two pages of close reasoning as to why this action could be justified. Since the formation of this lodge had such an immense impact on the whole of subsequent English Mark Masonry it is at least necessary to summarise Dr. Beveridge's argument.

He began by claiming that the Mark degree was really of Craft origin and not the Arch and instanced his own receiving of it in St. George's Lodge. Further, the Aberdeen Chapters positively refused to accept the 1845 Grand Chapter regulation requiring them to do so and the Grand SN after meeting them agreed to their traditional objection. In 1850 NO Aberdeen Chapter conferred the degree and Bon Accord was the first to do so. He especially stresses the *vacillation* of the 1842 granting of Chair Master Lodge warrants and their abrogating them in 1848 quoting the 12 March 1848 resolution: "... the power of granting these degrees shall be vested in Chapters only ...", and he continues.

"Had therefore the six Mark Masters in London applied to Supreme Chapter for a warrant they would undoubtedly have met with a refusal ... In fact in December 1851 Supreme Chapter did actually refuse an application for a Mark warrant from 'certain brethren and companions, Mark Master' in Newcastle, on the grounds that this 'was contrary to the existing laws' ". Beveridge thus pleads that as no English Chapter could – even if willing – accept power to confer the Mark "the only way in which the degree could be obtained in England was by the intervention of private Chapters from Scotland". He did admit to not approving one point in the proceedings of the London Brethren and that was their insistence on a special ceremonial for installing a Master into the Chair of a Mark Lodge when *clearly no such thing existed*. However, his general conclusion is clear:

"... the proceedings of the London Bon Accord Mark Master Lodge were, in themselves, perfectly valid. It is of no practical moment now (1879) discussing this point; for even our English brethren admit the validity of what they call 'time immemorial' usage: that is to say, that a body that has *gone on unchallenged* for a number of years practising a degree or degrees, acquires a sort of prescriptive right to do so, *no matter how irregular its procedure may have been at first.*"

Such was Beveridge's full account of what comprised this **cause celebre** and anyone who wishes can thus learn the full story of Bon Accord from the hand of one who alone could claim to know its every detail. Whilst the story was largely told by Grantham (1960) and Handfield-Jones (1969) it is interesting that that story was not recounted in the Lodge's official history which was published in 1951. The importance of having the full facts recorded here is surely clear. It shows that the Mark Degree at this time was alive and well and when re-discovered by senior Masons was regarded as a worthwhile part of ancient Masonry. It reveals the enthusiasm, not to mention *remarkable haste*, with which its extension in London was undertaken, and it also points up the serious matters that were involved when such eagerness was intertwined with a developing Supreme Grand Chapter of a neighbouring country and a distinctively different Masonic jurisdiction. Scottish Royal Arch Masonry was now to reveal itself South of the Border.

Before we come to the repercussions of this 'doubtful' project it will be as well if we complete the early history of Bon Accord Mark.

The continuing enthusiasm, or might it have also been anxiety, seems to be shown by the meeting of the members on 18 September to agree on their By-laws before the warrant had arrived from Scotland. Moreover they chose a different day, frequency and place of meeting from what would be found in the warrant and they even arranged to hold the inaugural meeting on **the next day** even though the warrant was still not to hand. The Bon Accord Chapter at least imposed its control to the extent of requiring all candidates to be regular Royal Arch companions and by claiming the right to examine the books of the Mark Lodge **at any time**. Of particular note in the warrant was the requirement 'That they shall not affiliate or admit into the Lodge or countenance any one made a Master in an irregular manner or *have any connection with any body of Mark Masters* working or pretending to work without a Warrant of Constitution from a duly authorised body'.

The Lodge was 'duly consecrated by the WM' because, as a Mark Lodge in Scotland was appendant to a RA Chapter, no such procedure there was ever necessary, and whilst Grantham presumed that the postponement of the formal officers' installation was due to shortage of time they still balloted for 18 candidates and advanced six of them. With their limited membership they just managed to fill the main offices, with Comp. Norton doubling up as Treasurer and Junior Warden for the early meetings. It should be noted that there were no Overseers in the working they adopted.

In the first two years meetings appear to have been called without any summons, at the pleasure of the Master and sometimes in his house at Portman Square. On 12 October 1853 the Minutes certainly record a most remarkable Installation of Dr. Jones's successor as WM. After the minutes of the last regular and several emergency meetings were read everyone else left the room and the Master installed his successor in private. Companion Surly, SGIG, of the 33°, was then introduced to the new WM and took his place. Comp. King and other illustrious members of the KH 30° were then introduced to the WM and having saluted in due form were conducted to their respective Chairs. The members of the 18° were then introduced and the WM having been proclaimed and saluted the sovereign Princes were then conducted to their seats *after which the Mark Masters were admitted* and the Master saluted again. The Master then appointed Wm. Tucker as SW, Lord Leigh as JW, and Sir John de La Pole, Bart. as Register (sic) of Marks. These three not being present proxies took their places.

By almost every present criterion the Bon Accord Mark Lodge had flaws of inception and procedure yet one has to admit that it was highly successful and evidently filled an unexpected need. Not a few of those who joined the long list of expectant candidates were Grand Officers of the Craft or Royal Arch, and recruits came not only from the London area but also from the Provinces. As Grantham so aptly phrased it: "Bon Accord was the only Mark Lodge in England which offered a *semblance* of warranty from a *recognised* source." There were, as we have seen, numerous groups of Brethren who were maintaining what they regarded as a time immemorial right to practice Mark Masonry. Without any kind of Grand Body to support their efforts there was always a possible sense that their work was transitory and perhaps not fully respectable. With the advent of this new and increasingly well-connected Lodge Mark Masonry emerged from the shadows and took a new place not only in London but in a wider world where it was already at home.

It is to that overseas world, especially on the other side of the Atlantic, that we must briefly but necessarily pass before this part of our story can be considered complete.

(iii) OVERSEAS

Early records of Freemasonry in India in any degree are not very numerous owing to the ravages of the weather, the insects and the serious losses sustained at the time of the 'Mutiny' but what has remained shows that our Masonic forebears there worked vigorously not only in the Craft but even in degrees that have long since fallen into disuse. The strong influence of military lodges was everywhere seen.

One interesting old Lodge was Social Friendship, No. 326 in Madras which had its 'Keystone Chapter' attached. About 1840 and in connection with the Chapter we find that the Mark and Royal Ark Mariner degrees were extremely popular. Reports in the Madras 'Freemasons' Herald' for 1848 reveal that this was the case and an extract for Friday 26 May helps to show what was common.

"Mark Masons and Royal Ark Mariners. Bro. Davidson admitted to the latter. The Brn. this evening, on the requisition (i.e. at the request) of the Worshipful Overseer, Bro. Pepell, to be relieved from the post he then held as Head of (both) these degrees. He having filled both offices for the past two years proceeded to the election of separate rulers of each degree. The votes were cast for the following:

W. Bro. WE Clarke: Wor. Overseer of Mark Masters.
Bro. W.Boyd. Head of Royal Ark Mariners."

This gives some indication of the frequency with which degrees occurred.

The Lodge Oriental Star, No. 619, Cannanote, worked the Royal Arch in its Chapter, 'Glory and Peace', but also Mark, Royal Ark Mariners, The Priestly Order (sic), KT, KM, Knights of the Mediterranean Pass and Council of the Symbolic Order of Knights of the Red Cross. Whilst in the early 1840s and thereafter we know that lodges in Calcutta, Cawnpore, Agra and Simla worked the Super-Excellent, Mark, and Red Cross of Babylon with the Royal Arch.

Turning to the West the reader may recall that the Bon Accord Lodge made use of a 'qualified Brother from the Bermudas' so let us look first at that quarter of the New World. At a meeting of Loyalty Lodge No. 358 (EC) on 11 November 1820 the minutes record that the Lodge was opened on the 4th Degree of Masonry and three brethren were exalted to the degree of Past Master, whilst in 1821 the Lodge is borrowing £13 from the Mark Lodge, which suggests that that aspect of the work was regular and flourishing. Whether it was here or in the Somerset (Antients) Lodge, which also worked the Mark, that our earlier English 'stand-in' belonged we are not told but it is clear that his claim to have the qualifications required had been possible.

We know too that the Minden Lodge which assisted in the formation of the Albany Mark Lodge in the Isle of Wight was stationed in Bermuda in early 1847 and by the end of that year was first in Nova Scotia and then Canada West. In both places it would be keeping this aspect of Freemasonry alive among the local population, and on 27 December 1848 we have a detailed description of how the brethren of this military Lodge "sat down in full Masonic costume, about 90 in number, to a sumptuous entertainment provided at Mr. Bramford's Hotel. After enjoying the good things of this life and the cloth being removed the presiding officer, W. Bro. Capt. South, gave these toasts: 'The GMs of *England, Ireland and Scotland*'; 'PGM of Canada'; 'Grand Masters of *United States* Lodges'."

These toasts remind us that Masons in these areas had a much wider canvas to work on and more than one's own Constitutional regulations had to be considered. When RW Bro. Simon McGillivray re-organised the Craft in Canada in 1822, he saw that masons from five jurisdictions could not be governed by the tightly drawn lines that would be thought right in their home Constitutions.

That the practice of the Mark degree was a factor to be reckoned with there can be no question. The number of ritual manuals produced in North America in this period is testimony enough to the prevalence of the degree and one of the earliest but perhaps less well known is "The Mason's Manual for the Government of the Most Ancient and Honorable Society of Free and Accepted Masons *in Lower Canada*" published by order of the Provincial Grand Lodge in 1818. Here is a manual issued by those who represent the United Grand Lodge in England and yet the book contains a full exposition of what was there and then considered the Mark Masons degree, amongst other post-Craft ceremonies. It was, of course, reflecting the true state of affairs.

Extant Minutes of some 'Antients' Lodges in the Eastern townships show how very much opposed some Brethren were to the dissolution of the Grand Lodge of Ancient York Masons at Quebec. They wished to remain "Ancient York Masons" and they not only objected to paying 'registration' and other *double* 'annual, initiation and joining fees' to the Grand Lodge of England but they were even more opposed to surrendering the right *to confer the Mark and other additional degrees.* Many Brethren even became unaffiliates. After several meetings of Caldwell Manor, No. 14, for example, only about $\frac{1}{4}$ of the members decided to become enregistered in England and petition for a new Warrant from there, whilst in another Lodge, Old Golden Rule, No. 19, such a move was approved but only with just more than half the members in agreement. As the original Minutes of many more Antients Lodges have been irrecoverably lost we shall never know fully just what the whole situation was like. What is certain is that when 'English' Craft Lodge members saw how some of their neighbours from other jurisdictions still made Mark, Excellent, Super-Excellent, Cryptic and Chapter Masons 'under the sanction of their Lodge Warrants' they were bound to wonder what had been preserved by the 1813 Union 'back home'. By the 1820s there was growing up that folk memory of when pioneers were levelling the primeval forests along the frontier that moved East and Brethren would go many miles on foot or horseback to attend Lodge meetings in the open air or the garret of some true and trusty Brother – no matter what his Masonic origins. Among such Brethren Masonry was Masonry and the distinctions of the Old Country faded in their fresh homeland.

Yet the Mark persisted. Even after the effects of the Anti-Masonic campaigns in America of the 1830s, which certainly had a knock-on effect in most areas, we read in 1843 of a certificate issued to a W. Bro. Hoy by the officers of St. George's Lodge of Mark Masters in Montreal. This assured the reader that this Brother 'received the **Honorary Degree** of Mark Master Mason in our Lodge on the 26th day of October, 5843'. We have already seen that there was understandable confusion between the terms 'Honorable' and 'Honorary'. There was no doubt about this being a real step forward, for Bro. Hoy told the author of one History of Freemasonry in Canada that having taken the Mark he was able to proceed to the Royal Arch.

In December 1844 a letter arrived on the desk of the Grand Secretary in London. It was postmarked Montreal and sent by a PM of St. Paul's Lodge, No. 514. He had written on some matter in October and now, as once again the chosen Master of this Lodge 'to re-establish that discipline ... which the members stated had been somewhat relaxed ... I am in need of some information'. He refers to 'the uniform mode of work as established after the Union of 1813' which Simon McGillivray had sought to introduce into Canada in 1823 but says that when a Br.Badgley returned from England 3 or 4 years ago he said that the situation in England had changed. The writer therefore wants to know what the position is regarding the three Craft degrees as "I am exceedingly anxious to conform **strictly** to what is established by the **only competent authority**, the UGL Eng.".

He continued, however, "Allow me to ask whether *you acknowledge the degree of* **Mark Master Mason**. It is said to be required by the Grand Lodges of Scotland and Ireland, and is so throughout the United States. The lodges in Canada, except ours, recognise it and confer the degree. Have they that right? Please let me know your opinion on the matter and also whether the *honorary jewels of that degree* and those of *Knights Templar* &c may be admitted to be worn by Masons in lodge, with reference to the Chapter on Regalia in the Book of Constitutions, where, according to my reading such Jewels are forbidden." The latter ends with concern about Royal Arch matters.

The enquiry was no doubt dealt with though we do not have a copy of the reply. What is important, however, is that in July 1845 there is another similar enquiry from the same city but from another Brother. He addressed the Grand Secretary and asks "that you will excuse my troubling you so often, but in the absence of authority in this part of the world it becomes the duty of every Mason who does not wish to see *the Constitution of Masonry trampled upon* to apply to you ... I shall thus be obliged if you will answer these (questions) fully so that I can shew them as Authority, vis:

(1) Can a Master of a Blue Lodge under the Constitution of England *work the Mark Degree under such warrant* and charge for Initiation and appropriate that Money to the funds of the Blue Lodge?

(2) Can the Master & Wardens of the Blue Lodge take upon themselves *to be Master & Wardens of the Mark*?

(3) In calling a Lodge of Emergency can they state in the summons 'And for other Masonic purposes' without having refference (sic) as to what those purposes may be?"

There are other questions relating to the Craft Installation but these we may leave aside. What becomes clear is that by this date there was arising a situation in which the practice of the Mark degree was not merely present but was causing real difficulties. The matter was rightly one that exercised the mind of any conscientious ruler under the English Constitution and these were but two examples of what we know was a growing number of enquiries in the years that follow.

What is also certain is that right up to 1853 the Mark continued to be practised in a number of ways. At a meeting in January that year a Chapter in Clarenceville 'exalted' a Companion to the degree of Mark Master, and at another Chapter with a High Priest in the Chair (clearly a Chapter of Irish origin) two brethren were 'raised' to the 'Sublime Degree' of Mark Masters. In June we have further examples of brethren being 'Marked, Passed, and Received as well as taking the Most Excellent Master's Degree before being 'exalted' into the Royal Arch. By October 1853 and principally on the grounds of not being allowed to regulate their own affairs promptly and appropriately, bearing in mind the need to allow intervisiting of Masons from different traditions in these still new territories, notice was given at the Provincial Grand Lodge of Quebec that a petition be forwarded to the GL of England requesting that the subordinate Lodges of this Province be permitted to form themselves into an Independent Grand Lodge and 'to exercise all the privileges appertaining thereto'. It was now evident that failure to deal with the kind of issues raised by the letters quoted above was likely to have even more far-reaching consequences. At just this time RW Bro. Thomas D.Harington wrote from Toronto to the Earl of Zetland:

"In this section of Canada the disaffection has been gaining ground principally because of alleged neglect in London ... Had their remonstrances and representations relative to misgovernment, or rather neglect of government, which had been felt to be a growing evil for some time past, been courteously attended to in some way (they say), and a desire at least evinced to meet the wishes of the Brethren, and place them upon some satisfactory footing in regard to the management of their own local affairs, it is exceedingly doubtful if such an event as throwing off allegiance would have been thought of. I feel sure that it would not, for old country feeling is very strong."

What all this meant for the government of the Craft in general and the place of the Mark Degree in particular we must now describe.

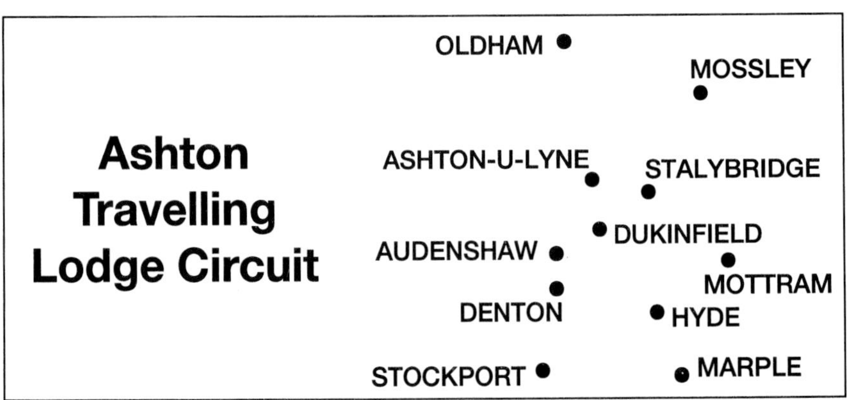

Chapter Eight

How did the Grand Mark Lodge come to be?

AS WAS MADE plain at the outset of our tale the Mark Degree in England and Wales is governed by an Institution which is unique in the whole existence of the Order. Nothing like it exists or has even been contemplated in the neighbouring Constitutions of Ireland or Scotland and yet each of them, in their way, had to devise a proper means by which the Mark Degree could be made properly available to regularly made Masons and held in relation to the other facets of Freemasonry. Only in England did circumstances arise which led some to seek another Grand Lodge – and that for what was long regarded as primarily 'part and parcel' of the Ancient Craft. Such a step in as august a body as English Freemasonry deserves to be explained and it is that part of our story to which we now turn.

We left off the account of how Mark Masonry was faring in the period up to 1853 with a serious situation beginning to appear in North American Freemasonry. On 28 August 1855 the Grand Secretary reported to the Board of General Purposes of the UGL of England "that circumstances had occurred, *more immediately* amongst Lodges in the *Canada's (sic) and Nova Scotia*, some of them holding Warrants from the Grand Lodge of England, and others from the Grand Lodges of Scotland and Ireland, in reference to *what is termed* the Mark Masons Degree, which is much practised *in America* and which circumstances have led to unpleasant feelings amongst the parties".

In order to consider, and hopefully to contain, this source of possible disaffection amongst members of the Grand Lodge overseas and of likely confrontation with sister Grand Lodges or Chapters the BGP "deemed it advisable to appoint a small Committee to consider the subject in conjunction with a Committee of the Grand Chapter ... with a view of communicating to the MW Grand Master their opinion, whether the said Mark Masons Degree may be deemed part of Ancient Free Masonry".

By 7 November 1855 the Grand Chapter was involved and a joint Committee was appointed as follows:

From the *Board of General Purposes*	From the *Grand Chapter*
The President: Alexander Dobie	William White
The Vice-Pres.: Henry L.Crohn	John Symonds
C.Locock Webb	W.H.Absolon
Algernon Attwood	J.H.Goldsworthy
J.Newton Tomkins	John Havers
J.S.S.Hopwood	Frederick Pattison

John Hervey Bonamy Dobree

Should this Committee have wondered whether their work was really needed two further incidents must have sharpened their awareness of how crucial their deliberations would be. The first happened on 10 November 1855 when Grand Lodge received an Address from the Grand Lodge of Ancient, Free and Accepted Masons of Canada. This sought to explain why the step of severance and independence had been taken and included these words from a circular issued in September 1855 in the City of Hamilton, Ontario. It ran: "The first and most important grievance is, the diversity of interests and the want of harmony in action and working, resulting from the growth in the Province, of Lodges hailing from the Grand Lodges of different Countries, thus perpetuating local and national feelings ... conflicting interests and consequent estrangement of affection, amongst the brethren of an Order that knows no country and is confined to no race." This made clear the problems arising from the Mark in the Colonies.

The second was, however, a problem on their doorstep and since three of the Joint Committee were personally involved it must have made an even greater impact.

We described in the last Chapter the formation of the Bon Accord Mark Lodge in London and noted that whatever the peculiarities of its foundation or operation it seemed to meet a very evident need. This is proved when we learn that by the autumn of 1855 it had 120 members. How some of those members came to know of the Lodge is revealed by a paragraph in the February 1855 *Freemasons' Monthly Magazine*. The magazine was edited by Richard Spencer, a founder member of the Bon Accord Lodge, and the paragraph was an answer to a earlier query. It told a RA Mason that if he wished to know about the Mark Degree he should apply to Bro. R.Spencer, 314, High Holborn, for all the particulars he required. The Mark Lodge, it was stated, was held under warrant from the Grand Chapter of Scotland. Such information was later repeated in March.

In case the above claim might seem a trifle ambitious it has to be said on the lodge members' behalf that as they bound themselves to 'Obey and Conform to all the Laws and Regulations that are or may be made by the Supreme Grand Chapter of Scotland' through the Bon Accord Chapter of Aberdeen it seemed logical that they might claim the latter's support and authority. Logical or not they were now about to face a serious problem.

In May 1855 another paragraph in 'Notes to Correspondents' replied to a Scottish Mason called W.GAYLOR who had clearly questioned the lawfulness of the Bon Accord's claim to a Warrant. The answer he was given was in part as follows:

"... it is working under the warrant, granted from Chapter No. 70, Aberdeen *before the abrogation of a law to which he alludes*. We have investigated the matter from the records and find that the Brethren of the London

Bon Accord are right and he is wrong." The law referred to was, of course, the one mentioned earlier regarding the warranting of Chair-Master Lodges which was abrogated in 1848.

In the June issue the First Principal of the Aberdeen Chapter made known that W.GAYLOR was the GSN of the Supreme Grand Chapter of Scotland and sought to calm any possible storm from that quarter by giving his reasons why the granting of the warrant was considered just by him and his fellow Companions. Simply put, he claimed that as the SGCS had stopped issuing warrants for Chair-Master Lodges and now allowed Chapters once more to grant the degrees of Mark and Past Master that is precisely what they had done in this London case.

A further comment by the Editor in this same issue was not, however, calculated to promote harmony. If Mr. Gaylor was not satisfied with the above explanation "he had better communicate with that gentleman in Aberdeen. It is our earnest desire to deal fairly by both parties, but we are not the proper instruments of analyzing *questions which hinge on mere dates*". Sadly this just added tinder to a growing fire.

On 20 June 1855 Gaylor reported the whole matter to the SGCS at their Quarterly Convocation, and the next day the Freemasons Monthly Magazine received another letter from Gaylor but this time in his full Masonic dignity as a spokesman for the Grand Chapter. The salient points were as follows.

Comp. Rettie of the Bon Accord Chapter "has applied to the Laws of Supreme Chapter *a meaning they are quite incapable of sustaining*". It was true that Chapters could confer the Mark Degree but "cannot *grant warrants to any other body* of Masons to confer the said degree, or *depute its own powers in any way whatever.*" That was a power vested only in the SGCS. Comp. Rettie was to withdraw the warrant immediately "and to report at next quarterly communication that the same had been so done, in order to avoid the necessity of ulterior measures".

What those 'ulterior' (i.e. disciplinary) measures might be and what effect they would have on their lodge and on the Masonic reputation of its many highly regarded members does not seem to have disturbed anyone unduly. A week after Gaylor's report to the SGCS the Rt. Hon. the Lord Leigh was inducted into the Chair of Bon Accord by Dr. Jones. The Minutes once more record that "the newly installed Master, being a member of the 30°, was first saluted *with the honours of the higher degrees* and subsequently the members of the inferior degrees being re-admitted he was declared duly installed in the Chair of KS (sic) and saluted accordingly".

There is no mention whatsoever of the impending squall in the Lodge Minutes but in the August 1855 edition of the Freemasons Monthly Magazine we see a report of the after-proceedings. During these and in a toast to the Bon Accord Chapter No. 70 *and its First Principal*, Dr. Jones spoke of the charge laid against the Lodge of "practising *spurious and illegal* Masonry" but re-played, and added to, the previous evidence in refutation of such a charge and went on to say that "the matter *still being under discussion* between the Mother and Daughter Chapters in Scotland he had little doubt the charge of the Lodge's illegality would be found untenable". At this point it is right to note that W.H.Absolon, a later Grand Chapter committee member, had belonged to Bon Accord since its formation and at this June meeting John Hervey, a member of the 1855 Board of General Purposes of Grand Lodge, was advanced. Despite the presence of these two members I cannot believe that what was still a matter 'sub judice' in Scotland could have played *any part* in creating the Joint sub-committees which were later formed. We have seen the declared cause of concern in the Grand Lodge BGP records and that was of far more importance than what was still a private matter between the SGCS and one of its Chapters.

Indeed the Committees were already being considered before the Bon Accord affair reached its more public climax.

As reported in the October issue of the FMM the SGCS had received no reply from the First Principal of the Aberdeen Chapter at their Sept. Quarterly Communication and the Chapter of Bon Accord was declared to be suspended from all their RA privileges until such time as they did what had been required and recovered the London warrant wrongly issued by them. By their **December** gathering there had been a complaint from Bon Accord Chapter about the treatment afforded them but the Supreme Grand Chapter re-affirmed that unless the Chapter complied with their June ruling the suspension would remain.

The SGCS, however, had obviously been giving thought to the needs of such brethren as formed the Bon Accord Mark Lodge and at this same meeting received a report from the General Committee on this subject. They then enacted a decision which would authorise the granting of Warrants for the conferring of the Mark Degree in other countries. This step was taken "on account of every Past Master being obliged never to acknowledge any Lodge that does not hold of some Supreme body, and the necessity of stepping forward to *the relief of the English Mark Masons* **until they can put themselves under a Supreme Body there**". The step was further justified on the ground that this Grand Chapter had already granted Royal Arch Charters to Masons in the Netherlands and Belgium and if they could thus authorise others in these countries to confer *all* the degrees then they could certainly do so in this case where *only the Mark Degree* was to be warranted. The phrase "until some other Body (than a Grand Chapter) be duly constituted in that country (i.e. England) to *take the superintendence* of the Mark Degree" was repeated. It will be seen shortly that this was putting ideas in people's heads.

In February 1856 the Bon Accord Chapter still met, claiming that it had only *adjourned at its last meeting*, and passed a motion of *censure on the Grand Chapter* couched in very strong terms, with a resolution to return the Charter received from that Body. What was more they declared that as the Knights Templar Encampments never gave up their even older right to work these degrees, the Companions would apply for another warrant to the St. George Aboyne Encampment in Aberdeen. It was only at this date that they declared that "these proceedings should be made *as public as possible*, and communicated to the Supreme Grand Chapter".

In receiving their communication at the March 1856 Communications the SGCS recorded their regret that the resolutions made by the Bon Accord Chapter were "unwarrantable, in so far as they are not only based upon a *total misunderstanding of the laws* of the SGC but contain statements *altogether at variance with the facts* of the case". It was also decided to suspend all the movers and seconders of the resolutions that had been forwarded. These included Dr. Robert Beveridge and five others of whom four, together with Beveridge, were already members of the Aboyne Encampment. To complete the Scottish side of this stormy episode it is worth noting that no attempt was made by Bon Accord Chapter to call for the return of the London warrant, no approach was made to the local Encampment for another RA warrant, the Bon Accord Chapter never met again but in 1864 Companions Beveridge, Houston and Mollison had their suspension removed.

Yet it is the London end of the incident that must still occupy us. To read the Minutes for this same period is again to have the sense that nothing untoward was taking place. In October 1855, Lord Leigh not being present, Dr. Jones took the Chair but no Minutes could be read because the Secretary was absent and there is no record of them being read subsequently. However, at the November meeting they agreed that 'a piece of plate not exceeding 10 guineas be obtained and presented to the Secretary for his services from the Lodge's formation' whilst in December the same gesture was made to the Treasurer. In April 1856 the presentations took place. Not a word is said about the activities that had taken place North of the Border. Bro. Spencer, of course, provided a full coverage in the FMM for April, July and October 1856 but there were then Mark-related events much nearer to home to report. (For the record Bro. Spencer was one of the later well known trio that formed the Toye, Kenning and Spencer firm of Masonic regalia merchants.)

The Joint Committee which had been set up to examine the purpose and place of the Mark Degree was meanwhile acting with commendable speed. One of its members, John Symonds, joined the Bon Accord Mark Lodge in November 1855 and in the same month William H.White and several others took themselves off to the Isle of Wight to receive the degree at the hands of the Albany Mark Lodge members. The remainder of the Committee became Mark Masons elsewhere but apart from John Havers who was advanced in Bon Accord in May 1856 the other Lodges have yet to be determined. What has to be admitted is that the Committee clearly took its task seriously and it was with considerable interest that Grand Lodge and Grand Chapter awaited the outcome in their next Quarterly Communications.

The report was not only prompt but brief and we should note that it has been "returned by the Grand Master, approved (by him), with (the) direction for its being laid before Grand Chapter and United Grand Lodge. It thus appeared first on 1 February 1856 at the Quarterly Convocation of Supreme Grand Chapter and was largely as follows:

"The Committee appointed... in relation to the Degree of Mark Mason, having jointly entered upon an enquiry and investigation of the matter referred to them (so far as the circumstance of the whole of the Committee not having been admitted into that degree would permit) came to the following unanimous Resolution, viz:– 'That after obtaining all the information in its power, this Committee is of opinion that the Mark Mason's Degree, so called, does *not form a portion of the Royal Arch Degree*, and that it is *not essential to Craft Masonry*, but they are of opinion that there is *nothing objectionable* in such degree, nor anything which militates *against the Universality* of Masonry, and that it might be considered as *forming a graceful addition* to the Fellow Craft's Degree.' "

It was then proposed by John Hervey (who was also a member of Bon Accord Mark Lodge) and seconded by Peter Matthews (who was not) that "As the Mark Degree formed no part of Royal Arch Masonry, the question of its introduction into Masonry be left to the Grand Lodge of England." On 5 March that is what happened.

The statement was succinct and graciously phrased and shows that some study of the subject had been undertaken. The fact that not all the members of the Committee were at that stage personally acquainted with the Mark *in some form* – and here let us recognise that the workings in the Bon Accord and Albany Mark Lodges were distinctly different – must have affected their viewpoint whilst the brevity of the experience of most of them has also to be weighed. Moreover the conclusions which they expressed were hardly calculated to be of much assistance in the overseas situations which had occasioned the enquiry. Some of the queries that remained were these:

(i) How could those belonging to Bon Accord not point out to the rest of the Committee the quite manifest link between the Mark and the Royal Arch in Scotland and as so clearly defined in their own warrant? (What practical steps could be suggested to English Masons abroad to deal with any who insisted on the Mark and wanted to share in that degree?)

(ii) Did the fact that it was *not essential* to Craft Masonry really imply that Craft Masons ought not to have anything to do with it or that it simply did not matter if they did? (What was the stance to be where rulers were faced with Craft Lodges that still insisted on their traditional right to confer the Mark Degree?)

(iii) When, in partial answer to the last question, they might endorse some participation in the Mark, what exactly was meant by speaking of it as 'a graceful addition'? (Did that mean that it should be an optional 'lecture' appended to the 2° ceremony, a brief conferral of words and signs for those who requested it, or should it be a special ceremony for Fellow Crafts administered once a year or from time to time?)

(iv) If there was nothing objectionable in the degree where did that leave all those whom we have seen were practising the Mark at home as well as in Gibraltar, Malta and India? (Were their activities now to be legally recognised provided they would relate it to the 2° or would there have to be an agreed ritual to which they would be called to conform if they wished to continue as Mark Masons?)

It can be seen that the statement left many more matters unresolved than it answered. Both in regard to not fully appreciating the situation of those overseas and either not being aware of, or not bothering about, any implications this might have for *what was*, for all its informality and diversity, a *living Mark Masonry* in many places, this Joint Committee had inadequately discharged its remit. Did the members ever ask themselves the really crucial question – *what is* Ancient Freemasonry? If, as one suspects, they took for granted the answer as meaning 'What the present United Grand Lodge of England and the Supreme Grand Chapter thereof consist' then of course they could give only one reply. Whatever its participants called this degree – and we notice that they do seem to have heard of two early parts, Mark Man and Mark Master – it was not allowed for in modern English Royal Arch practice. It would upset the sequence of progress to the Chair if it were allowed to be seen as an additional full Craft Degree, and yet, because it was interesting and inocuous, a place ought possibly to be found for it somewhere.

These, I suspect, were some of the reactions to the 5 March finding when it was printed and made known. The immediate response was another unanimous resolution in Grand Lodge:

"That the Degree of Mark Mason or Mark Master (but no one seems to have explained why there were two titles) is not at variance with the *ancient landmarks* of the Order, and that the Degree be an addition to and *form part of* Craft Masonry, and, consequently, may be conferred by all regular Warranted Lodges, under regulations as shall be prepared by the Board of General Purposes, approved and sanctioned by the MW the Grand Master."

Here at last was some more light but not a great deal. What had clearly been the case in some areas of English Freemasonry for almost a century was now acknowledged as having some legitimacy. The act of conferring a personal mark, its use in confirming one's best work, its value in helping to build and complete King Solomon's Temple and not least its virtue in signalling constancy through all difficulties – these were now recognised as fully consonant with the best that the Craft had to offer. Yet the permission to confer this 'honourable' degree was conditional and there was a wide margin of uncertainty as to how, when, for whom and with whom future English Mark Masonry might function. It was a breakthrough certainly but there would be many traditional Masons who would wonder whether yet another shake-up of United Craft Masonry was desirable and not a few Old Mark Masons who might suspect that what they had preserved in the Mark would be discarded by the regulations of those who knew it slightly or not at all.

Indeed we know that the reactions of many Mark Masons were varied. Some were openly delighted at the cachet of respectability that Mark had now acquired and with a statement that acknowledged Mark as a component part of Freemasonry. Some were so uncertain that they turned instead to the SGCS which had made known its intentions about issuing warrants for Mark Lodges in other countries – and we shall in due course see what happened in this connection. Some were just dismissive of the apparent recognition and determined the more to strengthen their own practice of the Mark and its appendant ceremonies, as we shall see was the case with the Ashton Travelling Lodge. There was also the line of thought that was now taken up by the members of the Bon Accord Mark Lodge.

If the steps taken by the Supreme Grand Royal Arch Chapter of Scotland against their 'mother' Chapter in Aberdeen took time to influence the Mark Lodge members the combined declarations of the SGCS in December and of the UGLE in March certainly alerted the wiser members of the Lodge to their precarious situation. If the Grand Chapter of Scotland was to become a recognised authority in England for chartering new Mark Lodges, then Bon Accord would be outlawed by that Grand Body and its new constituent English lodges. Their only future then would be to join the list of those many other Mark Lodges which were maintained by independent arrangements. Alternatively, they could submit to the Scottish Grand Chapter, renounce their allegiance to the Aberdeen Chapter, surrender their warrant and be re-advanced. Either course was unthinkable, especially for those many members of Bon Accord who were prominent and conscientious Masons in both Grand Lodge and Grand Chapter, as well as in the Knightly Orders. Was there another way?

It was thus that the idea of a separate Grand Mark Lodge was born. These Bon Accord members were shrewd enough to realise that if the UGL resolution went forward and was acted upon then their part in Mark Masonry would be side-lined. If, on the other hand, steps were taken to set up an entirely new Governing Body which would take charge of all the disparate Mark units around the country not only would that enhance and stabilise their position as promoters of the degree but it would also provide a new authority for Bon Accord to relate to; would preclude the SGCS from intruding into England further since there would now be a Supreme body, if not a Grand Chapter, which regulated the Mark in England; and above all would ensure that the Mark Degree was not relegated to some minor niche in the existing Craft structure. It was bold thinking but how might it be managed? From 6 March 1856 an agreed form of words was embodied on the Grand Lodge Minutes which so accepted the Mark Mason degree as to require that the M.W. the Grand Master should introduce new regulations by which this degree could be incorporated into the working of any warranted Craft Lodge. Surely the step in another direction had already been taken? Well, had it? Was there not another way out?

The cliquishness of English Freemasonry and its internal jealousies during the middle years of the 19th century are notorious and the Mark problem was seized upon as a *casus belli* by conflicting parties. But on one point, and for their own reasons, the Bon Accord Brethren – who were strongly representative of one of the factions – were in agreement with some of their opponents: that, *if possible*, the part of the minutes of the Quarterly Communications of 5 March 1856 dealing with the Mark Degree *should not be confirmed.*

It is at this point that we need to leave speculation and return to the facts for what now transpired has a curious pattern. We begin with a *special meeting* of the Bon Accord Mark Lodge on 21 May 1856 when Dr. Jones was again occupying the Chair. In the Minutes of that meeting there is a later inserted note which is in **different handwriting** to the rest. It states: "It was *at this meeting* that **final steps** were taken to *form a Grand Lodge* of Mark Master Masons, and the WM. Lord Leigh, was invited to take the *position of Grand Master* of Mark Masonry in England."

This at last confirms what was thought to have been a possibility. It will be noted that what took place in this gathering were *final steps* towards a premeditated goal. We know that in April contact was made with the St. George's 'Mark' Lodge at Bottoms to enquire what their position would be if a Grand Lodge of Mark Masons were to be erected. Their reaction was negative and they were not involved in the later negotiations but if this could happen in a remote corner of Yorkshire what went on in consultations with the Old Kent (London) and Old Cumberland (Bath) Lodges that were involved from the outset? It strongly suggests that after the March decision firm steps were taken to prepare the ground for the possibility of a 'new Grand Lodge' outcome. It would be very interesting if we could discover in the records of those old Mark Lodges that did cooperate in forming a Grand Mark Lodge evidence of similar approaches at this time.

We know for a fact that John Havers, who had been a member of the Joint Committee, was now advanced at this 21 May meeting, which means that at least 5 Grand Officers who would vote at the next Quarterly Communications in *June 1856* were already members of Bon Accord and could thus have been privy to the plan that was finalised on 21 May.

There is also the part played by Lord Leigh. At the time that all this was happening William Henry Leigh was 31 years old. His father, Chandos Leigh, was raised to the peerage in 1839 as 'Leigh of Stoneleigh' when William was at Harrow, and from there the boy went up to Trinity College, Cambridge. After starting what was to be an extremely happy marriage in 1848 William succeeded to his father's title in 1851 and in December that same year he was initiated into the Lodge of Light, No. 468 in Birmingham. Less than a year later, and with the personal approval of the MW Grand Master, the Provincial Grand Master for Warwickshire, Earl Howe, announced his resignation due to ill-health, and introduced Lord William Leigh, now 28, as his successor. He became the ruler of 12 lodges and 359 brethren.

Lord Leigh entered the Royal Arch on 9 March 1853 and on 9 July he was advanced in the Bon Accord Lodge of which he also became Master in June 1855. Of his personal integrity, obvious sincerity and single-mindedness in all he undertook there seems to be ample testimony. He was certainly hard-working and *carefully managed* all the concerns for which he was responsible. It is therefore extremely unlikely that he would have been privy to any activity that would have given cause to besmirch his reputation or that of the Craft, Mark or Supreme Council brethren with whom he so fully threw in his lot. If he considered it right to proceed with such an idea so innovatory in English or any other Freemasonry as a separate Grand Lodge for the Mark degree then he would have been the first to alert not only his peers in Grand Lodge but his personal friend, the Grand Master, as to what might be afoot. Indeed it is inconceivable that with his well-attested reputation he would have connived at unconstitutional measures to attain such a goal. Either before he accepted the role of a 'possible Grand Master of an as yet notional Grand Mark Lodge' or at least as soon as he did accept such an invitation he would be honour bound to inform, if not to consult with, his Chief and to think through such necessary steps as would have to be taken to permit that possibility. When it is realised that he had around him in Bon Accord members of the main Committees of the Grand Lodge and Chapter, and in the membership of Bon Accord **5** Provincial Grand Masters, who became senior Officers of the Mark Grand Lodge at its inception, it is even more certain that he would have insisted on legal steps being taken before any public announcement about a new Mark Governing Body for England was released. To see whether such a surmise might be supported by evidence the author made search through such of Lord Leigh's remaining Masonic papers as are lodged in the Record office at Stratford-upon-Avon but there is nothing there of any written kind between himself and the M.W. Grand Master at this time. On such a delicate issue however that is hardly surprising. With a new Mark Lodge just begun at Birmingham in 1851 (the Howe, named after his predecessor) Lord Leigh would be even more sensitive to the proper management of Mark affairs in the kingdom whilst also eager to put that degree on a firm and proper footing. That Lord Leigh was in charge of what subsequently took place in regard to a Grand Lodge is beyond question and it must be assumed that he was therefore both fully consulted and apprised of what was now about to transpire. What is interesting is that he was not present at the meetings of Grand Lodge in March or on 5 June 1856.

At this latter meeting, which is reported as being more than usually well attended, if not actually 'packed', the Minutes of the previous Communications had no sooner been read than V.Wor. Bro. Henderson, a Past President of the Board of General Purposes for the years 1836/7, when he was also Past Grand Registrar, rose and spoke. That his being a spokesman was not a mere coincidence is revealed by the compliment he received from a later speaker who expressed his delight at seeing this venerable Brother (he was in his 80s) in Grand Lodge again after a long absence. Nor is it without significance that in what was an able presentation he should emphasise that *when he was appointed by the Duke of Sussex* the latter had enjoined him to see that no innovations were made in the Order. Indeed, he continued, "he could scarcely conceive that the present Registrar (Alexander Dobie) had used sufficient authority in allowing this matter to be brought forward". He queried whether the Joint Committee *really knew* what they were dealing with, he feared that the previous decision would open the door to all sorts of new proposals and he thus called upon Grand Lodge not to consent to *any innovation* regarding their current ceremonies as otherwise *the most disastrous consequences* might result. He denied that "they had the power to make so great and constitutional a change as that of adding **a new degree** to the Order ... and he contended that no man, nor body of men, could make such innovation as *that now proposed*, without *endangering the whole stability* of the Institution".

Arguments in favour of and against the motion were heard at great length. They included a passionate plea from Bro. Aria who said that 'throughout the West Indies and other colonies the Mark was given as a preliminary to being exalted, *even under the English Constitution*, and would they stigmatise such Brethren as acting illegally?' whilst Bro. Dobie 'could not feel that he had not done his duty but would be glad to resign his position to the worthy Bro. if he would *again take it*'. The discussion was closed when the Earl of Zetland stated that *he upheld Henderson's proposal* and declared that he himself would record his vote of **non-confirmation of the minutes** that related to the Mark Degree. The vote was carried in that direction by a large majority and the Mark Degree was **rejected**, which might have been thought by some to be highly appropriate. It is no less ironic to note that almost immediately afterwards the Grand Lodge received a long address from the Grand Master regarding some Masons in Canada. "They asked", he reported, "that the Constitutions of the Grand Lodge should be altered so as to permit the Provincial Grand Lodge of Canada West to elect their Grand Master. Did they think that the Grand Master of England would propose such a measure to the Grand Lodge, so to alter the constitution of Free Masonry? It was so preposterous that he did not feel he could send an answer that could be respectful to that body ..." There was much more in the same vein.

The truth is, of course, that earlier in the year the MW Grand Master had already and formally approved a motion going to Grand Lodge that *would materially have altered the fabric* of the Craft had its openly agreed Resolution of March been confirmed in June. It was therefore at least unfair, if not downright incorrect, for any claim to be made that no suggestions of alteration to the Craft Constitutions could be made. For that matter what is supposed to have happened at the Union? The facts surely are that the Grand Master clearly had, or was encouraged to have, second thoughts about what *he had previously approved* and felt that he must firmly redirect the way that matters seemed to be going.

For those who perhaps find it odd that Grand Lodge at that time could fail to confirm, as a matter of course, something which had been properly proposed, seconded, and voted on with approval, and then correctly recorded it has to be said that apparently the custom *then followed* was different from today. Because the Craft were largely unaware of what was to be transacted at the next meeting of Grand Lodge, and there was delay in acting upon decisions made, the opportunity was provided for objections to decisions to be made when the Minutes had been read. What in effect happened was not that there was any denial of what had taken place but the chance was provided for another vote on a matter to be recorded. If it was contrary to the previous decision then the former resolution was lost *and not confirmed.*

What of course remains as a statement for all time is the judgement of two groups of serious-minded Grand Officers that the Mark was a part of Freemasonry that could not be objected to and might be regarded as some part of the Craft pattern. Those who have read this book will know that that is unquestionably true and what is even more intriguing is that on the 27 May 1856 the Board of General Purposes had gone so far as to make explicit arrangements regarding the conferring, the recording, the payment due and the insignia to be adopted when the Grand Lodge had confirmed and would authorise the commencement of this **new degree** of the UGLE. It must therefore have been at the very last moment that someone alerted the MW Grand Master as to the imminence and the implications of this action. Can we learn anything more about this matter?

We can start by noting that by this date **5** members of the Board of General Purposes were members of the Bon Accord Mark Lodge and the Grand Secretary was a member of Albany, IOW and therefore they could fully prime both the MW Grand Master and the prospective Mark Grand Master as to the imminence of the Mark degree's incorporation. There is more, however.

In the course of researching for this book the author was advised to see if there were any papers of the Earl of Zetland for this time or on this whole intriguing business. A search led to the Record Office in Northallerton, North Yorkshire, where the family have now permitted their ancestral papers to be retained and studied. A perusal of the Masonic documents for the 1850s produced the following information.

The first item (MIC 1986) is a Motion that was submitted to the Grand Master in the *summer of 1856* for his consideration. It came from John Symonds, a member of the Grand Chapter Committee and of Bon Accord Mark Lodge as well as PM of Lodge No. 275 (at that time). The motion has its own message.

"That Article 8 p. 27 be amended by addition of the following words:- 'No motion for the **non-confirmation** of any Resolution of a previous Grand Lodge can, however, be entertained *unless notice of such motion* shall have been duly communicated to the General Committee in conformity with Art. 8 pp. 19ff. The consideration of any such motion shall follow immediately *after the confirmation of the Minutes as entered correctly*'. Whilst this was to usher in the present arrangement it was also shutting the door after the horse had bolted but it at least reveals how some felt about what had taken place in June.

In September there began a series of letters from John Havers, member of the Joint Committee and also of Bon Accord, who reflects some of the feelings that surrounded the 'rejection'. The tone of the letters is respectful but intimate and very frank and it is clear that Havers had been in touch with the Earl of Zetland for many months previously. We can only select from this batch but some of the statements are revealing.

On Sept. 4th Havers, who was a Fellow of the Royal College of Surgeons residing at Russell Square, London, reminds the G.M. that he had previously suggested a special meeting of Grand Lodge and says now that the Grand Secretary recommended "that some notice should be taken on the summons of *the irregularity of the last (June) meeting*. I should say, by no means introduce one word more than is necessary. I may mention (and I am sure it will be received in confidence) that *Dobie feels himself hurt at being thrown overboard* by your Lordship on the Mark Mason's matter after you had *approved and signed* the recommendation. To this I could only reply that after the Committee appointed to report on this subject I had some chat with Dobie and left him with the full impression that he (letters here crossed out) felt as I did, *that it was quite absurd to recommend any such proceeding as its admission into the degrees of Masonry* – hence my astonishment to find on recovery from my illness that it had been carried in Grand Lodge, recommended by the Grand Registrar (Dobie) and yourself. It is unfortunate (and used not to be so) that the President of the Board and the Gd. Registrar are one and the same person – the very position gives & very properly so, an increased influence in Grand Lodge ... (He then ends by saying) Let us get every good man and true to the special meeting, get things moderately right and keep them so." (Author's italics) Two days later he sent the report of the Grand Lodge meeting on September 1st with his comments. (Mic 2004–2008) Very soon Havers was himself to be President of the BGP.

Even these short extracts reveal at least one of the Earl's sources of information and 'guidance' and since Havers joined the Bon Accord Mark Lodge on the very day when the 'final steps' were proposed for a possible Grand Mark Lodge it is clear that whether from Leigh or Havers the doings there would at last be made clear to the Head of the Craft. We also see that Havers, and doubtless others, had the impression that the March meeting was already 'sewn up' and that any motion of a positive kind in favour of incorporating Mark Masonry *would be lost*. When that did not happen other steps obviously had to be taken. We know that they were and that a damage limitation exercise was also contemplated. Perhaps the last word should be the

Grand Master's. On 25 November 1856 he wrote to Dobie privately to say that he thought he should resign as GM.

"Some measures have been carried of which I decidedly disapprove and notices have been given of several more which I think would, if carried, be injurious to the best interests of the Craft and trenching largely on the prerogatives of the Grand Master ... I see that great inconvenience must arise from a pro GM in the Chair interpreting the law in one way and the Grand Master upsetting his decision at the next meeting although I contend that he has a right to do so and that his duty compels him to exercise that right when he differs from a decision previously given." It was a gracious attempt at an apology.

Now that the Mark Degree had been rejected prepared alternative plans swung into action. Some looked at once for their Governing body in Scotland but others turned away from their Scottish origins and sought to erect their home-made Authority.

A NEW GRAND LODGE.

In September 1855 four journalists from London attended the Annual Meeting of the British Association in Glasgow. During this business trip three of them (Warren, Simmonds and Sharman) became members of the Glasgow RA Chapter No. 50. Hughes, the other member of the party already belonged having been admitted in 1853. Hughes would have then been made a Mark Mason and Sharman was already one having taken the degree in an Irish Chapter in Jersey in 1854. Immediately after the June U.G.L.E. meeting of 1856 Warren, Hughes and Sharman applied to the SGCS for a Charter which would enable them to hold a Mark Masters Lodge in London and there is an appropriate Minute in the Grand Chapter's records for 18 June 1856. They were granted their request and the name 'The St. Mark's Lodge of Mark Masters' with the rank of No. 1 on the Register of MkM Lodges holding under but outside Scotland. The Charter was received a few days later and on 15 August a meeting was held which was reported in the September FMM as follows:

"The Brethren of this Lodge met together on the evening of the 15th ult. at the Freemasons' Tavern ... The business of the evening consisted of the advancement of three Brethren ... It speaks well for the progress of the Lodge, and *marks the desire of the Brethren generally* to see the Mark Degree recognised by the Grand Lodge of England, to find that there are now on the roll of the Lodge, although only two months established the names of 30 Brothers, some of whom have been advanced *in the illegal assembly styling itself the Bon Accord Lodge of Mark Masons*, but who have renounced their allegiance to it and formally joined (was it 're-advanced in' also?) the new Lodge. There are, besides, as many as 17 Brethren on the list for advancement the next Lodge evening."

In October the Rev. Bro. Owen responded to a toast by expressing the hope "That as the success of St. Mark's Lodge would popularise the Degree in this country, and demonstrate the fact (which he never doubted) that Mark Masonry was part and parcel of the Craft, not only a graceful appendage to the Fellow-Craft Degree, as it had been styled, but an essential portion of it, and the link which connected it with the Third Degree, so the constituents of Grand Lodge would, when the question *was next brought before them*, be better acquainted with the subject on which they would be called to vote, and would not, *as on the last occasion, reject it because they knew nothing about it.*"

By March 1857 the FMM was reporting two more Charters having been issued to create Mark Lodges in England and concludes: "We have not heard to whom Charter No. 2 was granted (it was in fact to St. John's at Bolton, Lancashire) but it is stated that three of the Brethren of the London Bon Accord, having made their submission to the Grand Chapter of Scotland, are to have No. 3 (Thistle) – the meetings of which will be held at Radley's Hotel". The Scottish 'invasion' had begun in earnest.

Meanwhile the Bon Accord Mark Lodge was far from inactive. Ten days after the Grand Lodge meeting that 'rejected' the Mark the Bon Accord Secretary, William Collins, was writing from Maida Vale to the Lodge officers and members of the Permanent Committee. At the command of the 'illusts. Br. Lord Leigh' their attendance was desired 'on Monday the 23rd inst. at 4 o'clock p.m. precisely – To take into consideration the propriety of adopting the recommendation of the Permanent Committee "That a Grand Mark Masters Lodge for England and it's (sic) Dependencies be forthwith established…" '. The designation of the WM in this now curious way simply underlines what has already been noted, that in the lodge meetings Brethren were saluted with the highest rank in post-Craft Orders that they might possess. This letter alone shows that plans for this contingency were well prepared but there must still be amazement that such distinguished Masons as we know were involved could seek to so change the Masonic landscape simply through the medium of a single Mark unit.

The Lodge historian must be the spokesman for the remarkable event that now took place. "The members of Bon Accord, with the promptitude they had shown at the formation of their Lodge five years before, and in conjunction with 3 other Lodges – Northumberland and Berwick (Newcastle-on-Tyne), Royal Cumberland (Bath), and Old Kent (London), proceeded **at once** *to form the Grand Lodge of Master Masons of England and Wales*, and the Dominions and Dependencies of the British Crown." That is what is printed but of course he really meant *Mark Masters*. What this slip might suggest, as commentators since have often remarked, is that in a strange way the inauguration of the new Grand Mark Lodge was a form of re-play of the 1717 event in Freemasonry. Four existing lodges who sought a more stable organisation gathered in London to create the new body. Of course there were differences between the two events but the implications for the future of English and Welsh, and in some sense worldwide Masonry, were as significant on the latter as on the former occasion. How it came about was as follows.

A meeting of Bon Accord was held on 23 June 1856 just under three weeks after the 'rejection' meeting of Grand Lodge. Lord Leigh presided and 11 candidates were proposed with 7 being advanced that evening, among them being the later Earl Amhurst. *At the conclusion of this meeting* the members of Bon Accord 'with the assistance of the three previously mentioned Lodges proceeded to the formation of Grand Mark Lodge'. (LH p. 13) It was as simple and as straightforward as that.

The Rt. Hon. Lord Leigh was elected as the 1st Grand Master and held that position for 4 years, after which he was to be succeeded by another Bon Accord PM, the Earl of Carnarvon. The membership of Bon Accord at this period was about 150 and ALL the officers of the Grand Lodge were initially chosen from its ranks. If the other old Mark Lodges were 'assisting them in this venture' it is singular that not one of their members was appointed but not having scrutinised the Lodge's attendance book for that day I cannot be sure whether anyone was actually available to take office and clearly this new body had to officered from the outset. Nevertheless the attempt to either start modestly or keep a low profile created its own pack of problems.

On June 26th a correspondent calling himself 'Mark Master' wrote to the FMM having seen an advertisement in The Times which mentioned that a Grand Lodge had been established. "Can you favour those of your readers who take an interest in this Degree, with the meaning of this extraordinary announcement? Where has this 'Grand Mark Lodge' sprung from? What daughter Mark Lodges does it represent? Have any circulars been sent, or any announcement been made whereby those who are Mark Masters have been called together, and the present movement arisen out of such convention? If so, I, who read almost everything Masonic, have neither seen nor heard of any such assemblage. Or is this some *upstart self-constituted Grand Lodge* that has called itself into existence, dignified itself with a *Grand* name and by an act of usurpation, assumed to take the management of this interesting Degree in England?

"If you can give any information showing that this Grand Mark Lodge has been formed in the manner usually observed among Masons, that it is a genuine one and such a one as I can with propriety apply to for a warrant, and that it is not, as I suspect, a self-elected, and therefore a sham and spurious Grand Lodge, I shall esteem it a favour. I enclose my mark, &c, And Remain, yours fraternally . . ."

The notice that provoked this sharp response was repeated on 12 and 19 July though Collins was, in these latter insertions, referred to as '*Honorary* Grand Secretary'. This further exposure of what had taken place simply intensified the bitter reactions of many who were deeply troubled by what they regarded as a totally unwarranted and presumptuous claim by a minority of Mark Masons. It was now that there appeared a phrase used by the critics which has lingered in every report since. The Grand Mark Lodge just created was said to have been 'born in sin and shapen in iniquity'. This harsh judgement was particularly fostered when it was revealed that even the Aberdeen Chapter which gave the London Mark Lodge its name and support was not only under judgment but no longer even existed. How could authority and respect be built on such irregular foundations?

Of course there were those who as strongly supported the move that had been made. Mark Masonry in England and Wales needed a firm point of reference if, unlike the Irish and the Scots, English Craft or Royal Arch Masonry were not to be the 'home' of this ancient operative practice. Even the SGCS had recognised that Mark Masons in England needed a governing Body to which to relate, and had admitted that should there be a such a recognised Governing Body south of the Border then they would have no right to interfere with that Body's jurisdiction. Yet it has to be said that in their eagerness to encourage Lord Leigh and his officers in their aims even their supporters were occasionally most intemperate in their speaking and writing.

Grantham called all these expressions of anger and denunciation 'tedious' but there is another way of looking at what happened. Anyone who troubles to read the contemporary articles, letters, speeches and reports cannot but be exhilarated by the fact that English and Welsh brethren cared so much about how Mark Masonry should best be conducted in their countries. Here we have 'a powerful spotlight' on the character, sights, opinions and prospects of a fairly hard-pressed set of Victorian Freemasons. They spoke either as long-standing Mark Men who did not want their good name traduced or as eager new advancees who could glimpse the fresh possibilities for the degree. Above all, the heat of the controversy had its desired effect. The heat that was generated seared Lord Leigh's heart and mind.

The Grand Lodge he led was not progressing as had been hoped. None of the consenting 'Old' Mark Lodges were yet under its wing and only four had registered – the 'parent Lodge' of Bon Accord, No. 1; the ancient Phoenix, No. 2, that incorporated what remained from the famous Friendship Chapter of Dunckerley; Keystone, No. 3 and The Mark, No. 4, both of which were started by Bon Accord members. Something had to be done.

Yet some serious obstacles still lay in Lord Leigh's path. Unless these were faced and dealt with then the going would be very hard indeed. One had to do with the credibility of the Bon Accord team, another with the rapidly growing impact of warrants from Scotland, a third with the pretensions of the Ashton Travelling Lodge and a fourth with the way in which the new Grand Lodge was going to be managed. As long as these problems remained the future was extremely uncertain.

The Lodge of Fortitude and Old Cumberland, No. 12, is of Time Immemorial status and its Lodge History is full of the most fascinating detail. On 13 January 1851 we read that during a 2° ceremony a certain Bro. (Dr.) *Jones left the Junior Warden's Chair to converse with the Senior Warden.* After the ceremony was over the Master made the following comment: "Bro. Jones, with your knowledge of Masonry you must be fully aware that it is highly improper to vacate the Warden's chair in the midst of a ceremony." Jones replied that Bro. Norton called to him, having a communication to make.

Later in the same meeting a motion submitted earlier by Bro. Norton, the SW, questioning the hosting of musical entertainers at the banquet, was answered by the Secretary and Treasurer who between them showed that this had long been the practice and that charges by Norton and Jones (the latter having written a letter to the WM) of their violating the Bye-Laws were unfounded when 'Bro. Norton and Bros. Jones and Hall repeatedly (sic) and rudely interrupted Bro. Marriott (the Secretary) and would not allow him to explain'. Bro. Norton, on being called to order by the WM and requested to take his chair, *refused to do so*, and was reminded by the Secretary of the Laws of Grand Lodge that 'after having been three times called to order, etc., and been admonished the Master had the power to remove him from the Lodge. Whereupon, Bro. Norton *threw down the Senior Warden's Collar and Jewel* and left the Lodge with Bro. Hall. Subsequently they returned with their resignations which they handed to the WM. He could not properly decipher them and sent them to the Secretary to be read, who was at first also unable to make them out properly. Bro. Norton then rudely snatched them from his hand, read his aloud to the Lodge and then left, as did also Bro. Hall. The resignations of Norton and Hall were accepted.

The Master then addressed the Brethren as follows: "I plainly perceive that as long as I allow Bro. Dr. Jones to proceed in the improper manner in which he has for some time indulged, this Lodge will lose all its Masonic character and become a debating Society and from the dictatorial and improper letter I have received from him which contains unfounded imputations ... it is my determination to displace Bro. Jones from the office of JW ..." A vote was taken in favour and Bro. Jones replied: "WM I will resign and take my leave of you, but you will hear from me again" and left. On February 10 Bro. Hall apologised and asked to be allowed to return. On May 12 the BGP informed the Lodge 'That Bro. Jones had been *properly and justly expelled from the office of JW* but that he should have been sent a summons for the Lodge'.

If anyone wonders why the affairs of the Bon Accord Mark Lodge were conducted in so peculiar a manner in the years that followed we have in the characters of Jones and Norton a good measure of the answer. In October 1856 the same two Brethren were involved in another most unpleasant occurrence. With Comp. Jones in the Mark Chair Comp. Norton made a 'very forcible speech upon what he considered the unmasonic conduct of Comps. Kennedy, Hewlett and Pass (the latter a year before was on the BGP), in *having written and published* in the FREEMASON'S MAGAZINE charges against several of their Brethren, members of the Lodge, without having previously communicated with those Brethren individually or called the Lodge's attention to the subject'. That sounds most reasonable, if harshly put, until the substance of the letter is appreciated. The letter was addressed to Lord Leigh and dated 5 days after the new Grand Lodge was commenced in this very lodge. It made the following points:

(a) Great irregularities have been practised in your name and during your Mastership:

(b) Lodges of Emergency were called and held to advance Masons to the Mark but without the whole membership being summoned and only Jones, Norton, Collins and a few other officers being informed. The Bye Laws specifically state that new members can only be balloted for in open Lodge.

(c) When the writers of this letter turned up at a recent Emergency meeting of *their own Lodge, their presence was objected to* and when they refused to withdraw Jones and the Officers *retired to another room* and after an interval returned to advance the candidates without any open ballot having been taken.

(d) Your Lordship arrived, took the Chair and AFTER what had just taken place the Lodge was **opened**. We appealed to you but were told by Bro. Jones that *our presence was an intrusion*. Yet we are paid-up members with full rights and privileges in our own Lodge.

(e) When the Bye-Laws were read at our request to show that ALL must be allowed to ballot for new candidates Jones said that a Committee could meet between May and October to audit accounts and carry out 'other business' and that that permitted 'closed' balloting. When we appealed again to your Lordship you put it to a vote. Whose vote? Why, the very men and those only who had to justify their own illegal conduct. Yet vote they did and being outvoted thus 8 to 4 we left the lodge room.

(f) Surely the WM, PM and officers ought to be guardians of the Lodge funds and yet since the last Regular meeting there have been 2 illegal Emergency meetings and those present have banqueted at the heavy expense of the Lodge. Can such things be allowed?

The letter ended thus:

"We have the honour and prosperity of the noble Craft too much at heart to allow such proceedings to pass without seeking redress, and as they have taken place under the sanction of your Lordship's name as WM and whilst you were in the Chair we appeal to your sense of justice to have the legality of such proceedings thoroughly investigated, and not *allow the London Bon Accord Lodge to lay under the stigma* that must otherwise for ever attach to it.

"Originally founded, *though unknowingly, under an illegal Charter*, and having been repudiated by the Grand Chapter of Scotland under whose Constitution the Lodge professes to work, we cannot but think that the *utmost circumspection should be observed* to do justice to all its members".

In a discussion that ended this lodge meeting where Norton objected to the letter, the powers of the Permanent Committee were questioned and thereafter limited though there was also a resolution endorsing the 'honest intentions' of those who made up the Committee.

The impartial reader must surely appreciate why any step such as Bon Accord had now taken would be seriously questioned when its chaotic internal affairs were made so public. The fact that not one more mention of the whole matter ever occurred again but, equally, that Emergency Lodges cease and Dr. Jones's name begins to disappear suggests that, as he had to, Lord Leigh realised what a problem he had. If the Lodge No. 1 of the new Grand Mark Lodge behaved like this what possible confidence could any other Mark Masons have in the overall Body that was officered by its members. There was even direct imputation of his own incompetence.

In the FM for that month there appeared this item:

"Lord Leigh is, no doubt, a dupe to others. No-one who knows his Lordship will give him credit for having too great an acquaintance with Masonic laws, and nothing but his rank would ever recommend him to office. Any body of the brethren have an equal right to sell Masonic warrants as Leigh, Methuen, Jones and Co do. Should they do so, however, without the prefix of 'Lord' to the names of two of the firm, the BGP would most probably suspend them from their Masonic duties. In this case no such result can be expected as the greatest wrong-doers are, by virtue of the GM's appointment, members of the Board, and can overrule the opinions of those members elected by Grand Lodge."

It hardly matters whether this was fair judgement in all respect. It shows the growing scepticism about the new Grand Lodge and its first managers and it particularly highlights the need for Lord Leigh to restore confidence and re-arrange his henchmen. That he had to do and soon.

He also had to produce some answer to the obvious attraction of the warrants held out by the SGCS. Some papers recently recovered from the NOAR Collection in the Masonic library at Manchester reveal what happened in the case of a new Mark Lodge at Bolton nearby.

Bro. G.P.Brockbank, a PM of St. John's (Craft) Lodge No. 268 in that town, wrote in December 1856 to the now well-known Wm Gaylor in Scotland. Several Brethren like himself were anxious to have a Mark Masters warrant for their neighbourhood. He had taken the degree many years before 'but in a manner which would not be recognised by your Grand Chapter' and he was ready to take the steps to receive it lawfully again.

Gaylor told him that he must go either to London or Edinburgh and take the necessary obligation but in addition he had to renounce all other 'Mark' bodies not acknowledging a Supreme Body. On 4 March 1857 the brethren concerned were advanced in St. Mark's Lodge, London and the next day the Warrant was in their hands. 4 more joined on the 6th and the warrant dated that day has names of 13 more for the 11th.

By April there were 34 more members and it was about to sponsor two more lodges in Birkenhead and Liverpool. Meanwhile, at the Arnott Lodge No. 4, there were 40 candidates at the first meeting and by the end of 1858 the tally of Scottish warranted Mark Lodges had risen to 15. Not only was this *spate* of new Lodges impressive but so was its *spread*. Six were in London, 2 in Liverpool, and one each in Birkenhead, Bolton, Bristol, Cheltenham, Quebec, Whitehaven and Woolwich. Moreover it signalled to other groups of older or potential Mark Masons that so manifestly a regular Authority as the SGCS regarded the Grand Mark Lodge of England as irregular and illegal, since otherwise, by its own regulations, it would have had to withdraw from interference in another's territory. Somehow Lord Leigh had to break down this doubt about his Grand Lodge's activity and basis or else the manifest reservoir of interest in the Mark Degree would be channelled into the Scottish camp. There was also the horrid possibility that as Craft Masons had been torn in allegiance to two governing bodies in the 18th century so the same phenomenon might be repeated a century later. How could he avoid that division?

There was however a likelihood that the division might be even worse. On 19 October 1856 the Ashton Travelling Mark Lodge appointed a Committee 'to consider the present position of the Mark Lodge, and to report as to the desirability of forming from the Union a Grand Mark Masons Lodge together with such changes as may be deemed necessary to carry out the same'. The Committee reported at the next meeting on 18 January 1857 and recommended such a step with the drawing up of a Constitution and Code of Laws which would also control the Provincial lodges connected with it and that the name be 'The Honourable United Grand Lodge of Mark Master Masons of the Ashton-under-Lyne District'. That this was no pipe dream is shown by the fact that whilst we do not know exactly how many subordinate Lodges it ruled or formed it was to retain its own special identity until **1900**. RW Bro. Taylor, a later PGM of the Mark Province of Lancashire, once eagerly pointed out that this step by the Ashton brethren was not done in opposition to the Mark Grand Lodge since they were most unlikely to be aware of a Body in London that was only a few months old and itself finding its feet. What they were reacting to was the June announcement by the Grand Lodge that was confirmed in the September Quarterly Communications. Their reaction was in a strange way a full affirmation of what Lord Leigh and his colleagues had seen to be necessary rather than become a mere, if graceful, appendage to the Fellowcraft degree. One could almost imagine the Bon Accord folk giving a hearty cheer for this statement by the Ashton Mark Masters:

"That being fully aware of the present disorganised and unsatisfactory state of Mark Masonry in England, and convinced that the present is a favourable period to effect a restoration of this Degree to its ancient and honourable importance, do hereby agree and recommend to be formed from the Old Mark Lodge, a Grand Lodge of Mark Master Masons for England".

Though their appreciation of exactly what comprised the full ritual of the Mark would remain a matter of continuing debate there was here an unanimity of intention that Lord Leigh could work on in his earnest endeavours to rescue the situation. If he could prove that what had been begun in London was achieving its main goal of Mark stabilisation then at least the Ashton Brethren might reconsider their joint relations.

By the start of 1857 Lord Leigh was wise enough to have taken all these issues into account and begun a new appraisal of the situation. It is now that his best gifts as a Masonic leader began to emerge and whether or no it was because he was to be released from too close an attachment to some Bon Accord influences the truth is that in May of that year he wrote a letter which showed that that was his direction. It was sent to *every Mark lodge* which could be contacted regardless of whether it was in his Grand Lodge, under the Scottish Grand Chapter or completely independent of any outside Authority. Its principal and most endearing trait is that it shows a new flexibility and openness to all other parties that were interested in true English and Welsh unity. It was noticeable that he *never once* mentions the Bon Accord Lodge.

The letter began with a frank admission that he was "on a level with every other Mark Master who is a well-wisher of the Craft and it is from that level only that I desire to speak". That was the first very wise admission. He then briefly rehearsed the UGLE events of 1856 concluding that *had there been* a June assent "no other authority would have been desired for the government of Mark Masters". Then he showed the two converging factors that were in play: partly the conscientious objections of those upholding the 1813 principle and "partly from the disapproval of Mark Masters, Members of the Grand Lodge of England, of what they considered the *improper manner in which it was proposed to confer the degree*". Hence the 'rejection'. He therefore thought it desirable that *before* the next meeting of the Grand Lodge of Mark Masters in June "the *whole of the brethren* of the Degree in England and Wales should be invited to attend a general meeting for the purpose of *expressing their opinion* as to whether it is better to unite as a whole under a *constitutionally elected* body or to continue as at present, some under the English Constitution and some under Irish, Scotch (sic) or American Warrants, *each relatively to the other irregular*". That was the second and even wiser statement.

He then made a third wise concession by agreeing that if they met on 25 May 1857 at the Freemasons' Tavern and felt it right to place themselves under one constitution then he would be willing to put his own position in their hands and if need be *forego his continuing* as Grand Master. As a final wise offer he stated that should he be re-elected to his high office he would then appoint as Grand Officers "from amongst the most eminent members of the Craft, from a consideration only of the *well-being of the general body* and the *peculiar aptness* of the Brethren to be appointed".

Whether or no Lord Leigh wrote this impressive circular himself or with the help of some other author we shall never know. What we do know is that when the meeting took place, more conveniently for most, on Saturday, 30 May 1857, it at once began to change the complexion and the estimation of the new Grand Lodge. This was the fulcrum that worked the transformation. There were still problems ahead as with any large and widespread organisation but what had been the butt of derision and despite at last began to become a Masonic body with a serious purpose.

The attendance in itself was encouraging with almost 70 persons present and when Lord Leigh asked those who were already Installed Masters in a Mark lodge to join him, as the elected President for the day, at the top table he was joined by eleven Brethren who represented the GML, the GSCS and an Independent lodge. One of the main purposes of the day had been achieved already.

Several brethren urged the importance of re-establishing Mark Masonry as an integral part of English practice but then there was a revealing intervention by no less a person than *John Havers*, the confidant of Zetland, the Grand Master. He objected to the general proposal on the ground first of all that he *opposed the degree altogether.* Now at last one feels that perhaps the real 'eminence grise' that influenced the Earl of Zetland was showing himself. He denied altogether the antiquity of the degree and asserted that it was 'a recent and modern innovation and had never formed part of Ancient Free Masonry'. He virtually contended that it was entirely irregular to work the Mark *under any circumstances* whatsoever and to do so was a complete abnegation of the oath taken by every Installed Craft Master. He even took exception to Lord Leigh's claim that the degree had a wide influence across the country. This was opposition indeed and it could not have been better managed by someone eager to promote the cause. The last assertion provoked a number of replies showing what we have already seen to be the case across the land. Bro. Aria from Jamaica said that in the West Indies it was almost universally practised.

Bro. Burrell of Keystone No. 3 (EC) moved a resolution aimed to avoid confrontation on whether the English Craft should acknowledge the degree by stating: 'That this meeting, as a collection of brethren practising the Mark degree, is anxious to promote the **uniform working** of and general interest in the degree'. That was carried. A second motion deploring the differences between working authorities and organisations also urged 'unity and uniformity' and that was carried though it was remarked by the proposer that had this meeting been called a year earlier this whole enterprise would have been much easier to accomplish. That now seems only too self-evident.

This, however, led on to a third and most important proposal:

"That it was desirable to form a committee to ascertain and represent the views of *all parties practising the degree* in England with respect to the *means to be adopted* to promote such unity and uniformity and that the committee consist of 16 names (these followed)". What is now clear is that only 3 Bon Accord members were named, Lodges Nos. 1, 3 & 4 of the Scottish Constitution had representatives, and 4 Independent Lodges including Albany and Howe, the latter of course being in Lord Leigh's immediate Craft area. This was progress indeed, and more was to follow.

Bro. Warren who had made the third proposal urged that as this new committee could not usefully report before the Grand Lodge meeting on 10 June 1857 Lord Leigh would forebear to appoint Grand Lodge officers until that date. Lord Leigh not only agreed to comply with this idea but expressed himself **most anxious to consult the wishes of the Brethren in every respect**. It was eventually agreed that His Lordship should allow a maximum of two months from this meeting date before he made his next appointments. On this the most successful meeting closed.

At the Half-yearly Communication of the Grand Mark Lodge on 10 June the Grand Master confirmed his intention of postponing the appointment of new Grand Officers and he endorsed the idea of purchasing 250 copies of the report made of the May meeting which had appeared in the 'Masonic Observer and Grand Lodge Chronicle'. This was to be a most effective tool in helping to inform other Mark Masons of the new climate that had been created. Moreover the changes made in the first Book of Constitutions were helpful and positive. Briefly they were:

(i) To acknowledge the status of any Mark Lodge that could prove its existence as a working Lodge before June 1856.
(ii) Such a Lodge to be admitted to the Grand Lodge with a Warrant of Confirmation and to be entered **prior to** Phoenix No. 2.
(iii) Lodges that worked the degree under a Foreign Grand Lodge were equally welcome, they would be entered in accordance with the date on their Charters and their members would not be charged any registration fee.
(iv) Any Mark Master who could give proof of having been a WM or who had advanced two or more brethren before June 1856 would be recognised as a Past Master with all the usual privileges.
(v) There was now an agreed version of the Hebrew characters on the Keystone which is still the English standard form. An account in the Masonic Observer suggests that this form was probably the result of the work of John Staples Keddell, WM of the Adams Mark Lodge, No. 6 Sheerness.
(vi) There was now the first attempt to set up a Provincial network. The General Board were to draw up regulations to cover the work of whoever was appointed as a PGM by the Grand Master. All the 6 Lodges that then comprised the Grand Lodge were represented on the Board.

If such a meeting reflected the new spirit that was beginning to permeate the Grand Mark Lodge then the report of the Special Committee which appeared on 15 June 1857 added materially to that spirit's flow. Its recommendations were:

(1) That all bodies working the Mark degree should form a Union.

(2) That this Union should be represented by its Lodges' Masters, PMs and Wardens and should form its own regulations.

(3) That all proven PMs would be a part of this Assembly.

(4) That all Lodges desiring to so unite should communicate with Lord Leigh at his address, No. 30, Portman Square, London.

It really did look as though at last the way was being made for an entirely new beginning for the first much criticised Grand Lodge ... and then it was revealed that Bro. Warren, RW Master of St. Mark's Lodge No. 1 (SC) and the Editor of the 'Freemasons Monthly Magazine and Masonic Mirror', as well as the proposer of that crucial proposal about the Special Committee, was never consulted about when the meetings might be, was thus unable to attend when they met, and was left to learn about 'his' committee's findings from the rival Masonic journal. It was not only insensitive, it was nonsensical. The suggestion was not surprisingly made in the FMM that the June 15 Report was really the brain-child of the Bon Accord members on the Committee. It began to look as though matters might return to Stage One and certainly, as mentioned above, the spate of Charters issued by the SGCS was far from slowing down. Yet there was a change taking place. The Grand Mark Lodge in December 1857 had 15 lodges now on its books and three of these were 'old independent lodges'. Moreover, when someone raised the question as to why these old Lodges should be placed first on the Grand Lodge list the action was defended by Alexander Ridgway, Grand Registrar and a member of Bon Accord. His defence led Peter Matthews of the Old Kent Lodge to remark that it was the '*liberal and just terms* offered by the Grand Lodge that had *induced his Lodge* to join this union'. Samuel Lazarus of the Royal Cumberland, Bath, added his view after 36 years in the Order that "his Lodge could not have joined the Grand Lodge except on the terms offered which he must be permitted to consider as honorable to both parties". Even when the even more progressive terms of the proposed Articles of Declaration and Agreement could not yet be approved the effects of a more liberal policy were still evident. Not everything had been lost and the Grand Mark Lodge was on its way. How it *came to be* has at last been more fully uncovered. How it became the sole Mark authority for England and Wales is the last part of our story.

Chapter Nine

The Growth of the Mark Degree to today

Scotland and the Anglo-Scottish Lodges

Towards the end of the Grand Mark Meeting in December 1857 a member produced a document which purported to be a Scottish Grand Chapter Certificate of Exaltation. It stated that a certain Brother had been exalted in the Esk Dalkeith Chapter No. 42 on 18 November 1857 and, in *French*, that the Brother had entered into the usual obligation. It further purported to bear the seal of that Chapter and the Supreme Grand Chapter of Scotland (SGCS) and to be signed by the officers of the Chapter *including William Gaylor who also signed as* ***GSE pro Grand Recorder.***

The Brother who held up the document claimed that the person to whom it was supposed to have been issued *was never in a Scottish Chapter in his life*, had never, on the date stated, there or elsewhere, been obligated and had been *led into accepting* the document by a Scottish gentleman whom he had met in London. The apparent understanding was that this Certificate would show that he was a regular Scottish Mark Master and could thereby apply for a Warrant from the SGCS to work the degree in England. The brother who brought this matter forward suggested that 'for the good of Mark Masonry in general and this Grand Lodge in particular' it was essential to question every such document until this could be satisfactorily explained. As the Grand Mark Lodge (GML) had no direct contact with the Grand Chapter of Scotland nothing further at this stage could be done.

The matter was fully reported in the two Masonic journals of the day as was also the granting of Warrants for 3 more Mark Lodges by the SGC Scotland in December. One of these was to Peter Matthews, George Biggs and Henry J. Thompson to hold the 'Old Kent Lodge' No. 9 in London. The Freemasons' Monthly Magazine & Masonic Mirror reported, however, that Bro. Wm. Gaylor had visited London and through the introduction of Bro. Thompson had had an interview with Matthews or Biggs, both of them Past Grand Officers of the Grand Chapter of England. On his return to Scotland Bro. Gaylor sent them both certificates saying that 'they had each regularly passed the chair of a Master Lodge, were exalted to and instructed in the Mysteries of the Holy Royal Arch Degree of Freemasonry, in the Dalkeith Chapter of Edinburgh on 18 November 1857'. Yet these brethren had *never quitted England nor taken a step beyond* and it was supposed that they had simply paid a fee for such documents to be sent. What was Matthews doing when, in the last meeting of the English Grand Mark Lodge, he congratulated the Brethren on the union of the ancient lodges under that umbrella? Such playing fast and loose must stop.

As this report was made by that Bro. Warren whom we last saw as personally displeased with the new Grand Mark Lodge his words obviously merit serious consideration. He asserted that 'the Grand Chapter of Scotland must at once revoke the Charter to Old Kent and recall the Certificates, or the Scottish character will suffer and their Certificates he regarded as so much waste paper'. His words were unmistakable and by 6 January 1858 there were further comments from interested parties.

A Bro. Barnard, an 'old' Mark Master and presently SW of 'The Mark' Mark Lodge No. 4 (EC), confirmed that Gaylor had indeed sought to dissuade the English from continuing with the English Grand Lodge, had promised legitimacy by placing themselves under the SGCS and had, on his return North, sent them Certificates in three languages and stating that they had passed through several degrees of which they had no knowledge whatsoever. Matthews, who told Barnard all this, had *never seen* Gaylor and only responded to him because he thought his was the best way to go. He had been misled and wanted to make amends. Yet having with the two others received a Warrant from Scotland the issue was now a complex and difficult one. What may strike the reader as ironic is the fact that just as undue haste by the Bon Accord members in their attempt to form an effective body in England for the Mark Degree had almost led to disaster so the same was now happening to the Supreme Grand Chapter of Scotland which had benefitted from that situation.

Not surprisingly, many of the MMMs in the growing number of Anglo-Scottish Lodges were very disturbed by this affair and some of them wrote to the SGCS about it in January 1858. In this letter they even expressed indignation at the proceedings uncovered and looked to the Grand Chapter to institute a searching enquiry into all the details of what had happened. Above all they pointed the finger directly at Bro. Gaylor as making the Grand Chapter a party to such irregularity.

The Grand Chapter responded on 27 January by a limited recognition of responsibility and this was reflected in a letter from Gaylor to the Esk Dalkeith Chapter on 4 March in which he stated that though no blame attached to himself, or to the Chapter, yet it was the Grand Chapter's directive that the Warrant to Old Kent, and the Certificates issued to the three brethren, should all be recalled. This seems to have satisfied Bro. Warren but there were still many other members of Anglo-Scottish Mark Lodges who were far from pleased at the way the matter had been handled. For them, the more preferable way of English Unity in the Mark Degree began again to seem a possible alternative.

A first seed was sown when in April 1858 Henry Isaacs, the RWM of the Arnott Mark Lodge SC described a situation when his guest from the Albany Lodge, 'which had joined the Grand Mark Lodge' was refused entry to Arnott. He considered this state of affairs most unsatisfactory and his closing words in a letter to the FMM are worth noting:

"To Lord Leigh I consider unqualified praise is due for the very fraternal and conciliatory spirit in which he stepped forward to offer us the right hand of unity and good fellowship; and I therefore think it now behoves us in the same spirit to bestir ourselves for the purpose. I feel convinced that by these means we shall best consolidate this beautiful Degree, and thereby illustrate the old adage – 'Unity is strength' ..." The seed was to take some time to germinate but at least it was the first of several to be sown.

In July 1858 a Bro. Mott Thearle of London, who had been offered another Scottish Certificate for privileges not regularly obtained, wrote to the FMM:

"Instead then of dwelling upon the past, I would advise a union of all Mark Masons in England for the future. However objectionable the existence of the Bon Accord Mark Lodge was, there is no question but that the present Grand Lodge of MMMs have done *their utmost to create legitimacy.*" Thus was another public seed sown, and yet it has to be recognised that at the same moment new Anglo-Scottish Lodges were being established from Cheltenham to Cumberland, and in the case of the former we have the first notice of an elaborate Consecration ceremony. Even so in September 1858 the RWMs of the London SC Lodges wrote to all the other SC Lodges in the country remarking on the unsatisfactory position of the Mark Degree by having such opposed jurisdictions. They felt that 'the well-being of Mark Masonry' demanded the consideration of some kind of rapprochement.

Whilst this was to be welcomed the idea of once more re-designing another English Grand Mark Lodge and drawing in the other '4 or 5 others that exist independently in the country' was no longer facing reality. The reader will be aware that there were many more than 4 or 5 separate working Mark lodges in the land and Grand Mark Lodge was now much more stable and sufficiently democratic to permit of further re-organisation. However, it was good that these leaders in London should advocate 'our withdrawing allegiance from the SGCS and joining the other Brethren in the formation of a new Grand Mark Lodge, under whose jurisdiction we hope to see *firmly united the whole body* of Mark Masons in England'. They stressed that they had no hostility to Scotland, which had helped them to propagate the Mark Degree, but uniformity of working as well as overcoming the problems of fraternal visiting were now matters of even greater urgency, especially in the London area.

At first the Thistle Lodge returned a negative reply, still rehearsing their grievances regarding the initial arrogance of the Leigh 'faction', and Gaylor wrote a scurrilous letter attacking the 'self-constituted, surreptitious and irregular' Grand Mark Lodge – all under a *nom-de-plume*. By December 1858 however the Thistle Lodge had talked further with its London partners and was now much more amenable to the union proposal:

"The Grand (Mark) Lodge are willing to receive us on just, fair and equal terms ... we are to be accepted by them as having equal share in all their accumulated paraphernalia, books, documents, monies, &c and in the administration thereof ... Your Committee feel assured that the proposed union will materially tend to *popularise this ancient degree*, place it in a more elevated position, cement a better understanding amongst Mark brethren, and at the same time extensively promote the interest(s) of Freemasonry in its widest sense."

What was now of material interest and was commented on by Ridgway in the December Communications of the Grand Mark Lodge was that there were now *more SC Mark Masons in England than there were Companions in Scotland* and yet the fees paid by the English Masons obtained no special privileges whatsoever. By February 1859 the Thistle Lodge had led the way in receiving a Warrant of Confirmation from the Grand Mark Lodge and becoming part of that body. There was no ceremony of either consecration or rededication and all the existing officers were accepted, including a certain Frederick Binckes, their SW. He was to become an untiring and staunch supporter of the Grand Lodge thus joined and to render it devoted and most valued service for 30 years both as Asst. and then Grand Secretary. Surprisingly the other SC London Lodges did not as speedily follow this example though they had first suggested it. On the other hand by 1861 both the St. Mark's and Woolwich SC Lodges were declared 'Dormant' and Henry Isaacs of Arnott next appears as Lord Mayor of London in 1890 when he was also appointed Grand Junior Warden of Grand Mark Lodge. The SC Lodges in the West, largely led and promoted by the Canynges Lodge No. 7, steadfastly rebutted any idea of cooperation and in some cases that stance continued for more than a decade.

The effect of continuing disunity amongst Mark Masons in England and Wales seems in the 1860s to have led to some disgust amongst its members *and potential candidates* with the result that there was a very noticeable drop in attendance especially amongst the SC Lodges. This was not helped by another critical situation in Scotland.

In 1858, as we saw earlier (p. 41), the Grand Lodge of Scotland had accepted the proven fact that the conferring of the Mark Degree was part and parcel of the working of some of its oldest operative Lodges. To regularise the situation the Grand Lodge recognised the practice in its Constitution and this so incensed the SGCS that the latter threatened to authorise its Chapters to *confer the Blue degrees* under their Charters. It was only after a joint committee met in January 1860 that an agreement was reached which led to the compromise being assured whereby there was dual control of this degree. Thus was established the practice that obtains to this day (see p. 10). What needs to be emphasised is that this agreement made clear that whilst in the Craft the Mark is seen as a *second-part of the FC degree* it is regarded in the Royal Arch as a *fourth degree* and it is only in the Installation of a First Principal in the Royal Arch that the *secrets of the Mark Lodge Chair* are communicated. Even though a Craft Installed Master may confer the Mark upon his members he is not an Installed Mark Master and may not attend a Lodge of Installed Mark Masters in England without having first attained the Z. Chair in the Royal Arch.

In the period 1862 to 1870 nine of the 'Old' or Independent Mark Lodges joined the Grand Mark Lodge. These were in Hull, Bottoms, Devonport, Portsmouth, Stockport, Rawtenstall, Rochdale (2) and Hinckley, whilst in 1862 the Cheltenham & Keystone SC Lodge No. 13 followed the example of Thistle. By the autumn of 1864 the Grand Mark Lodge was in touch with the SGCS and was being asked for a statement which, if it could satisfactorily establish that the Grand Mark Lodge was a validly accepted Supreme Authority for the Mark Degree in England and Wales, would then allow the SGCS to consider the whole matter afresh. Indeed another hurdle was set up, namely that what the SGCS needed was for the UGLE and Supreme Grand Chapter of England to recognise the GML as the lawful head of the Mark in their territories. It was June 1865 before an official answer could be provided.

Naturally the UGLE declared that it did not "acknowledge the MMM's Degree to be part of ancient Freemasonry and does not recognise the Body styling itself 'The Grand Lodge of Mark Masters of England, Wales and the Colonies and Possessions of the British Crown' ". With such a reply before it the SGCS could hardly do other than decline to accede to the demands of the so styled GML, and this was reported at that Body's December 1865 meeting. There the General Board were able to report that the Grand Secretary had made a *private and unofficial* visit to Scotland to see the appropriate officers in the Grand Lodge and the Grand Chapter. The reception was friendly but no commitments were made on either side. It was therefore decided to 'memorialise', or present a case to, the other supreme bodies who might regard the Mark as an essential portion of ancient Masonry. This was to be the situation for the rest of that decade, though in London the Southwark, No. 11, SC in October 1866, and St. Marks late No. 1 SC in 1867, joined the GML, with Langley, No. 16 SC in Cardiff following in 1869. The principal petitioner for the 'Confirmation' of the revived St. Mark's was Robert Wentworth Little, a name to conjure with in connection with the appendant degrees. (see p. 399)

At the same time the SGCS issued warrants for new Mark Lodges in Burslem, 1862 and in Manchester in 1869. At the occasion in Manchester it is worth mentioning that the RW Master was a certain Bro. Charles Fitzgerald Matier and the consecration of the Lodge was 'permitted' by Scotland but carried out by the officers of No. 2 Lodge, Bolton. Bro. Binckes, now Grand Secretary, made another visit to Edinburgh in 1869 and this time spoke to the Grand Chapter in person. He had proposed a joint meeting which would include the Grand Chapter of Ireland and this was well received by the Scots. With that kind of initiative future progress looked momentarily hopeful but at the same meeting at which this was reported in London there was regret expressed that the SGCS counselled their overseas members not to countenance Mark Masons who were advanced under the GML. The Grand Master, the Rev. G.R.Portal, then asked for extra powers to warrant a Mark Lodge in Scotland if a petition from Glasgow brethren, as hinted, were requested. The power *was granted* but with every hope that favourable relations with Scotland would soon be such that this power would never be required. That was a hope that the events of 1870 seemed unlikely to fulfil.

On 15 June 1870 Bro. Matier of St. Andrews, No. 22 SC consecrated a new SC Lodge at Barrow-in-Furness and then, to cap all, the SGCS determined to extend its sphere of activities by establishing a Mark Province for Lancashire. This was applied for by the Lodges in Bolton and Manchester and was established on the same day as the Furness Lodge foundation. The effect was electric, and an immediate and strong protest was lodged by the Rev. G.R.Portal on behalf of the GML. At an Emergency meeting of this body in August 1870 he declared that he was ready to deal firmly with this open act of defiance. In a letter that was approved he expressed his irritation at the 'unwarrantable aggression of the last 15 years' though he still earnestly desired an honourable arrangement that might resolve the now almost complete deadlock. He even repeated the same kind of open-handedness as his predecessor, Lord Leigh. He wrote to the Anglo-Scottish Lodges as follows:

"Should any trifling difference in Ritual stand in the way of our most desirable Union I will at all times be ready and happy to meet your wishes to the utmost." Meanwhile he made plain that until some better settlement could be reached he would in no way allow his Masons to recognise the SC warrants or Certificates. Further, on 18 October 1870 Portal took the step of erecting a GML Province of Lancashire with the existing six lodges there and he himself, with a very strong team of Grand Officers, came to perform the impressive ceremony. Before the end of that year two more lodges had joined the GML Province. The Grand Master had certainly made his point.

The final breakthrough began with the recognition of GML Certificates by the Grand Chapter of Ireland in mid 1870. This meant that a body which was in friendly relations with the SGCS was making it possible for some kind of indirect communication to take place. Since the Irish Masons still seemed to think that either the UGLE or the SGCE might still take the Mark under its wing, as in their country and Scotland, they were as yet reluctant to recognise formally the GML as the only body which had supreme authority over the Mark degree in England and Wales. Moreover it was unwilling also to go too far at once to upset the SGCS with which it exchanged representatives at every level. There was not the same reluctance with the Grand Royal Arch Chapter of Canada which in October 1870 both recognised the GML and agreed to exchange representatives. By June 1871 the GML also had Conventions signed and agreed with the Red Cross of Constantine Council, the Supreme Council 33° and the United Orders of the Temple, Hospital and Malta. Whilst those treaties were sadly to have only a few years' existence at first, their effect whilst the conversations took place with Scotland and Ireland in 1871 was very worthwhile. It removed one of the main Scottish criticisms about the GML's non-recognition by others.

Thus we come to the gathering on 3 and 4 April 1871 which was to take place in the Library of Freemasons' Hall, Great Queen Street, London on the subject of 'The Position of the Mark Degree in England'. The Grand Lodge of Scotland, the SGCS, and the Grand Chapter of Ireland all agreed to send delegates but on the English side only the GML would be represented. Approaches were made to the UGLE and Grand Chapter of England but John Hervey, the Grand Secretary and Grand SE (and also a member of Bon Accord Mark Lodge), reported that having laid the matter of representation before the MW the Grand Master, the Earl de Grey and Ripon, the latter felt that whilst he wished the best at all times for the GML members, who were, after all, members of the bodies under his direction, he could not see that there was any need or point in further participation since the Mark Degree was not acknowledged by them. The *distinction* between not acknowledging the Mark degree as within their competence and not acknowledging the GML as if it were irregular, which was never intended, at last seems to have dawned on the Scots and they agreed that the Earl's decision was valid but not invalidating. The meeting was ready for action.

Binckes declared that the principal motive of their assembling was to decide on whether or no 'the English Grand Mark Lodge should be recognised as the *Conservator* of the Mark Degree in this Country'. This important and clear objective having been established and accepted the next two days were spent in a sharing of distant as well as more recent Masonic history in order to try and see, or show why, the English situation was so unique. The whole proceedings were recorded and are still preserved in a somewhat nondescript but precious pamphlet of some 50 pages which is preserved by the SGCS to this day. Of its contents Frederick Schnitzger of Newcastle has written in a foreword:

"It contains *more valuable information* re. the nature, position in regard to other degrees, the History of the degree and the actual status of the Mark English Grand Lodge (sic) – the Mark's position in Scotland and Ireland and the Colonies, per superficial inch *than all the Encyclopaedias put together* … No one should approach the investigation of the Mark degree without absorbing the intrinsic résumé of facts herein contained." Having read the booklet I am sure that *at that time* this claim was almost certainly true. All the points it makes have been covered in the foregoing pages but there has been evidence uncovered which is not reported in that booklet and of which even Schnitzger was probably not aware. Let us however summarise the main points that arose as the very pithy and practical discussion proceeded:

Real concern was expressed that when English Royal Arch masons visited Chapters outside their own land they were debarred from taking part in the **whole Royal Arch ceremony**. Could not the Mark, Excellent Master and Superexcellent Master degrees be somehow reintroduced so that this embarrassing situation need not arise? That *was* a leading question.

Throughout the main part of the meeting there was genuine puzzlement on the part of the Scottish participants as to why the UGLE or SGCE would not take the Mark or other degrees under their wing. They even requested that another attempt be made to seek such an outcome. It was only when Francis Burdett, representing the Grand Chapter of Ireland, was in the Chair on the 2nd day that he helped the Scots to see that not only had this already been decisively voted on but that to raise the matter again would cause a great deal of dissatisfaction.

It was only when this, to the Scots, strange state of affairs became clear, if undesirable, that a way forward out of the past difficulties began to emerge. A two-fold resolution was ultimately adopted in which (i) the parties agreed to report the proceedings of their Conference to their respective Constituents and (ii) that if, after that report, any of the parties approached the Grand Lodge and Grand Chapter of England and they refused to take charge of the Mark Degree **or** it was realised that such an approach was unnecessary then the Grand Lodges and Chapters of Ireland and Scotland would be recommended to recognise *a governing Body in England over the Mark degree.* It will be remarked what a careful wording was chosen as even after the cordial atmosphere of this encounter the GML and the SGCS still did not recognise each other's Warrants or Certificates and sought to expand their activity wherever and whenever the opportunity offered. One idea that emerged during the Conference does seem to have registered especially with the English Mark Masons. This was the concept of having the bodies that now administered the English equivalents of the pre-Arch degrees in other places united in some kind of way alongside the GML. Therein lies the origin of having the present Cryptic, Allied, Red Cross of Constantine and Knights Templar/Knights of Malta Orders all administered under one roof in London.

When in September 1871 the SGCS authorised the True Friendship Mark Lodge No. 26 at Maryport, Cumberland and then placed the brethren there under the supervision of the SC Provincial Grand Lodge of Lancashire the slumbering fires of disagreement were once more stirred into an active blaze. The fact that a Deputation arrived for this event led by one of the participants at the Conference only four months before seemed to be a direct act of confrontation and began to have, in both Cumberland and Lancashire, a clearly adverse effect.

In Cumberland the EC Mark Masons set about forming their own lodge in Maryport and another at Keswick, as well as petitioning for a Province of Cumberland and Westmorland and this latter step was taken on 29 July 1872. In Lancashire feelings began to run high. Most Mark Masons of both Constitutions began to feel that the constant disturbance to their fraternal relations – for two Masons who could visit freely in the Craft might find that they were so debarred in the Mark – was not only a nuisance but also a reproach to the general character of Freemasonry. By 4 June 1872 a report was made to the GML that steps were afoot to seek a means whereby the two rival Provincial Grand Lodges in Lancashire might be coalesced into one under the Grand Mark Master.

The actual day of the Lancashire 'Union' was 2 October 1872 when a Moveable Grand Lodge was held at the Freemasons' Hall, Manchester. It was to be the occasion for welcoming as members of the GML the greater part of the remaining SC Mark Masons in England. The Grand Master was there in person and he received the surrendered patents of the PGMs of both the Lancashire Prov. Grand Lodges. The retiring SCPGM, Bro. Entwisle (sic), then proposed and Bro. Matier seconded that Callender, the previous ECPGM, be now appointed the PGM of the new Province. The SC Lodges at Bolton, Manchester and Barrow-in-Furness were then presented with their Warrants of Confirmation and all the previous Provincial ranks held by brethren in these lodges were confirmed as Past ranks.

As a token of appreciation for the work done in bringing this new development to pass, one Brother from the SC and two from the English were immediately granted the rank of PGJW and in addition this rank was also conferred on Binckes, the Grand Secretary, for all his recent efforts to bring peace between the two Constitutions. Later in the meeting Charles F. Matier was appointed Junior Grand Warden. It was also a generous gesture that until 1910 the name of Entwisle as the first retiring PGM stood at the head of the Lancashire list. Lodges at Birkenhead and Llandudno were also admitted to the GML on this day. It was indeed a day to be remembered.

At the SGCS meeting on 19 June 1872 letters from the 'Lancashire Seceders' had been read but as the lodges had not approached Scotland about this action it was agreed that nothing further be done. In November 1875, but only after protracted correspondence to ensure that relations with the Grand Chapter of England would not be impaired, the Grand Chapter of Ireland at last took the step of recognising not just the Certificates of GML as hitherto but the Body itself. This was followed in August 1877 with the recognition by the Grand Chapter of the U.S.A., in 1878 by the Grand Chapters of the District of Columbia and then West Virginia, and finally in 1879 by the Grand Chapters of Illinois and Quebec. The GML was naturally delighted with each new step of acknowledgement and relations were speedily established with each other Supreme Body that communicated such acceptance. And yet . . . still the SGCS continued to stand aloof. In March 1875 it warranted yet another English Mark Lodge at Frizington in Cumberland and members of the EC looked on in astonishment and sadness at what seemed like continued aggravation. They had not long to wait however before the long desired and much needed change took place. In 1878 this Frizington Lodge had applied for and received an E.C. Warrant of Confirmation and the next year the SGCS at last deigned to consider a new relationship with the GML.

It really had little option by this time. The recognitions by Ireland and the U.S.A. meant that two of its closest allies had done what Scotland seemed incapable of doing, and yet had to do, to avoid utter confusion as regards its members' activities in those lands. In the U.K. a Scots Mark Mason might not attend a meeting with an English one. In so many other places that was now perfectly possible. What else could the SGCS do but comply with the general view. On 18 June 1879 it at last recorded its decision: to recognise the Grand Lodge of Mark Masters of England and Wales as *a lawful governing body of that degree in these countries*. It also agreed to issue no more Mark Warrants in that area though it reserved its right concerning those Warrants still held there. In the Colonies there was to be no restriction on who could issue warrants as requested there.

The exchange of Representatives did not happen at once but when it did it was a most appropriate occasion for the practice to begin. It was June 1884 and the occasion was the Installation of the Earl of Kintore as Grand Master of the GML. As he was also 2nd Grand Principal of the Grand Chapter of Scotland he had the very pleasant task of making known this final act of reconciliation between two parties with long standing difficulties. It had been a very arduous journey but it did at last seem as if the old wounds were about to be healed.

The Grand Mark Lodge: Its Secretariat and Meeting Places

Since the origin of the Grand Mark Lodge was in the Bon Accord Lodge it is hardly surprising that they both shared the first Secretary, William Louis Collins. Indeed the summons for the first meeting to discuss the GML venture was signed by him as Hon. Sec. and it is most likely that he conducted the first year's affairs from his home address.

In the summer of 1857 the Grand Registrar, Alexander Ridgway, very kindly offered more suitable accommodation in his office at 40, Leicester Square, London, and there it remained until 1861. Despite this helpful move it became increasingly clear that busily employed as Collins was in his own non-Masonic affairs, as well as still being the Bon Accord Secretary, the ever-increasing duties as Grand Secretary began to be seriously neglected. Without proper clerical help it is hardly to be wondered at that Collins began to fall behind in discharging essential matters. By 1858 there were complaints about correspondence not being promptly dealt with, as notably in the failure to send a Warrant of Confirmation to the Albany Lodge which then became disaffected and did not join the GML until 1896. Certificates were similarly delayed or just never issued and the summonses for the all-important Half-yearly Communications were not despatched in time or were entirely overlooked. In 1859, for example, a Special Meeting of GML at which the Earl of Carnarvon was due to be installed as the MW Grand Master was *never convened* and for the ensuing year no Grand Officers were appointed. Despite complaints and urging of the General Board to 'use its utmost exertions to have this matter rectified' there was still severe criticism in June 1860 when it was revealed that the members of the transferred Thistle Lodge had not received their GML

Certificates due after February 1859. This brought matters to a head, and a motion was carried that

"the Grand Master be empowered to appoint an Assistant Grand Secretary with a Salary not exceeding £30 p.a. & that an office for the transaction of the business of the Grand Lodge be provided at an annual rent not exceeding £20."

It was thus that within a few days Frederick Binckes of the Thistle Lodge was so appointed and he immediately applied himself to the task of arranging a system for the office work. It was to take some years before it was entirely complete and this also accounts for the early records of the GML still revealing many gaps.

The effects of Binckes's labours were soon evident and in the meeting of 12 June 1861 the General Board reported that "Much had been done during the past year to secure increased efficiency in carrying out the details of the official business of Grand Lodge. Improvement, however, may still be effected, and to this object the attention of the Board will be steadily directed, in the belief that the fruits of another year's exertions will be such as to afford unmixed gratification to every well-wisher of the Order." The language might be mid-Victorian and somewhat pompous by today's standards but it showed a healthy awareness of what was required and it was followed by deeds.

Bro. Collins did not appear at this GML meeting and his place was taken by Binckes. Collins received the rank of GJW and a vote of thanks duly inscribed on vellum and emblazoned. Binckes was also provided this year with a new office at 16A, Great Queen Street and this he was to occupy until 1867 when it was moved to No. 2, Red Lion Square, Holborn and from thence in 1881 to No. 8A also in the Square. In this latter property there was adequate and pleasant office accommodation but also a large hall which could be employed for both larger ceremonial occasions and for making separate lodge rooms. In 1887 Binckes, who had borne all the pressure of those difficult days which have been described earlier in this chapter, was joined by Charles Fitzgerald Matier as Assistant Grand Secretary, and together they had the very greatest delight in 1888 of moving into what was for 50 years the hub of GML activity – Bacon's Hostelry in Great Queen Street.

It had come to the ears of the General Board that this property was about to become vacant and a Committee reported that it would be eminently suitable for their purposes especially after some interior conversion. An approach to the Board of General Purposes of the UGLE who were the landlords was successful and a lease of 49 years was agreed. The premises obviously had good kitchen facilities and there was one assembly room that would provide a main temple, twice the size of what they had had already. There was a dining room to seat 150 people, there would be 5 adequate lodge rooms, and ample space to house the Grand Secretary and his staff. The UGLE agreed to a lease at £360 p.a., with a peppercorn rent for the first six months as alterations were carried out. The whole work, together with necessary furnishings, was completed for just over £7,000 and the first Half-Yearly Communication was held on 2 December 1890. It was the first real home of Mark Masonry in England.

In 1889 Binckes completed 28 years as Grand Secretary and received both the great appreciation of the GML and an annual pension of £125. He was succeeded by Matier who was to serve 25 years and whose experience of several kinds of Mark Masonry before joining the GML enabled him to help negotiate some of the difficult relations that still had to be resolved with 'Old' and Independent Lodges. His further experience as a member of several degrees and Orders also enabled him to guide his superiors in the formation of that wide-embracing organisation that those alive today are familiar with.

The temple in the new Mark Masons' Hall was in due time to be described as 'probably the nicest hall in London' but at first its walls were bare and the only decorative feature was the newly installed Organ that had been presented as a memorial to the late Canon Portal, Past GM. In 1893 the first step to remedy this state of affairs was taken when the Grand Master's Lodge presented a full length portrait of HRH the Prince of Wales, the Grand Master. Other portraits quickly followed and those who might wish to see what it was that adorned that first temple can still see these placed on the walls of the present Mark Masons Hall in London. They included: The Earl of Euston (from the Grafton Lodges); The Marquess of Hertford (Warwickshire); HRH the Duke of Albany (Grand Lodge); HRH the Duke of Connaught (Sussex); The Earl of Lathom (Lancashire); Earl Amherst (Kent); The Earl of Stradbroke (East Anglia); Lord Egerton of Tatton (Cheshire); and W.W.Bramston Beach (Hants and IOW). All of these distinguished brethren were or had been Past or Pro Grand Masters of the GML. It is both a delight and a necessary lesson in history that these fine pictures can be fully displayed again.

The task that now lay before the Secretariat was that of managing a much larger and growing list of lodges and their members, of servicing a much more experienced and therefore discriminating General Board, and maintaining a wide circle of contacts with lodges overseas, new Districts and those other Supreme Bodies with whom intercourse was now becoming common. Added to all that was the task of managing the Royal Ark Mariner Lodges (see p. 401) and servicing the Grand Master's Council that was to oversee the work of that degree nationwide and overseas. It was a most demanding task and one that has only increased as the years have gone by. What is so satisfying is the fact that as the GML has grown and flourished over the years the stature of the men who have been at the heart of its administration has been commensurate with the task.

In 1914 the long service of R.W. Bro. Matier came to an end with his death and many were the tributes paid to this very distinguished Mason who had helped to direct the Mark fortunes through so many varied years and events. He will perhaps be most remembered for his management of the Mark Benevolent Fund which will be described shortly (see p. 282f) for when he took it over its invested capital stood at £6,000 and when he relinquished the reins its capital was £60,000.

He was succeeded for the far from easy period of wartime by Bro. A.D.Hansell who died on 18 September 1923. He was a much quieter figure than his predecessor and the Board spoke of him 'as always kind and courteous and one who won the esteem and affection of his brethren as well as honourably and tactfully discharging his duties to within a few days of his death'. It was his thoughtful and gracious style which had been so appropriate at a time when Masonry, like all the national institutions, had to make many adjustments and withstand some grievous losses of membership.

His successor was a retired Army officer and thus made a distinct break from the previous line of men professionally trained as business administrators. The appointment of such a genial and sociable figure in post-war Britain was by way of being a stroke of genius. Major T.G.L. Lumley-Smith, DSO was well aware that the current policy must be to enhance the popularity of the Mark degree and extend its influence in the whole Body Masonic. This he was so well equipped to do and his great popularity not only in the Mark but in many other Orders meant that he achieved the general goal but also extended the influence exerted by the work done from Mark Masons Hall. He was made a Knight Bachelor in1937 and retired to Berkshire in 1955 where he lived until his death in 1961.

It was during his occupation of the office of Grand Secretary that GML had to move twice. The first time was in 1939 and the second was in 1954. The story of these two moves contains salutary lessons for all Mark Masons as well as revealing the responsibilities which have to be borne by those who are appointed as rulers in any Order.

As early as 1918 a Building Fund was inaugurated to assist in any future situation. It was realised that within 20 years the lease would expire on the existing hall at that time and it was thought wise to have funds that would enable the GML to purchase its own freehold site and property. In 1930 the UGLE gave notice that *it would not be able* to re-lease the site in Great Queen Street but it was prepared to extend the term until 1941. It signalled just the situation which the former far-sighted rulers had foreseen and shortly afterwards, following consultations with all the Prov. GMs and the Masters of all the Metropolitan Lodges as to how the necessary sum might be raised, the amount of £51,250 was spent to purchase a very satisfactory site opposite the Connaught Rooms. All looked fair and the 'Keystone Jewels' concept not only caught the imagination of the brethren but raised all the cash required. For those Mark Masons who may now come across this term, a Keystone Lodge, it needs to be explained that every lodge that raised a sum equal to an average of £5 or more per member within a given period was to be presented with a jewel for the reigning W. Master to wear, whilst every individual member of the Mark who gave 10 guineas or more before the end of 1932 was sent a personal jewel to wear.

The UGLE made it very clear on three occasions between 1930 and 1937 that there was *no chance* of their changing their minds and Mark Masons therefore prepared to move out into their purchased premises in due course. It was therefore something of a shock when the UGLE suddenly intimated in 1938 that there had been a *change of plan*, the reason for which was never disclosed. It would now be possible for a new lease of the existing premises to be granted at an annual sum of £800 and for a term of *99 years*, and with the option for the lessors to 'determine' the lease at 40, 60 or 80 years if they so wished. The offer was accepted with an alacrity which it is now extremely difficult to understand. There was the possibility of a new building, just a few yards away, and one that would have wholly belonged to the Mark Masons who had so generously contributed the means of purchase, and the extended present lease meant that they could have seen their new building complete before they had to forsake the present one. Whatever possessed those now short-sighted rulers of the Mark we shall probably never know. What is clear is that they made the wrong choice. They passed up what would have been, even despite the horrors of aerial bombardment that were to beset London buildings in the next five years – and to kill the Grand Secretary's wife and daughter in the Guards Chapel – a central 'home' alongside the Craft and Royal Arch Headquarters for all time. Their misjudgement was to cost the next generation dear.

There is also a mystery. As they had agreed to continue on the leasehold site they gave orders for the demolition of the old hall there and the building of a new one. Whilst this happened the Grand Secretary's office moved to 71, Kingsway in 1939. It stayed there throughout the war and continued there until 1954, when the Rt. Hon the Lord Harris, MC VL declared at his Installation that it had been decided to leave the Kingsway address and seek a new Centre elsewhere. What had happened to the site and the projected building in Great Queen Street? Limitations on supplies for construction up to 1946 were understandable but what happened thereafter? Did the UGLE change their mind about the lease or make conditions about the re-building style or time-table which could not be, or were not, met by the General Board? Was the money set aside for the project never enough to meet increased post-war costs or changed standards? Or was it a case of the money contributed not being used for the purpose for which it had been raised? No doubt there is somewhere an explanation of these things but there is none that I have been able to find. All that we are told is that inadequate accommodation was for too long accepted by the Grand Secretary and his staff and their options for a change were ultimately very restricted indeed. I, for one, can recall with some amazement the first time that I visited the headquarters of the Mark and other degrees to which I belonged. It seemed such a contrast to the ample surroundings of the buildings in Great Queen Street where we might have been.

The site chosen was a period property once thought to have been the home of the Dowager Countess of Derby and standing in Upper Brook Street, a busy side thoroughfare leading from Park Lane to Grosvenor Square. It was of limited usefulness though it had a certain grace and charm and it housed upstairs the staff who had to run seven Orders of Masonry. The stables at the rear were turned into the Library and Museum and thus provided a valuable facility in that area which is still not available today. Yet it was very small, and whilst some degrees benefit from intimacy others need room for manoeuvre. Above all there was no space for the GML meetings and many felt that the departure from Great Queen Street was a mistake, especially as it was never fully explained. Dining too was a problem as there was no provision on the premises or in the immediate vicinity. The previous disastrous decisions were beginning to show their effect.

In 1955 the post of Grand Secretary was taken up by Lt. Col. J.W.Chitty MBE and both in the post and later as the Grand Master of the Order of the Secret Monitor he was to be both a sound administrator and a much travelled promoter of the Mark and its connected degrees. For the next 35 years Col. Chitty was to be a name to conjure with and it was at his suggestion that in 1963 there was recommended to the GML as Deputy Grand Secretary another retired soldier who was to maintain the same standards of useful discipline and courteous ambassadorship for the Mark that were set by his superior. This was Lt. Col. the Hon. Michael G.Edwardes MBE who had in any case been Asst to Col. Chitty since 1957. What was achieved by these two men in the way of establishing foreign relations on a very happy basis and making a 'Council of Rites' operate efficiently from Upper Brook Street, despite its limitations, cannot be too strongly commended. They may have been somewhat short or slight in stature but what they lacked in physical girth they certainly made up for in terms of mind and character. Under their guidance and direction, with Col. Edwardes becoming Grand Secretary in 1968, the Mark grew and was stable, whilst its sister degrees also flourished.

When Col. Edwardes retired in 1976 he was replaced once more by a professional administrator who had served in the Middlesex Educational Authority, William Johnstone Leake. Active consideration again began to be given to the matter of acquiring a more suitable hall for the GML and the administration of those degrees which were now so associated with it. Finding such a property in a climate where the cost of building and buying was beginning to rocket, and inflation was a word in daily use, would not be at all easy. If the Order was to move then it had to be to premises that could more adequately supply many of the needs that were now required in a rather more affluent society. It had however to be in London and accessible to the many Masons who would need to come there for the various annual meetings or regular committees of the Mark, Royal Ark Mariner or other Orders. So the search began and it was only after 1976 that a fitting property was found.

The Constitutional Club at 86, St. James's Street had decided to merge with another club thus leaving the building there available for lease. A feasibility study was carried out and working plans were drawn up which would provide for 7 temples (one of them able to house 300 people) and 7 dining rooms. The fact that there was also a facility for offering meals to the public during the day, and that already it looked as though most of the 1,400 meeting slots a year would be taken up, added to the viability of this proposal.

Could the members of the Mark and other degrees provide the money with which this essential work could be done? The answer, as we now know, was that they could. Tour the building today and you will find on the doors of the various masonic suites the names of Provinces and Districts from the world over who secured that privilege by contributing the largest per lodge or per capita amounts from their members. It was a great cooperative exercise to provide a meeting point at which almost all the Orders administered from there could gather and which could yet provide for Craft Lodges and Royal Arch Chapters in London another place for their meetings.

The hall was first occupied on 21 July, 1979 and was formally opened and dedicated on 30 September, 1980. The ceremony, which included the naming of the six other rooms, was carried out in the fine new main Temple and the Provinces, Districts and unattached London Mark Lodge to be honoured were BRAZIL, BRISTOL, HONG KONG, RIVER PLATE, WARWICKSHIRE and JOHANN GUTENBERG, of which latter lodge the author was then proud to be a member. 26 Provincial and 3 District Grand Masters were in attendance as were also the Grand Secretary and Grand D. of C. of the United Grand Lodge of England. The presence of these latter brethren aptly symbolised the now cordial relations that exist between the two Grand Lodges. The Rev. A.B.Carver acted as Grand Chaplain and the Rev. Canon R.Tydeman gave the Oration.

In his own address the MW the Grand Master, the Rt. Hon the Earl of Stradbroke, made especial mention of the immense efforts made by so many to bring about this special occasion – the individual members of the Board, the 'skill, energy and unfailing good humour' of the Grand Secretary and the contributions of all the Freemasons throughout the world which had provided more than double the target of £300,000 which had first been decided. He closed with the words:

"Brethren, we can now look with much greater confidence to the future of our Order for having acquired, occupied and dedicated our own Mark Masons' Hall ... Like the ancient craftsman whose legendary experience gave rise to a great part of our ritual, each and everyone of us can say, 'Thanks be to God, I have marked well'."

In 1982 the Earl of Stradbroke had another very important duty to perform. At a Grand Lodge meeting that year he handed over the honour and responsibility of his high office to HRH Prince Michael of Kent. Before doing so he received an address by his Deputy, Dr. G.L.C.Colenso-Jones who spoke of the significant increases in Mark and Royal Ark Mariner numbers during the Earl's tenure of the Grand Mastership. At this date there were 1340 Mark and 672 Royal Ark Mariner Lodges which meant an advance of 192 and 181 respectively. He was thanked for setting up a new District Grand Lodge in West Germany, visiting two Districts in South America and instigating the ideas of London and Overseas Mark and Royal Ark Mariner Grand Rank in 1977.

When the Earl in turn addressed his successor he briefly reminded him of the history told in these pages and especially referred to Prince Michael's grandfather who had occupied the positions of Grand Master in both the Craft and the Mark. This had helped to cement the good relations between the two parts of Freemasonry. The future was no less promising with two blood brothers occupying those two important posts.

Following his Installation His Royal Highness appointed the Earl of Stradbroke to the post of Pro Grand Master, a position which his father had held under the previous Duke of Kent. Remarking on this fact of following in his father's footsteps Prince Michael repeated as his own the words spoken at that other Installation in 1939 – 'I can assure you that it will be my great endeavour during the time that I hold this high position to do all I can to promote the interests of the Order'.

Sadly, the Grand Secretary who oversaw this move took early retirement in 1986 before he could see the full development of what he had helped to bring about. His place was taken by a Professor of Economics from the University of Aberystwyth, Peter Glynn Williams, who had also shown his no mean skills as a Grand Director of Ceremonies in more than one Order. To this task of Grand Secretary he has brought administrative sharpness, enthusiasm and a readiness, like his predecessors, to be a widely travelled ambassador for all the degrees for which he has had to care. To the Mark and the Royal Ark Mariner he has given himself unstintingly and under a no less devoted Grand Master the two degrees can look forward to a promising future. It was as this book was about to be printed that this Grand Secretary's retirement was announced.

The Constitutional Task.

For Alexander Ridgway, the first Grand Registrar, to have presented his first draft of the Constitutions and Regulations as early as October 1856 means that he must have worked extremely hard. Doubtless he took his main cue from the existing patterns of the Grand Lodge of England documents but it was still a very heavy task that he had undertaken. This edition contains 111 clauses and covers every aspect of the GML activity. The 1955 edition had 156 clauses, so that in the course of the first century only 45 new regulations were added, excluding those that apply to the Mark Benevolent Fund, which did not exist when he began his work. On his basis the whole future work of the GML was, and was able, to be built. It was with these guidelines that the following issues could be settled:

(i) The Grand Mastership.

At first the occupant of this office was elected every three years so that in the first 30 years there were 10 Grand Masters. Then in 1886 HRH the Prince of Wales (the future Edward VII) was elected and he ruled until his accession to the throne in 1901. When he was succeeded by his brother, the Duke of Connaught, there began an occupancy of 38 years and in 1945 the Grand Lodge very properly deleted the rule which limited the reign of a Grand Master and that has since proved beneficial.

(ii) Moveable Grand Lodges.

Until 1891 the GML held only Half-Yearly Communications but in that year it was agreed that to arouse more interest in the Provinces and, as we shall see, make it more feasible for some Mark units to join the new Parent Body, the Grand Lodge meetings should be held in various points in the country. This also meant that the Grand Officers and their Provincial partners could meet and know each other better and the report of the first one ever held at Kingston-upon-Hull in 1868 speaks for itself: "The first Moveable Grand Lodge was held under the auspices of the Minerva Lodge No. 12 on Thursday 16th April last at which the Grand Master presided. The proceedings gave unqualified satisfaction to all who participated therein and the result must be regarded as in every way successful."

It was at the second such gathering in Worcester that Canon Portal as Grand Master raised the suggestion of inviting the ladies to dine at the dinner after the meeting. Whilst there was some support for the idea there were also those who opposed it vigorously and it took *two years* for the idea to be tried – but it has continued, now in the Mark Benevolent Fund dinners, ever since.

At the third such occasion in Cheltenham in 1869 a demonstration of the ritual was given and this enabled the members of the GML to consider the merits of what they saw, bearing in mind that a final form of the ceremony was not approved until 1872

It was in 1907 that the last Moveable Grand Lodge was held in Devon which was where the first Provincial Grand Lodge of the Mark had been set up. Indeed this occasion provided the opportunity for celebrating the Provincial Jubilee. A survey of the Province's history was given by the PGM and they were able to announce that 23 Lodges were now in existence.

Already in June 1890 it had been proposed that there should be Quarterly meetings of the Grand Lodge since access to the capital was increasingly easy. To have perpetuated the Moveable Lodges would have been to increase unnecessarily the duties of the Secretariat and to risk confusing those who regularly attended.

(iii) Aspects of the Ritual.

Those who have read what has already been written about the development of the Ritual, or rituals, for the Mark Degree will not be surprised to learn that when the GML came to the matter of deciding which working should be adopted in England and Wales it was not at all a straightforward issue. The

Bon Accord Mark Lodge had adopted the 'shorter' Scottish working and this was the one inevitably continued under the new Grand Lodge with its preponderance of Bon Accord members. The difference, let us recall, was that in this version there were no Overseers and the story of the 'rejection' was told in a lecture. The 'Longer' working used Overseers and dramatised the story. In 1858 the Grand Registrar, Ridgway, proposed that Overseers be appointed in the GML and that the longer working should be that adopted as the future official form. There were naturally voices raised from the Midlands and the West who said that this was only right because they had always used Overseers and could not understand how the degree could be worked without them. Herein was revealed the way in which Masonic ritual had taken hold of brethren's minds, for the truth is that in many early forms of ritual the use of catechisms, lectures and addresses was as valid as the now more usual custom of making a candidate act out a ceremony. Indeed one of the weaknesses of much modern Freemasonry is that whilst the acted ceremony is often well done the explanation or elucidation of what is being enacted is much underplayed. It is instructive to note that in American Freemasonry there is still a healthy balance, based on late 18th century European patterns, between 'doing' a ceremony and 'instructing' the candidate in what has been happening. It was and still is unhelpful to speak as if one manner of conferring a degree were more ancient or meaningful than the other. It is therefore also noteworthy that in Scotland to this day both the shorter and longer workings are available for use according to the needs of each Masonic occasion. In England and Wales the decision was thus early made to change from the one to the other and to retain a lecture which would materially assist the candidate to appreciate what it was that he had joined and shared in as a Mark Mason.

There was also much attention given in the early years of the GML to a feature that was most important for English Mark Masons since they operated as a unit separated from the Craft or Royal Arch. Whereas the Irish and Scots had logically employed those already placed in a Craft or RA Chair the GML had to ensure that there were strict rules of procedure to ensure that only qualified persons were permitted to confer the degree **or** be installed in the Master's Chair in a Mark Lodge. Great care had to be taken so as to avoid any suggestion that those occupying that position might either assume a similar right in the Craft – if not already installed there – **or** inadvertently convey in the Installation Ceremony any hint of what took place in the comparable Craft working. It was not until 1873 that a full agreement was reached and the first printed ritual could be issued to those entitled to it. This did not at first mean that it was official but from the point of view of those who now practise that rite it can be stated that what then was approved was very close to what is now the only agreed form. What is more the pattern adopted in England and Wales was later adopted and required, with slight variations, by Ireland and Scotland. The irony of all this is that the pattern which was first followed for this Installation Ceremony was that of an old Scottish rite. Explanation of that development cannot of course be given in this book but it would be a subject worthy of consideration for a lecture in the company of Installed Mark Masters.

From the outset the GML hoped that those who attained the Chair of a MMM's lodge would be already Installed Craft Masters. Yet it was soon appreciated that this might not be the case and therefore a Dispensation could be obtained for those who were otherwise entitled to this office in the Mark *before they reached* the Craft Chair. The obligation therefore had to be most carefully drafted and any study of this process will reveal what trouble was taken in this matter.

Moreover, there was also strict attention paid to the proper rules governing the tenure of the office, so that early examples of Masters only being in the Chair for ten or eleven months were seized upon and noted. Specific permission had to be granted for anyone not completing a full year to bear the title of Past Master and as time passed there were several cases mentioned in GML of such brethren whose cases were adjudicated upon and fines imposed. Irregularity, after all, was not something that this new Grand Lodge could happily live with in view of its early history.

Hence, when W.Bro. the Revd. C.H.Malden appealed against a suspension by the District Grand Lodge of Madras the matter provoked not a little interest. This clergy brother had protested that on at least three occasions to his knowledge Masons had been installed as Worshipful Masters in Mark Lodges when they had clearly not served the office of Warden. When the said clergyman failed to answer a letter from the District Grand Lodge asking for details but published the letter and his cases in an Indian Masonic magazine he was duly suspended. In dealing with the appeal the GML determined that whilst the clergyman should be reprimanded for blatant discourtesy in not responding to his District Grand Master's enquiry the DG Lodge was in error in suspending the brother without giving him a formal opportunity to make his defence. The case highlights the extent to which irregularities concerning Installation could occur but it also underlines the strict justice according to Common Law that the GML should, and now does, carefully maintain.

Another intriguing matter of ceremonial that arose in GML was in regard to salutes to the MW the Grand Master. It was in 1891 that a Bro. Stevens called attention to the fact that the salute to the Grand Master and other high-ranking Grand Officers had been altered on that occasion. He protested that old customs and usages had been changed without due notice or the permission of the Grand Lodge and he respectfully asked for an explanation. The Grand Director of Ceremonies replied that the salute hitherto given was that used after toasts at dinner and it was not thought sufficiently dignified. 'They' therefore thought it better to adopt a form of salute *similar to that used in the Craft*. Bro. Stevens was eager to know who 'they' were and not receiving any satisfactory answer he again protested that any proposed change should have first been considered by the whole Grand Lodge. When the President of the General Board added that no such idea had even come before that body the temperature nearly reached boiling point. Only an intervention by the Pro Grand Master, promising to have the matter brought up for proper review, helped to save the day.

Whilst this again reveals the constant vigilance that was kept on the practices that might be accepted we are regrettably still none the wiser as to exactly what were the types of salute which were involved. Copies of Craft ones might well arouse latent concern but it would be interesting to know what the previous actions were. Though it was clearly the case that Grand Lodge meetings could be lively affairs it is a shame that the records stopped short of providing just the detail that would make the occasion even more fascinating.

Connected with this matter of ritual, of course, there was the whole matter of the other degrees which were now closely associated with the headquarters of the Mark and Royal Ark Mariner. As the members of the Mark degree had learned a hard lesson regarding the control of Orders which were governed by Grand Lodges or Grand Chapters elsewhere it was proposed as early as 1870 that an English Governing Body be organised to administer those 'Universal' degrees which were elsewhere properly managed. The Grand Master stated that after communicating with Canada, Scotland and Ireland he knew it was their wish that those degrees should be worked in England and Wales 'in connection with this Grand Lodge'. Such was the measure of new respect and mutual progress that had at last been developed with those Supreme Bodies.

That agreements were reached by 1871 with the Red Cross of Constantine, the Orders of the Temple and Malta, and the Supreme Council 33° we have already mentioned but also that year a Deputation was received from America which had plenary powers to confer the degrees of Most Excellent, Royal, Select and Super-excellent Master upon suitably qualified Masons. By 4 May 1871 the Grand Council of Royal and Select Masters had been formed and another step had been taken towards that Council of Rites for which Canon Portal had longed. How it eventually emerged we have again mentioned above (p. 261) but at least the creation of still more Grand Lodges had been averted. Ritual was under control.

(iv) The remaining 'Old' or Independent Lodges.

Though the story of how both the Anglo-Scottish and Independent lodges joined the GML has already been touched on there were certain very well established Mark Lodges that persisted in their individual ways for much longer than any others. No story of how the full complement of the English lodges came at last under the direction of the GML Constitution would be complete unless we record what happened in the case of four of these – Minerva (Hull), Albany (IOW), Newstead (Notts) and Ashton District (Cheshire).

MINERVA

The year 1861 was a significant one for this ancient Lodge which was still noted for working five degrees – Craft, Mark, Royal Arch, Knight Templar and Rose Croix. Two brethren, Reynolds and Peck, were advanced in that year and Peck was appointed Secretary of both the Craft and the Mark Lodges a few months later. Though he was to remain the Craft Secretary for 26 years he handed the Mark office over to Reynolds in 1864 and the latter is recorded as never missing a Mark meeting in the next 30 years.

Under Peck's guidance the Mark Lodge contacted GML and in 1862 the articles of agreement with the Grand Lodge and a new code of by laws were adopted. It was at this meeting that the deputation came from Britannia Lodge, Sheffield, to demonstrate their form of ceremony which was at that time 'accepted' by GML. What exactly that was we cannot now know though the fact that the five founders of Britannia were themselves advanced in either the Phoenix Lodge of Portsmouth or the Albany Lodge at Newport, IOW suggests that they may well have imported their working from that area. If so that would account for a proposal in the Minerva Lodge in 1864 that the ceremony might be shortened, since we know that Britannia copied the older Southern forms by having both a lecture and a charge together with a form of examination and rejection. Certainly the Minerva Lodge has preserved features which show the older places of Overseers and an adherence to the old cypher alphabet.

If the Minerva Lodge had joined the GML it was not necessarily willing to adhere to all its requirements. There are several cases of proposals from London being firmly rebutted and when in 1880 it was suggested that a Provincial Grand Lodge be formed that was rejected on severely practical grounds. Indeed it was not until 1903 that they, along with the other Hull lodges, were willing to join what is the present flourishing province. Only then could Minerva be said to have come fully into the orbit of GML.

ALBANY

This Lodge which was to be the spawning ground for many Masons from elsewhere does not appear to have sent any representatives to the General Meeting which was summoned by Lord Leigh to form a Grand Lodge. On the contrary it asserted its independence in late 1856 by claiming *sovereign powers* and by issuing a Warrant to certain of its members who belonged to the Portsmouth Craft Lodge (then No. 717) authorising them to form a Mark Lodge and even appointing its first officers. It did not attempt to issue any other warrants and in 1857 it even applied for a Warrant of Confirmation from the new Grand Lodge. This, however, was one of the Lodges that suffered from the then inefficiency of the Grand Secretariat and the application was *never attended to until 1861*, by which time the Albany brethren were no longer interested. It was working in glorious isolation when it finally voted to adhere to the Grand Mark Lodge at the Provincial Grand Lodge meeting of Hampshire in *September 1893*.

NEWSTEAD

In 1858 a new Minute Book was purchased and was used until the Installation meeting in 1958. It was a signal of the new independence that the Mark now experienced as it became separated from the Craft Lodge whose officers and funds had hitherto been provided. When the 'new' Mark Lodge opened on 2 February 1858 a Past Master of the Lodge was in the Chair and among the 'initiates' (sic) were 12 from Nottingham, 3 from Radford and 7 from Leicester. It was decided to hold the Lodge twice a year in April and October and at the April 1858 meeting it was agreed that the Mark Lodge would be self-supporting. In the course of the next few years they decided to head the summons with cypher lettering and to produce a new style of Certificate if the old one could not be found, whilst in April 1862 the first Brother who had not been WM of the Newstead Craft Lodge was installed as WM of the Mark. On 21 October 1862 the Lodge was opened in the 'ancient form by Bro. W.Richards the principal (or Master) overseer' and this now continued to be the case.

In October 1863 the brethren were informed that the Lodge had given Warrants to Mark Masons in Leicester and Birmingham authorising them to hold lodges and confer the Mark degree in their respective towns. The name 'Newstead' was retained on the new certificates issued largely because Bro. Wm. Richards, the oldest member of the Lodge, recalled that "when he was admitted in 1831 it was known by the name of 'The Newstead' and that many of its predecessors spoke of it as belonging to Lodge 44 under the York Constitution and that it had always met in the lodge room of the old 44 Lodge and had used their furniture". It was also noted that various old Brethren had told him that there was even an older Minute Book before the last one that started in 1802. It was all this information which was ultimately to result in the Newstead Lodge being deemed a Time Immemorial one. Certainly by 1864 the Newstead Lodge of MMMs had its own Constitution, its own method of working, and its own style of officers, with the principal officer in April 1865 becoming the Worshipful Master Overseer. Even in November 1870 a second invitation to consider joining the GML simply resulted in the letters concerned being annexed to the Minutes, whilst in 1874 the Lodge ordered an extract from *a UGLE report* to be entered on the Minutes. It read:

"21 May 1872. The Grand Lodge *firmly forbids* all their Officials salaried from mixing themselves up in any way with other parties and especially *the schismatic body styling itself* the 'Grand Mark Lodge of England'."

In November 1872 the Lodge had appointed a Committee to settle the Mark Masons' clothing, and in May 1876 it was resolved to provide the Officers with collars. There was certainly no intention in Newstead of allowing others to direct their affairs, and the Lodge flourished. It met at Southwell in September 1877 with seventeen members present and 10 new candidates were then advanced and received their Certificates. The Lodge, incidentally, was now meeting four times a year and there was an interesting By-law: "None but present or past Masters (PMO) being eligible for 'Wardens' ". No one seems to know quite how this office fitted into the Overseers pattern of this old Lodge.

By November 1880 an important issue was raised by a Bro. Ward. He proposed that at the next meeting the Lodge should consider the anomalous position in which the Lodge stood in regard to Mark Masonry and decide what steps should be taken in the matter. By February 1881, with 28 members present, and four visitors including V.Wor. Bro. F.Binckes, the Grand Secretary, it was resolved at last that the Newstead Lodge of MMMs should ally itself with the GML and that terms for doing so should be brought to the next meeting. There were 22 votes in favour. An Emergency Meeting took place in March 1881 and the terms proffered were accepted. These allowed the Newstead Lodge to be entered as a TI Lodge before No. 1 on the GML Roll, the present members to be given free registration and a new certificate issued to each subscribing member so registered for the sum of 1/-. There were 20 members present and 15 gave their assent. On 1 June 1865 at the Masonic Hall, Nottingham, the first Installation of a WM in the Newstead TI Mark Lodge took place and again in the presence of the Grand Secretary and the GD of Ceremonies the lodge formally became part of the GML of E. and W.

That was not quite the end of the story. On 21 May 1884 a Bro. Benham was proposed as Tyler but before his election Bro. Benham was called into the Lodge and asked why he also tyled '*The Spurious Newstead Mark Lodge*'. He replied that he had done so in complete ignorance of the nature of the other lodge and he would solemnly promise not to tyle it ever again. He was elected. This at last accounts for the number of Masons who clearly dissented from the decision to join the GML and who thus worked an unrecognised Mark Lodge from 1881 to 1893. What is ironic is that the present Newstead TI Lodge is truly grateful that whatever we know of the older working of the Mark in Newstead was due to these 'spurious' Mark Masons preserving the older practices and their record of what was done, until such time as their documents could be lodged both with the Grand Mark Lodge collection and in their own safe.

ASHTON-UNDER-LYNE

The first extant Minute Book of the Ashton TI Mark Lodge begins on Sunday, 20 July 1856. That it was not the first time the Lodge existed seems clear from the first entry:

"This being a regular meeting, the Lodge was opened in due form at three o'clock in the afternoon ... Resolved that the WM and his Officers be allowed their expenses for attending the Special Meeting at Manchester."

We have, of course, shown in an earlier chapter that the lodge was indeed hard at work for at least three decades earlier and was at last apprised of what the Bon Accord Mark Lodge had been doing immediately after the June 1856 decision in the United Grand Lodge. As it had pretensions itself in the way of being a focus for Mark Masonry it is worth noting that on 19 July 1857 (another Sunday) the following resolution was agreed

"That a communication be made with the Mark Master Masons' Lodge, held at London, to know the basis on which they proposed to form a Grand Lodge for England." There was no further mention of the outcome later.

In 1861 we read that the 'salaries of the WM and Treasurer be discontinued' and that the latter office be even dispensed with as the moneys collected could be put straight in the bank. It is also clear that from this date the term 'initiated' is replaced by the word 'inducted' though in October 1864 the phrase used became 'admitted into Mark Masonry'.

In January 1865 there was another tentative proposal for 'the Secretary to obtain all particulars against the next meeting to see whether it would be advisable for the Society to be enrolled under the Grand Lodge of Mark Masons, England' but by April it was felt that the replies to the Secretary's enquiries not being satisfactory more time should be allowed for him to obtain further information. Meanwhile they thanked a Bro. Vernon for 'restoring and writing the Mark Ritual'. No enquiries were going to disturb their way of doing things.

On Sunday, 16 July the Secretary read correspondence from the Grand Lodge of Mark Masons, England, the Secretary of the Grand Lodge of England *and from* the Grand Lodge of Mark Masons of Scotland (sic) and it was decided that 'no change be made in the working of the Mark, as it cannot be shewn that we should derive any benefit by so doing'. At the October meeting, however, two extra mid-week gatherings were planned to deal with the number of candidates and to satisfy those who now began to *object to Sunday meetings.*

It was the assiduous Bro. Binckes who next approached these Ashton Masons. In June 1866 he arranged to meet a deputation from the lodge in Manchester and from the Notice of Motion that was given at the July Lodge it seemed that all was going according to Binckes's plan.

What had been proposed in Manchester was that the lodge should continue to be a travelling one but holding a Warrant of Confirmation from the GML, and its members would be registered free up to the date on the Warrant. There would of course be a half-yearly due of 1/-from all members and the existing benevolent fund run by the lodge would need to be adjusted 'to bring it in accordance with Masonic usage'. When this proposed agreement was presented at the next GML meeting it was fully endorsed but on Sunday 21 October the Ashton brethren decided to postpone any action for six months to allow time for further enquiry. What had apparently stuck in their throats was the insinuation that their Lodge Funeral Fund might possibly not be managed in a Masonic manner. London Masons still had something to learn about dealing with their Northern cousins. Certainly the way that these Ashton brethren conducted their affairs was different – as was also the practice of the other lodges mentioned above at this date – but Handfield-Jones's comment that this was simply 'a Friendly Society with a Masonic Dress' shows the kind of attitude, still prevalent a century later, that prompted these proud contenders for the Mark to look askance at these 'Grand Lodge fellahs'.

In March 1868 the lodge admitted 21 brethren of the De Grey and Ripon Lodge No. 1161 including their WM, and was then treated to an Address 'with respect to the *benevolent object of Mark Masonry*' – not, let it be noted, on the object of Friendly Societies. In April there were 23 more candidates with 6 from Liverpool, four from Hyde and the rest covering many districts in between. There could certainly be no doubt that Ashton Lodge was serving the cause of Mark Masonry very strongly and producing the brethren who would maintain it in Lancashire and Cheshire in the future. In May there was even the granting of a warrant to the Liverpool brethren to hold lodges and confer the Mark degree there because of the apparent interest aroused.

In October 1870 the Deputy Provincial Grand Master, Romaine Callender, attended their meeting and again sought to encourage the Ashton Travelling Lodge to amalgamate with the GML. He stressed the need for **uniformity** of working and for **freedom** amongst Mark Masons to visit each other. He also added, significantly, that their Funeral Fund would *in no way be interfered with* nor their *Sunday meeting pattern* but of course there would the Grand Lodge levy. Since Bro. Callender did not specify whose working of the ritual these brethren should conform to and since he clearly had full freedom to come to the Ashton Lodge the points he made must have fallen on fairly deaf ears. The Ashton men must have realised that maintaining their independence brought concessions and that their contribution was one that GML obviously coveted. They, in fact, had nothing to lose and therefore, after two more visitors had been courteously heard, they tendered a cordial vote of thanks for their attendance and said their committee would report at the next meeting. The Committee did report and a decision was deferred yet again and when the report was repeated in April 1871 with Romaine Callender present, but now as Prov. GM, it seems that pressure was really being applied. Why else should such a busy Mason spend time with what, by his normal standards, was a wholly irregular body of Mark Masons? Had he had strong directions from London or was it a similar Northern determination not to be outdone by these persistent 'outsiders'? Whatever the circumstances that led to the visit the outcome was decisive. They voted by 11 to 7 '*that this Mark Lodge remains and goes on working as it has done hereto fore*'. Thanks were tendered to the Prov. Grand Master and the rest of the Provincial officers for coming and they left, no doubt disappointed and also bemused.

One then wonders if the Masonic authorities in other quarters were asked to help? The rules of the new Oldham Masonic Hall forbade its *use on*

Sunday, there were rumours that the police might interfere with their meetings, on the ground that they were held at times when worship was taking place, and in 1873 a deputation waited upon the Deputy Chief Constable of Cheshire to ask if they might meet at the Clarendon Hotel in Hyde. There was even an attempt to prevent them meeting at all in hotels on the grounds that they might be breaking the licensing regulations. From April 1874 it was even agreed that to show their desire *not to upset family life* the ladies were always welcome to attend at the festive board. Those who today think this practice is a dreadful break with tradition might be amazed to see this 120 years ago.

The Lodge even began to discuss in October 1881 whether those belonging to the GML should be allowed to stay in the lodge when the ceremony was being performed as they had not been through the Ashton ceremony. This immediately resurrects the issues mentioned above. Any Mark Mason had hitherto been free to attend at Ashton's meetings but Grand Lodge was now raising fences against return visits. The working at Ashton was also distinctive and they were not wanting it to be altered. There was no sign of that or any other change throughout the next decade.

William Fitton, whose copy of the Ashton ritual we considered in Chapter 6, became WM in October 1888 and then Secretary in 1890. He was to hold the latter post until 1916 and thus brought stability and continuity at a very important stage in the lodge's history. He was not alone. In 1894 there died a lodge member whose daughter recalled her father becoming a Mark Mason in 1841. What that member did not see was the new By-Laws 'for the Government of the Honourable *United Grand Lodge of MMMs of the Ashton-under-Lyne District*', and even the Minutes are headed 'The Grand Mark Master Masons Lodge'. When the members turned up, as their traditional way had been, at a Craft Lodge the WM now welcomed 'the members of the Grand Mark Master Masons'. That must surely have upset the GML and its Provincial representatives.

It puzzled others and recalled them to the pretentions of the Bon Accord almost half a century before. In the 'Masonic Journal' of 1898 the Editor recognised that here was a Mark Lodge of more than a century of existence, and by many years pre-dating any other Mark Lodge in the counties of Lancashire and Cheshire, but he could not understand how it could be a Grand Lodge without constituent Lodges.

This query was quickly answered by a Dr. Foreman who pointed out what has been mentioned above, that there were many lodges working in the two counties that owed their very existence and warrant to this 'Grand Lodge'. The Editor countered by questioning this very practice. How could this Travelling **Lodge** issue warrants? He was voicing the very thoughts of the rulers of the Mark Degree in the GML.

A letter written by C.F.Matier and dated 3 March 1899 was then received by Bro. Fitton. It was peremptory:

"The existence of a Body styling itself the Grand Lodge of Mark Master

Masons, Ashton District, and *professing to work* the Mark degree, has been reported to this Grand Lodge, and I am directed by the General Board to inform you as the Secretary of the *so-called 'Grand Lodge'*, that they will have no alternative but to declare this body to be a **Clandestine Lodge** and to prohibit all members of this Grand Lodge from visiting or holding *any Masonic intercourse* with those who profess to be members of the so-called Grand Lodge. This edict will not be published until the 1st May in order to give your members *ample time to consider their position in Masonry, which will be seriously affected*."

Whilst appreciating the offence that must have been felt by the rulers of Mark Masonry at its Headquarters by this further apparent arrogance of a solitary Northern lodge it has to be said that not only was this statement a judgement before giving proper means of hearing from the accused – a course which it had so wisely condemned in India some years before (see p. 273) – but it threatened sanctions which it surely had no right to impose or even implement. That it could limit *all Mark* masonic intercourse was possible but to threaten ALL Masonic interchange was not in its right to claim. Nevertheless this was war. One wonders whether the Officers of GML ever pondered whether what they now felt could perhaps have been the same feelings once felt by the Grand Chapter of Scotland? Who were these people to behave like this?

A special Ashton Lodge meeting was held on 14 March 1899 and the Secretary was directed to reply. His reply was quite a salvo.

"*United Grand Lodge* of MMM, Ashton District. 21 March 1899.

Dear Sir and Bro.

Replying to your letter of the 3rd inst. we have had a special meeting *of our Board*, and after a lengthened discussion it was resolved to write to you, that this MMM Lodge has been in existence for at least 69 years, according to our records, which date to July 11th, 1830, and we believe there is strong and reliable proof of its existence for over 100 years.

We fail to understand why we should be designated a **"Clandestine Lodge"** and are strongly of the opinion *the word should be withdrawn*. There is not, nor ever has been, anything clandestine about our working. The lodge was *in existence before* the Grand (Mark) Lodge of England. Many thousands have been advanced therein, and at present its membership is nearly 100. We only admit Master Masons of good character who are well recommended. We have had correspondence *with your Lodge* many years ago in the lifetime of Bro. Binckes (sic) and Bro. Romaine Callender, and in 1860 both of these brethren visited us with a *view to inducing us to join* your Grand Lodge, but were unsuccessful, as a large majority voted against such a course. An edict such as you threaten can only very slightly affect a small number of our Brethren, not a dozen, and probably not half that number. We should be pleased to know what you wish us to do, and what you have to suggest.

Yours faithfully and fraternally, JAMES FITTON, Secy."

Matier, to whom this was addressed, replied on 7 April 1899 stating that he had nothing more to communicate but that anything further from them should arrive by April 30th.

When the Ashton Lodge met on 9 April the Grand Secretary's letter was read and it was resolved to take no further notice until a further communication might be received. On 6 June the GML met and pronounced the Ashton District Grand Lodge to be a spurious and clandestine Body and all members of GML were 'hereby prohibited from visiting or countenancing such Body, or from receiving any member thereof as a visitor or otherwise' in any of their lodges. This decision was sent to all their subscribing lodges on 13 June 1899. The harsh comments made in the Mark Prov. Grand Lodge of Cheshire and in London were reported in 'The Freemason' magazine but the Ashton brethren took strong exception to suggestions of 'silent contempt' and on 26 June Fitton wrote a very long letter to Matier with copies to the Cheshire PGM and a Bro. Loveland in London, stating that *they did not close* the correspondence and adding at the end "although we were then, as we are now, fully prepared *to negotiate allegiance* to the Grand Lodge..."

To that Matier replied on 30 June agreeing that the statements in 'The Freemason' were *not strictly correct* but expressing his delight at the sentiment expressed in the last paragraph. He would help in any way he could. The final stage of this remarkable story began on 15 July when the Prov. Gd. Secretary of Cheshire suggested an interview. This was followed by a letter from Matier explaining that they needed to apply for a Warrant of Confirmation 'and *surrender all powers* they possessed *or were supposed to possess*'. One of the last surprises is that within a few months of showing their continuing metal they now accepted this total surrender without any apparent opposition. One part of that reason for acceptance was, it appears, that a Dr. Foreman took charge of the negotiations for the lodge and he must have been very forceful in his persuasion. He became the first nominated WM and on the Grand Master's *personal recommendation* he was, at the Consecration and Re-Constituting of the Ashton District TI Lodge, made Past G. Overseer of England. He it was, certainly, who got through GML a motion which not only withdrew the words 'spurious and clandestine' but had them *expunged* from the Grand Lodge record. Thus came into the Grand Lodge the last of the 'Old' Mark lodges, almost half a century after GML's own formation from an independent and solitary unit.

The Mark Benevolent Fund

Its origin lay in the idea of *promptness* and this is still intended to be its key-note. Its motto – 'Bis dat qui cito dat' – expresses just that sentiment – 'He gives twice who speedily responds' – and when on 3 December 1865 an appeal for help came to the General Board from a widow in Plymouth, whose husband had been advanced in Gibraltar, the first opportunity arose for the principle to be applied. They promptly gave her £3. The fact that the lady had already been relieved from the Fund of Benevolence of the UGLE only served to emphasise the point that perhaps there might be a need for Mark Masons to provide a channel by which urgent cases of their distressed members or dependants could be speedily assisted even if there were still the Craft funds to provide longer and more lasting aid.

Prior to 1868, in fact, it was naturally assumed that as all Mark Master Masons were contributors to the Craft charities, as first of all Master Masons, that particular aspect of Masonry need not figure in any post-Craft degree. To those who claimed to be brothers of him who was 'the son of a widow' the appeal from Plymouth was an unexpected reminder that what was done elsewhere might be delayed as proper enquiries were made, might be inadequate when granted and would not reflect the further bond which could now be expressed by those in another Grand Lodge. How wise that widow was, who presumed that if one Grand Lodge could help her, so could the other to which her husband had also paid dues. It did not take the Revd. G.R.Portal and the indefatigable Frederick Binckes long to devise a plan that would meet any such 'call upon their charity' as MMMs in the future.

By May 1866 the Grand Lodge had confirmed the proposal for a Benevolent Fund to be started by asking each subscribing member to *add 6d annually* to his dues and topping it up with the '*fines levied on Grand Officers* for non-attendance without due cause given'. All seemed set fair for the launch of the project when rumblings from around the country caused there to be second thoughts and in December 1866 the Deputy Grand Master, on the advice of the General Board, suspended that approved action until fuller enquiry had been made of the Provinces and Lodges. We have, of course, seen above how a body like the Ashton Lodge were put off GML membership by an annual addition to their existing Masonic dues. That Mark Masons should have these second dues further increased was asking too much and there was early evidence of their reaction.

V. Wor. Bro. Hughan, whose name was to become one of the most well known as a Victorian Masonic historian, made a special journey from Devon to warn the Grand Lodge Board of the likely consequences of their proposal. In particular he made plain that it was not the idea of just any increase in dues that was the problem. By *adding 6d* the brethren in the Provinces would be contributing to the GML *a larger sum* than that they were called upon to contribute to the UGLE. That was thought to be unnecessary, undesirable and objectionable in principle. He felt that such an increase would prejudice the interests of Mark Masonry abroad as well as at home just at the time when the Mark needed agreement and cooperation to establish itself in English Freemasonry. As his was far from being a lone voice, and he used his known eloquence and thoughtful presentation, the Board gave way. It withdrew the idea of a levy on each member and donated £50 from GML funds to meet any immediate distress. No sooner was the money available than the object of this Fund was met – £5 was sent to a Mark brother who had lost almost all he possessed as a result of shipwreck. If one may be forgiven the pun he and the Fund idea had been 're-launched'.

Yet this was not quite the whole story of the Fund's origin. That there were reasons for special 'Mark' help might be true but there was also a case for saying that if this were so then surely there could be grants made occasionally by the Board, as had already happened, or some officer could make them in between their meetings and in their name. That was not thought to be fitting or adequate, even though it attempted to meet Portal's point about prompt response. There must surely have been some other ground for pressing, as in the Communication of December 1867, for a Mark Fund of Benevolence. It may have been the realisation that once grants began to be made speedily the rate of them might increase beyond either the capacity of one man to deal with them or that the funds might just not be adequate. On the other hand one suspects that there was also a sense of pride involved here and not least as far as the dignity and status of this still evolving GML was concerned. Let us remember that this was the period when the GML, with Portal very much involved, was struggling to become firmly established and yet faced with Anglo-Scottish Lodges which were as yet unwilling to break their links with the North, where the SGCS continued to regard this Grand Lodge with disdain. Everything possible that could be done must be done to enhance the position and purpose of the GML. It seems logical to believe that amongst those plans for developing and strengthening the appeal of this burgeoning Body a fresh and specifically Mark charitable endeavour would be an added bonus. Yet whatever the thinking behind it, and certainly there had been some thinking this time about its effect on the troops, the plan now devised was still not quite the one that would stand the test of time.

The 'GRAND LODGE OF MARK MASTERS' FUND OF BENEVOLENCE', to give it the proper title, was to have a separate Account with the Bankers of the GML and it was to be funded by occasional donations from the General Funds of Grand Lodge supplemented by voluntary contributions from private lodges and individual brethren. It was to be administered by the Grand Lodge on the recommendation of the General Board and the Grand Treasurer alone was to have authority to sign cheques in payment of the grants authorised.

However, whilst the operation of the grants and their funding were laid down, there was no mention in this somewhat hastily prepared document of what conditions were required of those who sought the relief, whilst the amounts of £5 for a distressed brother and £3 for a widow cannot even in mid-Victorian terms be thought to have been over-generous: but then there was no guarantee that the 'voluntary gifts' would come soon or in sufficiently large enough amounts to make greater generosity a possibility. 10 appeals would swallow up the sum granted from GML and, in the event, half the money had gone by June 1869. In response to an appeal to all the Provinces and Lodges under their authority **not one single penny** had been received. Something had to be done urgently and thus the Festival idea connected with the MBF was born. It was in fact *a double birth* for at the same time Portal and others contended, against strong opposition, that this was also the time and opportunity for the bringing of the ladies into the picture.

Ladies had indeed already begun to attend at the Charity Festivals organised in the Craft but this suggestion in the Mark immediately caused a split in the Grand Lodge camp. The Grand Master, Bramston Beach, said in no uncertain manner that 'he felt this innovation would be fraught with *inconveniences of no small character*'. Quite what this impressive phrase was meant to mean, other than that having the ladies around at dinner was an inconvenience anyway, we do not know but though uttered by the Grand Master he was overruled at the Moveable Grand Lodge on 21 October 1868 and when it came up *for confirmation* at the December Communication it was again approved if only by *one vote*. This was so narrow a majority that the Grand Treasurer moved that the whole matter be reconsidered six months later but Portal had two more strings to his bow. He suggested that there be a Board of Stewards to arrange a **special** Charity Festival to which the Ladies would be invited, and he agreed that if this did not prove successful or was found to be too difficult to manage then he would move the discontinuance of the whole idea. In the event the arranged event proved a great success and from that year to the present time it has been accepted that the ladies will be invited to join their companions for the MBF Festival dinner.

The above record of events shows that as with the UGL decision in 1856 the practice of not taking things for granted *until they were later confirmed* was still customary, though in this case it was a decision by the same people about their own affairs. We also see that the Grand Master did not just have to speak and it was done. Matters were judged by all the Grand Lodge members on their merits.

From this beginning progress began to increase in speed. A Charity Jewel was devised and was in early days presented by the MW the Grand Master himself. Contributions began to grow, there was investment of the funds and there was a readiness not simply to help individuals but also whole groups of Mark Masons, such as those suffering from a hurricane in Curaçao in 1877. An Educational Fund was started and then revised in 1880 and at least one Headmaster, who was also a Mark Mason, promised one place at his school if the Fund would care to nominate a pupil.

It was from 1880 also that recognition was given to the fact that some kind of control had to be exercised over who could apply for help. Hence were introduced the rules which have been steadily adapted up to the present day but which have remained the same in principle. This was especially important as the Fund got into the area of Annuities.

Each applicant has to be able to produce a Certificate which confirms his status as a regular MMM who has paid all his dues and is able to be supported in his claim by the lodge in which he was advanced and to which he contributed for two years. A similar proof is required where a widow or dependant is concerned. A petition has to accompany the certificate and this petition has to be with the Grand Secretary 2 clear days before the meeting of the General Board. The finer points of procedure are of course all laid down in GML Regulations and may be slightly altered as national, economic and social circumstances vary but the main principle of ready help for Mark Masons, regardless of whatever other help may be applied for, has been retained and can still be provided. If there is a problem it may be that, due to the generosity of the voluntary gifts made by the Provinces through the Annual Festivals on behalf of the Fund, there may at times seem to be a shortage of really needy cases that can be referred to the Board's attention.

What has certainly been given over the last 125 years is the answer to the query, "Is the MBF really necessary?" The amounts swiftly but carefully distributed, the complementary service provided *alongside* and *also to* the other Masonic charities, the additional and sometimes unique help given to some overseas brethren in particular distress, and above all the pride that Mark Masons have had in contributing to a Charitable Fund that is, and always has been, uniquely their own – these are unquestionable benefits. On the other hand some of the factors foreseen by our predecessors have also had to be recognised. The danger of trying to draw from *the same source of giving* at too frequent and, in some cases, identical periods, as when Provincial Craft and Provincial Mark appeals are too closely linked; the limitations that may present the results of generous, not to say sacrificial, giving being as fully used as it might be; and the possible danger of creating an *unnecessary sense of competition* between Provinces that leads to ambitiously high targets being sought, without perhaps any appreciation of what the money is for and whether it is really needed. All these are real matters that Mark Masonry may have good reason to heed for the future. Giving to the true needs of others is commendable: giving for the sake of merely satisfying someone's sense of achievement could be self-defeating. Making the celebration of passing one's sensible target a cause for self-congratulation and excessive Festival indulgence could become, and maybe has already become, a serious problem for some.

Relations with Mark Masonry Overseas

As has already been mentioned the desire to have the approval of, and agreeable relations with, Supreme Bodies overseas who controlled the Mark degree was very much the desire of the GML of England and Wales and it was the goodwill extended from an increasing number of such quarters that helped in the final recognition and acceptance of the GML as itself a legitimate Governing Authority. Yet the world in which the GML was set up was one in which the British Empire was still a living reality, bringing with it both its benefits and its own peculiar difficulties. It is to some of these that we must refer in this last stage of our story.

In 1884 the Grand Chapter of Quebec made it known that all intercourse with the GMLEW would cease until the warrants of certain Mark lodges in that Province were withdrawn. They claimed that they had the right to demand that any minority of units in their midst should cease or accept their local sovereignty. This invasion of minority rights in another land had always been resisted hitherto and in this case, where the Mark had been worked independently in that place **before** the Quebec Grand Chapter existed, the GML, to which two of the lodges now owed allegiance, continued that prior right to administer the Mark degree in such places where **English** Masons desired to do so. Furthermore, said the Grand Secretary, though some, but by no means a majority of, American Grand Chapters have expressed support for the Quebec action, "I cannot but express my surprise that they should so far have overlooked one of the fundamental landmarks of Masonry as to attempt to oblige English Mark Masters to join a *so-called Masonic body* meeting in defiance of the State in which it finds itself". This crushing circular was pointing out that the Parliament in Montreal still refused to legalise the lodges and chapters holding under the Quebec Masonic bodies. Nothing further was heard on this point.

In June 1889 the Grand Registrar moved that the title of what had hitherto been Provincial Grand Lodges in "the Colonies and Dependencies of the British Crown" should now be described as Districts and that powers should be given to them to regulate their own fees subject to the approval of the General Board. This was largely at the request of the brethren overseas and was, in any case, following the pattern already set by the Craft.

Some of course were eager to press on from even that distinction and in that same year the District GM of New South Wales informed the GML of his State MMMs' desire to form a new Grand Lodge there. The original warrants issued were allowed to be retained so that the ancient historical links could be remembered and both bodies appointed representatives to each other. That example was repeated in 1901 in Victoria, Australia, though in this case the lodges that belonged to the English, Irish and Scottish traditions were to combine in a *United* Grand Lodge of MMMs. The GML was requested to recognise the new body as a Sovereign Authority and this was granted with the proviso that should there be any individual lodges of Mark Masons who wished to retain their links with England directly they should be allowed to do so. The same proviso was made when in 1906 South Australia took the same step.

A happy and wise example of how relations could best be fostered abroad arose in 1915 when certain First Principals in a Jamaica Chapter of the SC requested advice on how it might be possible for them to be present at the Installation of the Master of an English Mark Lodge, when they themselves did not have those secrets, although they were, of course, Mark Masons. The Grand Registrar came up with a simple solution. He suggested that the RW the District GM of the Mark in Jamaica should authorise a meeting of a Board of Installed Masters within the local Lodge of Instruction and therein, by rehearsal, communicate all the necessary information to those who would need it. The Grand SE of Scotland replied to this suggestion by expressing his "many thanks for the courtesy and kindness which you have shown in this matter ... We will endeavour, in any case in which we are able to do so, a similar service to return your help". Relations even with Scotland were very different from earlier days.

In the years after the Second World War the visits of the Grand Secretary and other senior Mark Masons to many Overseas areas manifestly created a new climate of understanding and cooperation in a rapidly changing Commonwealth. Ghana and Nigeria, New Zealand and South Africa, Rhodesia and India, the West Indies and even South America, all revealed issues that needed careful attention and in some cases wise guidance. Such was the case, for example, in 1966 when there had been a far from easy tour in the islands and countries south of Panama. The whole trip with all its many stops and changes of climate and residence must have seemed the more worthwhile when the Grand Secretary of the Grande Oriente do Brasil wrote subsequently:

"The Grande Oriente ... has no objection of any description to the working of the following degrees which we understand are regularly conducted, viz. the Mark Master Mason and Royal Ark Mariner. Once again with the kindest regards and warmest fraternal greetings..." What is even more remarkable about this letter is that it was written to the Deputy District Grand Master of the *Craft in Brazil.* The days were passing when there might be any lasting antipathy between the Craft and its close relation, the Mark.

Latterly, and in a Europe that has been not only changing but coming into closer and more regular association with Britain the work of taking the Mark degree into Holland, Belgium, France and Spain has occupied the attention of the Mark Secretariat. What the future will be as even more European countries resume some kind of Masonic association only the future will tell. What is certain is that the GML under its Royal leader is well able to cope with all eventualities. It has, after all, had enough storms to weather in its passage to the present.

Chapter Ten

A Mark Miscellany

IN THE PREVIOUS chapters we have travelled through the many scenes of the Mark degree story. We have looked at its meaning and management, its origins and development, both of the organisation and the ritual, and we have seen how the Grand Mark Lodge came about and what happened as it strove to become the recognised and respected Masonic Body that is today. Much has been said about many of its features in the course of that journey but there are still some aspects of the Mark which were deferred for later attention and others which could be easily overlooked and yet which are essential parts of modern Mark Masonry. It is with these remaining Mark features that this chapter is concerned. My hope is that what now follows will answer questions that even some long-serving Mark Masters have sometimes wondered about and which they have not known how to respond to.

REGALIA IN THE MARK DEGREE

What did the early Mark Masons wear when they took part in the first ceremonies we have earlier described? The chapter on the development of the ritual will have provided some clues in answer to this query but there is no single pattern to which we can point. It has to be remembered, after all, that those who engaged in some kind of Mark degree did so in ways that determined already what they would wear. Several rituals indicate that the candidate enters as a Fellow Craft, a Master Mason or even a Past Master and there were other occasions when some forms of Mark degree were clearly taken by those who were already Royal Arch Masons. In addition to the retention of the clothing of the 'parent' degree to which they had to belong we have, however, several other glimpses into this fascinating field. We have the evidence of some candidates coming into the Mark setting with no apron, an apron with one lower corner turned up or wearing a long leather apron as in an Operative yard. We have the candidate in the Mark Man ceremony that bears Dunckerley's name coming in with a square and compasses tucked into his apron band, whilst in the ceremony described by Carlile in his 'Manual of Freemasonry' he enters as a Fellow Craft but with the 'additional characteristics of this degree' on his FC's apron. Those characteristics are 'the 10 mathematical characters, to correspond with the nine figures and cypher in arithmetic, the signature of Hiram Abiff and the mark of this degree'. In Dunckerley's rituals there is a token or jewel that begins to resemble this description and might have given the idea for, or have been drawn from the same source as, that which was used in supplying Carlile with information. We also have jewels mentioned by the 19th century and these also were to be appropriately marked. Examples of these early jewels are still extant in Norwich and further examples are preserved in the Grand Lodge museum in London. (See pictures).

Of all the early forms of apron that related to the Mark alone the most distinctive are those of the Albany (IOW), St. John's (Bolton) and Southwark (London) Lodges. These were in due time so established that their shape was used on at least two sets of summonses or certificates (Albany and St. John's) though we have no detailed information as to exactly when they began to be used or when they were surrendered. These aprons have the usual Craft colours but the sides have been tapered somewhat so as to suggest a keystone (see Picture). In the case of the Albany apron the flap bears the number of the Craft Lodge to which it was originally attached (151), and the centre is occupied with a keystone shown in perspective. At the top of the stone is a square over a semi-circle of cypher letters that spell 'Albany Lodge' and flanking these words are a chisel on the left and a mallet on the right. In the centre of the stone's face is a large circle with the now usual 8 letters but in cypher, on a band round the perimeter, whilst at the heart are the initials of H.A.B. but again in cypher. Beneath the circle are the words 'Albany Lodge Newport I.W.' in clear writing. On the exposed underside of the keystone are the joined letters 'T over H'. There is in this instance a Minute of 7 March 1850 mentioning 'suggestions relative to the Clothing and Ceremony which were unanimously adopted' but whether this form was continued until Albany joined the Grand Mark Lodge we do not know. It is a matter for further research as to whether Southwark and Bolton copied this Albany pattern or whether there was some other common source. Were there different designs or were there other mid-19th century Mark Lodges that also adopted this style for a time? What, for example, were the Ashton Travelling Mark men thinking of adopting when, as we recorded earlier, they considered distinctive dress for the Mark?

When we come to the subject of the present dress adopted for English and Welsh Mark Masonry we naturally enter upon a much better documented terrain. When the Bon Accord Mark Lodge was warranted from the Chapter in Aberdeen it owed no allegiance to either a Craft lodge or Royal Arch Chapter. Yet they desired a distinctive regalia. Again, this was not needed in Scotland because the brethren taking the Mark were either inevitably moving on to the Royal Arch, and would in due course be clothed with that regalia, or they were members of a Craft lodge who wore their lodge regalia even when they took this appendant degree. The Bon Accord brethren therefore asked Brother Rettie of the Aberdeen Chapter *to design something* for them, thus indicating that they wanted to have an apron that was entirely distinctive for a 'separate' degree. That they were pleased with the result, which incorporated the blue of the Craft and the crimson of the Arch, is shown by the minute of the new GML General Board for 29 October 1856 when 'it was resolved that the jewels of Grand Lodge should be obtained from Brother Rettie of Aberdeen, the design of those supplied by him to the Bon Accord Mark Lodge having been so much approved'. Not too much should be read into this approval for we have to recall that at this stage the Grand Mark Lodge and the Bon Accord Mark Lodge were composed of much the same people but the choice of craftsman was obviously a sound one for the colours he devised have remained the same until the present day and only the shape of the Grand Lodge jewels have had to be adapted. At first the encircling gold band was a perfect circle, but in 1897 it became a quatrefoil, the dove on the Deacons' badge became a Mercury in 1886 and a quite new device had to be introduced when the office of Overseer became the norm.

In April 1884 a much more noticeable change took place when it was decreed that 'Grand Officers of the Year (excepting Grand Stewards), Provincial Grand Masters and their Deputies will wear chains when attending Grand Lodge or Provincial Grand Lodge or on any occasion when the Grand Master or a Provincial Grand Master shall command'.

As far as Past Masters in the Mark were concerned there was no plan at all for their wearing a distinctive collar until 1932. At that date it was declared that 'Past Masters of Private Lodges, so long as they continue to subscribe to some lodge, shall be entitled to wear, on all occasions when Mark clothing may be worn, collars 4" broad, light blue in the centre with 1" of crimson on each edge with silver braid $\frac{1}{4}$" in the centre. The PM jewel to be suspended from the collar'.

It may be remarked by some brethren that in certain Mark Lodges, even today, gloves are still worn. This is undoubtedly another instance of the early association of these or connected, earlier Mark gatherings with a Craft Lodge that wore gloves. It seems perhaps a little unusual in a degree with such clearly operative foundations and the great majority of Mark units have dispensed with them. It is sometimes worth pondering the fact that in truly Operative days it was only the Master Architects who exercised this privilege of having their hands covered.

The Jewel worn by all Mark Master Masons consists of a white keystone, generally made of mother-of-pearl, ivory or white cornelian, with a silver-coloured Lewis (or cramp) at its head, and the whole suspended by a silver bar to a blue and crimson ribbon 1" wide. The obverse of the Jewel is designed to bear the mark of the Brother to whom the jewel belongs within an equilateral triangle that is surrounded by a double circle bearing certain Hebrew characters. On the reverse is engraven a double circle bearing the letters H.T.W.S. S.T.K.S., synonyms of the Hebrew characters, whose significance the MMM will already know. Of the full importance of the keystone in the past and present of the Mark degree anyone who has read thus far will be fully aware. Some words of a Past Grand Chaplain in New York, however, are too apposite to be missed here and will perhaps remind the reader of why this jewel is so important to the MMM. He wrote:

"Often what is heresy in one age is found to be truth in another, ... whether it be the teaching of Socrates, the Fatherhood of God, the theory of Galileo, the property of steam or the awareness of human rights ... In each case the keystone, though rejected at first, was afterwards eagerly sought and applied to its intended use, binding together some arch in the great temple of human progress, adding something to the strength, glory and beauty of the fabric, something to the enlightenment and welfare of mankind, and bringing home to every honest heart the comforting and inspiring conviction that truth is mighty and will prevail".

Most of the remaining items that adorn the Mark Masons and their lodge are taken from the pattern of their Craft predecessors. The appropriate working tools, the wands or batons, the warrants or even record boards, but there is one feature of Craft lodges that is fast becoming a much more frequent part of Mark regalia and that is the lodge banner. Here again tradition has reigned, and the privilege of such an item with all its significance as a centre of allegiance and an evident mark of unity has mostly been seen as a Craft item. Nowadays the banner is even being sought by Chapters, and Mark lodges too are following in the wake of some of their number who have had a banner for many years. The design of such an item needs careful thought and happily there are some fine examples already to be consulted. It is to be distinctive of the Order as well as being informative of the lodge's name and origin. Here is a field where the Mark Masons of the future can add materially to Mark regalia. It might even spur more to research and revere their particular lodge's background.

MARK TRACING BOARDS

It is neither possible nor desirable in this book to enter into the whole matter of why we have tracing boards at all and how they came into existence and general use in the Craft. That is a truly fascinating subject and one which any informed Mason ought really to be aware of. What must occupy us here is the story of how the tracing board developed in this degree and why we have the board that is displayed in our lodge room today.

Just because the tracing board was a Craft feature in regular use and of constant importance it is hardly to be expected that there would be a demand for a Mark board when the link between the two usages was still close. Moreover the number of Royal Arch boards was minimal until the Harris board appeared in the middle of the 19th century so there was no likelihood that that would serve as a stimulus to those Mark Masons who were admitted to the degree in a Chapter setting.

What is interesting however is the fact that the oldest Mark board of which I am aware, that once used by the Albany Mark Lodge, appears in a Mark unit that was so closely linked with the Craft in its early days. The board still extant is, not surprisingly, somewhat indistinct in some of its features but it is so striking and vivid in its conception that it deserves to be better appreciated by MMMs at large. (See picture).

The board is surrounded by what looks like a form of trellis-work but which, on more careful examination, shows itself to be a series of 'lines parallel' with a St. Andrew's Cross in between. These two items form, of course, the basis of the cypher alphabet and one is left with the distinct impression that this is what is meant to be conveyed. The board has a meaning that is veiled but decipherable.

In addition to the border however there are four items at the corners. The top left is an open book, which is probably the Bible; at the top right is the silhouette of a cock; at the bottom left are crossed keys, whilst at the bottom right is a ship's anchor. No one today can easily interpret these symbols in relation to the Mark Degree though it would be possible to understand them as meaning that 'the Word of God reminds us that the secrets retained or unlocked herein give ground for hope'. That they had some specifically Christian significance I would doubt.

There are four distinct scenes revealed in the body of the board though three of them are shown as parts of one whole in the mediaeval manner of portrayal i.e. showing various activities as though happening at the same time and in the same place when in fact they happen seriatim and in different locations. I shall describe these in turn in a moment but first let us consider the scene set apart at the top of the board, which has a vague but evident line dividing it from what is below.

On the left of this scene is a quarry with some of the rocks prized away from the rest and lying in various states of shaping. On the right is a huge tree revealing its abundant foliage and stretching over the figures that occupy the lower centre. The most prominent of these is a camel with a rider which has its head directed towards a tiny kneeling figure in white who faces a bush. This latter is surely a representation of Moses at the burning bush. Behind the camel there is an elephant which is carrying a great sawn trunk of a tree on its back. This and the spreading tree would represent the Cedars of Lebanon whilst the quarry could be that of Tyre. Certainly this would begin to fit well with the succeeding scenes below.

Here we see first the glorious rayed sun and beside it a huge rainbow overarching the rest of the picture. Below the rainbow is a dove with an olive branch and on the horizon of the sea beneath we just make out the Ark. In addition we see a line of vessels crossing the water past a wooded promontory (are these the ships from Ophir?) and round the first of four bays below there comes a procession of camels that are obviously carrying loads from the wooded area (Lebanon?). In the same bay we see rafts being loaded with timbers where the camel line ends. A little lower down and in the second bay we see a raft rounding a tall promontory with figures directing operations as the fully laden raft comes to the foot of a cliff-like shore which must be Joppa. Men are handling tree trunks up the side of the steep incline. At the lower end of this bay is an empty raft moored below even higher cliffs.

Meanwhile and inland the unloaded timbers are being cut up and made ready for use whilst on the headland above the empty raft a man is seen trying to get his camel to rise bearing a huge load of white stones. Opposite the third and empty bay we see four smooth ashlars standing on the ground and two apronned figures, one dressed in crimson and the other in blue, lifting a fifth ashlar to the foot of the new temple wall behind them. A further ashlar is being raised above their heads by a bracket and pulley that protrudes from the top of the wall. Even more fascinating are the peacock and the large pot (of spices) that stand alongside the stones. Is this a reference to the biblical description of the merchandise from Ophir – peacocks, spices and precious stones?

Further down again and in the fourth bay a complete ship appears with carved prow, large rudder, mast and rigging as it lies at anchor. On its deck is a golden casket that looks very like the Ark of the Covenant. Here may well be one of those earlier ships shown coming from afar or Ophir. On the hill above the vessel is the Temple in the course of being constructed. It has three broad steps to its portico and standing at the foot of the square pillars that flank its entrance are the two men already described. On the top of the nearest pillar is a tripod with a smooth ashlar suspended within it. To its right is an arch of the portico and in the centre of the arch there is a keystone. Below that arch we see the inner door of the Holy Place and that too has an arch and a keystone marked with a level.

At the foot of the whole picture are more human figures standing amongst the huge stones which lie ready for use. The figures here are all dressed in either crimson or blue, the Mark Master Mason colours. Together with the sacred vessels of the Temple – the Laver with its lion legs, the anointing vessels, the cups and plates and candlesticks, all the stones have marks on them and the stones are cubes or rectangular blocks. Three figures on the left are testing the stones and discussing them, two on the right are deciding where they will be placed and they are helped in this by the central individual (surely Hiram) who has an unfolded plan of the whole Temple like a scroll to which they are pointing.

As a lovely final touch we see in the very bottom and centre of the picture the crossed maul and chisel, with another smaller copy of this same tracing board, which tell the discerning viewer the purpose for which this work was created. The whole panorama, especially when you consider the date and circumstances for which it was prepared, is a remarkable work. It has all the items needed to instruct the candidates for the Mark as well as its present or past attached degrees – the Ark Mariner, Mark Man, Link and Mark Master. As you might well expect on a board that would be inspired by the Minden teaching, which was of Irish derivation, there are the hints of the Excellent and Super-Excellent degrees in the scenes with Moses and the vessels of the Temple.

What is most surprising is that no-one hitherto seems to have drawn attention to this recorded treasure other than the historian of Mark Masonry in Hampshire and IOW and he simply noted its existence. Handfield-Jones said that he could find no evidence of any Mark board in use before 1862 for had such a board been in use in the London Bon Accord Lodge surely the Grand Lodge would have adopted it. There is no reason of course why the London Mark Masons should have known of the Albany Board since none of them had visited there. One of the Grand Chapter Committee set up to investigate the Mark went down to Albany but we have little evidence that he ever returned there and no reason why he should have specially remembered the board in his brief stay or mentioned it to those who were Bon Accord members when there were other members of their Committee who were NOT Mark Masons.

It is true that it was not until 1862 that the General Board first thought of the matter and then their attention was drawn to the question of whether a board was necessary by seeing the design executed for the Minerva Lodge No. 12. Search is still being made by that lodge to see if by any chance the design or a description of it has survived but so far we are unable to determine what were the 'several unacceptable features' which caused it to be referred to a Grand Officer for his opinion. Could it have been that like the Albany Board it had symbols that seemed to link it with Christian degrees, for we know that Minerva had KT and Rose Croix connections as well as having a Craft lodge and Royal Arch Chapter? Did it also have the intimations of Ark, Link and Wrestle or intimations of the Red Cross degree? Whatever it was it did not last but it had served its purpose. It created a line of thinking about what should be the principle on which a Mark board should be designed. There was much talk about it and doubtless many ideas and suggestions were made: that it should have the First Temple as its focus, that it should incorporate the symbols of the degree, that it should highlight the idea of a stone rejected and of wages rightly paid, of the cypher alphabet and the Arch completed. These must have been the necessary themes because all the boards that followed made their own attempts to present these same subjects.

In May 1870 the General Board at last solicited designs for their consideration and at the same time the older lodges and experts in the field of the cypher were asked for advice on how best to interpret and instruct it. With this latter subject we shall deal shortly. In November 1871 there appeared the design of a Board by Bro. Rosenthal. It was much admired and in May 1873 it was purchased for £120, which included 100 copies and three stones of the style shown in the drawing.

This was not a totally official production for though GML informed all its lodges of the board's availability and many were purchased there was no regulation about its having to be used in private lodges. Nonetheless it began to set a pattern of dignity and fine draughtsmanship and not only was it used but other lodges began to create their own forms of the board using the 'Rosenthal' as their basis.

The Rosenthal board focuses the viewer's attention on the Temple forecourt with its Porch of Solomon (or arcade) surrounding it on three sides and the whole raised on the semblance of the Temple mount. At the far end of the forecourt is the archway entrance to the Holy Place and this archway is flanked by two tall representations of the 5 tiers of side-chambers and topped by a gallery of ten pillars. There are seven steps leading up to the main doorway. Behind this broad facade a ray of sunshine emerges from the clouds and strikes the top of the dome that presumably represents the roof of the Sanctum Sanctorum. (See picture).

In the countryside depicted around the Temple we see the mountains and forests of Lebanon, the stone being brought from below the Temple mound and the rafts carrying the wood across the sea. Around the picture is an arch of several stones with a large keystone at its apex and on the latter the circle of Hebrew letters around an equilateral triangle. The symbols on the stones are:

Left, descending: Open book, chisel, maul, hour-glass, calipers, lines parallel and St. Andrew's cross.
Right, descending: All-seeing eye, trowel, ladder, anchor, Axe or hatchet, lines parallel and St. Andrew's cross, both with dots.

In the foreground we have on the left 3 Middle Eastern robed figures around a gabled wicket on a pedestal. They are the persons usually expected there. On the right are the three stones: a cube with a square on it, a rectangular ashlar with a plumb on it, and a keystone with its lewis and the same device as on the keystone of the arch. To complete the board there are Hebrew words in the two spandrels between the top curve of the arch and the frame.

Of the variations that followed three deserve our attention. One was from the Holmesdale Lodge of Ramsgate (HLR), one from the Duke of Connaught, London (DCL), and one from the Star of the East, Scarborough (SES). There were two others held by the Stuart Lodge at Bedford but one of these is the same as the DCL and the other was unfortunately stolen, along with the other heirlooms of that lodge, in the early 1990s.

The HLR Board was obviously painted by a local artist and departs at once from the more sober browns of the other paintings by being done in the Mark degree colours. The spandrels at the top are crimson and bear the Latin words: LAPIS REPROBATUS CAPUT ANGULI. These reproduce in another language the sentiments of the Rosenthal Hebrew. There is a similar arch with symbols though there is no semblance of stones. The sequence here is different though the central keystone is identical.

Left descending: Open book, chisel, mallet, ladder, square & compasses, anchor, axe, dotted lines parallel & St. Andrew's cross.

Right descending: All-seeing eye, plumb, trowel, 24" rule, hour-glass, level, triangle, Lines parallel and St. Andrew's cross.

The arrangement of the picture within the arch is noticeably different in that there is no view of the interior of the Temple court. The viewer stands at the foot of a long viaduct that leads from 6 steps, and under a richly decorated classical canopy on six pillars, to the main entrance of the Temple in the background. There are four more steps before one enters the temple itself. Above the pediment of the midway canopy we glimpse the dome of the inner temple and it is here struck by a diagonal ray of sunlight emerging from the clouds.

On both sides of the viaduct there is steeply sloping ground suggesting a valley below the viaduct but on the right slope there are seen some palms to indicate the Middle Eastern nature of the site. At the foot of the front steps stands a plinth on which is set a wicket with its hand-holes clearly marked for the appropriate workmen, with the sign of the level in the gable space. At the base of the plinth stand 3 stones of the same size and decoration as in the Rosenthal board.

On the HLR board we now have below the main picture some scenes referring to incidents that are connected with the Mark story. They are in the form of a plaque with 4 panels:

Top left: The stone being approved and marked, with another figure ready to lever it into position towards the scaffolding close by.
Bottom left: 3 Eastern garbed figures, of whom one shapes a large stone, whilst the others consult about either its size or purpose.
Top right: One figure poles away an empty raft whilst another assists a third to ascend the very steep shore line.
Bottom right: Three figures are involved in preparing timber. Two are using a large hand-saw to sever a beam whilst the other is holding a frame into which the sawn timber will be placed.

The plaque is signed L.B. and this would seem to link up with the Wor. Bro. L. Browning whose name is on the small metal plate at the foot of the board and which states that he presented this work to the lodge.

The D.C.L. board is of the same pattern but has three different features. The board is in that sepia colour beloved of early Victorian photographers, the arch is clearly composed of marked stones and the scenes that were shown at the foot of the picture in HLR are here more skilfully inserted on what were the bare slopes alongside the central walkway. Indeed, despite being smaller in this position, the four events have more detail and show much greater mastery of portrayal. One is left with the conviction that the DCL board was done by a professional artist whilst Bro. Browning was doing his best to provide a board at less expense. Only in the scene at Joppa has he more vividly portrayed the proper meaning of the event.

The board at Scarborough is clearly of the same derivation but shows the effects of being produced by someone who had fewer detailed skills. The result is that there are no figures grouped around the left-hand wicket and the landscape alongside the processional way leading to the Temple building is dark and featureless. Whilst this sharpens the whole composition it means that several useful pointers for those giving the lecture are omitted. This again was a locally produced board which, whilst it revealed a desire of Mark Lodges to have their own copy, emphasized the point that some variations could be less than satisfactory. (See picture).

Having seen these variations on the Rosenthal theme one is eager to see any others that might somewhere be uncovered. This subject needs still more research and discovery.

At the meeting of GML in September 1892 a new tracing board was revealed to the members of Grand Lodge. It had been painted by W. Bro. Arthur R.Carter who had registered it under the Tradesmark and Design's Act at Stationers Hall. He had then transferred his rights in it to the Trustees for GML. The Grand Registrar moved that this design be adopted as the official tracing board of the degree and this inevitably led to a spate of questions and an animated discussion. On whose authority had it been undertaken? Was any brother entitled to paint and present a new board for adoption? What was wrong with the previous one? Were they not in danger of doing away with established landmarks? What was the lecture on the new board and who would be able to give it?

It was pointed out by the Grand Registrar that nothing new had been added to this board and *nothing had been omitted* from the old. It had been made more colourful and attractive but as *the symbols were the same* and *all the essential features* of the Mark were present there was no reason why the existing lecture could not be continued. The work had been done with the full sanction and approval of the General Board and it had been submitted to them from time to time for approval as the work progressed. The Rev. J.S.Brownrigg, a P.G.Chap., remarked that as he had *rarely seen any previous board in use* in a lodge, as the previous ones were not *officially recognised*, he hoped that this one, if it were made the official one, would be wisely displayed and explained. A large majority then voted to make it the official tracing board for the Mark degree and an unanimous vote of thanks was passed to the designer. The debate which this new item generated was not of course principally concerned with the board as such but with the underlying and constant concern as to whether the General Board were trying to usurp the rights that belonged to Grand Lodge alone. There would be some Masons returning from London that day who would still be somewhat uneasy at how this new step had come about.

That the new board was purchased by lodges is unquestioned though there were some lodges that still felt that the board they had already was good enough for them and there was no need to incur extra expense by obtaining another. Indeed there were some that would feel that from a teaching point of view the earlier boards were more appropriate as indicating clearly the various stages of the building process. The nonchalant figure with an axe who stands near the porchway of the present board does not seem to be clearly related to the important lesson that any Mark Masonic tracing board is meant to convey. His dress alone may be authentically Eastern but is hardly such as conforms to accepted Biblical costume. He looks more like a porter than an Overseer or the officer that he is meant to represent.

Mention of the main discernible character on the new board leads an inquisitive student to ask himself just what it was that specially commended the new design to the General Board. Was it that this board seems to start from the faulty inference of the 19th century Harris boards that gave us two great pillars at an **exterior** entrance on the south side of the Temple. Is that meant to convey some kind of link with the Fellow Craft degree? What then is the edifice on the hill in the far background for if that too is the Temple then why do we have two representations of it? Was that because, as with the earlier boards, we need to see the sunlight on it? What is the significance, if any, of the 8 steps that lead from the mosaic flooring to the porchway entrance and does it matter that there are 9 rungs on the ladder above with its three winged angels stationary upon it? It is true that the Hebrew characters with their words from Psalm 118, verse 22 are prominently displayed but how many know that reading from right to left they may be set in English letters and meaning as follows?

Eben	mah-asu	hab-bo-nim	hay-thah	l'rosh	pinnah.
A stone	rejected by	the builders	became	as head	of the corner.

We have retained the All-seeing eye, the forms for the cypher alphabet, the mallet and chisel, the hour-glass, the anchor and the square and compasses, as well as the wicket (but with no holes), the three stones as hitherto, cedars of Lebanon and the steep shore of Joppa. Where, though, are the cramp, the 24" rule and the open book? The scroll in the foreground can hardly be said to replicate the latter. The border moreover is more reminiscent of a carpet with the irradiated symbols of the Royal Arch. One only mentions these matters to show that there was some natural concern at first by older Mark Masons as to whether this board did match the preceding ones and that it created questions in their minds. It may also suggest to MMMs today that there are still unexplained portions of the board that the lecture does not cover.

That, however, raises another question. Is the lecture on the degree delivered or the explanation of the board given so that the full measure of the Mark degree is savoured by all who join? In 1968 the General Board had reason to observe that many lodges did not even appear to *have a board* and they therefore directed that the tracing board was an official and essential requirement of lodge furniture. Yet to have a board is not enough. To understand what the board represents, and to have a panel of Past Masters who are able to present the appropriate address on it at least once a year, would seem to be the best and most fitting accompaniment to the mere acquisition of the item. The same system for delivering the Mark lecture will be found to bring benefit. What is clear is that there are still too many Mark Masons who undervalue this hard earned addition to their Mark tradition.

MARK TOKENS

In almost every form of Mark ritual that we have examined earlier in this work there has been some kind of emphasis on the duty of the candidate to recognize his responsibility to assist a brother in distress *if his own mark were not already pledged*. If however he is free to receive a brother's mark he is committed to assisting him. By underlining this duty, and sometimes in the most bizarre ways, the formulators of the degree revived, albeit in a modern dress, an ancient practice known as the 'Tessera Hospitalis'. This 'ring of caring' was regarded in ancient times as a most sacred duty. Individuals entered into contracts of friendship, binding themselves and their descendants to assist and protect each other when trouble might arise. Amongst the Greeks it took the form of breaking a ring into two parts so that each possessed a half. A strange visitor would be kindly received, clothed and entertained for up to nine days but thereafter he would be asked who he was and whence he came. If he could show half a ring then he would be invited to stay as long as he was able. Otherwise he must leave or pay his way.

Therein lies one possible origin of the idea of having a token that could be used to pledge friendship and aid. There is also something else.

If there is one feature that distinguishes the Mark degree today from all others it is the fact that as well as underlining the constant duty we have to be of kindly service to others the MMM *receives wages* in the shape of a perceptible **Token**. Nowhere else in Freemasonry does this happen for though the Fellowcraft Freemason is told about his predecessors going 'without scruple or diffidence' for such a purpose he is never himself engaged in that practice and all he may recall are the words he had to recite before he entered a MM's lodge.

In many of the rituals that have been shared earlier in this book the reader would have noticed references to Mark coins and shekels and as the ceremonies have changed steadily over the last century and a half so has the design of these items. Yet whilst the design might change, the part it had to play was invariable. It confirmed the MMM as a member of the degree, it often revealed his particular lodge, it reminded him of virtue at last rewarded, and it was sometimes a firm link with Mark practices of the past that are now only a memory. It is fair to say that in Scotland and North America there was more emphasis on, and development of, the token than in England, and it is therefore not at all surprising that it is in an exposure with those influences that we have the fullest early description of what a Mark Token might be like. It comes in the ceremony of 'Mark Men' as given in Carlile's 'Manual of Freemasonry' of the 1820s.

"W.M. What was the pay of each Mason in this degree per day?
S.W. Nine shekels, equal to £1.2.6d of our money...
W.M. What was delineated on this ancient coin?
S.W. On one side, the **pot of manna**, and the words, **Shekel of Israel**; on the other, **the rod of Aaron budding**, with the word, **Jerusalem the Holy**.

This description is paralleled by a similar passage in the 'Mark Master' degree that follows:

W.M. What was the pay of each Mark Master per day?
S.W. Twenty-five shekels, equal to £3.2s.6d. of our money...
W.M. What was delineated on that ancient coin?
S.W. The same as on that of the Mark Man, with the addition of the proper signature.

Whilst there is not the slightest doubt that the kind of coin which Carlile describes was in existence at that time, for there is one lying in front of the author as he writes, there is still no explanation of what he meant by 'the proper signature' in the MMM degree nor do we have any certain interpretation of the symbols shown of a pot of manna and the flowering rod of Aaron. What these latter symbols were associated with were the intermediate degrees that linked the Mark to the Royal Arch, and that in itself is interesting, but still does not explain why they should appear on a Mark coin used in the Mark ceremony. Of course Carlile mentions the use of the pot of manna employed in the ceremony of testing whether a Mark Mason has his full five senses.

"In the fourth round the *pot of manna* was presented to me, and having *partaken of its contents*, and declared the same good, the proper officer acknowledged my possession of the faculty of *tasting*."

Yet this does not explain why the symbol appears on a coin of a degree that comes before this happens nor why it is accompanied by this other Aaron reference. Of course it is the case, as any present MMM can testify, that we have still a reference to the 'hidden manna' in our ritual but the reference here from the Book of Revelation has much more relevance in the Christian degree of the Knights Templar than to the shekel of Ancient Israel. That a Templar connection still persists in the Mark degree is intriguing when we realise that it was the Grand Encampments that kept some of these appendant degrees in existence. Enough on that score has already been written above.

It may, of course, simply be the case, as suggested by one writer on the subject, that the Secretary of an American chapter happened to see a silver shekel of the period of the first Jewish revolt and thought how fitting it would be for his Mark ceremony. If that is what happened then his speculation is pointless. There was such a coin mentioned in Exodus chapter 30 as a ransom during the census, and called the Shekel of the Sanctuary, since the money paid was handed over to the 'Tabernacle' or Tent of Meeting. Titus brought a number of these coins to Rome after his destruction of Jerusalem and its worth was about $13\frac{1}{2}$ pence, which might create echoes of some older Mark rituals.

The American seeing one of these might explain the modern coins but not the Carlile one.

The subject of Mark tokens however must not be restricted to one particular though intriguing Jewish style coin. Much more common today is a token made of bronze, or perhaps some substance made to appear like the original bronze, of the same size as the old English penny and with other distinctive features on the two sides. A familiar type of this kind of token has on one side the word 'ADVANCED' with a space in the outer circle where the date of one's own admission to the Mark degree may be engraved. In the centre is a representation of the mallet and chisel linked and the words around them 'SON OF MAN MARK WELL' which will be understood by anyone taking the degree.

The reverse of this token bears a representation of the keystone with its cramp and the circle of 8 letters but this time surrounded by the MM's mark of approval, along the three sides of which are letters in one of the cyphers used by Mark Masons. When read in a clockwise direction they comprise

i) The password used in the Ceremony of Advancement today.
ii) The ancient word of the degree.
iii) The words substituted for the above where English is spoken. On a token designed by a Major Irwin of Bristol well over a century ago there is, around the above, a serpent with its tail in its mouth thus symbolising the perpetual circle of eternity or lasting life.

Another similar token, and one used in the Irish Mark ceremony, has on one side a keystone surrounded by the words 'THEY RECEIVED EVERY MAN A PENNY' (or 'TO EVERY MAN HIS WAGES') which, as we again saw in the ritual review, was part of a reading of the Scriptural parable when there was a 'simulated' dispute amongst the Mark Masons over what was their just due. It is still part of some American workings and on the penny of Ousatonic Chapter in New Milford, Connecticut, there is even a pictorial representation, on one side of a man sent into the vineyard, and on the other the workers complaining about their treatment.

There are of course Mark tokens of many different designs under other Constitutions and especially in Scotland. There the Mark is administered under lodges and Chapters and with their well-known wide variety of dress there goes a no less wide variety of tokens. Some show the emblems of the individual lodge or Chapter and others have local portraits, buildings, railway engines or coats of arms, whilst on the reverse they show the mallet and chisel with a thistle below and the usual band for inserting personal details. In the U.S.A. they became so numerous that in 1925 there was commissioned a 'House of the Temple' collection in Washington D.C. That is so far the largest known collection of Mark tokens anywhere.

Whilst it is true that the vast majority of tokens are circular there are also tokens in the shape of a shield, a keystone, a triangle, an oval, a heptagon and a heart. They are also made of copper, brass, iron, lead, nickel, silver, gold and wood. The *seven sided token* is very much encouraged in Scotland where it is thought that the keystone was such a shaped 'plug' and that is how it appears in the roof of most Scottish vaults. Not to be outdone for variety there are even some Scottish lodges that present their Mark candidates with a *paper token* that resembles a banknote.

As far as England is concerned there seems to be no official policy in regard to them and they are certainly not referred to in the Book of Constitutions. For that matter they are not mentioned by name in the ritual and when given they are transmitted discreetly from behind the Senior Warden's wicket. That they can become an item of much value personally is undoubted and there are many MMMs who regard the token with as much affection as their jewel.

We started with one possible source of the token's purpose and it may be as well as if we close this section with a tale that perhaps proves that origin to be true.

In the 1960s a Past Master of an Mark lodge was employed as a corrosion engineer by a company in Kansas City. He and his crew had been working in Dixon, Illinois when they were transferred to Whiteside County in Iowa and booked into a small hotel. When pay day came round, the wages had not arrived from Head Office and following a phone call it transpired that their pay cheques had been sent to Dixon. The Past Master went to the proprietor of the hotel and explained his plight. He was asked rather oddly if he had 'his penny'. He replied that he had 'a penny' and produced from his wallet the token of Liberty Chapter No. 3 Missouri. The hotel proprietor made no more ado. He assured them that they could pay their bills later and meanwhile he loaned them enough to cover their immediate needs.

MARK MUSIC

It may come as a surprise to some Mark Masons to learn that this aspect of the degree is quite differently viewed by their brethren around the country. In some areas there is hardly any music at all whilst in others there is a very complete musical accompaniment throughout the ceremony. This is a subject which needs much fuller treatment than it will receive here but as it has not even received mention in most books on this degree it will be a step forward if I here give some information to help forward further study.

In the book by Herbert F.Inman entitled 'Mark and Ark Working Explained' we read the following:

"The appointment of an Organist in a private lodge is not essential. The WM will be well advised to remember that *music is not essential* to our ceremonial... Nonetheless, it is an indisputable fact that where the services of an expert musical Brother are available those services will *enhance the beauty and impressiveness* of the ceremonies. This truth applies with greater force in the Mark degree than in the Craft. Probably none will deny that the impressive effect of an Advancement Ceremony where the 'Mark Masters' Song' and the Chants are *expertly accompanied* on the organ is *incomparable* to that which obtains when such accompaniment is lacking."

That reflection, together with some wise words about incidental music, unsuitable tunes and the hiring of artistes, constitutes the whole of what has hitherto been contributed on the subject, but as hitherto it was considered unwise or indelicate to refer to more than the lineaments of our ceremonies perhaps it was thought that further specific details would be to violate an obligation. In what follows I do not think that we are likely to communicate any vital secrets.

As samples of the variations that can occur in three parts of England I am going to quote from a Mark lodge in Birmingham (B), Chesterfield (C) and York (Y). We shall proceed through the ceremony with brief indications to enable those familiar with the ceremony to note the alterations.

Whereas C and Y begin with the usually adapted Craft opening hymn B has something different. Since it may be unknown to many I append it here:

O grace this Lodge, Great Overseer,
With all Thy pure and earnest truth,
That it may flourish through all time,
In strong and undecaying youth.

Bless the advancing ones this night,
That more and more their lives may be
Made glorious by increasing light.
Acknowledged and derived from Thee.

Their mark in hand, Thy mark at heart,
O may they ever constant prove,
And in all time and circumstance
Unite in brotherhood and love.

In B and Y there is a chant before prayer is offered – 'let my prayer come before Thee: incline Thine ear unto my cry' and at the words 'Patient Industry and Merit' B uses the chant – 'It is your reward for your service in the tabernacle of the congregation' – whilst C. and Y. have – 'And he causeth all, both small and great, to receive a mark in their right hand'.

B has a chant **before** the Ob. – 'Deliver my soul, O Lord, from lying lips and from a deceitful tongue' – whereas C and Y have one **after** it – 'That which is gone out of thy lips, thou shalt keep and perform, as thou hast vowed unto the Lord thy God'.

At the moment of *rejection* B has the single line chant – 'Have mercy upon me, O Lord, for I am in trouble' whereas C and Y have a three line one –

> 'Hear me, O Lord, for thy loving kindness is good: Hide not thy face from thy servant for I am in trouble

> Reproach hath broken my heart; and I am full of heaviness; dishonour and shame have covered my face.
> I am poor and sorrowful; Let Thy salvation, O God, set me up on high.'

In the use of the Processional Hymn B and Y use three verses and C two. They all use 'Mark Masters' for the first, B and Y use 'Those who have passed ...' for the second, B. uses 'Hiram ...' for the third and C and Y use 'Now to the westward ...' for their last one. Variation reigns supreme.

For the search B and Y employ the words – 'Seek and ye shall find, knock and it shall be opened unto you.' and before the first sign B sing 'He that hath **ears** to hear ...' whereas C and Y sing 'He that hath **an ear** to hear, let him hear'. The second sign is preceded in all by 'The stone which the builders (C builder) rejected has become the headstone of the corner'.

In B alone they sing at the transmission of the Word – 'Except the Lord build the house, they labour in vain that build it; Except the Lord keep the city, the watchman waketh but in vain' and in B again, at the investiture, they alone have – 'To him that overcometh will I give to eat of the hidden manna' before the others join in like B with 'To him that overcometh I will give a white stone and in (C and Y 'on') that stone a new name written which no man knoweth (C and Y 'knows') saving (C and Y 'save') he (C and Y 'him') that receiveth it'.

In B there now follow 2 more chants during the lecture. One is after the words '... correspondence with a Brother MMM' when they sing –

> 'By this I know that Thou favourest me because mine enemy doth not triumph over me.
> And as for me, Thou upholdest me in my integrity and settest me before Thy face for ever.
> Blessed be the Lord God of Israel from everlasting to everlasting. Amen.

whilst at the end of the lecture the chant is

'Glory be to Thee O Lord most high'.

Even at the closing of the lodge all of them are different. C uses the adapted version of the Craft closing hymn, 'Now the evening shadows closing', whilst Y has the two unused verses of the MMMs' hymn, 'Hiram, the widow's son' and 'Now to the praise of those ...' but B once more uses a completely different hymn which I here reproduce:

"Have we worked well, Great Overseer,
  A work to last beyond all time;
Each his allotted task fulfilled?
  The Glory and the Praise be Thine.

In this degree we find the truth,
  On earth below, in heaven above;
The corner-stone of every work
  Should be unselfish, lasting love.

Still will we work, and working, pray;
And trust that in a better land
Our mystic keystone may be raised,
And fitted by Thy Master Hand.

Enough has been produced here to show the unexpected diversity of usage even in this matter of the hymns and chants. A much longer and more detailed study would have to consider the variations even within the MMMs' hymn and its wording not to mention the settings that accompany the words. There are also some Mark songs that have been composed from time to time and that need more careful consideration. What is clear is that here is yet another area of Mark practice that has been too long neglected. I would hope that readers will themselves be able to contribute to that study by providing other evidence that they may have regarded as normal and therefore not worth reporting. Could it be that in the South-west, the South and the North-west there are still further and pleasant surprises in Mark music still waiting to be uncovered?

THE CYPHER ALPHABET.

It again needs to be said that it would be impossible as well as unnecessary to attempt any complete explanation of codes and cyphers in this book. Yet there are some questions about the topic, and especially in regard to the Mark degree, that need to be asked and answered. In order to tackle these questions we shall have to travel back a little in time so as to appreciate the source, or sources, from which the various forms of cypher alphabet derive. Anyone who then wishes to pursue the matter further can begin with the material noted in the booklist.

Cryptograms, codes or cyphers are not new. Ever since human beings first learned to make marks on clay to convey their messages they also appear to have occasionally practised the art of concealing, as well as revealing, what they wanted to say. By adopting a secret arrangement of, or substituting alternative arrangements for, letters or hieroglyphs they have conveyed their signals to those who should know and kept them from those who need not. Even the chatter of Morse on a telegraph is 'Double Dutch' to those who are unfamiliar with the code.

Our investigation in this field will most usefully begin with *Henry Cornelius Agrippa* who was born in the city of Cologne on 14 September 1486. He was descended from a *noble* family and was renowned for his many talents and far-ranging genius. As a youth he *served as Secretary to the Emperor* Maximilian and after some time as *a soldier* in his service he was knighted for valour in the field. He studied law and medicine and duly received a doctorate in both these fields. Of his literary attainments we know that he *spoke six languages* so fluently that he could deliver a discourse or translate at sight in them and he was also able to understand and communicate simply in eight others. He was known as a skilful debater in many abstruse studies and was generally learned in other than his main sciences. He travelled a great deal in Europe and was a renowned warrior not only in military skirmishes but in those of a philosophical kind as well. In 1509 he was lecturing on a book called 'De Verbo Mirifico' (*The Remarkable Word*) by Reuchlin and in 1515 he lectured on 'Mercurius Trismegistus', both of which occasions so upset the Church authorities that he had to flee, and by 1521 he was a very poor refugee in Geneva.

From 1524 he was a court physician to Francis I but he quarrelled with him over the use and the misuse of astrological predictions, which he had steadfastly tried to avoid making. In 1528 he was appointed as *historiographer to the Emperor* Charles V but after writing another book 'Concerning Occult Philosophy' in 1530 he was imprisoned in Brussels on suspicion of heresy but was soon freed and died in Grenoble in 1535.

To record his life though briefly is important because it shows how he had **access to the highest levels of government** in more than one country, was obviously skilled in many arts, knew what it was to have to act very discreetly and *communicate cautiously*, whilst also revealing a prodigious knowledge of *ancient as well as contemporary languages* and their use. It is with his book 'Concerning Occult Philosophy' that we most need to be concerned.

In Volume 3 of that work Agrippa gives *several curious alphabets* and for our purposes it is worth remarking that many of the letters which he exposed either closely resemble, or are identical with, some of the Masons' marks of the period. Agrippa made due acknowledgement of the debt he owed for information on this subject to Porphyry (sic), an authority on secret writings, who died in 305 AD, Peter of Abano, a philosopher who died about 1300, and to Honorius the Theban who gave his name to one of the alphabets examined. Whatever the sources, however, it is in these pages of Agrippa that we find what is almost certainly the earliest example of a *9 chambered cypher system* which is now best known from its association with the Masonic Mark degree.

Cyphers, as Agrippa was only too well aware from close personal experience, grew out of the *then new* custom of keeping at foreign courts resident ambassadors who had, of necessity, to be discreet and even secret in their making of reports to their masters. The oldest reference we have of any code system being thus employed is an instruction to a 15th century Venetian ambassador at the Court of the Emperor in Austria. In his despatches he is ordered to refer to the Doge as 'V', the King of Hungary as 'P' and the Pope as 'Q'.

It is hardly surprising, therefore, to find Agrippa producing what must have seemed like a 'ready reckoner' for those eager to devise more and more ways of disguising their actions and reactions. Whilst Agrippa was not the first to produce such a work – that claim belongs to G.di Lavinde with his 'Trattati in Cifra' (or Discourses on Number) – it is Agrippa who specialises in letters rather than mathematical signs.

His substituted symbols were written, not only one after the other, but were also able to be combined to form a compound symbol which was almost certainly the origin of the Monogram. He gives an example with the name MICHAEL, in Latin, Greek, Hebrew and Cypher.

in Latin. *in Greek.* *in Hebrew.* *in Cypher*

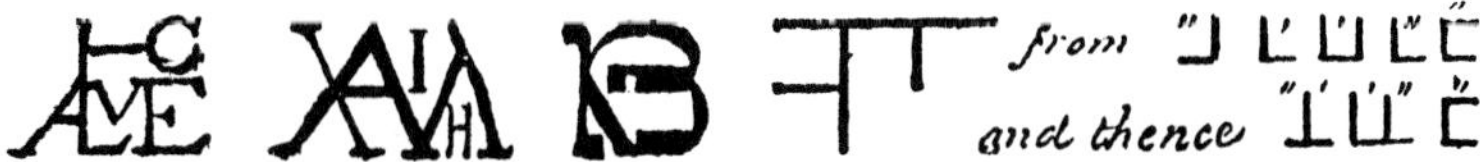

The transliteration into cypher, I must remark, is in this example from the Hebrew letters, Mem, Yod, Kaph, Aleph, Lamed, corresponding to the English MIKAL and not MICHAEL.

What is especially fascinating for the Mark student is that exactly this idea of *combining the chambered cypher letters* was what was done in the 19th century on the Ashton Mark Lodge summons. Unless one knows this principle of conjunction outlined by Agrippa that summons is quite unreadable since no patterns of the basic letters give anything that appears there.[1]

For the record we should note that the alphabets that Agrippa revealed were called 'Transitus Fluvii' (Crossing the River), which would have appealed to some Irish and Northern English Mark Masons, the 'Celestial' and the 'Malachim'. Those who care to examine these in detail will be struck with the similarity between these symbols and those employed by medieval masons to sign their work, as well as remarking that the letters have a clear relationship to the forms of some cypher systems.

Though Cornelius Agrippa was a source for much subsequent reflection and writing on the subject it was *Giovanni Baptista della Porta* of Naples who wrote the book on cyphers that most influenced their use in the 16th century. In his book he mentions secret communication by bells, torches, invisible writing, *gestures and signs*. The latter can be seen to have been put to ample use by the Freemasons. Most especially he was the first to point out the frequency of certain vowels and the need to differentiate between vowels, consonants and double letters, all this leading to his most important adaptation of the earlier NINE CHAMBERS framework as follows:

ALU	BMX	CNZ
DO	EP	FQ
GR	HS	IT

The nine groups were distinguished by nine fundamental characters thus:

These characters stood for the first letters in the groups whilst the second letters were indicated by *one dot* added in the angles and the 3 other letters by *two dots* added in the angles. The use of dots was almost certainly taken from Agrippa. Thus ⌊=C; ⌊·=N; ⌊:=Z. This artificial alphabet was used extensively, but also with different variations in the letters, throughout Tudor times. Cardinal Wolsey used a modification of it – interspersed with writing in the clear – when he was the English ambassador in Vienna in 1527. It is therefore highly likely that copies of this cypher system would have been available in the library at Hampton Court when, as stated earlier, Thomas Dunckerley was in residence there. That Dunckerley was a student and well-read person we know already and that he was not only familiar with the 9 chamber or 'lattice' form of cypher construction but was aware of, and ready to employ, old Operative forms for his cypher we have again hinted at. More will be said about that shortly.

Meanwhile we might note that another writer was at work – the Duke of Brunswick-Luneberg – and he published a book called 'Cryptographiae' under the pseudonym of Gustavus Selenus. Since 'Selen' is the Greek word for Moon and Luneberg means Moon-town we see that he was of a cryptic turn of mind. In his book, which has several much more complicated cypher methods, he also refers to an invented alphabet which he attributed to King Solomon. It is remarkably like the forms from Agrippa's combined alphabets and the resemblance between this and any set of operative masons' marks is striking. Another person, of course, who kept both the name of King Solomon *and* cyphers alive in the early 17th century was Francis Bacon, the philosopher, scientist, essayist and author, not to mention Lord Chancellor of England. It was whilst acting in that office that he introduced into his charge of treason against the Earl of Somerset the fact that the accused communicated with his friends in cypher 'a process reserved for Kings and Princes in their affairs of State.' Was this already part of the Royal Art?

The prevalence of cipher in state circles is confirmed by the claim of some that it was in fact the letters in cypher that Charles I wrote to his wife that eventually led some to demand the ultimate penalty. The letters and other papers were captured at Naseby field, deciphered by a Dr. Wallis and were said to contain such denunciation of the King's enemies, and details of plots against the Parliament, that extreme measures were deemed urgent.

Before we come to the end of the 17th century mention must be made of John Wilkins, the remarkable scientifically-minded Bishop of Chester, who produced plans for a submarine but also wrote a short manual on cryptography. This manual included many methods but one of them was his version of the Porta system. He called it the 'pig pen', or Rosicrucian cypher, whether from the 'fence' arrangement of the letters or because it most frequently emerged in books connected with the latter system of thought. In his arrangement we have the following

ABC	DEF	GHI
JKL	MNO	PQR
STU	VWX	YZ

The use of this system was similar to Porta's so that 'COME HERE' was: [cypher symbols]. The system was known by early American settlers and one of the first gravestones in Trinity churchyard, New York City, bears an inscription in this cypher form. It was used during the American Civil War by northern prisoners in southern camps to communicate with those outside and it is still used in the 'mysteries' of certain negro secret societies. It should be noted that already we have *two apparently identical but distinct* cypher processes.

For our purposes it is now necessary to see how several strands at last came together to provide a new and emerging degree of the Antients lodges with the alphabet that was to distinguish it for at least a century. First and foremost there was the growing interest in early 18th century England, and London in particular, in the art of shorthand. The recent biography of John Byrom has revealed at last how a known teacher of the art was employed by politicians and professional men, not to mention some of the nobility and the Royal Family, so that they might speedily and secretly record and share information of importance. Byrom was himself a Freemason and Martin Foulkes of the Premier Grand Lodge was one of his pupils. So also was Thomas Gurney, who in 1740 published the Mason system of shorthand. Even today Messrs Gurney are the official shorthand writers of the Houses of Parliament. John Byrom's method was finally published in 1767 and being regarded as the best was eventually purchased by Isaac Pitman who made his own improvements towards the system so well known today.

This interest in the art of 'secret writing' was expressed by Laurence Dermott, at one time the industrious and influential Secretary of the Antients Grand Lodge. In some portion of his personal writings we find that he was fond of using cypher and in the Holy Royal Arch Grand Chapter Register he drew a pedestal and then added these lines **on it**:

> Hail mysterious! royal art,
> What wonders! does thy sons impart:
> Who, with two **squares**, can make appear,
> That hands can speak. and eyes can hear!!!

He then reproduced his own form of cypher method as follows, but now introducing not just the 'pig-pen' but also the St. Andrew's cross:

A	C	E
G	I	M
O	Q	S

B.	D.	F.
H.	L.	N.
P.	R.	T.

U
Y Z
W

This introduces *a third variant* into the still apparently similar basic pattern albeit it now uses some acute angle 'letters' as well.

The next factor that has to be considered is that in the Early French Exposures, so excellently edited by Harry Carr, we have ample proof that the use of cypher patterns was part of contemporary Masonry there. We cannot here examine all the examples but in 'Le Sceau Rompu' (The broken seal) of 1745 we have the following commentary:

"One of the most ingenious practices of Masonry & one which is least noticed by Masons themselves, is our Writing … Masonic Writing combines, with that same simplicity, the advantage of being an universal Writing & suitable for use in all Languages.

"This marvellous Alphabet consists of two *parallel* perpendicular *lines*, crossed by two horizontal lines also parallel, forming a proper square in the middle, four open squares, & four equal angles. All these divisions form nine compartments, either open or shut, five of which contain two letters each, & four others three."[2]

All that sounds very familiar, but then we come to the distribution of the actual letters –

f q.	a. i	o. u
g p.	r.s:t	d h.z:
c n.	e.x:l	b.m y:

"Hence the French word 'Compas' is ┐⌞┌⊐⊔⊡: it will be seen, without stressing the point, that the Masonic Letters are very similar to those of the Hebrews, & the Analogy is striking. The dots which distinguish the letters make the resemblance even closer, & they doubtless owe their origin to the vowel-points invented by the Massoretes."

To mention but one other case. In 'le Maçon Démasqué' (The Mason Revealed) of 1751 we have a chart which shows us clearly how that alphabet was formed and we now have yet another form. Is it any wonder that when Dr. Oliver in the first half of the 19th century wrote about this subject he could produce at least **SIX** different forms of the cypher – Original English, Improved English, Another variety (English), Original Continental, Improved Continental, United States – and he went on to say that these were *a few of the most usual.* All of these incidentally use the 'pig-pen' and Andrew's cross, with or without dots, to form the whole English alphabet. He also added some perhaps surprising words, though we should remind ourselves that he was describing what he believed was the '*old manner* of Masonry':

"You are also, my Brethren, *entitled, as Master Masons, to the use of an alphabet*; which our venerable Grand Master, HAB, employed in communicating with King Solomon, of Jerusalem, and King Hiram, of Tyre. It is *geometrick* in its character and is therefore eminently useful to Master Masons in general. By means of two squares and a mallet, a Brother may make the whole alphabet, and silently convey his ideas to another at any convenient distance ..."[3]

It will, I trust, now be clear to the reader that any idea that there was, or was ever intended to be, **one special Masonic cypher** is mistaken. When, therefore, I or others are approached by puzzled brethren who cannot interpret some form of cypher writing, though they have what they think is *the one key*, the response has to be, 'Possibly you are not using the right code'. I for one have to say that the range provided by Dr. Oliver has hitherto solved every cypher problem on which I have been consulted. These are reproduced in an Appendix and, together with the ones already given in this chapter, should make any transliteration possible. I therefore repeat: the forms of cypher alphabet which have been used in connection with the Mark degree around the world have been much more diverse than most of us have been ready to admit or accept. In this respect Dr. Oliver was misleading when he completed the passage mentioned above with these words:

"That this geometrick alphabet may be easily learned and remembered, I will entrust you with the key thereof which is as follows:

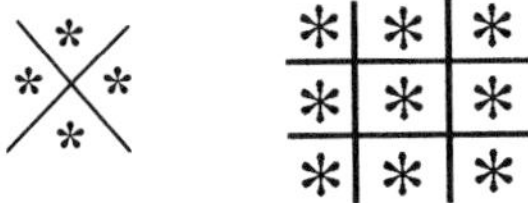

The fault in this statement was the suggestion that one form of this arrangement was sufficient to answer all de-cyphering needs. That is the message that was widely transmitted. The fact remains that Oliver *did not supply any letters to go with his drawings* and he could thus rightly claim that he had merely indicated a method but **not supplied the whole key**.

Though it is in one sense no part of this work to examine and explain the principal remaining use of the Masonic cypher as we look out on to the 21st century – its appearance on the 3° Tracing Board – it is nevertheless interesting to reflect on what we now know. It would seem that there was one firm tradition that *gave to Master Masons* the right to understand and employ a cypher method of writing. It was their due as Geometrick Masters. Accordingly it is not surprising if at the very heart of that degree's secrets that type of writing should be employed even if no-one today ever explains it in open lodge.

On the other hand, as Oliver implied, this *was a secret manner of writing* that is now not conveyed to MMs but has been lost or taken up by Masons elsewhere in the system. By his date it certainly had been resurrected elsewhere in the whole Masonic system. It was taught in the rituals of the old Independent Mark lodges or Craft lodges conferring the Mark degree. Before too long a key would be reproduced on the Mark tracing boards. As Canon Tydeman once wrote:

"The Mark degree logically precedes the Master Mason's, since it is necessary to study the key on the TB of the one, in order to understand the writing on the other!"[4].

It only remains to tackle one more important strand in the 18th century story before this section is complete. I refer to the cypher system which Thomas Dunckerley attached to his form of the Mark Man and Mark Master ceremonies and which was used by the Friendship Chapter for almost a century after he visited them in 1769. Reference to this system has been made in the chapter on Dunckerley but we can now examine it in still more detail with the background of the cypher alphabet's history before us.

It now becomes even more clear that not only did Dunckerley **not invent** the Mark degree but neither did he create the Mark cypher language that he said should accompany it. That form of communication was already there in the Antients' armoury and the point so constantly made earlier about the part played by military lodges must underline the fact that this would suit brethren in that milieu. That Dunckerley acquired the idea of the cypher along with the notion of a Mark ceremony seems the most natural and obvious development.

What further convinces me that this is what happened is that when we meet the cypher alphabet in several old Mark lodge rituals the form that they employ, and sometimes teach explicitly, was much more like the forms we have seen above referred to by Dermott and Oliver. If the Mark cypher had been Dunckerley's innovation then surely there would have been some who would have copied his first essay in the field.

The truth is that Dunckerley acquired the idea of a cypher language but being the person he was he did not leave it as he found it. Indeed we know that he certainly must have done something to the method of cypher communication because his is a **unique form** of that medium. In the chapter on his connection with the Mark degrees I even went so far as to show how he took the basic 9 chamber or 'pig-pen' basis, added the St. Andrew's cross, put in a diamond shape that gave equilateral triangular letter forms, and then topped it off with a Swastika facing left. No other cypher system in Freemasonry is so complicated or 'rich' and *nowhere else* but in the Friendship records at Portsmouth have we found anything comparable. If there were to be anything similar it would surely be in the *Fortitude Mark Lodge* archives at Plymouth where Thomas Dunckerley is known to have devised some of his degree **improvements**. So far that discovery has not been made though as this chapter was being written there arrived from that very source one of their early Mark certificates showing just the kind of lattice wicket window, with a round hole in the centre pane of NINE, that was later copied assiduously in North American manuals and practice. The Certificate also states that a beloved Brother had 'received the order of MMM in the order of the **holy St. Mark**' which answers the question by some as to where that phrase comes from. On the matter of the cypher we have not yet found any 'parallel' to Portsmouth.

The only query that still needs more attention is why did Dunckerley introduce the Diamond and the Swastika? To those of us who even now fear the resurgence of groups who display the form, or comparable forms, of the latter this question is doubly important. We need to satisfy our search for past truth and we need to be reassured for the present reputation of our Masonic practices. Happily I believe we can do both with impunity.

The answer lies in that very area with which we began in Chapter 2. We learnt there that at the head of the Operative masons were three Grand Masters. These rulers each bore a rod and those rods were in a strict relation to one another. That relation was 3 to 4 to 5 according to any scale that might be appropriate. In order to create or test the perfection of any form, and that was surely the final responsibility of the Rulers of a Building trade, those rods were employed. *Their use was the ultimate secret of masonry.* The forms they could jointly create were the perfect forms of all created matter and two of those forms were (i) a triangle and (ii) a square. For our purposes the technical explanation of these combinations are irrelevant but the results of this capacity to form these items helps to answer our present query. When FOUR triangles of 3:4:5 rods are made they can create a diamond. When FOUR squares of 3:4:5 dimensions are joined they form a Swastika. If I tell you that on the Holy Bible in an Operative lodge, as on the VSL in a Speculative one, there is a Square then you will understand why the 3 Grand Masters with their own squares were able to form the four-legged symbol.

It will be for the reader to make his own more intimate study of the Swastika if he so wishes but there are three brief facts that must be recorded before this Mark portion of our book closes. The name of this figure is in Sanskrit, one of the very oldest languages in the world. SU-or SW-meant good or goodness, well, well-being or prosperity; ASTI-means 'May thou, he or she be'; and the suffix -KA turns the whole thing into a noun or substantive. Thus it really means 'This is that which represents good or well-being for you'. Its original and proper use is to suggest all that is good and beneficial.

The sign was universally employed with that idea in mind on the bricks of the Chaldeans, the Egyptian and Roman altars, the Temples of India and China and Japan (where it is still prevalent), on Runic crosses in Scandinavia and on 13th and 14th century brasses in British churches. It was particularly related to the Pole Star which was an absolute fixed point for mediaeval building plans. Hence its value to the rulers of the Operatives and their possession of the means to create a symbolic form of their important building guide. Though we cannot pursue this further here let it be said that in due course the Sun overtook the Polar Star as the most important luminary. Suffice it to say that the mediaeval theory was that this sign originated with the Turanian or Mongolian people and that is why the cypher language was once said to have begun with the Turanian form.

Nowhere else in the whole of Speculative Freemasonry is the Swastika known or employed because, as was said at the outset of our story, Dr. Anderson was just not advanced enough as an Operative mason to know anything about it. Only the delving of a Moderns Mason who appreciated the richness of

Antients ways, one Thomas Dunckerley, re-introduced this old Masonic feature and made it work for the Mark. What was good was that he knew which way round it had to face – to the left – in order to be well meaning. Turn it the other way and it meant the reverse – all that was evil. What Dunckerley did for the Mark was, we believe, for its good. Its place in Freemasonry today would seem to have proved him right.

Chapter Eleven

The Royal Ark Mariner Degree: its origin & development

OF ALL THE most noteworthy stories in the world's history that of Noah and the Flood must surely be one of the most memorable. The fact that on the threshold of the 21st century we know so much more about the background to this biblical event – that it is recorded in other ways and in other cultures than those of the Hebrew and Christian Scriptures, that the Flood was not what we now regard as an universal inundation, and that the mathematical figures stated are not according to present scales – all this has no bearing whatever on our present purpose. To those who first conceived the idea of an Ark Mariner degree, in which the story of Noah and the Ark are central, and who pursued and developed that idea until its firm emergence as an ordered part of English Freemasonry in the latter 19th century, such critical researches were quite unknown and therefore have no relevance to our story. For our masonic forebears the story of Noah was true and trustworthy as it stood. It is to that story that we must therefore first turn our attention. Whilst we cannot here attempt an exhaustive commentary on the Bible account there are several key points in the narrative that demand our notice and about which some useful things can be said before we turn our attention to the rituals of the degree that eventually emerged. It is only as we appreciate how the story was understood **in early times** that we can see the relevance of the symbols, tokens and forms of words used by Masons in their Ark Mariner ceremonies. For the sake of clarity we shall deal with the story under the following heads:

Noah's ancestry;
His family and their names;
His character;
His occupation and skill;
His 'experience';
His deliverance and new life;
His descendants;
His story's significance.

NOAH'S ANCESTRY

That Noah was the son of **Lamech** there seems to be no doubt whatever. The varied authorship of the Bible, however, gives two lines of descent to Lamech though both of them link him with **Adam**, whose name meant 'from the earth'. The first of these lines, found in Genesis chapter 4, is through **Cain**, 'the acquirer', who founded a city and gave it the name of his first born, **Enoch**, 'a teacher'. Enoch then fathered *Irad* whose son was *Mehujael* and he in turn bore *Methushael*, who was, by this tradition, Lamech's father.

In the second explanation of Noah's ancestry (Genesis chapter 5) Adam's wife is said to have given birth to a third son named **Seth** whose name means 'compensation' (for Abel's death?) or 'further sprouting' and from him descend in order Enos 'mortal', Cainan, Mahaleel 'God is splendour', Jared, 'the descendant', Enoch, and then *Methusaleh*, who is again the father of Lamech. It is no part of our task here to try and unravel this apparent confusion of traditions though it might be remarked that there is a surprising similarity of most of the names, even if not in the same order, and since these lists were for a long time simply recalled by memory it is singular that they are not more dissimilar than they now appear. What will be immediately clear to the member of the Ark Mariner degree is that the *second* line of descent in the Bible source was preferred to the other whilst the reader who has not yet acquired this degree may be assured that many of these names and their meanings are more than simply a list of ancient personal or tribal titles. The use of them leads the candidate on into more truth and light. What we shall also see in due course is that the line leading from Adam to Noah was determined in Freemasonry long before anything that resembled our present ceremony was fashioned. The ancestry of Noah was, in fact, part and parcel of Freemasonry's most treasured 'memories'.

As a sidelight on this linkage of Noah with other masonic personages it is worth noting here that Lamech has two wives, Adah and Zillah. By the first he reared Jabal, whose name meant 'leader', and Jubal 'a horn' whilst by the latter he bore **Tubalcain** 'the metal acquirer' or 'smith'. We are not told whether Noah was born of either of these wives or of another woman altogether but the fact remains that to Freemasons of old, both Operative and Speculative, Noah was some kind of blood brother to these well established figures of Craft Masonry. His appearance on the Masonic scene is no accident.

HIS FAMILY and THEIR NAMES

What was true of his ancestors was also true of himself and his family. Their names were of especial significance – though it may have been remarked by the reader that *Methusaleh/Methusael* do not appear to have had any special meaning. Thus **Noah** means 'rest' or 'comfort' and that name was appropriate for one who so trusted in, or walked with, God as to have an ultimate peace of mind and know that as he did what God commanded he would have comfort and security. What is noteworthy in the biblical record is the fact that the compiler or editor of the ancient record adds to the crucial verse – "Noah found grace in the eyes of the Lord" – the names of his three sons. That there was a bond of real affection between father and sons seems to be suggested at every stage of the story but there is something else. R.H.Mottram, in his study of Noah, suggests that no historian would add a list of sons if they were weak and unsuccessful characters. Much more likely would have been scant mention of their existence, if any, and sole emphasis on the principal character and his salvation – as is the case earlier with Enoch. That is not what happens here. The earth – or such part of it as they know and are concerned with – is cleared so that Noah's line, led by his sons and their wives, can re-populate it with a righteous folk. Their names are names that matter and are worthy of record.

Shem, which means 'name' or 'renown', was the youngest of the three sons, and the significance of his name is emphasised by the fact that to this day respectful reference to Almighty God in Jewish circles is by using the term 'Shem Haphoresh'. Yet this son appears to have earned respect simply because he did not rest on his name but diligently applied himself to the tasks which his father set him. The position he had in the family, as the last successor to his father and the junior of his two brothers, does not seem to have concerned him unduly and the position in which we find him when the present Ark Mariner ritual begins to be formed shows that the lessons taught by him are simply a reflection of his principles in action. As far as the Flood event was concerned he was a loyal and obedient subsidiary of the Patriarch.

Ham, or **Kham**, came next and his name meant 'swarthy' or 'dark coloured'. The tendency to regard this second son as in some way especially ill-favoured is difficult to sustain when one recalls that the whole pattern of the Flood event is that God selected one man and his family as worthy of saving because of their evident righteousness. There is no question in the biblical account of Ham being any different from his brothers in obeying and assisting their father in the task set by God. There is also no evidence for excluding him from the blessing that all the family of Noah enjoyed in being kept safe from the waters of destruction and he was delivered to the life after the Deluge along with the rest of the family. It was to him, as to all Noah's family, that God spoke the most reassuring words, "I am now establishing my covenant with you and **with your descendants to come** ... that never again shall all living things be destroyed ... nor ever again shall there be a flood to destroy all the earth". It is only one incident, and that described in the most neutral manner – 'he saw his father naked and told his brothers outside' – that seems to effect any change in his status. That is all. It is the father who seems to react with remorse at his condition, with anger at being discovered, with bitterness towards him who reported it and with unbridled harshness in his punishment. One is bound to reflect that either we are not being told the half of what really happened or that somehow the 'dusky skin' of this offspring was the ground for his being set apart as a much less favoured progenitor of race than his brothers. When one also learns that the other name of Ham was 'Canaan' and we recall the subsequent conquest of the people of that area by the Israelites, the descendants of Shem (the **Semites**), there must be a possibility that this rejection of Ham in Genesis was part of the justification of that later history. To the society of the 18th century, in which this 'Deluge' degree was to emerge, the subservience of the 'dark coloured races' was part of the natural scene. What the name HAM really teaches is that there is always a danger of despite and prejudice being merely skin-deep and superficial. We need to base our convictions on much more solid and deep-rooted truths.

Eldest of the sons is **Japhet** or **Japheth**. His name, contrasting with that of Ham, means 'the fair one' and we shall see the implication of that a little later in this survey of the Deluge account. His name also meant 'the enlarger' and here the tradition of him as the oldest son adds the suggestion that he was the 'front man' or 'odd job member' of the male crew and that not only was he given the extra tasks to perform but was the first to set foot outside the Ark when it came to testing whether the ground outside the Ark's resting place was fit to set forth on. The Bible, in Genesis chapter 9 verse 27, even reveals a play on his name and yet recognises his primacy of place: "May God *make space* for Japhet that he may live in the tents of Shem and let Canaan be his slave". This might also be called the future scenario for these sons of Noah. They were set in an almost fixed relationship to one another but they were also freely related. Whatever the future might hold they felt bound to one another – the renowned, the dusky and the fair. What is also clear is that initially they were all still close to each other even after the Flood subsided. They belonged to each other as a family.

Mention must be made of **Noah's wife**. She is, after all, specifically referred to in the Bible account, as indeed are the daughters-in-law. Of Noah's wife we seem to know more because, as will be noticed later, she appears as a distinctive personality in the Mystery play of the Deluge that was performed for more than two centuries in English city streets. We even learn from Arab sources, which tell us that they also performed religious plays, that her name was, in their language, **Wa'ila**, which meant 'lamenter' or 'contender', and it may well be that it is precisely this aspect of her character that was seized upon by the Christian playwrights and used in their presentation. What is clear is that whilst she may have protested her own doubts about what her husband was foretelling, and the uselessness of forsaking the homestead which she and the other women had worked so hard to create, she was still at heart an accepting and loyal partner to Noah and, once aboard, she is heard of no more as she set about the new tasks that would await her in the floating farmstead. What is so appealing about the whole story is that God the Father apparently appreciates that even so stout a heart as Noah possessed needed the affection and companionship of his wife and children as they set forth on the deep.

HIS CHARACTER

We have already hinted at the quality of Noah's faith and dependence on God but there are other traits which issue from this foundation of belief and which materially affect our story. When, today, we set the biblical account of a flood alongside those from other Middle Eastern sources, from India,

Greece and even Ireland, we notice that Noah seems to stand out as a very special individual. He knew what was coming and he pledged himself to meet it. He even undertook to confront ridicule and scorn as he strove to complete his building project by a determined date. He showed not only strength of arm but strength of character. He was charged with a task and he would see it through. As Mottram again remarks, "he must have been a man by race, nature and avocation of outstanding bodily presence ... and of dignified demeanour. There is no hint of hurry, but every sign of long and careful preparation ... there is every reason to consider him a man of ripe experience, and (without any) inclination for petty thought and pointless clamour".

The astonishing thing about this story of Noah is that whilst half of what we read is possibly legend – the distant memory of a time when men were said to have done this or that – and much of what was written was certainly symbolical – which is why it lends itself so naturally to Masonic usage – yet there emerges this very human and understandable man, a countryman, the head of a household, a refugee, a hero in a moment of crisis and something of the explorer and innovator. As Mottram rightly concludes: "Small wonder that the hardy race that colonised the Americas and Africa and Oceania read the Bible with a strong sense of its literal accuracy. It not only gave them the support of the finest religious poetry in the world but it also described, in such narratives as those of Noah and Abraham and Moses, just the *sort of people* those colonists were, and just the sort of circumstances in which they found themselves."[1] Noah especially was their exemplar – a man of God, a pioneer and a founder of new races.

HIS OCCUPATION AND SKILL

How could Noah be anything at first but a peasant farmer? Centuries after his time the descendants of Shem are revealed as the keepers of flocks and dwellers in tents. Where else did Noah and his sons acquire their knowledge of and care for the animals that they were to assemble in the Ark?

The story of the Flood comes at a significant turning point in human history. Instead of hunting animals and killing them on the spot man now kept them alive and took care of them. He let them breed and multiply under his direction. He had meat but he also collected wool and eggs and milk. He had begun to learn how to manage plants and crops and as the story of the Ark demonstrates Noah was aware that even olives can grow under water. That is why he was not surprised when the 'messenger' returns with a leaf from a plant that is still growing after the Flood. Those who were most involved with animals found that they had to be more or less on the move since new pastures had to be found and from the Greek word for 'pastures' we now speak of them as 'nomads'.

Noah and his extended family were past this stage for they were more stationary. They had begun to build permanent dwellings near their fields of crops and to work in cooperation at the strenuous tasks of planting, watering, weeding, protecting, tending and harvesting. They learnt how to preserve food until the next season, to store seed and to propagate it. It was this new concentration of families working at the same process in certain areas that led to the establishment of villages and then small towns, small at least by present-day standards. It was in those communities that the first and primitive trades also appeared – the potters, the smiths, the builders and the carpenters.

What is now so much more certain is that all this first began to happen in the area which we call the Middle East. "The traveller in the region today", says a very recent writer, "might have difficulty believing that any great cities could ever have survived in these regions. Nevertheless, it is clear that in the past these lands were very fertile and well husbanded, for they produced sufficient food and materials for the sustenance of thousands of communities ... It was a region of intensive farming and breeding, truly a garden of plenty, as the Old Testament records: 'And a river went out of Eden to water the garden ...' The ancient Sumerian word for the open pastureland of the lower Mesopotamian plains was **eden**, and it is probable that these ever fertile lands formed the basis of the early legend of man's origins."[2]

What could not be controlled satisfactorily was the tendency of the four great rivers of the area to flood unpredictably and it is in that context that stories of a special Great Flood could arise. What is of particular concern to us is the fact that besides being by tradition a herdsman, by contemporary usage a farmer and crop-breeder, Noah seems to have acquired skill as a major carpenter and builder.

That Noah had the basic knowledge of how to erect a shelter for his family may easily be granted and it was Dr. Oliver who so graphically described how "The first Pillars used by the primitive inhabitants of the earth were merely trunks of trees, placed upright on stones to elevate them above the damp, and covered at the top with a flat stone to keep off the rain. On these the roofs of their huts were placed, covered with reeds and plastered with clay to resist the effects of tempestuous weather."[3] Such were techniques that many others than Noah were able to apply. Yet in the task that was now set before him Noah was expected to be more than a simple village carpenter.

Could it be that he had already encountered something similar in the variable conditions that faced people in that region? Had there been a previous occasion when he had constructed something more than a mere raft that would float. Had he made a vessel into which he packed his family and farmyard stock so as to cross a surging flood in the Delta or crossed some arm of the waters we now call the Persian Gulf?

Whatever the background two things are abundantly clear. One is that the catastrophe for which Noah was now advised to prepare was going to be far more serious, far more demanding and unexpected than anything he and his family had undergone before. The second is that whatever we may make of the dimensions which it is reported that God laid down for him the construction task was quite beyond anything that he can have previously imagined or planned. Noah was faced with a very large building project in conditions that in no way seemed to warrant it and involving an assembling of materials and manpower that could jeopardise his normal daily programme of husbandry. This would test his skill to the limit.

"Anyone", says R.H.Mottram, "who has attempted or even watched less arduous efforts at boat-building would know that there are few tasks more onerous. The timbers of a small boat are heavy and cumbersome to handle. And there is a curious opposition between building a boat and building a house. The farther one proceeds with the latter, the more the half-finished erection supports itself and aids the constructor. With a boat the reverse is the case. The initial steps are comparatively easy but the addition of each strake adds to the difficulty. Until the boat is launched it is in its wrong element. The more complete it becomes the more out of place it is on the ground, which is not its natural basis. Until it is launched, its ill-distributed weight requires more and more artificial and dexterous support. It may be that the Ark never was launched in the exact meaning of the term, but was allowed to float on the rising waters. That did not ease the task of construction. The fact remains that, however much it may have resembled a floating house of very primitive shape – something between a floored barn and a wooden tank or crate – (and that is how many early Masonic documents portray it) – it lay on the ground and was not steadied by dug and banked foundations."[4]

The building of the Ark was manifestly a major work of construction in antiquity. It required a basic acquaintance with **Geometry**, the gift of being able to draw a plan, even if only on the ground, the knowledge of how to select and manoeuvre large tree-timbers, to know how to attach and preserve such timbers in water, and lastly, though nothing of this is mentioned in any account, to fashion and employ such primitive tools as were available.

To stay for a while with these problems is, I believe, important. Royal Ark Mariner Masons today can become blasé about Noah's practice but we shall do well to recall that the art of metal-making or working had only just begun to emerge with his half-brother, Tubalcain, and wasn't he now among the drowned? For Noah the main implement was **Stone**. As an HMSO booklet on 'The Sheffield of the Stone Age' puts it:

"... ancient man was dependent on stone, more especially on flint for axes and picks ... heavy choppers of flint were also used. The size and weight of these tools required the use of both hands ... and axes had blades with oblique ends and a chisel-like cutting edge called a 'tranchet' ..." There were no cross-cut saws to assist the sizing of timber, the screw was not discovered until Roman times and there were no iron spikes, just wooden wedges to help split logs. Water and fire and sensible use of sheer muscle power were the main assistants. And how could Noah be sure that he was laying the timbers or rough planks true? He had the sun overhead and he had a stone attached to a cord for a *plumb-line*. With great effort he made his wooden pegs and hammered them into the hard-won holes and then he seems to have known of some resin or gum, or perhaps the precursor of that bitumen that was to herald the oil sheikhs' paradise in these parts, and 'within and without' he secured the frame as God desired.

From then there was the whole complicated business of ensuring that the internal plan was correct. The stalls for the different kinds of creatures, 'clean and unclean' as the record calls them, the farmyard beasts, the local wildlife, the birds and the insects, and all the fodder or green herbage that they would require. All this, without attempting to enter the fairy-tale world of elephants and giraffes, hippopotami and ostriches. Pigs, cows, sheep, goats, mountain rabbits and grasshoppers were quite enough for anyone to cope with – and to muck out.

It is quite true, to emphasize a earlier point, that he does not seem to have had the problem of providing any means of steering or propulsion for there is not the slightest mention of any attempt to sail, row, punt or tow the Ark. There is however the reasonable deduction that he built this vessel away from the 'cities of the plain' – and there is a moral there – and in some more elevated position where trees were more at hand not only for the building but for the women to use to fire and stoke the cauldrons that cooked food and prepared the pitch. It was after all a truly corporate undertaking. Perhaps the women also had something to say about how the doorway and the window should be constructed for they were things they used constantly, and did they not also advise on how and where to catch and keep drinking water?

When the skill and dedication of the builder, the scope of his task and above all its ultimate purpose is considered it is in no way unreasonable to regard this project as at least comparable to that of building King Solomon's Temple. What is interesting is to discover that in Masonic tradition just such a view was held. Noah was an ancient and early prototype of Hiram. This is not the point at which to compare the two in detail though it is interesting to note that neither of them was initially prepared for the task that ultimately occupied their main attention. For Noah certainly it was a test of his innate and no doubt unsuspected talents.

HIS 'EXPERIENCE'

"The same day were all the fountains of the great deep broken up and the windows of Heaven opened." What it must have been like for Noah and those with him on that fateful occasion it is difficult to imagine exactly though anyone who has undergone a tropical thunderstorm on land or a major storm at sea will have some impressions not easily forgotten. It must have seemed as if a tidal wave and several cloudbursts had taken place at the same moment. Whilst the rain descending was more like a set of solid objects the surge from below must have been like a sort of earthquake shudder. Even today and in places well known around the Mediterranean it is still the case that what have been apparently stone-dry riverbeds become in a flash formidable torrents sweeping everything before them. Yet however familiar those living in that countryside might be with this sort of phenomenon they met here something quite outside their normal experience. Here was something that threatened not temporary but total devastation. Life of every sort was under the sort of threat that Noah had predicted. Could it be that even Noah wondered, 'Can the Ark survive?'.

Like many a boat-builder in the centuries that have succeeded his Noah must have waited almost with baited breath to see how she took to the water. R.H.Mottram has described this moment as few others could. "Noah was quite helpless now. If he had done well, he was safe. If he had made the least slip, even to the distribution of his largely living freight, and the tethering of animals or the ordering of humans, he would soon feel her heel and list, if he did not hear the straining and cracking of displaced timbers and the rending of fastenings as they parted ... The water still deepened. Then suddenly, and so secretly that at first he dared not believe it, he felt, not so much beneath his feet as in his stomach ... the new-born life of his craft. The Ark was afloat."[5]

"The waters prevailed and were increased greatly upon the earth; and the Ark went up upon the face of the waters." That is how the Ark's life began and perhaps already Noah and his family had less time than we think to wonder about the outcome. There were the animals to be fed and watered. Even if their menagerie was less exotic than has sometimes since been fancied the crew would have had little time for gazing out on the growing blankness of the scene around them.

At first, of course, the scene would not be quite so blank. The familiar surroundings began to disappear but there were desperate scenes as people rushed up the hillsides, climbed rocky heights and tall trees, or sought to swim or even paddle something that might lie to hand. But the force of the Deluge, the persistence of the downpour and the relentless rise of the water gave way to floating corpses and scattered debris, even of the most substantial erections of the 'Cities of the Plain'. What must the families of Noah and his sons have felt as they realised how slender was the line between those who died and those who rested in the Ark. It is not in the least surprising that ever since this time the event of Noah's Ark has been a cause of significant human reflection. As the loneliness of these few human beings became complete – a fearsome loneliness such as we know wracked the very spirits of Columbus's sailors – Noah's one task was doubtless to keep his folk occupied, to maintain the flame of purposeful living, to re-assure those whom he had helped to stay alive that the life they still enjoyed was theirs for a purpose.

"Human faith is a flame that flickers all the time and will easily go out. Noah kept his alight and burning and therein, as much as in anything, lies his claim to be the first great human hero."[6] Therein also lies one strand of the claim made later that this was a prototype of another Master of fishermen or the teacher on the sea of Galilee.

HIS DELIVERANCE AND NEW LIFE

Did someone call Noah's attention to a shift in the wind? Did he catch a change in the breeze as he paused in the midst of doing some task with the animals or checking the stores? God at least, says the Bible, "made a wind to pass over the earth and the waters were assuaged. The fountains of the deep and the windows of Heaven were stopped and the rain from Heaven restrained". Could it be that the whole dreadful experience was to end and that their lonely vigil was over? Yet just because the rain ceased and the waters no longer rose or were troubled did not mean that all was well. Noah's faith must have included the recurring awareness that God would not have preserved him, his wife and their children just to leave them on the untroubled waters. Their food stocks were not inexhaustible and what may already have begun to be the progeny of at least smaller creatures amongst them would soon need more space to dwell in.

What first gave him the sense that not only was the deluge over but that the Flood might be about to subside? Was it that for the first time in months he could count the stars and with some simple knowledge of the main ones recognise roughly his position? Was it that he began to pick out small pinpoints of land, the tops of the highest mountains, though as yet they were like small outcrops on the surface? Was it that he watched the flotsam of debris and could tell by its motion that there was a settling of the waters? Who knows? What is made clear is that on the 'seventh day of the month' the Ark rested on '*Ararat*'. The excitement that had attended the sudden lift-off of the Ark onto its watery bed was now equalled by the thrill of feeling it subside into inactivity. It ceased to be a boat and became a building once more. And where it rested was what we otherwise know as **Urartu**, the independent kingdom of Van of which the Armenians were to be the heirs. Its Persian name was **Kuh-i-Nuh**, the Mountain of Noah. What is also intriguing is the fact that to this day in Maltese, a language related to that Semitic language spoken by Jesus, the words '**ar-a-rat**' mean 'Land is there'. It was a place that seemed appropriate for God to have chosen.

It is here, settled in some nook of the upper mountain, that Noah does what any sensible countryman might think of doing – he selects the birds that will tell him if the waters are indeed subsiding and if there is land to graze on, fruit to feed on, or trees to build with. He selects first what is called a 'raven' but may have been any of those scavenging birds of black plumage that can still be seen hovering over tropical cities. Its disappearance showed that it had much carrion to feed on and perhaps enough rocky spots on which to devour its discovered prey. This was a sure sign that visibility was good, the waters were at least rising no more and a raven could exist without any other aid. No doubt Noah saw to it that the raven's mate soon joined its partner.

Noah, however, needed to know about grain or seed-bearing plants. He sends forth the dove and back comes the bird with the proverbial olive branch in its mouth. This was progress indeed. The olive furnishes the sub-tropical peasant with food, a means of cooking, lubrication and sustenance for some animals. Noah and his family would never starve even if this was all there was to begin with. At least it was a sign that life was possible outside once more. It was the presage of peace from the tempest and its effect and it has ever since been the symbol of that blessing. Yet still the dove had nowhere to rest or nest for long, and since the dove was nothing like as far-ranging as the 'raven' Noah knew that in the Ark's vicinity there was still not enough land to use. The time for disembarking had still not arrived.

It was *symbolically* the first day of the first month of the 601st year in the life of Noah that that great day came. The doves had at last flown out and never returned and the kindly welcome that old Father Noah had extended to them as they flew in before was no longer required. If the dove could rest and eat and begin to multiply then so could all the other creatures in Noah's care. He could begin to open the door of what may have already begun to resemble a farmyard more than a boat and allow the animals to depart. Getting them in may have been somewhat difficult but letting them loose was much more easily done. One imagines that the scribe who wrote that God said, "Bring forth every living thing that is with thee" must have had a tongue in his cheek. With the scent of the ground, the sight of some fresh greenery, however battered, and the liberation of the open-air most of the 'cargo' would need no second invitation. They may have needed some policing to prevent them crushing one another, the pigs, the poultry and the sheep might have required herding and the frightened horses special words of calm and control but for the great majority it would be a case of out and away.

What of the humans? They too had to leave. If Wa'ila and her daughters in law, who would have arranged things to their liking in their cramped home, objected yet again to a further move we have no mention of it, save that, as for Noah himself, the command of God was clear. 'Go forth out of the Ark, thou and thy wife and thy sons' wives', and there is no mention of the boys. Were they already poised to depart or even leading the first cattle and pack animals, the camels, the donkeys and mules on to dry ground? What was clear was that the sooner the whole 'community of the Ark' left and started to procreate the happier the Almighty would be. Though there was something else.

Noah's first act, when he found some satisfactory place for himself and his dependants to settle, was to build an altar and return thanks for their safe deliverance. Notice first that Noah here acts as any ship's Captain might act today, taking upon himself the responsibility of a priest, to offer prayer, to render thanks and to commit the dead. Noah does it naturally as the Patriarch of the people just as his notable ancestors, Abel and Enoch did. Though done grudgingly in his case, it was even the act of Cain.

Further we note that Noah raises an altar of stone. This was probably no specially hewn or carved affair but the taking of the very earth on which they had safely landed and the making of it into a pedestal or flat-topped cairn on which a beast could be laid. This was itself to be a pattern for the generations to come, and the raising of stones to recognise the presence of God and become, if only temporarily, meeting-places between God and his chosen people, is a fact that any Masonic student and reader of the Bible must be aware of.

Does the very fact that he offers burnt sacrifice mean that there had been fresh progeny born in the Ark so that there were additional sheep and goats and other flesh for use in this way? Does the making of a large fire for their roasting and burning mean that he had already begun to dismantle the Ark's timbers and use them for kindling and heating in their new settlement? This is no place to discuss the nature of early Scriptural worship and to wonder at the apparently childish way of giving thanks to the Almighty. What is important is that God had promised their deliverance, he had provided the means by which they and the creatures of the land could be preserved and could now multiply once more, and the only visible manner in which Noah, his contemporaries and successors could both reach God and show him their gratitude for continuing life was to take something of what he had given them and to surrender it as a return of thanks to God. That is not only a practice that was still being followed in the days of Abraham but was practised in the courts of Solomon's and Herod's temples. In principle it is still the same today in Hebrew and Christian religion.

Moreover it is declared to have been effective. The sweet-smelling savour of the sacrifices made was appreciated as a token of human thankfulness and God responds: "I will not again curse the ground for man's sake. Neither will I again smite any more every living thing as I have done." God is giving the go-ahead for life to resume and we have pictures of the Ark's timbers being fashioned into sledges and drag-carts such as the early American Indians used and the caravans of families and domesticated beasts starting to wend their way down to the drying plains to set up the Mesopotamian dwelling places which would emerge at last into written history.

That this promise of God was to last was confirmed by an astonishing phenomenon that must have impressed itself as never before on the minds and hearts of Noah's race. No-one pretends that in a landscape where rain and sunshine can be intense and follow swiftly upon one another there had *never previously* been a **rainbow**. What matters here is that at last, after incessant and prolonged rain, after much darkness and the utter desolation of a featureless journey under leaden clouds, there bursts upon the grateful sight of Noah and his children the glorious vision of that brilliant, five-banded arch which spans the heavens, what someone has called 'that celestial ribbon of watered silk'. Here, and for ever, is recorded the sensation that this perfect shape, the model of all that is best in the things that man might make with his hands, is the sign that God is sealing his words of promise with his own special mark. And could it be that on this day, as if to underline the unique occasion which it accompanied, this wonderful sweep of pure form was duplicated, as some of us can still very occasionally behold, by its repetition with an 'echo' in the sky above and beyond it.

However he and his dependants saw 'this bow in the cloud which shall be for a token of a Covenant' Noah recognised it as a visible response to all his wondering about the future. It was striking, it was unmistakeable and it was reassuring. Yet it did not linger. Just when you begin to appreciate it and examine it it fades. It is, as it was then, a reminder of beauty and design in the universe but it demands the faith of knowing that it was really there and that it can come again when it is fitting. It is in that setting of trust that we have the words:

"I establish my covenant with you and **your seed after you** ... and every living creature ... neither shall all flesh be cut off any more by the waters of a flood..."

That this beholding of the rainbow was imprinted in the folk memory of mankind there cannot be the slightest doubt. "The Rainbow", says Dr. Oliver, "was an emblem common to every species of religious mystery; and was probably derived from an old Arkite tradition, that the divinity was clothed in a Rainbow. For thus is he represented by Ezekiel the prophet ... St. John saw in a vision, the throne of God encompassed by a Rainbow." The Brahmins of India saw Vishnu arrayed as the rainbow when a harbinger of peace, whilst in the Druidic traditions of Britain "When the destruction (by the flooding of Lake Llion) was complete, the Avanc or Beaver, a symbol of the floating Ark, was drawn to land by the oxen of Hiw Gardarn; Gwidion (the British Mercury (or Hermes)) *formed the Rainbow*, as a fair attendant of the Sun; and an assurance was given to the man and the woman, by whom the world was to be repeopled, that the Lake should burst no more."[7]

It was no wonder then that Noah and his folk could set about the task of establishing a new life for themselves. There must have been pasture or the command to be fruitful and multiply would have been of no avail. Either they brought wood from the Ark or there were trees drying out that could be cut up to make dwellings for man and beast. Fences were needed and poles to hang the washing on though laying the latter on stones might first suffice. There had to be land to till and re-channelling of the essential waterways to keep it fruitful. There had to be attention to weeds and rubbish, the selection of new seeds, the watching of calving cows and mares in foal. And there was the discovery of something fresh.

"A climbing plant, with broad serrated leaves, pushed up shoots from its solid stock, that clung by its tendrils to trees and bushes of the wilder margin around the cultivated land. On these, in the fierce sun, ripened a small, globe-like berry, greenish yellow, in some cases turning to a rich purple, almost transparent, but with drops of sweet juice enclosed in its fine skin, and covered with a delicate bloom ... The juice plentiful and crushed, by hand or by accident or by the weight of the clusters, would bubble, and seethe, throw off a fine scum and then, if kept, the liquor lay in the bottom of the receptacle cleared again, had a pleasant odour, a fine colour, a delicious taste."[8]

When Noah first sipped the remains it became one of the epoch-making acts of all human history and ensured that Noah was to be later regarded as the original patron of the Vintners Company of London. That discovery was also part of God's gracious provision for we now know that the slight tilting of the earth as it spins has the curious effect of shifting the line by which the vine can reach its wine-producing maturity. That is why there are fields in Eastern England known as 'old vineyards' that have not produced for half a millennium, and why Noah could taste 'the grape' in a situation that today seems frankly impossible. What we have already seen of Noah's skill shows us that he was both a man of great common-sense but also a fast learner from experience. When it says that Noah 'planted a vineyard' it means that he had the time to give to a demanding occupation, enough knowledge to know the special requirements of the crop, the improvement of tools to tend it and enough relaxation to be able to appreciate the results. "He thought it tasted nice. It made him feel jolly. He liked it. The more he had, the more he wanted. His hard open-air life and great physical strength endowed him with a head of prodigious resisting powers ... but that which danger and difficulty could not do, comfort and prosperity did. He went down before the easy luxury of a summer afternoon."[9]

"He drank of the wine and was drunken" says the Bible, and there in his tent he dropped like a log and fell fast asleep, unconscious of his attire in the privacy of his own home.

Whether or not the sequel of this outcome to his now aged pursuits of wine is history, folklore or simple allegory to explain what followed we shall never know. What is striking about the story at this point is the fact that all three sons are within reach of their father. Were they gathered for a celebration, and hence Noah's indulgence beyond his normal enjoyment? Did they need to greet him before they departed again with their wives and grandchildren? Did Ham offer to seek out the 'old man' and alert him to the time? At all events he lifted the flap of the tent, he peered inside and hastily withdrew. Was he so overcome that he laughingly drew his brothers aside and shared with them the state their father was in? Certainly the others responded with filial respect and laid a covering on the old man whilst keeping their eyes firmly averted. What seems clear is that they neither woke him nor told on their brother.

Yet Noah was a man of common-sense. When he woke his mind would clear but some things were far from clear. Where did the covering come from? Who brought it? Why did they need to? Who penetrated his tent to see his state? Somebody must have told him what had happened but who it was does not matter. What seems evident is that he became self-conscious and may even have felt that his status as Patriarch was jeopardised. He doubtless felt that he had a dignity to maintain and it was in danger of being undermined. He thus rouses himself from the natural lethargy of a nonagenarian and seeks to show that he is still in charge. "Cursed be Canaan, a servant of servants shall he be to his brethren. Blessed be the Lord God of Shem and of Japhet and Canaan shall be their servant." The traditional status of the peoples of Ham, at least until the third quarter of the 20th century, was being established on the basis of one flash of an eye, one nervous laugh, and one unguarded comment. He who had drunk rain-water caught in skins was discovered in drink of a more potent kind and a sad and sorrowful slice of history is made. At least it shows the potency of the Noah narrative amongst biblical readers.

HIS DEATH AND DESCENDANTS

"All of the days of Noah were nine hundred and fifty years, and he died." Whatever we may make of the Bible's numerology, and here is not the place in which to consider it, Noah died at a truly great age. He was, by the same reckoning, still some 19 years younger than Methusaleh but both of them were legendary by reason of their longevity, quite apart from their other exploits.

Very soon, if we only consider the early age at which girls are married and conceive to this day in the Middle East, there were children born who had never seen him, to whom he was someone, or almost some *thing*, that your elders talked about with awe. Here was this great, slightly shadowy Father-figure who had helped to save the whole of the known world, had directed the making of a boat in which grandpa and grandma had sailed and from which they emerged with all their cattle and the other creatures so that our tribe, our extended family, our settlements could begin afresh. As time passed this clever old ancestor became a holy figure, the earthly father of the whole human race who knew better than to let his children be drowned like the rats they saw caught in a seasonal wadi surge. This demi-God had been on God's side all the time, so the story now ran, and of course those who were not in Noah's tribe, as present people were, were unheeding strangers so they had deserved to die. The legend in outline was already complete.

Of his actual dying and his body's whereabouts there was nothing known by those who now wrote down the Hebrew story. For those who had stood round his bed at the last it was almost certainly the same as for grieving relatives of long-living folk ever since. It was well-nigh impossible to imagine a time when he was not there. This was not credible because he had always been there directing operations. They had looked up to him, obeyed him, needed him and now he was gone. Could it be so? Yes, it was all true just because they were there. It was history that he had made. If Noah had not lived they would not be grieving now. The truth was that already the human race around them had grown so much that his death was lost in the fresh pursuit of life.

The story now moves on to the descendants, the sons and their offspring who set up establishments of their own, which from family units became tribes and then nations. Whatever may have been the case prior to Noah's death there seems to have been a steady progress both over and away from the Mesopotamian basin in the century that followed. Japhet was the accepted progenitor of the peoples that dwelt in the lands of the North from Britain to

Russia. As we read the names of his successors in chapter 10 of Genesis we are given glimpses of the far flung limits to which his children's children roamed. Gomer and Magog, Tubal and Meshech and Tiras (of northern Syria) and Madai and Javan (the king of the Ionians). Amongst the sons of Gomer was Ashkenaz (founder of Armenia and father of the Ashkenazi or Jews of Central Europe) whilst one of Javan's children was Tarshish (the later Biblical name of Spain). He also had Kittim (part of Italy) and Dodanim (much of France). "By these (tribes) were the isles of the Gentiles divided; everyone after his tongue, after their families, in their nations." (Gen. 10:5)

The sons of Ham were the acknowledged forebears of the inhabitants of the African continent starting from Cush (in Mesopotamia and later Ethiopia) and **Mizraim** in Upper Egypt, but including Canaan and Phut as early coast dwellers of the Levant. Cush was to bear Havilah and Raamah, from whom came **Sheba** and Dedan, the areas later associated with the Upper Nile and the Horn of Africa, but he also "begat **Nimrod** who began to be a mighty hunter before the Lord, and the beginning of his kingdom was **Babel** and Erech (Iraq), Akkad (of the Akkadians) and Calneh in the land of Shinar." Of Nimrod we must say more shortly.

From Canaan there came Sidon and Heth, and then that unforgettable list of tribes which have bemused many a reader – the Jebusites, Amorites and Girgasites, the Hivites, Arkites and Sinites, the Arvadites, Zemarites and Hamathites and "afterward the families of the Canaanites were spread abroad".

From Shem there came all the children of Eber (the Hebrews), but also others whose names breathe of the very Middle East, Elam (the Elamites) and Asshur (Assyria), Arphaxad (or Ur of the Chaldees) and Lud (from whom the Lydians) and Aram (whose language was the Aramaic that the Jewish exiles brought back to Galilee). Here we must note that "unto Eber were born two sons, the name of one was **Pelag** (or Phaleg), a Chaldean, and his brother's name was Joktan (whose offspring reached India) and from the latter came **Ophir**.

Of all the nearer descendants of Noah the most recorded one is Nimrod who, as Dr. Anderson once remarked, was engaged 'in the large and fertile vale of Shinar along the banks of the Tigris, in building a stately tower and city, the largest work that ever the world saw, and soon filled the vale with splendid edifices'. But they over-built it, and knew not when to desist, till their vanity provoked their Maker to confound their design by confounding their speech; hence the city was called Babel, confusion."

One tradition has it that Ham and Japhet led some of their families to Shinar in order to erect a tower which would prevent them ever being overcome by any other flood. It was composed of huge stone slabs, said to have been $19\frac{1}{2}$ feet long, 15 feet broad and $7\frac{1}{2}$ feet in thickness and 3 years were spent in making them. It is hardly likely that estimates of 4 or 12 miles to its summit are correct but one figure of 600 feet to its observatory there does begin to seem more likely. In the main body of the structure were apartments with *arched roofs* supported by pillars and here was an intended temple for idolatrous worship.

Of that tower, Dr. Oliver tells us further "that as the lower apartments were dedicated to the purpose of initiation into the (Cabiric) mysteries so the uppermost tier was appropriated solely to astronomical researches; for the first arrangement of the fixed stars into constellations was effected before the dispersion of our brethren from the plains of Shinar; and Nimrod was placed in the heavens under the name of Orion." Moreover "the token of union on the plains of Shinar (for Japhet's, Ham's and Shem's families all inter-married there) was a broad Banner on which a Dove bearing the Branch of Olive in its mouth, encircled by a Rainbow, were curiously embroidered". It is in this same work that we have the explanation of the Tower's shape as fundamentally a circular figure "from its similarity to the spiral flame; for it was dedicated to the sun as the great agent . . . employed in drying up the waters of the deluge."

These builders, continued Anderson, "were forced to disperse about 53 years after they began to build, or after the flood 154 years. When the general migration from Shinar commenced they went off at various times and travelled North, South, East and West, with their mighty skill and found the good use of it in settling their colonies. But Nimrod went no further than the land of Assyria and founded the first great empire at his capital, Nineveh, where he reigned. Under him flourished many learned mathematicians, whose successors were long afterwards called Chaldees and Magicians . . ."[10] And there we may leave the Flood story.

THE STORY'S SIGNIFICANCE

This telling of the story of Noah, the flood and its aftermath, may seem to have been in overmuch detail but it needs to be emphasized that if we are to understand the origin and development of the Masonic degree then acquaintance with the whole story is essential. For our Masonic forebears of the 18th and 19th centuries the biblical and traditional events connected with Noah were much more common knowledge than can be assumed today when nothing of this sort can be taken for granted. When we pass shortly to the facts of subsequent history it will now be easier to refer to the above review of the evidence from which presentations of the story were derived. It only remains in this section to try and uncover some of the strands of meaning that the recounting of this story was meant to convey to both hearers and readers.

The major difficulty which any present Masonic student of the Royal Ark Mariner degree has to face is the undeniable fact that since 1872 the context of the Flood narrative has been completely changed by the discovery that was then revealed by a 36 years old engraver of bank notes. The full story of the unravelling of the 'Epic of Gilgamesh' has been amply given elsewhere and is only important here as a reminder that **up to that date** the universal impression among Masons, as of the general Western European and North American public, was that the references to the Flood in the Bible were the origin and source of all mentions of that phenomenon elsewhere. Noah's experience was therefore a fundamental facet of all theological, moral and social instruction and its various parts, as outlined above, were all of crucial significance for human behaviour.

At much the same time as the deciphering of the cuneiform tablets took place biblical scholars made a further discovery which showed that the accounts of events in the early chapters of the Book called 'Genesis', including the Noah story, were compiled from at least two separate sources which were two centuries apart. Again, the details of this intriguing study do not need to be reproduced here but the same reflection has to be made that **prior to that time** the biblical account was regarded as ONE whole description which derived from ONE source, the Patriarch Moses, even if not actually written by him. Of its intrinsic value and reliability there could not be the slightest question. As was said by Pontius Pilate in another context, "What is written, is written".

Whilst there are those who today seek to lecture on this Antients degree by displaying their ample awareness of the scholarly advances made in the last century the question that has to be faced is this. What precisely is the relevance of such textual studies to the Royal Ark Mariner degree when the latter was developed and shaped to virtually its present form in a period when such information was not available?

The answer, I suggest, is none at all. If the legends and ceremonies of Freemasonry constituted a corpus of historical or moral theology which depended on their strict conformity to proven fact then, as in the Hebraeo–Christian tradition, we would need to adjust to this kind of new evidence. The fact is that Freemasonry does not pretend to be such a system nor does its validity rest on whether or not it conforms to the latest textual scholarship. Significantly, such critical new assessments of the Bible or related documents have very little effect on most religious people in any case. What they have been taught to believe they believe.

What matters therefore to the Masonic student in this particular area of the Science is what lessons have been inculcated in the brethren who practice this particular degree. There would seem to be four of these – the Lordship of the Creator, the importance of an Ark of Safety, the place of the Arch as a covenant and the value of true humility.

The Lordship of the Creator

Whilst it is evident from the very first verses of the book of Genesis that there is a Divine Creator behind the emergence of the universe it is only in the stories of Adam and Noah that we have the abiding sense of this Creator as a living, present and personal Lord who seeks a relationship with his human creatures. In both cases it is with those who are clearly 'new creations' – the one from the earth and the other from water. In both cases also the communication is intimate and direct. Indeed, one of the striking characteristics of the Noah story that led its analysts to distinguish its divided authorship was the way in which the so-called 'J' or 'Jahweh' compiler stressed in his verses the primacy of God (Jahweh) in all the events that make up the Flood story. Jahweh decides to destroy humanity, warns Noah of the approaching cataclysm, opens the heavens to let forth the deluge, determines the end of the downpour and its effects and responds to the 'sweet-smelling savour of sacrifice'.

What is perhaps ironic is that it was probably *because* the Hebrew patriarchs brought the Flood story from a Mesopotamian source that it had so pronounced an emphasis on the personal relationship between God and a man. That there was such an intimate link is perhaps the most memorable feature of the whole episode and has made it so ripe a subject for verse and plays and pictures. The fact that God cared about his world and the kind of creatures in it, that if his first effort was unsatisfactory he would try another method, and that he was so pleased with the second outcome that he undertook never to obliterate man again – all this led to a most significant insight. It was that the Great Creator, the Architect and Builder of the whole universe might even invest one of his creatures with divine Lordship.

After all, what did Noah do. He was willing to risk his life on the word of his God. He was cast forth in a form of coffin on the watery waste and passed through a world of death and destruction. He comes forth alive after his symbolic 'death' and he has 'saved' all living things. Is it any wonder that he was regarded as holy and venerable. "Noah", wrote Dr. Oliver, "was esteemed, and actually was, according to the flesh, the great father of mankind. He was at once the seed of a woman, born of the virgin Ark, without the intervention of any human creature, and hence Noah was elevated into an object of idolatrous worship, and became the chief deity of the gentile world." Not only so, he continues, but "Noah was considered an incarnation of the divinity". He and the Lord of Creation were one. By the turn of the first millennium of the Christian era Noah has become a direct prefiguring of Christ himself.

The Ark of Safety

This strand of meaning in the story naturally developed from the first. If legendary status began to be accorded to Noah as a 'saviour' figure so also there grew up legends about the vehicle which he created and used in this act of salvation. R.H.Mottram expressed it as follows:

"Far away and up above their own fathers and mothers dwelt this over-father, nearer to God than anything else they could conceive of. Had he not taken their fathers and mothers into the Ark that he had made? As to what that Ark was, they could have only the remotest and most fantastic ideas. Some of the younger ones may already begun to say that it was **a box, a chest, a magic casket** into which God had put all the animals."[11]

From this idea there grew up the practice in antiquity of carrying about small navicular shrines and of constructing temples in the form of an ark. The historian Diodorus Siculus records that Sesotris built an ark which was 280 cubits long and made of cedar wood. It was covered with plates of gold and silver and was dedicated to Osiris and by reason of this dedication and the temple being in the inland City of Theba it was clear that it was never intended to be used for any voyage. It was, in fact, an immense place of worship that imitated an Ark and the ceremonies that were solemnly performed there were designated 'the diluvian mysteries'.

It was no great step for the Greeks to start describing a temple and an ark by the same word 'naus' or 'naos' and what may well be a relic of the primitive Arkite rites is still preserved in the calling of the body of a Christian church the 'nave', as distinct from the eastern end which is called 'the chancel'. That the 'nave' was where the great body of the ordinary people (the 'laos' or laity) sat adds to the imagery.

Meanwhile in Latin literature we find many references to the idea of a chest or 'cista', not least in relation to the Eleusinian processions or the rites of Dionysus. Virgil is on record as describing this chest that bore the sacred fruit of the vine – and the allusions to the later events surrounding Noah are here quite obvious – as a 'basket' or 'wicker hamper' which was borne aloft on the shoulders of the participants. Hence the word 'cistoferi', which was later adapted by Christian allegorists as 'Cristoferi', showing the infant saviour being borne on the shoulder of a giant figure to keep him 'safe' from dangers on his way. That figure became 'St. Christopher'. This needs to be compared with a picture of a Dionysiacal procession shown in the 'Antiquities of Herculaneum' where a woman carries on her shoulder a square box with a projecting roof, and what suggests that it was a form of Noachic Ark is that it has the 'door' in the side. The Bacchic Ark was regarded as so sacred that, like the Jewish Tetragrammaton or name of the Deity, the term referring to it was considered unpronounceable. One author, Oppian, even described the ark of firwood that contained the representation of the infant Bacchus, and which was carried by a sacred choir, the 'arca ineffabilis', whilst Homer reports that after the sacking of Troy the booty given to Eurypylus was such an 'ark' with a statue of the infant Bacchus inside it and when he tried to look inside it he was deprived of all his senses. One cannot but compare this ancient experience with what happened to the men of Bethshemesh in the Bible (1 Samuel chapter 6, verse 19) when they profaned the Ark by trying to look into it. To bring the matter down to late Roman times we have pictures showing the use of the ark in the worship of Diana, Ceres and Isis.

By the end of the first century we have in the letters of Peter the parallel proposed that the waters of the Flood prefigured the waters of Christian baptism. Tertullian in his renowned work on baptism speaks of the Ark as a symbol of the Church and Justin Martyr declared that Noah, awaiting the return of the dove with the olive branch, was quite simply a figure of Christ.

This was to be a constantly repeated idea and by *1713* one French religious writer was expressing the idea in this way:

"The Holy Fathers have observed that this ark was visibly the figure of the Church, which is the *sole Ark* in which a man may find salvation, and without which he is lost eternally. The mighty size of this construction which was borne upon the water, and this assembly of all manner of clean and unclean beasts, represented the extent of the Church throughout all the earth, and the calling of many nations and peoples differing among themselves in the diversity of their habits and customs, whom God, whose will it is that all men should be saved, would one day join together in this refuge, in order that they might find a like salvation and escape a like shipwreck.

"The wood and the water visibly represent two great mysteries: the water, that Baptism which washes us clean of sin, as the Flood purified the world of its abominations; and the wood of the Cross of the Saviour, who has saved the whole world, and who is still today the only hope of Christian folk, who look for salvation only through its infinite cost. Thus did it please God to prefigure His Church in the Ark, which served for the mending and renewing of the world."[12]

That there were comparable writings in English at exactly the same date there can be no doubt for this was a very prevalent 17th and 18th century form of Bible exegesis. Indeed it would be a most useful adjunct to Masonic study if research were done into the biblical studies that were being conducted in the period 1660 to 1730. It might reveal some very interesting parallels with Masonic allegories used at that time.

What is clear is that by the time that Masonic catechisms were beginning to appear there was a long pedigree of reference to Noah and the Ark as the symbol of Christian safety and salvation. That too is a factor that we shall have to bear in mind as we come to the emergence of the Ark Mariner degree.

The Arch as a Covenant

"I do set my bow in the cloud, and it shall be for a token of a covenant between me and the earth." This is the clear indication in the remaking of human kind that God the Creator has some kind of lasting relationship with and concern for his creatures. This is, in fact, the first of a series of such covenants that were to be declared and made visible throughout not only the Hebrew period of the Bible story but even into the early years of the Christian era. Indeed the original Greek words used to describe the books that we call 'The New Testament' really mean 'the new covenant' and when a sacred feast was inaugurated for the early Christian community its elements were described as those of the 'new Covenant'.

What is important for the reader to know is that in the Babylonian and Egyptian forms of the Flood narrative there is **no mention whatever** of any rainbow and we must therefore now deduce that the insertion of this feature and its obviously shaped message that God and man were bound in some sort of relationship was a priestly Jewish addition. We know, as was said above, that the link of divinity and the Arch of Heaven was more than just a Jewish idea though the latter race were probably alone in giving it this special meaning as a token of some lasting and timeless undertaking between God and his people. As God is reported as saying to Noah: "This is the token of the covenant, which I have established between me and **all flesh** that is upon the earth." (Gen. 9:17)

At some stage in the Jewish memory this connection of the rainbow arch with God's promise of salvation from the danger of flood or some similar destruction was removed to the margin of their tradition. They became a desert, pastoral people as Abraham led them from the Euphrates basin to the grazing lands of the Levant. Following Isaac, Jacob and Joseph they find themselves in the sandy countryside of lower Egypt. When Moses leads them out from 'captivity' in an alien land God's Covenant is there renewed first by ascending a mountain which is crowned with an arch of cloud that will later descend also upon the Tabernacle and then by giving Moses the two arched stones upon which were inscribed the precepts that we call the Ten Commandments.

Moses also, by God's command, as with Noah, constructs an Ark on dry land, one that can be borne on the shoulders of Aaron's priestly band and planted in the midst of the Israelites when they camp in and around the peninsula of Sinai. It is a chest or box to contain the symbols of God's saving acts, the rod of Moses that brought water from the rock, the box of manna that fed the Hebrews in the desert, and the tablets of God's will and direction. Over that ark were the arched wings of the two cherubim and over the whole tented structure that enclosed the Ark and its resting place, the Holy of Holies, there came the arch of cloud that was called the Shekinah, from which God spoke to his people. It need hardly surprise us to learn that there was one persistent tradition that when eventually the ark was reinstated in a more permanent Second Temple after the exile in Babylon it was placed, empty though it might be, in an arched and vaulted chamber that had been where the Temple's first builders had secretly assembled. The Arch, the Ark and the Covenant were, it would seem, closely intertwined in Jewish tradition. The significance of this and the other strands we are describing for later Masonic interpretation may already be beginning to strike some readers.

The Virtue of Humility

"Noah was a just man and perfect in his generations, and Noah walked with God." It might almost be a repeat description of the first of God's recorded human creatures, Adam, when the latter was engaged in the happy days of walking and talking and working under God's direct control. Yet if Adam seems to us to be something of a 'type', or even an 'idea' of primitive mankind, Noah is remarkably real by comparison. In a quite discernible sense Noah is a husband, a father, even a father-in-law, a neighbour, a farmer and a craftsman. "He stands out even more distinctly", writes Mottram, "by the fact that he does not chatter. He has no tricks. He does not desire to attract attention, nor to gain some small advantage over others. He does not laugh easily, but when he does, it is with gusto. He pays far more attention when he sees something practical being done ... Men like him lasted well into our own historic era."[13]

This is the mark of the man as he is recorded because he came of a line of 'giants' and 'mighty men'. The very arithmetic by which he and they are surrounded seems to have been devised to suggest that they were more than normal life-size. With Noah the astonishing thing is that the more he can be seen to havc achieved the more human and explicable he becomes. As he could reasonably have begun to think what a good provider for his family he was, what a great constructor of such a vessel, what an imaginative prospect he had hung on to, what a land developer he became, the more we appreciate the verse, "But Noah found grace in the eyes of the Lord". In wise fashion he seems to have kept his sense of proportion. Whether in the deep awareness of what was about to happen to his neighbours or in those moments when he saw them suffering the results of their cynical indifference to his warnings we can imagine him thinking, "There but for the grace of God, go I."

It is not without discrimination that the writer of the original story records how even the patriarchal figure can so enjoy the results of his husbandry as to fall drunkenly asleep on his bed. The god-like figure shows just ordinary reactions to well-supped wine. But was this episode part of the original folk-memory or interpolated here by a master story-teller? Whatever the manner of its coming to us the effect of this portion of the story is to keep Noah human and to show that whilst he might recognise his responsibility to keep his family in order he was himself only what he was by the direction and support of Almighty God.

This continual recognition that whilst he might have been successful and revered he yet owed everything to God, his maker and his Lord, is the lasting feature of the story that has been preserved to the present day. When all the intriguing facets of the story are forgotten the lasting memory is that in order that God's plan and purpose might be achieved a man had to do what he was told. To rejoice that one is that man, to give thanks that what one did was beneficial and to go on to enjoy some of the pleasures of that successful outcome were all legitimate because it was all done in the right context. Man does not arrogate to himself the right of the knowledge of God, as Adam did, but knows his place at last. The lesson of the danger of pride had unhappily been shown in the Garden of Eden, and will be repeated on the plain of Shinar where the Tower of Babel was attempted. The lesson here is that of proper humility. The message here is that honest and obedient work brings its due recognition and the seeking for status or dominance is not the right path. One other tradition which emerged in the late 18th century was the story that Noah carried the coffin containing Adam's body with them in the Ark. Was that so that he might ever have the results of pride constantly before his eyes or was it so that the ancestor who suffered the consequences of arrogance might behold the salvation that humility could enjoy?

THE TRANSMISSION OF THE STORY

The Flood and Noah's Ark are among the most frequently depicted of all biblical themes. The oldest representations would be those found in the Catacombs in Rome dating from the 2nd century AD and, linking with the 'burial' or 'coffin motifs' already referred to, we find the story shown on many early Christian tombs and even in a mosaic form in the 5th century (C.E.) synagogue of Gerasa. Significantly the main feature preserved intact in this latter instance is the dove perched in a tree holding a branch in her beak and close by the names 'Shem' and 'Japheth'.

By the late 11th century there is an ark shown in the cycle of paintings at St. Savin in France and here the vessel is seen advancing confidently across savage waves. Its figurehead is a mastiff with flowing mane whilst its three-storied superstructure reveals not only the animals but Noah, his wife and the other three couples. They seem calm and unperturbed. A like realism begins to occur in carving at the same period, as for example in the Collegiate Church of Beaune or at Autun Cathedral and some English Cathedrals also have bosses which show Noah clutching his ark as Solomon holds his temple. What therefore became clear is that there were always some carving stonemasons who were fully aware of the story of the Flood as a subject for instruction of the faithful.

It is precisely this use of picture in some form that explains the wall paintings in many an English parish church and this was of course to lead eventually to the works of Raphael in the Vatican 'Stanze' or the inclusion of Noah in the incomparable drawing of Michelangelo in the Sistine Chapel. In this latter work we note how the great designer chose the moment of thanksgiving after the Flood subsided as that most conducive to his patron's taste. Titian and Carracci were to produce their own versions of the Ark story and by the 17th century Cardinal Richelieu commissioned the artist, Poussin, to represent the Four Seasons. He did so by using the Garden of Eden for Spring, Ruth and Boaz for Summer, the grapes carried from the Promised Land for Autumn and the Flood with the Ark for Winter. In this latter work the theme is that Nature is in danger of being obliterated and the serpent who caused the disaster is shown sliding over a rock. Above the surging current rides the Ark as the affirmation of hope.

Whilst these more sophisticated forms of picture were being devised for wealthier Church members there was in England a more plebeian audience to be served. In the 14th century we see the production of a remarkable book that had, for its day, a quite large circulation. It was called the 'Biblia Pauperum' – The Bible for the less well-to-do" – and its aim was solely to instruct the reader in the remarkable parallels that were then thought to exist between the great figures of the Old and New Testaments. The book was for a wide audience for it consisted of pictures rather than words and the two parallel scenes were on each pair of facing pages. The connection between the Tree of

Knowledge in Eden and the Tree of Calvary outside Jerusalem and the making of sour water drinkable by Moses compared with the turning of water into wine at Cana give easy samples of the type of instruction provided and it is therefore hardly to be wondered at that Noah and Joseph, the carpenter husbands, making necessary objects; Noah the sailor bridging the Flood and Jesus the fishermen's leader calming the storm; or the Ark being compared to the Church sailing serenely along with its faithful aboard, were all useful items for the devisers of this work. No-one was likely to be unaware that the activities of Noah had lasting and orthodox importance for the ordinary church-goer.

We have in the traditional story-telling of the County of Norfolk a most instructive form of Noah and the Flood. Whilst most people imagine that the Ark finally ended its voyage on Mount Ararat this version records that it really came to rest on Dunham Common which is about 320 feet above the western part of that County. This is how the version is recorded:

"When old Master Noe felt her fetch aground on Dunham Common, he opened one of them portholes, and he loosed out his ole Dowe. The old Dowe that flittered, and that fluttered, and that couldn't find no place to light on, and that flew right out o' sight. Ole Noah he kept looking for that.

Now, the ole Devil, he was in a rare taking all because he hadn't bin able to git aboard the ark. So he kept scullin' round in his punt, hoping some chanst would come his way. When he see old Noah open the porthole, and stan' there starin' round a'ter his Dowe, he reckoned his chanst was come, so he sculled a little nigher and a little nigher, and presently he hollered out:

"Morn'n, Master Noah; hazy morn'n.

"Ole Noah he couldn't think who that c'd be that'd have the sauce t' call out t' him like that, so he looked up, and he looked down, and presently he spied the ole Father o' Lies scullin' in his punt. He didn't want t' have nothin' t' du with him, so he turns his head away and says,

"You be damned. Japhet, shut the winder."

This piece of folk-lore reveals as few things can how the story of the Flood and the Ark penetrated to the least articulate and simplest of our forebears. It is a piece of ordinary English life from the past that can stand alongside the opinion of an early 17th century citizen of Kendal – at the other end of the land – who declared that all he knew of God's salvation of mankind was what he had learned from the pageant plays that he had seen portrayed in the streets of that North-western town. For the part played by these 'mystery plays' in conveying the great truths of the Creed and of the Scriptures during 250 years up to about 1620 cannot be too strongly stressed. One of the plays that was constantly performed was that of 'Noye's Fludde'.

As I have more fully explained in the Prestonian Lecture for 1974 the Masons' Guilds were regularly involved in the processions of Mystery plays that took place from Aberdeen to Coventry and from Chester to Norwich, and the similarities of incident, and, in specific cases, of interpretation, can be shown from the texts that have been preserved.

Three issues have to be reckoned with in any investigation of the Guild involvement with these Corpus Christi performances. The first is the differing order of precedence of the Guilds in each place; the second is the desire of the separate Guilds to have a play which was as nearly appropriate to their particular traditions as possible; whilst the third was the general awareness of the participants as to the Cycle in which they were sharing. They were neither just play-makers nor business-men looking for extra advertisement.

The Mystery Plays connected with Noah were performed annually at the following places:

Chester:	'Noe's Floode' by the Watter Drawers (or Watermen) of Dee.
Coventry:	'Noah's Ark'.
Cornwall:	A play about the Ark.
Hull:	'Noah's Ark' performed on Plough Sunday.
Newcastle:	'Noah and the Ark' given by the Shipwrights (up to 1556).
Wakefield:	'The Building of the Ark and its voyage on the Flood'
York:	i) 'The Building of the Ark' played by the Shipwrights;
	ii) 'Noah and the Flood' by the Fysshers and Maryners.

To attempt to survey the whole subject of even these performances in any detail is not possible in this book but we should notice some sidelights on the various forms of the plays which may be seen later to have a particular relevance.

At Chester we have the best known example of the wife who has no desire to enter the newly-completed 'Shippe' and in shrewish manner roundly abuses Noah as a pig-headed fool whose threats of deluge are wholly misguided. Moreover she has others' welfare besides that of her family to consider:

"But I have my gossipes everychone,
One foot further I will not gone;
They shall not drowne, by Sante John.
And I maye save ther life.
An thou loven me full well, by Christe.
Do but thou lett them into thy Cheiste. (Cista, chest, Ark)"

Eventually son Japhet persuades his mother to come aboard whereupon she greets Noah with a sound box on the ears. Apart from the dramatic effect of this popular style there is the subtle use of this apparent virago to express, without a large caste of players, the sentiments that would have been in the mouths of the original individuals who scoffed at Noah's enterprise. Noah's wife was but the mouthpiece of a whole unseen array of doubters. Her last-minute surrender highlighted the disaster that was about to engulf those she had been representing.

In the Cornish play the wife is merely late for the sailing but her role as a protester is taken in that setting by no less a person than **Tubalcain**. In the 20th century negro version of the same play the protestor is called 'Cain VI'. At Wakefield we have the reverse of the Chester version for Noah's 'mastership' is emphasized by his giving his wife a sound beating before she will agree to embark. One feels that here she may be representing some of the animals rather than humans.

At Hull the play was carried out on a moveable stage that was built in the form of a ship and since this was on an agricultural festival the emphasis was on Noah and his family as husbandmen and vintners. At Newcastle there was reference to the art of building the ark and this was illustrated by alluding to the working tools with some appropriate gestures. In York the Shipwrights remind the audience that the 'ark was to be made of light wood' whilst in the second play the Mariners refer to Noah being in his ark with his wife and **three** children. It is in the York version that Noah seeks to corroborate the news that the waters are abating by casting a lead and holding it in a most plumbline-like fashion.

Whilst it is true that there are mentions of trades above which were clearly associated with shipping or water activities the fact is that some of these Flood plays were not linked with such bodies. The truth was that plays were allocated in each city or large town according to the local precedence of the Guilds that practised there. If when your turn came a play that specially suited your avocation or patron Saint was still available then you thankfully accepted it but the fact that Masons or Wrights (i.e. Carpenters) did not always have plays to perform that they would have first chosen says nothing about their lack of interest in or close association with these dramatic events. I have shown elsewhere that wherever the Masons performed they took what was available and turned it in some fashion to their purpose. What would be worth examining but cannot be pursued here is what plays the Carpenters and Wrights took up where the Ark play was already bespoke by another Company. This may not seem to have much relevance to our present Masonic subject until you take seriously the fact that Masons, Carpenters and Plumbers had to be closely allied throughout the Middle Ages, as in some building projects they still are today. Scaffolding, supports for arches, frameworks for raising implements and doorways are but a few of the essential joint works that such a technical amateur as this author can think of. When it is also recognised that by the 17th century some Guilds or Companies of Crafts had been compelled by economic necessity to combine the suggestion that there was a kind of total exclusion between separate disciplines seems to belie reality. In so far as the building trades were concerned there had always had to be some kind of cooperation even if the innermost trade skills were still a matter of proud privacy.

It is therefore not irrelevant to mention here that even when Masonry took on its official Speculative guise this relationship between the trades was acknowledged. In the 1723 Constitutions we read the following:

"Nor should it be forgot, that **Painters** also, and **Statuaries**, were always reckon'd good Masons, as much as **Builders, Stone-cutters, Bricklayers, Carpenters, Joiners, Upholders** or **Tent-Makers**, and a vast many other Craftsmen that could be nam'd, who perform according to **Geometry** and the rules of **Building**."

It is therefore quite unnecessary to have to prove that if the Masons never participated in a play about Noah and the Flood they were unmoved by or unaware of the lessons that such a play conveyed. On the contrary, the fact that those jointly employed in a complicated building trade *were often performers of it* would have interested the Masons greatly and since they themselves were especially attracted to plays that spoke of death and restoration to life the peculiar theme of the Noah legend in the teaching of the mediaeval Church would have further arrested their attention.

It has further been suggested by a Geo.Bullamore that 'the earlier church builders, using much timber, might have based their traditions on the sons of Noah and Bezaleel, one of whom built a wooden vessel and the other the wooden structured Tabernacle for Moses. But a later invasion of stone cutters . . . might promulgate a legend connected with the Temple of Solomon, built of stone, (and when they) were well established the secrets of the sons of Noah could be made to coincide with (those) of the Temple craftsmen'.

Not, of course, that that factor was in the end the crucial one. It is no part of this writer's belief that we owe *all* our present Speculative legend or allegory to the traditions of the Operative freemasons or even the Operative carpenters and shipwrights. What is important to grasp is that by a host of different channels the story of Noah and the Flood became an embedded part of British folk-lore. It may well be true that Operative 'arch' masons saw in the Noah story elements that served their purposes but what is equally significant is that any well-read gentleman or traditional citizen of the 17th century was fully aware that Noah and his 'experience' had important lessons to teach society.

Mention was earlier made of the pictorial impact of a book like the 'Biblia Pauperum' but there were to be other views of the Deluge that would add their own weight to making this story one of the best known ever. Professor Coulton, whose work we considered earlier in another context, described the coming of the Franciscan Order into England in this way: "All men had known that Noah's Ark was the type of God's Church. To this Church the black-robed Benedictines had done service in their time; these were prefigured by the raven. The soft-grey dove, with her olive branch and her message of divine comfort, was naturally the Franciscan – the 'grey friar', as men called him from his peasant frock of homely wool."[14]

"It is a matter of common knowledge", wrote Bernard E.Jones, "that 'black art' stories relating to **Ham** go back into early history. Herbert de Losinga, the first Bishop of Norwich, who died in 1119, is believed to have written: 'The Ark was of small compass; but even yet there, Ham preserved the arts of magic and idolity (sic)'."[15]

A French Dominican monk of the 13th century reflected gloomily upon the character of Noah's second son, whilst learned writers of the 15th century and Reginald Scot in the 16th still associated Ham with the 'black arts'. There were even works in 1677 and 1681 which argued with great seriousness whether Zoroaster, who was alleged to be the inventor of magic, was really 'Noah's wicked son, Ham'. Whatever may or may not have been the connection of Ham with necromancy there is certainly no doubt that he gave his family a sharper profile in medieval times.

There was also Chaucer. Anyone who would appreciate how Noah and the Deluge he surmounted became real to the mediaeval reader should turn to the 'Miller's Tale'. In portraying a rascal who sought for a stratagem with which to bamboozle a village carpenter, Chaucer was able to draw on an event that was regarded as intimately real and eternally true.

We have already seen how Norfolk folk regarded Noah's voyage. The carpenter was here warned of another Flood by Heaven (through the mouth of a cunning clerk) and prepared to escape with his wife from the impending visitation, not in an Ark, but a set of large kneading-bins. He set about provisioning them, taking Noah for his model. What is intriguing is that the carpenter's plan is here based not on the original Bible narrative but on the more popular understanding of this story as shown above in some of the Town Plays. Nicholas the clerk asks the carpenter

> "Hast thou not heard the sorrow of Noah with his fellowship
> Ere he might bring his wife to ship?
> Him had been liefer, I dare well undertake,
> At that time, then all his weathers black,
> That **she had** had a ship **herself alone**."

If she could not have her own ark at least she could have her own bin.

By the end of Queen Elizabeth I's reign the level of literacy had begun to rise appreciably and it is therefore not surprising to find a private book of prayers produced in 1609 which is entitled "Foure Birds of Noahs Ark". It was composed by Thomas Dekker and his symbolism is not lost on a Masonic reader. He chose 'The Dove' for comfort, with simple prayers for the younger and meaner sort; 'The Eagle' for courage, being supplications on behalf of Kings and Rulers; 'The Pelican' for health, and prayers against deadly and capital sins; and finally 'The Phoenix' for life, being mainly thanksgivings.

It is not possible here to consider extracts from the extensive 17th century Bible commentaries that looked in depth at the Genesis stories but all this literary use of the Noah story is paralleled in Masonic tradition by the regular appearance of the event in those manuscripts which were directly related to the practice of the building craft. As early as c.1390 we have in the Regius Poem (line 537) a reference to Noah and the Flood and this is repeated in every Masonic Constitution that follows up to the 18th century. What is fascinating in this regard is the context in which this mention of the Flood occurs. It is in connection with what are called the ante-diluvian pillars.

The legend surrounding these pillars has a long-standing pedigree. Frazer, the author of the 'Golden Bough', records elsewhere that the great flood took place in the reign of a Babylonian king to whom the God Cronus appeared, warning him that all men would be destroyed. "Therefore the god enjoined him to write a history of the world from the beginning and **bury it for safety** in Sippar, the city of the Sun. He was moreover to build a ship..."[16]

By the second century AD the Jewish writer Josephus tells a similar tale but places it in a biblical context.

"They (the children of Seth) were the inventors of that peculiar sort of wisdom which is concerned with the heavenly bodies and their order. And that their inventions might not be lost before they were sufficiently known, upon Adam's prediction that the world was to be destroyed at one time by the force of fire, and at another by the violence and quantity of water, they *made two pillars*, the one of *brick*, the other of *stone*; they inscribed their discoveries on them both, that in the case the pillar of brick should be destroyed by the flood, the pillar of stone might remain, and exhibit those discoveries to mankind ... Now this remains in the land of *Siriad* to this day."[17]

In 1527 a famous publication called the 'Polychronicon' contains its own version of the Josephus record. It spoke of *books* that Seth's descendants had made with great effort and which were *enclosed* in the two great pillars of *marble* and *burnt tile*. "Men sayeth that the pyler of stone escaped the floode and yet it is in *Syrya*."

By 1687 the William Watson MS shows that the story had developed further: "& these here brethren had knowledge before that God would take vengeance for Sin, either by fire or by water, & they had great care how they might do to Save the Sciences that they had there found ... & by all their wits they said that there were two manner of stones of Such virtue that the one would never burn (named Marble) & another Stone that would not sink in waters (called *Laterus*) and So they devised *to write all* the Sciences that they had found *in these two stones* (which was done by *Jaball*)." It continues by saying that *both pillars* were later found, the one by 'a great Clerk that men called Pythagoras' and the other by Hermes.

Whilst the Old Constitutions gave the honour of making these pillars to Noah's father, Lamech, Dr.Anderson in the 1723 Book of Constitutions selected Enoch, Noah's earlier ancestor. However, in 1738, Anderson made a further slight amendment and we have this explanation:

"Some call them *Seth's Pillars* but the Old Masons always called them *Enoch's Pillars* and firmly believ'd this Tradition, nay Josephus (Lib.I, Cap.2) affirms the Stone Pillar remain'd in Syria to his Time."

What all this plainly reveals is the persistence of the Noah's Flood theme as part of the background of English Freemasonry. Its continuance is very clearly seen in an 1820s Masonic Lecture that was used in an Atholl Lodge in Northumberland.

"Q. Please inform us how the names of those two Pillars originated.

A. After Noah had built *the pillar or altar of sacrifice* upon his coming out of the ark, and received the blessing of God on the spot, he called it J. which signified 'to E ...' *in commemoration of the Rainbow* which God established in the heavens, and three times declared it to be established. This pillar was in after years greatly increased in size and ornaments by the descendants of Noah, and considered a most sacred Treasure, and in every country *where they so sojourned* they built one in imitation thereof..."

The narrative continues until the usual B. and J. are set up and explained but that cannot engage us here. The line of continuity between the Noah event and the establishment of the English Grand Lodge was steadily drawn as the following series of references clearly shows. What has to be noted is that whilst some writers highlight many features of the story there are some who only dwell on one or two. What may be a real surprise is the persistence in the *early* 18th century of what many readers may imagine to be a *late* 18th century theme.

When we turn to the oldest of our *Old Charges*, the *Regius MS* said to date 1390–1420, we find that the 'first most excellent Grand Master' is declared to be King Nimrod and it was he and not King Solomon who gives the Masons of his day their first Charge.

This is still more pointedly brought out in some later versions. By 1700 we have in the Sloane MS the following question and answer: "Where was the first word given? At the tower of Babylon" whilst in the Dumfries MS of a decade later (c.1710) the usual history of the antediluvian pillars has a reference to the fact that the mortar used in building King Solomon's Temple was the same as that employed in constructing Nimrod's Tower.

In 1722 we have the Hudibrastic Poem which was referred to in regard to the Mark degree but which here continues the earlier tradition.

"If Hist'ry be no ancient Fable,
Free Masons came from **Tower of Babel**:
When first that Fabrick was begun,
The Greatest underneath the Sun,
All Nations thither did repair,
To build this great Castle in th'Air;
Some thousand Hands were well employ'd,
To finish what was ne'er enjoy'd;..."

It is against this background that we come to the fuller account set forth by Dr. Anderson in his first Book of Constitutions of 1723. (Author's italics)

"No doubt Adam taught his sons Geometry, and the use of it, in the *several Arts and Crafts* convenient at least, for those early Times; for CAIN, we find, built a City, which he call'd CONSECRATED, or DEDICATED, after the Name of his eldest Son, ENOCH ... until at length NOAH, the ninth from Seth, was commanded and directed of God, to build the great Ark, which tho' of Wood, was certainly fabricated by Geometry, and according to the *rules of Masonry*, NOAH, and his three Sons, JAPHET, SHEM and HAM, *all Masons true*, brought with them over the Flood the Traditions and Arts of the

Antediluvians, and amply communicated them to their growing offspring; for about 101 years after the Flood, we find a vast Number of 'em, if not the whole Race of Noah, in the *Vale of Shinar*, employed in building a City and Tower, in order to make to themselves a Name, and to prevent their Dispersion…"

In 'A Mason's Examination' of the same year or in 'The Grand Mystery of Free-Masons Discover'd' of 1724 we have a further question and answer that has often seemed strangely out of context. "Whence comes the pattern of an Arch? From the Rainbow." In the light of what the reader will already have learned in this book it is possible that this simple extract will begin to have more relevance than hitherto, especially in pointing up three things – the persisting reference to the Flood as of Masonic significance, the awareness that there was an arch aspect, as well as a square one, in ancient Freemasonry, and the connection of both arch and rainbow with the principles of morality.

The elements of morality are shown in 'The Grand Mystery of Free-Masons Discover'd' of that same year. The catechism there states:

"Q. How many particular points pertain to a Free-Mason?
A. Three; Fraternity, Fidelity & Tacity (sic).
Q. What do they represent?
A. Brotherly Love, Relief, and Truth, among all Right Masons; for which all Masons were ordain'd at the Building of the Tower of **Babel**, and at the Temple of Jerusalem."

This was a passage that was repeated the next year in the 'Institution of Free-Masons'.

The flood connection is still further emphasized by a section of the 'Briscoe Pamphlet' of 1724 which states:

"Adam caused a beautiful Monumental Stone to be form'd for the depositing of his Body, on which was carved all the Geometrical Figures, and *Hieroglyphicks*, afterwards used by the Antient Egyptians, together with the particular Signification of the letter *Tau*, which was the Mark put upon Cain, lest anyone should destroy him, and was the Mark afterwards used by Moses to protect the Israelites from the destroying Angel.

Now it happened when Adam was fore-warn'd of his approaching Death, that he delivered this Stone Coffin of his … to his son *Seth*, with this Charge, that upon his Decease, his Body should be there deposited 'till at such Time there shou'd be found a Priest of the most high God to interre it, which was verified in that of Melchisedec; for Adam's Body was safely convoy'd to Noah, who placed it in the *centre of the Ark*, and daily offer'd Prayers upon this Monumental Tomb as an Altar raised to God upon the Faith of his Father Adam…"

We have already had an inkling of this tradition and it is one that is met with in more than one place. A newly uncovered 1805 Ms. booklet on 'the Porphyry Stone' will be discussed shortly but a MS book that was compiled as late as the mid-19th century in Rochdale, Lancashire, has the same story and some other familiar, and not so familiar, details about the Stone.

"Upon this Stone, did Noah make his first offering to the Lord for his safe deliverance; and desir'd it there to be fixed till the first of his descendents (sic) should be call'd from above to travel again either by Land or Water; and this falling some few years after to the lot of Abraham, he took it with him when he left his native country.

"Later – This Stone was in the form of a true Double Cube ... A cube has always six sides or faces and so had this Stone – and on each side was delineated, with various instruments made or designed for that purpose, the **Six most remarkable circumstances, relative to this famous Ancient Stone**.

"First, belongs to Royal Arch Masonry...

Second, Was made by Noah, when he made his exit from the Ark, and thereon was describ'd with a **Porphyry Tool**, that remarkable event of the Deluge..."

Interestingly, and as an aside, it is worth noting that in the same note-book there is a Royal Arch catechism which has the following words:

> "Q. Here's 2 Arks depicted on our tracing Board. What are they call'd?
> A. Noah's Ark, and the Ark of the Covenant."

The reader will note once more the natural link between the 2 Arks at this time whereas we would firmly distinguish between them.

In 1725 we have 'The Whole Institution of Free-Masons Opened' and the declaration that "We differ from the Babylonians who did presume to Build to Heaven, but we pray the blessed Trinity to let us build True, High and Square, and they shall have the praise to whom it is due". Whilst in the so-called 'Letters of Verus Commodus' we are informed that a "New Lodge will be open'd at the St. Alban's Tavern, in St. Alban's Street, for *regulating the Modern Abuses, which have crept into the Ancient Fraternity* of Free-Masons; where 'tis desired, that all the old real Masons will be present to accompany their Founders, vis. Jabel, Jubel, Tubal Cain, and their Sister, Nahama, also Nineveh (or Nimrod), Marcus, Gracchus, Euclid, Hierom, Charles Martin, Athelstone, and their good friend St. Alban who loved Masonry well." Two strands of Masonic development are here held together rather than separated and restricted and the evident persistence of links with a Noachic, as well as a Hiramic, form of Masonry was to become very evident in the year that followed.

In his Inaugural address to the Quatuor Coronati Lodge Sadler, the Librarian of Grand Lodge, drew attention to an advertisement of 1726 which was headed "Antediluvian Masonry" and which was mentioned briefly in our examination of the emerging Mark Degree. It announced a lodge to be held at the *Ship Tavern* in Bishopsgate Street, on the Feast of St. John the Baptist. There were to be 'several lectures on *Ancient Masonry*, particularly on the Signification of the Letter G, and how and after what Manner the *Antediluvian Masons* form'd their Lodges, showing what *Innovations* have lately been introduced by the Doctor (Desaguliers) and some other of the Moderns...'

One cannot but be intrigued by what those attending this Lodge would have heard for the Notice continues:

"There will likewise be a Lecture ... shewing that the two Pillars of the Porch were *not cast in the Vale of Jehosaphat* but elsewhere; and that neither the Honorary, Appolonian, or Free and Accepted Masons know anything of the matter; with the *whole History* of the Widow's son killed by the Blow of a Beetle..."

It is not for us to discuss here the pros and cons of this argument though it is relevant to my present theme to point out that such a reference to innovation would have been pointless had there not been some kind of recognised comparison between an older and a newer system.

For the record we might note that Sadler himself commented: "Whether there ever was a Society of Antediluvian Masons I cannot positively say, but I have been told by one of our members, who is not likely to be mistaken, that he has seen mention of them somewhere." (AQC 23: p. 326)

Looking at the matter from a reverse viewpoint we have 'The Freemasons Accusation and Defence' in which the writer of certain Letters to the Craft asks the author of the Book of Constitutions –

"To what purpose does he set out in that pompous Manner, and Deduce Masonry from *Noah* and his three Sons, *Shem, Ham, Japhet*? or as he inverts the Words 'and Japhet, Shem and Ham, all Masons true'? To what purpose does he make *Masons* of Noah and his Sons, who *never handled a Trowel* in their Lives, and were, at best, but *Shipwrights*?"

The matter was clearly one of significant current interest for Masons and in York that year (1726) a Bro. Drake made a well-known speech in which he referred to Seth's Pillars prior to the Flood and the Tower of Babel following it, whilst also mentioning that the walls of Babylon, built 1000 years before King Solomon's Temple, gave cause for believing that 'three parts in four of the whole earth might then be divided into E – P, F – C & M – M'. Yet even this insistence on the extended antiquity of the Craft was as nothing when compared with another document that probably originated that year though it was not to be fully revealed until it appeared, also in York, over 200 years later. I refer, of course, to the Graham Manuscript.

We touched on this important evidence when we were examining the emergence of the Mark Degree in English Freemasonry but it is in its references to Noah and his sons that the greatest importance of the document lies both for Freemasonry in general and our particular concern with incipient Ark Mariner Masonry.

Opening with a salutation followed by an examination the reader quickly comes upon those same words that have just been quoted in 'The Whole Institution' – 'we differs from these baballonians who presumed to build to heaven but we pray the blessed trinity to Let us build trueLy (sic) and square and they shall have the praise to whom it is due ...'. The reader may have noted the use of capital Ls as Squares. It then continues:

'But how came (it) that the works of the Baballonians stood before all this or yet the brightness of the gospell – . . . because the presumption of the Baballonians afforesaid had vexed the God head in so much the Language was Confounded ffor their sake so that no mankind ffor ever was to do the Like again without a divine Lisiance which could not be had wtout faith and prayer – . . . we have it by tradition and still some refferance to scripture (what) cause shem ham and Japheth (had) ffor to go to their father noahs grave for to try if they could find anything about him ffor to Lead them to the vertuable secret which this fameious preacher had for I hope all will allow that all things needfull for the new world was in the ark with noah.'

(It is worthy of remark that the Graham MS has no mention of 2 pillars.)

Thereafter the three sons agreed that the first thing they found should be 'to them as a secret' and then they attempted to raise Noah's dead body in a manner that involved five points of contact. What is striking is that the very moment when it is now generally accepted that the Hiramic legend was beginning to be adopted and incorporated into the English Speculative process we have this clear evidence, albeit from the North of England, that an almost identical story was told about Noah. It is at this point that Alex Horne has some very revealing things to say.

"The (Graham) manuscript presents numerous ideas, practices, and symbolical allusions as of the period in question; and, associated with the Noachic Legend itself, there is a Legend which comes immediately after, connected with 'Bazalliell', the builder of the Tabernacle of Moses in the Wilderness." Horne is thus pointing up the evident link between one builder of an Ark and the later builder of a dwelling for the Ark, and he continues:

"It is perhaps additionally significant that the story of the building of King Solomon's Temple, as it comes down to us from all the Old Charges since the Cooke MS, comes in immediately after these stories of Bezaleel and of Noah, while elements of all three stories are now found telescoped into one, in our present Legend."

He pointed to a comment of Dr. Poole who asked, "Is it possible that we have here an earlier version of the story which was later (say, during the 17th century) transferred to Hiram?" One thing seems to him to be settled beyond any reasonable doubt and that was that the import of the 'five points of fellowship' was known at least by the time of the 'Edinburgh Register House MS' of 1696 whether it still had a Noachic or already a Hiramic dress.

There is another twist to the story illuminated by the Graham MS. This is prompted by some words from Knoop and Jones who remark that 'the five points of fellowship may have originated in practices connected with witchcraft or some other superstition, of which there was then no lack in Scotland'. Is it not conceivable that in order to provide the Fellow-crafts with some kind of corresponding 'history' or even to explain the **five points** for the benefit of growing numbers of non-operative members there, the Noah story was adopted or adapted? Let me remind the reader that we have already met traditions –

beside the Graham ones – that spoke of a coffin at the heart of the Ark, of the necromantic rites attributed by Churchmen to Ham, and the overall link of Noah with a risen Master because he and his were saved from death to live again. To quote Knoop and Jones further:

"The stories of Noah and Hiram call to mind the fact that in biblical instances of the miraculous restoration of life, the prophet or apostle lay full length upon the body and breathed into its face."

Any Scot would be both well aware not only of Noah and his sons but even of Elisha and the son of the Shunnamite and if, of course, the dating of the Graham MS is 1672, as some experts at the British Museum have suggested is quite possible, then another scenario opens up. Heron Lepper is on record as declaring that this was 'a genuine Masonic production of a period not later than the early 17th century' and very possibly of Scottish origin. We might bear this in mind when we come to Stirling a little later on.

What is not so surprising is the introduction of so definite a Noah story bearing in mind the chain of 'Noah' references that both preceded and now follow it. Whether one can go as far as Handfield-Jones in saying that this evidence suggests "that in the earliest days of Grand Lodge the Noah story was of *more importance* than the Hiramic legend" is less certain but from this book's point of view it is essential to note that there was a strong and undying emphasis on the Noachic aspect of Masonry.

In 1730 the theme is still there. In the first notable Masonic exposure, 'Masonry Dissected' by Samuel Pritchard, we have reference to the basic importance of the Liberal Arts and Sciences and especially the 5th, that of Geometry. "For at the Building of the *Tower of Babel*, the Art and Mystery of Masonry was first introduc'd, and from thence handed down by Euclid ..." Even more complete is an extract from 'The Perjur'd Free Mason Detected':

"*Ham, or Cham*, the second son of NOAH, having a Genius to Architecture, is said to have practised it in the Antediluvian World, before the Deluge, for he was 90 Years of Age when the Flood came upon the earth.

"Fame tells us, that after the Flood he communicated the Knowledge of it to the Great Council or Meeting upon *the plains of Shinaar*, where it was proposed to build a Tower up to Heaven: ... But the History imports, that his Workmen growing wearing of mounting that stupendous Stair-case, and at last being divided in Speech, mutinied and left him. and so the Work was broken off; but the mighty ruins of that Fabrick shews to this Day the Skill of the Master Mason; the immense *Arches*, the vast *Pilasters*, the strong *Basis*, which are still to be seen, are a lasting Testimony as well to the Greatness of the Work as to the Genius of the Workman." In the Catechism that then followed there was the question: "Who was the first Master Mason in the World?" and the answer first given is: "He that built the Tower of Babel."

'A Collection of the Songs of Masons' was produced in 1734 in London and included was *The Master's Song*, by no less a person than Dr.Anderson.

The intriguing fact is that nowhere in the libretto is there any mention of Solomon's Temple and the name of Hiram, whether as king or craftsman, is also absent. Following two stanzas that tell us of Adam, Cain, Seth and Enoch we come to the core of the work:

"Our Father **Noah** next appeared, A **Mason** too, divinely taught;
And by divine Command uprear'd The **Ark** that held a goodly Fraught;
'Twas built by true **Geometry** A piece of Architecture fine:
Helped by his Sons, in number Three, concurring in the Grand Design.

So from the gen'ral Deluge none were saved but **Masons** and their wives;
And all Mankind from them alone descending, **Architecture** thrives;
For they, when multiply'd amain, Fit to disperse and fill the Earth,
In Shinar's large and lovely Plain to MASONRY gave second Birth.

For most of Mankynd were employ'd to build the City and the Tow'r;
The **General Lodge** was overjoy'd, in such Effects of Masons Pow'r;
Till vain Ambition did provoke Their Maker to Confound their Plot;
Yet tho' with Tongues confus'd they spoke the learned **Art** they ne'er forgot.

There was also a Chorus that had its own contribution to make:

"**Who can unfold the** Royal Art? **Or sing its** Secrets **in a** Song?
They're safely kept in Mason's Heart, **and to the** *antient Lodge* **belong**."

It is therefore not surprising to learn that in 1733 a very similar song was used at a specially convened meeting in Dublin, already the home of 'antient practices' and that contained the following verse:

"The Reason that **Babel** succeeded so ill,
Was because they knew nothing of **Mason's** Skill;
For still their Tower standing would be
Had they known Rules of **Masonry**."

It was time for Dr. Anderson to revise the Constitutions of Masonry and what is now noticeable is that in 1738 he makes two very distinctive additions to the First Charge. To the words "A Mason is oblig'd by his Tenure, to obey the Moral Law" he joins, and then it is only in the second edition of that year's printing, "as a true Noachida", and even later in the same Charge: "For they all agree in the 3 great **Articles of Noah**, enough to preserve the cement of the Lodge".

That this was not a mere whim on Anderson's part is obvious when we recall that he was, after all, simply the spokesman for the Grand Lodge, which had to authorize whatever he submitted. The term 'Noachidae' was by no means peculiar to him. We see it being used in a letter of 1735 by no less a person than the Grand Secretary of the day, John Revis. The latter was writing to the Provincial Grand Master in Calcutta:

"Providence has fixed your Lodge near those learn'd Indians *that affect to be called Noachidae*, the strict observance of his Precepts taught in those

Parts by the Disciples of the great Zoroastres, the learned Archimagus of Bactria, a Grand Master of the Magians, whose religion is much preserved in India." Quite apart from the intriguing reference to Zoroaster in connection with the sons of Noah, bearing in mind the earlier suggestion that he and Ham might be identical, this letter also requested information as to the 'possible Remains of Old Masonry' (did the writer mean ante-diluvian?) which might be found in that area. (AQC xi. 35/6) Does that imply that even the senior members of the Premier Grand Lodge seriously entertained a desire for pre-Hiramic Masonry?

How much earlier the term 'Noachidae' began to be used we do not yet finally know but the Old English Dictionary tells us that the word 'Noachian' was certainly employed in *1678*. The parallel existence of these terms and the prevalence of the Noachic aspects of Freemasonry cannot be a mere coincidence, especially when we come to examine the associated subject of the **Noachian Precepts** or Articles of Noah.

These titles presumably had some definite significance for Anderson and his readers and Woodford, in Kenning's Cyclopaedia, submits that the 3 Articles were (i) abstain from idolatry and worship the one true God: (ii) honour God's holy name and not to profane it or take it in vain; (iii) not to commit murder. Begemann was of the opinion that the three Articles were the familiar 'Brotherly Love, Relief and Truth', whilst Vibert thought that it referred to a Mason being 'a good man and true and strictly to obey the moral law'. He saw this as being the right deduction from the verse in Genesis: 'Noah was a just man and perfect and walked with God".

There is a problem for us today, however, since Hebrew scholars, and a Chief Rabbi who was also a Freemason, have pointed out that the commandments given to the descendants of Noah were SEVEN in number namely, (i) the establishment of Courts of Justice; (ii) the prohibition of blasphemy; (iii) no idolatry; (iv) no incest; (v) no bloodshed; (vi) no robbery; and (vii) no eating flesh cut from a living animal. The Chief Rabbi specifically stated that 'these constitute what might be called Natural Religion' and no three of them were any more important than the other four. To be fair to Woodford's previous description he did add that four other prescriptions were later joined to the first three which he named. These others were: to avoid incest, not to steal, to be just, and not to eat flesh with blood in it. It may be seen that these related fairly closely to the Jewish definitions.

That the Talmudic or Scriptural list *of 7 items* above is likely to have been what Anderson's Charge was referring to seems more probable since both he and Dr. Desaguliers would be well aware of such teaching as being the moral law binding on Gentiles as descendants of Noah. The very term 'Noachidae' was, says one Masonic commentator, the name applied to members of other nations who practised the great principles of religion and morality, without accepting Jewish doctrine and ceremony.

It was not only in the Charges, however, that the term appears. The

1738 traditional history also has a much more detailed account of this part of the Masonic story.

"After the Flood, Noah and his 3 sons, having preserved the Knowledge of the Arts and Sciences, communicated It to their growing Off-spring, who were all of one Language and Speech. And it came to pass, as they journey'd *from the East* (the Plains of Mount Ararat, where the Ark rested) *towards the West*, they found a Plain in the land of SHINAR, and dwelt there together *as NOACHIDAE* or sons of NOΛH; and when **Peleg** was born there to Heber, after the Flood 101 years, Father Noah partitioned the Earth, ordering them to disperse and take Possession..."

This historical statement was to be repeated in all the English editions of the Constitutions until the time of the Union. The term 'Noachidae' was dropped *from the Charge* after this 1738 edition but it was still retained in the **Irish** editions.

As we reflect on this surprisingly steady and persistent flow of material which obviously kept alive both a knowledge of and interest in the part played by Noah and his descendants there are three thoughts that perhaps merit consideration.

The first is that if this aspect of Biblical 'history' was so constantly repeated it must have been done because it had real significance, at least for contemporary Masons. Perhaps here is yet another field for more intensive study in the future. What evidence can be discovered in contemporary theology, scripture studies, ethnology or antiquarian researches which might point to reasons for this emphasis?

A second thought must be that despite the growing concentration on the Hiramic and Solomonic aspects of the basic Speculative degrees from about 1725 the Noachic or Nimrod approach to Freemasonry still continues in some form. The decrease in the latter between 1740 and 1755 might in fact be explained by just such a determined Hiramic 'take-over'. What we have to note, however, is that in Scotland and Ireland the Noachic or Ark theme did not disappear and it was the Military Lodges, as in the case of the Mark Degree (or its related ceremonies), that were to bring this section of Freemasonry back to the mainland.

The third thought is, as again expressed in the early part of the Mark story, that once a legend, a symbolic way of thinking or acting, or a form of teaching, have established themselves somewhere in the Masonic 'corpus' then it is more than likely that sooner or later that material, if laid aside by the mainstream of the Craft, will re-emerge in some form, under another guise, available for an instructive purpose. That this happened in one way or another with the material associated previously with the Flood story is what I hope to show in the section that follows.

Before we can start on that journey however there is one more literary reference to which attention should be drawn. I refer to the issue of what were in fact the Constitutions of the Atholl or Antients Masons. These were compiled by Laurence Dermott, the dedicated Grand Secretary of that body, and they were given the distinctive title of **Ahiman Rezon**. The work first appeared in 1756 and contained, as in future editions, an Introduction, General Remarks, Charges, Prayers, General Regulations and Masonic Songs. It is in three of these sections that we can usefully observe the approach adopted to the Craft's traditions.

In the Introduction we read:

"The Royal Art was ... carefully handed down by Methuselah, who died but a few days before the general deluge, and who had lived 245 years with Adam, by whom he was instructed in all the mysteries of this sublime science, which he faithfully communicated to his grandson Noah who transmitted it to posterity... From the flood to the days of King Solomon the liberal arts and sciences gradually spread themselves over different parts of the globe ... It has been the custom of most writers on the subject to give us an elaborate history of Masonry from the creation to their own time, viz. from Adam to Noah, from Noah to Nimrod, from Nimrod to Solomon, from Solomon to Cyrus... (giving an account of the building of temples, towers, cities, pyramids, bridges, pillars, etc). Nothing is thereby intended to impeach the veracity, or to offend writers of historical truths. Our intention being only to expose ridiculous innovations, and fabulous accounts of Grand Masters, whose masonical authorities never existed.

"It is certain that Freemasonry has existed from the creation, though probably not under that name; that it was a divine gift from God; that Cain and the builders of the city were strangers to the secret mystery of Masonry; that there were but *four Masons* in the world when the deluge happened; that one of the four, even *the second son* of Noah, was not master of the art; that neither Nimrod, nor his Craftsmen, knew anything of the matter; and that there were but *very few masters of the art* even at Solomon's temple; whereby it plainly appears that the whole mystery was communicated to very few at that time..."

What this extract highlights is a continuing recognition of Noachic Masonry and this is underlined by the fact that as late as 1813 an 8th edition of 'Ahiman Rezon', like the Irish Constitutions, contains the sentence in the Charges:

"A Mason is obliged by his tenure to observe the moral law as a true NOACHIDA."

Furthermore the songs in this work confirm the same emphasis. In a Royal Arch Song the second verse reads as follows:

> "Then Noah found favour and grace in his sight,
> He built up an ark by the help of our Light;
> In clouds, GOD his rainbow then set, to insure
> That his mercies and cov'nants should ever endure."

There was even a Song composed by Dermott himself which seemed to mitigate his queries about Nimrod's men:

> "As Masons once on Shinar's plain,
> Met to revive their arts again,
> Did mutually agree,
> So now we're met in Britain's isle,
> And make the Royal Craft to smile,
> In Ancient Masonry."

And there was also an Oratorio called 'Solomon's Temple' in which one unaccompanied recitative declared:

> "Upon the surface of the waves,
> (When God a mighty deluge pours)
> Noah, a chosen remnant saves,
> And lays the ark's stupendous floors."

Whatever may have been a reason for the silence of the 1740s in England there was no question about the awareness of Noah for Antient Masons throughout the remainder of the century. It is to the events in that period that we now have to turn.

THE EMERGENCE OF A NOACHITE DEGREE

The point must surely by now have been established that the stories surrounding Noah and his immediate descendants were too well known and revered to be allowed to disappear altogether from the Masonic scene. If it is true, as has begun to seem likely, that one strand of Noachic legend – the discovery of the dead Master and his attempted resuscitation – was taken over by or surrendered to the new Grand Lodge Masons then other aspects of the Deluge story and its aftermath would need to be preserved and even developed. In **1754** we have some interesting evidence to suggest that just such a process was possible.

In a paper presented by J.T.Thorpe in 1907 we are introduced to a curious pamphlet entitled 'Freemason Examin'd'. On the title-page the doubtful claim is made that herein is revealed how Masons are made 'in all the Lodges round the Globe' and even the declared author seems to be unreliable as his claim to be 'Late Master of 3 Norwich Lodges' cannot be verified by any lists of the oldest lodges there. Nonetheless the interest of this work for our present purpose is that it is entirely based on the construction of the *Tower of Babel.*

The officers are the 6 sons of Cush, the eldest son of Ham and hence the grandson of Noah. The names here given are those as reported by Josephus rather than the forms found in Genesis chapter 10, Sabas, Evilas, Sabathes, Ragmus, Sabactas and Belus, which latter name was an alternative for Nimrod.

The form of the lodge was circular, following the previously mentioned ground floor plan of the Tower of Babel, and the officers were arranged with Belus, the Master, facing across the circle to Sabas, the Superintendent. Evilas and Sabathes, the 2 Wardens, likewise faced their two Deacons, Sabactas and Ragmus. The Master wore the Compasses pendant by a white ribbon about his neck whilst the Superintendent wore a Square. The Wardens had respectively the Level and Plumb Rule, whilst the Deacons each held a 24" gauge in their hands. There were 3 degrees.

1. **The Minor's Degree** which claimed that Freemasonry began about "one hundred and fifty four years after Noah's Flood, at the Building of Babel's Tower". It was held in the 'pleasant plain of Shinar' by the Tigris and Belus instructs his Men in conversing by Signs. Silence, Secrecy and Brotherly Love are enjoined, the Candidate is clothed in a long white garment 'of Holland, or some other fine Linnen, and sometimes of Silk', obligated on a sword and then re-clothed with a white leather apron. When accepted he receives a signet ring

"That he may to great **Babel's** Tow'r repair
And on him take a Major's Character...
'tis then my Will and Pleasure, that he may
Begin to work, and enter into Pay."

2. **The Major's Degree** in which the candidate undertook to behave "as a true Noachidae (sic), and instruct the younger Brethren, using all Endeavours to encrease Brotherly Love". It takes place in a secret Arbour beside the River Tigris, an Arbour, the candidate is told, being another name for the Shed which Operative masons use for keeping their curious tools and for examining strange Brethren as well as retiring to at Noon.

There follows an examination by Sabas who then leads the new brother "round the Tower, and then knocked at the Brazen Gate 9 times ... In order that the Watchman of the Gate might know, that he had been with me round the Tower which was 9 miles." The candidate is then told that the diameter of the Tower is 3 miles and its height 5146 paces. The Passage that went to the top was on the outside and like a winding staircase, of a very great breadth so that Camels and Carriages might turn with ease. The reason that this Tower was built to be so extensive was 'to make them a great Name, and also to save them from a second Deluge'.

The degree words are 'Eureka' and 'Philadelphia'; the sign was traced to Sampson (sic) in Judges, who, after slaying a lion with an ass's jawbone, received water from a Rock and wiped his mouth in appreciation. Most striking of all is the note to this degree: 'A Tower is raised in the Lodge room, about 8 feet high, and in some of the Grand Lodges it is really a very curious Piece of Workmanship; it is made of wood and, though in many pieces, it can be raised in about 2 hours'.

3. **The Officer's Part** or **Ceremony of Installment**. This takes place in the Observatory at the top of the Tower. Here the Plan laid out by Belus is

explained to the assembled company. Taken on bended knees the new officers receive the secrets of their office:

> "The Word is **Belus**, be it known to thee,
> 'Twas that great Man gave Birth to Masonry."

Whilst Bro. Thorp himself thought that this seemed like a Parody of true Masonry and others agreed, it is noticeable that Bro. Songhurst could not align himself with that view. He commented on the fact that the Tower of Babel was portrayed on certain old tracing-boards and jewels in such a manner as to leave no doubt as to its importance at some stage. He ventured the opinion that 'it may hereafter be found that the history of the building of the Tower of Babel played a prominent part in early Masonic ritual'. Since Slade's entry into the Craft was by carefully perusing documents left by his father, who was initiated in **1708**, Songhurst thought that Slade's publication might contain something that had been worked at an earlier period. Whether there were many lodges working this kind of Nimrod Masonry at this date is a matter needing much more investigation but there are factors that allow for this being a possibility. Even Thorp in his reply admitted that Songhurst might have a point. Though not then referred to the tower motif in the Royal Order ceremonies from 1735 onwards this idea might merit consideration.

Mention was also made in comment on this paper that there existed a degree known as that of the Noachites or Prussian Knights. We know that there was a ritual of **1768** which was part of the West Cornwall series and with which John Knight, who claimed to receive certain degrees through Thomas Dunckerley, was closely connected. That form of the ritual was headed as follows: "Royal Ark Marioners or Noachides also sometimes called Prusian Masons". Let me assure the reader that these spellings are the original ones. We know that a form of the degree appeared in the several editions of Carlile's 'Manual of Freemasonry' and was still being promoted in the Early Scottish Encampment at the close of the 19th century. What we also know is that in the list of degrees attributed directly to Dunckerley's influence and use, and from which we earlier selected the Mark ones, there was a degree named Royal Ark Masons, but as yet no papers conveying the contents of that ceremony have been located in the United Grand Lodge library. To discover that would be yet another step forward in the future.

The West Cornwall or Redruth version (RED) begins by describing the dress worn by those already members of the degree. They wear swords, aprons and gloves trimmed with yellow, and jewels pendant to a black ribbon attached to a waistcoat button. The Worshipful Master's jewel is triangular with an arrow pointing to the earth.

The lodge is to be held in the light of the full moon and the three principal officers are Noah, Shem and Japhet. The presiding officer and Past Masters are referred to as Most Venerable Brothers and others as Venerable Sire. At the Opening Noah gives 7 sword beats, Shem 5 and Japhet 4. To alert the lodge members and prepare them for the admission of a candidate 8 slow and 2 quick knocks are given with the word **Phaleg**.

The candidate, who is hereafter called 'Proselyte', is now led round the lodge room *16 times* and is then offered a glass of wine. He lies flat upon the floor and Shem and Japhet throw a cloth over him. They also perambulate *16 times* and after this the Proselyte rises to his feet to stand between Shem and Japhet before the Most Venerable. The latter then says:

"You now represent Noah who, being drunk, was mocked by Ham. You will therefore repeat as follows: 'Cursed be Ham and he shall be a slave to his Brothers for his mocking. Blessed be Shem, and Ham shall be his slave. Blessed be Japhet, and Ham shall be his slave.'

All the officers now point their swords towards the Proselyte, whilst the Most Venerable asks: 'Will you renounce *Pride* for ever hereafter, for you plainly see the external Habit does not gain you admittance into our most Sacred Lodge?' Proselyte responds, 'I will'.

MV 'Shew me an act of your humility. Kneel and give three obeisances and then kiss the pummel of the sword.' Proselyte does so.

MV 'I now administer an obligation which you will repeat: 'In the awful presence of the Most High God who showered down his vengeance upon us I will keep from all the children of Adam the secrets now to be revealed to avoid a like transgression as that of the second son of Noah. If I transgress may my spech be confounded as at the building of Bable (sic).'

The Proselyte having taken the obligation the MV then communicates to him the three signs with the words, and the grip.

1st Sign: The arms extended towards the sky but with face to the earth. The words are uttered: 'I, even I, that have done it.
Noah that pronounced it.
Pheleg (sic) that drew it on himself.'
2nd Sign: Throwing out an arm as if throwing off a Garment.
3rd Sign: Pointing up to Heaven.

The Grip is given by clinching the hands 3 times and saying

'Shem, Ham, Japhet.'

There now followed a Catechism:

Q. What caused the Deluge?
A. The wickedness of Mankind.
Q. What caused a curse to be set on Ham?
A. Ham finding Noah naked and mocking him.
Q. Who proposed the building of the Tower of Bable?
A. Pheleg.
Q. When was the design finished?
A. On the night of the full moon.
Q. What became of Pheleg?

A. He travelled secretly into Prussia, by night, subsisting on wild roots, so we eat nothing but roots and shrubs in this degree.
Q. Who told you this?
A. An intelligent brother.
Q. In what Lodge?
A. In a Lodge where the moon gives light.
Q. Why was the Tower never completed?
A. Because the foundation was laid in pride.
Q. Is it to imitate the children of Noah that you retain it in the memory?
A. No, it is to avoid that empiety (sic).
Q. Where were the remains of Pheleg deposited?
A. In a tomb.
Q. Was he considered a reprobate?
A. He was not, for his Epitaph is – 'Here repose the Ashes of the Grand Architect of the Tower of Bable (for) that the Lord had pity on him because he became humble.'
Q. In what manner were you received as Noachites of Prusian Masonry?
A. By 3 Humiliations, kissing the pummel of a sword and then taking an Obligation.
Q. Do you know the children of Adam?
A. I know three of them.
Q. Who are they?
A. Shem, Ham and Japhet.

The MV then says: 'May Wrath be turned away from us all', the Lodge is darkened, the verse 25 of Genesis chap. 10 is read, and the words "REMEMBER PHELEG" are solemnly pronounced. The ceremony is over. (Gen. 10.25: And there were born to Eber two sons; and the name of the one was Peleg; and in his day the world was divided.)

Such was the original, hand-written and 'primitive' form of the earliest **Ark Mariner** ritual of which we have evidence in England. What is of interest in our present quest for the antecedents of the degree as it is practised today is the fact that we have printed versions of the degree as it continued to be recognised in the period from 1820 to 1850 though the title under which it then appeared was 'The Masonic Degree of Noahites or Prussian Knights'. That it was basically the same degree is clear but with the usual 19th century efficiency the forms that were then produced were more rounded and comprehensive as an actual ceremony. I shall now run through the degree again and will this time insert the portions that were added in Carlile's 'Manual of Freemasonry' (CMF) or an American Monitor of the Scottish Rite (AMSR).

Before addressing the content of these workings, however, it is worth noting the position of this step in the series to which it is said to belong. In the series of degrees used in Cornwall that of 'Prusian Blue' comes after the Link and Wrestle, but immediately before 'Red Cross Knight'. In CMF/AMSR it comes between 'The Degree of Provost and Judge, or Irish Master' and the 'Red Cross Sword of Babylon'. The Irish Master degree concerned the discovery of the monument erected to the great architect Hiram A.B., whilst the Red Cross covered the journeying of Zerubbabel from the court of Cyrus across the bridges of the two rivers, Euphrates and Jordan, to reach his native land where he might begin the re-building of the Temple. This positioning is not only of interest because of the apparent resonances between the three ceremonies but also because it will be relevant to our examination of 18th century practice in Scotland and Ireland later.

We are told in CMF that 'The origin of this degree is deduced from the Tower of Babel, or from a son of Noah' and both versions now have the following officers: 1st. A Grand **Commander**.
2nd. A Knight of Introduction.
3rd. A Knight of Eloquence.
4th. A Knight of Finances.
5th. A Knight of Chancery, and
6th. A Knight of Defence.

CMF then has an extended introductory commentary which was clearly no part of the acted ceremony but which provides interesting information on how the degree was regarded at the time.

This degree is said to have been first conceived by the Prussian Knights during the Crusades and to have been used to initiate Christian Princes and their attendants. The apartment for the reception was not to be confined as it needed access to the light of the moon. The form of the Chapter was **triangular** and the symbol of the degree was an arrow pointing to the earth.

In opening the chapter the GC struck thrice with the blade of his sword and returned it to its scabbard. He then raised his hand towards the moon, the brethren copying him, and he thus declared the chapter to be lighted. The Knights then examine a drawing until the candidate is prepared. The drawing shows two apartments: the ground of one is blue with a silver moon and golden stars on it, whilst the other is black with a triangle and golden arrow delineated.

The candidate, led by the Knight of Introduction, is bare-headed, without a sword and wearing a white apron and gloves. Three strokes on the door are given and the Knight of Defence who has arranged the knights within along two sides of the triangle leading to the GC at the apex facing East, and hence the moon's rising, enquires at the door, asks for the password and then with one knock from inside the closed door reports to the GC that a Master is without desirous of becoming a Prussian Mason.

There is no representation of the drunken Noah incident in these forms of the degree before the candidate is faced with the array of swords. The GC says: 'I declare, brave knights, that he is worthy of your countenance' and the candidate shows his humility as hitherto but before he again rises the Knight of Eloquence addresses him on the subject of Vanity and uses the cases of Peleg and Solomon as examples. The obligation follows which now also includes a willingness to associate with the Knights of the Order and to prevent any unauthorised person wearing the jewel but there is no penalty.

It is at this point that a completely new address is inserted, to be given by the Knight of Eloquence, and it will be instructive to consider some of its passages. After mentioning the Flood as God's vengeance it continues: "Notwithstanding the Deity had given the **rainbow** as a sign of reconciliation, vouchsafing that favour declared that the world should not again be destroyed by waters, the descendants of Noah, from their want of faith in the divine prediction, being apprehensive of a second deluge, said, Let us build a city whose top may reach the heavens ... To accomplish their designs, they began to erect a high tower in the plain of Shinar ... but this enterprise being displeasing in the eyes of their Maker ... he obliged them to discontinue the project, by confounding their language, so that one could not understand another ... It was on the night of the full moon that the Lord worked this wonder, in remembrance of which the Noahites held their lodges at this season. The architect was named Pelag ... As a punishment for his contumacy, and the presumption of his brethren, he was deprived of his speech; and to avoid the outrages of his companions ... he travelled into countries remote from Shinar, and from thence only by moonlight, as he was fearful of massacre if his person were recognised. His place of retirement was Prussia, where having erected a **triangular** dwelling, he, by humiliation, ... obtained remission for his sins, and had his speech restored to him. This dwelling of Peleg's was discovered 15 cubits deep from the surface of the earth, in the year 553. In it was found a *stone of white marble* on which was inscribed in the Hebrew tongue the particulars I have related' and the epitaph given earlier was nearby.

The GC declares this the 'grand secret' and adds: 'Misfortune to you if you are weak enough to transcribe it. Be circumspect, and for that purpose practise humility, after the example of our grand architect.'

The knights sheath their swords, the candidate receives his, the jewel is attached to his waistcoat, his apron and gloves are decorated with yellow borders and the sign (previous 1st one only), grip, word and password (Pheleg)) are given. The GC ends the ceremony by observing that the lodge is obscured and that it is time to retire. Following that declaration a candle-lit table is brought in and if supper follows it is a vegetarian one. A Catechism is attached to the ritual which has several of the questions that appeared in the earlier one though again the mention of drunken Noah is omitted. Of special interest are the following items:

Q. Do you know the children of **Noah?** (Not **Adam** as previously)
A. I know three of them.
Q. Who are they?
A. I particularise them by their initials **S H I**. (In the preceding 'Irish Master' degree the letters are **I H S**)
Q. (Can you) Present the signs? (Note the plural but only one given: is this a relic of the earlier practice?)
A. The arms extended towards the moon, and the face towards the **East**. (Not towards the **earth** as previously).

Q. Why is the face towards the east?
A. Because it is the part in which the moon rises. (The remainder is almost identical with the previous catechism but there is a different ending) -
Q. Why do knights wear a triangle?
A. In memory of the temple of Peleg.
Q. Why is the arrow reserved in the centre of it?
A. In remembrance of the remission that took place from his contrition and that the cup of wrath has turned from him.
G.C. So may it be turned aside from all his successors, and with this sentiment I close the lodge of Noahites.

Almost the same ritual was recorded in the 1883 Early Scottish Encampment but here the title of Ark Mariner is given to another degree which is still placed immediately before the Red Cross of Babylon degree.

Today the Prussian Knight or Noachite degree is the 21° of the Scottish Rite in America and it too has some interesting variations from what preceded it. The meetings are called Grand Chapters and the officers are a Lieutenant Commander, 2 Wardens, an Orator, Treasurer, Secretary, Master of Ceremonies, Warder and Standard Bearer. The apron is yellow with an arm holding a sword and the Egyptian figure of silence. The order is black and the jewel a full moon or the triangle traversed by an arrow. The legend describes the travels of Peleg from Babel to the north of Europe and the triangular building was discovered in trenching the rubbish of the salt mines of Prussia. At the side of the column of white marble was a tomb of freestone on which was *a piece of agate* which bore the familiar epitaph. The thorough dispersion of the races of mankind and the virtue of humility seem to have been the constant lessons of this degree which also found a home as the 35° of the Rite of Mizraim.

To show the persistence of the theme maintained by these Noachite ceremonies we ought also to record that in **1816** there was founded in Paris an 'Order of French Noachidae'. It was composed of the partisans of Napoleon and its Grand Master was General Bertrand who was with Napoleon on St. Helena. It consisted of three degrees: Knight, Commander, Grand Elect. In the First degree the candidate was told that he worked under the architect **Phaleg** who was a cunning workman who came to direct the building of the 8 storeys of the Tower named: **A**dam, **E**ve, **N**oah, **L**amech **N**aamah, **P**haleg, **O**ubal, **O**rient – which initials formed 'Napoleon'. The 2° centred on a veiled urn containing the ashes of Phaleg brought from an island. The degree was practised for but a short time.

With this aspect of Diluvian masonry amply provided for there was only one other facet of the story that was not apparently served and that was the more central fact of the Ark itself and its human voyagers. It is to this aspect that we can now turn.

The Ancient Stirling Lodge (Scotland) possessed two brass plates of about 3" by 9" which it is claimed dated from about 1745. One has Craft emblems on both sides whilst the other has Craft emblems on only one side. On the other are (i) 'Redd Cros or Ark' showing a dove emerging from the Ark, (ii) 'Sepulchcre' (sic), (iii) Knights of Malta' (iv) 'Night Templer' (sic) and (v) An Arch made up of six concentric bands (hence resembling a **Rainbow**) with a rough keystone at its apex. No one has yet been able to explain satisfactorily the precise origin or purpose of these plates but that they are very old and clearly relate to the previous practices of this ancient Scottish Chapter does seem to be the most likely reason for their existence and retention.

There are several deductions which it seems reasonable to make from the Stirling plates. The first is that all the drawings seem to be by the same hand and that therefore to establish the date of the brasses is to suggest that not only the plates showing the Craft degrees, but the one with appendant orders, is of the same period. For this to be claimed is very significant indeed and when W.J.Hughan states in his paper on the brasses that 'the singular figures (are) not in my opinion older than about the middle of the last century' (i.e. c.1750) he is still saying something of consequence. Where else have we any evidence that by 1750 there were ceremonies being acknowledged such as are shown here? Even if we allow that these brasses were produced a decade or so later it would still be remarkable.

What has further to be said is that by the time these degrees are being so recorded we note that the Ark Degree has something to do with a vessel and a dove. We are no longer in the area of Shinar and Babel. That, as we shall soon see, was by no means impossible, and what is of no less interest is the juxtaposition of the Ark degree with the Red Cross which is signified by a form of the Cross of Lorraine, a definite knightly symbol. We have already had occasion to note this connection.

Further to these indicators we have to reflect again, as we did in part in the earlier Mark section of this book, on the only possible reference on the brasses to the Royal Arch. It is made by stressing three features. First, the semblance of an arch without pillars, as if the arch of a bridge; secondly, the clear indication that this arch was also like a rainbow; and thirdly, the prominence of a keystone at the apex of the arch, but a keystone that does not pierce the arch. In case the reader may be thinking that this is too detailed an assessment of very simple drawings may I suggest that the skill of this artist is precisely that in very few lines he has summed up the very heart of each Order and what he drew he meant to draw. The figure for the Knights Templar is subtlety itself.

If this **is** an intended drawing referring to the Royal Arch degree as the Stirling **Antient** Lodge understood it then what it is saying is that the Ark, Mark and Arch degrees were all part and parcel of that significant 4th Degree. That tells us a very great deal for it suggests that already there was in Stirling a Masonic body that was similar to, if not connected with, Irish Freemasonry of at least 1765.

I have no intention of re-tracing the steps through Irish Freemasonry which I took in the earlier parts of this book save only to highlight some facts not then mentioned which relate to Ark Masonry. It is, for example, evident from an extant Youghal seal that by the late 1750s the Mark, Ark, Red Cross, and Arch ceremonies (even if they were only or mainly in the form of lectures) were linked with the Holy Royal Arch. A seal from Lurgan in the 1770s shows the Dove on one side and the hand and trowel on the other, whilst seals from Leitrim show the ark sailing on the waters, the dove with the olive branch, the Red Cross 'bridge' and the four armed cross of that Order. That that was an accepted format for the linked degrees is then confirmed when we find aprons and floorcloths as well as certificates by the end of the century. One of these at Limerick is addressed to all 'Red Cross and Noachides', and is signed by a High Priest, a Royal Arch Captain and three Grand Masters (of a Lodge). We know moreover that by 1790 the Irish Encampments were regularly conferring the degree of Noachida and by 1810 the Ark, Mark and Link.

It has to be accepted that whereas the Mark Degree started on a new lease of life with the advent of John Fowler after 1810 the Ark, Link and Wrestle degrees did not and though we see the 'Sublime Degree of Ark Masonry' still being communicated in 1828 it soon after faded away and was no more practised.

Nonetheless we do have an example of an Ark, Link and Wrestle degree as worked in Rock Lodge, No. 325 (IC) and it will, I believe, be quite instructive to see the pattern that had been established in that land by the early 19th century.

The lodge room is decorated with a transparent Rainbow and the Ark sailing on the waters. The **Grand Master** addresses the Master of Ceremonies and asks if the Assembly of Ark and Link Masons is duly guarded. The MC checks that all present are duly qualified by receiving the word and grip. The following prayer is rendered:

"Almighty God who art ever present, cast thy eye of compassion on this assembly and preserve us who put our trust in Thee, who once for the sins of the world didst drown all mankind, with the exception of Thy servant Noah and his family. We pray Thee as in those days of old to support us as Thou didst the Ark in the wilderness of the waters, and conduct us to Thy celestial Haven of rest where the olive branch of peace flourishes for ever and ever. Grant this, O God. S.M.I.B."

The Grand Master declares the Lodge open with 3 × 2 and 9 knocks. The Holy Volume is opened at Genesis chapter 7, the minutes read and candidates ballotted for.

The Ceremony proper begins with the MC announcing the presence outside 'the door of the Ark' of 2 Master Masons who desire to 'obtain the shelter of Ark and Link Masonry' and he duly gives the password for them. The two candidates are then led 'thrice around the Ark' and kneel for prayer before advancing to the East 'as if ascending the inclined plane that led to the

Ark'. They set their hands on the Bible and take an obligation. The ancient penalty here was to have 'a heavy stone tied round my neck and be thus hurled into the depths of the ocean' It is sealed 4 times on the Holy Volume.

The first 7 verses of Genesis 7 are read and at verse 7 there are 'intimations of Thunder, lightning and rain', after which verses 8 to 13 follow. The candidate is now blindfolded and verses 14 to 17 are read. The candidate is placed in a chair and 'lifted up and down, as well as rocked to and fro' throughout the rest of the chapter and for the first four verses of the next one, when the rocking stops. At verse 9 a sign is imparted, at verse 11 an olive leaf is given to him and at verse 13 the blindfold is removed with the reading continuing until Chapter 9, verse 17. A pedestal is now brought in and set up, after which prayer is offered to the All Wise God.

Whilst solemn music plays everyone now rises and joins the candidate in proceeding round the room once. All but the candidate sit and the secrets are exchanged: The Word is **Enoch**: the password is **Methusaleh**. The sign is as if throwing the dove out of a window with both hands and is answered by stretching forth a hand for the dove to alight on.

The following Lecture was then delivered:

'Now God commanded Noah to make an Ark of Gopher wood, instructing him how to fashion it, denoting the length, breadth and height thereof, with 1, 2 & 3 stories (sic), door and window. It took Noah 100 years to complete it – he was 500 years old when he commenced this great work, consequently he was 600 years old when it was finished. He entered it with his wife, his three sons and their wives. His father **Lameach** (obviously an Irish pronunciation) had died a short time before at the age of 777 years.

'There were no ancient Patriarchs at the time of the Flood, with the exception of **Methusaleh**, the Grandfather of Noah, who attained the age of 959 years and is supposed to have perished in the Flood as no mention is made in Holy Writ of his death. The Ark being finished agreeably to the commands of the Most High, Noah and his family entered and also two and two of all flesh, wherein was the breath of life, and they went in male and female.

'The Flood took place in the year of the world 1656 and destroyed most of the superb monuments of antiquity. **Enoch** had erected two pillars, one of brass and one of marble. The brass pillar withstood the rage of the waters, but the marble pillar fell a prey to them. On the brass pillar was engraved hieroglyphics, signifying that it was the depository of the **liberal arts and sciences** as well as of all the traditions from the fall of man to Enoch's death, which would have been lost had it not withstood the overflowing waters.

'We find that the posterity of **Shem** were the Persians from Elam their Father, the Syrians from Aram, the Hebrews from Eber. The posterity of **Ham** were the Cainites (sic), the Philistines and the dwellers in Africa. The sons of **Japhet** were Gomer, Javan, Meshech and others. The Germans sprang from Gomer, the Greeks from Javan and the Muscovites from Meshech. It is supposed that the family of Shem was the most favoured of God for in Genesis chapter 9, verse 26, we find, 'Blessed be the God of Shem'. Also the family of Japheth received a similar blessing, for which see verse 27 of the same chapter, but Ham received the curse of his father Noah, "Cursed be Canaan, a servant of servants he shall be to his Brethren"

The Lecture thus ended the Grand Master called for the business and labour to be transferred to the Link and Wrestle degrees with the same knocks as he had opened.

The reader will appreciate that attention was given earlier in this book to the Link and Wrestle degrees so there is no need to repeat that detail here. After the latter was completed the Grand Master gave 9 knocks and said: "My Brethren, let us close these Lodges in the firm assurance that the covenant which the Lord made with Noah after the Deluge will never be forgotten and may the blessing which Jacob gained from the Angel ever rest upon you. Amen." All present gave the signs of both degrees and in the name of Noah and Jacob the Grand Master ended the proceedings with 3 × 2 and 9.

Yet the seeds had been sown by Irish warranted military lodges in North America and then in England. The bird may have flown as far as ongoing Ark Mariner Masonry in the Emerald Isle was concerned but the branch had been transplanted and was to bear lasting fruit elsewhere.

It is to North America, as one of the areas where an infant degree was planted, that we now turn. It has already been shown in this book that Antient Freemasonry was flourishing in the American colonies and by 1755 it is claimed that there was already a ceremony called 'The Ark and the Dove'. One 19th century Monitor there says of it:

"This degree, though short, can boast of as ancient and honourable a pedigree (**if masonic tradition be true**) as any other" and to show where it was related it continues, "It cannot be legally conferred on any but royal arch Masons; upon them (if they are found worthy) it is conferred as an honorary degree". A ritual tells us the following:

The Lodge room has four lights in the East, three in the West and one in the South. The North being the place of **Ham** must be in darkness. A transparency with a Rainbow should adorn the East end and an Ark of curtains should be in the centre of the room. **8** Ark Mariners are required 'to form an Ark'.

The Master represents Noah and is called Venerable Patriarch; the SW representing Shem is called the Ark Mariner and the JW as Japhet is called the Ark Mate. The other officers are Secretary, Treasurer, MC, Asst. MC, Inner Watch and Tiler. The Sec. sits to the right of the Patriarch and the Treasurer to his left. The MC sits on the right of the altar.

Since this ceremony is unknown to most British Ark Mariners I shall present it fairly fully but will pass more quickly over sections similar to present British practice. The letters N., S. and J. will be used to designate the main speakers though in America the longer titles prevail.

"N. Shem, my son, what is the hour?
S. My father, it is gray dawn.
N. Shem, my son, what seest thou?
S. My father, I have looked, and lo, the waters are rising over the face of the earth, and if they abate not, all flesh shall perish.
N. Japhet, my son, is the ark made ready, that we may take shelter therein?
J. It is, my father.
N. How is it made ready, my son?
J. All that the Lord God has commanded thee to place therein are even as he has commanded.
N. What now remaineth to be done?
J. To see that none enter the ark save those who are Ark Mariners.
(All come to order with the salutation sign and are proved)
J. My father, with your permission we shall enter the ark.
(Here all enter the ark and the curtains shall be drawn)
N. Is all secured?
J. All is secured.
N. Let us pray: O Lord God, keep us, we beseech Thee, from the perils that assail the wicked world. Give to us who are in the ark peace and harmony. Grant, that we being freed from the sins of the evil age, may so pass through the waves of a stormy life, that we may be finally grounded safely on the Ararat of everlasting peace. S.M.I.B.
N. Shem, my son, is the sacred **O**(live) **L**(eaf) on the altar?
S. It is, my father.
N. Then give notice that I am about to launch a Lodge of Ark Mariners.
(This is done and the Brethren give the r-st-g sign)
N. The ark being shut up and launched upon the great deep, I declare this Lo. of brethren of the Ark and Dove launched and open in due form.

The *reception* of the candidate required 3 apartments: One hung with green and with a table carrying choice food and wine lying east and west, the Patriarch at the head, the Ark Master at the foot and the Ark Mate halfway down one side. The Patriarch invites the newcomer to partake of the food: "Do we not live that we may eat? Tomorrow death may come and we can enjoy the delight of food no more." The Ark Master similarly invites him to drink heartily: "To him that is a fool it giveth wisdom. From the sorrowful it taketh away sorrow, It filleth the veins of the old with the blood of youth. Look, my brother, on the wine when it is red in the cup." Whilst the Ark Mate tries another ploy: "Foolish is the man who saith: restrain thy passions and keep a rein on thy desires; for the desires were given to men that they might have pleasure thereby."

(At this point there should be great confusion and noise and the roof should fall in, with the lights going out. Wailing and groaning arise.)

1st Voice: Alas, alas; we are undone.
2nd Voice: Lo, we are eating and drinking, marrying and giving in marriage and the flood hath come and we shall all be destroyed.

(The candidate is now hoodwinked and unshod as he comes to the second apartment. This is the Ark of Noah lit with 2 windows and a moveable board at its centre. The sound of waves and noise of many creatures should be imitated. The Patriarch has white hair and beard and wears a yellow robe whilst the other principal officers have brown beards and white robes. The Inner Watch (IW) asks who comes.)

MC A poor inhabitant of earth who hastens to escape the great destruction.

IW (To candidate) Dost thou believe that a man should eat to live but not live to eat? Cand. I do.

IW Will thou ever seek to be temperate, lest wine should make thee to err, or strong drink compel thee to sin? Cand. I will.

IW Will thou earnestly seek to be pure in thy life and to govern thy passions and appetites? Cand. I will.

(IW reports to Ven. Pat. who demands password of entrance which is duly given by MC. The candidate enters on the angle of an **equilateral triangle**, has his hoodwink taken off and stands in the East.)

J. The waters prevail, my father: what shall we do?

N. Send forth the dove. my son, and peradventure if she return no more, we shall know that there is yet room for the foot of man upon earth.

(J. releases the dove from a window, more waves and cattle are heard and MC takes the candidate to the South-west corner.)

J. My father, lo. the dove that thou sentest out, she hath found no rest for the sole of her foot, and now she hovereth to and fro near the window of the ark.

N. Stretch forth thine hands, my son, and take her in.

(J. does so, goes to his place, whilst S. looks out of window and repeats the same procedure with N., with the candidate being taken to the North-west.)

S. The waters must be abating, my father, and the tops of the trees must be above the surface for the dove hath an olive leaf in her bill, which she hath plucked in her journeyings.

N. (making the h . . . sign) Praise be to God, my son, the waters are indeed abating; stay yet a little while and send her forth again.

(N. does this himself, the candidate moves to the east and stands on the moveable board. S. remarks that the dove has not returned and N. perceives the summit of a great mountain. The board is pulled away so that the candidate falls and, as if the Ark grounds, all cry, 'Hallelujah')

N. Once more shall we feel the earth beneath our feet. Let us go forth that man may once more be fruitful and multiply upon the earth.

(All leave the ark and enter a third apartment, like the first save that there is **no green cloth or Olive Leaf** on the triangular altar. The MC leads the candidate

8 times round the apartment as N. reads Genesis chapter 8 verses 21 and 22 followed by chapter 9 verses 13 to 16.)

> N. My brother, do you desire to be elevated to the degree of the Ark and Dove, and to be made an Ark Mariner? Cand. I do.
>
> N. Stand then perfectly erect; look upon the rainbow in the east; hold up both hands (H … S …) (and the obligation is taken)

This latter refers to the name of the Grand Patriarch of the Universe, the God of heaven and earth, and to 'this Venerable Lodge of Ark Mariners opened on the Olive Leaf'. It does not state the nature of the penalty but it contains this moving affirmation:

"that I will make every endeavour to be temperate in meats and drinks; that I will seek to lead a pure life and speak no evil of my brother man; that in affliction I will pray for patience to endure, in hope, for whatever it may please God to bring about; that I will avoid, as far as possible, the company of wicked men, nor will I follow the multitude to do evil; but will seek earnestly to be with the right, when the many desert it, and the few uphold it."

The Candidate seals the OB and the Patriarch requests him to hold the Olive Leaf in his right hand as N. recites a passage from Isaiah that will be familiar to any Royal Ark Mariner today. After this the signs, words and tokens are communicated but are not here outlined. The newly admitted Brother goes to the west to be invested and S. says:

"My brother, this apron of white bordered with blue should ever warn you that the purest life cannot escape the waves of trouble. The ark in the centre reminds you of that Only Refuge for the soul – Almighty God, in the hour of death and before the throne of judgement."

(S. sends him to N. for further investiture.)

> N. Receive this collar which by its colours will ever remind you of the promise that God has made to you, and that He who hath promised will surely perform.
> Receive the jewel, the emblem of gentleness and peace. It bids you ever to be at one with your brethren, and to remember that the Ark Mariner ought always to be lowly in heart and to bear himself towards his brethren with courtesy and urbanity.

(The brother is then re-shod in the ante-room and returns to the East where the Patriarch delivers the Lecture, parts of which deserve our thoughtful attention and especially the opening historical section.)

"Those of our Ancient brethren, who attribute to Freemasonry a very great antiquity, tell us, that when, on account of the inquities of man, God determined to visit the earth with a deluge, Noah and his family, among the male members of which the true Masonry existed, were saved from the destructive waters. Thus was the secret art preserved and handed down through the ages to that Most Wise Grand Master, King Solomon, who will ever be esteemed, by the Craft, as the true patron of Freemasonry.

"The Masonry, however, of King Solomon being of an architectural character, and its symbolical language derived from the instruments of architecture, it was but natural that a degree so peculiar in its legend and symbolism as that of the Ark and Dove, notwithstanding its great antiquity, should have become neglected amongst the Jews who were never, in the true sense of the word **a maritime people**. We are therefore indebted, say our ancient brethren, for this degree, to Hiram King of Tyre who had received his Masonic knowledge independently of King Solomon and through a different channel. Tyre being a seaport this degree was conferred upon many seafaring brethren whence, it is supposed, the title Ark Mariner was derived. Through them and their successors the degree has come down to later days."

The axe, the auger (sic) and the saw are now presented and explained but the moral implications are different to British ones today. Hence the axe 'reminds us that we ought to fell down, from the very root, all evil and corrupt habits within our souls, so that we may bear in our lives the fruits of righteousness'. The auger 'by the rents that are made in our hearts by afflictions, more closely unites us to our brethren, in sympathetic friendship and brotherly love'. Whilst the saw 'has the more noble purpose of reminding us that while we are all derived from the one great parent tree of humanity, yet is each man responsible for his own soul to God, and for work, sympathy and help, to his fellows. And as the plank is separated by the saw from the tree so ought we to be separated from the evil that is in the world, and live as good men, and true Masons'.

Finally N. speaks of the **Equilateral Triangle** whose angles are Beauty, Strength and Wisdom and its sides represent God 'in his threefold relation of Self-existence, Revelation and Redemption'. The usual point about attendance follows with this piquant addition:

'If those reasons (for absence) are good, he will respect your position but if they are trivial and unimportant you must be prepared, at the next meeting of your Lodge, to receive a reprimand from its Patriarch.'

The new brother now takes his seat and the Lodge is closed as follows:

N. Shem, my son, what is the hour?
S. My father, the sun is in mid-heaven & shines with exceeding brightness.
N. What seest thou, my son?
S. I have looked, and lo, the heaven above and the waters over the face of the earth.
N. Shem, my son, how long is it since the dove that brought us the olive leaf of hope went forth from the ark?
S. Seven days, my father.
N. Japhet, my son, what seest thou?
J. I have looked and lo, there is a dark line upon the waters as though the highest hill were above the surface.
N. Then let us offer thanks to God.
(Prayer) We thank thee, O God, for thy mercies; we bless thee for thy tender

care, and we pray thee to go with us into a renewed world that we may walk therein as thy children. S.M.I.B.

(There is a GRAND SHOCK)

N. The ark is grounded.
All. Hallelujah.
N. Since the Ark is grounded let us prepare to land, but before we do so let me see that all here are prepared to make themselves known as Ark Mariners. (The signs are given)
N. Shem, my son, give notice that I am about to moor this ark of A.Ms.

(S. and J. both do this)

N. The ark is moored; let us go forth to be the servants of God.
(In more modern versions of this ceremony there is a closing rubric which states that all candidates have to be Master Masons in good standing and each elevated brother is exhorted to become a Mark Master Mason – 'if he be not already such'.)

With this illuminating ceremony before us it is time to re-cross the ocean and resume the story in England.

We left off our story of the prevalence of the Noah legend in public or Masonic writings in the decade following 1750 and it will be worth noting that by that time there were at least two areas of masonic ritual activity that merit our special attention. Whether they relate to any emergence in England of something like the present ritual of Royal Ark Mariner it is impossible to claim but they are important because they show that in any comprehensive approach to Masonic knowledge the traditions that attached to the Noah story were already present and acknowledged. The first of these rituals had been practised in the City and environs of London from at least 1740 and by 1744 a Chapter was operating at Deptford in Kent. It is nowadays known as the ritual of the Royal Order of **Scotland**, for reasons that cannot here be gone into, but its official title is that of 'Heredom of Kilwinning and Rosy Cross'. From one of its various sections we have the following catechism:

Q. What was the first building erected under divine direction?
A. Noah's Ark.
Q. To what intent was it built?
A. To preserve the elect from the Deluge.
Q. How many persons were preserved?
A. 8: four men and four women.
Q. Name the men.
A. Noah, Japhet, Shem and Ham, all masons true.
Q. How many pieces of work by men's hands were called Wonders of the World? A. Seven.
Q. Name them. A. The Tower of Babel...
Q. What things ought Freemasons chiefly to commemorate?

A. Three great events: the Creation of the World, Noah's Flood and the Redemption of Man.

Q. To what intent? A. To the Glory of God."

That this was no purely private and secret practice is shown by known advertisements in the public press. In 1743 notice was given that the Brethren of the Scotch H-d-m, or Ancient and Honourable Order of K-n-g, are desired to meet the Grand Master of the Order and his Officers at the sign of the Swan in Great Portland Street, whilst in 1750 members are similarly informed that the Grand Lodge and Chapter of the Order are to move from the Swan to the Thistle and Crown in Chandos Street, which sounds highly suitable. Men like Dunckerley and Sibley would have been amply aware of its existence and activities.

Meanwhile there was a group of travelling ritualists who were carrying a **Harodim** form of Masonry around the area of the Tyne if not also as far afield as Alnwick, Sunderland, Durham and Hexham. We are now fairly well aware of their forms of working and reference was again made to this influence when we pursued the emergent Mark degree. What is of interest though obviously less in extent is the couple of references that relate to Noah and Nimrod in the Harodim lectures. They are these.

In the Third Section of the Fellowcraft Degree Lecture the well-known question as to what struck the attention of those who sought the middle chamber by way of 'the famous porch' was answered by giving the names of the two great Pillars there. The wording continues:

"Please inform us how the names of those two Pillars originated.

After Noah had built the pillar or altar of sacrifice upon his coming out of the ark, and received the blessing of God on the spot, he called it J . . . which signifies E . . . in commemoration of the **rainbow** which God established in the heavens and three times declared it to be established. This Pillar was in after years greatly increased in size and ornamented by the descendants of Noah and considered a most sacred Treasure, and in every country where they sojourned they built an imitation thereof."

In the Second Section of the same Lecture we are reminded that Masonry and civilization have gone hand in hand, since Cain was not only the first to practise agriculture but was also the first Architect who built a city called Enoch. The lecture continues:

"The next remarkable Masonic period was that of our Grand Master Nimrod employing his masons in the valley of Shinar, when he built a strong city and tower which they called Babel, signifying confusion. From this period of time we date the origin of signs and tokens. Hence our antient brethren dispersed themselves East, West, North and South . . ."

It was Shum Tuckett who, as long ago as 1919, made the proposition that before 1717 there was a store of legend, tradition and symbolism from which only a limited amount was drawn to create what we currently regard as the basic and essential degree. It was, he claimed, from the residue of that store that additional degrees were formed and not only did he set about showing how this took place but he insisted that it was from Britain outwards that Masonry developed rather than by initial importation from abroad. As readers of the earlier parts of this book will by now be aware I would accept this thesis provided that we talk about *British* Freemasonry and recognise that sometimes the seed that originated in these islands had to travel to be further germinated. I have already suggested that whilst all the ingredients for a Mark degree were present at home it was the military lodges with their travelling warrants who probably contributed most to developing and disseminating the additional ceremonies. It seems to me to be very likely that Thomas Dunckerley was first made aware of the emergent Ark Mariner ceremonies during either his last voyages to North America or through his known associations with certain military units and their Antient or Irish connections. As should become obvious when we look shortly at the ceremonies that he and Sibley took part in, Dunckerley might well have had a hand in adapting to English usage ideas and ritual that originated elsewhere. He was a man with his own ideas and the authority to implement them. What we as yet lack is the written evidence which would settle once and for all what part he played in shaping the Ark Mariner degree for home consumption. That someone after 1760 and within 2 decades had done such work is clear. To discover exactly who was the creator of what follows is a continuing research project.

The other figure who has been only briefly mentioned so far, and whom Eric Ward believed might well have been the chief architect of the form of the degree that developed into today's practice, was Ebenezer Sibly. It will be worthwhile to review his life and then consider why his connection with the Ark Mariner degree might support Ward's claim.

Exactly when Sibly was born is still not known but on his own admission it must have been in 1759 and it seems likely that he was the son of Henry Siblys who was noted in the Poll Book for Bristol as a weaver of St. James Parish in 1754. We know that Ebenezer had an elder brother, Manoah, who was born in 1757 and who by 1776 was able to teach Hebrew, Greek, Latin and Syriac as well as shorthand and published 'A Critical Essay' on the Hebrew text of Jeremiah chapter 33 verse 16 – a Messianic verse concerning post-exilic Judaism. The brothers lost their mother in 1768 and it could well be that the older brother felt a sense of responsibility for the younger boy. It is interesting that Ebenezer was in his 21st year before Manoah had married, setting up a bookshop in Bristol and even started a school in which books on alchemy and astronomy were studied. He was later to become a Swedenborgian minister with a permanent place of worship built for him near Ludgate Hill, London, in 1803. It is only a coincidence that his brother Ebenezer was also a student of astrology and surgery, and that both of them moved to the South-east of England. That Ebenezer would have been well-grounded in the Scriptures seems equally clear.

Ward tells us that "Sibly was throughout almost the whole of his adult life first and foremost an author of astrological works, the earliest being published in 1784 when he was about 23. One of these works ran into 12 editions and others continued to be published, mostly in weekly parts, for long after the author's death." He also wrote supplements to the *Herbal and English Physician* by Culpepper and for *The Magazine of National History.* The Culpepper books had a dedication to Thomas Dunckerley. Ward adds: "Whatever value may be placed upon the end product of Sibly's works, it is obvious from their contents that the author knew his subject. Considering the very early age at which he started publishing it seems likely that as a boy he possessed (for his time) a gift for mathematics."[18]

It was also in 1784 that Sibly began to interest himself in Freemasonry for we know that he was initiated in No. 79 (Antients) at Portsmouth on June 7 that year and would thus become immediately aware of the name of Thomas Dunckerley. Something of what this step meant to him is revealed in a foreword which he wrote for a book in 1784 and which was addressed to "Gentlemen and Brethren,

"The Antiquity of your excellent Fraternity, the universality of its plan, and the moral rectitude and purity of its design, claim a decided pre-eminence over every other Bond of Society into which mankind have ever formed themselves ... To you I commit this venerable pile of ancient Astrology; a fabric obviously constructed by the Great Architect of the World, ... and inseparable from one of the grand subjects of your official contemplation ...

"Sheltered, therefore, under the wing of your fraternal regard, and patronised by every sober admirer of the secret works of Nature, I shall attempt to lay the Foundation-stone of an illustrious building, sacred to Urania, upon which some more able and ingenious Workman, sanctioned by your patronage and protection, may hereafter raise the edifice to out-top the skies, and, like Jacob's ladder, pierce the starry regions, leading the intellectual faculties of the soul to the most sublime contemplations of God and Nature.

"I have the honour to profess myself, GENTLEMEN,
Your Accepted Brother ..." (from Portsmouth Common).

A year later he was back in Bristol and his Masonic experience grew rapidly. He was exalted into the Chapter of Charity No. 9 on April 1, joined the Sea Captains' No. 445 (Moderns) on 16 June, and in July became a Knight Templar of the Bristol Encampment (now the Camp of Baldwyn). It is clear that Sibley was assiduous in everything he undertook.

His secular interests were revealed in Felix Farley's *Journal* for 25 September 1784. Under the heading *'To the Curious in Futurity'* we read:

"Mr Sibly's work on the science of Astrology ... with physical observations on the progressive tendency of the earth to its dissolution and an elucidation of the signs and tokens in the sun, moon and stars (etc.). With infelt satisfaction the author informs his Masonic Brethren, to whom this work is dedicated, that the late attempts to suppress his publication, under the vague pretences of its dangerous tendency ... are now removed by total repeal of that statute." This quarto volume was said to contain 'all the secrets of an Art' and was published and sold by W.Nicoll in St. Paul's Church-yard, London.

By September 1785 there was a further advertisement in the same Journal under the heading, 'RICHES AND HAPPINESS'. The content was much as before but on this occasion it had a fuller ending:

"London: Printed for the Author, and may be had at his Historical, Novel and Philosophical Circulating Library, No. 39, Castle Street, Bristol: where are bought and sold Periodical Publications and Books in all Languages – Stationery, Book Binding in all its branches.

"Nativities calculated, pupils instructed and all lawful questions answered with accuracy and honor."

Less than two months after joining the Bristol lodge Sibly served as SW *pro tem.* and in the same evening was appointed Secretary. It was in this capacity that in October he recorded the visit of 'Hanam' (Hannam) with whom we find him later associated in the Ark Mariner venture in London.

At a time when the idea of a National Lottery has once more been accepted by many in English society it is not such a shock to learn that from 1694 to 1826 this form of fund-raising was a regular feature of Government finance and town-life. Nor is it quite such a surprise to discover that Bro. Sibly was an agent for the sale of Lottery tickets. That he was not exactly moving in unsavoury company is confirmed by discovering that William Meyler, Provincial Grand Secretary and later Dep. PGM for Somerset, was also a ticket agent, as was Joseph Winpenny, another Bristol bookseller and fellow Mason. In Sibly's case his expert knowledge of futurity, so claimed, ought surely to have been invaluable in this role but its outcome was all the more humiliating for that same reason.

On 31 December 1785 Sibly advertised a service for country folk of issuing 'certain numbered certificates' as members of 'The Equitable Society of Lottery Adventurers'. This not only used a name that seemed to resemble the 'Amicable Society of Lottery Adventurers', thus angering that body, but gave them the chance (14 January 1786) to warn the public that "a most AUDACIOUS IMPOSITION is now practised at Bristol, under the title of the Equitable Society &c Edward Hoare, Esq. president, to which a Mr. Sibly No. 39 Castle Street Bristol appears as Agent – The Managers of the Amicable Society having every reason from good information to suspect a fraud in this case, sent to the said Mr. SIBLY'S to purchase some certificates."

This uncovered some unhappy facts, such as issuing tickets that were still in the Bank of England, using Hoare's name but it *not being* the reputable Banker, and having a fictitious 'payer of dividends'. It was all very unfortunate to say the least and on 23 January Sibly replied in the Press saying he was away when the attack was made, he would write to the firm concerned and he would re-fund any money so desired or he would place such money as had been paid with another reputable Society. He was writing as 'E.Sibly. Agent to the

Societies'. On 31 January he issued an Affidavit made before the Mayor of Bristol affirming his ignorance of the spurious Society but it was, of course, the end of his activity in this role. It also meant that on 2 March he resigned from the Sea Captains Lodge and he also appears for the last time on the pages of the Chapter of Charity on 5 January 1787.

That he thereafter left Bristol for the South East is revealed first by his advertisement in Farley's Journal for 9 August 1788 stating that the 40th number of 'Sibly's Display of the Occult Sciences' was that day published and on sale at Sellick's of St. James's Back. On 21 April 1789 he was a Founder and First Master of the Lodge No. 253 (Antients) in London (now Lodge of Joppa No. 188), and we also know that he was now studying surgery in a hospital there.

Yet by 1790 he was in Ipswich, Suffolk, and it is here that we first encounter him as associated with the name of Ark Mariners. In Davy's Suffolk Collections (post 1800) we read: "Of this individual (Sibly) I have met with no particulars, except that in the year 1790 he was for some time resident in Ipswich, for the purpose of assisting in support of the interests of the Yellows, or Whig Party, in the then approaching election of Members for the Borough", Davy also quoted from the Ipswich Journal of January 1800: "Lately died in London, Dr. Sibly, better known here by the name of **FATHER NOAH**, from the conspicuous part he took in Sir John D'Oyly's election".

This intimation is expanded by an extract from Clarke's 'History and Description of the Town and Borough of Ipswich' (pp. 116 and 117):

"On the 17th of June, 1790 74 freemen were admitted and ten more the next day (when) 4 candidates were put in nomination as members for the borough ... A great deal of money was spent at this election. Sir John D'Oyley (sic), the personal friend of the governor, had just returned from India with a handsome fortune and he, in a most honourable manner, paid off the debts of his deceased father, who had but a very small estate: this praise-worthy conduct added much to his popularity, and a stratagem was resorted to that tended greatly to secure the freemen in his favour:– a person of the name of Noah Sibley (sic), a man of some parts and oratory, established a club or society, at a house in Saint Clement's, purporting to be a particular branch of freemasonry, called the Good Samaritans, or the **Ark Masons**: the oath of introduction was binding upon every member to unite together in brotherly love and friendship, and to assist each other as much as possible on every occasion: the young freemen in particular were artfully seduced and wheedled to enter as members into this fraternity, and, as Sir John D'Oyley was a **brother Samaritan**, they became bound by their oath to support him: their public exhibitions were attended with much ceremony in their various processions through the different streets of the town, when a **model of Noah's Ark** and a variety of insignia and banners were displayed, and bands of music played before them ..."

Whilst it has to be appreciated that Clarke did not write the above until 1830 the extract does suggest that he had to hand something more than just a vague remembrance of what took place 40 years before. As we have already seen, the title **Noachidae** or **Noachite** had already been in use throughout the 18th century and the Ark, Rainbow, Dove and Triangle were already well known as attributes of Noah Freemasonry. Whilst it seems clear that Sibly, with his ingenious turn of mind, started some politically-directed club or society in Ipswich and tacked on to it both a Masonic name and trimmings, the fact remains that he was able to do so because either he was already engaged in such a Masonic body elsewhere or was sufficiently aware of such a body as to want to adopt its name and purpose. It is somewhat singular that after being brought up in a seaport town he passed through the City and Port of London to produce in yet another port the semblance of a maritime, as well as quasi-masonic, society. To try and discern what might have been his relationship with Ark Masonry in and after 1790 we must here pause before pursuing his final decade of life, and try to discover what had been happening elsewhere.

In the list of Degrees that we have good reason to believe were both commended, amended and practised by Thomas Dunckerley from 1769 onwards – and from which we have earlier illustrated the Mark Man and Mark Master ceremonies – we find, listed **after the Sublime Degree of the Royal Arch** and its Five Points, the degree of Royal Ark Masons. That this was in existence in 1778 is endorsed by the fact that in the list of degrees required of Knights Templar in West Cornwall by that date, and taken by Bro. John Knight, was one with this same name. Let me repeat that John Knight personally acknowledged his debt to Dunckerley for his progress in Freemasonry's further reaches. What exactly the ceremony was that is so described we still do not know because the pages relating to the Royal Ark Mason are apparently not with those for **all** the preceding ones. To discover that must be our aim. What is not directly related to our main story here, but is revealing of then current masonic thinking, is the fact that there was in 1778 a degree known as 'The Knight of the Royal Axe' in which the principal theme concerned the Sidonians who cut down and dressed the Cedars of Lebanon so that they could be used, not in the erection of the Temple at Jerusalem, but for building Noah's Ark. This is but another pointer to the persistent idea that that piece of construction had its necessary Masonic place.

We know, of course, as will shortly be seen, that Dunckerley had a personal interest in Ark Mariner Masonry and linked it with his intense involvement in both the Royal Arch and Knight Templary. It is therefore not impossible that by 1772 there was already some embryonic attempt by London Masons to encourage this further 'adornment' of the Masonic edifice.

On the hitherto available information it certainly seems that Handfield Jones was correct in his assessment that the claim made by some 1871 Statutes of 'the self-styled Grand Lodge of Royal Ark Mariners' was unreliable and inadmissible as evidence. This claim was that 'it has been discovered that, in the year 1772 a Grand Lodge was *re-constituted*', that 'This Grand Lodge has been in existence down to (1870) and the warrant has been transmitted *from one to another*', and 'In London it has been *worked from the year 1772*'. It is rightly objected that these assertions carry no corroborative details to support them and the whole idea that what must have been an infant degree, if it did exist at all at this stage, could sport not just a Grand Lodge but a re-constituted one is seemingly ridiculous.

On the other hand it has to be said that whilst we discard the attempt to give this burgeoning form of Freemasonry too mighty a status there may be a glimmer of truth in the last statement of 1871 above – '*In London* it has been worked from 1772'. Perhaps this is something further that needs to be more closely researched.

What we do know is that by 1780 there is a report, in one of the Masonic Provinces over which Dunckerley had already been a Ruler, that a lodge was practising Ark Masonry. Covey Crump, though giving no detailed information, claimed that some form of Ark ceremony was being worked in Portsmouth. It must have been by the mid 1780s at least that the Ark Mariner degree began to be developed in Bath where the influence of Dunckerley was strong and in 1790 there is actual evidence of a William Boyce having this degree conferred upon him by the KT Camp of Antiquity No. 1, as if this were an already normal event. It is worth noting also that in the same entry at Bath Boyce took 'all the degrees of ye Red Cross' so the association of these degrees is again confirmed.

What may also be more relevant to our search for Ark Mariner degree origins than hitherto thought is the fact that in 1790/91 Dunckerley took the step of 'collecting the scattered Camps (of Knights Templar) and soon had four which he termed 'time immemorial' conclaves, vis. *London*, Observance of Seven Degrees; *York*, Redemption; *Bristol*, Eminent of the Seven Degrees; *Bath*, Antiquity.' (AQC XXVII p. 88) In the light of this coordination it would be worth further study to see whether the new relationship of these degree-conferring bodies led to cross-fertilization between them and whether the fact that working one less well known degree in one Camp led to this being done in the others. Is this how Ark Mariner came from London to Bath or the other way round? The proposition might be worth pursuing further and it will be interesting to consider the new history of York Redemption 'B' Conclave that has just appeared.

As we now return to Bro. Sibly it seems more and more certain that by 1790 or soon thereafter an attempt was being made to do for the Ark degree what Dunckerley was doing for the Knights Templar. Indeed it seems as if Dunckerley was also closely involved in this exercise as was his eventual successor, Lord Rancliffe. Their participation was all the more intriguing because they were prominent 'Modern' Masons whereas the Ark, like the Mark, degree emerged from a definitely Antients source. I have, however, already explained what was probably Dunckerley's strategy in this regard so we need only concern ourselves here with the fact of his involvement.

If Dunckerley found himself dealing with brethren who, like himself, already had some concept of both the value of, and the need for, an Ark

Mariner ceremony as part of ancient Masonry, we still have to discover some kind of link between him and Sibly. There were two possible points of contact. We have seen that in 1785 Sibly became a Knight Templar and in the same year he recorded the visit by a Bro. Hannam in his Bristol lodge. Hannam, however, had by 1790 become Dunckerley's Acting Grand Master in Knight Templary. The link was possibly made there.

Alternatively, Dunckerley was PGM for the area that covered Ipswich in 1790 and he might well have had occasion to summon Sibly to explain what he meant by bringing Masonry into the political arena, and above all by adopting the terminology of the Ark Mariner Masons. We know that Sibly was a good talker. Did he work his charm on the old sailor by explaining his own ideas of how this struggling degree could be even more effectively presented and developed? We do not know, and can only surmise. What is *not surmise* is that from this year onwards Dunckerley and Sibly are close collaborators, a whole ritual for the Ark Mariners appears which is said to be largely Sibly's work, and which shapes the degree in the form we now associate with the term 'Ark Mariner'. Even special jewels and regalia are produced. These latter items will be explained in the last section of this chapter.

Let us therefore turn to the ritual which now appeared. The copy from which I shall quote is dated 1790 but is copied from Bro. Purday's MSS of 1861. It bears the following title on its first page:

> "Royal Ark Lodge or the (**PILLAR**) of an ARK MASON
> Laid open in the form of a **LECTURE** as handed down from Noah to the present time and carefully transcribed from Ancient Records
> By Ebenezer Sibly D(eputy) G(rand) N(oah). 1790."

It opens with a squared drawing of the Nine stairways up the 9 storeys of the Tower of Babel, opposite an 'Address to the Worthy Fraternity of Royal Ark Mariners' which starts as follows:

"Brethren,

In early ages when necessity taught Man the use of Society and the rapid progress they made thereby in Arts and Sciences, it led them to mark and contemplate the nature and properties of **lines, figures, superficies, and solids** and thus by degrees **formed the science of Geometry and Architecture** …". Could this wording be due to the influence of Dunckerley in person or was this copied from his so-far undiscovered version of this degree? It is strangely like the start of his Mark Man ceremony. (see p. 119f)

We next meet Methuselah "who lived 255 years with Adam, by whom he was instructed in all the mysteries of the Sublime sciences, which he faithfully communicated to his grandson Noah, as he died a short time before the deluge". Those possessing this 'Art' after the Flood were called Noachidae or sons of Noah and later, Sages or Wise Men who had been instructed by Moses in the wisdom of Egypt and the Chaldeans. A whole tribe was set aside called 'the children of Issachar' and they were named 'Masters in Israel' and afterwards

'Philosophers'. The 'Art they were in possession of was esteemed Royal as it was practised by Kings and Princes.

"Noah, finding what superiority Geometry and Architecture had over the rest of the Sciences, put Shem to Asia and Japhet to Europe, whilst he himself continued in the city of Apobatarion (sic), built at the bottom of Mount Ararat, and convened Lodges under them with full powers and Instructions in all the Orders and degrees of Masonry. The officers of the first Royal Ark Lodge, having expelled Ham to Africa, who carried his curse and mark with him, at this time began to consider how a permanent Ark Lodge might be established, when immediately were presented to their view Brotherly Love and Immortal Fidelity..."

These qualities having helped form the Fraternity then it had persisted to the present. (At this point, however, I suspect that there is inserted a slice of deeply felt contemporary history.) "It is true that Ark Masonry, like every other part, met with calumny and slander, easier hit off than Praise, for Satire will sooner procure a name for those employing it than (will) Panegyrick. These sordid souls look through all Societies of this kind, and through false and narrow mediums (glasses?) form a judgement of them from their trifling selves in direct contradiction to the Apostle Paul in Phillippians chapter 4, verse 8: "if there be any praise think on these things".

"Unmoved therefore by envy or lucre the Champions of Royal Ark Masonry still persevere in keeping up this laudable Institution and live in affection and friendship with each other ..." and the passage concludes with reflections on Brotherhood, the standards of an Ark Lodge and the fact that 'The man of shining abilities and those unblessed with such ornaments are all equally admitted".

The conversation of Ark Masons is claimed to be 'Wisdom in good humour for all' and the antiquity, universality and moral purity of its design give it 'pre-eminence over every other bond of Union'. It is on this high note that the Candidate is asked to take his obligation. The secrets and mysteries are those of 'this *Supreme Degree of Ancient Freemasonry* denominated *Noachidia* or Ark Mariner' and the penalty is the same as that administered today.

Isaiah Chapter 54, verses 8–10 are now read with some words about 'comfort' that are used today but with this addition: "for the stability of the Lodge is Brethren joined together by Truth and covenanted by Love". Then, after reading the last verse of the Isaiah chapter the hailing sign is given in remembrance of the Rainbow.

The Master, Noah, now delivers the well-known passage: "A Brother's distress may arise from three different causes..." though certain extra phrases and sentences were then included. The Conductor then shews the *Equilateral Triangle* to the Candidate and Noah speaks of its use as again we do today. A 'clean lambskin apron' is now presented 'as the badge of innocence and virtue' but without any mention of Emperor or King. Thus clothed the Candidate is permitted to withdraw with the words: "May the peace of God which passeth all understanding be with you and direct you in all your ways." He is told that on his return the ceremony will be proceeded with.

After his re-entry Noah starts the presentation of the working tools with this sentence: "I inform you that as an Architect and a Mason all the tools of a **Carpenter** and a Mason *belong to you*, but as an Ark Mariner you are only to use such tools as Noah worked with in building the Ark." The axe, saw and auger or borer are now introduced in a manner very similar to that currently used.

There follows a Lecture in the form of a catechism which begins with words about the original land and journeying of Ark Mariners that is now used at the outset of a meeting. Thereafter we have something rather different which is applicable no longer:

Q. What are you, Brother?
A. A Master Architect. (This was a degree that is not now practised).
Q. What is your name?
A. Nechodie (sic). (Should it be 'Noachida'?)
Q. Where did you receive that name?
A. In a regular Lodge of Architecture with a grip and salute belonging thereto.
Q. Are you an Ark Mason?
A. I am taken and accepted as such.
Q. How do you know yourself to be an Ark Mariner?
A. By being admitted a regular Architect and joining a Lodge as such.
Q. But how shall I know you to be such?
A. By strict examination as an Architect?
Q. Bro., how were you prepared?
A. In my mind, and (then) admitted by a friend to a Lodge as a Master Architect where I was ordered to give a certain and distinctive knock.
Q. What was asked from within?
A. Who comes there?
Q. What was your answer?
A. A Master Architect truly proved.
Q. What was your name?
A. Nechomoe. (No search in 'Architect' degrees yet reveals this name.)
Q. What was then said?
A. Enter Nechomoe.
Q. What did you enter upon?
A. The point of a Triangle presented . . . (and then as today).
Q. Into what did you enter?
A. The body of a R. Ark M's Lodge.
Q. How were you then dealt with?
A. I was taught to stand erect **upon a square** with my right arm up in the posture of an Architect giving his salute and then to **step around** the beautiful form of the Lodge which is a **Triangle**. After which I heard a prayer.
Q. How were you then dealt with?
A. I was told to stand erect with both hands on **the VSL** and to take an obligation.
Q. What was next given to you?

A. The hailing sign (as today).
Q. After you received this H.S. what were you next informed?
A. That by my voluntary engagement I was bound to answer all lawful s. and s. if I was found within my cable tow.
Q. What was the Mark on your summons?
A. A Triangle marked on the inside with the initials **N.J.S.** and on the outside with **G.L.M.**
Q. How long is an Ark Mariner's cable tow?
A. Its length is not known for it comprises the time of the Ark floating and that of the Ark resting on Mount Ararat in Armenia.
Q. How were you next dealt with?
A. I was told to be seated and was presented with a clean lambskin apron (and the words as used earlier).
Q. What were you next presented with?
A. The working tools (and they are now fully described as above and today)."

Whilst this completes the ritual proper there are 2 additional sheets with the MS. One shows an ark at rest with its one door closed and its triangular window in the roof. Below this is a triangular arrangement for the 'ARK' as a lodge with **N** at the apex, and **J** and **S** at the left and right corners respectively of the base. The Treasurer is placed to the right of J and the Secretary to the left of S. The rest of the Ark Mariners line the sides of the triangle and three lights are placed, one inside each angle.

The other page shows an ark sailing on the waters with the dove and rainbow above it. Around the rainbow it reads "Royal Ark Mariner Lodge", whilst beneath the ark is 'No. 9'. There is then another triangle which is divided up internally into 7 other triangles with letters attached to the lower three. All of this is accompanied by wording that shows this to have been a model 'Certificate' to be given to any elevated brother by his lodge officers.

It can thus be seen that as early as 200 years ago the lineaments of our present ceremony were already in place and if, as was suggested earlier in this book, a certain manner of stepping along a figure **Y** was transferred to this degree, since it was not taken up in the Mark ceremonies, then all the main features were available *other than the Porphyry Stone* which was only introduced at a much later date. More will be said about that in the latter part of this chapter.

We can now resume the story of Sibly and others' involvement with the degree and it would seem that in 1793 Dunckerley became the Grand Commander of the Society of Ancient Masons of the Diluvian Order of Royal Ark and Mark Masons. The year is significant because the later Statutes of 1871 were to claim that in November of 1793 a Warrant or Charter 'sanctioned by the Grand Lodges of England under the old Constitution before the Union in 1813' showed that HRH the Duke of Clarence had been pleased to accept the office of Grand Commander. Several Masons of distinction appended their signatures and certain seals were also attached making this 'a curious and valuable document'.

Handfield-Jones remarks that though one of the seals bearing the device of the Ark, Rainbow and Sun on a red background seemed to show a genuine Ark Mariner style the other two were very suspect. One of these has the words 'The Ancient Grand Lodge of the Ancient Freemasons of England' but with an attempt to block out the first 'Ancient'; whilst the second has a circular piece of paper with a rainbow ribbon, the words 'Union of Ancient and Modern Masons' and 2 interlaced triangles that are almost covered by a seal that has a 2 pillared arch. Whilst this latter combination creates a real sense of confusion with its pre-Union designs and its post-Union words it would at least accord more with the last words on the document which are "This Royal Warrant Revived in the year of Royal Ark Mariners 4165 i.e. 25 years later signed" John F.Dorrington, Grand Commander. The fragility of this document as evidence, however, is here again revealed by the fact that if this final clause is meant to substantiate the dates '1793 in the year of Masonry 5793 and of the Grand or Royal Ark 4142' then the difference is not **25 years** but **23**. Of Dorrington we shall hear more before long.

That Clarence was head of the Royal Arch at this period and that this would accord with the RA style seal seems reasonable but quite what the point of this document was, other than to claim a later doubtful tradition of authority, is a mystery. That it was a fabrication seems clear. What we can more surely repeat is that not only in 1793 but also in 1794 Dunckerley was Grand Commander of the Ark Mariners as he was also Grand Master of the Knights Templar. These two bodies were referred to by him as 'the United Orders'. Was this perhaps **the Union of Ancient and Modern Masons** that was mentioned above? What is certainly worth reflecting on is the suggestion by Eric Ward in his AQC paper on the Baldwyn Rite that the link of the two Orders perhaps reflects a desire of Dunckerley to have Ark Mariners as a naval version of the Knights Templar. That theory certainly gains credence when we consider the 'Grand Royal Ark Vessel' plan below.

In October 1793 Sibly joined, or was re-exalted in, Lodge No. 240 (Ancients) in London and was now practising as a surgeon and Doctor of Medicine. He had graduated with that degree at Aberdeen University the previous year. In Wilke's 'Directory to the Nobility' (sic) we note that he was residing at 12, Grafton Street, Tottenham Court Road, and by now was probably separated from his wife, Charlotte Thomas Sibly.

The degree was certainly developing in 1794. It was being worked in the Baldwyn Chapter at Bristol and also in the Old Kent Lodge in London where it was conferred alongside the Mark and Cryptic degrees.

On Sunday 12 January 1794 5 brethren were **dubbed Ark Bro.** in this Kent or No. 8 Lodge and this was a special meeting at which Isaac Moseley as Deputy Grand Commander Noah appointed a Bro. Durisk as Noah, 2 other brethren as Japhet and Shem and yet others as 'officers of this Royal Ark Vessell' (sic). These officers appointed a Bro. Hoare as 'Captain' and Bro. Lewis as 'Watcher'.

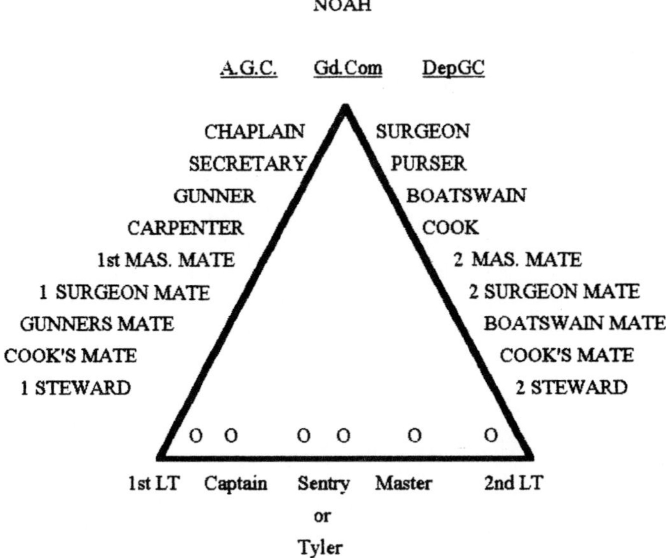

There is evidence also that a lodge was held at the Bedford Arms, Bedford Square, London, where the names of Isaac Moseley as Acting Grand Commander Noah and Charles Sinclair as a member appear. It is of interest to note that the same fee of 5/3d was charged here for the Ark Mariner, Mark Man, Mark Master, Master, Excellent and Super Excellent, whilst the Red Cross and Knights Templar candidates paid 10/6d.

On August 16 being the birthday of his Royal Highness the Duke of York, it was celebrated with all the honours of Masonry by 'The United Orders' assembled at the Surrey Tavern in the Strand, being summoned by Thomas Dunckerley. An elegant supper was provided and the Grand Master gave the following toasts:

The King and the Craft:
The Prince of Wales, Grand Master of Symbolic Masonry:
HRH The Duke of York, with a **thrice hearty** wish that HRH may be blest with health and happiness, and long remain a **terror** to the enemies of Great Britain:
The Duke of Clarence, Grand Patron of **Royal Arch Masons**:
Prince Edward, Grand Patron of Knights Templar:...
Lord Howe, and the wooden walls of Old England. (The naval theme again)

To add an authentic touch to this occasion we might here record two verses of a song that was probably sung on that night and which was composed by 'NOAH' Sibly as he was now known.

"Thus to us is given the cause of the Flood,
And how all true Masons together combin'd,

To enter the Ark for they well understood,
For protection no other place ever could find;
    Where every want
    Was quickly supplied,
    Joy, Peace and Contentment,
    So freely reside.
That Noah e'en after the Flood did agree,
The Ark should be sacred to free Masonry.

Then let us like Noah the Ark enter in,
And keep up the Lodge so justly renown'd,
For we as descendants of **Japheth** or **Shem**,
The **Sciences** love, and with us are found
    The true principles
    That lead to delight,
    That make us like Noah,
    Stand truly upright,
Then fill up a Bumper and toast it around,
To all true ARK MASONS, like NOAH of old."

Was it at such a gathering, or with such brethren as would there be assembled, that Dunckerley might have tried out his idea of what he thought the style of lodge and officers ought to be? We have no reason to believe that this 'blue-print' was ever acted upon but it is so very **naval** and so precisely thought out that it bears the mark of Dunckerley. Could it be that had he lived longer than the following year this kind of imprint might have been more fully set upon the future Ark Mariner ceremony? What is certain is that the Grand Commander had plans to enhance the Ark Mariner contribution to Masonry and especially to give a much more maritime and Service flavour to what might otherwise be considered a purely land-based Society.

Dunckerley died in 1795 but not before he had appointed Sibly as his Deputy. It was in that capacity that Sibly welcomed Lord Rancliffe as the next Grand Commander and the former was to continue in the same office until he himself died at the age of 40 in 1799. It is also in November 1795 that we have a letter written by W.Hannam announcing Dunckerley's death and recommending Lord Rancliffe as the Grand Master of the Knights Templar, 'the more so from his being a Colonel in the Army'. Indeed Col. Thomas Boothby Parkyns, as he was first known, was in Ireland with his Regiment when his ascendancy to the Peerage was announced.

Lord Rancliffe is represented as being a middle-sized man, with pleasing and expressive features. He was well-made and active, being slender and with the deportment of a man of fashion. He was known as a zealous Patron of Freemasonry and, somewhat in the mould of his better known predecessor, he was Provincial Grand Master of Nottingham in 1783, Derbyshire from 1789 to 1792, Rutland from 1789 to 1798 and of Leicester from 1793, being succeeded there by his son in 1812. He was also Prov. Gd. Superintendent of Leicestershire and Rutland from 1793.

This was the brother who followed Dunckerley as Grand Master of the Knights Templar and whose pro-Grand Master was William Hannam, Provost Marshal of His Majesty's Foot Guards. This too was the Irish Peer who now became the Grand Commander of the Ark Mariners, with Ebenezer Sibly as his Deputy and Robert Gill as Assistant Grand Noah. That he took at least as much interest in this Order as in the Midland Provinces was shown in the following year when we have a Charter of Warrant issued by him. This empowered Robert Gill, Isaac Moseley, Charles Sinclair, William Jones and William Cooper to grant Dispensations and Warrants to regularly registered Ark Mariners *to command such vessels* as are appointed and commissioned to them. The fuller description of this well embellished document is given in the section on regalia in the last part of this chapter.

That this system worked is revealed by just such a dispensation as follows:

"A Dispensation granted **on board the Grand and Royal Ark Vessel** moored at the Surrey Tavern, Strand, London.

I do hereby authorize and empower our Trusty and well beloved Brother Charles Sinclair from this time to assemble and *hold a Royal Ark Vessel* under this dispensation on all lawful occasions and reasonable times, to *Enter Ark Mariners on board* until they are qualified to receive a Warrant from the Grand and Royal Ark Vessel, provided the above Brothers pay a due respect thereto, otherwise this Dispensation be of no force or virtue.

Given under my hand and seal this 5th day of the 9th month from the year of the Flood 3348 and the 26th of October in the year of our Lord 1796. AGCN Robert Gill."

This brother was no mean person. In 1795 he was Junior Grand Warden of the Antients Grand Lodge and Senior Grand Warden in 1796. He was a real Traditioner being not only a member of several Antients lodges but belonging also to a Moderns lodge. He was to be Senior Grand Warden at the Union of the Craft Grand Lodges in 1813 and he was also in high office in Great Priory. His name is also well remembered because due to a fire which burned his house to the ground many priceless records were lost which might have thrown further light upon these early days of the Royal Ark Mariner degree.

As an indication of the progress of the degree we have what is stated to be a form of the ceremony which dates from 1797. It is copied from the William Watson Manuscript of West Yorkshire and is interestingly attached to a contemporary form of Royal Arch working as well as to a Knight Templar certificate. We now know that this kind of connection would then have been both natural and expected.

The ritual here considered has at last a definite Opening but no Closing ceremony. The triangular shape of the lodge is drawn at the head of the document and is identical with the drawing at the end of the 'Sibly working' given already. There is then the following dialogue:

N(oah). Sons, be upright. It is my will and pleasure that the Royal Ark Lodge (note, not Vessel) be opened for all business that may come before it.
Sons. Thy will be ours, Father. So let it be.
N. Glory to God on high, and peace to us on earth.
(He strikes pedestal with **axe** and opens the Sacred Volume on Isaiah chapter 54, verses 5, 9, 10.)

Though the VSL is nowadays replaced by the 'Porphyry Stone' it is worth remarking that later in this ritual, as at present, verses 8 to 10 are used. The substitution of verse 8 for verse 5 is very appropriate whilst also providing a continuous passage.

This document also shows that on the VSL are placed the square and compasses in the 3° position. There is also this diagram

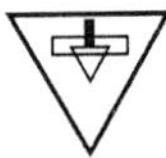

without any comment but whether this means that a triangle is now changed round to have its apex facing West with an ashlar and trowel upon it has not yet been revealed.

After the present opening query by Noah and response by Shem, it is the latter (for there are **no deacons**) who is detailed to go and prepare the candidate(s) 'according to our Ancient clothing . . .'. The candidate is prepared as for the 3° and when enquired of at the door says: 'A Master **Architect** tried and proved' and also gives his name as today, to which N. responds 'Enter N . . .'.

Immediately J. carries out the same practice as today, the candidate does not salute but makes certain steps to form a triangle before a prayer which, whilst containing the elements of that now used also reveals significant differences and much greater biblical detail.

'O thou Great and Glorious Architect of Heaven and Earth, who spoke and it was done, who commanded and it stood fast; we the creatures of thy Power preserved by thy Grace and Favour, humbly beg the fulfilment . . . this evening to initiate a Brother . . . from the overwhelming deluge. Endow him with the Grace of Thy Holy Spirit that he may prove a true and faithful Brother and be able to enforce the spiritual mysteries of Masonry. May he be as constant and industrious as Noah, as faithful as Abraham, as upright as Jacob, as patient as Lot, and may the purity of him who was separated from his brethren and the wisdom of Solomon dwell in him.

O Thou who did meet Jacob by the way, Gideon in the field, and Moses by the bush, meet and bless him. Bless him in his going out and in his coming in, in his basket and in his store, may he enjoy the upper and the lower spring blessing, so as to be rich in faith and good works, given to hospitality, so that the blessing of those ready to perish may come upon him.

May he love the brotherhood unfeignedly. May a **Ham** never be found amongst us but may we by well-doing so conduct ourselves . . . called forth by our Supreme Grand Noah we may find a Blessed Asylum in the Mansion of Eternal Rest. S.M.I.B.'

Careful consideration of this one prayer alone is sufficient to alert the student of this degree to the richer masonic context within which the Ark Mariner degree had arisen and taken its place. Each of the names used in it could evoke some aspect of late 18th century practice between the sacrificial mountain top of Moriah and the burning bush of the Sinai desert. For anyone who may have then wondered where the Ark Mariner degree fitted such a recital must have provided many answers.

Noah now addresses the candidate:

'As you have been presented to your Master, the Maker of heaven and earth, for his blessing, there is no objection to initiating you amongst the brethren by a solemn engagement which I presume you are willing to take or enter into?'

On receiving the candidate's assent the obligation is administered. It is shorter than the one now used and has two phrases of interest – 'in the presence of God and before this worthy and worshipful Royal Ark Lodge ... this supreme degree of Ancient Freemasonry denominated Noachidia'. It ends after 'lawfully assembled' but the penalty is the same.

Noah now reads the Isaiah passage and follows it with another variation from present practice:

"You may with truth now meet Brethren with that promise of God in your right hand, a promise that will comfort ... all Eternity, for the Stability of the Lodge is brethren joined by Truth and cemented by love. He has given us a promise collectively in the same Chapter and the last verse thus (and he reads: No weapon ...)."

The grip now exchanged is not one used today but the word is the same. The only other sign indicated is the Hailing sign and this is the one nowadays reserved for the ceremony of Installing a Worshipful Commander. The purpose and property of this latter sign is now explained and is seen to be similar to the present day purpose of the 6th sign.

As we saw in the Sibly ceremony N. now gives the discourse on the 3 causes of a Brother's distress. Whilst the first section is almost identical the second has a further verse of John's Epistle inserted and ends with the words 'and the **sign itself** cannot fail to obtain relief unless the Brother's heart has turned to stone'. The later dropping of this clause can be well understood when we hear the same third section as today. The sign that is now pointed out and its import is identical with ours.

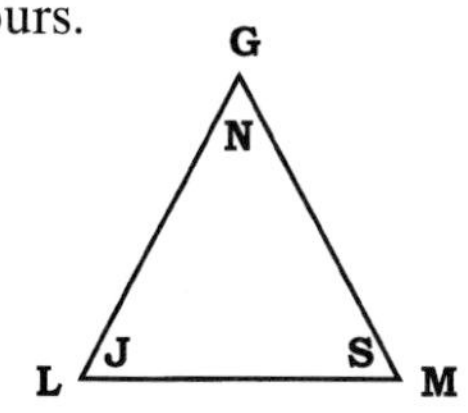

G
N
L J S M

The candidate receives a clean lambskin apron and its use is described in familiar terms save that it is still the 'badge of innocence and virtue' and no Rulers are mentioned. With the delightful words from Noah "May the peace of God which passeth all understanding be with you and direct you in all your ways" the candidate withdraws.

On his return Noah presents the tools in a form very close to our present practice save that the distinction between being a Master Architect and an Ark Mariner is again underlined and a Borer replaces the Auger. The following Lecture is still in the shape of a Catechism and is a reproduction of the one earlier given.

Such is the nearest we can yet discern of what happened in the Ark Mariner meetings over which Sibly, now generally known as 'Noah' Sibly, would preside or which he would expect as he visited in his office of Deputy Grand Commander of the Order.

Of his work as an author there is still further evidence. Two volumes of 'A Complete Illustration of the Astrological and Occult Sciences' appeared in 1796 and 1797 and they reveal that his address was now No. 1 Upper Titchfield Street, Cavendish Square. As in one of his earlier works Sibly called himself 'Astro-Philo' and was clearly eager to be associated with a gallery of notable astrologers including Nicholas Culpepper and William Lilly. As a writer he composed not only books but also songs and it was to him in this guise that the writer of a letter in the Monthly Magazine referred to in December 1798.

"Let our worthy Noachite speak, or rather sing, for himself and his fraternity.

> 'They entered safe – lo. the deluge came on,
> And none were protected but masons and wives,
> The crafty and knavish came floating along,
> The rich and the beggar of profligate lives;
> It was now in woe,   For mercy they call,
> To old Father Noah,   And loudly did bawl,
> But Heav'n shut the door, and the ark was afloat,
> So perish they must, for they were found without.'

There is (continued the correspondent) doubtless something affecting and tragical in this composition ..." and the reader may indeed reflect that the author of this song was not unknown in East Anglia from where we obtained a dramatic folk-tale version of this same Deluge scene.

The contributor to the Magazine also made two other observations which are pertinent to our study. The first had to do with the reference to 'Masons' in the Ark. He says: (Author's emphasis)

'With Brother Sibley's (sic) leave, I should suppose that these venerable and ingenious builders of the ark ought rather to be called **carpenters** or **shipwrights** than masons; but perhaps they will plead as an apology for adopting that appellation, that Noah was commanded to **pitch**, or rather as the Hebrew expresses it, **plaster** the Ark. Genesis chapter 6 verse 14. But this kind of plastering is very different from mason's work, so called. I am afraid, then, that the modern **Noachites** have no grounds for calling themselves Masons." The reader of an earlier passage in this book will perhaps see why some attention was given to this repeated query as to the link between two allied Crafts.

In the body of his letter the correspondent spoke of 'one of the new degrees in Free Masonry which has not been noticed by any writer on that subject. The brothers of this institution are distinguished by the high-sounding appellations of 'The Fraternity of the Royal Ark Mariners, Mark, Mark-Master, Elected of Nine, Unknown, Fifteen, Architect, Excellent, and Super-Excellent Masons, Etc.

You must observe that they profess themselves to be followers of Noah (and in ONE respect they doubtless are so. See Genesis 9: 21); therefore they call themselves **Noachidae or sons of Noah** ... These brother mariners wear in lodge time a broad sash ribbon representing a rainbow, with an apron fancifully embellished with an ark, dove, etc...'

It can thus be seen that Ark Masonry was not entirely hidden nor was it so insignificant that it could escape attention by the public. The Order which Sibly served in the necessary absences of the Grand Noah was alive and well. Albeit its days of being managed by a Grand Lodge were fast coming to a close the degree was now firmly established as a facet of English Freemasonry and it would, as we shall see, persist in some form or another throughout the next century.

Meanwhile Sibly moved to New Bridge Street in the City of London and joined or, as this owed allegiance to the Moderns, was re-exalted into Caledonian Chapter No. 2 on 24 April 1799. It was his last masonic step for by the end of that year he had died. We learn from his will that he had a daughter called Urania and she was left certain proceeds from his patent medicines and tinctures and, until she was of age, in the guardianship of a Mr. Chamberlain. If she died the money was to go to the children of his **two** brothers, Manoah and Job. His whole estate realised less than £2000.

Of the other brethren with whom 'Noah' Sibly was associated by the 1793 Interim Warrant **Isaac Moseley** first continued in his calling as a publisher and as a member of the Ark Mariner Lodge attached to the Old Kent Lodge No. 15. His name also appears, however, at the head of the list of those who printed two warrants (Nos. 1 & 2) which were used in America. These documents had obviously been prepared before 1799 since they both bear the name of Sibly who was not alive after that year. Moreover they were both issued for the formation of Knight Templar Encampments, one at New London, Connecticut and the other in New York State.

The names of the recipients of No. 2 warrant were, interestingly, 'our well beloved *Isaac Moseley, MD, Past Acting Grand Master*; the Rev. Samuel Peters, LLD, and Stephen Thorn of Granville, County of Washington, State of New York'. Quite of what Moseley had been Acting Grand Master is not clear but it certainly seems that he had left the London scene to pursue his life on these foreign shores.

Charles Sinclair was also a member of the same Kent Ark Mariners, in 1784 declined the office of Grand Secretary in the Antients Grand Lodge and then became tyler in a Moderns lodge and even Grand Tyler in the Premier Grand Lodge. It is again interesting to note that not only does his name appear as one of those printing this No. 2 warrant but he is named as the 'Secretary' to 'Rancliffe CGM' who authorised it. He was later to fall on evil times and in July, 1810 he was even minuted in the Kent Lodge records as having tried to sell the Royal Ark Mariners warrant for £3.

Robert Gill was a member of an Ark Mariners Lodge No.6 meeting at The Crown, Wapping Wall, in September 1799. He also appears after Rancliffe on the above 1803 warrant with the initials A.F.C.H. His further progress we have already mentioned. **William Hannam** likewise figures as one of the printers of the warrant but was prominent only in Knight Templar circles.

Was it perhaps the removal of such determined characters as Dunckerley and Sibly that led to the demise of the 'Ark Mariners Grand Lodge', especially as Lord Rancliffe was to die in 1802 and Bros. Gill and Sinclair clearly moved into the Moderns camp? On present evidence we cannot know but what we shall now see is the emergence of the Ark degree in provincial and private settings and without the input from London.

THE CONTINUING SCENE

In the well-known Chapter of Friendship at Portsmouth eight brethren were elevated to the degree of 'Mark Mariner' in 1801 whilst in 1802 we have evidence that the ceremony was worked in Leicester and nearby Hinckley. An Antients lodge, No. 91, in Leicester has an Ark Mariner seal which is preserved in the Museum there and that dates from the early 19th century, but in Norwich for 1802 there is a seal of the Perseverance Lodge.

It is at this point that the work of William Finch has to be looked at and in his book 'Masonic Treatise' (1802) there are letters of appreciation from various sources and the first from Thomas Ashcroft who describes himself as RWM of the Mariners Lodge No. 362, Liverpool. We know also from Finch's 'Freemason's Heureka and Guide' that this degree was portrayed in the same sequence of ceremonies as those which had already been associated with Dunckerley. Royal Ark Mariners comes after Mark Man, Mark Master, Architect, Grand Architect, Pass Master (sic) Red Cross of Babylon, and the Holy Royal Arch (in 11 points).

Of the Ark Mariners Finch wrote: "This degree, though generally given long after the Craft and Arch ought to precede the whole, for it is antecedent to all the Orders of Masonry. It consists of four points, and is very sublime. It ought to be known to every Brother who has been raised to the degree of a Master Mason."

We do not only have this brief commentary on the rite. We also possess a specific work by Finch relating to the degree and yet, as we have just seen, set within a much greater framework. As the Preface to this ritual he says that the key to Freemasonry 'represents from the Creation, the **Logos** or great name – from the Garden of Eden to the Deluge, and from the wise Master Builder Noah, to Moses in Egypt, and the Exodus from that bondage – the passing the Red Sea, giving the law from Mount Sinai, sojourn in the Wilderness, gaining possession of the Holy Land, building of the Temple, destruction and re-building – the Advent of our Saviour, Incarnation, Resurrection and Ascension, – and ends with the triumphs of the Prophecies'. It is quite a scenario.

This form of Ark Mariner ceremony resembles the Sibly one in that it begins with a catechetical form of lecture before any semblance of what we would regard as a working today. Where the content is similar to, or the same as, that presently used, it will be abbreviated but there are some passages that need reproducing for masonic study.

Q. What do the T(riangle) and P(oints) represent?
A. Noah and his two sons, Shem and Japheth.
Q. Why is Noah's second son excluded?
A. For exposing his Father to his Brothers, which occasioned that heavy curse falling on his posterity; for about 800 years after, the Israelites, descendants of **Shem**, took possession of Canaan, destroyed most of its inhabitants and laid heavy Tributes on the Remainder; and afterwards the Greeks and Romans, the descendants of **Japheth**, brought into subjection the Relicks of Canaan, who settled in Tyre, built by the Sidonians, in Thebes, built by Cadmus, and in Carthage, built by Dido; so that Canaan and his posterity became slaves to both their brethren, Shem and Japheth.

We now learn that Ham's folk went South and Japheth's North and West, 'and possessed not only all Europe, and lesser Asia, but Media likewise, and part of Armenia, Iberia, Albania, and the vast regions towards the north now inhabited by the Tartars'. Shem's folk went East.

The triangle and points further indicating the Sun, Moon and Stars is because 'Those who move in the highest sphere have ... power equal with the Stars of the firmament'. There is now a 'full definition of Noah's Ark and likewise the nature, cause and consequence of the General Deluge'. Having given the measurements in *yards* the explanation continues

"It is highly worth being mentioned, and reflected on, that notwithstanding the experience of above 4000 years since, yet human ingenuity cannot now contrive any proportions better adapted than those of the Ark were, not only to resist the force of the waters and the winds, but also for all the purposes it was intended for."

There now follows a long dissertation on the prevalence of sea creatures in the highest mountains such as the Alps, the Appenine, the Pyrenees, Libanus, Atlas and Ararat (where search hath been made), from Japan to Mexico. Moreover the Moose-deer of America is buried in Ireland, Elephants of Africa in central England; Crocodiles of the Nile in Germany; and large trees 'with their roots and tops, at the bottom of Mines and Marles'. How all this could be is only answered by recognising that 'these events perfectly demonstrate Moses's account of this matter to be incontestably true'. This all happened because the fountains of the deep were broken up and then shut up again by God. Such is a tradition all over the world.

"And the inhabitants of all parts give some account of the manner of the restoration of mankind through the indefatigable exertions of ROYAL ARK MASONS…"

There now follows a meditation on the vast numbers lost in the flood – '2 millions of millions of souls, which they think a greater number than what is at present on the earth' – and the awareness of their sinful foolishness in the face of Noah's being saved. The passage closes with this peroration:

"And that man might know that this was so, He (God) publicly declared that He would destroy all the inhabitants of the earth, and the manner in which he intended to do it, 120 years before he put it into execution, that all succeeding generations might know that it was HE, even HE, that had done it; and from hence learn to fear HIM, before whom all the **Nations are as a drop of the bucket, and are counted as the small dust of the balance; yea, even are less than Nothing and Vanity**.'

The G.Commander now puts an obligation which is the same as Sibly's, and on receiving its affirmation says, "You are at liberty to make known the history of our excellent order.

To every Royal Ark Mason (sic), be it known, notwithstanding the recent vengeance (or that) the Deity had given the Rainbow as a sign of reconciliation … the descendants of Noah, from their want of faith in the divine prediction, being apprehensive of a second deluge, said: Let us build a city whose top may reach the heavens, and let us make a name lest we be scattered abroad upon the face of the earth – To accomplish their designs they began to erect a high tower in the plain of Shinar but this enterprise being displeasing in the eyes of their Maker … he obliged them to discontinue the project by confounding their language.'

We are now given a 'Form of Examination' that reveals how a ceremony was developing.

'How do you and I meet?	On the Square.
How do we part?	On the Level, I hope.
From whence came you?	From Armenia.
And where are you going?	Where the Gd.P. pleases to direct.
What are you?	An Ark Mason
Advance to me as such.	(Done)
Do the steps demand anything else?	Yes: a sign, token and word.

Give them to me. (Done, but not specified)
What is the meaning of that Word? ⊏⊐V⌐LL ⌐⊏Λ⌐□
What is the meaning of the Grip? At the time Noah and his family entered into the Ark they helped each other with this grip. (The grip is exchanged and the candidate declared 'a just Bro.')
Have you that solemn engagement? I have.
Pray repeat it. (The obligation repeated)
What was then said to you? I was informed that I had then made a covenant with the Brethren, and the Grand Geometrician of Heaven and Earth had condescended to make a covenant with me as proclaimed by the Prophet Isaiah in chapter 54 verses 8 to 10. And that *the square and compasses and triangle were always laid upon these verses* whenever an Ark Lodge was opened.
What was then given you? The Grip and Word.
Have you that Grip and Word? I have.
Then you will be good enough to give them to the Bro. on your right.'

Finally there is a section entitled 'Reasons' which is a series of Questions and Answers referring to various actions or teachings in the ceremony.

Q. When you were made an Ark Mason you informed me that you were an **Architect** and that in that manner you were led to the door of an Ark Lodge where you were taught to give one certain & distinct knock: Why?
A. Because it was the first Ark Lodge.
Q. There is another reason?
A. Because there was but one man employed by God in building the Ark and but one God worshipped at that time.
Q. You told me you were passed into the Lodge by the name *Nichodian*: what does that mean?
A. The first Mason is the son of Noah.
Q. You were ordered to stand erect to receive the benefit of prayer: why is prayer made use of in an Ark Lodge?
A. As all men are intimidated when they are about to be made Ark Masons prayer is made use of to take off that fear as well as to crave the approbation and benediction of God in the candidate for Masonry.
Q. You then told me you took 3 regular steps & stood erect to receive an Ark Mason's voluntary engagement with both hands on the Holy Word: why?
A. The reason of the steps is the form of the lodge & standing erect to enter into the engagement is the form Noah stood in when he offered up the sacrifice to God for his safe deliverance from the Deluge. His sacrifice having been accepted & his prayer heard it was certainly the most proper position to place me in.
Q. Where is an Ark Lodge to be held when duly erected?
A. On a high hill or in a low valley.
Q. Why on a high hill?
A. Because the Ark was built on a high hill & rested on a high hill in Armenia, called Mount Ararat.
Q. Why in a low valley?

A. Because Noah rested in a low valley at the foot of Mt. Ararat.
Q. What was Noah's first duty?
A. To offer up a sacrifice to God of any clean beast for his safe deliverance, to beg His protection & instruction in what he was further to be employed.
Q. What were God's instructions to Noah and his family?
A. The sacrifice having been offered God was pleased & made a covenant with Noah, and all Ark Masons, that they should stand as long as time should endure; and commanded them to multiply and replenish the earth.
Q. What was thc cause of the Ark being built?
A. SIN.

There now follow the details of the time and size of the Ark's building, and we continue:

Q. How was it secured from the weather?
A. By being pitched within & without with pitch.
Q. Why was it pitched?
A. To keep the waters free from penetrating it, it being over hardened by God's love.
Q. How was it divided? A. Into 1st, 2nd and 3rd stories (sic).
Q. What entrance was there A. One door.
Q. Where was it placed? A. In the centre of the side.
Q. What form was the door? A. 12 cubits high & 10 wide.
Q. Why was it placed in the side?
A. That whatsoever entered and turned to the right hand or the left would be safe.
Q. Is there another reason why?
A. There is but one way to God & but one entrance into Heaven.
Q. How many windows were there? A. One only.
Q. Where was that placed? A. In the centre of the top.
Q. Why so?
A. As the eye of God is in the centre & He beholds all things, so the window was constructed in the centre to light every part of the Ark.
Q. What form was the window? A. A Triangle.
Q. Why so?
A. Because it represented the Ark Lodge & the triangle supporting it. The occupants of the 3 storeys – Family, clean and foul beasts – having been described.
Q. What was the year, month and day on which the Ark floated?
A. On the 17th day of February in the year from Adam 2256.
Q. How many years since the commencement of the Flood? A. 3.
Q. How long was the flood on the earth or Noah in the Ark?
A. One calendar year and 10 days. For he entered the Ark on the 17th day of the 2nd month in the year from Adam 2256 and quitted it on the 27th day of the 2nd month 2257.

There is now a short discourse on the subsequent events including Ham being expelled to Africa 'with his curses marked upon him'. The other sons went North and East whilst Noah rested in the valley APOBATERION.

'The officers of the Grand Royal Ark Lodge being thus dispersed,

Provincial Grand Warrants were given to them, and wherever they settled they were to act as Gd. Masters and convene lodges under them with full powers & instructions in all the orders and degrees of Masonry. Thus dispersed Masonry began to flourish all over the Earth and has continued to the present era and so may it continue until time shall be no more.

Q. Is Noah's Ark still suffered to rest on Mt. Ararat?
A. It still rests on its summit.
Q. What was the capacity of the Ark?
A. 2,731,782 cubic feet or about 20 times larger than a first rate man of war, i.e. a 120 gun ship.
Q. What is the height of Mt. Ararat?
A. 17,260 feet above the level of the sea. Its summit has never been troden (sic) by the foot of man since the days of Noah.'

It can be well understood why almost the whole of the foregoing section has been omitted from present day Ark Mariner working. Its detail would be tedious, quite apart from the issue of veracity, and it would add little to the symbolic morality conveyed by the ceremony of today. It shows however the stage of verisimilitude through which the developing degree passed and the attempt made to keep as strictly as possible to the biblical basis.

This is not the last of the links between Finch and the Ark Mariner story. If we examine the four crests at the corners of the Interim 1793 warrant already referred to we shall find that they are the same as those used on the Finch certificates and charts. There was an attempt made to try and associate these symbols with family emblems but only the one in the top left corner could be directly joined to the Johnstone family of Annandale. We shall look again at these in the later section on regalia but the connection with Finch is an intriguing matter for more research in the future.

During 1806 we have the book of the St. John of Jerusalem Field of Encampment in Redruth which confirms that nine knights had taken the Ark Masons degree amongst others, and one of them, James Andrews, shows a Noah's Ark as his personal mark on June 17. Another 4 were elevated in 1811, 2 in 1814, 1 in 1815, 4 in 1816 and 9 in 1819.

By 1807 the degree surfaces in Liverpool and Dukinfield and the details of the 'Sunday Mark Lodge' given earlier in this book will largely apply to further practice of the Ark degree in that area. One such entry is the following: "The business of the night (14 September 1807) was Royal Ark Mariner and 5 brethren were admitted to that degree." Mention of the Ark degree also appears shortly afterwards in Manchester.

In the Friendship Lodge of Blackburn, Lancashire, we find an entry for 13 September 1809 which reads 'The Companions received the degree of Royal Ark and Mark Mariners', whilst in Bottoms, just over the Yorkshire border, we read that in 1812 the Prince George Lodge practised the 'Ark Mariners', 'Mark, Ark and Link', and 'Old Mark'.

That there was a hiatus in most places around the period of the Union of the English Grand Lodges is perhaps understandable though from 1815 lodges in Bolton, Bury and Farnworth in Lancashire have minutes which show that the Ark, Mark, Link and Wrestle degrees were still being regularly if not frequently conferred. Further instances of such extra-Craft activity at this stage and especially in the Eastern counties or the Midlands would be a very useful 'find'. After all, we do know that when the Bon Accord Founders were seeking a quorum of Mark Masons to form their first Mark Lodge they encountered in London a brother from the Midlands who spoke of the Ark degree that he had received there many years before even though the body that conferred it was now acting more like a charitable Friendly Society.

Bro. Noar (sic) has shown in his collected private papers that there were brethren from Yorkshire attending the Royal Lancashire Lodge, Colne to see several degrees, including the Ark, in 1815 whilst the first known reference to the 'Ark, Mark, Link and Wrestle' degrees in the St. John's Lodge No. 325 of Bolton, is a minute of 29 April 1821.

Any British military or naval mason passing through Gibraltar in the decade after 1820 would have been able to discover the Rocksavage Lodge No. 325 (IC) where another version of the Ark Mariner degree was carried out whilst in England in that same period we have numerous examples of Ark ceremonies. In 1823 Samuel Lazarus of Bath took the Ark degree in the Royal Sussex Lodge and as was stated earlier he was to assert that this took place under the Mark warrant held by that lodge. In the same year Richard Pearce was elevated 'by the Most Venerable Master and Venerable Wardens of a Lodge of Royal Ark Mariners or *Noachides* held under the sanction of the Druid's Lodge of Love and Liberality No. 127 by the light of the full moon at the Foot of the Mountains of Arrarat (sic) 9 June', and the Knights' book for the Encampment in the same place continues to record 1 Elevation for 1820 and another for 1826.

The Prince Edwin Lodge at Hythe in Kent gave the Ark degree to two military members, Johnson and Long, in 1829, whilst in April 1831 the Social Lodge, No. 145, of Norwich held an Ark Mariner ceremony and five brethren were admitted. It was also in Norwich in 1833 that we have a Sunday evening meeting in January at which 3 brethren were admitted to the Mark and Ark degrees whilst in 1834 the degree was being worked in the Cross of Christ Knight Templar Encampment and the Royal Clarence Lodge in Bristol. The entry for this latter occasion states that the 'Ark Mariners or Ark, Mark and Link Masons met and renewed the objects of their Order'.

That there could be confusion still about what exactly the Ark Mariner degree was is revealed in the 1881 edition of Howe's Manual of Freemasonry. We read there that "Some of the degrees now embodied in the Ancient and Accepted Rite continued to be separately practised up to a very recent period, and a little over forty years since (circa 1840) were conferred at the Crown Tavern on Clerkenwell Green ... We are unable to learn what degrees were conferred, for, excepting as to the Ark Mariner **or Noachite**, and the Rose-Croix, we have no knowledge." Those who have followed our story thus far will now know that this form of Ark Mariner degree was somewhat different to that which is known by that name today.

Yet it was in 1843 that a very significant step indeed for our present degree was taken by certain brethren in Hoxton Square, London. At the home of a Bro. Barnes and under the presidency of Bro. John F.Dorrington several candidates were inducted as Royal Ark Mariners. At this same meeting, with many more of the existing Ark Mariners present, an attempt was made to resurrect the old Grand Lodge, with Dorrington being elected as the Grand Commander. Indeed there is evidence of a Body meeting in London in 1844/5 at which Dorrington is again noted as GC and the degrees of Royal Ark, Mark and Excellent Master were conferred. The attempt at a revival was premature and by 1850 any printed notice of the degree in this connection seems to have disappeared.

In this regard it is worth noting that all this was happening as soon as the Duke of Sussex had died and by 1846 the Knights Templar and the Ancient and Accepted Rite had set up their own controlling bodies, with the Mark Degree following suit a decade later.

Meanwhile we have references in the Edinburgh Chapter for 1840 showing that 'Ark, Mark and Link' were being practised, whilst in 1843 the Knight Templar Encampment of Glasgow was admitting a Bro. Morris Leon to the RAM degree. The Ark Mason degree was already agreed as a responsibility of the Supreme Grand Chapter of Scotland and its relationship to the Red Cross of Babylon degrees was then established, as is still the case today. The various forms of ceremony in Scotland will be looked at shortly but there was not the necessary re-adjustment of control of the degree such as had still to happen in England.

In England forms of Ark Masonry were to be found alive and well right up to 1850. In the Lodge of Relief at Bury an ornament for Ark, Mark and Link was purchased in May, 1844, and on the following 11 November brethren took the degree and others did the same in 1847. Yet the future of the Mark degree was now the topic that would occupy the attention of many English Masons and it is hardly surprising that we have little mention of any of the other appendant degrees until the future of the new Grand Mark Lodge had been settled in the 1860s.

It was in 1870 that the next attempt to restore a Grand Lodge of Royal Ark Mariners was begun. It may be said to have started with a meeting of the St. Mark's Lodge of Mark Master Masons reported in the 'Freemason' Magazine of 7 May:

ROYAL ARK MARINERS

"A vessel of the Most Ancient and Honourable Fraternity of Royal Ark Mariners appeared off the George Hotel, Aldermanbury about seven of the clock p.m. on Monday the 2nd of May 1870 under the command of Father Noah, and having on board RA Mariners – Marsh as Shem, Hubbard as Japhet and Vesper as PN.

The vessel being properly moored the Ark was opened in due form and the following brethren, after taking the AOB of this Honourable Fraternity, came on board as RA Mariners, viz. Church, **G.Kenning**, Warr, Kierman, Levander, **M.Edwards**, T.C.Davison and Gilbert. The Ark **was then** opened in the degree of Shem and Japhet and these chairs were occupied in rotation by RA Mariners Marsh, Cubitt, Church, Levander and **M.Edwards**.

After an interval and on the retirement of the rest of the RA Mariners Hubbard, Levander and Edwards were passed into the Chair of First Principal. The 'Gill' warrant of the Fraternity was on the Scribe's table during these ceremonies. The Ark was properly closed, the vessel unmoored, the Ark Mariners adjourned and, after an evening spent very agreeably, separated."

The Morton Edwards who has been highlighted here was advanced in the Thistle (Mark) Lodge No. 8 on 1 October 1869 and joined the Northumberland Lodge on 22 September 1870. He was made Grand Junior Deacon in the Grand Mark Lodge in 1871 and being a sculptor by profession he was invited to model a bust of both the Grand Master, the Revd. GR Portal, and the Grand Secretary, Bro. F.Binckes. He was thus well known in Mark circles.

His rapid rise from **Elevation** to the **Chair of Noah** in one day, in what was in any case an interesting Installation ceremony involving 3 Chairs as in the Royal Arch, was carried out under the gaze and direction of the ageing John Dorrington who still claimed to be Grand Commander of the Order and usually presided over meetings in London. The next stage of events was therefore of special interest.

Not surprisingly it took place in the home of John Dorrington at Bow, in East London. On 13 May, 1870, he appointed and invested Morton Edwards as Deputy Grand Noah and Grand Scribe of the Order, handed over to him the 1793 warrant, and the declaration was made that a Grand Lodge should be revived. Edwards was further charged by solemn promise to do his best to restore this portion of Ancient Masonry to its former position. His task would not be at all easy for it was with difficulty that the requisite number of Grand Officers could be found when in July Dorrington signed a new warrant reconstituting 'A Grand Lodge of Royal Ark Mariners of England and Wales and the Dominions and Dependencies of the British Realm'. Edwards was now nominated as his successor though it was barely three months since the new Grand Commander had entered the Order.

These actions involving a senior Mark Mason could not but disturb deeply a Grand Mark Lodge that had only just recovered from a period of severe testing as to its own legitimacy and authority. In May 1870 it was moved in GML that 'a Committee be appointed to take into consideration the working of the degrees of **Ark, Link and Wrestle and Most Excellent Master** and report' and a group of 12 members was so appointed. At a meeting of the Old Kent

Lodge TI on 14 June the Grand Master, now **Canon** Portal, was elevated to the degree of Royal Ark Mariner along with several other high-ranking Mark Masons. They were also 'installed in the Chair of Noah' and made privy to the secrets of that office. They at least now knew more fully what was being considered and could both advise and direct the Committee in their deliberations. The Committee reported in August.

The main points of their findings were as follows: –

A) The degree appeared to have been worked since 1790 either under a jurisdiction **purporting** to exercise authority or in Mark lodges of Time Immemorial constitution.

B) Though worked in other countries it nowhere seems to have been considered essential and had on occasions seemed prejudicial to those degrees that are 'deemed integral portions of Ancient Masonry – prominent amongst which must be reckoned the degree of Mark Master'.

C) That the Mark Degree – with its two divisions of Mark Man and Mark Master – is a degree complete and entire in itself.

D) There was nothing in the Ark Mariner ritual to prevent it being worked under the authority of the Grand Lodge of Mark Masters, for the existing machinery for working the Mark was adequate for the Ark Mariner.

E) That those Mark lodges which wanted to work the Ark ceremony should apply to the Mark Grand Secretary for permission from the M.W. Grand MMM after referral to his Royal Ark Lodge of Advice. If agreed a warrant to that effect would be issued. Fees payable for any stage were stated.

These arrangements seemed to provide a stable basis for the future progress of the Ark Mariner degree on a national scale but at the next half-yearly meeting of the Grand Mark Lodge it was reported that the proposals could not be quite so simply effected as 'other bodies' which claimed the right to regulate the Order demanded to be consulted. The 'other bodies' referred of course to the 'so-called Grand Lodge' revived by Dorrington and Edwards.

By now this latter body had an imposing list of Grand Officers and Inspectors General of Counties together with representatives to India, Canada, USA, South America, Germany, Sweden, Norway and France. Yet there were only 28 lodges on their Roll, some of which were actually described as being 'in the course of formation'. A great effort was apparently being attempted to coordinate all the units that practised Ark Masonry and there was even a Lodge of Instruction held at the Lyceum Tavern in the Strand.

There can, however, be little doubt that the Grand Mark Lodge was correct in stating that it was extremely unhelpful to encourage the formation of additional Masonic Supreme organisations at that time. The fact that certain Mark lodges, now under the jurisdiction of the new GML, were themselves accustomed to conferring the degree of Ark Mariner and that Morton Edwards was himself a senior Mark Master Mason, meant that some resolution of the affair had to be found and found quickly.

After much correspondence and several meetings Morton Edwards was disowned by Grand Lodge, a sum of £15 was paid for equipment brought from the 'so-called GL of RAM' and in June 1871 the Grand MMM announced that the RAM degree was being taken under the protection of the Grand Mark Lodge and he was elected Grand Commander of the degree.

If the arrangements that now regulated the practice of the Royal Ark Mariner degree in England and Wales were largely satisfactory and conformed to the plans formulated by the GML, there were, as is often the case when major change is planned, individuals who were far from pleased by its new management. As early as 9 August 1871 a special meeting of the earlier 'Grand Lodge' thanked the member bodies for their vote of confidence and added some further resolutions urging them to continue to practise the Ark Mariner and add the Excellent and Super-Excellent Master degrees if they so desired. They even went on to ask for more fees.

Morton Edwards himself proved to be a constant irritant and so awkward did his interventions prove that he was at one point suspended. At last, in 1884, his agreement to surrender all rights in the degree was secured and he was paid a final sum of £25 on surrender of all his claims to act as Grand Commander, and the documents and properties belonging to the previous Grand Lodge. It is worth noting that in the 'receipt' for this transfer, which is in Edwards' own writing, the words 'so-called' are attached to the title of the earlier Grand Body. This only serves to endorse the conviction that even its supporters were aware of its doubtful legitimacy as the inheritor of the late 18th century phenomenon. Morton Edwards himself emigrated to America in 1885. A new stage of Ark Mariner Masonry began.

The two significant steps that were immediately taken to advance the fortunes of the degree were that the former Lodge of Advice became the Grand Master's Royal Ark Council, and each Ark Mariner lodge was henceforth no longer 'moored' but 'attached' to the Mark Masters lodge which was its parent. As the Ark Mariner lodge took the number of the parent Mark it can no longer be assumed that an Ark Mariner number represents its antiquity.

However, there have been other steps taken over the intervening century which have still further attempted to raise the Ark Mariner degree from the level of being regarded, as some still consider it, the 'poor relation' under the GML. In the late 1930s certain brethren from the North of England suggested that there might be some form of recognition for Past Commanders who had given continued valuable service to the degree. The idea had to be shelved whilst a war intervened but after the Centenary of the GML in 1956 the idea was revived and serious thought began to be given to the notion.

The main problem was that there was no Provincial or Grand Lodge structure, as with the Mark, in which recognition and acknowledgement could be progressively expressed. At last, however, it was decided that on the pattern of the London Grand Rank procedure a new pair of grades could be introduced – Royal Ark Mariner Provincial (or District) Grand Rank and subsequently RAM Grand Rank. The former would wear a rainbow coloured collarette from which would be suspended a model of Noah's Ark on a silver triangle whilst the latter would have the same but with the model and triangle made of gold or gilt. This arrangement has been in use for over 25 years and has certainly commended itself as a further incentive to Ark Mariner service as well as increasing the interest of the Provincial Grand Lodge meetings.

In 1991 the GMR Ark Council took a still further step by deciding to hold its November meeting as a purely Royal Ark Mariner occasion. This meant that the MW the Grand Master could devote one day in the year to this degree alone and present, in a gathering where all the officers would be dressed as Ark Mariners, a report of the Grand Master's Royal Ark Council whilst the honours bestowed that year upon the brethren so designated could be conferred. It would, I am sure, have delighted Bros. Dunckerley, Rancliffe, Sibley, Dorrington and even Edwards to see their Ark Masonry thus displayed once more in such august surroundings. Certainly the growth in the number of RAM lodges founded in the last 50 years, and the recognition which it has been accorded by its parent body must provide some answer to the continuing impression of some that this is but 'trivial and second-rate' Masonry.

THE LATEST RITUAL DEVELOPMENTS

We left off our description of the growth of Ark Masonry ritual with the mention of earlier 19th century practice. Just as the control of the Mark degree by the GML meant that that Body had to apply itself to the task of agreeing a future Mark Master ceremony so the appointed Royal Ark Mariners Council had to do the same in regard to Ark Mariner Masonry. That there were patterns to consider and adapt we already know but it is worth looking one more time at what happened after 1871 to realize how our present form of ceremony was arrived at. Whilst using the term 'present ceremony' it is recognised that even as this book was being prepared still further adjustments to the Mark and Royal Ark Mariner degree ceremonies were being suggested but these were comparatively minor changes and not such as to alter substantially the content and style.

In 1873 a new form of ceremony appears but there are some interesting variations. In the Opening we note that the brethren are referred to as **Ark Masons**, the shorter opening is replaced with today's catechism but there is no Chaplain mentioned and after prayer to the Gd. Comm. OTU Noah says: "Glory to God on high and peace to us on earth" and opens **the Bible** at Isaiah chap. 54, placing the **triangle and compasses** upon it. There is no mention whatsoever of the Porphyry Stone.

In the Ceremony of Elevation the following points are worth noting:

i) 'Is there anyone *among you* to join this Royal Ark Lodge?'.
ii) 'Go Shem, and instruct the Deacons to prepare him according to our ancient custom'.

iii) The candidate is additionally prepared with a Cable Tow three times round his neck and both feet slipshod.
iv) The entry is almost the same save that the Guardian merely reports to the Wor. Commander and gives no password.
v) Prayer is offered after the three addresses at the points of the triangle and is much longer than at present, reproducing in fact the 1797 form given earlier.
vi) The obligation is also introduced as in 1797 and taken on the Book of the Sacred Law. The penalty is more gruesome than is now known and the Isaiah passage is read before light is restored. There is no mention of removing the Cable Tow.
vii) An olive branch 'or myrtle if olive is not to be had' is now given and the previous words of 'You may now with truth meet Brethren in Ark Masonry with that promise of God in your right hand...'.
viii) In the same number of signs that now follow (N.B. no steps yet) the Pass sign is differently described as 'usually given at the Door of the Lodge and has improperly been called by some a Pass Grip'. The Penal sign is what we now regard as the Hailing sign whilst the Hailing sign described here is that used in today's Installation. The last two signs are as used today.
ix) The Pass Word is as today, the 'Common Word' is our present Sacred Word, and the Sacred word here is T ... d.
x) It is Shem who now delivers the same instructive three point address as today but in the 1797 form.
xi) It is therefore Japhet who invests the candidate with his apron. The words are still those mentioning King and Emperor as earlier.
xii) It is **now** that the candidate is taught the steps that lead as today to the East where Noah presents the working tools. A borer still appears in preference to an auger and an additional phrase is still kept in this connection: '... afflictions to make holes and uneasiness in our minds, that the axe of God's goodness may cut out promises as pins, and drive them into our remembrance so as to keep us in one family dependent on Him, and as the Ark...'.
xiii) A long interpolation after mention of the Bow in the heavens takes up the points made in the Finch working – explaining the '9 unequiformed steps as denoting the signs timely given by the SGC OTU to warn Noah that the time was coming to build the Ark'; the Triangular pedestal; and the details of the dispersion after Shinar.
xiv) It is here that the explanation of the steps used today appears for the first time, and this is immediately followed by two fuller explanations of the Grip and the Hailing sign with Scottish and American variations.
xv) In the closing we have virtually the same ceremony save that the prayer ends '... his Covenant made with the children of Noah, who passed from the old to the new world', and the sign of fidelity is as in the 3° of the Craft.

A lecture was provided for the occasions when there was no candidate and the content would be familiar to readers of the earlier ceremonies which have been recorded.

There was also a full ceremony for the Installation of a W.Commander Noah for it had been decided in 1870 that there should be provision for such a situation. The ceremony devised was almost identical to the present one except that it contained at this date and for some time to come an historical section which explained the parts played in the Flood story by Methuselah, Lamech, Jared and Enoch, as well as the 2 pillars of brass and marble of which so much has been said already.

In 1888 a new version of the Mark and Royal Ark Mariner ceremonies was produced by A.Lewis of London and already we can see the changes that were taking place. A frontispiece shows the Ark as a floating barn of two visible storeys with the dove fluttering above one end and the mountains appearing below a rainbow.

The tradition of a Porphyry Stone is now recited in the opening and it is upon such an object that hands have to be placed at the taking of the Obligation. It would seem that following the 1884 settlement with Morton Edwards this new form was adopted. Was it to distance the new Ark Mariner ceremony from what had gone before or was it because some overlooked 'tradition' discovered in the transferred papers could now be employed afresh? Research just carried out amongst old Royal Arch documents in the Grand Lodge library in London reveals that in 1809 the tradition of a Porphyry Stone in connection with that order did exist. Being discarded in that context it now looks as if it was re-used here.

Referring to the numbered items of the 1873 working we now note that i), iv), vi), viii), and xv) have disappeared completely whilst the following alterations have occurred elsewhere:

- v) Prayer is in the present position but still of 1873 content.
- vii) An olive branch or sprig of myrtle is given but not the 1873 words.
- xii) The steps are in their present position and the tools the same, but we still have the 'borer' and the later words of 1873.
- xiv) The explanation of the Grip and Hailing sign with foreign variants has now disappeared.

There is the insertion of a description of the Jewel and apron of the degree which is somewhat different to today.

An early 20th century form of the degree compiled by Bro. Cook of Derbyshire gives us further insight into the transition stage of the ritual. The Opening is as at present but the Candidate is still prepared as in 1873, Shem still instructs the Deacons and the prayer still has the same older and longer form. The signs are all as today and so are the Pass **or Ancient** Word and the Common **or Covered** Word but it is Shem who still delivers the lecture on a Brother's distress and Japhet who invests a new Brother. The Borer is still one of the tools but the words additionally used in 1873 have now been dropped though the portion on the 'warning nature' of the 9 steps and the dispersal of the sons across the earth are retained. The Lecture that was previously provided for use in the event of no candidate being available is now used for each meeting but in a shortened form.

By 1926 the transformation is almost complete. Brother Ark Mariners now assist in opening the RAM Lodge, Son Shem is still to direct the Deacons to prepare the candidate but before doing so the SD reverses a triangle on the floor and the candidate is attired as today and not as in 1873. A possible office of Chaplain is now mentioned and the prayer addresses the deity with a name we are familiar with, and also ends the same, but still has the continuing reference to the 1873 biblical figures.

The olive or myrtle is now given without any words, and whilst the Pass or Ancient Word is given we now speak of the Covered Word only and that is the one we use today. Moreover the word 'borer' has now been replaced by the more familiar 'auger'. Surprisingly the now much valued passages explaining the steps and the value of humility in service are here marked as **optional.** The rest and the Closing are also as today.

Whilst all this was happening in England the Early Grand Encampment of Scotland was still printing its ritual called 'The Green' and this gives an idea of how the present Scottish ritual was to develop. The Royal Ark Mariner degree comes 11th in the series of 31 degrees that comprised this Encampment's working and it takes its place in the following sequence:

6th Marked Master; 7th Architect; 8th Grand Architect; 10th Master of all Symbolic Lodges; 12th Fugitive Mark; 13th Link and Chain; 14th Sublime Master; 15th Order of the Scarlet Cord; 19th Most Excellent Master; 20th Excellent Mason; 21st. Super Excellent Mason and 22nd Holy Royal Arch.

The opening is of the shortest form:-

Three separate knocks by the principal officers:

N(oah) Sons: Be upright. (All rise)
N. It is my will and pleasure that a Royal Ark Lodge be opened for all business relative to this Order.
S(hem) Thy will, father, be ours. S.M.I.B.
N. All glory to God on high, and peace to us on earth.

He opens the VSL at Isaiah 54 verses 9 and 10, and sets the Square, compasses and triangle on it. (The Lodge is open and proceeds at once to the ceremony because it is only held if there is a candidate.)

The Candidate is attired as in the 1873 English working and comes to the door with Shem who was deputed to this work. (NB. No deacons) It is J. who goes to receive them at the door. In the prayer on entry the words of 1797 regarding blessings on his 'basket and his store' and 'the upper and lower spring' are here retained and the mention of 'such a one as Ham' is still present.

In the obligation occur the interesting words regarding answering summonses duly marked 'and I am found in my cable tow'. It is sealed by saluting the Book and the triangle. In explaining the significance of the Isaiah verses which lie exposed we hear: "The Lord therein, by the mouth of the prophet, makes another and a greater covenant with us than he did with Noah – the one being the type of the other – the endurance of His church as long as the world shall last".

The Equilateral Triangle is also described as "of that shape to remind us of the threefold personality of the Deity – a knowledge which was imparted to the patriarchs at a very early period". Furthermore there is a very specific passage, now no longer employed, which students of the degree should be acquainted with.

"The marks or signatures placed on the summonses in this degree are 3 parallel Triangles with their respective initials, and three concentric (or embracing) ones over them. (This is exactly the design that was attached to the 'Sibly' papers but without the explanation which is at last given here.) Those on the right signify ancestors of Noah – Methuselah, Lamech and Jared, the three words combined being a prophecy that death and destruction was about to come upon the miserable inhabitants of the earth. Those on the left represent the Master and Wardens of the **first** Ark Lodge – Noah and his eldest and second sons, Japhet and Ham; those in the centre, our present patrons ... Ham being excluded for exposing his father to his brothers ... Japhet is placed before Shem because he was the elder brother (but) Shem is usually mentioned before Japhet, because the promised Messiah was to be descended from him." This is followed by the usual passage on 'he who performs his part best'.

The 'auger or borer' is mentioned in the presentation of the tools but this is followed by some further paragraphs taken from the 18th century working. There are no steps, no commentaries on Distress, no morals at the points of the Triangle, and the Closing is as brief as the Opening.

It would be as 'ultra vires' to speak of the current Royal Ark Mariner ceremony in Scotland as it would be to reveal that used in England and Wales but in his small History of this degree Handfield-Jones states certain features that can thus be mentioned here.

'They used to invest their candidates with an apron of unshorn lambskin but now they use a dressed skin; they wear a sash over the left shoulder either rainbow or **green**; they do not have the porphyry stone but the VSL, and the Triangle is chalked or marked by tape on the floor. These are really quite trivial (differences) and the ritual itself is nearly identical with ours.'

If Handfield-Jones meant that the general tenor of the degree in Scotland is similar to our own then I would heartily agree but anyone who is allowed to read their text carefully cannot but be impressed with the fact that the Scots have retained many allusions and wordings which we have seen revealed in the Sibly and Watson documents. The dress of the candidate is as in 1873 form and there are also direct quotes from 'The Green' which have had no place in our working during the last 100 years. Whilst it is granted that there are instructions regarding optional or alternative usages the fact remains that the Scottish ritual has preserved features that would have been natural to Dunckerley and Dorrington but which would be unknown to anyone joining the Royal Ark Mariner south of the Border today. By the same token the Scots RAM might be surprised indeed by the beautiful ritual that takes the candidate in England and Wales around the sides of the Triangle. What we must be grateful for is that between them these two continuing ceremonies have preserved enough to remind us of our origins and cause us to be properly grateful for the retention of this aspect of a Masonry which may be much older than many have often imagined.

THE PORPHYRY STONE

For just over a century Royal Ark Mariners in England and Wales have been accustomed to the place of this feature in their ceremony and have perhaps imagined that such a stone was a long standing part of their traditional way of doing things. Accordingly, those not familiar with the history of the degree, or the manner in which it has developed both here and elsewhere, may have been surprised to learn how singular has been its use. As was evident in a previous part of this chapter, in which we traced the development of earlier and other rituals, there is still no sign of a stone being used in the RAM ceremonies of either Scotland or America up to the present day. Whilst this gives the present English/Welsh ceremony a distinctive cachet it has to be admitted that the use of such an item does raise intriguing questions for any serious student of our 'mysteries'.

The first question has to be when and why the Porphyry Stone was brought in to use. Without any further information than we have at present it would appear that when in 1884 Grand Mark Lodge finally obtained the whole of Bro. Edwards's documents there may have been amongst those papers some intimation that led the Mark authorities of the time to consider such an innovation but clearly, without access to those private papers, it is impossible to say whether this would solve our problem. Stuart Richardson has referred to an unofficial ritual of 1873 that showed 'the Degree, as practised by the old Grand Lodge, being very similar to that of today though certain sections were given in greater detail . . .'. Having earlier examined this ritual the reader will appreciate the main differences that it revealed and above all that no porphyry stone had yet appeared in the RAM ceremony. What seems certain is that if there were old associations of Porphyry with Noah, as we saw in the old Rochdale notebook mentioned above (see p. 347f) and it was linked with the prevalent idea of some sacred stone in Noah legends then the basis for our present practice was available. As already indicated we now have further evidence to show where a basis for present practice comes from. The relevant passages from the Grand Lodge library document signed "c.b." are reproduced below. What cannot be denied is that in the first available ritual after the 'buying out' of Morton Edwards the porphyry stone had come to stay. The Grand Mark Board must have been fully persuaded that this feature was both appropriate and legitimate.

Yet questions must remain as to why this was considered so essential and I have found it intriguing that no previous commentators on the Ark Mariner degree such as Pick, Inman or Handfield-Jones have felt it necessary to investigate this aspect of the ceremony. It might be contended by some that surely the whole raison d'etre for the Porphyry Stone is laid out in the current ritual and therefore there is nothing further to be said. Whilst that appears a reasonable stance it does not wholly satisfy a serious enquirer.

The first observation on our present situation must be that the usual explanation of the Stone is clearly tacked on to what would otherwise be, and was, a quite satisfactory Opening ceremony. Why, one is bound to wonder, was this extra ritual felt to be necessary? Was it that this was such an innovation that it had to be specially pleaded and that those agreeing to its inclusion were only able to do so if there was some explanation given for this new departure? Again we do not know but the truth is that, even for those very familiar with Ark Mariner ritual, one of the odd little hiccoughs in Opening the Lodge is precisely at this point when, having completed the first part of the procedure, one has to start all over again, as it were, and answer the question, 'On what is a Lodge of R. Ark Masons **properly** opened?' Does this mean that all other kinds of opening were, or are, **improperly** conducted or is this simply the cue for giving what purport to be the solid grounds for now having this peculiar item in our ceremonies?

If the first interpretation is the correct one then one wonders what that is saying about our relations with Ark Mariners elsewhere who do not adopt our 'proper' practice, but perhaps it is unfair to raise such issues. If, on the other hand, the second interpretation is correct then we are still left with some intractable questions.

Why, for example, do we say that the use of the Porphyry Stone is essential and more correct 'because at the period whence we deduce the origin of this degree the Sacred Words were not in existence'? This means either that the degree is to be thought of as beginning from the time of the Flood which surely no-one claims, or that when the degree **was first conceived for use** sometime in the 18th century there was no VSL available, which is also not true. Moreover, if the SWs are to be thought of as being something produced **after** the Flood experience, which is here presented for our instruction, why are portions of them both used and referred to in our ceremony? These must be **proper** questions because it is quite evident that for the previous century at least the members of the Ark degree never doubted that the VSL was quite a satisfactory vehicle for endorsing an obligation.

There have often been queries about the 'many traditions' to which reference is made. The only stone 'associating it with this degree' of which I was for long aware was either the stone coffin containing Adam's mortal remains and which he is said to have set in the centre of the Ark during their voyage on the waters, or the marble stone of which mention is made in the Noachite degree of Prussian Knights. Both these were referred to earlier in this book. Neither of these easily fit the rough, cubic or triangular porphyry stone.

When it comes to the matter of an anchor or the stone of sacrifice, where again Adam's coffin was sometimes thought to have been used, we may also be into other Talmudic or Hebrew writings and the stories they relate and which we now give, but the query still persists as to why any or all of these accounts are thought to have a relevance to a **Porphyry Stone**? That is an issue to which we will finally have to address ourselves.

The Talmud tells us that in the Creation God cast a great stone into the Abyss and it was upon this foundation that the world was created. The question asked of God in the Book of Job, chapter 38 verse 6. 'Whereupon are the foundations of the earth fastened, or who laid the cornerstone thereof?' may well be an allusion to that belief. Moreover the legend continues with Abraham carrying a fragment of that very stone to Mount Moriah when he went there to sacrifice his son Isaac, whilst another fragment was used by Jacob as a pillow when he had his remarkable dream of a ladder leading from earth to heaven. Again, Moses was said to have sat on part of this stone when he prayed to the Almighty at Rephidim with his hands supported and uplifted. Could it indeed be that in these three incidents alone we have the bases for what was said about Noah **resting** and **reposing upon a stone** as well as using one **for an anchor** and **an act of sacrificial thanksgiving**? Why that should be when these events were subsequent to Noah, and only recorded in the later SWs, is a further paradox to be faced.

The stories continue with a sacred stone that was said to have oracular power, similar to that associated with the Urim of the later High Priest. It was inscribed with the Sacred Name of God in an **equilateral triangle** and a circle, and this same stone was that north-east **corner stone** of King Solomon's Temple. This would immediately separate it from the **anchor or foundation stone** at the south-east corner, where such a stone still lies buried and is manifestly not made of porphyry.

One writer has suggested that the most likely connection with the present use of the porphyry stone is the one mentioned in Zechariah chapter 3, verse 9, and chapter 4, verse 7. The prophet is there told to behold a certain stone upon which 7 eyes were engraved and which was apparently intended to be the 'headstone' at the summit of the Temple mount. The Jewish Fathers maintained that it was placed "in the **centre of the Sanctum Sanctorum, occupying the spot where the Ark would have stood**". On this stone the Blood of Atonement was annually sprinkled by the High Priest on the Great day of Expiation and it could be that the idea of **bloodstains** could have given rise to the idea of the reddy, purplish stone, Porphyry.

Stress should not of course be laid unduly on the strict geological necessity of porphyritic stone and that is why some lodges today use any kind of purplish marble. It may also be why there was some slender link with the marble stone mentioned in the Noachite degree. The fact that, though the true Porphyry was only quarried and squared by the Egyptians, the stone was abundant in Sinai does seem to provide grounds for so much of the Hebraic legend.

It was only when this point had been reached in the consideration of the matter of the porphyry stone that a story related by Dr. Oliver in his mini-encyclopaedia of Masonic Antiquities struck the attention. This relates that in order to preserve the 'secrets and mysteries' which had been communicated to his ancestor, Adam, Enoch took the step of inscribing what he knew on a '**white** porphyry stone' and concealed it in an underground cavern. This cavern was eventually sealed up and the entrance hidden but in order to mark the spot two pillars were erected near the entrance and these were the pillars which are familiar to all well instructed Freemasons.

This legend is not proposed as the solution to what we have seen to be an enigma though it has certain features that commend it as a possible means of shedding light on our problem. It sets a porphyry stone firmly in the ante-diluvian period and it makes it an object of revered antiquity for a descendant like Noah. Its connection with Enoch has relevance when we reflect on the contents of the now approved Ark Mariner tracing board discussed in these pages and there is also the suggestion of an Arch connection that is appropriate in much of Ark Mariner history. Finally, it connects the porphyry stone naturally but uniquely with the more established legend of the mysteries and secrets retained by the two pillars. Moreover Dr. Oliver was a collector of strange traditions but he was not a fabricator.

When I first made my preparations to complete this part of my work I was of the opinion that the introduction of the Porphyry Stone was perhaps one Ark Mariner mystery too far. It was certainly a mystery that one could heartily wish would be settled. It now looks as though that wish has been realised. What would apear to have happened is that someone recalled a discarded pre-Union Royal Arch tradition, and one that actually used words that seemed entirely relevant to the subject of this ancient degree. Though the whole text, entitled 'The Famous Royal Arch Porphyry Stone', cannot be reproduced here the following extracts will serve to show why those who now controlled the RAM degree in England and Wales were drawn to its use:

"Placed as the Centre Stone of Solomon's Temple, and in Zerubabel's (sic) Temple etc ... On this stone did Adam sit to name and number all the animals sent to him for that purpose by the Almighty ... Upon this stone the good old Patriarch Noah reposed when he daily returned from his pious labour in building the Ark, and when finished took and placed it in the centre of the said Ark. With this stone as an Anchor of Hope did Noah fix the station of the Ark on Mount Arrarat (sic) when himself and family came out.

Upon this stone did Noah make his first offering to the Lord for his safe deliverance and desired it there to be fixed in the valley of Arrarat till the first of his descendants should be called from above to travel again either by land or water ..." All this, let us recall, in a text recorded in 1809 but based on the information provided in 'A History of the Jews' by C. Buxtorff. And that is not all.

In a later section we read: "Such Chapters as like to go to the expence (*sic*) have 3 Arch canopies .. with the following devices painted thereon ... 2) Adam sitting on (the stone) pointing to the animals in pairs ... 14) Noah sleeping on it – Ark building at a little distance (night scene); 15) Noah lets down the stone out of the Ark on Mount Arrarat, when he comes out ..." This is no invention of the future Royal Ark Council members. They are exercising that principle of Masonic economy which does not allow traditions to be wasted. If not used in one degree then they can be profitably resumed elsewhere. One hopes that as this part of our ancient ceremony is now so much better understood brethren will at least never call it the 'porfry' or even the 'palfrey' stone.

AN ARK MARINER TRACING BOARD

If, as we saw in the section on the matter of a Mark Tracing Board, there was some hesitation regarding the selection of an acceptable design then such hesitation certainly seems to have been displayed in regard to any possible board for the Royal Ark Mariner degree. Indeed the absence of such a board for this ceremony has become so commonplace that, as with the Holy Royal Arch, the display of such an item is never considered especially if, as is generally the case, there is no board to display anyway. When one discovers that Royal Arch tracing boards were actively used, and in various designs, in days gone by, it is really quite a shock. That is exactly the experience I had when the same happened in this degree.

It was during the time that I was serving as Provincial Grand Master for the Mark Province of Surrey, England, in the 1980s that a Past Master of Dorking Lodge asked whether I would agree to an explanation of such an old RAM board being given one evening when there happened to be no candidate. On the understanding that this could not be deemed any kind of legitimate addition to the ritual, but might prove to be of historical interest, I assented to the idea and was duly introduced to what we now know as the Board preserved by the Gladsmuir Lodge of Royal Ark Mariners, No. 367 in the Mark Province of Hertfordshire. Unknown to myself the Past Master who had made the request was himself a Past Commander and Treasurer of that Hertfordshire lodge and had helped to compile this explanation for its first presentation as long ago as 1960.

What is of permanent importance is the fact that the original board is similar to a Warrant of the so-called Grand Lodge of Ark Mariners, issued to a Charles Sinclair, and as this Warrant was dated 1796 the board must have been painted about that time. An independent view as to the state and nature of the varnish later confirmed that opinion.

Because this board was a legacy of Antients' working, when many more than simply the basic degrees were worked, it is hardly surprising that this board contains some features that refer to more than simply the Ark Mariner degree as we know it. That will not surprise the reader of this book as by this time he will have become used to hearing that both the Mark and the Ark degrees were part of a larger sequence of ceremonies such as Past Master, Architect, Link, Wrestle, Red Cross and even the Royal Arch itself.

In the explanation that I was first introduced to that evening and which will be generally outlined shortly there were evident links with these other degrees and to make the board even more meaningful the modern explanation has even added items relating the Craft and Mark degrees to what is here shown. One further point also became clear. The amount of instruction that could be given on Freemasonry generally in making clear the board's contents was such that it could immediately follow an Elevation. Taking it steadily and meaningfully would occupy nearly 20 minutes and certainly that long if, as also seemed desirable, it was a piece of work that could be divided up between three competent brethren. To expect that kind of concentration regularly after each ceremony was hardly sensible and in any case its overuse would only depreciate its obvious benefit as part of Royal Ark Mariner instruction.

Such considerations were of course not in mind when the board was first introduced to Surrey in this way and would not be relevant unless there were authorization for its regular use by lodges. The first task was to become acquainted with its contents and its message. (See picture).

Within a border that contains a series of cypher characters there are some 20 separate scenes or clusters of symbolic items each very finely drawn. To distinguish this as an Ark Mariner board we have five very different scenes along part of the top, above the centre and along the base. These are: the cities of the plain with trees and fields, the Ark being constructed and held upright on stilts, the Ark sailing majestically on the face of the waters with a white dove poised above it, the figure of Enoch against an arcade of six pillars, and finally, the Ark perched on the summit of Mount Ararat with a procession of animals and their attendants descending to a plain with four erected bell-tents, whilst Noah and his sons kneel in thankfulness as a sacrifice is offered on a stone altar over which the **rainbow** is displayed.

I shall now select portions from the normal explanation given and add to that presentation some guide to the parts of the Board that may not have been fully covered.

At the head of the board there is the Mountain of Vision which is a symbol of that insight and prophecy which was exercised by 'righteous men of old', here represented by Noah who holds in his left hand an **equilateral triangle** and in his right the faint but upright shape of an axe. "The Book of Genesis tells us that 'he walked with God' and to him upon the Mountain of Vision was shown the destruction which awaited the wickedness of Mankind. Being desirous of preserving the principles of the Sciences for the posterity of those whom God should be pleased to spare, Noah's ancestor, Enoch constructed two pillars . . ." of brick and marble. In them he created a secret hiding-place to hold the Archives of Wisdom.

"Those pillars were securely placed in a cavern and were approached by a system of nine arches, here shown only notionally since the secret of their actual arrangement, and of the means of access from one to another, was communicated only from father to son and is now lost." The marble pillar did re-emerge after the Deluge but only a long time later.

"The Vision of Enoch was brought to pass in the days of his great-grandson, Noah. Now we are told in the Book of Noah that when he was born 'his hair was as white as wool and his eyes beautiful, and when he opened his eyes he lighted the whole house – like the Sun – and the whole house was very bright'. And Noah became a man and found grace in the eyes of the Lord . . ." Thereafter we follow the usual story with the help of the first four scenes showing Noah and the Ark. It ends with the words: "hence also the dove and the olive branch are the universally accepted symbols of peace".

The episode following the Flood is now related, as shown at the foot of the board, and we are reminded that the 'rainbow, with the dove and the olive branch, symbolise the origins of the degree and together form the jewel which is worn.' Thus, we are told, were Wisdom and Righteousness preserved and Noah, Japheth and Shem commemorated, 'but Ham, Noah's **third son**, fell from grace and has no place among us'.

Towards the bottom of the board there is a simple reproduction of the veils of the Tabernacle with three sets of 3 pillars supporting them. The narrative now takes us to the Mosaic stories connected with those veils and we are thus being introduced to the Excellent Master degree which preceded the Holy Royal Arch, as it does to this day in Scotland. The events concerning a serpent and the crossing of the Red Sea are here depicted and the 'Lecture' speaks of the latter event thus:

"Now this episode is not a part of the origins of the RAM Degree, but it cannot escape your notice that here, for the second time, the Almighty used the power of the great waters for the destruction of evil, and provided the means whereby His Chosen were preserved in safety."

Whilst in this proximity to the 'Antients' form of the Royal Arch we might note the Ark of the Covenant, the trowel, and the three squares which were found in the vault along with other items. The link between RA and RAM Masonry could not be more closely portrayed.

Other scenes shown are of a man laying a building's foundation and craftsmen dressing stones for use. The latter scene is explained as the marking and numbering of the work with that perfection which 'has ever been the standard demanded of the Operative Mason'. Here shown are the contemporary jewels of the Worshipful Master, his Wardens and the Past Masters whilst there is also the **key and sword** which remind the Mason to be discreet and faithful in fulfilling his obligation.

The Mark Degree is now clearly revealed with the three stones – a cube supporting a mallet, the keystone a chisel and the rectangle a vase of consecrating oil. These items are all given moral interpretations as are the three squares of the Overseers that are also shown.

"The Winged Hour-Glass denotes the flight of time, reminding you of the admonition of the Brother who raised you to the Sublime Degree of a Master Mason – to be careful to perform your allotted task while it is yet day. The Anchor, the Symbol of Hope, will ever encourage you to hold fast to that aspiration which should be the central aim of every Freemason – to achieve within yourself that perfection which is here significantly represented at the very centre of the Board by the Perfect Ashlar." It should be noted that this Ashlar bears the very same symbols of the triangle and circle which were mentioned in connection with the Porphyry Stone above and it may therefore seem logical that the next sentence is as follows:

"You will observe that the Porphyry Stone on the Wor. Commander's pedestal is a Perfect Ashlar".

Since mention was made when we began looking at this Tracing Board that it was of some considerable antiquity the inference might be made that similarity of shape between PA and PS supports an ancient basis for the latter but it should be recalled that whilst the contents of the board are indeed of some 200 years ago the explanation was compiled a mere 35 years ago and therefore assumes the presence on the W.Comm's pedestal of the PS. There is not the slightest reason for believing that such an item was in the mind of the board's draughtsman and the long exposition that now follows has wholly to do with perfect ashlars and nothing else.

As to the triangle within a circle that adorns this central feature on the board the Lecture is quite explicit. "Their conjunction teaches you the fundamental truth that Deity pervades Eternity, and as this combined symbol **also relates to another Degree** (the Holy Royal Arch) you are again reminded that there is still greater knowledge to which you may attain."

The impact of this well phrased explanation on the first occasion that it was given has hardly dimmed in the years that have since passed. Combined with the graphic and well arranged contents of the board itself it is good to know that here is an item that has just been accepted and authorised by the whole of Ark Masonry. It not only covers all the essential aspects of the degree as at present conducted but it relates it to the Mark with which it has for so long been connected and also reminds any Ark Mariner of the older setting within which this degree existed from its inception. It thus tastefully and adequately links the past with the present, tradition with current practice. It is to be hoped that it will have a yet longer contribution to make to Royal Ark Mariner Masonry.

Yet it has not been the only contender for filling the gap that some see as unfilled for this ancient degree. In 1968 another form of Royal Ark Mariner board was designed and painted for use by certain lodges in the Province of Kent. There does not, as far as I am aware, exist any older drawing on which this design might be based though there are some representations of the Ark that would suggest this as a possible form of that vessel, albeit this one seems of remarkable length. This board was never submitted to Mark Masons Hall for approval and the then Prov. GM, RW Bro. F.W.Friday, was always insistent that if on display this scene should be called a 'Pictorial Representation' and must never be moved or even referred to during the Ark Mariner ceremony. It was allowed as a decorative reminder of at least some of the features that were connected with the story of the Flood but it was never given any explanation in the course of lodge evenings. It was thus hoped that whilst it helped to bring the degree visually alive it did not transgress any Ark Mariner landmark. What it did do was to show that there was a latent longing in at least another Province for this piece of lodge furniture and raise the awareness that, if there were no official Board, then there was always the likelihood that diverse attempts to produce one could arise. (See picture).

This particular board does have the merit of being solely connected with the degree it illustrates and of being economical with its contents. It displays the basic tools of the degree, and in a possibly unconscious manner it retains the old Ark degree connection with the Link degree by its suggestion of Jacob's Ladder, though the original design here was that the ladder should have the letters F H C on the separate rungs, thus linking it with ancient Craft working.

The three pillars below with their moral 'adornments' certainly underline that connection though the words on the central pillar do not immediately suggest 'Aude Vide Tace' as they are intended to do. Whilst the dove is reasonably presented the Rainbow is of quite the wrong colours and the apparently limestone altar of sacrifice seems to call in question the ritual's assertion that it was meant to be of porphyry. Noah also seems to be the only human on the scene though a magnifying glass shows that someone else is shepherding the animals near to the Ark's ramp. Of all the detail the 'weed line' around the Ark gives the most realistic impression and one assumes that the anchor rope is also snaking towards the same stone as that at which Noah is kneeling. It should if the ritual is to be believed.

Such then are two examples of what an Ark Mariner board has been or could be. That a well-designed board would enhance the practice of the degree I had become more and more convinced. It is a matter for great satisfaction that the Grand Master's Royal Ark Council have now been able to give a lead.

ARK MARINER REGALIA

As was mentioned when the matter of separate regalia for the Mark was considered the practice in regard to the appendant degrees was ruled by the fact that these additional ceremonies began within the orbit of Antients lodges and it was thus simply a matter of adding one or more symbols to the Craft apron. Strangely, this does not appear to have happened to any extent in regard to the Ark degree and the symbol of an Ark on 18th century aprons might just as well have referred to the 3° in the Craft as to any incipient Ark Mariner practice. After all we still have in lodge rooms as far apart as Bath,

Somerset and Llandudno, North Wales 3° tracing boards that display the Ark clearly as part of their symbols.

To this day many Scottish lodges use the Ark as a significant symbol in their explanation of the 3° and reference to their often unpublished rituals, as also to Monitors in American Masonry, will reveal something like the following:

'The ark, an emblem of that which survived the flood, reminds us of that ark of safety which will waft us securely over this sea of troubles; and when arrived in a celestial harbour, the anchor of a well grounded hope will moor us for ever to that peaceful shore where "the wicked cease from troubling and the weary are at rest".'

It may even have been because there was this existing link between a major feature of any new ceremony and the Craft that encouraged those designing a new degree to think not only of the ritual but also of its attendant dress. It may be recalled that as we considered the 'Noahite or Prussian Knights' degree there was mentioned the yellow bordered gloves and aprons that were meant to be worn by those who took that step.

What is certain is that when in the **1790s** the Ark Mariner degree begins to take a recognisable shape it is immediately accompanied by an 'authorised' apron for officers that was to be ornamented with an Ark and the Dove whilst a **sash** of rainbow ribbon was also worn with it. Not only so but there are in the Grand Lodge Museum in London fine examples of the jewels that were designed to accompany this regalia. (See picture.) Yet even this is apparently not the whole story. There is more evidence from this period to consider.

Eric Ward drew attention to the fact that in the Museum of the Grand Lodge of New York there is an apron made of silk which is similar to the one that is preserved in Melbourne, Australia and described below. The New York apron bears an inscription stating that it was printed by the same group that produced the Granville warrant and that was signed by Moseley, **Sibly**, Sinclair and **Hannam**. The design of these aprons is worth noting.

The designs on the Melbourne apron are printed in dark blue and on a cream (once white) background, but long use with consequent wear and tear, and the fact that the apron was folded right through some of the scenes depicted, means that most of them are illegible. Happily, of course, we have a very good representation of the Interim Warrant that is kept in Mark Masons Hall, London, and thus we are able to identify some otherwise vague areas of the apron.

The border of the apron is composed of a series of ellipses each containing an emblematic figure and Bro. Byatt (AQC XXII) tells us that this is a design used on aprons engraved by Newman. The emblems are as follows:

Top row: Level, plumb, 7 stars, Sun with a keystone, Crescent Moon with face, Square and Compasses in the FC position.

Left side: Winged Spur (with semicircle of illegible wording above), crossed quill pens, trowel, St. Andrew's cross, beehive, ladder, cross pattee, crown and anchor, something illegible.

Right side: Winged globe (also with semicircular band and words above), crossed keys, hour-glass, wavy sword, Euclid diagram, scythe and mallet, entwined cross, Paschal lamb, pot of manna, and a winged wheel.

Bottom row: Beast, eagle, altar, lion, man.

The scenes across the top and bottom of the apron are exactly the same as on the Gladsmuir Tracing Board and therefore need no description. Between them are two rows of four pictures and as these partly differ from, and amplify, the scenes on the Board I will explain them in order.

Left side (descending):

1. This shows three Craftsmen shaping and marking stone.
2. Here the builder is laying the corner stone of his foundations.
3. Appears to be a prison with a crowned figure having his fetters loosened whilst two soldiers with spears stand looking on.
4. This is 'The Bridge' of three arches, with a serpent-entwined cross above the centre of it and foliage or figures to the right.

Right side:

1. Moses before the burning bush, on one knee and with the reverse FC sign, and a serpent in front of him.
2. Moses raises his rod to command the Red Sea to part.
3. On the left of a dark room, whose door is being opened by a winged angel, there is a cock and a triangle with 12 lights which has a skull and crossbones at its centre.
4. This looks like the risen Master with either the soldiers at the tomb or the disciples on the shore.

The significance of these pictures is very plain. It shows to the knowing Mason that the Royal Ark Mariner degree which surmounts and underpins this apron is also related to the Mark Degree, the Red Cross of Babylon, the Holy Royal Arch and the Knights Templar Order. It is thus a most illuminating and distinctive garment though not one that would have been relevant to post-Union English Freemasonry. It is most instructive to note that the Gladsmuir board has no representation of anything that is connected with the Red Cross or Knights Templar.

In addition to this interesting sidelight on the regalia which some of the leading Ark Mariners (and Knights Templar?) might have devised there is another matter which needs to be aired before we leave this particular period. Whilst there had been a positive and apparently final provision for identifying those who would henceforth join the Ark Mariners the uncertain and fragmented progress of the degree in the first half of the 19th century meant that no widespread use of its dress was promoted. Indeed, as we have seen, any activity at all connected with Ark Masonry was to appear in wholly unconnected areas of the country and with very little exposure to many of those who now began to join and expand the Craft.

What is therefore both curious and apparently inexplicable is that just at the point when all trace of 'Noah' masonry seemed to have dropped from view a step was taken which seemed the reverse of that trend. When at the Union of the Grand Lodges the new shape and personnel of a lodge was determined the office of Deacon, hitherto formally approved only by the Antients, was adopted under the new Regulations. Regalia for the office had to be approved and since the former insignia, mostly used by Antients Lodges, was a Hermes or Mercury carrying a caduceus, or staff entwined with a serpent, it was decided to introduce another device – the dove bearing an olive branch. Whilst in no way questioning its appropriateness as a peaceful bearer of important tidings the question that persists is bound to be – why was this particular 'Noah' emblem chosen and why at the point when its significance had begun to be freshly enhanced as part of another Masonic ritual? Was the intention to pre-empt any widespread use of the symbol elsewhere? Was it simply that this was the most helpful answer to a neutral replacement of the Antients practice? Or could it have been, as happened more recently with the return of the Trowel, that the Grand Lodge of England has a capacious memory and somewhere in that vast recollection was the awareness that Noachite Masonry was part of its oldest traditions and this would be a proper recognition of that connection? Is that merely surmise, or could it be that somewhere there is the record of why that decision to use the Dove and Olive Leaf was taken? It would settle a matter that otherwise remains a mild mystery. When, however, the Ark Mariner degree reached its much safer haven under the flag of the Grand Mark Lodge it was in the hands of that Order's leaders that a decision about such matters as future regalia lay. The outcome, in the shape of the present Rainbow edged and rosetted apron, with a Rainbow coloured collar for those entitled to such an addition, and the breast jewel of a rainbow and dove, is now part of what we trust is settled practice. What is pleasing is the fact that despite the uncertain passage which the Ark degree endured in the 19th century it has re-emerged with clothing that would have been both recognized by, and amenable to, its early promoters.

FURTHER TOPICS FOR RESEARCH

1.	p. 14, 27	The state of pre-1717 English Operative Masonry.
2.	p. 36f	Further examination of the Graham MS.
3.	p. 96	Irish influence on 18th century English Masonry.
4.	p. 100, 211	Northumbrian Freemasonry in the period 1750 to 1850. (Was there a Travelling Lodge or did Harodim persist?)
5.	p. 130	A picture or drawing of Carlile style Mark apron.
6.	p. 128, 141	The "Lighthouse of Lebanon" & "Trumpeter at the Sea-side".
7.	p. 147	More evidence of this type of stone.
8.	p. 163	Is there further evidence of such Christian forms of ritual?
9.	p. 187	Can we discover the Irish Mark Fellow Mason theme?
10.	p. 188	More evidence of the "Arch" degree in Devon Masonry.
11.	p. 197	Further clarification of early Bristol practice and origins.
12.	p. 197	Can the fuller story of 18th century Bath Masonry be found?.
13.	p. 199	The present whereabouts of the Minden Mark keystone.
14.	p. 203	The origin and foundation of the Ashton Travelling Lodge.
15.	p. 295	What was meaning of Grantham's "Cypher" remarks?
16.	p. 207	Can we learn more about a Bolton "Travelling" Lodge?
17.	p. 210	The life and practice of the Sunderland Joppa Encampment?
18.	p. 212	The presence of early appendant degrees in East Anglia.
19.	p. 233	Where did other 1855 Committee members view the Mark?
20.	p. 235	Why were two titles for Mark degree used at this stage?
21.	p. 237	What other Independent Mark "lodges" were approached regarding a possible new Grand Mark Lodge?
22.	p. 290	Further information about the origin of "Keystone" aprons.
23.	p. 298	Any further variations of Rosenthal tracing boards known.
24.	p. 303	A complete survey of Mark degree music, even if within a definitive work on Masonic music generally.
25.	p. 336	Study of later 17th and early 18th century Bible exegesis, ethnology & antiquarianism to discover allegorical sources.
26.	p. 342	The Mystery plays performed by the Carpenters and Wheelwrights and the reasons for those choices.
27.	p. 358	Any evidence or content of Dunckerley's early R.Ark.M. degree.
28.	p. 358	What was the origin of the "Tower" section of the Royal Order (of Scotland) ceremony?
29.	p. 374	Who worked on the R.Ark.M.ceremony between 1760/ 80?
30.	p. 379	Did the Early Encampments cross-fertilize to produce degrees?
31.	p. 392f	Further evidence of R.Ark. M. degree in period 1800–1820.
32.	p. 397	What more is there to discover about the Finch connection?
33.	p. 398	The extent of early non-Craft degrees in the East Midlands.

Appendix

(The following extract appears on pages 120 and 121 of the Revd. Dr. Oliver's book *The Discrepancies of Freemasonry*)

THE ANCIENT MASONIC CIPHER.

"Are you acquainted with the process by which this was accomplished?"

"I am. This was effected by the agency of the ancient Masonic cipher, consisting of simple squares and angles, but I cannot think that two squares would furnish sufficient machinery for the purpose, unless one of them had a joint at the angle to reduce the two limbs to one when necessary. A square, two 24-inch gauges, and the gavel, appear to be the most efficient implements. But although Dermott boasts that the secret was known only to a few intelligent members of his own schism, yet it is quite evident that he himself learnt it on the Continent, where it was used by the Craft long before the time when he flourished; and it had been promulgated a hundred years earlier by the Marquis of Worcester in the following words: 'A method by which, at a window, as far as the eye can discover black from white, a man may hold intercourse with his correspondent, without noise made or notice taken; being according to occasion given, or means afforded *ex re nata*, and no need of provision beforehand; though much better if foreseen and course taken by mutual consent of parties, and may be carried on by night as well as by day, though as dark as pitch is black.'"

"It was, in fact, a telegraph," said the D.P.G.M.

"You are right," Bro. Gilkes replied; "it was a telegraph, and in existence before that wonderful invention was known to the public."

Original English. *Improved English.* 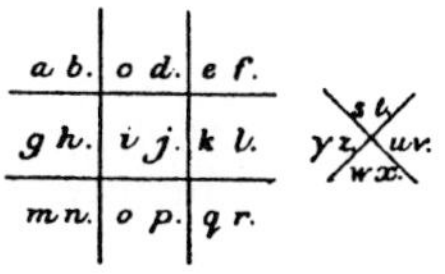 *Another variety—English.*

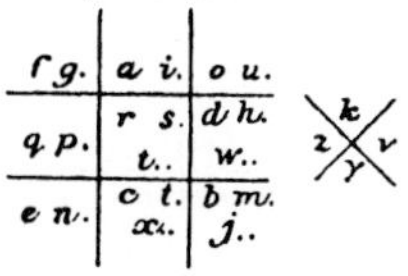

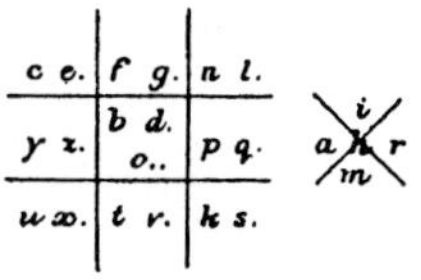

Original Continental. 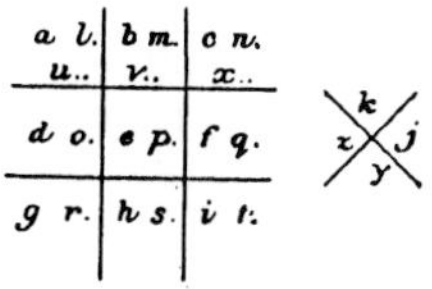 *Improved Continental.* 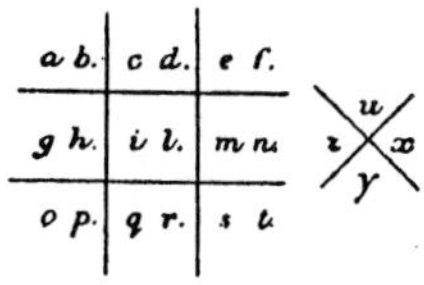 *United States.*

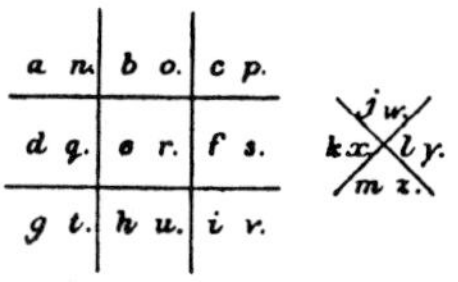

Booklist

D.C.Allen, "The Legend of Noah" (University of Illinois Press) 1963

Revd.Dr.Anderson. "Constitutions of the Freemasons (1723)" (Spencer, London) 1871

E.H.Buckeridge. "History of the Kent Lodge No.15" (London) 1903

R.Carlile. "Manual of Freemasonry" (Wm. Reeves) 1820 edn.

H.Carr (ed.) "The Early French Exposures" (Q.C. London) 1971

T.Carr. "The Operatives" Manchester Association of Masonic Research

R.Chudley "Life of Dunckerley" (Ian Allan) 1988

F.S.Collier. Humber M.M.M. Lodge Centenary Booklet

G.G.Coulton. "Art and the Reformation" (Blackwell) 1928

W.J.Chetwode Crawley. "Caementaria Hibernica" (Dublin) 1897.

P.Crossle. Lodge of Research Transactions Vols. (Dublin)

G.W.Daynes. "200 years of Freemasonry in Norfolk Masonry" (London)

F.R.Eaton. "An Outline of the History of the Provincial Grand Lodge of Norfolk" (Norwich) 1960

S.Forster. Research Lodge Transactions (Dublin)

J.G.Frazer. "The Golden Bough" (Papermac) 1987

R.F.Gould. "Military Lodges" (Aldershot) 1899

Grand Lodge of Scotland. "The Mark Master Mason" (Edinburgh)

J.A.Grantham. "History of the Grand Lodge of Mark Master Masons". (A. Lewis) 1960

J.A.Grantham. "Introduction to Mark Masonry" (Clark) 1935

R.M.Handfield-Jones. "A New and Comprehensive History of the Grand Lodge of Mark Master Masons" (London) 1969

F.G.Harmer. "The Mark Degree and Masons' Marks" 1919

H.F.Inman. "Mark and Ark Mariner Working Explained" (Spencer) 1934

A.S.H.Johnson. "Wisdom, Strength and Beauty" (Buenos Aires) 1949

Bernard E.Jones. "Freemason's Guide and Compendium" (Harrap) 1956

F.Josephus. "The Works" (trans. Wm. Whiston) (London) 1878

D.Knoop and R.Jones. "The London Mason in the 17th Century" (Manchester University Press) 1935

J.Heron Lepper & P.Crossle. "History of Grand Lodge of Ireland" 1925

A.G.Mackey. "A Lexicon of Freemasonry" ('Mark' section.) 1860

A.J.R.Milborne. "Freemasonry in the Province of Quebec" 1960

R.H.Mottram. "Noah" (London) 1937

Newstead Lo. of Mark Master Masons T.I. (1792–1973). Bicentenary Booklet

Revd.G.Oliver. "The Origin of the Royal Arch" (Spencer, London) 1867
Revd.G.Oliver. "Revelations of a Square" (London)
J.G.Osborn. "History of Freemasonry in West Cornwall" (1765–1828) 1901
A.Parrot. "The Ark and the Flood" (SCM Press) 1955
W.H.Rylands. "Masons' Marks" (Liverpool) 1893
H.Sadler. "Thomas Dunckerley: His Life, Labours and Letters" (London) 1891
C.J.Schott. "The Tradition of the Old York T.I. Lodge of Mark Masons 1713–1783" (Bradford) 1912
F.Smyth. "Brethren in Chivalry" (Ian Allan) 1991
B.H.Springett. "The Mark Degree" (A.Lewis) 1931
J.Stokes. "Britannia Lodge of Mark Master Masons No.53 1861–1920".
J.Strachan. "Northumbrian Masonry" (London) 1898
Canon R. Tydeman. "The Fourth Regular Step" (London) N.D.
T.B.Whytehead. "Notes on the History of the Mark Degree" 1880

References

(The full titles of works referred to as 'op.cit.' are in the Booklist)

1/1	p. 12.	Johnson, A.S.H. op.cit.
2/1	p. 15.	Carr, T. op.cit. Vol. 5 (1915) p. 9f.
2/2	p. 16.	Coulton, G.G. op.cit. p. 168.
2/3	p. 17.	Coulton. op.cit. p. 171.
2/4	p. 19.	Springett, B.H. op.cit. p. 13.
2/5	p. 20.	Coulton. op.cit. p. 158f.
2/6	p. 20.	Coulton. op.cit. p.161f.
2/7	p. 21.	Coulton. op.cit. p. 147.
2/8	p. 22.	Rylands, W.H. op.cit. pp. 44–7.
2/9	p. 22.	Cockburn, Sir John. Masonic Record. pp. 254/255.
2/10	p. 23.	Harmer, F.G. op.cit. p. 45.
2/11	p. 23.	Whytehead, T.B. op.cit. p. 6f.
3/1	p. 32.	Carr.T. op.cit. Vol. 5 p. 5.
3/2	p. 33.	Knoop, D. & Jones, R. op.cit. pp. 17, 18
3/3	p. 33.	Grantham, J.A. Introduction. p. 1.
3/4	p. 35.	McLeod, W. Ars Quatuor Coronatorum (A.Q.C.) Vol. 107 (1994) pp. 14, 19.
3/5	p. 37.	Moss, W.E. A.Q.C. Vol. 51 (1938) p. 223f (See also Poole, H. AQC Vol. 50 (1937) for the text of the MS.)
3/6	p. 37.	Moss. op.cit. supra.
3/7	p. 37.	Harvey, J.M. AQC 80 (1967) p. 100.
3/8	p. 38.	Jones, Bernard E. op.cit. p. 316.
3/9	p. 39.	Mackey, A. op.cit. (Mark section).
3/10	p. 40.	Ward, Eric. A.Q.C. Vol.LXXV (1962) p. 130f.
3/11	p. 42.	Inman, H.F. op.cit. p. 31.
3/12	p. 42.	Hughan, W.J. A.Q.C. Vol. VI (1893) p. 108.
3/13	p. 43.	Crawley, W.J.C. op.cit.
3/14	p. 44.	Lepper, J. Heron & Crossle P. op.cit. Vol. 1 p. 40.
3/15	p. 44.	Grantham, J.A. Introduction. p. 18
3/16	p. 45.	Crossle, P. Lodge of Research Transactions (LRT) for 1923 (Healy, Dublin) 1929 pp. 161, 207.
3/17	p. 45.	Crossle. op.cit. pp. 210, 217.
3/18	p. 46	Crossle. op.cit. pp. 224, 225.

3/19 p. 45. Grantham, J.A. Introduction p. 91.
3/20 p. 47. Crossle. op.cit. p. 182.
3/21 p. 48. Crossle. op.cit. p. 243.
3/22 p. 48. Parkinson, R.E. Lodge of Research Trans. 1959 p. 119f.
3/23 p. 49. Gould. op.cit. p.126.
3/24 p. 51. British Army Records. Public Record Office, Kew.
3/25 p. 51. Crossle. op.cit. p. 272.
3/26 p. 52. Waples, W. A.Q.C. Vol.LXII (1949) p. 89.
3/27 p. 54. Todd, T.O. (compiler) Phoenix Lodge History.
3/28 p. 54. Schnitger, F Unpublished Ms. (Library of the Province of Northumberland, Newcastle upon Tyne).
3/29 p. 55. Collier, F.S. op.cit.

4/1 p. 58. Milborne, A.J.R. op.cit. p. 38.
4/2 p. 59. Chudley, R. op.cit. p. 18.
4/3 p. 60. Lepper, Heron A.Q.C. Vol. LVI (1943) p. 166.
4/4 p. 60. Lepper, Heron op.cit. p. 169.
4/5 p. 61. Sadler, H. op. cit. p. 52.
4/6 p. 61. Lepper op.cit. p. 168.
4/7 p. 61. Sadler op.cit. p. 49.
4/8 p. 62. Chudley op.cit. p. 21.
4/9 p. 62. Henderson, T.R. Freemasonry in the Royal Scots. 1934. p. 18
4/10 p. 65. Chudley op.cit. p. 23.
4/11 p. 66. Lepper op.cit. p. 163.
4/12 p. 67. Oliver, Rev.G. Revelations. p. 151.
4/13 p. 67. Sadler op.cit.
4/14 p. 74. Oliver Revelations. p. 298.
4/15 p. 75. Chudley op.cit.
4/16 p. 82. Osborn, J.G. op.cit. p. 176.
4/17 p. 82. Smyth, F. op.cit. p. 24.

5/1 p. 91. Osborn op.cit. p. 91.
5/2 p. 92. Grantham, J.A. History p. 103.
5/3 p. 93. Newstead op.cit. p. 9.
5/4 p. 93. Newstead op.cit. p. 10.
5/5 p. 95. Noar, C.P. MAMR 1916 p. 22.
5/6 p. 95. Pick, F.L. MAMR "The Ashton Travelling Lodge".
5/7 p. 96. Taylor, Canon. MAMR "Marks of Antiquity" p. 124.
5/8 p. 96. Rogers, N. AQC Vol. 75 (1962) pp. 37–51.
5/9 p. 97. Pick/Hughan MAMR "Freemasonry in Oldham".
5/10 p. 98. "Masonry at Bottoms" booklet. p. 12.
5/11 p. 99. Schott, C.J. op.cit. p. 17.
5/12 p. 100. Stokes, J. op.cit. p. 8.
5/13 p. 102. Daynes. op. cit. p. 18.

5/14 p. 103. Buckeridge, E.H. op.cit. p. 31f.
5/15 p. 108. Forster, S. op.cit. Vol.XIX p. 167f.
5/16 p. 108. Forster, S. op.cit. Vol.XIX p. 178.
5/17 p. 109. Forster, S. op. cit. idem.
5/18 p. 111. Dashwood, J.R. A.Q.C. Vol.LXXII (1959) pp. 127–133
5/19 p. 111. Graham. Outline History of Quebec. p. 81.
5/20 p. 113. Graham op.cit. supra p. 150f.

6/1 p. 131. Carlile, R. op.cit. pp. 190ff.
6/2 p. 153. Schnitger op.cit.

7/1 p. 211. Strachan, J. op.cit.
7/2 p. 213. Forster op.cit. Vol.XVIII pp. 134ff.

10/1 p. 308. Grantham Introduction. pp. 73, 83
10/2 p. 311. Carr, H. (ed.) op.cit. p. 215.
10/3 p. 312. Oliver Royal Arch p. 96.
10/4 p. 313. Tydeman, Canon R. op.cit. p. 7.

11/1 p. 320. Mottram, R.H. op.cit. pp. 64, 66, 193.
11/2 p. 321. Baigent, M. Babylon.
11/3 p. 321. Oliver. The Antiquities of Freemasonry.
11/4 p. 322. Mottram op.cit. pp. 64, 65.
11/5 p. 324. Mottram op.cit. pp. 102, 103.
11/6 p. 324. Mottram op.cit. p. 118.
11/7 p. 328. Oliver A Dictionary of Symbolical Masonry.
11/8 p. 328. Mottram op.cit. pp. 179, 180.
11/9 p. 329. Mottram op.cit. p.185.
11/10 p. 332. Anderson, Rev. Dr. 1738 Constitutions.
11/11 p. 334. Mottram op.cit. p. 169.
11/12 p. 336. Parrot, A. op.cit. p. 70f.
11/13 p. 336. Mottram op.cit. p. 23f.
11/14 p. 343. Coulton op.cit. p. 316.
11/15 p. 343. Jones, Bernard E. op.cit. p. 316.
11/16 p. 345. Frazer, J.G. "Folk Lore" journal.
11/17 p. 345. Josephus, F. op.cit. p. 32.
11/18 p. 375. Ward, Eric A.Q.C. Vol.LXXI (1958) p. 50.

Index

(Variant forms or related items are shown in brackets)

Index

D

E

F

G

H

I

J

N

O

Q

R

S

T

Y

Z